Investment in Uncertainty

Applied Optimization

Volume 21

The titles published in this series are listed at the end of this volume.

Investment in Uncertainty

by

Jaime Gil-Aluja

University of Barcelona,
Faculty of Economics & Business Administration,
University of Paris IX Dauphine

KLUWER ACADEMIC PUBLISHERS

DORDRECHT / BOSTON / LONDON

A C.I.P. Catalogue record for this book is available from the Library of Congress.

ISBN 0-7923-5296-3

Published by Kluwer Academic Publishers,
P.O. Box 17, 3300 AA Dordrecht, The Netherlands.

Sold and distributed in the North, Central and South America
by Kluwer Academic Publishers,
101 Philip Drive, Norwell, MA 02061, U.S.A.

In all other countries, sold and distributed
by Kluwer Academic Publishers,
P.O. Box 322, 3300 AH Dordrecht, The Netherlands.

Printed on acid-free paper

Printed in the Netherlands.

This book is dedicated
to Mario Pifarré

Index

SECOND PART
Selection

> Life is an eternal adventure, but the world is not for the adventurers but for those who even knowing how to assume the necessary risks are capable of limiting and directing them in order to crown their profoundest wishes with success.

Introduction

Any period in time would appear to be suitable for tackling the task of taking an inventory of the situation through which an institution, association or company may be passing, in short, a co-ordinated nucleus of people seeking certain objectives. During latter times this healthy exercise has become more frequent due to the doubtless effect caused to citizens by the imminent advent of the end of the century.

We can stand and contemplate as imposingly large buildings rise from nothing. We can marvel at the way machines and installations of complicated mechanisms operate. In front of a computer, by only pressing a few keys, financial empires change hands. With every minute that passes, the maelstrom of our times shows us, as if it were a cinema picture, numerous scenes that because they have become so frequent they now form a part of our lives.

By the very nature of things, there is a particular interest in separating the occurrence of events into watertight compartments. This nearly always cunning separation struggles with the continuous rhythm of events, which forms a consubstantial part of life itself. But nobody can doubt that the realities of today are consequent upon what happened yesterday and that current actions will condition the future, to a greater or lesser degree. To put this another way, things are not as they are just because, but because there has been <<somebody>>, an active subject, who by contributing intelligence or his hands has with his actions made the realities of each moment possible.

A part of these realities has the vocation for permanence, in the sense that its use and enjoyment is prolonged during an interval of time that goes beyond the periods in which it is customary to separate economic activity. But it so happens, as it does in all human work, that the estimate, by those holding or those who can obtain ownership of it, is weakened in the course of time as a consequence of its physical ageing and/or because its use, relative to other enjoyment alternatives, is less. The ingenuity of those to whom the custody and control of the values of the economic units of production and distribution fall, has period after period, allowed for following the evolution of this <<collective appreciation>>, through the creation of a concept, depreciation, the mission of which is to regulate underestimating <<assets>> by assigning their just price at every moment. This then is as it should be.

Precisely due to their long life, these assets are known as fixed assets and their management includes a whole set of particularities, which makes them quite different from the rest of the elements that form what constitutes patrimony. Based on this, people, companies or institutions of the most diverse nature, seek profitability, stability, permanence, survival or any combination of these objectives. But if this management has at no time been easy it is certainly less so at present, where complexity has hidden itself in every corner of economic activity, due to the rapid and very often unexpected evolution of events. The time effect, that plays a fundamental role, today requires that we reconsider the studies accepted over many years as basic elements for taking decisions relative to these fixed assets.

These works, gathered under the common denominator of <<investments>> have captured the interest of researchers and executives for several decades. However, economic-financial relations within an environment of globalisation are undergoing a spectacular change and those schemes which a short while ago were valid for facing reality at every turn have become inoperative, and their distancing from the problems that concern those in responsibility have again opened up gaps between events and their formalisation. In spite of this evidence we are witnessing with profound disillusion certain manifestations loaded with conformity and indulgence by groups of specialists whose training and capacity is outside all doubt. With this an attempt is being made to hold on to the past and continue in this way with positions where security is guaranteed by years and sometimes centuries of experience. We understand these positions, but to understand is not to consent and we feel the moment has come to give an about face to traditional approaches, although to do this is to run the risks of an adventure, occasionally with untried instruments. It is particularly true to say that to live is a permanent adventure, but this world does not belong to the adventurers but to those who are capable of controlling and placing limits on events by directing them at those most intimately sought after objectives.

These latter observations will appear to some as obvious, but to the greater majority perhaps they are unorthodox, disconcerting and even challenging. The author who has had the audacity to write the same, in the hope that someone will read them, has no other intention than to awaken concern in those who are uneasy faced with the impotence to fight, with any possibility of success, before uncertainty that is ever more present in the consequences of our acts. We are at a crucial moment for the design of our society, our economy and our businesses. Many things are changing and many more are going to change in forthcoming years. In order to be able to face up to the important challenges that are emerging, large doses of experience and imagination will be required, but above all the availability of instruments that are suitable for explaining the world in which we live in a better way, an essential condition for carrying out a treatment that is efficient for obtaining such longed for results.

With our work we intend to take a step forward, even though this is minute, in the search for solutions to the problems arising for those who possessing or able to obtain sufficient financial means, desire to invest the same under the best conditions in accordance with their needs or desires, in a world governed by uncertainty. For this, we have resorted to a wide range of techniques that are supported by certain numerical and non-numerical mathematics, which are all the time becoming more firmly entrenched in the seats of learning where new lines of investigation for the future are being engendered. From the arithmetic of confidence intervals to expertons, passing through fuzzy numbers, fuzzy sub-sets and their multiple extensions, on the one hand and resorting to new theories such as those as forgotten effects, affinities and neural graphs, among others, we have constructed a wide range of models and algorithms capable, we feel, of giving a satisfactory response to the challenge of investment within a context of uncertainty. Some of these have been drawn up based on classical works, transferring the traditional elements in the sphere of certainty and probability to uncertainty. The results obtained have allowed us to verify better adaptation to current reality. Others, however, have had to drink from the waters of the new paradigms of the theory of decision. It is here that non-numerical mathematics has appeared in all its fullness, as the central axis around which the new concepts rotate, and also other old travelling companions, requiring reformulation.

It is particularly well known that economic systems undergo fluctuations causing speculation of a diverse nature in the agents acting in the same. Although it is true to say that it is easier to manage investments in a company or institution in times of plenty than in times of want, it is also true to say that opportunities always exist, if one knows how to find and take advantage of them. This perhaps is one of those values that are subject to being associated to a good manager. But the best of managers require a stimulus, help or support of <<something>> that allows them to improve their prospects, confirm their hopes or put a stop to dangerous impulses. The loneliness of those responsible for decisions at decisive moments is only comparable to that of hermits. The singularity of this fact is that the latter are always surrounded by people. If with our work we manage to supply them with a little company, our hopes when we started out will be more than amply fulfilled.

This work has been dedicated to one of our dearest teachers, Professor Mario Pifarré. He it was who gave his assistance to us during the more difficult times at the commencement of our academic activity. My debt to him obviously is not settled with this modest work, because gratitude goes much further than the works carried out in his honour, materialised in just a few hundred pages. When life begins to decline with its inexorably accelerated rhythm, it is comforting to be able to feel that we can still count on the invisible and imperceptible protecting shield of those who have preceded us in the knowledge of science and introduced us along the paths of teaching and research. Many years, perhaps too many, have gone by, but time cannot make us forget our own roots, without which the merest breeze would leave us to the mercy of the ups and downs that are the scourge of our coexistence.

JAUME GIL ALUJA

PART ONE

Preparing the investment

1 Investments in the company

The decline of stability

For some time now, economy and management researchers have been attempting to find a new course for their anxieties to resolve the serious problems that social, economic and business systems are causing as a consequence of the situation of uncertainty which is characteristic of our day and age. Emerging thus, within scientific spheres, are a large number of proposals which, in different senses, are converging to give new treatment both to old problems as well as to those which arise from the complex framework of economic-financial relations.

The belief is dawning, and growing stronger all the time, that scientific knowledge should not explain and discuss the universe we would like to live in, but that in which we are really living[1]. This leads to the conviction of the need to put an end to <<sacred>> knowledge of the true laws which describe a stable world and to create a new rationality based on instability leading to uncertainty, although to encroach upon these laws requires revising the principals on which science is nourished. Also, it will be necessary to find a language that allows for answering all the profound questions that are being asked in these last few years of the century.

Traditionally, western science has been based for many centuries on one idea, in itself, original: the idea of the laws of nature. According to these, nature is obliged to follow certain rules that lead to structures based on certainty. This is particularly obvious in the laws of Newton, and curiously, those which were considered as great revolutions of the XXth. Century, <<quantum mechanics>> and <<relativity>>, have done nothing else but confirm this vision. In spite of this, all the time it is becoming more evident that these theories are in contradiction to the phenomena which have emerged from the reality of our time, subject to a universe in constant evolution, which concurs with the also evolutionary appearance of the human being.

Today this path does not appear to be acceptable as a basis for investigation activities. We feel that a Darwinian idea of the evolution of the universe must be arrived at, and that a geometric idea must be left aside. It is necessary to give a good explanation of the universe and as a consequence of the fact that this universe is unstable, this gives rise to uncertainty. But even from uncertainty certain patterns of conduct can be extracted, which in the majority can be expressed by means of possibilities, some of them by probabilities and a very few by certainty.

Therefore it would not be honest to close ones eyes and say that one believes in certainties, even though these were not to reside in our world, above all taking into account that uncertainty may give rise to a new way of representing instabilities and through this to better understand the role they play in certain new rules which explain nature. It would thus seem that a door has opened which perhaps is very narrow, but is sufficient for leaving the determinist world which is alienating since in it all is predetermined and recorded in the Big Bang. On passing through this door a new uncertain world will appear which will allow for an explanation of new habits, new rules of conduct, new phenomena.

Economic systems, which are always characterised by a tight network of interconnections, obviously do not escape from these reflections. Apart from this, the configuration of our very existence, is being attacked by over information that is very difficult to assimilate and control, and also by very profound changes in unpredetermined directions, which make us look to the future surrounded by a haze of nebulous uncertainty. It would seem that the time has come for the decline of stability and security. Economic and business activities, professions and jobs, which in the past were immobile and transmitted from generation to generation, are finding that the interest which they aroused before has now ended and they no longer arouse the enthusiasm of those making up the new strata of our society. It is impossible to admit that those persons acquiring or who may have acquired training in any sphere of science or technical subjects, can aspire to carry out their work throughout life without nearly permanent updating of their abilities. Faced by a world of instability and uncertainty, rigid specialisation no longer has room, but this is replaced with the phenomena of imagination, the creator of flexible and adapting spirits.

Unlike former times, in which events took place in a much slower way and evolution occurred over long periods of time in which the capacity of reaction to changes was practically total, nowadays social activity is at permanent boiling point. And above all else it has been during these latter decades when the changes have been more important, not only relative to facts and phenomena, but also in behaviour and ideas. Thus, traditional values such as hard work, perseverance, patience, which for so many years constituted a monolithic whole and were a guide for being immersed in a society, have exploded into a thousand pieces to be substituted for other values such as audacity, the competitive spirit, etc, and the so called <<kingdom of the image>> has appeared. Faced with this context, it would appear to be permissible to ask oneself how one can conceive a scientific activity when human thought, charged with a high degree of subjectivity, can attempt to find the objective, among so much change. Explaining these changes and giving reason to the consequences of these changes has awakened the interest of the most restless souls. One should not forget the idea, frequently repeated by François Perroux: <<science develops through the needs of reality at any given time and as a consequence of the same>>, and he continued by saying, <<social structures act and condition economic thinking>>. It should not come as a surprise, therefore, that stability in progress of economic knowledge has taken a step in the hatching of new ideas which, in very different directions, seek to give an answer to the numerous problems which current society has raised.

The economy, perhaps the youngest of social sciences, appears rather late, and the thought that revolves around it is initially structured based on mechanist mathematics, between 1880 and 1914 with the General Equilibrium (Walras, Pareto, Cournot, Edgewort....). Faced with a reality, the basic characteristic of which was a certain stability in social life and economic relations, groups of scientists attempted to formalise the processes taking part in it. The classical mechanics of Lagrange are used, which gives an impression of seriousness, before what Perroux liked to call <<the laxism of economic reasoning>>. But, on the other hand, human thinking remains trapped by certain laws, which unfailingly leads it to a predetermined future. Perhaps because of this, the mathematics of determinism had a great influence and has prevailed and even today continues to prevail, in many spheres of scientific activity within the economy and management.

But on the initiation of great changes within society, which all the time gain more presence in the economic field, certain voices were raised crying out for a new way of tackling the problems and underlining the insufficiency of mechanist mathematics for describing the new society which was emerging. This radical change commenced after the Second World War. The figure of the <<robot-man>> is cast aside, time is considered irreversible, formalisation of the fatalism of predestination is avoided, giving to man the opportunity to freely elect his future, a future of which he is an active participant and not a mere cog in a predetermined chain.

The current situation, characterised by certain abrupt and unforeseen changes in very often opposing directions, has brought us, during the last few years, to reconsider the use of those techniques which are normally used for handling a reality, which has become so changeable as to have been converted into uncertainty.

Firstly in this sense, it would appear convenient to consider a concept, that of decision, which, within the spheres of economic science, constitutes one of the most often used terms. It is obvious that it is not possible to detach the concept of decision from the estimate of those economic parameters located in the future which will be affected by the consequences of the decision itself. Therefore, given the fact that in economic systems acceleration and deceleration processes are taking place which do not always pull in the same direction, certain pressures of a diverse nature take place in their midst, which provoke important problems for an adequate quantitative assignment of said economic parameters. These problems are provoked, in general, by the absence of a platform for the future with sufficient stability in order to be able to establish selection processes based on the estimate of economic parameters which allow for conveniently limiting the outcome of these events.

And this is so, because those responsible for companies and institutions must adopt certain decisions with an economic and financial repercussion which are not limited to the moments when they are taken but stretch out, in many cases, over several years. The difficulties of foresight and estimates, consubstantial in every executive, increase all the time as a consequence of a recent climate of uncertainty. It is obvious that <<the very facts of nature are uncertain; the economic, social, financial environment of companies changes unceasingly; the acts of man -because he is free and provided with imagination- and relationships between men because they are not robots, are the profound causes of uncertainty>>[2].

Our concern, and the work we have carried out, is directed at bringing to light the fact that, in the sphere of investments, even without being able to measure in a formal manner or by probabilities, one can also aspire to rational conduct. The attempt to carry out any adequate handling of investment problems requires certain reflections[3] on the study of historical evolution of scientific thought which has favoured explanations of diverse nature, and on many occasions opposing, relative to the fact that substitution of certain theories for others occurs. In this sense, the echo has not yet dimmed of the confrontation between the positions of Popper[4] and Khun[5]. Without intending to make an in depth analysis of this fundamental element for every investigator and not even take up a position in the debate arising, it would seem opportune to point out, at a time such as this in which society is undergoing profound changes, that during long periods investigation works carried out in different spheres of knowledge have accepted a basic body of principals on which certain theories have been elaborated, which have permitted development of scientific activity.

However, the outcome of events, on the one hand, and the new approach to investigation, on the other, have brought to light the difficulty of providing an adequate explanation to a large number of phenomena, which have been accumulated in the << corners of anomalisms>>. But these corners have become so big that they have reached a point of occupying an important part of many of the buildings which constitute the different segments of knowledge. The fact is that these accumulation processes that have been arrived at in this way are now untenable for those attempting to supply answers to the problems that the different strata of society have raised.

Sets of rules (or suppositions) which have made up the support of investigative work, universally accepted within the different areas of knowledge, are first questioned and later substituted, by others. These new rules have given rise to changes in processes, from which models, techniques, algorithms... may emanate, which are liable to provide the solutions the scientific community is clamouring for.

Within the sphere of economics and management, attempts have been made, and we believe partially achieved, of creating certain elements that are capable of arriving at an adequate handling of the phenomena which are taking place at the centre of States and companies, when their knowledge takes place in a not particularly precise manner. For this, the theories of errors, of confidence intervals, fuzzy numbers, fuzzy sub-sets have been used and also all the proposed generalisations which we have already employed[6]. The difference between the treatment of these problems with these elements and those of classical schemes is important. Faced with the impossibility of accepting the complex and uncertain economic reality with any degree of precision, recourse was made to an initial simplification for carrying out later developments based on these simplified elements. The possible initial deviations were accumulated and expanded as the operating process advanced. Also information was lost from the outset which was now impossible to recuperate.

We prefer to accept economic and management phenomena with their uncertainty, to carry out the pertinent developments, by preserving the lack of precision (and also all the information) in order for it to <<fall>> as late as possible, since it is always possible (by loosing information) to reduce the uncertainty.

From all the works carried out new elements have arisen which are situated in four different spheres of knowledge: logic, mathematics, operative investigation and economy and management. In this sense, and from a perspective of logic, <<the excluded middle principle>> appears, in conjunction with others, dominating the thoughts of the investigator, who has continued to use a mathematical language derived from the same and the maximum exponent of which (but not the exclusive one) has had the binary system and mechanist mathematics as its support. Overcoming this principal and its substitution by another, which we have called <<the gradual simultaneity principle>>, has allowed us to pass from <<the>> boolean logic to <<certain>> multivalent logic, among which, fuzzy logic, stands out. From these a mathematics of uncertainty is developed (fuzzy arithmetic and non-numerical mathematics) which is presented with a new axiomatic, as rigorous as that which is to be found in determinist mathematics and in probabilistic mathematics. Following this line of analysis, it is not difficult to see that from this conception of mathematical language, a work method has been developed which has given as a result a set of decision models, with hundreds if not thousands of variations.

In place of the contents of traditional operating investigation with concepts such as profitability, economic viability, productivity... expressed by means of cardinal functions, the notions appear of assignment, order, comparison, affinity ..., which now acquire a new sense. This movement is essential, because it signifies the transfer of non-arithmetical elements, in traditional studies considered complementary, to the privileged position they currently occupy, in what would appear to be a new paradigm.

All we have just mentioned, has as its object the bringing up of certain reflections[7] on the profound changes taking place in the spheres of study of the problem of decision in companies and institutions in our times. We feel that, in an imperceptible but continuous way, investigators are accepting bases on which to support new decision techniques. It should be recognised, however, that the transfer, from a situation in which the scientific community was comfortably entrenched to another which requires substantial efforts of adaptation, is not easy, without taking into consideration the risk inherent upon taking a new path of which as yet so little is known.

Therefore, it is convenient to bring to light from the outset, that not all the concepts, methods and techniques that are being used, arose spontaneously and suddenly. Some of them, even, have already been in use for decades, although in other contexts and can be found in works that have been considered, justly, as classical texts. Perhaps it was the inroad of fuzzy sub-sets which was the trigger that raised the level of their interest and use, converting them into the axis of the new movements relative to the theory of decision taking.

The lengthy lethargy, into which operative techniques for the study of the economy and management had sunk, appears to have reached an end with the incorporation of these new elements. The lack of any adequacy between models and reality, had, all too often, mutilated the latter, so that in this way they fitted into the models selected for handling them. This practice, repeatedly exposed by a number of investigators desirous of greater honesty in works, has gone to make up the attempts that are crystallising into this profound change in concepts, methods and objectives[8].

In fact, the path towards knowledge followed by the works of classical investigators, starts out from an estimate in exact terms or by means of laws of probability[9], of a determined number of economic parameters. This <<data>> is incorporated into the models and the use of adequate algorithms drawn up based on determinist arithmetic, or in the event, to the calculation of probabilities, permits obtaining certain objective numerical results, that is to say of certain <<measurements>>. With the change of paradigm, provided by the new society arisen from uncertainty, the way towards knowledge now does not start off from the estimate of future economic parameters in terms of certainty or probability, but from the perception of elements, inherent to or surrounding the process under study, the very nature of which is not principally measurable. What we are talking about are concepts obtained by means of subjective numerical estimates, that is to say <<valuations>> which, as such, do not permit the use of operators from determinist and/or probabilistic arithmetic. Thus, on a first plane, appears an arithmetic and non-numerical mathematics strengthened by the theory of fuzzy sub-sets and their many variations.

It is as from this moment, when the frustrations and concerns of so many researchers of management problems, appear to have found a way out with possible authentic transformation to new forms of knowledge, much more in line with current and future needs.

Now, all that has been mentioned should not induce in one the false belief of the uselessness of those models based on instruments arising under cover of the classical paradigm. What is more, the undoubted advances that their application has undergone in latter years, have permitted an improvement of quantitative studies aimed at handling decision phenomena, thus resulting, in the validity of these methods, on many occasions fortunate. Only when it is not honestly possible to consider <<objective>> estimates, should recourse be made to different principals and manners of acting. But in a confused world such as we live in today, it would not appear that uncertainty were about to remit, and only by living with it will the acceptance of new rules be easy. When the scientific community in its great majority have assumed them, the birth of the new decision paradigm will become a reality.

The change in direction of studies on the investment process

All too often it has been considered that the financial problem of the company can be considered as solved at the time when the means of payment enter within the sphere of the same. But the financial means are not an end in themselves, but they have as their object the attention of certain cash and bank balance needs caused in some way by the production process, taking the latter in its widest possible sense.

As management studies consider the end to which financial resources are destined, it is customary to establish a separation of the same by taking the theory of accounting by periods as a basis. From this the concept of investment that arises from consideration of the resources that are not to be totally materialised in one and the same accounting period is born. On the other hand a certain amount of payment means are destined for the acquisition of those factors of production which, to put it in this way, <<are consumed>> in the accounting period itself. Because of the periodic appearance of the same and because of the difficulty arising from their estimation, the production means, which constitute the material object of the investment process, require special attention. As we have already pointed out, investigation works within the sphere of company decisions, have been upheld by certain paradigms, which have impregnated the development of the different objects of knowledge. One of these, which is now deserving of our attention, is colloquially known by the name of <<investment selection>>. For those, even from varying points of view, who have advanced along the path of seeking models that are suitable for handling the problem of optimum placing of financial resources, have generally shared certain rules and principles which are located in the different levels of knowledge.

It is not difficult to verify that from the concept of traditional mathematical language, accepted for a long time by the scientific community, a work method evolved that gave as a result a set of decision models for those controlling in certain cases the <<so called>> genetic principle of yield[10] and for others, the preference for the liquidity principle, from which concepts have been generated such as, financial capital, financial equivalency and financial operation[11]. These elements have allowed for a very solid technical body, which is suitable for handling the problems brought up under a <<determined>> reality.

Perhaps the most important aspect of these investigations, can be found in the fact that with them the basic objective is reached which certain authors[12] identified by means of the name <<economic viability>>. In short, what this means is trying to measure a certain <<profit>> (expressed by means of different units, either presented in absolute or relative values) for each investment object, so that in this way select the one which gives greater profit to the shareholders. Thus, the object which the models attempt to arrive at, and the objective nature of data to be considered, operators to be used and results to attain, appear clear. The other aspects, considered very often as qualitative, are normally relegated to second place.

The incursion, let us say somewhat traumatic, of rapid acceleration in economic and social systems, which have given rise to profound changes in economic-financial phenomena, have brought to light the inadequacy of the instruments used with this paradigm for handling an uncertain reality. The lack of adequacy between the model and reality has gone to make up certain attempts that now are crystallised into profound changes.

In fact, basic concepts relative to classical studies such as financial capital, financial system, income ..., which constituted the axis on which rotated the calculation of economic viability of investments in an economic system governed by certainty, no longer play an essential role, although they continue to be fundamental when the study reaches the sphere of analysis of the monetary currents of collections and payments arising from the decision to invest. In their place appear the notions, which we have already pointed out, of grouping, order, comparison, affinity ... This displacement is fundamental. And we insist on the fact of <<displacement>> and not on that of <<substitution>>.

The path towards knowledge followed from classical studies, uses a determined number of economic parameters such as: monetary currents, collection and payment futures arising from the decision to invest; estimated rates of inflation; monetary incidence rates from technical progress, etc... This <<data>> is incorporated into selection models constructed from diverse financial systems. The use of suitable algorithms drawn up on the basis of determinist arithmetic or, in the event, the calculation of probabilities, allows for obtaining certain objective numerical results, that is to say certain measurements of <<profit>> which the investment object should bring to the investing subject.

The final objective, in many cases the only one, consists in a quantitative maximisation, which can be referred, <<roughly>>, to the wealth of the investor. Obviously, the search for a multi-objective cannot be excluded, although optimisation of profit is omnipresent.

But the change in the abundance of information available, relative to the investing reality requires a new development of the models which leads to a different path, the start of which is the grouping of heterogeneous information which allows, in some way, a summary of diverse criteria without mixing them. From there, certain groups of objects of similar or related characteristics are established at a determined level and after this the problem of ordering these groups is tackled. The decision takes place, in general, not by means of quantitative comparison, but through different ways, not excluding the assignment of <<weights>> to each of the criteria.

From all that has been mentioned, it can be deduced that the final solution no longer is expressed by a measurement and when not alone, is represented by one or several ordered successions of objects of the investment, which constitute the basis for the selection which will fall to one or another object, in accordance with the priority of the considered criteria.

The scheme that we present below shows the changes occurring in the studies for the selection of investments.

Traditional Paradigm	*New Paradigm*
Fundamental elements	
Excluded middle principle	Gradual simultaneity principle
↓	↓
Binary logic	Multivalent logics
↓	↓
Mechanist mathematics	Mathematics of uncertainty
Operative elements	
— Applied mathematics	— Management operating techniques
• Financial Mathematics	• Uncertain numerical mathematics of finances
• Operational research	• Non-numerical techniques of uncertainty
↓	↓
Classical theory of investment	Investment theory in uncertainty

We have repeatedly talked about investment and perhaps it would be useful now to determine what is understood by investment. The concept of investment appears in classical studies, both for making reference to the <<decision to invest>> and to the <<object of investment>>, sometimes indicated and others not, is which of these two aspects reference is being made to.

It would therefore be useful to establish a definition in which both these elements appear in a clear manner. In this respect we propose the following:

> <<The decision to invest is that act of choice by means of which certain economical-financial effects take place of an opposing tendency, materialised into certain periodic currents of payment and collection, both the consequence of the use of a physical or mental object. >>

Traditionally, studies related to investment activities centre their attention on the monetary effects that the acquisition of an investment object has caused and give rise to the existence of magnitudes located at different moments. This connection between the past and the future of the investment activity allows for consideration apart from the subject of the same, of three principal elements: the object of the investment, the cost of the investments and the income arising from the same.

Faced with this context, it should come as no surprise, for the study of the investment process from an economic point of view, that recourse should have been made to the concept of financial capital, frequently used by applied mathematics. The advantage of its use arises because, in itself, it comprises two elements: monetary mass and instant of time in which it is located, either because it is received or because it is delivered.

Independently of this aspect, of a formal value, a fact exists on which the reality of companies rotates: executives see themselves in the need, prior to taking a decision, of carrying out a study which allows them to invest their financial resources under the best conditions.

This decision can be directed at:

1. The making of investments in new objects

2. Renewal or change of those already existing.

In either one of these suppositions, certain monetary masses come into play which mean, for companies, a disbursement which it is hoped will give good results. The problem which arises is, therefore, fundamentally a problem of selection.

Selection can be centred, on the simplest hypothesis, between the alternative of acquiring a determined asset (object of the investment) or not to do so. However, in a situation such as this, characterised by multiple possibilities of placing monetary masses, it is not a risk to assume as most frequent the existence of various investment objects to which the decision to invest may fall.

In this way an attempt is being made to know which specific object will fulfil a series of conditions, which must be determined, in order for it to be more suitable than the others from the economic point of view. In order to arrive at a solution to this matter it is necessary to consider a whole series of elements concerning these objects, which, once systemised, will constitute the basis of all studies relative to the sphere of investments.

Investigators who have worked in the management field, with the object of assisting the essential genius of the businessman, draw up certain formal schemes which it is intended will be a representation of the real investment process. For this they take into consideration and draw up models.

Considering the enormous complexity which is shown by the investment phenomena, it is obvious that it is very difficult that the models which are traditionally drawn up on the same, to be an adequate reflection of reality.

Recognition of the impotence of the classical elements, for handling economic phenomena was clearly made obvious in Boulding's observations:

> <<The method of the economic analysis consists in commencing with simple hypotheses on human behaviour and then go on to talk on what consequen-

ces will be deduced from the economic system overall if such hypotheses were to be true. *«In this way we can create a picture of a simplified economic system»*.[13]

Once we are completely aware of this simple picture we can proceed to place it in a more intimate relation to real life, introducing additional modifications into our original hypotheses and verifying how they have an influence on the said picture, just as we see it. *But we will never arrive at «real life»*>>[14].

As we have repeatedly mentioned, our alternative, for treatment more in line with reality[15], consists in estimating this just as it is, with all its imprecision, in order to maintain it throughout the process, and carry out, if this is essential, suitable simplifications at the end of the same.

It should be pointed out that handling by means of the concept of probability requires the need to know certain information which is included in two different categories: the first refers to possible situations (it is the denominator of a fraction, the limit of which defines probability); the second is constituted by the favourable cases. This <<objective interpretation considers that all the announced numerical probabilities express something on the relative frequency with which an event of a certain type takes place within a succession of events>>[16]. The introduction of the concept of probability into models has allowed for the appearance of numerous problems which were latent in the investment process, but their applicability is limited by the nature itself of management problems, given the changing context in which companies operate.

The sphere of formalisation, supported on hypotheses based on certainty and probability, very common until recently in micro-economic models for investments, has been completed, from recent investigations, with the handling of uncertainty, initially by means of numerical mathematics using, among other elements, fuzzy numbers, in general, and their more operative simplification, triangular fuzzy numbers, in particular.

But in more recent works[17] we have continued incorporating, all the time with greater insistence, elements of non-numerical mathematics, which has allowed for handling situations, all the time more frequent, in which uncertainty did not even allow representation of investment phenomena based on uncertain numbers.

In this way, the growing importance can be affirmed of the consideration of new investment models, based on new rules, adopted with ever greater insistence by the scientific community, because they represent reality in a better way. With this, immersion is sought into a new-world, in which uncertainty no longer constitutes an impediment for efficient handling of investment decisions.

Basic elements for arithmetical study of selection

It is indisputable that during these latter years studies relative to the investment process have undergone a profound change taking into account the incorporation of new mathematical elements that have served for introducing a change in method to the directions existing to date.

In a first phase the models established constituted an adaptation of those already existing in the sphere of certainty, for which they were valid in an uncertain context. The fundamental elements continued to be the same as those in classical studies, but their generalisation permitted covering a much wider spectrum of real situations.

Estimates, for each investment object, of the two monetary currents of contrary tendencies: collections and payments, this no longer is expressed in crisp magnitudes but by means of uncertain numbers (confidence intervals, triplets or fuzzy numbers, nearly always triangular).

The fact that these monetary streams were not to be limited to a single period, but may belong to different moments in time located in the future, abandoned these new elements. Each one of these currents had at any given moment, a force expressed in monetary units by unit of time.

In this way and at certain times, certain currents could be conceived which were expressed, in the simplest of cases, of uncertainty, limited but not structured, by a surface between two curves. Thus, for each estimated current for collections and payments a figure such as that reproduced in Fig. 1.1 could be conceived.

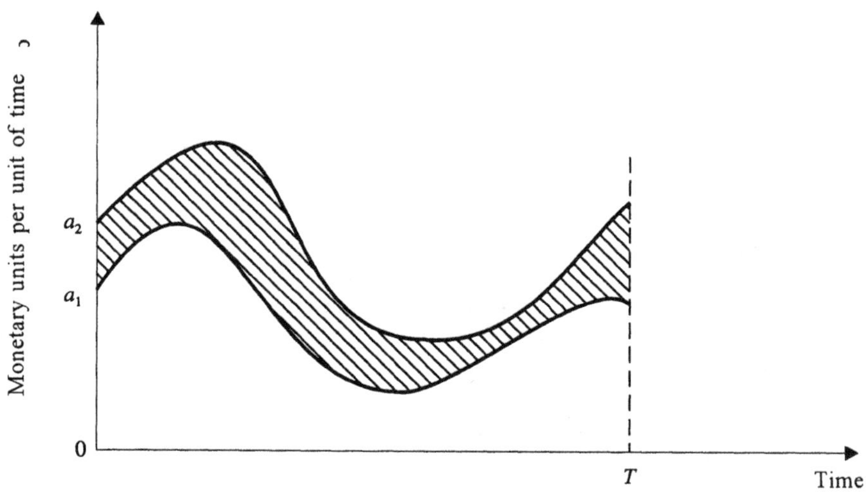

Figure 1.1

But for most cases another simplification of reality was adopted, on assuming that the monetary current of collections and/or payments was discontinuous and, although in an uncertain manner, took place at a determined number of times such as t_1, t_2, ..., as shown in Fig 1.2.

In this way, it is considered that future economic parameters can be expressed by confidence intervals $[a_1, a_2]$, $[b_1, b_2]$, $[c_1, c_2]$, ...

With the object of providing this problem with a structure in order for it to be formally expressed, the habit had been adopted of considering the sum of the payments and/or collections estimated for each period, assuming that the respective amounts were paid and/or collected at the beginning or end of the same. In this way t_1, t_2, t_3, ...,

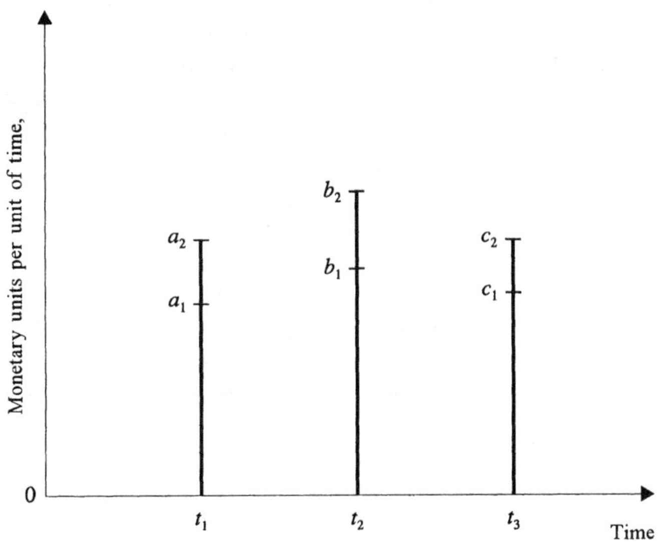

Figure 1.2.

of our figure would correspond to equal lapses of time, substituting a real current of unequal cadence by a series of theoretical streams with constant time periods. In the event of discontinuity, the strength of the current at the interior of each period would be equal to zero. It can be concluded, in short, that in that context, when making estimates for payments and/or collections the distribution of the expiry within each period was disregarded.

One cannot conceal the fact that, on attempting to obtain <<quantitatively>>, and even if this were to be done by means of uncertain numbers, the extension of these streams brings up serious difficulties which are due, principally and among others, to the misty shroud surrounding events in the future, which have an influence on both collections and payments as well as on other elements related to the same.

Starting out from this basis, in the near past, certain models were drawn up with the intention of getting closer to complex realities. And this, as a consequence of a look through the classical studies of investment selection, has permitted observation of certain criteria the operability of which, under other circumstances unquestionable, have been proven inadequate in the current complex world.

We are now going to make a very short reference to criteria, which are considered as classical, with the object of making comprehension easier of the transfer from the mathematics of certainty to the arithmetic of uncertainty. For this we will mention in the first place, the criterion with the *well-known name of minimum recuperation time*. The basis of this criterion can be found in the calculation, for each investment object, of the moment in which the difference between the accumulated currents of collections and payments, initially estimated in an exact manner, becomes positive. The decision should fall to the one nearest the time when the process was initiated. The objective consists, therefore, in determining the <<exact>> time when payments already made as a consequence of the acquisition and operation of the investment object, are recuperated. The comparison between these times, relative to each investment object will point out the lesser, which will become, in its turn, the determinant of the most favourable investment.

As can be seen, this criteria does not take into account the profits arising out of the operation of the investment object after the moment in which the difference of accumulated currents passes from being negative to positive, on taking into consideration the useful life of the object. From this it can be deduced that there is only a partial interest in that supposition in which the sole objective is to determine the liquidability of the investment. We know of the existence of no works for transferring this criteria from the sphere of certainty to that of uncertainty.

Let us now go on to list those models which attempt to give a reply to the quantification of profits, either in absolute terms or percentages, answering, at one and the same time, the question as to whether an investment is convenient. Traditionally three paths have been followed.

The first consists in calculating the net current value (NCV), also called capital value of an investment, which refers to a moment in time and to a rate of interest. That is to say, the sum of all payments and collections occurring after the time of reference and discounted at that time. The decision to invest should fall to that object the capital value of which is the greatest. Another path consists in comparing, for each object, the mean annual income and mean annual expenses. This is the so-called method of annuities. And lastly one can also determine the suitability of an individual investment by the so-called method of the internal interest rate or internal yield rate (IYR). In fact, it can be stated that, with a different type of calculation, all three paths constitute one and the same method, on the basis of which one can begin to see the generic income principle. It has been from these elements that the first attempts were made for structuring a set of models in which the incorporation of uncertainty were first incorporated in one or several of the components which give rise to up dated collections and payments, on occasions based on the interest rate[18], others on estimates for collections and/or payments, or on both aspects at the same time.

In an attempt to come closer to economic reality, with an already visible evolutionary process, and try to reflect the incidence of the changes in models for investment selection the idea was reached to consider, within the classical methods of selection, certain elements which it was considered had a notable incidence on future collection and payment monetary currents. In this sense among others were included, *technical progress and inflation rate*. The introduction of these new elements, which did not change the essence of existing models, on the other hand allowed for an extension of the same. Likewise it was found that the passage to consideration of uncertainty did not cause any greater problems.

But classical handling of the investment problem does not end with the mere use of techniques established in determinist mathematics. In fact, specialists on the subject had come to the conclusion that the future was being generally considered in an imprecise and uncertain manner and, therefore, it was very difficult to estimate the economic parameters relative to the investment process with total exactitude and certainty. This circumstance lead to the introduction of the concept of risk, which meant technical problems on reviving the old problem of the validity in the decision taking field of objective probabilities, by the traditional difficulties arising from the need to know, alternatively, the favourable cases and possible cases; that all cases were equally probable; that one were to have available a series of observations of a repeatable phenomena. This gave rise to the possibility of incorporating, in the handling of investments, subjective probabilities, that is those that stem from psychological axioms.

The difficulties in method that these considerations mean, however, did not prevent certain attempts of a systematic use of the calculation of probabilities for investment selection, with particularly estimable formal results.

In this context, the incorporation of techniques should be pointed out which, in certainty, but above all by probability, allow for the development of sequential handling[19]. With this, new objectives were achieved, but the problem of <<quantification>> of probabilities continued latent, which in our understanding is obviously a basic necessity. Also in this field, passage towards uncertainty from a probabilistic stand point has occurred very slowly but continuously, giving rise during the last few years to a substantial advance, thanks to the use of the theory of fuzzy sub-sets allowing for more efficient handling of the problem of investment selection. Within this new investment decisional framework there has been a passage from contingency to fuzziness, formalising imprecision by considering that the occurrence of the studied phenomena may be explained in a different way on allowing a grading between the truth and falseness of any given proposal.

As is well known, the theory of fuzzy sub-sets is a part of mathematics that adapts itself very well to the study both of the subjective and the uncertain. In this sense it should be pointed out that the investment process frequently brings up problems which require taking decisions in an environment in which the objectives which it is intended to reach, the limitations to which they will be submitted, and even the consequences for each of the alternatives brought up, appear in an imprecise manner.

All we have just pointed out allows for entering into the heart of the classical elements making up the investment process. Let us remember, once more, the monetary currents arising from the decision to invest are not indifferent when conceived at different points in time. For this reason, it is said that one and the same monetary unit is considered as if it were two different economic assets when located at different times. This is the reason why additions or other arithmetical operations cannot be done directly.

To get over this difficulty recourse is made to something that is like a price system. In fact, when handling problems in which the economic parameters must be considered at different times, this type of price, which plays a fundamental role, is constituted by the interest rate, which can be considered as the joint between the present and different stages of the future.

The existence of a determined interest rate, has a doubtless influence on the decisions of the businessman. In effect, there exists, in principal, a tendency to request loans when the interest rate is low, while the decision taker will hold back or limit or limit the productive activity when these are high, among other things because a good<<profit>> can be obtained by placing the same in the capitals market.

In this way it has become obvious that a determined amount of money available at any given moment is not indifferent to this same amount of money when it is available over n periods. For this, in the sphere of numerical mathematics, it is necessary to find a tendency capable of <<quantitatively>> establishing the comparison between series of capitals (both if dealing with collections or payments) which by common sense it is not possible to do.

Let us now see how traditional studies resolve this problem.

Starting off from the criteria according to which, in the capitals market, 1 current monetary unit is changed within a year for $1 + i_1$ units. The number i_1, interest rate for the first year, is positive in the majority of cases, because normally <<a current monetary unit>> is preferred to a <<monetary unit within one year>>.

In the perfect forecast hypothesis it is assumed that the annual rates of interest $i_1, i_2, ..., i_n$, which will be in force during years 1, 2, ..., n is known. On many occasions, the interest rate is considered as constantly equal throughout all the years, that is to say, that it complies with: $i_1 = i_2 = ... = i_n = i$. In this case the value of 1 monetary unit after n years will be $(1 + i)^n$.

Now then, if the interest rates in force in the market are i_j, and $j = 1, 2, ..., n$; then 1 current monetary unit will be changed for $(1 + i_1)$ units after one year, $(1 + i_1)(1 + i_2)$, within two years, $(1 + i_1)(1 + i_2) ... (1 + i_n)$ after n years. By means of the rule of three it can be concluded that 1 monetary unit held after n years is equal to:

$$\frac{1}{(1 + i_1)(1 + i_2) \cdots (1 + i_n)}$$

monetary units available at moment zero.

When starting out from the hypothesis of a stationary economic system, it is admitted that the interest rate is constant throughout time, that is, $i_1 = i_2 = \ldots = i_n$, and therefore one monetary unit placed during n years is equivalent to:

$$\frac{1}{(1 + i_n)} \text{ current monetary units}$$

Therefore, in the hypothetical event of a single interest rate, up dating coefficients would be successively:

$$1, \frac{1}{(1+i)^1}, \frac{1}{(1+i)^2}, \ldots, \frac{1}{(1+i)^n}$$

forming a decreasing geometric progression of $(1 + i)^{-1}$.

Let us say in passing that the transit of this average reasoning to another in which continuous economic parameters are considered should lead to an exponential form. In fact, if starting out from a period of a year and this is divided by a large number, p, of elemental periods, and if ρ is the continuous interest rate, ρ/p is, by definition very large for p the interest rate given by 1 monetary unit during a very reduced period $1/p$. At the end of one year the application of compounded interest will have transformed the amount 1 into $(1 + \rho/p)^p$, the limit for $p \to +\infty$ is e^ρ.

Those works drawn up under classical schemes consider that, on reducing a series of monetary masses available at different periods in time to one single value, using the technique of up dating, the problem is resolved of the order of preference between a series of capitals.

From this certain reasoning is initiated tending toward giving a solution to the different situations which can arise. Thus, in the simplest of events, when for each period the difference between collections and payments corresponding to an object is greater than the others, there can be no doubt relative to the selection based on economic criteria. In fact, <<when two incomes A and B are such that at all times when accumulated income from B is, at least, equal to that from A and that at certain times is greater, nobody would hesitate to prefer B to A>>[20]. But this is just one particular case and the true problem of selection arises when it is necessary to compare investments which imply greater differences for one object, in certain periods, and lesser than any of the rest, in others.

This is the reason why the need to homogenise values arises, which, as they correspond to different periods in time, appear at first sight to be heterogeneous. As we have already pointed out it is precisely the rate of interest, basis of the up dating concept, which takes on this converting role.

In a modern economic system, it is unthinkable to totally accept a case such as that we have just looked at, among other things, because the existence of a single interest rate cannot be considered invariable over a period of time, nor can it be estimated in certain terms, above all when the economic horizon covers several years.

These obstacles have stimulated the study of the nature, characteristics and effects of the use of an interest rate. This then is one of the most important problems arising when facing a study of investments.

It can be observed that, traditionally a large proportion of works on the subject, adopt either explicitly or implicitly the hypothesis according to which one can request or offer any quantity of money at an interest rate which has become known as <<calculatory>>. This statement can be translated into classical terms as:

- The existence of a perfect capitals market.

- The calculatory interest rate corresponds to an equilibrium between capital offer and demand.

The hypothesis that at the calculatory rate of interest any monetary quantity can be given or taken is difficult to admit in reality, and its sense is open to discussion. In effect, if we are dealing with an economic unit which is willing to deliver a monetary mass at a determined rate of interest, the calculatory rate, the conclusion is reached that there is a preference for the monetary mass, plus the interest rate within a year, to the monetary mass today, since to the contrary the loan would not be made. This reasoning reflects, apart from the fact that at lower interest rates there would be moneylenders who would also be willing to hand over their money and there must be others, who could acquire the category of <<marginals>>, for whom the calculatory interest rate is a limit situation. For this, and only for strictly theoretical effects, it is possible to admit the validity of this calculatory interest rate and even then, only in the long term, when the corresponding adjustment to the system were to have been made, and all moneylenders were to be in a marginal situation. This then is the situation which implies indifference to giving or taking the quantity of money at this interest rate, and also the indifference between a monetary mass today and the same mass plus the corresponding interest after a few periods.

From the strictly formal point of view, the study of the determination of an interest rate, as well as the functions which the same fulfils in economic systems, gave rise to the birth of the so called <<capital theory>> and the division of the <<theory of distribution and prices>>. In his study Böhm-Bawerk, with the publication in 1889 of his Positive Theory of Capital as well as by the formulation of the three reasons for the existence of interest, points out:

- The economic subject hopes to find himself in the future in a better position than he is in today, which makes him give a higher value to current assets than to those of the future.

- For a set of reasons, the economic subject systematically underestimates the needs of the future.

- Lengthy production methods are more beneficial than short ones, and therefore, having consumer goods available today, allows for subsistence while initiating more drawn out production processes.

Also important in this field was the publication of the work by Irving Fisher in 1907, The Rate of Interest, handled methodically in a very exact manner, bringing to light, among other important questions, the fact that the interest rate is determined by the interaction of two factors:

- The opportunity for investment, which has its correspondence with the third cause of Böhm-Bawerk.

- The <<temporary preference>> or impatience to spend, which corresponds to the second cause of Böhm-Bawerk

It is known that the theoretical determination of the rate of interest does not presuppose the possibility of use of these techniques to the changing reality of today. A quick glance is sufficient at the financial activity of companies of any developed country to see that these have recourse to certain sources of outside financing of very different kinds which go from reduced rates of interest, to others of an emergency nature and nearly always with a high cost in order to avoid the fact that the incidence of the lack of bank liquidity were to cause irreversible situations.

All this leads to the conclusion that one of the most important problems which are brought up in the study of an investment project is the setting of the interest rate which must be taken as the basis for calculation. These difficulties, which are forewarned about in the traditional models, acquire greater importance now as a consequence of the variety and changing natures of the rates existing in the market, according to the time and the company which must decided on the investment.

For this, within the numerical sphere of uncertainty, right from the very start, the consideration of the rates of interest expressed by means of uncertain numbers has been included, in this way managing to reduce the possibilities of error in their estimating but knowing full well that the results will be uncertain, although in the very worst of cases with limited uncertainty.

The study of selection from non-numerical elements

The handling of problems which include the decision to invest, fortunately do not end with the use of elements arising from the arithmetic of uncertainty. Beside these, there is emerging new theoretical and coherent contents, capable of facing those ever more frequent situations, in which it is very difficult even to numerically limit uncertainty. And this is so, because the classical concepts, nearly always subject to an objective or subjective numerical quantification are not adequate for the profoundly changing world of today. It is true to say that the reformulation of traditional concepts adapted to this new context allows for certain solutions, but there are still far too many dark spots to allow us to be in agreement with the, on the other hand, interesting findings of numerical mathematics. The appearance of new concepts and displacement of those already in existence to new places, are allowing for the covering of a wide range of problems of the decision to invest.

Thus it can be said that under the current situation of scientific investigations on investment processes, traditional concepts still play a role as a support to the necessary developments for handling the problems entailed, but new concepts have emerged with strength which are occupying ever greater space, relegating the existing problems to ever more secondary places. Among these we would like to point out relation, correspondence, grouping, resemblance, similarity, affinity and order, among others.

In this way it can be seen that those concepts which inevitably require to be numerically expressed (in certainty or uncertainty) are becoming less of a leading light, because of the difficulties of expressing them objectively and even at times subjectively, taking into account the ever growing uncertain context in which they are included.

For all this it is inevitable, in the study of investments, that a fundamental change in method is taking place, both in all that is relative to the collation of information, and its handling and the manner of its results. In effect information is collated in total even though in an imprecise manner maintaining it throughout the whole process or *until such time as this is possible.* When the information can be expressed numerically, in an uncertain manner but limited, it is always possible to pass over to certain numbers, which implies establishing restrictive hypotheses that can cause errors. Sometimes it is possible to reach the end without making the entropy fall, and then the results occur in an uncertain but not erroneous manner. On the contrary, numerical results are crisp and therefore less erroneous when uncertainty, and the information inherent to the same, have been maintained for a longer period.

We have referred to numerical information and, as a contrast we can talk about non-numerical information. Therefore we can see that the transformation of traditional models of a numerical nature to the sphere of uncertainty, substituting crisp numbers for uncertain numbers, tends to generalise the same and make them more apt for handling reality, but in itself this transformation does not justify the change of paradigm. But, on the other hand, the uncertain models developed based on the concepts emerging from non-numerical mathematics, means a clear break from precedent, even when in their development, elements from classical studies were to be used.

Today, co-habitation of numerical and non-numerical models can be found for handling investment decision problems in uncertainty.

All that we have stated above makes one think on the possibility of the change of paradigm of the theory of investments, even though today, the scientific community in total has not taken the final step in this direction.

Perhaps it would be suitable at this point of the study we are making, to bring to light how the basic concepts show themselves in what could be the new paradigm of the theory of investment. For this we shall make recourse to the use of combinatory mathematics, the basic elements of which form what is becoming known as non-numerical mathematics. On the basis of this one of the more usual activities of this thought can be found: relation.

It is precisely from this idea of relation when advancement is made along the path of the new decisional elements. For this recourse is made to pre-topology, generalisation of topology, to the theory of graphs, to the lattice theory and to many other aspects which go to make up combinatory studies. We are not talking about bits and pieces taken at random from here and there with no connection, but of elements which are intimately related among themselves. Take into account that a graph is a combinatory topology, a lattice is a graph and an algebra, be it boolean or fuzzy, takes on the lattice structure.

A start is made from the existence of two sets or referentials E_1 y E_2, such that:

$$E_1 = \{a_1, a_2, ..., a_n\}; \quad E_2 = \{b_1, b_2, ..., b_m\}$$

The <<correspondence>> or <<relation>> between the elements of these two sets can be represented, among other ways, by an arrow form or in the form of a matrix. Thus, in the case of the existence of a relation between a_1 and b_2, a_1 y b_m; a_2 y b_1; a_2 y b_2; ..., a_n y b_1; ..., a_n y b_m, we would find (Fig. 1.3):

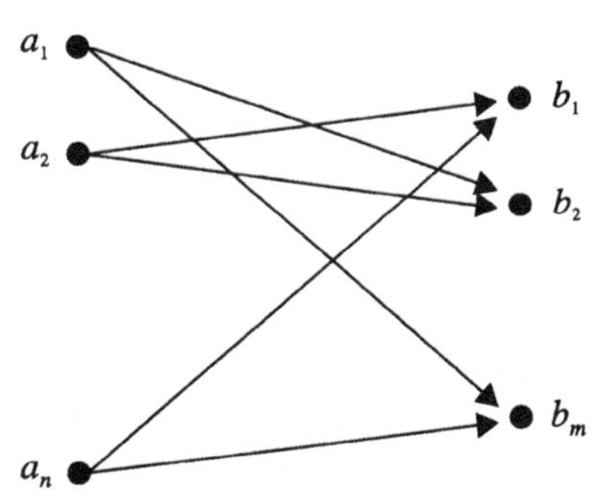

Figure 1.3.

	b_1	b_2		b_m
a_1	0	1	...	1
a_2	1	1	...	0
	...	...	...	...
a_n	1	0	...	1

The use of $\{0,1\}$ as values of the elements of the matrix (does not exist if there is correspondence) can be generalised by substituting the set $\{0,1\}$ by the interval $[0, 1]$. On taking this step, something so important for the mechanism of human thought such as <<nuances>> is obtained. Thus we arrive at a <<fuzzy relation>> such as:

	b_1	b_2		b_m
a_1	μ_{a_1, b_1}	μ_{a_1, b_2}	...	μ_{a_1, b_m}
a_2	μ_{a_2, b_1}	μ_{a_2, b_2}	...	μ_{a_2, b_m}
	...	...	...	...
a_n	μ_{a_n, b_1}	μ_{a_n, b_2}	...	μ_{a_n, b_m}

where $\mu_{ij} \in [0, 1]$ is the valuation of the pair (a_i, b_j), with $i = a_1, a_2, ..., a_n$, $j = b_1, b_2, ..., b_m$.

In a general event, the decision to invest in an object is based on a finite number of <<criteria>> or <<decision elements>> of a diverse nature which require, for their quantification, different measurement or valuation units. The consideration of these aspects which have an influence in the decision to invest will give rise to the <<E_1 set of criteria>>, which in our matrix could be given by the elements of rows $\{a_1, a_2, ..., a_n\}$.

Normally, these criteria belong to different spheres and are collected by means of many information channels. This means that in a very general case, there is a high degree of heterogeneity in them. Thus, and only as an example, as criteria for decision on the acquisition of industrial equipment, elements could be considered such as the life of the machine, its degree of capitalisation, financial conditions, economic viability, quality of technical assistance, etc.

These criteria are useful in order to <<reason>> on the convenience of acquiring a number, also finite, of <<investment objects>> in order to obtain the desired objective or objectives.. Thus appears the second set of elements $E_2 = \{b_1, b_2, ..., b_m\}$ which correspond to the columns of the fuzzy relation.

The degree to which each object complies with the respective criteria, will be expressed by the values k_{ij}, $i = 1, 2, ..., n, j = 1, 2, ..., m$.

But the concept of relation acquires special significance when it appears as involved in the notion of a graph. Mathematically a graph is defined from a bipartition of a product of n sets. Thus, given the referentials $E_1, E_2, ..., E_z$, if a product is obtained as follows:

$$P = E_1 \times E_2 \times \cdots \times E_z$$

and a bipartition of P is found:

$$G \subset P \quad , \quad \bar{G} \subset P$$

in such a way that:

$$G \cup \bar{G} = P \quad , \quad G \cap \bar{G} = \emptyset$$

it is said that both G and $\bar{G}$ are graphs of P.

If, as we have done before, only 2 sets are considered for E_1, and E_2, a graph is obtained which expresses the existing fuzzy relation. The advantage of working with the theory of graphs is obvious, as it permits the use of a large number of properties which are inherent to this theory, it facilitates presentation and simplifies developments.

One of the most frequent stages arising in the process of multi-criteria investment selection, consists in carrying out a grouping of the investment objects possessing similar properties. Within each group we will arrive at, then, the indifference between all the objects making it up. Let us now develop this idea. We start off with a fuzzy relation such as:

$$[\underset{\sim}{R}] = \begin{array}{c|c|c|c|c|} & b_1 & b_2 & & b_m \\ a_1 & \mu_{11} & \mu_{12} & \cdots & \mu_{1m} \\ a_2 & \mu_{21} & \mu_{22} & \cdots & \mu_{2m} \\ & \cdots & \cdots & \cdots & \cdots \\ a_n & \mu_{n1} & \mu_{n2} & \cdots & \mu_{nm} \end{array}$$

With the object of doing the study[21] of $[\underset{\sim}{R}]$, it is customary to breakdown this fuzzy relation in α-cuts, by a determined system, for example the hendecadarian system, where $\alpha = 0, 0.1, 0.2, ..., 0.9, 1$, and a level is selected which is called the threshold from which the existence of affinity is accepted. This system has given rise to the birth of the so-called <<theory of affinities>>[22].

Having established one or in the event several thresholds, a boolean matrix $[B]$ is obtained from:

$$\mu_{ij} \geqslant u \quad : \quad \beta_{ij} = 1$$
$$\mu_{ij} < u \quad : \quad \beta_{ij} = 0$$

where u is the established threshold and β_{ij} the elements of the boolean matrix $[B]$.

To put it into other words, when the valuation of a row of the fuzzy relation $[\underset{\sim}{L}]$ is equal to or greater than the corresponding threshold, it is considered that the investment object has the required level of the considered criteria.

Treatment of matrix $[B]$ can be done starting out from the notion of a Galois lattice.

As is well known, there exist an important variety of algebraic structures in the form of lattices, which correspond to peculiarities of their configuration. One of the most interesting for the handling of groupings by affinities is due to Evariste Galois.

The properties of Galois lattices give rise to maximum sub-relations, which permit bringing to light in an explicit manner how all the <<affinities>> are situated, taking into account criteria and objects, that is to say the elements of one set in relation to those from the other. The use for grouping of the investment objects is doubtless. According to the importance assigned to each criterion, in relation to the others, the decision can be taken to invest in one of the objects from each group (to be determined).

The consideration of diverse decision criteria means, in a general hypothesis, the investing subject considers each of these at a different level, that is to say that implicitly or explicitly an order of preference takes place. In this sense, it can be stated that if there is a modification in the order of the criteria, a change in the selection of the investment object may follow suit.

There is a wide range of techniques which are suitable for materialising the different appreciation that the investing subject has of the various criteria, from the classical forms of weighting through the notion of the mean, to the processes of subjective comparison of each one of the criteria with all the others, which we have used with interesting practical results[23].

For this brief summary on the problem of harmonious grouping let us say that, there is in existence a particular assumption of the concept of affinity. That is the notion of similarity. When the sets E_1 and E_2 are such that $E_1 = E_2 = E$, the graph obtained of the product $P = E \times E$ this is a <<graph in the sense of Berge>> which will reflect a relation of the referential with itself. The representation of this type of graph in the arrow form and the matrix form has given rise to an interesting development of certain relations, such as that of <<resemblance>> and <<similarity>>.

In effect, when a fuzzy graph expressed in the matrix form represents the relations of resemblance:

	a_1	a_2		a_n
a_1	μ_{11}	μ_{12}	$\cdots$	μ_{1n}
a_2	μ_{21}	μ_{22}	$\cdots$	μ_{2n}
	$\cdots$	$\cdots$	$\cdots$	$\cdots$
a_n	μ_{n1}	μ_{n2}	$\cdots$	μ_{nn}

where $\mu_{ij} \in [0, 1]$, $i, j = 1, 2, \ldots, n$; $\mu_{ij} = 1$, $i = j$; $\mu_{ij} = \mu_{ji}$.

Initially the concept of resemblance acquired, with the development of the mathematics of uncertainty, special importance, above all for processes of comparison for the effects of groupings or separations. But, on many occasions, the concept of resemblance is not useful for grouping, as a consequence of the non-existence of the property of transitivity. In effect, if one has available a group of concrete or abstract objects, A, B, C, and the following is complied with, that is to say A and B resemble each other at a certain level, as well as B and C resemble each other, also at this level, it does not mean to say that the specified level has to be had by A and C. For this to be complied with the intervention of the property of <<transitivity>> is necessary.

From a graph of resemblances (reflexive and symmetric) transitive sub-graphs can be obtained which express <<relations of similarity>> between some of the elements of the referential forming the largest possible <<group>> with similar characteristics: these are the so-called maximum sub-relations of similarity. For obtaining them certain algorithms have been drawn up among which should be pointed out that of Pichat[24] and that of Lafosse-Marin-Kaufmann[25].

The presentation of results by means of Galois lattices, permits expressing in a visual manner all the affinities existing at the considered level. From this point onward to obtaining an order for the effects of a decision is only a very short step. The variation of the lattice as there are changes in the selected level, gives rise to an interesting panorama of information which is particularly useful for decisions on investments.

Let us now move on to the last of the concepts that we consider as important. This is the concept of order. We have made a special mention of the concept of order because, in a social and economic system marked by uncertainty the concept of order occupies a privileged position for taking decisions. To order investment objects, the sources for their financing, the resources necessary for carrying the investment forward, ... is the prior step to taking decisions. When it is impossible to obtain a <<valued>> chart of objects, recourse is then made to a<<non-quantified order>> of the same and this may be sufficient for a rational decision.

The theory of graphs supplies interesting schemes for establishing a relation of order. The concept of <<ordinal function of a graph>> is in this case significant. In effect, if the<<heavily connected>> graphs are excepted which, represented by matrices with only one kind of equivalency, do not permit finding an order among their vertices, all the other assumptions allow for an ordering.

Thus if we assume[26] the case of a graph with no circuits, that is to say that each vertex is at one and the same time a type of equivalence, then the order by levels is practically immediate. In fact let us assume a graph such as the following (Figure 1.4):

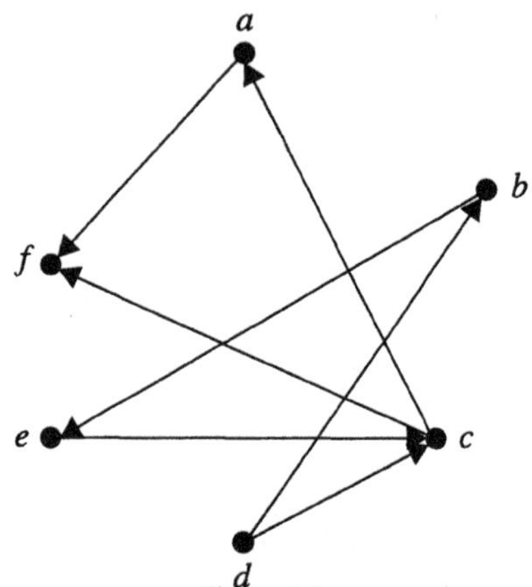

Figure 1.4.

If the set of objects on which the decision to invest may be taken is {*a*, *b*, *c*, *d*, *e*, *f*} the order of preference will be (figure 1.5):

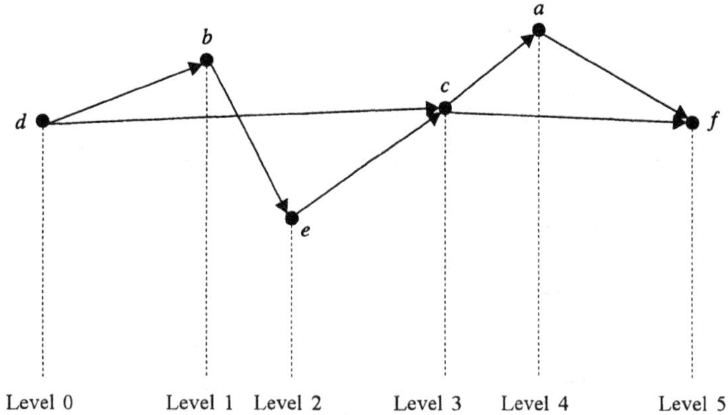

Figure 1.5.

Now, when the graph is not particularly connected and each element does not by itself form a kind of equivalence, the possibility exists of breaking it down into heavily related sub-graphs or types of equivalency which, some of them at least, include several elements (investment objects). This has opened the door to ordering when there are no vertices, at least of sets of vertices (which make up each type of equivalence or heavily connected sub-graphs). For this there are available algorithms, among which we would highlight that of Malgrange[27].

Once all the kinds of equivalencies or heavily connected sub-graphs are obtained, the most important stumbling block which could avoid ordering has been overcome. Now, when it is impossible to order vertices by the existence of circuits, it is possible to order by kinds of equivalence, that is to say, of groups of real or mental objects. Once again we are dealing with the traditional problem of obtaining the <<ordinal function of a graph>>.

Let us now look at the following graph that is not heavily connected (figure 1.6):

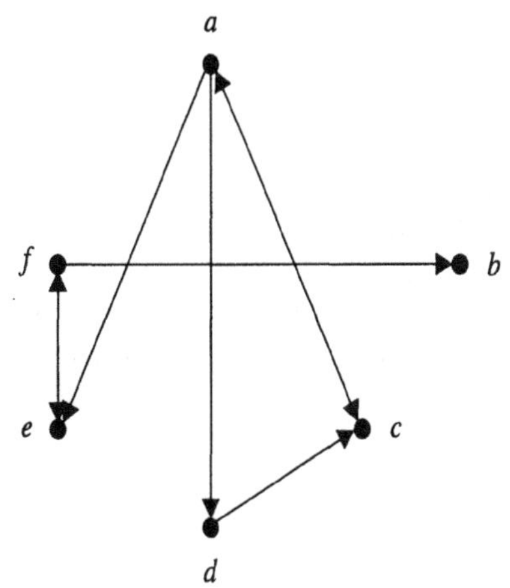

Figure 1.6.

From establishment of the heavily connected sub-graphs and having found the following order among them we arrive at (figure 1.7):

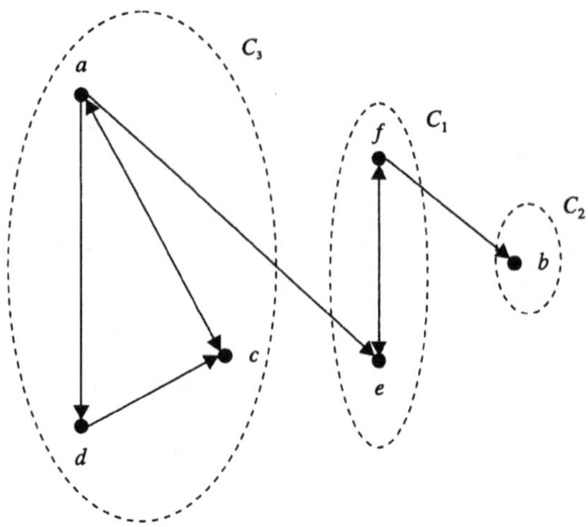

Figure 1.7.

Therefore we have been able to see, that the ordinal function can be found both for the kinds of equivalence and for the vertices, although in this latter case only in the event that in the graph no circuits exist. Also for this algorithms have been thought up, which are valid for both cases, since both the vertex and the class play the same role. We mention among these that of Kaufmann and Gil Aluja[28] on the one hand and that of Demoocrom[29] on the other.

We have mentioned certain concepts such as relation, grouping, resemblance, similarity, affinity, order..., but we could mention many others which have emerged in the new handling of the renewed theory of investment. They will appear throughout the subjects making up this work, in this way seeking a place in modern studies on the decision to invest.

REFERENCES

1 J.Gil Aluja: <<La incertidumbre en la economía y gestión de empresas>>, Proceedings of the IVth. Congress of the Spanish Association on Technology and Fuzzy Logic, Blanes, September 14, 1994, pages 9-14.

2 R. Barre: Prologue of the work by A. Kaufmann and J. Gil Aluja: *Técnicas operativas de gestión para el tratamiento de la incertidumbre*, Hispano Europea, Barcelona, 1987.

3 These ideas were expounded upon in J. Gil Aluja: <<Towards a new paradigm of investment selection in uncertainty>>. *Fuzzy Sets and Systems*.Vol 84, number 2, December 9, 1996, pages 187-197.

4 K. Popper: *La lógica de la investigación científica*, Tecnos, Madrid, 1971. The first edition of this work dates from 1934 and in it he inaugurates his philosophy of science, by formulating the well-known theory of falsibility.

5 Th. Khun: *La estructura de las revoluciones científicas*, Fondo de Cultura Económica, Madrid, 1981. This work was written in 1962 and it is one of the many works this author has written on this subject.

6 A. Kaufmann and J. Gil Aluja; *Introducción a la teoría de los subconjuntos borrosos a la gestión de las empresas*, Milladoiro, Santiago de Compostela, 1986.

7 J. Gil Aluja: <<Spre o noua paradigma a teoriei deciziei>>, acceptance speech into the Rumanian Academy, September 27, 1995, *Revista Académica*, Bucharest, October, pages 20-21.

8 J. Gil Aluja: <<Les approches connexionistes dans le changement du paradigme de la théorie de la décision>> À 3rd. International Meeting of ACSEG, Nantes, October 25,1996.

9 Observe the at least apparent contradiction which exists between the use of the term probability (even in the event of it being a subjective probability) with its strict axiomatic and the estimate of economic magnitudes which it is hoped appear in later periods.

10 See the work by F. Insolera: *Curso de matemática financiera y actuarial*, Aguilar, Madrid, 1950. The original Italian edition (2nd.ed) was published in 1937 under the title of: *Corso di matemática finanziaria*, although his first work on this subject dates from 1916.

11 We would like to point out, relative to this aspect, the works of A. Rodríguez, among which is found: *Matemática de la inversión*, Romargraf, Barcelona, 1983.

12 We should mention among these E. Schneider: *Teoría de la inversión, Cáculo de economicidad*. The first edition in German, entitled: *Wirtschaftlichkeitsrehnung*, dates from 1951. The Spanish edition is by Ateneo, Buenos Aires, 1956.

13 The words in italics are ours.

14 H. Boulding: *Análisis económico*, Rev. de Occidente, Madrid 1962, second edition page 81. The fragment written in italics is ours.

15 A. Kaufmann and J. Gil Aluja: *Introducción a la teoría de los subconjuntos borrosos a la gestión de las empresas*, Miladoiro, Santiago de Compostela, 1986, pages 76-83.

16 K. Popper: *La lógica de la investigación científica*, Tecnos, Madrid, 1962, page 141.

17 See for example our works: <<La selección de inversiones en base a criterios diversificados>>, Proceedings of the AEDEM Congress, Cáceres, June, 1994; <<Criterial Selection of investments within a context of uncertainty>>, Symposium Fuzzy Systems and Neural Networks, AMSE Press, Lyon, July, 1994, pages 83-93; <<Selección multicriterio de inversiones mediante retículos de Galois>> included in the work, Dirección de empresas en los noventa,Civitas, Madrid, 1995, pages 139-157.

18 A. Kaufmann and J. Gil Aluja: *Introducción a la teoria de los subconjuntos borrosos a la gestión de las empresas*, Milladoiro, Santiago de Compostela, 1986, pages 76-83.

19 J. Gil Aluja: <<El estudio dinámico de la selección de las inversiones>>, *Revista Técnica Contable*, February, 1967, pages 41-66.

20 P. Masse: *La elección de las inversiones*, Sagitario, Barcelona, 1963, page 7.

21 For effects of simplification we have substituted m_{a1b1} for m_{11}; μ_{a1b2} for m_{12}, ...

22 This theory was drawn up at the outset by A. Kaufmann and J. Gil Aluja: *Selection of affinities by means of fuzzy relations and galois lattices*, Porceedings of the Euro XI Congress O.R., Aachen, July 16-19, 1991.

23 J. Gil Aluja: <<Criterial Selection of investments within a context of uncertainty>>, Symposium Fuzzy & Neural Networks, AMSE Press, Lyon, July 1994, pages 83-93.

24 E. Pichat: *Algorithm for finding the maximal elements of a finite universal algebra, Inform Processing* 68 Publ., North Holland, 1969.

25 A. Kaufmann: *Modéles mathématiques pour la stimulation inventive*, Albin Michel, 1979, page 62.

26 The suggestive examples described below have been taken from J. Gil Lafuente: *Marketing para el próximo milenio. Técnicas comerciales para el tratamiento de la incertidumbre*, Pirámide, Madrid, 1997, chapter 3.

27 Y. Malgrange: <<Décomposition d'un graphe en sous-graphes fortement connexes maximaux>>. Cie. Machines Bull internal memo, 1967.

28 A. Kaufmann and J. Gil Aluja: *Técnicas de gestión de empresa. Previsiones, decisiones y estrategias*, Pirámide, Madrid, 1992, pages 351-374.

29 M. Demoocrom: Work submitted to Compagnie de Machines Bull, 1964.

2 Programming investment activity

Classical programming techniques

Investment processes include a set of tasks or activities that can be done successively or simultaneously, normally signifying a certain cost which, at some given time or another, will be converted into a payment. One of the initial problems to arise, is when the possibility of investing in an investment object crops up, refers to the duration of the investment process. In this sense what is intended is that the total duration of the project will not extend beyond a determined date. In order to reach this objective it would appear convenient to watch the activities which make up the project carefully so that they take place at the most opportune moment.

Now then, in an investment programme there normally exist a large number of tasks for which on many occasions it is awkward, if not to say the least, difficult, to carry out a permanent and exhaustive control. In reality it is frequent to see for this that the experience of specialists on the subject leads them to carry out a follow-up <<by exception>>, in the sense of taking into account, for these effects, only those points which they consider as special or <<critical>>. But, if one of the characteristics of the investment process is its singularity or exceptionality, experience or routine can be fatally deceptive. The incorporation of new techniques has all the time become more convenient as these allow for establishing which are the tasks requiring special treatment from a perspective of time.

Nevertheless, the requirements of time are not the only things that prevail in the investment process. The mere fact that the carrying out of a task requires a payment is sufficient for the introduction of an aspect of financial management. Throughout the development of the investment activity certain means of payment will be necessary in order to cover the payment that any task carried out incurs. Investment involves, therefore, a programming of financial needs that must be covered by means of ones own or external capital.

Time-cost, or time-payment to put this in another way, makes up the two pillars on which the argument of the programming process is built. At this point would it not be possible to ask what are the techniques that economic science proposes for giving an adequate answer to these problems?

If we go back some way in history, it will be seen that during a long period that commenced with our century, the programming instrument most used was the GANTT[1] diagram. It is basically used in production processes, with the object of knowing the time when events take place and the speed in which a task is carried out. Its object then is to establish a relation between events and the time in which they take place. There can be no doubt as to the advantages which this technique provided at the time, since to the clarity of representation of the project is added exactitude and precision, the fact that it has a synthetic nature and allows for perfect control of activities and, therefore facilitates the detection of any eventual deviations between estimates and execution[2].

But in spite of the doubtless advances made with the Gantt diagram, its use decreased as companies grew in dimension and their surroundings made its handling more complex. One of its principal defects consists in the fact that the diagram does not show the interdependence existing between different activities. <<The mere fact that they may have been programmed in overlapping or simultaneous times, does not necessarily mean that they are related or are interdependent>>[3].

Perhaps the problem of interdependence was the reason why at the beginning of the 60's a group of techniques known generally by the name of PERT acquired notoriety, although since then there has been a wide range of variations such as CPM (Critical Path Method), ALTAI (Analisis Livellamiento e Tempificazione Automatice e Integrato), among others.

The letters PERT correspond to the expression <<Program Evaluation & Review Technique>> and also <<Program Evaluation and Research Task>>, both being accepted indistinctly. This technique was created and used in order to reduce the duration of the POLARIS (American nuclear submarines) ballistic project by the Navy Special Projects Office, Aircraft Corporation and consulting firm Booz-Allen and Hamilton.

The mathematical basis of PERT is arrived at by the theory of graphs, which as is well known, constitutes an interesting part of the theory of sets. A graph is perfectly identified by a set of vertices and the interconnections existing between them.

If the elements taking part in a programme: events and activities, are capable of being represented by knots (vertices) and arrows (arcs), then the result is a graph in the arrow[4] form that would constitute an adequate expression of a project. In fact, every project is made up of a set of tasks or activities, which are framed within certain events or incidents that constitute the commencement and end of the same. On many occasions, the activities are represented by the arcs and the events by the vertices. But it does not always have to be this way.

Now, for a graph to be considered as a PERT it is necessary for it to comply with certain requirements[5] that can be summarised as follows:

1. Existence of a finite number of vertices (finite graph).
2 A single initial vertex and a single final vertex.
3. Non-existence of circuits (all the classes of equivalence possess a single vertex)
4. Every arc forms the part of a path leading from the initial vertex to the final vertex.

When in an investment project the activities making it up are known and it is possible to establish, for each one of the latter, when they are susceptible to being carried out simultaneously or, on the contrary, when commencement of one requires another or others to have finalised, the construction of a network of interconnections, that is to say a graph, appears to be obvious. The concept of interconnection arises, therefore, as an outstanding element in the structure of the graph. Thus, in order to form a network it is necessary to know the order in which the activities should be carried out and any parallelism that may exist between them. At this stage in the description of the subject, it would appear convenient to direct our attention to the fact that, an activity can nearly always be broken down into others, in accordance with the degree of detail that may be required for effects of analysis and control. This statement leads to the conclusion of the possible construction of several PERT in order to represent one and the same project. The degree of subdivision will be determined by the number of elemental activities which may have been established, and these, in turn of the person to whom they are directed and of the specific objective which it is desired to reach.

All that has been mentioned before takes us to the first phase of programming consisting in the construction of the network. For this, it is convenient to establish the outline of the project, determining the principal operations required for this. Following on this the analysis of each one of these in order to fix the specific activities taking place, which will be represented by the arcs of the graph. Determining the specific activities is equivalent to deciding on the extension of the PERT.

With the object of facilitating the shaping of the relations existing between activities, that is to say in order to form the architecture of the network, it is particularly useful to take any given activity and answer the following questions:

- Which are the activities that follow on immediately after the one under study.
- Which are the activities that immediately precede the one under study
- Which are the activities that can be carried out simultaneously with the one under study.

Any activity, represented by an arc of the graph, should be able to be identified in an unequivocal manner, so it is customary to describe the same by means of the two vertices which limit it. These, in turn, are identified, each one of them, either with the letter (*A*, *B*, *C*, ...) or with the whole number (*0*, *1*, *2*, ...). When a numerical identification of the vertices is adopted, it is established that a vertex (incident or event) prior to an arc (activity or task) should have a lower number to a later vertex. Thus, an activity represented by the following arc (figure 2.1):

Figure 2.1.

expresses that it has its origin in vertex (event) m and its end in vertex (event) n. It will be read as arc (m, n) and $m < n$ should be complied with.

The second phase of programming would be the numbering of the vertices of the graph. For this we have proposed a very simple algorithm consisting of:

1. The lowest number, which can be one, is placed at the single initial vertex.
2. Draw a line for all the arcs leaving the initial vertex.
3. Find the vertex/vertices in which all the arcs arriving are marked and are assigned the following number/s.
4. When there are several vertices to which all the arcs arriving are marked consecutive numbering is assigned in an arbitrary order.
5. Continue with these criteria until all vertices of the graph are completed.

This simple algorithm allows for numbering in accordance with the requirements of the PERT. Let us now take a look at an example (figure 2.2.):

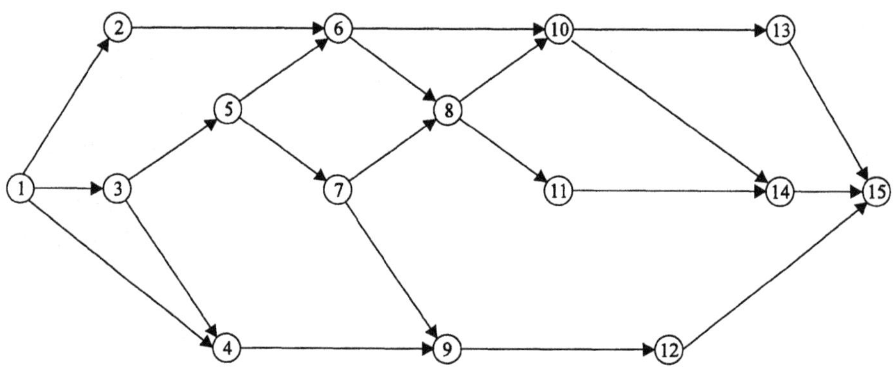

Figure 2.2.

Having finalised the vertex numbering process, which automatically includes the arcs, since these are described by the vertex from which they leave and the vertex to which they arrive, we pass on to the third phase relative to the assignment of the EARLIEST times for each vertex starting out from the time estimate for each activity.

If we establish zero as the EARLIEST time for the initial vertex, the time for the following vertex/vertices to which a single arc arrives will be equal to the time for the activity represented by the arc which joins the initial vertex with the one under study. Therefore for example, when the time estimated for activity (1, 2) is 20, the EARLIEST time of vertex 2 will be $0 + 20 = 20$.

Now, to any given vertex it is possible that more than one arc may arrive. In this case the EARLIEST time for this vertex is taken as the HIGHEST value of the sum of times for each of the arcs and the time corresponding to the vertex from which it leaves. Let us look at an example. If the EARLIEST time of vertex 2 is 20, that for arc (2, 6) is 12, that for vertex 5 is 26 and for arc (5,6) is 4, then we will have (figure 2.3):

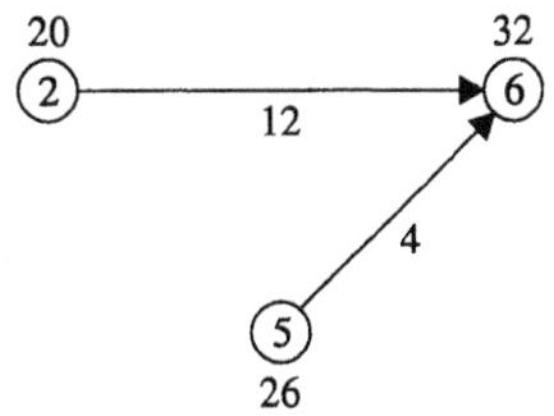

EARLIEST time for vertex 6 = Max {20 + 12, 26 + 4} = 32

Figure 2.3.

The assignment of times to each of the activities (arcs) can be done by means of crisp, probable or uncertain numbers, with which the duration of the project will be established with exactitude, by means of probabilities, or intervals, confidence triplets, etc.

The fourth phase consists in the assignment of the AT THE LATEST times to each vertex starting out from the time in which it is really desired that the whole project be finished. This is the time established as the AT THE LATEST time in the final vertex. Therefore this assignment is initiated by the last incident and from it one moves back to the beginning, following the reverse numbering of the vertices. It is normal, although not necessary, that the EARLIEST time and the AT THE LATEST time of the last vertex coincide since if a project can finish in x periods it is required to finish within this time limit.

Let us now continue with our example and assume that the EARLIEST time and the AT THE LATEST time of the final vertex 15 is 200, and that for carrying out activities (13,15), (14, 15) and (12, 15) are, respectively 10, 8 and 6, the AT THE LATEST time for vertex 13 will be 190, for vertex 14 it will be 192 and for vertex 12, 194. In this way it can be said that the AT THE LATEST time of the vertex is equal to the next one less the value of the arc (activity) linking them.

But when we want to establish the AT THE LATEST time of a vertex from which more than one arc originates, then we calculate for each arc the difference between the AT THE LATEST time of the vertex of arrival and of the corresponding arc linking them, choosing the lowest value. Let us look at an example. Leaving vertex 10 are two arcs (10, 13) and (10, 14). If the AT THE LATEST time for vertex 13 is 190, for the activity (10, 13) is 18, the AT THE

LATEST time for vertex 14 is 192 and for activity (10,14) 25, then we will have the following (figure 2.4):

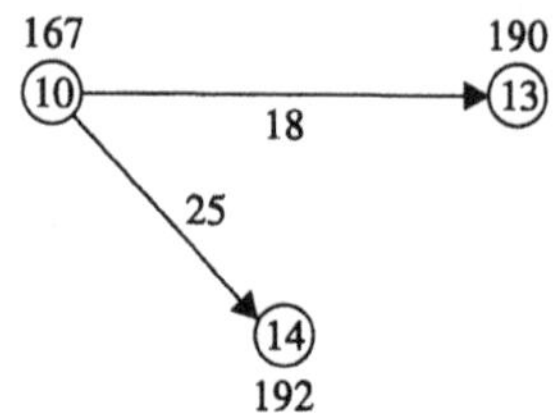

The AT THE LATEST time for vertex 10 = Mín {190 − 18, 192 − 25} = 167

Figure 2.4.

The assignment to each vertex of a time or <<margin>> EARLIEST and a AT THE LATEST time allows for the incorporation of the notion of <<floating time>> for an incident (vertex) as a difference between both times, with which we arrive at the fifth phase. Determination of the floating times for the vertices of the graph is simple (simple subtraction). Their significance is important as they show the maximum accumulated time by which the incident can be delayed without which, by doing this, stretching out the project beyond the AT THE LATEST time of the final vertex, also, assuming, that the later activities will be executed within the foreseen time limits.

When equality is established between the EARLIEST and AT THE LATEST times in the final vertex, then there will be a set of vertices with zero floating time. The path joining these vertices is called the <<critical path>> and the corresponding tasks require special care. When a non-zero floating time exists for the final vertex, the vertices of the critical path have the same floating time as the floating time for the whole project.

With the object of making visualisation of the information relative to the vertices of the graph (incidents of the project) easier, we propose dividing the representative circle into three parts (figure 2.5):

Figure 2.5.

The number of vertex r will be placed in the lower part, the EARLIEST time t_p in the upper left and the AT THE EARLIEST time t_d in the upper right. In this way, the difference between the figures in the upper part gives us the floating time for the event. In order to make this description easier, we are going to continue with our example by assigning exact times in an arbitrary way to each arc of the graph:

Arc	*Time*	*Arc*	*Time*	*Arc*	*Time*
(1, 2)	6	(5, 6)	4	(8, 11)	10
(1, 3)	4	(5, 7)	10	(9, 12)	14
(1, 4)	7	(6, 8)	2	(10, 13)	1
(2, 6)	8	(6, 10)	8	(10, 14)	5
(3, 4)	1	(7, 8)	4	(11, 14)	8
(3, 5)	5	(7, 9)	5	(12, 15)	6
(4, 9)	12	(8, 10)	1	(13, 15)	3
				(14, 15)	4

Let us now reconstruct the PERT we presented previously, with the new time established for each activity, by placing these over each arc and presenting the vertices with all their information (figure 2.6):

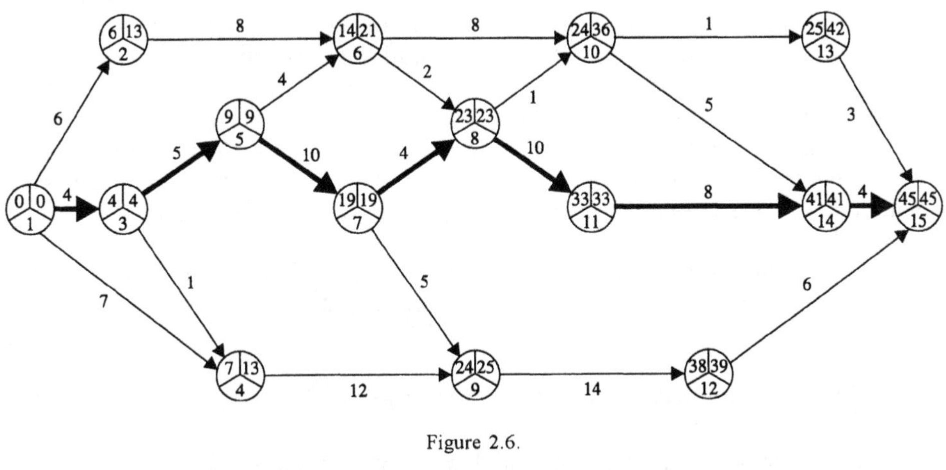

Figure 2.6.

We have drawn those arcs (activities) linking the critical vertices (events) with a thicker line, in this way highlighting the <<critical path>>. These activities will require careful watching, because the delay in only one unit of time in one of them, also means the delay at the end of the programme of one unit in time.

We are now going to leave the technical aspects of the PERT-time, which we will pick up again in the following section, to make a very brief reference to the cost of the activities.

It has been seen that the execution of the activities which go to make up a programme normally means the passing of time and this signifies cost (certain activities commonly known as fictitious, which have as their object the applicability of the graph, are excepted). The existence of these two important economic parameters has lead us to believe in the possibility of the use of the structure of the graph, suitable for programming and time control of the project, in order to carry out an analysis of the costs of the elements which go to make it up.

There are several alternatives arising relative to costs, according to the objective it is desired to attain. Those who have handled this problem in depth have suggested certain models, the application of which has given us some interesting results. We are going to limit ourselves at this point to mention two aspects that are, perhaps, the most frequently used in specialised works. On the one hand, in those works intended for immediate practical use: it is considered that costs (and in the even their payment) are independent or proportional to the duration of each task, it is assumed they are known with certainty, by means of a law of probability or through an uncertain number and they accumulate throughout all the sub-paths of the graph, right up to the final vertex. In this way we have available an instrument that allows for estimating <<ex ante>> the financial needs and for later control. But it has also been considered that the PERT graph could be useful for obtaining optimisation (minimisation) of all costs borne by the programme. And so interesting models[6] have appeared which show that on many occasions starting from a functional relation time-cost in such a way that when the attempt to reduce the duration of an activity is greater, the cost of the same will be higher. The notion arises of a normal and accelerated programme and based on the floating times of the non-critical activities an attempt is made to carry out the project in the established time reducing the cost to the minimum, assuming the risk that new critical activities may appear. Linear parametric programming has been the frequent recourse for finding a solution to this problem.

We are not going to dwell any further on these technical aspects since out interest is centred on programming an investment project.

Handling of an investment programme

The investment process, considered in its widest sense, includes a whole range of interconnected activities, which go from the moment that the <<light is lit>> for the need of an investment object or of placing a monetary mass, right up to when the object commences its normal operation or the financial means have begun to give a response by collecting the first interest payment. Obviously that after this phase, the monetary currents of collections and payments arising from the decision to invest, follow on or may follow on. But let us consider that these activities form a part of the normal financial tasks of the company and their follow-up and control is more an act of financial management than an investment. If one thing particularly stands out in the investment process it is its singularity compared to the regularity of any other process. In any event, we do not question acceptance of this principal. What we are interested in highlighting is the statement that the process if formed by a <<set>> of activities and the <<interconnection>> between the same, because definition of both elements will allow us to define a graph.

In effect, given a set E, if the product set $P = E \times E$ and a bi-partition G is made such that:

$$G \subset P = E \times E$$

then G and also $\bar{G}$ are a graph.

Graph G is then defined by the pair formed by the set of elements E which form it and the corresponding connection Γ which exists between them. This can be written as:

$$G = (E, \Gamma)$$

The <<signal>> has now been lit and the investment process commences with the search, by the different <<actors>> of the company, for information that will serve as the basis for the eventual selection of the type of investment. Each of the actors can study one or more markets for assets, machinery or financial markets, in which case there may be an overlapping between several agents (actors). Once the corresponding information is available they meet with the object of deciding, in a specific and individualised manner or by groups if necessary, which are the objects on which, because of their technical characteristics, the decision to invest may fall. With this the first activity of the programme has taken place. Let us assume that it has been considered suitable to invest in machinery for the manufacture of certain products.

Every investment in production equipment includes, principally, three types of activities; financial, productive and market. Therefore it will be in these three directions that the tasks of the programme will continue in a simultaneous manner.

From a monetary perspective, the possibilities of the financial market will be investigated in order to ascertain what the external capacity is for arriving at the means for defraying the requirements of the project. This activity not always requires a significant period of time for carrying it out, since many firms are permanently aware of their possibilities in this field. The knowledge, therefore, of outside or auto- financing capacity, will be an invaluable piece of information for determining the financial viability of an investment project. Also the knowledge of the financial products existing in the market, will be sufficient for commencing steps tending toward obtaining external funds, which later will be necessary for defraying payments arising from the decision to invest.

As is sufficiently well known, the availability of external financial means may partially take place throughout a certain period of time or at one single instant. An adequate financial strategy should allow for lightening the burden and therefore reduce the price of the project.

From the commercial point of view, activities commence with the relative market survey of the needs of the manufactured product with the object of the investment. Once the sales centres are known, it will be necessary to determine the capacity for absorbing the product to be manufactured in the market. With this it is possible, on the one hand, to estimate an invoicing figure and, on the other, commence studying distribution and sales channels, in this way continuing in the strict sense with the commercial activity, which in fact will have its continuation, once the investment object (equipment) is selected, with the approval of those commercial actions tending toward the setting up of a distribution and sales network. Estimating and consequent invoicing proposal then is the second support, in conjunction with financing, on which the selection study of the investment object is based.

From the technical-productive point of view, activities commence with the search in the equipment market for the investment objects that are suitable for carrying out the foreseen necessary productive activity. This task will lead to the individualised determination on the investment objects on which the decision to invest may fall.

The knowledge of the financial, market and technical-productive possibilities should be sufficient elements for carrying out the survey which, once approved by the corresponding executive levels of the company, will allow commencement of the action phase within the three already mentioned spheres, financial, commercial and technical-productive. Therefore, the <<analysis and survey>> stage, prior to the <<action>> stage has been covered. The executives commence action.

While the financial people take steps for obtaining funds with which to make the payments arising from the decision to invest, and marketing set up or organise the distribution and sales network, in order to adapt it to the incorporation of the products manufactured with the investment object, those responsible for the technical-productive activity commence the work tending towards installation and start up of the investment object (equipment). For this they direct their attention to three particular areas: selection of the personnel to be in charge of the machine and their later training, drawing up the purchase order for the machine for its later reception, and also drawing up the orders for works and installations, with the consequent jobs that will allow them to set up the machine in its final place. Once installed and duly connected with the corresponding power inlets, testing the different prototypes can commence.

If we adopt as a working hypothesis the fact that payment for the investment object, as well as costs arising from the financial, commercial and technical-productive activities, take place once the machine is installed, the commencement of tests will coincide with the need to have the external financial means available. We could ask ourselves at this point what could be the real validity of this hypothesis. Well, although this is only a working hypothesis, we have seen, throughout our professional life, that it is not too far removed from reality. There are many companies which assign part of their own funds to finance the study and handling phases, and leave outside financing to totally or partially cover payments necessary for the payment of the investment object. And this is even truer still if we take into account the fact that many of the study and handling tasks are carried out by company personnel and therefore their cost does not imply the payment of additional amounts more than sporadically or partially, it even being difficult to make an exact estimate of the same. It is obvious, however, that other hypotheses can be made, adoption of which would not lessen the validity of the scheme we are proposing.

Having made this observation, let us get back to the main point of our exposition to finalise by saying, once testing has been done, and the specific products for distribution and selling selected on the one hand, and the commercial network set up, the product is now ready for being sent out into the market for its sale and later payment. We can now consider the cycle which commenced with the <<signal>> of the need to invest as closed.

Throughout this short story, we have insisted on the possible simultaneity and successiveness of activities or tasks of which the investment project is made up. The objective of this insistence is to facilitate the construction of an arrow form graph representing the structure of the project in a coherent fashion.

Below we have shown a PERT graph which has been drawn following the above indications, and also establishing the corresponding numbering of the vertices (figure 2.7).

The setting up of a programme relative to an investment project normally seeks two objectives: time and money. The first of these, seeks the carrying out of the project in the shortest possible time compatible, obviously, with the carrying out of the tasks which comprise it at the desired quality level, but taking advantage of the possibilities of carrying out activities simultaneously whenever possible. The start up of a control system should allow for follow-up during the whole process, thus avoiding disagreeable surprises during the latter and final stages of the project. With the second, what is desired is the knowledge, as reliable as possible, of the total cost of the process and also of the rhythm with which payments will take place, and in this way, to be able to estimate cash requirements at all times. We are conscious of the difference existing between cost and payment, but a correct organisation of the programme is sufficient for arriving at a good idea as to when one and the other should take place.

We are now going to pass on to the time study of the project. For this, we will assume that an expert for all activities, or several experts, each one competent in one or several activities, express their opinion on the duration of the same by means of an uncertain number which, in order to simplify matters, they choose as a confidence interval. In this way we are entering into the realm of uncertainty.

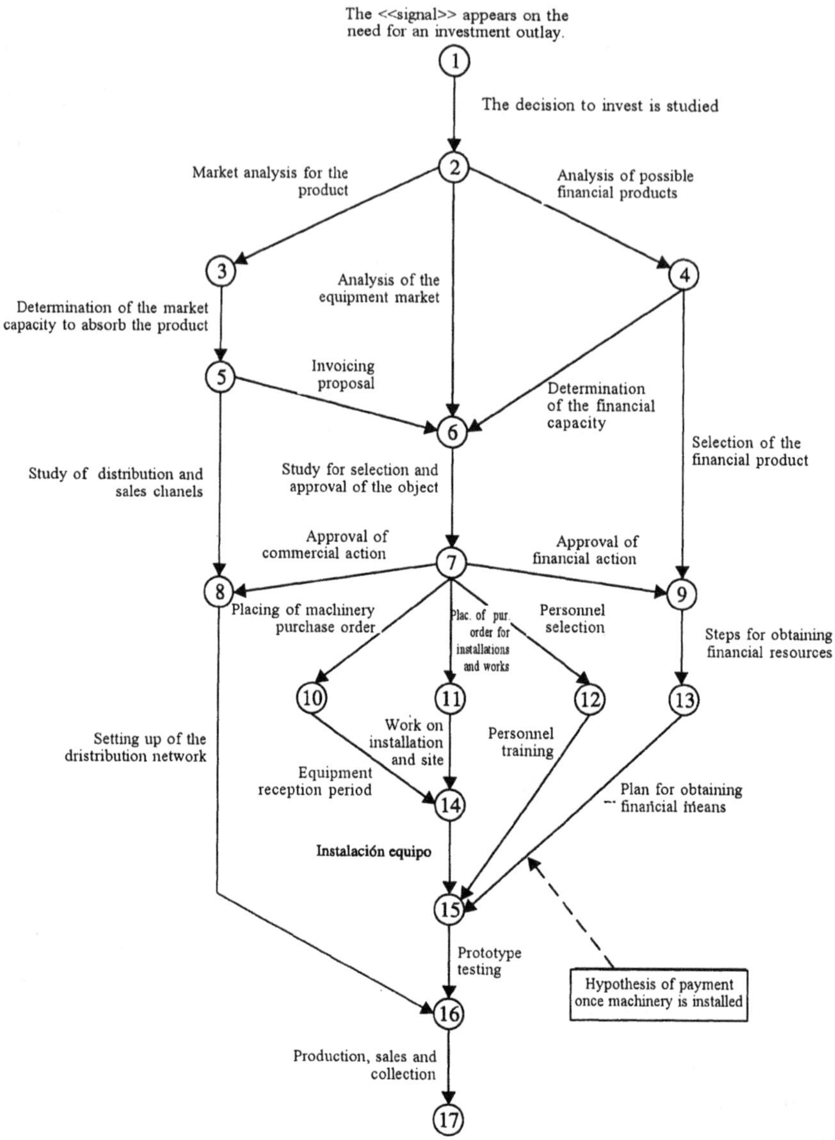
The <<signal>> appears on the need for an investment outlay.
1
The decision to invest is studied
2
Market analysis for the product
Analysis of possible financial products
3
4
Analysis of the equipment market
Determination of the market capacity to absorb the product
5
Invoicing proposal
Determination of the financial capacity
6
Selection of the financial product
Study of distribution and sales chanels
Study for selection and approval of the object
Approval of commercial action
Approval of financial action
7
8
9
Placing of machinery purchase order
Plac. of pur. order for installations and works
Personnel selection
Steps for obtaining financial resources
10
11
12
13
Setting up of the dristribution network
Work on installation and site
Personnel training
Equipment reception period
14
Plan for obtaining financial means
Instalación equipo
15
Prototype testing
Hypothesis of payment once machinery is installed
16
Production, sales and collection
17

Figure 2.7.

As a mere didactic example, we have reproduced below the results obtained for the consultation. The numbers in brackets show an unmistakable activity, from its vertices of origin and arrival.

Arc	*Valuation*	*Arc*	*Valuation*	*Arc*	*Valuation*	*Arc*	*Valuation*
(1, 2)	[3, 4]	(2, 3)	[6, 8]	(2, 4)	[3, 5]	(2, 6)	[10, 14]
(3, 5)	[12, 15]	(4, 6)	[2, 4]	(4, 9)	[5, 6]	(5, 6)	[1, 3]
(5, 8)	[14, 20]	(6, 7)	[15, 18]	(7, 8)	[2, 3]	(7, 9)	[2, 3]
(7, 10)	[1, 2]	(7, 11)	[1, 2]	(7, 12)	[20, 28]	(8, 16)	[30, 34]
(9, 13)	[8, 10]	(10, 14)	[32, 36]	(11, 14)	[16, 18]	(12, 15)	[20, 26]
(13, 15)	[10, 15]	(14, 15)	[8, 12]	(15, 16)	[6, 8]	(16, 17)	[12, 14]

In accordance with the previous section, and with the object of making the EARLIEST and AT THE LATEST times visible at each vertex of the graph, we are going to divide the representative circle into three parts, in order to identify the number of the vertex, the EARLIEST time and the AT THE LATEST time. For greater clarity, beside each arrow representing an activity (arc of the graph), the interval estimating the duration of the same will be noted down.

As is well known, the option of an interval as an uncertain number representative of the duration of each activity, has given rise to different ways of resolving the problem of estimating the AT THE LATEST and THE EARLIEST times of a graph[7]. Taking into account the end we are seeking, on this occasion we have chosen a scheme known as the traffic-light method[8]. For applying this method, we will proceed to separate each interval, taking from it, on the one hand, the lower extremes and, on the other, the upper extremes, representing, respectively, the optimist hypothesis (all activities take place in the shortest possible time) and the pessimist hypothesis (all activities take place in the longest time). This is equivalent to considering two graphs with the same architecture and numbering, but with different EARLIEST and AT THE LATEST times. In this way we will arrive at the most optimistic and the most pessimistic graphs.

For assignment of the AT THE LATEST times, as is normal but not unavoidable, we will choose for the finalisation time for the project, the same as the EARLIEST time corresponding to the last vertex. In this way critical events will have a floating time equal to zero. On the following pages we have presented the representative graphs for the optimist position (figure 2.8) and the pessimist position (figure 2.9).

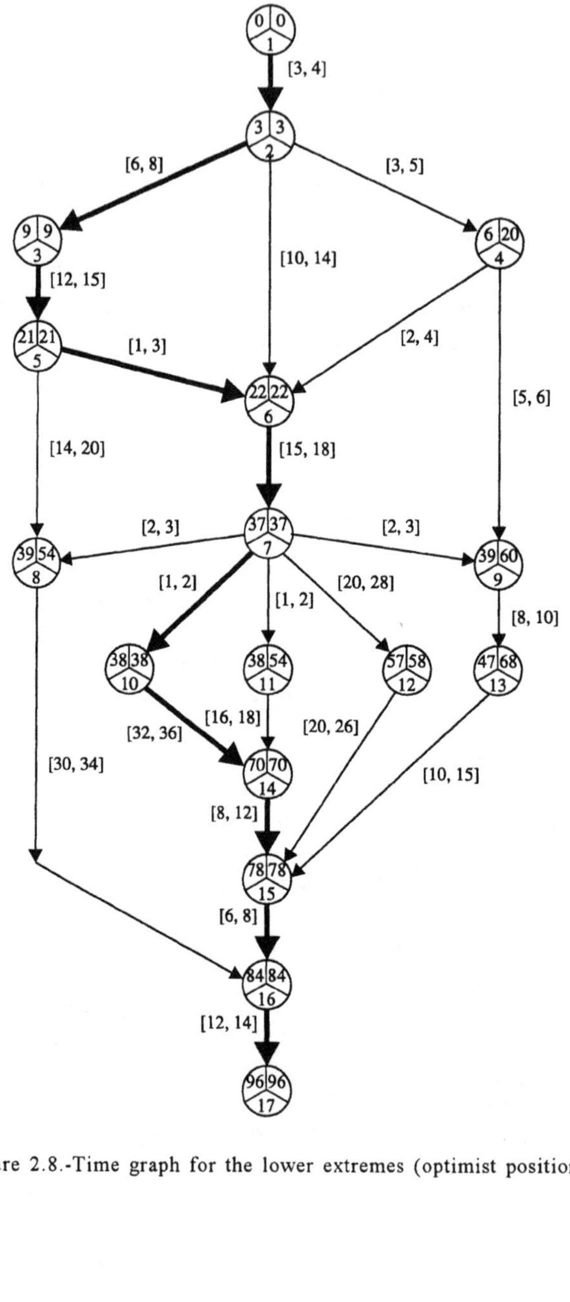

Figure 2.8.-Time graph for the lower extremes (optimist position).

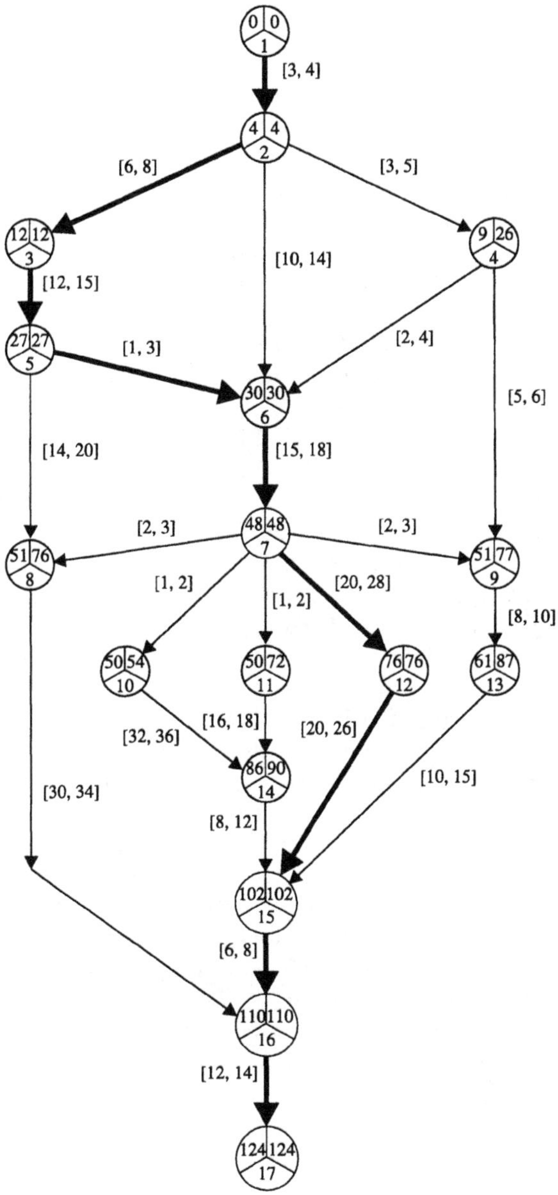

Figure 2.9.-Time graph for the upper extremes (pessimist position).

Bearing these graphs in mind we can now make certain considerations, among which we would point out the one relative to the existence of a <<critical path>> in the optimist position, which in a part of its path differs from the pessimist position. If, as is known, the activities to be found on the critical path are those which require special care when it is desired that the project finishes in the established time, the important question now crops up to determine which of these should be the object of special control, those of one extreme or the other. For some perhaps, the reply would appear to be obvious: of we align ourselves with the optimists, it will be certain ones; but if we align ourselves with the pessimist then it will be others; if we position ourselves in an intermediate situation, that is in a cautious position, then both. But this does not appear to be the definite solution.

The traffic-light method, highlights a path, in a certain way different, which allows by means of the image of traffic circulation, the use of PERT programming with greater flexibility, taking into account all the events (vertices of the graph), the EARLIEST and AT THE LATEST times of the optimist position and the AT THE LATEST time of the pessimist position. With this we arrive at, in the first place, the best times which can be taken for each event (if circumstances are always the most favourable). Therefore, when an event (incident) takes place during this time, it can be assumed there are no hitches since, at a first approximation, there appears to be no problems (green traffic light) for the operation of the project. In the second place, on choosing the AT THE LATEST times of the optimist position, if the execution time for the activities take an event up to this time, an alarm will have to ring because this is a limit situation for the optimist case (amber traffic-light)[9]. Finally, in third place, the worst is taken into account for the pessimist position. This is if the time of an event arrives at this limit, the situation is serious for the execution of the project within the established time and drastic measures will have to be taken (red traffic light).

It can be seen from this scheme, that the EARLIEST time is omitted from the pessimist position. It would seem that the sense this time can adopt for each event, the most optimistic of the pessimist position, has a far lesser significance than that of the AT THE EARLIEST time of the optimist position which we have taken as the yellow traffic-light. We leave it up to readers to decide in their opinion if we have got out choice right.

For greater ease, we will place the time relative to each event in the table below, in order later to select those that form the traffic-light.

Floating time of the optimist and pessimist positions.

Events	Optimist position		Pessimist position	
	Lower extreme	upper extreme	Lower extreme	upper extreme
1	0	0	0	0
2	3	3	4	4
3	9	9	12	12
4	6	20	9	26
5	21	21	27	27
6	22	22	30	30
7	37	37	48	48
8	39	54	51	76
9	39	60	51	77
10	38	38	50	54
11	38	54	50	72
12	57	58	76	76
13	47	68	61	87
14	70	70	86	90
15	78	78	102	102
16	84	84	110	110
17	96	96	124	124
	a_1	a_2	b_1	b_2

Finally in order to form the traffic light, columns a_1, a_2, b_2 of the above table are chosen. We arrive at:

Events	Green light	amber light	Red light	Events	Green light	amber light	Red liht
1	0	0	0	10	38	38	54
2	3	3	4	11	38	54	72
3	9	9	12	12	57	58	76
4	6	20	26	13	47	68	87
5	21	21	27	14	70	70	90
6	22	22	30	15	78	78	102
7	37	37	48	16	84	84	110
8	39	54	76	17	96	96	124
9	39	60	77				

Once we have arrived at the above table, we are in a position to establish control of the project, relative to its time aspect. But, logically, the problem of programming an investment project does not end with the construction of a structure (graph), nor with the determination, follow-up and time control of the activities of the same. In an investment project, material means have to be used (which provoke monetary requirements) and certain financial means. Either one, or the other, require availability to a greater or lesser degree throughout the whole project and normally generate a cost that gives rise at <<certain times>> to a payment. Here we have two important factors to be taken into account, normally linked to the duration of the project (time aspect) but with their own substantiveness.

At this point we would like to make a very brief reference to the problem of the means. This arises due to the fact of considering that for carrying out any activity the assignment is required of certain means (personnel, instrumental, financial..) that the company posses in limited quantities and also, because the optimum duration of a project requires, when by its very nature this is possible, the simultaneous carrying out of two or more tasks, as we have already seen. We highlight the expression <<by its very nature>> because in order to be able to carry out several tasks simultaneously it is also necessary to have the means available in sufficient quantities in order for them to be assigned to the same. This is an interesting aspect of the programmed task, which acquired a certain technical notoriety in the 60's[10] and which obviously could cause waiting modifications (lengthen times for certain activities - arcs of the graph - through lack of means) and a breaking down of a single task into several. We are going to avoid this aspect, by asking interested readers to consult the specialised literature on the subject.

Incorporation of costs into investment projects

In our opinion introducing costs into the activities making up a project means a certain change in the concept of time for those programmes constructed with the object of finalising, all the tasks which go to make them up, in the least possible time. In effect, when assigning an uncertain time to an activity (in our case by means of a confidence interval) the extremes or limits are established the difference of which indicate the degree of uncertainty, outside of which (neither before or after) the expert feels their duration will not occur. Therefore, when in a graph the floating times are calculated for an event <<for one or another extreme>> of the interval, what we are in fact doing is assigning the possibility or not (critical events with a floating time of zero) to carry out one of the activities of a sub-path in a greater time than that which is set for the corresponding extreme, which can be even higher than the upper extreme. If this were to happen an interval would be exited which by definition is considered as closed.

A particularly revealing example is given by the floating time of event 4 (6, 20) of the graph relative to the lower extremes. In fact, if the uncertain times for the activities are added (1, 2) and (2,4) we arrive at: [3,4] (+) [3, 5] = [6, 9]. The floating time for the referenced event is (6, 20) in the graph for the lower extremes and (9,26) in that for the upper extremes. In this way a longer time can be used for the upper extreme. We could well ask ourselves when would we have any interest in it being this way and the answer appears when the cost is inversely linked to the duration of an activity (longer time less cost) as a consequence of the concept of forced acceleration of a task. As we have already mentioned, this aspect of economic programming has been studied, following the current of certainty[11], by means of certain schemes, which presuppose a certain development of the function linking time and cost (lineal, non-lineal monotonous decreasing, existence of a minimum within the floating time..)

It is quite obvious that, when introducing uncertainty into the time factor, and if necessary into the cost factor, by means of confidence intervals, in which, by definition, the behaviour of the corresponding economic parameter in them is absolutely unknown, to establish a functional correspondence time-cost would seem at the very least risky, and the practical use of the scheme that would arise from this hypothesis, very doubtful. Then, let us now restate the question by attempting to simplify the proposed development to the maximum degree.

Let us say, in the first place, that activities exist for which the passing of time is related to their cost (independently of their functional form). There are also others, the time for which could be considered as <<waiting>> (delivery date for the equipment, for example) and, as such, have no implicit cost but on the other hand their realisation will give rise to a payment with no connection to the time passed (payment for the equipment) and it is even possible to imagine others which give rise to no cost whatsoever (simple waiting times).

With this preamble, let us now include the cost for each activity, in accordance with its nature, taking into account the sphere of uncertainty that presides over this work.

We will start off with the hypothesis according to which there is a homogeneous unitary price for the activities of study and analysis and a different one, but also homogeneous, for activities relative to decisions and management. Within this context we are also going to assume that there is no surcharge for acceleration and, therefore, the cost will be proportional to the time used for carrying out an activity. For greater generality of the model, these prices are also going to be considered as uncertain and expressed by confidence intervals. There will be activities that will not depend only on the work of humans and in this case these will be assigned the corresponding costs with no strict relation with the previously mentioned prices. Let us arbitrarily set as a price for study time [12, 15] monetary units and as a price for the tasks of decision and management [10, 14]. These prices will not vary throughout the project.

Let us now go on to establish costs for all activities.

Arc	*Valuation*	*Arc*	*Valuation*	*Arc*	*Valuation*	*Arc*	*Valuation*
(1, 2)	[36, 60]	(2, 3)	[72, 120]	(2, 4)	[36, 75]	(2, 6)	[120, 210]
(3, 5)	[144, 225]	(4, 6)	[24, 60]	(4, 9)	[60, 90]	(5, 6)	[12, 45]
(5, 8)	[168, 300]	(6, 7)	[180, 270]	(7, 8)	[20, 42]	(7, 9)	[20, 42]
(7, 10)	[10, 28]	(7, 11)	[10, 28]	(7, 12)	[200, 392]	(8, 16)	[300, 476]
(9, 13)	[80, 140]	(10, 14)	[0, 0]	(11, 14)	300[12]	(12, 15)	[100, 130][13]
(13, 15)	[0, 0]	(14, 15)	[1500, 1600][14]	(15, 16)	[60, 112]	(16, 17)	[120, 168]

For financial effects we are going to assume that all payments are made immediately following the end of each activity. On the other hand, if the generosity of the estimates for each activity is accepted, that is to say the competence of the expert or experts is recognised, finalisation of the project will be estimated by an interval formed by the sum of the EARLIEST times of the critical paths, that is [96, 124].

With the object of acquiring this information easily, we are going to assign an interval at the end of each arc before it reaches the corresponding vertex, which will be the result of adding to the interval corresponding to the vertex of origin of the arc, the interval corresponding to it (time for the activity). When several arcs arrive at a vertex, as the time for this vertex we will assign the maximum interval that can be formed with those arriving at it. As is known, if we have three intervals:

$$\underset{\sim}{A} = [a_1, a_2]; \quad \underset{\sim}{B} = [b_1, b_2]; \quad \underset{\sim}{C} = [c_1, c_2]$$

we arrive at:

$$\text{Max}\,\{\underset{\sim}{A}, \underset{\sim}{B}, \underset{\sim}{C}\} = [a_1 \vee b_1 \vee c_1, a_2 \vee b_2 \vee c_2]$$

As an example let us look at the assignment of the interval to vertex (15). Arriving at it are activities (14, 15) with a time of [78, 98], (12, 15) with a time of [77,102], (13, 15) with a time of [57, 83]. The maximum of these three intervals is:

$$[78, 98]\ (\vee)\ [77, 102]\ (\vee)\ [57, 83] = [78, 102]$$

It can be seen that on this occasion, as on many others, the optimum (maximum) does not coincide with any of the intervals taken as data, but that these have had to be destroyed in order to form the result. This is one of the characteristics of the maximisation and minimisation processes that makes them different from other operators such as the one for establishing an order.

We will now show the graph in which the interval of time calculated in accordance with the previous indications has been placed at the end of each arc. Below the circle representing each vertex, the interval of time assigned to the same has been placed. In this way we show that, for calculating the time when payment takes place for carrying out each activity, consideration should be given to the interval of time relative to the end of each arc, while in order to accumulate times recourse will have to be made to the maximum interval, that is, the one placed immediately below each vertex.

The corresponding graph showing time assignment appears as (figure 2.10).

Once we have found the times at which each activity ends, we are in a position to accumulate costs (which in our case we have identified as payments) moving conveniently throughout the network following the numbering of the vertices. Acting in this way will allow us to take into account something as important as the notion of financial capital and the consequent fact that it is not possible to add monetary masses located at different periods of time. To express this colloquially, this is equivalent to taking into consideration the existence of rates of interest. Our aim consists in proceeding with this accumulation by means of a process of updating. For this it will be necessary to establish a unitary rate of interest that is invariable throughout the process which is also considered as uncertain. As is well known, assuming a unitary rate of interest per unit of time $[i_1, i_2]$, a certain monetary mass $[m_1, m_2]$ will be, after discounting 1, 2, ..., n units of time, respectively, from the following expressions:

$$\underset{\sim}{M}_1 = [m_1, m_2] \, (\cdot) \left(\frac{1}{1 \, (+) \, [i_1, i_2]} \right)$$

$$= [m_1, m_2] \, (\cdot) \, \frac{1}{[1 + i_1, 1 + i_2]}$$

$$= \left[m_1 \left(\frac{1}{1 + i_2} \right), m_2 \left(\frac{1}{1 + i_1} \right) \right]$$

$$\underset{\sim}{M}_2 = \left[m_1 \left(\frac{1}{1 + i_2} \right), m_2 \left(\frac{1}{1 + i_1} \right) \right] (\cdot) \left[\left(\frac{1}{1 + i_2} \right), \left(\frac{1}{1 + i_1} \right) \right]$$

$$= \left[m_1 \left(\frac{1}{(1 + i_2)^2} \right), m_2 \left(\frac{1}{(1 + i_1)^2} \right) \right]$$

....

$$\underset{\sim}{M}_n = \left[m_1 \left(\frac{1}{(1 + i_2)^n} \right), m_2 \left(\frac{1}{(1 + i_1)^n} \right) \right]$$

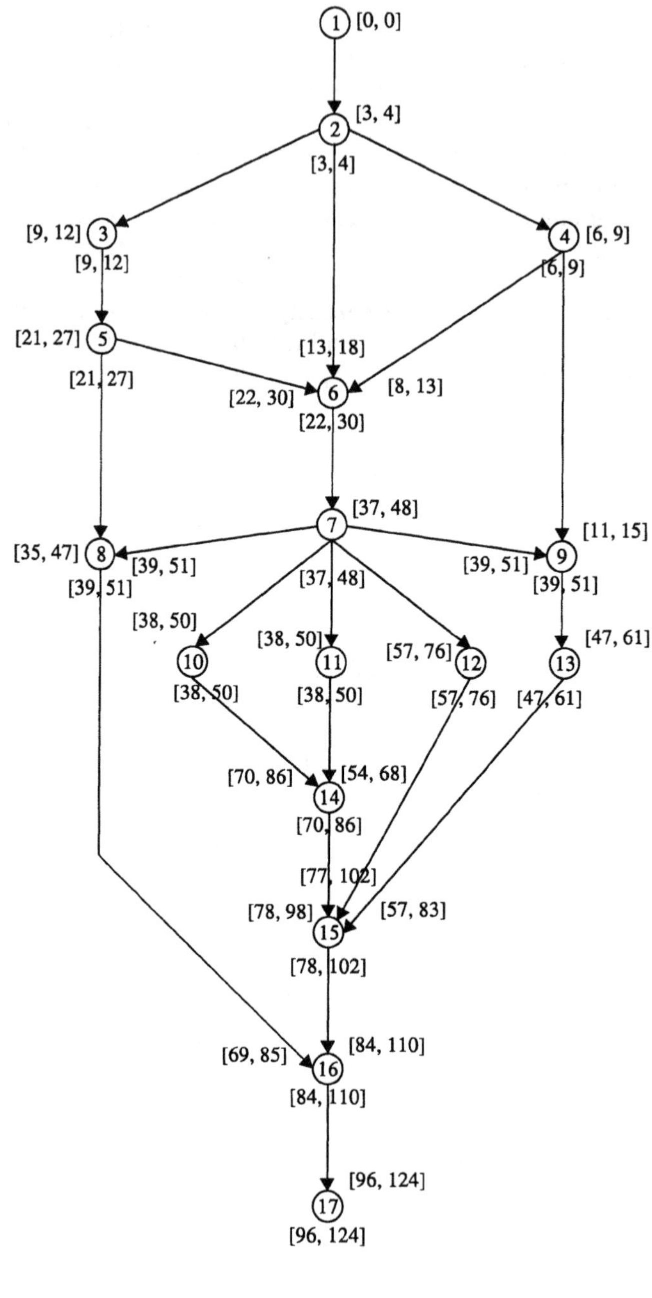
1
[0, 0]
2
[3, 4]
[3, 4]
3
[9, 12]
[9, 12]
4
[6, 9]
[6, 9]
5
[21, 27]
[21, 27]
[13, 18]
6
[22, 30]
[8, 13]
[22, 30]
7
[37, 48]
8
[35, 47]
[39, 51]
[39, 51]
9
[11, 15]
[39, 51]
[39, 51]
[37, 48]
[38, 50]
[38, 50]
[57, 76]
[47, 61]
10
11
12
13
[38, 50]
[38, 50]
[57, 76]
[47, 61]
[70, 86]
[54, 68]
14
[70, 86]
[77, 102]
[78, 98]
[57, 83]
15
[78, 102]
[69, 85]
[84, 110]
16
[84, 110]
[96, 124]
17
[96, 124]

Figure 2.10.

This process allows for carrying out additions and any other operation, with monetary masses located at different periods of time, and therefore, to proceed with accumulations of updated payments. For this we will take as a reference the time of commencing the programme, in such a way that we will <<transfer>> all payments just as if they had to be made at moment zero.

Let us now go on to develop this scheme by using the estimates of the presented supposition. For this it will be necessary to estimate an interval that reflects the uncertain rate of interest that we are going to use.

In this sense, we propose the use of a daily compounded rate of interest for which, merely as an example, we could take $\underset{\sim}{i} = [0.0002, 0.0003]$. In this way the updating rate will be, for an activity (r, s):

$$\underset{\sim}{\omega}_{r,s} = \left[\frac{1}{(1+i_2)^{t_2}}, \frac{1}{(1+i_1)^{t_1}}\right]$$

where:

$$\underset{\sim}{i} = [i_1, i_2]; \quad \underset{\sim}{T} = [t_1, t_2]$$

On using this formula[15] we will have, in our case, for each of the activities:

$$\underset{\sim}{\omega}_{1,2} = \left[\frac{1}{(1+0.0003)^4}, \frac{1}{(1+0.0002)^3}\right] = [0.9988, 0.9994]$$

$\underset{\sim}{\omega}_{2,3} = [0.9964, 0.9982]$ $\quad$ $\underset{\sim}{\omega}_{2,4} = [0.9973, 0.9988]$ $\quad$ $\underset{\sim}{\omega}_{2,6} = [0.9946, 0.9974]$

$\underset{\sim}{\omega}_{3,5} = [0.9919, 0.9958]$ $\quad$ $\underset{\sim}{\omega}_{4,6} = [0.9961, 0.9984]$ $\quad$ $\underset{\sim}{\omega}_{4,9} = [0.9955, 0.9978]$

$\underset{\sim}{\omega}_{5,6} = [0.9910, 0.9956]$ $\quad$ $\underset{\sim}{\omega}_{5,8} = [0.9860, 0.9930]$ $\quad$ $\underset{\sim}{\omega}_{6,7} = [0.9857, 0.9926]$

$\underset{\sim}{\omega}_{7,8} = [0.9848, 0.9922]$ $\quad$ $\underset{\sim}{\omega}_{7,9} = [0.9848, 0.9922]$ $\quad$ $\underset{\sim}{\omega}_{7,10} = [0.9851, 0.9924]$

$\underset{\sim}{\omega}_{7,11} = [0.9851, 0.9924]$ $\quad$ $\underset{\sim}{\omega}_{7,12} = [0.9775, 0.9887]$ $\quad$ $\underset{\sim}{\omega}_{8,16} = [0.9748, 0.9863]$

$\underset{\sim}{\omega}_{9,13} = [0.9819, 0.9906]$ $\quad$ $\underset{\sim}{\omega}_{10,14} = [0.9745, 0.9861]$ $\quad$ $\underset{\sim}{\omega}_{11,14} = [0.9798, 0.9892]$

$\underset{\sim}{\omega}_{12,15} = [0.9699, 0.9847]$ $\quad$ $\underset{\sim}{\omega}_{13,15} = [0.9754, 0.9887]$ $\quad$ $\underset{\sim}{\omega}_{14,15} = [0.9710, 0.9845]$

$\underset{\sim}{\omega}_{15,16} = [0.9675, 0.9833]$ $\quad$ $\underset{\sim}{\omega}_{16,17} = [0.9634, 0.9810]$

Taking into account that the costs for each of the activities of the project $\underset{\sim}{C}_{r,s}$, are known, and given updating rates of $\underset{\sim}{\omega}_{r,s}$, established from an estimated interest rate $\underset{\sim}{i}$ and to certain payment times relative to the end of the activity $\underset{\sim}{T}_{r,s}$, in order to obtain the overall cost of the project, it will be enough to calculate the sum of the products $\underset{\sim}{C}_{r,s}(\cdot).\underset{\sim}{\omega}_{r,s}$. The supposition illustrating this scheme will be:

$$\underset{\sim}{C}_T = \underset{\sim}{C}_{1,2} (\cdot) \underset{\sim}{\omega}_{1,2} (+) \underset{\sim}{C}_{2,3} (\cdot) \underset{\sim}{\omega}_{2,3} (+) \cdots (+) \underset{\sim}{C}_{16,17} (\cdot) \underset{\sim}{\omega}_{16,17}$$

$$= [36, 60] (\cdot) [0.9988, 0.9994] (+) [72, 120] (\cdot) [0.9964, 0.9982] (+) \cdots (+)$$

$$(+) [120, 168] (\cdot) [0.9634, 0.9810] = [3491, 4858]$$

In this way we arrive at the conclusion that the updated cost of the investment project will be no less than 3491 monetary units, and no more than 4858 monetary units.

Having arrived at this estimate, making us aware of the overall financial needs, it would appear to be suitable to bring up the convenience of knowing the financial tying up that will take place throughout the whole process and will not commence to be recuperated until the project is completed and commercial activity begins with the consequent collections and payments arising from exploitation. What we are attempting to get to know is the cash and bank balance requirements at every moment so that if it were necessary internal or external funds could be found to allow for adequate *liquidity* and also for subsequent control of the same.

A quick look at the previous time graph, draws attention to the difficulties that a simple accumulation of updated costs would cause by following the direction of the different paths leaving from the initial vertex to the final vertex, and specifically when from one and the same vertex several arcs originate (as occurs for 2, 4, 5, and 7 of our case). To add the accumulated cost at any given vertex to those that follow, would mean doubling, tripling or quintuplicating the accumulated costs right up to that specific vertex. It is convenient, then, to find a procedure that avoids falling into this trap.

Estimating financial needs throughout the process

There are many technical possibilities for carrying out a development based on the elements described above. On this occasion we are inclined towards the incorporation of those elements arising from neuronal graphs which, we believe, will permit clarification of the problem and will provide a fluidity of method to the process. For this, we are about to consider that the PERT that has been established constitutes a neuronal graph with regard to the following simplified correspondences between the nervous system and a graph[16]:

- Neuron and its axon: vertex of the graph
- Entry dendrites: arcs having an incidence towards the interior of the vertex
- Exit dendrites: arcs having an incidence towards the exterior of the vertex

As is sufficiently well known, the nervous system of living beings is governed by the brain, in which there are hundreds of thousands of millions of <<neurons>>. A neuron is a cell composed of a soma (cellular body of the neuron) and a nucleus, which narrows down at one end to form a terminal called an axon. A number of conducting filaments reach out from it and end up at other neurons. Each neuron, then, has a number of dendrites that enter it and other dendrites that leave it. A very simplified drawing may be useful in helping to visualise the neuron and its surroundings (figure 2.11.

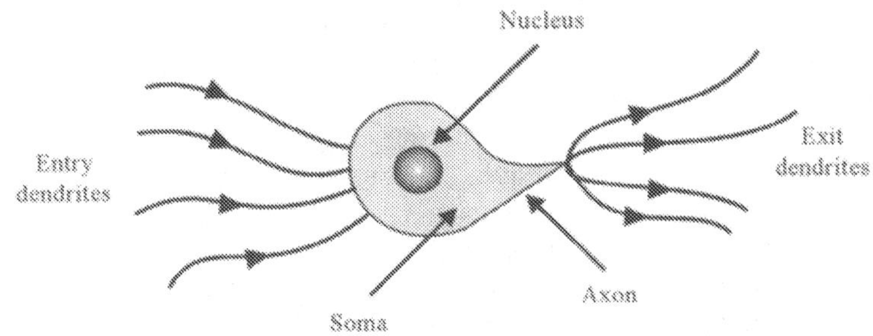

Figure 2.11.

Through the entry dendrites (sometimes called synaptic dendrites, since the union of one neuron with another takes place in the synapses) <<information>> arrives by means of certain electrochemical potentials of little known characteristics (other names are also used such as signs, signals, ..). In the cellular body of the neuron a process of addition of the received potentials takes place, in several ways, giving rise to a new potential that struggles to leave the neuron by way of the axon. Along this path it finds itself up against a membrane, wall or simply a barrier which can stop the passage of the potential, and which is known under the name of <<threshold>>. If the potential is <<stronger>> than the threshold it passes through and it expands in the same intensity along all the axonic dendrites (equal to the total passing through the threshold). On certain occasions, the impact, of the potential struggling to leave, with the threshold gives rise to a weakening of the potential which is about to expand, while on other occasions it leaves unharmed. If a neuron emits a potential, it is said that it is active and inactive if the latter dies at the threshold.

The simultaneous or successive operation of hundreds of thousands of millions of neurons allows living bodies to carry out the most diverse functions. Certain neurons receive information from the exterior, which allows then to give rise to activities such as sight, smell, etc., other receive signals from the interior which very often are stored in certain parts of the brain and give rise to memory, dreams, etc.

In their passage along the dendrites, the potentials, signals, information, may undergo a modification in their intensity or strength in such a way that the exit potential of a neuron is not always the same as the potential arriving at the next neuron. These variations can give rise to either positive or negative effects, either strengtheners or weakeners.

This then is the elemental operation of a natural neuron system described colloquially, without it being particularly meticulous, but sufficient, we believe, for the objectives of the subject we are about to develop. Let us now see how we can include it into our problem.

Before proceeding with any consideration about the incorporation of the principals of neuron networks to management problems, it should be taken into account that it is not always possible, nor at times expedient, to totally adapt the systems which govern nature to economic systems. Advances that have taken place throughout centuries, have occurred by taking advantage of the assumed or real properties of the beings and objects which surround us. But the human mind, precisely due to the gift of imagination, has been able to adapt, modify and change beings, objects and phenomena and in this way make them more suitable for satisfying his needs or desires. Important advances in technical matters have been possible thanks to substantial changes in natural functions. The high speeds that have been reached with the creation of the wheel which do not exist in the movements of living beings. Man has always wanted to fly, but he has not been able to do this by moving himself with wings similar to those of birds, but in a rigid manner and with propulsion. And so on, the examples multiplying themselves.

In the scheme we are proposing, the intention is to <<copy>> nature to some extent, but only in some of its aspects, separating ourselves from it when we feel that in this way, we arrive at a desired advancement for reaching our objectives.

We will start off by putting our PERT graph on the same level as neuronal architecture, according to the already mentioned equivalencies. Now then, just as in the graphs used up to now, each of the activities has been represented by an arc and expressed by exit and entry vertices, from now on, consequent upon the incorporation of the notion of the neuronal graph, each activity, on normally causing a cost, will be represented by a vertex, while the arcs will have as their sole (but highly important) significance, the connections existing between activities. This change will allow us to identify the vertex (activity generating a cost) with the neuron (emitting a potential), and the arc (connection) with the dendrite (transmitter of the potential).

Below we have established the correspondence between the arcs of the previous graph (activities) with the vertices of the new graph, which are also a representation of the activities.

Arcs	*Vertex*	*Arcs*	*Vertex*	*Arcs*	*Vertex*	*Arcs*	*Vertex*
(1, 2)	1	(4, 9)	7	(7, 10)	12	(11, 14)	18
(2, 3)	2	(5, 6)	9	(7, 11)	13	(12, 15)	19
(2, 4)	4	(5, 8)	8	(7, 12)	14	(13, 15)	22
(2, 6)	3	(6, 7)	10	(8, 16)	16	(14, 15)	21
(3, 5)	5	(7, 8)	11	(9, 13)	20	(15, 16)	23
(4, 6)	6	(7, 9)	15	(10, 14)	17	(16, 17)	24

On acting in this way, a variation of the PERT graph, with which we have been working up to now, occurs, giving rise to another graph which we show below, and from which we have placed, alongside the denomination of the activity (vertex in this case) the estimated cost for the same (figure 2.12).

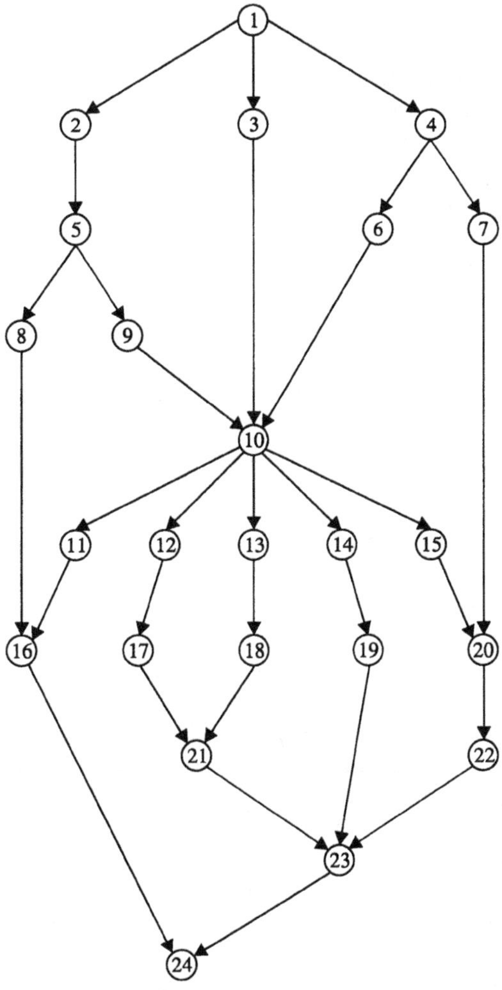

Figure 2.12.

Vertex 1: The decision to carry out the investment is studied [36, 60].
Vertex 2: Market analysis for the product [72, 120].
Vertex 3: Market analysis for equipment [120, 210].
Vertex 4: Analysis of possible financial products [36, 75].
Vertex 5: Determination of the capacity of the market to absorb [144, 225].
Vertex 6: Determination of financial capacity [24, 60].
Vertex 7: Selection of financial product [60, 90].
Vertex 8: Survey of distribution and sales channels [168, 300].
Vertex 9: Proposal for invoicing [12, 45].
Vertex 10: Study of selection and approval of object [180, 270].
Vertex 11: Approval of commercial action [20, 42].

Vertex 12: Drawing up of equipment purchase order [10, 28].
Vertex 13: Drawing up works purchase order [10, 28].
Vertex 14: Personnel selection [200, 392].
Vertex 15: Approval of financial action [20, 42].
Vertex 16: Setting up distribution network [300, 476].
Vertex 17: Equipment delivery [0, 0].
Vertex 18: Installation and works tasks [300, 300].
Vertex 19: Personnel training [100, 130].
Vertex 20: Steps for obtaining financial resources [80, 140].
Vertex 21: Equipment installation [1500, 1600].
Vertex 22: Time limit for obtaining financial resources [0, 0].
Vertex 23: Test with prototype [60, 112].
Vertex 24: Tasks for commencement of production, sales and collections [120, 168].

In this graph, 24 vertices can be observed, corresponding to as many activities that make up the project.

Let us now pass on to speak in the new terminology arising from neuronal networks. In a first approximation, it could be said that the neuronal architecture is composed of 24 neurons, each one of which possesses its synaptic and axonic dendrites, except for the first (only axonic dendrites) and the last (only synaptic dendrites).

Having made these general statements, it would now be useful to introduce ourselves into the structure of the neuronal graph with the object of making it represent the phenomena under study, as accurately as possible. In this sense it is necessary to take into consideration two aspects which prevent automatic consideration of the above graph.

The first of these refers to the architecture of the network itself. In fact, if the objective consists in finding at each of the vertices of the graph, the costs (payments) accumulated up to the end if this activity, it will be necessary that at the vertex that represents the accumulation, there should be an incidence not only of the costs accumulated at the end of the previous activity, but also its own costs should be included. This means <<breaking down>> each vertex (neuron) into two: one that emits its own impulses and another that collects and emits the result of adding these and those coming from previous vertices (neurons). In this way what we will have is that each activity is represented by two neurons (vertices): one emitting its own potential and the other emitting the accumulated potential. We will designate the neurons sending out their own potentials by $r \in \{1, 2, ..., 24\}$ and those emitting previously accumulated potentials by $r' \in \{1, 2, ..., 24\}$.

The second is caused by the possibility that a neuron possess more than one axonic dendrite (exit dendrite). If the accumulated value is transmitted more than once to the following neurons, what happens is that the accumulation is multiplied by the number of dendrites which leave from each neuron. With the object of solving this problem we can make use of the effects caused by the << impact>> on the threshold of the potential struggling to exit. As a consequence of this, intervention takes place of a function that could be given by the opposite of the number of dendrites leaving each neuron. This would be equivalent to assigning to the threshold a reducing function on the exit potential. It is obvious that the concept of a threshold could be done away with and it could be assumed that the exit potential is divided into equal parts for all the neurons, but we are reticent about this way of tackling the problem which, we feel, moves away far too much from the essence of the operation of neuronal graphs.

All this allows us to make the following suggestion. We will call:

- $\underset{\sim}{C}_{e'_j}$ the accumulated cost of the entrance of a neuron proceeding from e_j.
- $\underset{\sim}{C}_{s_i}$ the cost of the activity i (potential emitted by neuron i).
- $\underset{\sim}{C}_{s'_i}$ exit cost (accumulated) in neuron i (potential emitted by neuron i).
- $\underset{\sim}{\omega}_{s_i}$ the updating rate applicable to the cost of neuron i (weight of the dendrite).

Into the nucleus of neuron i enter the potentials that have been transported by the entry dendrites. Here an addition takes place which, in this particular case, requires the use of the addition operator. This then will be:

$$f(\underset{\sim}{C}_{e'_i}) = \underset{\sim}{C}_{e'_1} (+) \underset{\sim}{C}_{e'_2} (+) \cdots (+) \underset{\sim}{C}_{e'_n} (+) \underset{\sim}{C}_{s_i} (\cdot) \underset{\sim}{\omega}_{s_i} = \underset{\sim}{C}_{s_i} (\cdot) \underset{\sim}{\omega}_{s_i} (+) \sum_{j=1}^{n} \underset{\sim}{C}_{e'_j}$$

assuming that in a neuron n dendrites proceeding from the accumulation of the costs of the preceding activities, plus that corresponding to activity i, which is been handled.

The potential struggling to exit is therefore $f(\underset{\sim}{C}_{e'_i})$, but in the attempt to pass through the threshold, a modificaction[17] takes place to this potential which, to our effects, can be reflected by a function F:

$$F(f(\underset{\sim}{C}_{e'_i})) = f(\underset{\sim}{C}_{e'_i}) (\cdot) \frac{1}{d} = \frac{1}{d} (\cdot) \left(\underset{\sim}{C}_{s_i} (\cdot) \underset{\sim}{\omega}_{s_i} (+) \sum_{j=1}^{n} \underset{\sim}{C}_{e'_j} \right)$$

d being the number of exit dendrites.

All and each of the exit dendrites will lead a potential equal to the function of function $F(f(\underset{\sim}{C}_{e'_i}))$ towards another (or other) neuron(s).

Having made these considerations, we are now ready to tackle the problem by means of neuron architecture. For this we are going to present a network in which we will place beside each emitting neuron r, its exit potential multiplied by its weight (updating rate). This product gives rise to the entry potential to the neuron in which the corresponding dendrite will arrive. In this way we arrive at the potential or signal arriving at an accumulation neuron r' proceeding exclusively from neuron r (this is the product $\underset{\sim}{C}_{s_i} (\cdot) \underset{\sim}{\omega}_{s_i}$ of our formula). The sum of the 24 potentials will give rise to the total updated cost of the project.

But as we have said, apart from this information what is interesting is the information relative to costs accumulated at each moment. The incorporation of the accumulation neurons r' to the previous neuronal graph gives rise to the following network, in which the potentials representing the accumulated costs of the previous activity have not yet been incorporated (figure 2.13).

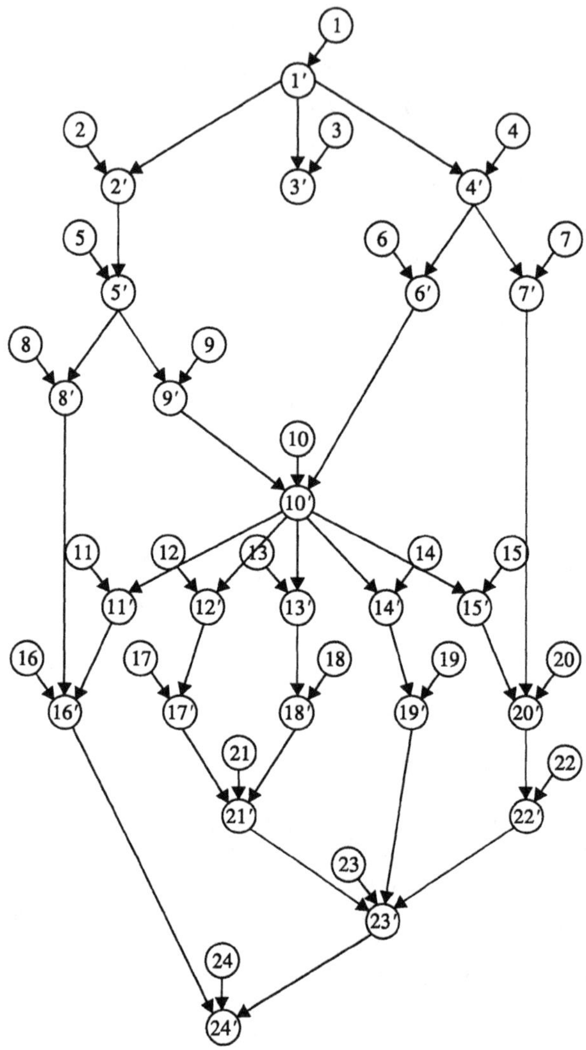
1
1′
2
3
4
2′
3′
4′
5
6
7
5′
6′
7′
8
9
8′
9′
10
10′
11
12
13
14
15
11′
12′
13′
14′
15′
16
17
18
19
20
16′
17′
18′
19′
20′
21
22
21′
22′
23
23′
24
24′

Figure 2.13.

Vertex 1: [36, 60] (·) [.9988, .9994] = [35.9588, 59.9640]
Vertex 2: [72, 120] (·) [.9964, .9982] = [71.7408, 119.7840]
Vertex 3: [120, 210] (·) [.9946, .9974] = [119.3520, 209.4540]
Vertex 4: [36, 75] (·) [.9973, .9988] = [35.9028, 74.9100]
Vertex 5: [144, 225] (·) [.9919, .9958] = [142.8336, 224.0550]
Vertex 6: [24, 60] (·) [.9961, .9984] = [23.9064, 59.9040]
Vertex 7: [60, 90] (·) [.9955, .9978] = [59.7300, 89.8020]
Vertex 8: [168, 300] (·) [.9860, .9930] = [165.6480, 297.9000]
Vertex 9: [12, 45] (·) [.9910, .9956] = [11.8920, 44.8020]
Vertex 10: [180, 270] (·) [.9857, .9926] = [177.4260, 268.0020]
Vertex 11: [20, 42] (·) [.9848, .9922] = [19.6960, 41.6724]
Vertex 12: [10, 28] (·) [.9851, .9924] = [9.8510, 27.7872]
Vertex 13: [10, 28] (·) [.9851, .9924] = [9.8510, 27.7872]
Vertex 14: [200, 392] (·) [.9775, .9887] = [195.5000, 387.5704]
Vertex 15: [20, 42] (·) [.9848, .9922] = [19.6960, 41.6724]
Vertex 16: [300, 476] (·) [.9748, .9863] = [292.4400, 469.4788]
Vertex 17: [0, 0]
Vertex 18: [300, 300] (·) [.9798, .9892] = [293.9400, 296.7600]
Vertex 19: [100, 130] (·) [.9699, .9847] = [96.9900, 128.0110]
Vertex 20: [80, 140] (·) [.9819, .9906] = [78.5520, 138.6840]
Vertex 21: [1500, 1600] (·) [.9710, .9845] = [1456.5000, 1575.2000]
Vertex 22: [0, 0]
Vertex 23: [60, 112] (·) [.9675, .9833] = [58.0500, 110.1296]
Vertex 24: [120, 168] (·) [.9634, .9810] = [115.6080, 164.8080]

Let us now go on to calculate the potential leaving each neuron. For this it will be necessary to add all the potentials arriving at the neurons and modify them with the threshold reducing function.

Taking into account that in the neuronal graph only four vertices exist from which more than one dendrite leaves (1′, 4′, 5′ and 10′) the reducing effect of the threshold represented by the function of function F is only manifest in these. Just as an example let us take a look at the intensity of the impulses of neuron 1′ towards 2′, 3′ y 4′.

The potential struggling to leave neuron 1′ is [35.9568, 59.9640] but as $d = 3$, the one actually leaving each dendrite will be:

$$\frac{1}{3}(\cdot)\ [35.9568,\ 59.9640] = [11.9856,\ 19.9880]$$

One can see that acting in this way is equivalent to assuming that the previous accumulated cost is distributed in equal parts to the following neurons, in such a way that the accumulated cost in a vertex (potential struggling to exit from a neuron) $f(\underset{\sim}{C}_{e_i'})$ is equal to its own cost plus the corresponding part of the costs of previous activities. And this always taking into consideration the updating rate.

Before going any further with the calculations, it is necessary to take into account that, given the fact that neurons r' only have an accumulated function of already updated costs, their exit dendrites will always have as their weight $\underset{\sim}{\omega}_{s_i} = 1$ which implies that the potential travelling along the dendrite linking a neuron r' with a neuron s' does no undergo any modification in its path. As an example let us look at the potentials arriving and leaving neurons 2′, 3′ y 4′.

Neuron 2′: [71.7408, 119.7840] (+) [11.9856, 19.9880] = [83.7264, 139.7720]
Neuron 3′: [119.3520, 209.4540] (+) [11.9856, 19.9880] = [131.3376, 229.4420]
Neuron 4′: [35.9028, 74.9100] (+) [11. 9856, 19.9880] = [47.8884, 94.8980]

Below we have reproduced the results obtained for the accumulated costs for each activity, that is to say, the exit potentials from neurons r' (figure 2.14).

Vertex 1′: [35.9568, 59.9640]
Vertex 2′: [83.7264, 139.7720]
Vertex 3′: [131.3376, 229.4420]
Vertex 4′: [47.8884, 94.8980]
Vertex 5′: [226.5600, 363.8270]
Vertex 6′: [47.8506, 107.3530]
Vertex 7′: [83.6742, 137.2510]
Vertex 8′: [278.9280, 479.8135]
Vertex 9′: [125.1720, 226.7155]
Vertex 10′: [481.7862, 831.5125]
Vertex 11′: [116.0532, 207.9749]
Vertex 12′: [106.2082, 194.0897]
Vertex 13′: [106.2082, 194.0897]
Vertex 14′: [291.8572, 553.8729]
Vertex 15′: [116.0532, 207.9749]
Vertex 16′: [687.4212, 1157.2672]
Vertex 17′: [106.2082, 194.0897]
Vertex 18′: [400.1482, 490.8497]
Vertex 19′: [388.8472, 681.8679]
Vertex 20′: [278.2794, 483.9099]
Vertex 21′: [1962.8564, 2260.1394]
Vertex 22′: [278.2794, 483.9099]
Vertex 23′: [2688.0330, 3536.0628]
Vertex 24′: [3491.0622, 4858.1380]

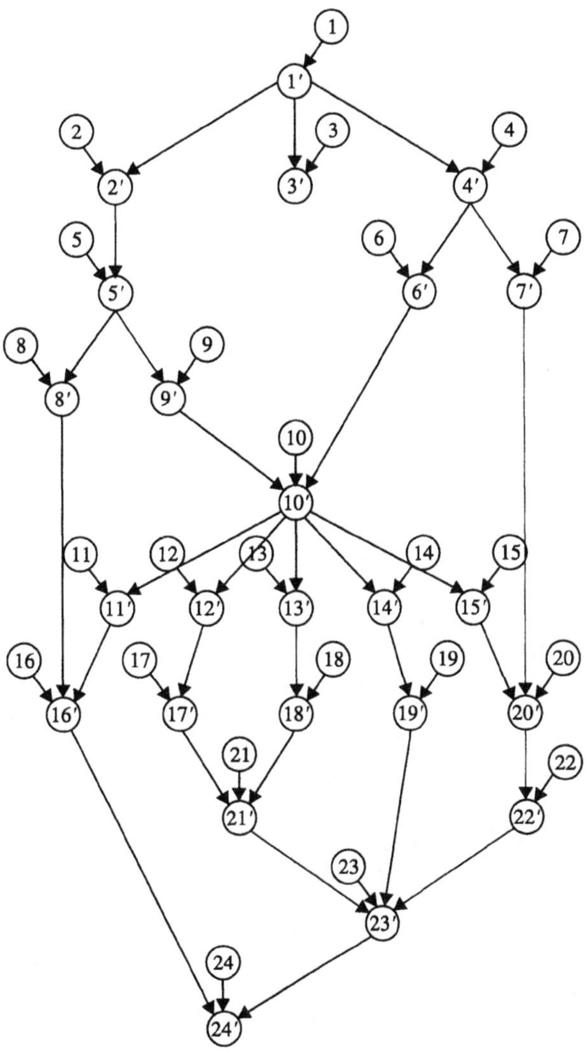

Figure 2.14.

As was only to be expected we have arrived at the same final result as we found before, taking into account that in one and the other process the same calculations have been made, but from different conceptual perspectives. The hypothetical advantage of the use of the neuron method can be found in that the ease of assimilation of economic phenomena with the notions relative to neuromimetics offers a sequential development that allows for great clarity of the scheme, being particularly useful for effects of follow-up and control of an investment project.

Having arrived at this point and with the object a avoiding possible incorrect interpretations, it would be convenient to show that the incorporation of a threshold that divides the potential for an equal quantity to the axonic dendrites, is in reply to a scheme for the distribution of certain <<common costs>> between several <<users>> corresponding to the activities that were necessary in order to be able to commence the following tasks. Obviously, equal distribution has sense when this hypothesis does not move away from the reality that the model intends to handle. When a circumstance were to arise which were to prevent its acceptance, recourse should be made to the incorporation of some element permitting distribution to take place in such a way that the arrival of the potentials at the following neurons is different, depending on the dendrite bearing them. In this event, we suggest assigning weights, differing from the unit, to each of the axonic dendrites of neurons r', when the number of these is greater than one. We can also think of other procedures. From a financial point of view, a precipitated reading could lead to thinking about an apparent misinterpretation in the event that the monetary means were to arrive at the company at moment [57, 83], when payments updated to that point already reached [2688, 3536], having been made throughout the process. It is precisely this fact that brings into evidence the financial interest of the scheme, because on being aware of the needs of payment means for carrying out activities at all times allows us to know if the situation of the company will permit it to fulfil its undertakings and, therefore, if the investment project will be completed successfully. We will assume it is unnecessary to insist on the fact that, if required, the entry of money from external sources could also occur by means of partial draw-downs, while the activities of the investment programme were taking place. In any event, to all intents and purposes, this is a mere problem of financial management.

All too frequently the concept of an investment process is compared to the selection of investments. Even assuming the risk of wanting to << turn the tide>> on attempting to limit the activities which comprise the investment activity, we have presented a set of interconnected tasks which form, in our opinion, a basic framework for the investment process, by means of an arrow form graph, the nature of which has allowed us to use the properties of the PERT graph.

In the sixties and seventies the development of the PERT, CPM, ALTAI, etc. techniques made possible the solution of a large number of time and/or economic programming, by using estimates of economic parameters located in the future, in terms of certainty or probability. The current situation of economic systems, subjected to constant coming and goings due to uncertainty, which is con-substantial to the times we are living in, have made it necessary to revise certain elements with the object of adapting them to new needs. In this sense we have developed the part of this work basing ourselves on previous works, carried out in co-operation with much missed Professor Arnold Kaufmann.

But the birth of the new concept of neuron graph at the end of 1995, as a result of the publication of the work *Grafos Neuronales para la economía y gestión de empresas*, was the focal point of suggestions for renewing concepts and methods. In this way we have tackled the task of transforming the PERT graph into a neuron graph attempting very carefully to maintain a total parallel between traditional techniques and the new proposal, with the object of being able to see, through a numerical example, the identity of the final result obtained following both paths, but highlighting the advantages that can be achieved with the development of neuromimetics. From an economic-financial point of view, it has been seen that the activities making up the programme can be classified by following two aspects: study and handling on the one side, both of which require different aptitudes and knowledge, and marketing, organisation or financing on the other. In this way, if the graph is separated into sub-graphs it will be seen that a bi-partition in a vertical direction will provide the separation of study-action and a tri-partition (not always disjunctive) from left to right will give rise to a division of the functional tasks. This then is a not an insignificant aspect, above all from the controlling perspective of the process.

Finally, we would like to record that the subject that has been developed has not run out on finishing these pages, but all to the contrary. This is an open door to more profound studies, in which the developments from these neuron networks can provide highly interesting elements. We are convinced that imagination, this precious gift to mankind, put to the service of investigation, will give rise to new models which will ease the difficult task of preparing, selecting and executing investment projects.

References

1 The name comes from its creator Henry L. Gantt.

2 W. Clark, W.: *El gráfico Gantt en la dirección de empresas industriales y comerciales,* "2nd. Ed, Montesó, Barcelona, 1944, pages 16-17.

3 H. F. Evans: *Introducción al PERT,* Sagitario, Barcelona, 1965, page 32.

4 A graph can also be represented by boolean matrices, latin matrices, by means of multivocas relations, etc.

5 See in this respect, the interesting work by A.Kaufmann and G. Desbazeille: *Método del camino crítico,* Sagitario, Barcelona, 1965, page 22.

6 See the work by A. Kaufmann and G. Desbazeille: *El método del camino crítico*, Sagitario, Barcelona, 1965.

7 A. Kaufmann and J. Gil Aluja: *Técnicas operativas de gestión para el tratamiento de la incertidumbre,* Hispano-Europea, Barcelona, 1987, pages 195-203. A. Kaufmann and J.Gil Aluja: *Técnicas de gestión de empresa. Previsiones, decisiones y etsrategias,*Pirámide, Madrid, 1992, pages 123-129.

8 A. Kaufmann and J.Gil Aluja: <<La programación de actividades por el método del semáforo>>. *Revista Europea de Dirección y Economia de la Empresa,* vol. 1, April 1992, pages 7-13.

9 In the critical events of the presumption we are studying, both times coincide. The green and amber light would be on at one and the same time. An elemental rule of caution would advise always to consider the most unfavourable situation and therefore in these cases the amber light would prevail.

10 As an example we mention the work by C. Lapoureau: <<Evaluation des changes de contrôle de l'avancement des travaux par la méthode du cheminement critique>> *Revue de Gestion*, October, 1965, pages 556 and following.

11 See the interesting work by A. Kaufmann and G. Desbazeille: *El método del camino crítico,* Sagitario, Barcelona, 1965. The original French version was edited by Dunod, 1964.

12 These are works done by closed contract and finished works, so the price has been set in advance.

13 Including salaries for new personnel and for their trainer and does not cover the total hours of the day.

14 Included is payment for the equipment and its installation.

15 The $\underset{\sim}{T}$ corresponds to the interval of time it is estimated that the activity will finish.

16 A. Kaufmann and J. Gil Aluja: *Grafos neuronales para la economia y gestión de empresas,* Pirámide, Madrid, 1995, page 33.

17 A. Kaufmann and J. Gil Aluja: *Grafos neuronales para la economia y gestión de empresas,*Pirámide, Madrid, 1995, page 83.

3 Financial risk of investment

Financial aspects of the investment process

The activities required in order to materialise an investment process, commence with the decision to invest and include the need to have available a certain financial capital, that is to say certain monetary masses at certain points in time. The financial aspect of the process, in the strict sense, has as its main objective obtaining these resources in order for them to be placed at the disposal of those making payments.

In specialist works on the subject, it is quite normal to find the concept of investment risk, defined relative to the capacity of the object acquired to generate profit, that is to say, that in a certain way, for the notion of financial risk, one of the measurements or valuations of the eventual economic benefit, is taken as a basis. We have no intention at this stage to indulge in a debate on the adequacy of the words <<financial risk>> for representing this phenomena, but to propose a different notion which we feel has been little studied and which deserves special attention.

For this we will commence by saying that the normally extraordinary nature of the investment task, in general, makes one's own financial sources insufficient for attending to the required payments. From this arises the need for resorting to external financial sources.

On many occasions we have mentioned that one of the most important aspects of investment programmes is the possibility of making time estimates for the amounts of money required for complying with undertakings made at the beginning of the process. It is obvious that modern programming schemes constitute a solid support for financial management, but they cannot be considered as an impassable barrier to possible non-payments, caused by the many aspects susceptible to causing friction in the system. From this the existence of a certain financial risk arises from the investment activity.

Let us define the financial risk of an investment as the <<possibility existing of not being able to satisfy the necessary payments in order for finalisation of the process to take place at the previously established time>>.

In studying the financial risk of an investment two fundamental aspects appear. The first of these refers to the availability at the correct time of the monetary means necessary for *each one* of the activities which comprise the programme, and the second to the accumulation of the financial possibilities of *all* the activities, which will constitute the degree of risk assumed at commencement of the process. These two aspects bring to light the dependence of the concept of risk relative to the time for carrying out the tasks. It should be taken into account that the lack of monetary availability at any given time does not inevitable impede its incorporation into the company at a later date and that, therefore, the project can be finished with a certain delay. From this the need arose for the intervention of the notion of <<insolvency>>. Insolvency would imply the definite ceasing of activities and, therefore, the breakdown of the investment process.

All we have mentioned above just goes to show that the most elemental rules of caution would tend to advise an << economic-financial diagnosis>> of the company prior to commencing is the activities involved in the project, and in this way to verify if the company in a reasonable condition to undertake the same.

On introducing ourselves is into this aspect of the problem it is particularly useful to choose the correct technique for drawing up the programme, since from this, it is possible to get to know the amount of payment means required for handling, at every moment, the payments for carrying out the tasks making up the project. In this way, there will be certain immediate, short term, medium and long term requirements. How to meet each one of these and the degree to which it will be possible, will determine the level of risk that is assumed if the project is undertaken. The <<health>> of the company, at any given moment, can very well tend toward <<sickness>> of a certain seriousness as a consequence of assuming the more or less high risk that every investment signifies.

There are certain paths which can be followed with the object of getting to know the economic-financial situation of a company. We will now propose a method that we already developed on other occasions, giving us good results[1].

In order to be able to continue along the path we have commenced it would appear to be convenient to attempt to establish the fundamental elements that determine the solvency of a company faced with the financial requirements of an investment. The duality health-sickness in living beings offers certain parallelisms in the corporate body. As an indication we list:

Health		*Sickness*
A. Adequate liquidity	→	Lack of immediate liquidity
B. Sufficient discount lines	→	Discount lines covered
C. Solvency relative to suppliers	→	No credit with suppliers
D. Extendable short term credits	→	Short-term credit at maximum level
E. Long term accessibility	→	Long-term credits depleted
F. Option to mortgage loans	→	All assets mortgaged
G. Recourse to guarantees	→	Impossibility of new guarantees
H. Facility extension own funds	→	Own funds not extendibles.

Having established the above financial pathologies, which we have no intention of saying includes all the possible weaknesses of the company, we propose listing as is done for medical diagnosis, all those <<symptoms>> by means of which we can make a clear diagnosis. On many occasions, these symptoms are expressed by the fact that a certain economic parameter does not reach a determined limit, on others the sickness is discovered because it passes certain limits which are considered as dangerous, and also when these are outside a certain interval. The nature of these economic parameters is diverse. On occasions we are dealing with absolute parameters and on others relative parameters; they can be estimated by means of measurements or valuations; but always, wherever possible, by means of numerical assignments.

These considerations lead us to the question relative to where to *look for* these symptoms. If we take into account the fact that the diagnosis is made at an initial period in time and refers to one or several stages in the future (period in which the investment process takes place) it would seem not to be particularly unreasonable to extract them from the accounting books and from the information which directly or indirectly arises from the same. Let us now detail, only as an example, the ones we are going to use below:

a) Available
b) Definitely realisable
c) Conditioned realisation
d) Generated Cash Flow
e) Quotient between current assets and short term liabilities
f) Short term debt ratio
g) Medium and long term debt ratio

Each of these elements is susceptible to being valued by diverse units. In our case we will consider that *a, b, c, d* are expressed in monetary units and *e, f, g* by means of ratios.

We feel it is unnecessary to insist on the fact that the listed symptoms are not unalterable either relative to their concept or to their amount. Certain others could be considered, adding to the same those we feel are more important or cancelling any of them thought to be superfluous.

Also, considering the fact that in order to obtain the risk of the investment it is necessary to check a company or institution relative to several <<diseases>>, because it could happen that certain symptoms were to be highly significant for some of them and on the other hand, were not to be too important for others. In another sense, it would be quite normal to think that the level that each symptom should reach in order to detect the economic-financial health or in the event sickness, can be very different in one or other of the <<health>> manifestations.

Let us now go on to study the set of activities which make up the project and let us tackle the economic-financial diagnosis. For this we shall use the graph we have shown below, which corresponds to the investment programme developed in the previous chapter, on which the genuinely financial activities <<zone>> has been marked (figure 3.1).

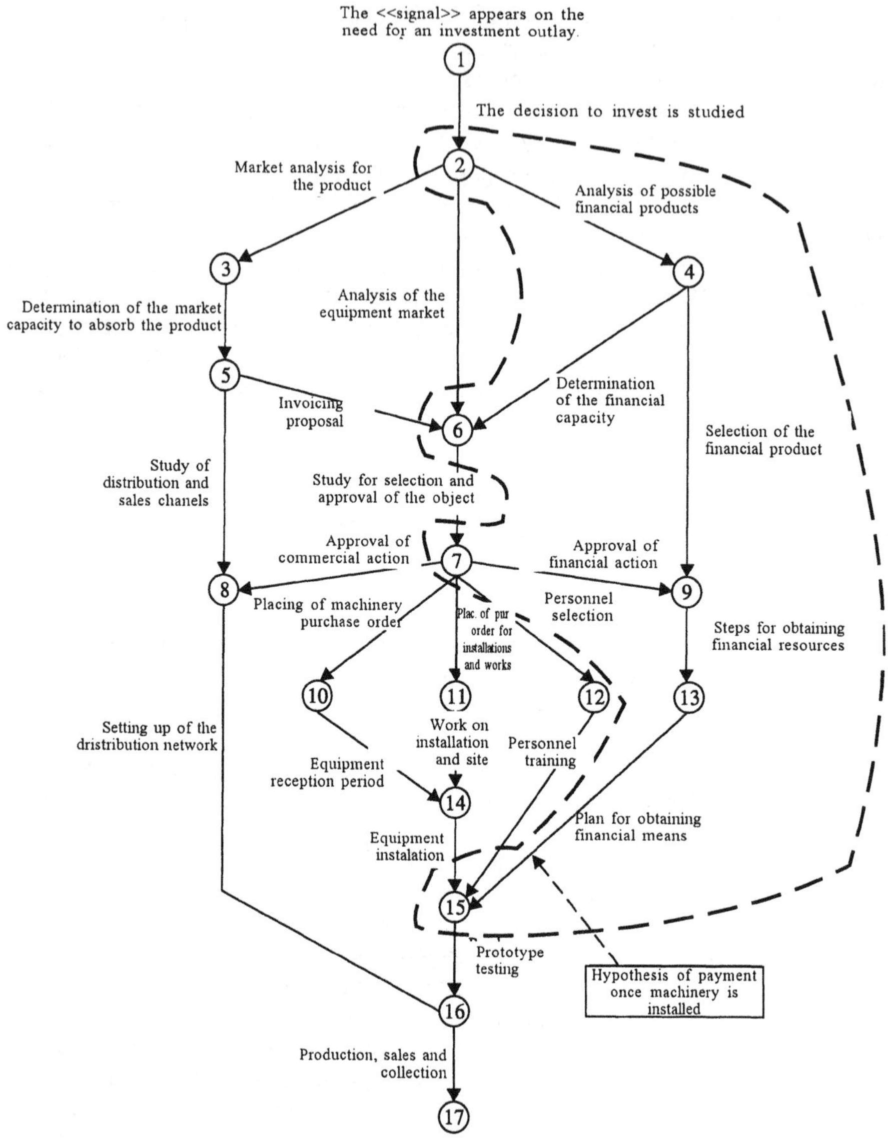

Figur6 3.1.

In this graph, we have started out from the hypothesis according to which the steps taken for obtaining outside resources are intended for financing the total or partial acquisition of the investment object (the resources arrive as a consequence of vertex (13, 15), once the equipment is installed). From this it can be deduced that the rest of the activities of the project is financed by in-house capital. However, there is no problem in extending this scheme to the assumption in which the needs of payment means obliges seeking an understanding with financial institutions, successive partial draw-downs when in-house funds are not sufficient or it is not convenient to put them to use for these purposes. In this case there would be a modification in the architecture of the graph in the arcs affecting the financial tasks of the process.

Having made this point, it is now convenient to point out, that to make recourse to <<extraordinary>> financing (internal or external) in order to be able to handle the investment, requires certain tasks prior to finding the money. These are activities (2, 4) <<analysis of possible financial products>> and (4, 6) <<determination of the financial capacity>>. The first of these, means knowledge of the financial and monetary markets from which knowledge has been gathered of possible products that they offer and which are open to being used by the company, with their corresponding price conditions, time limits, guarantees, etc. Only when this information is to hand, is it possible to start the activity of determining the financial capacity from a diagnosis. This task constitutes the fundamental part of activity (4,6) of the graph.

Now, as has already been mentioned, with the object of setting the level that each symptom must reach or not exceed in order to be able to talk about a healthy situation of the company, it will be necessary to take into account the activities relative to the times in which payment is required.

Determination of the financial capacity of the investment

In order to reach the objective of getting to know the financial capacity with which to be able to satisfy the payments included in carrying out the activities, we will start off with the existence of two sets: R, which will include the elements representing the health of the company required for commencing the tasks of the project, in our case:

$$R = \{A, B, ..., H\}$$

and S, which corresponds to the symptoms which allow for detecting the degree of health. Here we will have:

$$S = \{a, b, ..., g\}$$

Below we are going to establish for each of the elements of set R, which identify the economic-financial health for starting the investment project, those levels that each symptom must exceed, or not reach (the case could also exist where they should be positioned between two of them) in order for the absence of financial risk to be considered. Let us take a look at these elements one by one.

A. Immediate liquidity:

a	*b*	*c*	*d*	*e*	*f*	*g*
⩾200	⩾350	⩾400	⩾500	1.3⩽	⩽0.6	⩽0.8

B. Sufficient discount lines:

a	*b*	*c*	*d*	*e*	*f*	*g*
⩾50	⩾250	⩾500	⩾550	1.5⩽	⩽0.5	⩽0.6

C. Solvency relative to suppliers

a	*b*	*c*	*d*	*e*	*f*	*g*
⩾100	⩾300	⩾600	⩾600	1.5⩽	⩽0.4	⩽0.7

D. Extendable short term credits

a	*b*	*c*	*d*	*e*	*f*	*g*
⩾80	⩾400	⩾600	⩾600	1.6⩽	⩽0.4	⩽0.6

E. Long term accessibility

a	*b*	*c*	*d*	*e*	*f*	*g*
⩾40	⩾200	⩾500	⩾700	1.4⩽	⩽0.5	⩽0.3

F. Option to mortgage loans

a	*b*	*c*	*d*	*e*	*f*	*g*
⩾40	⩾200	⩾500	⩾650	1.3⩽	⩽0.5	⩽0.4

G. Recourse to guarantees

a	*b*	*c*	*d*	*e*	*f*	*g*
⩾150	⩾300	⩾600	⩾550	1.5⩽	⩽0.5	⩽0.7

H. Facility extension to own funds.

a	*b*	*c*	*d*	*e*	*f*	*g*
$\geqslant 50$	$\geqslant 150$	$\geqslant 500$	$\geqslant 800$	$1.2 \leqslant$	$\leqslant 0.6$	$\leqslant 0.5$

Let us move on and express this data in unitary a form by using a matrix in which we will place as elements of the rows, the <<symptoms>> and as columns, the elements representative of the economic-financial <<health>> of the company for undertaking the investment. For this we are going to place the above rows one alongside the other as columns.

$[M] =$	*A*	*B*	*C*	*D*	*E*	*F*	*G*	*H*
a	$\geqslant 200$	$\geqslant 50$	$\geqslant 100$	$\geqslant 80$	$\geqslant 40$	$\geqslant 40$	$\geqslant 150$	$\geqslant 50$
b	$\geqslant 350$	$\geqslant 250$	$\geqslant 300$	$\geqslant 400$	$\geqslant 200$	$\geqslant 200$	$\geqslant 300$	$\geqslant 150$
c	$\geqslant 400$	$\geqslant 500$	$\geqslant 600$	$\geqslant 600$	$\geqslant 500$	$\geqslant 500$	$\geqslant 600$	$\geqslant 500$
d	$\geqslant 500$	$\geqslant 550$	$\geqslant 600$	$\geqslant 600$	$\geqslant 700$	$\geqslant 650$	$\geqslant 550$	$\geqslant 800$
e	$1.3 \leqslant$	$1.5 \leqslant$	$1.5 \leqslant$	$1.6 \leqslant$	$1.4 \leqslant$	$1.3 \leqslant$	$1.5 \leqslant$	$1.2 \leqslant$
f	$\leqslant 0.6$	$\leqslant 0.5$	$\leqslant 0.4$	$\leqslant 0.4$	$\leqslant 0.5$	$\leqslant 0.5$	$\leqslant 0.5$	$\leqslant 0.6$
g	$\leqslant 0.8$	$\leqslant 0.6$	$\leqslant 0.7$	$\leqslant 0.6$	$\leqslant 0.3$	$\leqslant 0.4$	$\leqslant 0.7$	$\leqslant 0.5$

It is necessary to take into account that the values of the accounts of the balance sheet representing the liquidity or liquidability of the company, cannot only be used for the tasks of the investment, but must also be available for payments arising from the normal activity of the company.

The above table, in the form of a matrix, brings to light what could be called the <<standards for financial comfort for an investment>>, valid for a wide range of companies located in a particular geo-economic space and during a determined period of time. It will constitute the basis on which comparisons can be made of the real situation of the company wishing to invest. What should be done then is to establish a confrontation between what *should be* and what *really is*. For this the financial analyst will take from the potentially investing company, the data and estimates in the form of a <<verification>>. Let us now suppose that this has already been established and that the information received for each symptom has given rise to the following vector:

	Company Z
a	[160, 180]
b	[320, 340]
c	[530, 580]
$[P] = d$	[660, 720]
e	[1.3, 1.4]
f	[0.2, 0.3]
g	[0.8, 0.9]

With the object of generalising our scheme wherever possible, we have resorted to establishing estimates relative to the data of the company by means of confidence intervals. The supposition with crisp numbers would mean a very special case.

Now, comparison of the health standards with the situation detected in the company takes place. For this several paths can be followed. Among these we have selected one that consists in looking for each one of the symptoms relative to each illness, the intersection between requirements of health and estimated situation of the reality. This means considering each of the columns of matrix $[M]$ and comparing these to vector $[P]$, the use of the $(\cap)$ operator will give rise to the following result:

	A	*B*	*C*	*D*	*E*	*F*	*G*	*H*
a	∅	[160, 180]	[160, 180]	[160, 180]	[160, 180]	[160, 180]	[160, 180]	[160, 180]
b	∅	[320, 340]	[320, 340]	∅	[320, 340]	[320, 340]	[320, 340]	[320, 340]
c	[530, 580]	[530, 580]	∅	∅	[530, 580]	[530, 580]	∅	[530, 580]
$[M] \cap [P] = d$	[660, 720]	[660, 720]	[660, 720]	[660, 720]	[700, 720]	[660, 720]	[660, 720]	∅
e	[1.3, 1.4]	∅	∅	∅	1.4	[1.3, 1.4]	∅	[1.3, 1.4]
f	[.2, .3]	[.2, .3]	[.2, .3]	[.2, .3]	[.2, .3]	[.2, .3]	[.2, .3]	[.2, .3]
g	0.8	∅	∅	∅	∅	∅	∅	∅

What we have just developed should allow for the transformation of matrix $[M] \cap [P]$ into a fuzzy relation $[\underset{\sim}{B}]$ observing the following rules:

1. The elements of matrix $[\underset{\sim}{B}]$ will be expressed by means of the hendecadarian system
2. Segment [0, 1] of valuations will be separated into sub-segments starting out from certain values α y β and which will be set up into thresholds.

   a) Threshold α will let manifest sickness pass on to ever better states of health
   b) Threshold β will constitute the passing from a state of relative health to full healthiness.
3. For those relations (x, Y) in which a strict inclusion exists valuations in $[\beta,1]$ will be assigned, in accordance with a determined criterion.
4. For those relations (x, Y) where *non*-strict inclusion exists a valuation in $[\beta,\alpha]$ will be taken, also in accordance with a certain criterion.
5. For those relations which are located in a limit position, a value equal to (α) will be assigned.
6. Values $\emptyset$ of matrix $[M] \cap [P]$ will be substituted by valuations in $[0,\alpha]$ in accordance with a criterion to be established.

Let us now take a look at the more specific aspects and criteria to be adopted in this transformation algorithm, from an overall perspective.

In the first place, we will establish the semantic hendecadarian scale that will relate segment [0, 1] with the words normally used for designating the degrees from overflowing with health, to the galloping sickness, of the company or institution:

0: galloping sickness
.1: very sick
.2: quite sick
.3: relatively sick
.4: more sick than healthy
.5: neither sick nor healthy
.6: more healthy than sick
.7: relatively healthy
.8: quite healthy
.9: very healthy
1: overflowing with health

As we have mentioned on previous occasions, the correspondence we have just presented is not intended to be imposed as a single and rigid rule. The uses and customs of every country, and even of every person, may very well advise the use of different rules. We ourselves have used different words for the cases of the extremes of section 2, *a*) and *b*).

In second place let us move on to separating segment [0, 1] into three subsets $[0,\alpha]$, $[\alpha,\beta]$, $[\beta,1]$, by means of Figure 3.2

For each specific assumption, what we are doing is assigning to α and β the convenient values within segment [0, 1], in accordance with the sense we wish to give to the words of the accepted semantic scale. We are well aware of the hypothetical difficulty of knowing (in people and in companies and institutions) when there is a passing from good health to sickness and, therefore, in determining the value of the threshold relative to the limit situation α. However this act, inevitably impregnated with subjectivity, posses in this case, less of an impact than if done in the boolean field.

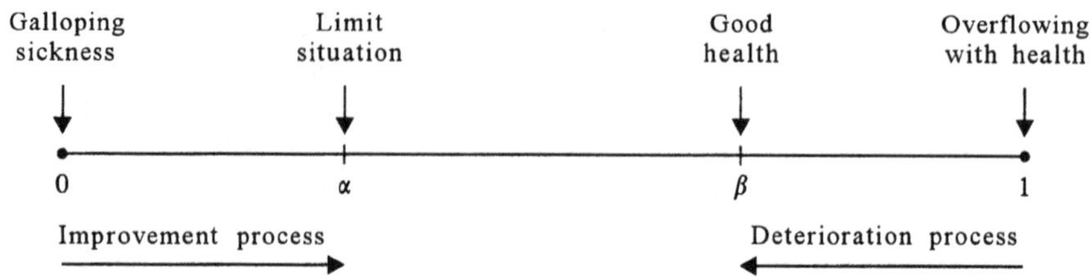

Figure 3.2.

Having supposedly established the values of α and β we can now pass on, in third place, to assignment of valuations to segment $[\beta, 1]$, for which it will be necessary to establish the corresponding criterion. But before tackling this aspect it is important to mention that two differing cases could occur according to the whether the symptoms of normality are expressed in confidence intervals or by means of a limit (crisp number) which it is necessary to exceed, in some cases, or not to reach in others. This would be the cases in which the health were to be conditioned as to whether the results of the verification were to be situated within the interval $[m_1, m_2]$ or that the health condition should give rise to the fact that those results were higher (or in the event less) than m, limit desiggnated in the matrix as accepted normality. We will now establish for each one of these cases the corresponding criterion of numerical assignment.

a) The relation symptom-health of the normality matrix is given by a confidence interval. In this case it can be accepted that the healthiest condition is located in the mean point of this interval $[m_1, m_2]$. The verification is also expressed by means of another confidence interval $[p_1, p_2]$[2].

As a prior step let us obtain an index expressed in [0, 1] which later will be transformed into a number in $[\beta, 1]$. For this the entropy found at the mean point of the interval $\underset{\sim}{m} = [m_1, m_2]$ that is to say $\overline{\underset{\sim}{m}}$ giving rise to the perfect situation, will be made to fall. The closer the result of verification is to this point, the better will be the health condition. If the real situation of the company or institution is given by $\underset{\sim}{p} = [p_1, p_2]$, the mean point of this interval $\overline{\underset{\sim}{p}}$ can also be taken as a point of comparison, as it is its best representation in the crisp sphere. From these considerations we now propose as an index the complement to the unit, of double the difference between $\overline{\underset{\sim}{m}}$ and $\overline{\underset{\sim}{p}}$ referenced relative to the extent of the interval $\underset{\sim}{m}$ in absolute values. Let us take a look at it.

Since:

$$2\left(\frac{m_1+m_2}{2}-\frac{p_1+p_2}{2}\right)=(m_1-p_1)+(m_2-p_2)$$

on referencing it with the extent of the interval it will be:

$$\frac{(m_1-p_1)+(m_2-p_2)}{m_2-m_1}$$

but taking into account the fact that the deviation to the right is as important as the deviation to the left, this value must be taken in absolute terms. The need to give higher values to the proximity of $\underset{\sim}{m}$ will require complementation to the unit. In short it will be:

$$J_{(x,Y)}=1-\left|\frac{(m_1-p_1)+(m_2-p_2)}{m_2-m_1}\right|$$

By the construction itself $J_{(x,Y)}$ is a value in [0, 1]. In order to pass on to a valuation $K_{(x,Y)}$ in $[\beta, 1]$, it will be sufficient to use the linear form:[3]

$$\boxed{K_{(x,Y)}=\beta+(1-\beta)\cdot J_{(x,Y)}}$$

b) The relation symptom-health of the normality matrix is also given by a limit which must be exceeded (interval $[m, \infty)$), or not exceeded (interval $(-\infty, m]$, when the field is R)[4].

When these circumstances arise, it is acceptable to use the notion of distance which, also, provides an index of remoteness relative to a limit. Therefore the greater the distance of a value the closer it is to the unit and better <<health>> situation. The distances obtained, obviously in [0, 1], should be converted later into valuations relative to segment $[\beta, 1]$. Let us take a look, in the first place at the case of the interval $[m, \infty)$ (limit m must be exceeded).

The absolute distance is:

$$d_{(x,Y)}([p_1, p_2], m)=\frac{(p_1-m)+(p_2-m)}{2}$$

And with the object of having a distance value which is open to being compared with other distances, a relative distance will be obtained, taking as a reference the subtraction between the higher value of the limits and the upper extreme of $\underset{\sim}{p}$ and the lesser value between the limit and the lower extreme of $\underset{\sim}{p}$, that is:

$$\delta_{(x, Y)}(\underset{\sim}{p}, m) = \frac{d}{\text{Max}\,\{p_2, m^{(j)}\} - \text{Min}\,\{p_1, m^{(j)}\}} = \frac{(p_1 - m) + (p_2 - m)}{2(\text{Max}\,\{p_2, m^{(j)}\} - \text{Min}\,\{p_1, m^{(j)}\})}$$

$$j \in \{A, B, C, ...\}$$

Now let us move on to the case of interval $(-\infty, m]$ (limit m must not be exceeded).

The absolute distance will be:

$$d_{(x, Y)}([p_1, p_2], m) = \frac{(m - p_1) + (m - p_2)}{2}$$

and the relative distance:

$$\delta_{(x, Y)}(\underset{\sim}{p}, m) = \frac{d}{\text{Max}\,\{p_2, m^{(j)}\} - \text{Min}\,\{p_1, m^{(j)}\}} = \frac{(m - p_1) + (m - p_2)}{2(\text{Max}\,\{p_2, m^{(j)}\} - \text{Min}\,\{p_1, m^{(j)}\})}$$

It is obvious that both cases can be summarised into one single formula, considering the distances $p_1 - m$ and $p_2 - m$ in absolute terms. In short we arrive at:

$$\delta_{(x, Y)}(\underset{\sim}{p}, m) = \frac{|p_1 - m| + |p_2 - m|}{2(\text{Max}\,\{p_2, m^{(j)}\} - \text{Min}\,\{p_1, m^{(j)}\})}$$

In any case by construction it will be:

$$0 \leqslant \delta_{(x, Y)}(\underset{\sim}{p}, m) \leqslant 1$$

for this, it will be necessary to convert the corresponding values into others located in segment $[\beta, 1]$, for which we will use the following linear form again:

$$\boxed{L_{(x, Y)} = \beta + (1 - \beta) \cdot \delta_{(x, Y)}}$$

Now let us move on, in fourth place, to establishing a criterion for obtaining a valuation in $[\alpha, \beta]$.

It would appear that, when this case arises, the greater or lesser possibility that the symptom implies the existence of sickness, be calculated. For this several procedures can be worked out. We propose one that adds to its simplicity, easy practical use. What is done is to set up an index $H_{(x, Y)}$ such that, as it comes closer to the unit it is considered that the symptom induces one to think in a increasingly healthy condition. The removal from and consequent proximity to zero leads one to think in the precariousness and approach of an illness situation. In general, this index could be expressed, as always:

$[p_1, p_2]$: the interval resulting from revision
$[m_1, m_2]$: the interval of accepted normality

and by carrying out the intersection of both intervals:

$$[p_1, p_2]\ (\cap)\ [m_1, m_2] = [n_1, n_2]$$

by means of the following expression:

$$H_{(x, Y)} = \frac{n_2 - n_1}{p_2 - p_1}$$

The substitution of m_1 or m_2 by $-\infty$ or $+\infty$, that is to say these are values which must not exceed m_1 or exceed m_2, brings up no problem since the intersection of the intervals $\underset{\sim}{p}$ and $\underset{\sim}{m}$ automatically leaves the infinite limits of one or the other limit outside.

Now all that has to be done is the transfer of segment [0, 1] to segment $[\alpha, \beta]$. For this once again we will use the linear expression:

$$\boxed{I_{(x, Y)} = \alpha + (\beta - \alpha) \cdot H_{(x, Y)}}$$

In fifth place, we pass on to the assignment of valuation α that has been previously established for those relations (x, Y) which are located in the situation which we have qualified as limit.

It is easy to see that this phase is a special case of the previous one since when $m_2 = p_1$ or $m_1 = p_2$ the intersection takes place at $\emptyset$ and, therefore, it can be considered that $H_{(x, Y)}$ is equal to zero and $I_{(x, Y)}$ is equal to α.

Let us now take a look at, in the sixth and final place, how to situate in what could be called the sickness interval $[0,\alpha]$ the $\emptyset$ of matrix $[M] \cap [P]$. In this case there is total domination of interval $[m_1, m_2]$ or of the crisp number m over the confidence interval $[p_1, p_2]$ or inversely. The concept of distance can be a good criterion for obtaining the corresponding values which allow for the corresponding valuation. And this, both for the case of the intervals of normality and for the crisp numbers to be exceeded or not to be arrived at. Let us now pass directly on to the formulas of relative distance we arrived at previously.

In the case of intervals:

$$\delta_{(x, Y)} = \frac{|p_1 - m_1| + |p_2 - m_2|}{2(\text{Max}\ \{p_2, m_2^{(j)}\} - \text{Min}\ \{p_1, m_1^{(j)}\})}$$

Now then given the fact that the greater distance in relation with $[m_1, m_2]$ means a lesser health condition, in this case the complement to the unit of distance, that is to say, an<<index of nearness>> should be used. Thus, we will consider:

$$\bar{\delta} = 1 - \delta_{(x, Y)}$$

In the case of a crisp limit:

$$\delta_{(x, Y)} = \frac{|p_1 - m| + |p_2 - m|}{2(\text{Max}\ \{p_2, m^{(j)}\} - \text{Min}\ \{p_1, m^{(j)}\})}$$

For the same reason the following will now be taken into consideration:

$$\bar{\delta}_{(x, Y)} = 1 - \delta_{(x, Y)}$$

where

$$\bar{\delta}_{(x, Y)} \in [0, 1]; \quad j \in \{A, B, C, ...\}$$

In order to pass over from [0, 1] to [0, α] it will be sufficient to do the linear transformation:

$$F_{(x, Y)} = 0 + (\alpha - 0) \cdot \bar{\delta}_{(x, Y)}$$

$$\boxed{F_{(x, Y)} = \alpha \cdot \bar{\delta}_{(x, Y)}}$$

In this way what has been proposed are certain criteria that will allow us to obtain the fuzzy relation $[\underset{\sim}{B}]$. Once again we repeat that the adoption of these criteria is not absolutely essential. Obviously there exist others that in certain cases may be more useful and which we have on occasions used[5]. What can be stated is that their use is very easy. As a sample of this let us take a rapid look through matrix $[M] \cap [P]$ of our example. In it what is brought to light is the fact that there are four types of results relative to their elements.

Let us assume that the experts have adopted as values for α and β, respectively:

$$\alpha = 0.3, \quad \beta = 0.7$$

a) The first concerns those symptoms that are within accepted normality, interval $[\beta, 1]$, and which, therefore, do not induce us to believe in the existence of the illness but on the contrary that health is evident. In these cases it may be interesting to see the <<degree of comfort>>. Since in this case normality is given by limits, the notion of distance will be used, which will allow a numerical assignment in this respect. Let us take a look at, for example, some of the cases that have arisen in our example.

Let us start with box (a, B), We have as an overall distance:

$$d([160, 180], [50, 50]) = \frac{(160-50)+(180-50)}{2} = \frac{110+130}{2} = 120$$

and, as a relative distance, if we take the difference between Max {50, 100, 80, 40, 40, 150, 50, 180) and Min {50, 100, 80, 40, 40, 150, 50, 160), that is, 180 - 40 = 140:

$$\delta([160, 180], [50, 50]) = \frac{d}{140} = \frac{120}{140} = \frac{6}{7}$$

Let us now take a look at box (a, G):

$$d([160, 180], [150, 150]) = \frac{10+30}{2} = 20$$

$$\delta([160, 180], [150, 150]) = \frac{d}{140} = \frac{20}{140} = \frac{1}{7}$$

If the distances obtained are compared, it will be seen that in the case of box (a, B) the relative distance is far greater to that corresponding to box (a, G), which indicates a greater degree of comfort and, therefore, a greater movement away from the risk through symptom a in pathology B than in G . And so on, one could in this way go through each and every one of the boxes.

Let us now transform the values of the distances in [0, 1] to valuations in [0.7, 1]. We will arrive at:

$$L_{(a, B)} = 0.7 + 0.3 \ \frac{6}{7} = 0.957$$

$$L_{(a, G)} = 0.7 + 0.3 \ \frac{1}{7} = 0.743$$

b) The second appears when the corresponding symptom is only normal in an <<area>> (optimist) while the rest of the interval (pessimist area) indicates the existence of an illness.

Let us look at this in relation to (*d, E*).

For this symptom and illness, normality requires that the symptom be located at 700 or above this number, while the check-up of the company has given us an uncertain amount [660, 720]. Only if reality situates the symptom in the area given by interval [700, 720] can the company consider itself as healthy. If we divide the difference between the extremes of the healthy zone by the difference between the extremes of interval $[p_1, p_2]$ obtained through the check-up, we will have:

$$H_{(d,E)} = \frac{720 - 700}{720 - 660} = \frac{20}{60} = \frac{1}{3}$$

The transfer of the value of $H_{(d,E)}$ in [0, 1] to $I_{(d,E)}$ in $[\alpha, \beta]$ is immediate:

$$I_{(d,E)} = 0.3 + 0.4\,\frac{1}{3} = 0.433$$

c) The third refers to those symptoms which are at the limit considered as normal relative to a sickness. In our example two cases have appeared and they correspond to boxes (*e, E*) where only the optimist position (which in this case corresponds to the upper limit of the interval) permits concluding in precarious normality, and (*g, A*) in which normality, also precarious, only occurs in the optimist case, represented this time by the lower level.

d) The fourth concerns elements of $[M] \cap [P]$ which have been designated by $\varnothing$, that is those sunken in sickness. As an example, let us take a look at the assignment of valuations to (*a, A*) and (*b, A*). We arrive at for (*a, A*), $\text{Max}\,\{p_2, m^{(j)}\} = \text{Max}\,\{180, 200\} = 200$ and $\text{Min}\,\{p_1, m^{(j)}\} = \text{Min}\,\{160, 200\} = 160$, therefore:

$$\delta_{(a,A)} = \frac{|160 - 200| + |180 - 200|}{2(200 - 160)} = \frac{60}{80} = \frac{3}{4}$$

therefore:

$$\bar{\delta}_{(a,A)} = 1 - \frac{3}{4} = \frac{1}{4}$$

Given that for (*b, A*), $\text{Max}\,\{p_2, m^{(j)}\} = \text{Max}\,\{340, 350, 400\} = 400$ and $\text{Min}\,\{p_1, m^{(j)}\} = \text{Min}\,\{320, 350, 400\} = 320$ we will have:

$$\delta_{(b,A)} = \frac{|320 - 350| + |340 - 350|}{2(400 - 320)} = \frac{40}{160} = \frac{1}{4}$$

Then:

$$\bar{\delta}_{(b,A)} = 1 - \frac{1}{4} = \frac{3}{4}$$

In order to pass on to interval [0, α] the following is done:

$$F_{(a,A)} = 0.3\,\frac{1}{4} = 0.075$$

$$F_{(b,A)} = 0.3\,\frac{3}{4} = 0.225$$

Having seen these examples, we feel it is unnecessary to reproduce all the calculation which take us to the fuzzy relation $[\underset{\sim}{B}]$, so we will pass directly on to the results obtained, which will give rise to the following pre-diagnostic matrix:

$[\underset{\sim}{B}] =$	*A*	*B*	*C*	*D*	*E*	*F*	*G*	*H*
a	.075	.957	.850	.893	.979	.979	.743	.957
b	.225	.826	.747	.037	.905	.905	.747	.984
c	.958	.791	.107	.107	.791	.791	.107	.791
d	.959	.891	.823	.823	.433	.754	.891	.064
e	.775	.150	.150	.050	.300	.775	.150	.925
f	.962	.887	.812	.812	.887	.887	.887	.962
g	.300	.175	.225	.175	.025	.075	.225	.125

We consider that this fuzzy relation $[\underset{\sim}{B}]$, constitutes the materialisation of the financial pre-diagnosis of a company or institution. In fact, if it is taken into account that each of the columns represents a fuzzy relation, relative to the corresponding illness, of the symptoms referential, one will be able to see to what degree, from 0 to 1, the symptom makes one think of the healthy situation of the company or institution. Thus, in the case we are developing, pathology *A* which concerns liquidity, would give rise to the following fuzzy sub-set (first column of the matrix):

	a	*b*	*c*	*d*	*e*	*f*	*g*
$\underset{\sim}{A} =$	.075	.225	.958	.959	.775	.962	.300

It can be seen that the state of liquidity is practically optimum, if we consider symptoms *c, d, f,* good as from symptom *e,* but is at the limit relative to *g.* Symptom *b,* and above all *a* indicate serious health problems.

This example brings to light a fact that may very frequently occur in reality: not all symptoms lead unmistakably to a clear conclusion on the degree of health relative to a pathology. This is a general case that includes the supposition of clarity in the pre-diagnosis as if it were a specific case.

From pre-diagnosis to diagnosis

The indecision that such situations can induce makes it impossible for us to halt this study at this point. We are now going to propose a scheme which will allow, we feel, advancing from pre-diagnosis to diagnosis. For this we would like to state that in all sickness, either in living beings or in companies or institutions, the set of symptoms that are capable of detecting it do not always have the same importance, because some can be more significant than others. This fact needs to be formalised in order to incorporate it into the model we are developing. Several paths can be followed in order to reach this objective. The greater part of these converge in the need of assigning a weight to each of the criteria relative to an illness.

But the problem does not stop here, since the objective sought cannot be forgotten, that is the determination of the risk of not being able to make the payments arising from the investment process. It is for this reason that there are certain pathologies linked to each one of the activities, subject to whether they mean immediate, short term, medium or long-term payments. It is quite normal to think that certain financial sicknesses will severely affect payments made after several periods (long-term) and which have little incidence on immediate payments, for example. Thus, *each expiry date* will be found to be related to the *different financial pathologies.*

In the first place, we will tackle the establishment of weights for each of the pathologies. We will continue with our example, in which there are seven symptoms and we will centre out attention on one pathology, for example, A, which is relative to the existence or not of sufficient liquidity. We are now going to establish the importance of each symptom relative to the others, by stating the number of times one symptom is worth more than another. Let us assume that we accept the fact, beginning with *a,* that *a* is worth 3 times *b*, 5 times *c*, 8 times *d*, 2 times *e*, 2 times *f*, 10 times *g*. Continuing with *b:* that *b* is worth 2 times *c*, 3 times *d*, 1/2 times *e*, 1/2 times *f*, 4 times *g*. We follow on with *c:* c is worth 2 times *d*, 1/3 times *e*, 1/3 times *f*, 2 times *g*. We now pass on to *d*: *d* is worth 1/4 times *e*, 1/4 times *f*, and is equivalent to *g*. Now we look at *e*: *e* is equivalent to *f*, is worth 5 times *g*. And finally *f* is worth 6 times *g*.

We have assigned certain valuations to these correspondences that are not strictly coherent, since reality makes it difficult for this assumption to be complied with. Even so, certain totally coherent relations not only would confirm the scheme but would constitute a special case. Using the previous estimates we are now going to construct a reciprocal matrix such as the following:

	a	*b*	*c*	*d*	*e*	*f*	*g*
a	1	3	5	8	2	2	10
b	1/3	1	2	3	1/2	1/2	4
c	1/5	1/2	1	2	1/3	1/3	2
$[T] =$ *d*	1/8	1/3	1/2	1	1/4	1/4	1
e	1/2	2	3	4	1	1	5
f	1/2	2	3	4	1	1	6
g	1/10	1/4	1/2	1	1/5	1/6	1

This matrix is reciprocal by construction, but not totally coherent[6]. We are now going on to calculate the dominant value and corresponding vector. For this we will do the multiplication $[T] \cdot [1]$ arriving at:

$$\begin{bmatrix} 1 & 3 & 5 & 8 & 2 & 2 & 10 \\ 0.33 & 1 & 2 & 3 & 0.5 & 0.5 & 4 \\ 0.2 & 0.5 & 1 & 2 & 0.33 & 0.33 & 2 \\ 0.125 & 0.33 & 0.5 & 1 & 0.25 & 0.25 & 1 \\ 0.5 & 2 & 3 & 4 & 1 & 1 & 5 \\ 0.5 & 2 & 3 & 4 & 1 & 1 & 6 \\ 0.1 & 0.25 & 0.5 & 1 & 0.20 & 0.166 & 1 \end{bmatrix} \bullet \begin{bmatrix} 1 \\ 1 \\ 1 \\ 1 \\ 1 \\ 1 \\ 1 \end{bmatrix} = \begin{bmatrix} 31.000 \\ 11.330 \\ 6.360 \\ 3.455 \\ 16.500 \\ 17.500 \\ 3.126 \end{bmatrix}$$

We are now going to normalise this result in the sense that is given to this term in the theory of fuzzy sub-sets (divide each element of the vector by the highest value of the same). We now arrive at:

$$\begin{bmatrix} 31.000 \\ 11.330 \\ 6.360 \\ 3.455 \\ 16.500 \\ 17.500 \\ 3.126 \end{bmatrix} = 31 \cdot \begin{bmatrix} 1 \\ 0.365 \\ 0.205 \\ 0.111 \\ 0.532 \\ 0.564 \\ 0.103 \end{bmatrix} = 31 \cdot [U_1]$$

We now do the product of $[T]$ with the normalised vector $[U_1]$, that is to say $[T] \cdot [U_1]$. The result is:

$$\begin{bmatrix} 1 & 3 & 5 & 8 & 2 & 2 & 10 \\ 0.33 & 1 & 2 & 3 & 0.5 & 0.5 & 4 \\ 0.2 & 0.5 & 1 & 2 & 0.33 & 0.33 & 2 \\ 0.125 & 0.33 & 0.5 & 1 & 0.25 & 0.25 & 1 \\ 0.5 & 2 & 3 & 4 & 1 & 1 & 5 \\ 0.5 & 2 & 3 & 4 & 1 & 1 & 6 \\ 0.1 & 0.25 & 0.5 & 1 & 0.20 & 0.166 & 1 \end{bmatrix} \cdot \begin{bmatrix} 1 \\ 0.365 \\ 0.205 \\ 0.111 \\ 0.532 \\ 0.564 \\ 0.103 \end{bmatrix} = \begin{bmatrix} 7.23 \\ 2.398 \\ 1.376 \\ 0.836 \\ 3.9 \\ 4.003 \\ 0.707 \end{bmatrix} = 7.23 \cdot \begin{bmatrix} 1 \\ 0.332 \\ 0.190 \\ 0.116 \\ 0.539 \\ 0.554 \\ 0.098 \end{bmatrix}$$

$$= 7.23 \cdot [U_2]$$

We continue with the product $[T] \cdot [U_2]$:

$$\begin{bmatrix} 1 & 3 & 5 & 8 & 2 & 2 & 10 \\ 0.33 & 1 & 2 & 3 & 0.5 & 0.5 & 4 \\ 0.2 & 0.5 & 1 & 2 & 0.33 & 0.33 & 2 \\ 0.125 & 0.33 & 0.5 & 1 & 0.25 & 0.25 & 1 \\ 0.5 & 2 & 3 & 4 & 1 & 1 & 5 \\ 0.5 & 2 & 3 & 4 & 1 & 1 & 6 \\ 0.1 & 0.25 & 0.5 & 1 & 0.20 & 0.166 & 1 \end{bmatrix} \cdot \begin{bmatrix} 1 \\ 0.332 \\ 0.190 \\ 0.116 \\ 0.539 \\ 0.554 \\ 0.098 \end{bmatrix} = \begin{bmatrix} 7.04 \\ 2.328 \\ 1.345 \\ 0.817 \\ 3.781 \\ 3.879 \\ 0.691 \end{bmatrix} = 7.04 \cdot \begin{bmatrix} 1 \\ 0.330 \\ 0.191 \\ 0.116 \\ 0.537 \\ 0.551 \\ 0.098 \end{bmatrix}$$

$$= 7.04 \cdot [U_3]$$

The process is now continued with $[T] \cdot [U_3]$:

$$\begin{bmatrix} 1 & 3 & 5 & 8 & 2 & 2 & 10 \\ 0.33 & 1 & 2 & 3 & 0.5 & 0.5 & 4 \\ 0.2 & 0.5 & 1 & 2 & 0.33 & 0.33 & 2 \\ 0.125 & 0.33 & 0.5 & 1 & 0.25 & 0.25 & 1 \\ 0.5 & 2 & 3 & 4 & 1 & 1 & 5 \\ 0.5 & 2 & 3 & 4 & 1 & 1 & 6 \\ 0.1 & 0.25 & 0.5 & 1 & 0.20 & 0.166 & 1 \end{bmatrix} \cdot \begin{bmatrix} 1 \\ 0.330 \\ 0.191 \\ 0.116 \\ 0.537 \\ 0.551 \\ 0.098 \end{bmatrix} = \begin{bmatrix} 7.035 \\ 2.327 \\ 1.344 \\ 0.816 \\ 3.778 \\ 3.876 \\ 0.691 \end{bmatrix} = 7.035 \cdot \begin{bmatrix} 1 \\ 0.330 \\ 0.191 \\ 0.116 \\ 0.537 \\ 0.551 \\ 0.098 \end{bmatrix}$$

$$= 7.035 \cdot [U_4]$$

At this point we stop the process because $[U_3] = [U_4]$. Taking into account that the order of the matrix is $n = 7$, the relation $(\lambda - n)/n = (7.035 - 7)/7 = 0.005$. It is assumed that 0.5 percent is sufficiently small for accepting the fact that the dominant value is $\lambda = 7.035$ and the corresponding vector in the form of a normal fuzzy sub-set is:

	a	b	c	d	e	f	g
$\underset{\sim}{K}_A =$	1	.330	.191	.116	.537	.551	.098

If each of these valuations is divided by the sum of all the others, that is 2.823, the corresponding weights of a convex weighting (probabilistic normalisation) will be arrived at:

	a	b	c	d	e	f	g
$\underset{\sim}{Q}_A =$	.354	.117	.068	.041	.190	.195	.035

These weights, shown as a fuzzy sub-set of the symptom referential, just go to show the relative importance of each one of these. The joint observation of $\underset{\sim}{A}$ and $\underset{\sim}{Q}_A$ constitutes, in our opinion, a good support for the diagnosis. But if it is desired to assemble in one single number the representation of the degree of health of a company or institution relative to a determined pathology, in this case A, it will be sufficient to make the entropy fall by calculating the composition of the ordinary-product addition of vectors $[\underset{\sim}{A}] \cdot [\underset{\sim}{Q}_A]$. We arrive then at:

$[\underset{\sim}{A}] \cdot [\underset{\sim}{Q}_A] =$

a	b	c	d	e	f	g
.075	.225	.958	.959	.775	.962	.300

$\cdot$

a	.354
b	.117
c	.068
d	.041
e	.190
f	.195
g	.035

$= 0.503$

The result obtained brings to light the fact that the analysed company or institution, in spite of the fact that in matrix $[M] \cap [P]$ only two symptoms of sickness, a and b were detected, is in a difficult position relative to <<adequate liquidity>>. And this is due to the great importance of symptom a, <<available>>, and to a lesser degree b, << definitely realisable>> (the major indecision).

In short the number that summarises the state of health relative to pathology A, in this case 0.503, can be expressed in words, by making recourse to the semantic scale, saying: <<The liquidity of the company or institution is in a situation that it is neither sick nor healthy>>.

We feel it is important to point out, as it appears clearly in the example, the essential difference between the results obtained in $[M] \cap [P]$, $[B]$ and $[\underset{\sim}{A}] \cdot [\underset{\sim}{Q}_A]$, three stages towards this important objective which is the attempt at an economic-financial diagnosis of companies and institutions.

It goes without saying, that from these same elements, we could successively obtain $[\underset{\sim}{B}] \cdot [\underset{\sim}{Q}_B]$, $[\underset{\sim}{C}] \cdot [\underset{\sim}{Q}_C]$, ..., $[\underset{\sim}{H}] \cdot [\underset{\sim}{Q}_H]$. With this we would have completed the analysis on the economic-financial state and we would find ourselves in a position to tackle one last aspect, in this case the crux of the matter of this study, that is the risk which the entity assumes on taking on an investment process.

Numerical determination of the financial risk of an investment

Before passing on to this aspect of the problem, let us just say that the diagnosis, as it has been presented, has an interest which goes further than the sphere in which we have now placed it. Its use, we feel, covers a wide range of situations in which profound knowledge of the company is essential for taking financial decisions. Having made this comment, let us now pass on to determine the risk, as it was initially defined. For this, account must be taken of two aspects: the moment at which payments must be made, and their amount. The first of these is related with the set of pathologies, the second with the degree of health of the same.

In fact, we have been able to see throughout this subject that certain pathologies exist that affect financial needs in the short term and on the other hand others affect the medium and long term. Therefore, according to what investment activity is studied, one or another of these pathologies should be considered. In this way, the existence is accepted of a relation <<time at which an activity-pathology, under consideration, ends>>.

With the object of not making this study unnecessarily complex, we are going to develop this idea by means of an example. Let us suppose we are going to analyse activity (6, 7) of the graph presented in the first section of this chapter, which represents the <<study of selection and approval of the investment object>> commencement of which is estimated in the interval of time [22, 30] and it is hoped it will end in interval [37,48]. Its cost and consequent payment has been valued at [180,270].

The first question that is asked is, taking into account that the estimated payment should be made at the [37,48] units of time after commencement of the project, what are the pathologies that affect this particular payment. If the unit of time corresponds to the concept of days, then it is obvious that we are talking about a short term payment and the most suitable pathologies for getting to know the possibility of doing this are *A, B, C, D.* To make things easier we have practically done without the others.

With regard to the second, in order to be able to determine the degree of risk that is assumed at the commencement of this activity, it is necessary to consider the level of payment of the same. In this respect it is necessary to take into account that this can be done *indistinctly* by any of the four health indicators (liquidity, discount, supplier credit, short term credits), therefore the possibility of making the corresponding payment will be influenced by the levels of health relative to these particular concepts. If the influence is accepted of the level of health over the possibility of payment, the problem has an easy solution by means of the use of logical inferences.

In fact, the relation existing between the level of health in relation to a pathology and the possibility of making the payment of an activity, can be established from a logical reasoning, taking into account proposals P, S and the inference $P \rightarrow S$. Therefore, for pathology A:

P_A: Adequate liquidity
S_A: Possibility of payment of activity (6, 7)
$(P_A \rightarrow S_A)$: *If* there is adequate liquidity, *then* the possibility exists for paying activity (6, 7), by this channel.

As an experiment we will now use, the Lukaciewicz inference:

$$v(P \rightarrow S) = 1 \wedge (v(\bar{P}) + v(S))$$

$v(P \rightarrow S)$, $v(P)$, $v(S)$ being valuations of the inference and of propositions P and S respectively.

We have seen that for this pathology A we have obtained $v(A) = 0.5$. We are now going to assume that the corresponding calculations have been done and that $v(B) = 0.8$, $v(C) = 0.7$ y $v(D) = 0.8$ have been found, that is to say the valuations corresponding to $[\underset{\sim}{B}] \cdot [Q_B]$, $[\underset{\sim}{C}] \cdot [Q_C]$, $[\underset{\sim}{D}] \cdot [Q_D]$.

With the object of obtaining the valuations corresponding to inferences $(P \rightarrow S)$ recourse is made to the opinion of experts, who express the same by means of the following values[7] :

$$v(P_A \rightarrow S_A) = 1$$
$$v(P_B \rightarrow S_B) = 0.9$$
$$v(P_C \rightarrow S_C) = 0.7$$
$$v(P_D \rightarrow S_D) = 0.8$$

These four expressions bring to light the following reasoning: << *If* adequate liquidity exists *then* the possibility of payment is total>>, << *if* there are ample discount lines *then* the possibility of payment is 0.9>> ...

With this data we are ready the use the chosen inference. Let us take a look at it then.

In order to obtain $v(S_A)$:

$$1 = 1 \wedge (0.5 + v(S_A))$$

where $v(S_A)$ is the valuation of proposition S proceeding from proposition A.

We arrive at:

$$v(S_A) = [0.5, 1]$$

For $v(S_B)$:

$$0.9 = 1 \wedge (0.2 + v(S_B))$$
$$v(S_B) = 0.7$$

For $v(S_C)$:

$$0.7 = 1 \wedge (0.3 + v(S_C))$$
$$v(S_C) = 0.4$$

For $v(S_D)$:

$$0.8 = 1 \wedge (0.2 + v(S_D))$$
$$v(S_D) = 0.6$$

Now, as we have mentioned before, payment for activity (6, 7) can be done by means of A and/or B and/or C and/or D, therefore the operator to be used will be the maximisation of the valuations. Therefore:

$$\begin{aligned} v(S) &= v(S_A)\ (\vee)\ v(S_B)\ (\vee)\ v(S_C)\ (\vee)\ v(S_D) \\ &= [0.5, 1]\ (\vee)\ [0.7, 0.7]\ (\vee)\ [0.4, 0.4]\ (\vee)\ [0.6, 0.6] \\ &= [0.7, 1] \end{aligned}$$

If the risk is valued as a complement of the unit of possibility of payment, this finally results in that the financial risk of operation (6, 7) which we shall call $R_F^{(6,7)}$ will be:

$$R_F^{(6,7)} = 1 - [0.7, 1] = [0, 0.3]$$

In this specific case what we have is an uncertain but limited result, by means of a confidence interval. This is due to the use of the Lukaciewicz inference. We can now ask ourselves, what would have been the valuation of the risk of this same operation (6, 7) if in place of the inference we were to use another such as the Lee inference. It is very well known that the operator of the Lee inference is written as:

$$v(P \rightarrow S) = \bar{v}(P) \vee v(S)$$

So that for $v(S_A)$:

$$1 = 0.5 \vee v(S_A)$$
$$v(S_A) = 1$$

For $v(S_B)$:

$$0.9 = 0.2 \vee v(S_B)$$
$$v(S_B) = 0.9$$

For $v(S_C)$:

$$0.7 = 0.3 \vee v(S_C)$$
$$v(S_C) = 0.7$$

For $v(S_D)$:

$$0.8 = 0.2 \vee v(S_C)$$
$$v(S_C) = 0.8$$

We will finally arrive at, for $v(S)$:

$$v(S) = v(S_A) \vee v(S_B) \vee v(S_C) \vee v(S_D) = 1$$

The use of the Lee inference leads us to a different result, as it could not be otherwise, in which the uncertainty of the interval does not exist. Under this supposition, the conclusion is reached that there is no financial risk for this operation because:

$$R_F^{(6,\,7)} = 1 - v(S) = 0$$

The practically unlimited possibilities which versatile logic offers give this scheme great flexibility and adaptability to the needs of each specific case, in which it is possible to choose the inference which better adapts to the conditions reality presents.

To summarise and in the way of a brief conclusion, we can say that the development of this subject has been done in three stages. The first, the object of which was to obtain a <<pre-diagnosis matrix>> which by itself allows us to get an idea on the situation of the analysed entity (company or institution). But this information, is not always sufficient for giving a responsible opinion, on not taking into account the degree of importance of each symptom over the different pathologies.

With the object of reaching this second objective we passed on to a second stage, in which we showed a way for finding certain<<weights>> that allow us to take into account the relative importance of each symptom in the different pathologies, and at the same time to obtain an overall result, summarised in a number (in certain cases it is possible that this is a crisp number and other an uncertain number) that represents the degree of health in a certain pathology. We have shown that the operation of composition, ordinary-product addition is a way of making the entropy fall.

At this point, we have introduced an important hypothesis, for the effects of the developed model, which consists in accepting that there exists a relation of inference, between the concept of the degree of health of a pathology with that of <<the possibility of making the payment>> by means of the element represented by this pathology. Having accepted this hypothesis we are in a position to pass on to the third and final stage.

In this we found a valuation for the degree of possibility of making the payment that an activity means, by an element subject to an eventual pathology with a certain level of health. For this we chose to represent the reasoning linking two propositions by means of an inference extracted from versatile logic. This aspect acquires a special orientation, given the existence of several inference operators within the sphere of uncertainty that, as is quite normal, do not exactly lead to the same result. In each case the decision will have to be taken of choosing one or the other according to the circumstances surrounding the problem to be tackled. Having obtained the possibility for each one of these elements subject to a pathology, and, taking into account that the payment can be made by one and/or the other, the overall possibility is obtained with the use of the maximisation operator. Continuation follows on almost automatically, on considering the degree of risk as a complement of the unit of the possibility of payment.

One of the aspects which deserves special consideration, and which makes this model the instrument of conceptual and technical interest, can be found in the fact that only on very rare occasions does the financial sickness of an entity appear with total clarity, consequent upon the fact that all the symptoms point unequivocally at it. In short, the absolute truths or falsehoods only arise in those minds that, arising from unreality, behave like robots. The economic-financial context in which society is submerged at the end of this century makes human beings, as well as organised groups, capable of reasoning from quasi-infinite nuances, and this thanks to the golden box that is our boundless imagination.

References

1 J. Gil Aluja: <<Ensayo sobre un modelo de diagnóstico económico-financiero>> Proceedings of the Hispano-Portuguese Conference on Scientific Management, Vigo, September 1990, pages 26-29.

2 In the event that it were to be possible to express the result of the verification by means of a crisp number, there is no problem as this would be a special case (a crisp number is also a confidence interval).

3 It is not essential, but useful and practical, to use the linear form. In the case of need any of the sigmoid forms could also be used.

4 In the event that the validity sphere were to be R+ the interval would by [0, *m*] and we would find ourselves in the previous case.

5 J. Gil Aluja: <<Ensayo sobre un modelo de diagnóstico económico-financiero>>. Proceedings of the Vth Hispano-Portuguese Conference on Scientific Management, Vigo, September, 1990, pages 26-29.

6 For a theoretical justification recourse can be made to T. L. Saaty: <<Exploring the interface between hierarchies, multiple objectives and fuzzy sets>> *Fuzzy Sets and Systems*, volume 1, number 1, 1978, pages 57-68.

7 This is obviously a pedagogic example and therefore this data is arbitrary.

4 Analysis of financial products for the investment

Aspects prior to product analysis

To take on an investment process with any guarantee of success means not only an in depth financial knowledge of the company or organisation itself, but also of the environment that will have to be resorted to in order to obtain the necessary means for making external payments. This leads to an analysis of the financial products available for making payments arising from the decision to invest, all of which are offered by different financial institutions.

The procedure to be followed means, in the first place, collecting information relative to the products of the different banks and other credit organisations, as well as carrying out their corresponding collation and screening with the object of making available genuine date inherent to each product and discarding the superfluous or those that are merely commercial advertising.

Once the initially possible products are on the table, in second place one proceeds to their dissection to determine if they posses or not, and to what degree, the necessary characteristics or properties for the investment process. This is a task which means a certain thoroughness and knowledge of the conditions under which the programme should develop, from commencement to termination.

The assignment of the corresponding characteristics or properties to each of the financial products can take place in very different ways. We feel that it is adequate for our purposes, to construct a fuzzy sub-set for each of the financial products, the referential of which would be the set of characteristics or properties. In this way, if we have n possible products $P_1, P_2, \ldots, P_n$ and m characteristics or properties have been considered, $C_1, C_2, \ldots, C_m$, we would arrive at, $\mu_i^{(j)}$ being the degree in which the financial product i posses characteristic j:

$$
\underset{\sim}{P}_i = \begin{array}{ccc|c} C_1 & C_2 & C_3 & C_m \\ \hline \mu_i^{(1)} & \mu_i^{(2)} & \mu_i^{(3)} & \mu_i^{(m)} \end{array}
$$

$$i = 1, 2, ..., n$$

In this way we would arrive at n fuzzy sub-sets, each of which would be the descriptor of the corresponding product by means of its characteristics or properties. The adequate analysis of these fuzzy sub-sets would allow for knowledge of the adequacy of each product or group of products to the end that is sought, in our case, financing of the investment process.

As of this point, there are several paths to follow for reaching this objective. Perhaps the one most used, with verified success in several spheres of management study[1], consists in finding the greater or lesser approach of a product relative to all the others by means of an index. In this respect the notion of distance (Hamming's distance being useful and simple) has been frequently used. With this a fuzzy relation of non-resemblance is obtained, with its complementation that of resemblance and, by choosing an adequate level, a squared and reflexive boolean matrix. By means of an algorithm constructed for this[2] the maximum sub-relations of similarity can be found that allow for a good homogeneous grouping of financial products and, therefore, the corresponding separation into groups which, at the established level, have the different characteristics or properties.

Models drawn up based on this path have been particularly useful for the objectives sought in each case. For us, we are not renouncing to their use further on, when we handle other aspects in this work, above all when the time comes to obtain a criterion for selection of investment objects, under determined conditions of uncertainty. But on tackling the specific problem with which we are now occupied, we have preferred to follow other paths, which should allow us a better adjustment to certain needs in which analysis prevails over selection, as corresponds to the subject. We have used two supports for this: the theory of clans[3] and Moore families[4].

In order to make this exposition clearer and to avoid excessive abstraction, we will develop the proposed model from a didactic example which we assume is sufficiently general for its representation.

Let us assume that once we have done the preliminary tasks, we are left with 6 financial products P_i, $i = 1, 2, ..., 6$ that are subject to being used in the investment process. In this way we arrive at the referential:

$$E = \{P_1, P_2, P_3, P_4, P_5, P_6\}$$

Each of these products posses (or not, in the event) certain characteristics or properties C_j, $j = 1, 2, \ldots, 5$, to a greater or lesser degree. Therefore we can do:

$$C = \{C_1, C_2, C_3, C_4, C_5\}$$

These characteristics are, for example:
C_1: Flexibility in time availability
C_2: Adaptability to the possibilities of reimbursement
C_3: Compatibility of the financial cost with the needs of the investment.
C_4: Agreement of the financial institution with the project (for effects of possible renewals, deferment of expiry dates, etc.)
C_5: Adequacy of the grace period to the estimate of collections arising from the investment.

Let us now see to what degree each product has the listed characteristics or properties. We obtain, then, certain fuzzy sub-sets $\underset{\sim}{P}_i$, $i = 1, 2, \ldots, 6$ which in our case could be:

	C_1	C_2	C_3	C_4	C_5
$\underset{\sim}{P}_1 =$	.4	.7	1	.8	.2

	C_1	C_2	C_3	C_4	C_5
$\underset{\sim}{P}_2 =$	.8	.6	.9	1	.4

	C_1	C_2	C_3	C_4	C_5
$\underset{\sim}{P}_3 =$	.9	.8	.4	.6	1

	C_1	C_2	C_3	C_4	C_5
$\underset{\sim}{P}_4 =$	.5	.9	.8	.2	.7

	C_1	C_2	C_3	C_4	C_5
$\underset{\sim}{P}_5 =$	1	.4	.9	.9	.6

	C_1	C_2	C_3	C_4	C_5
$\underset{\sim}{P}_6 =$	.3	.9	1	.5	.9

It is obvious that all the characteristics or properties not always have the same importance for the satisfactory development of the investment process. This fact can be formally materialised by requiring a different minimum level for each characteristic, from which it is considered that the financial product is satisfactory, relative to the specific characteristic or property. Thus, for example, we could estimate:

For C_1 a minimum level of 0.8. The requirement of monetary availability throughout the duration of the financial product is high.

For C_2 a minimum level of 0.7. The fact of being able to adapt repayments to the development of the investment project is considered of substantial importance.

For C_3 a minimum level of 0.9. This then is the most important characteristic, according to the experts, since the price of money constitutes the most determining aspect of the decision to invest.

For C_4 a minimum level of 0.6. Although harmony with the financial institutions is important, this is considered as relative taking into account the changes in personnel that take place in the same.

For C_5 a minimum level of 0.7. Special interest has been shown by the experts by the fact of being able to harmonise the period from commencement of repayments to the commencement of entry of financial means from the investment process.

If a proposal is accepted of which this example is only a sample (obviously many others could be made) the problem is resolved of the relative importance of each characteristic or property. From these levels a sub-set of limits can be established, known as <<a sub-set of thresholds>>. In our case this is as follows:

	C_1	C_2	C_3	C_4	C_5
$\underset{\sim}{U} =$	.8	.7	.9	.6	.7

Now, we establish that when the level of a characteristic or property possessed by each financial product is equal to or greater than that required in the fuzzy sub-set of thresholds, it is considered as sufficiently adequate for the investment process and when not reaching the level, then it is *not.* With this we pass on from the fuzzy sub-sets $\underset{\sim}{P}_i$, $i = 1, 2, ..., 6$ to the following boolean sub-sets:

	C_1	C_2	C_3	C_4	C_5
$\underset{\approx}{P}_1 =$	0	1	1	1	0

	C_1	C_2	C_3	C_4	C_5
$\underset{\approx}{P}_2 =$	1	0	1	1	0

$\underset{\sim}{P}_3 =$

C_1	C_2	C_3	C_4	C_5
1	1	0	1	1

$\underset{\sim}{P}_4 =$

C_1	C_2	C_3	C_4	C_5
0	1	0	0	1

$\underset{\sim}{P}_5 =$

C_1	C_2	C_3	C_4	C_5
1	0	1	1	0

$\underset{\sim}{P}_6 =$

C_1	C_2	C_3	C_4	C_5
0	1	1	0	1

We are now going to collate for each of the characteristics or properties C_j, $j = 1, 2, \ldots, 5$, those financial products which posses them to the required degree. For this a boolean matrix is formed with the sub-sets $\underset{\sim}{P}_i = 1, 2, \ldots, 6$, in such a way that the characteristics or properties form the rows and the products, the columns. We arrive at:

$[B] =$

	P_1	P_2	P_3	P_4	P_5	P_6
C_1	0	1	1	0	1	0
C_2	1	0	1	1	0	1
C_3	1	1	0	0	1	1
C_4	1	1	1	0	1	0
C_5	0	0	1	1	0	1

The study of this matrix can take place from several angles which will differ according to the current it is desired to give the analysis of the products.

Analysis by means of the clan concept

In the first place our objective is to gather extensive information on the financial products, in the sense of getting to know all their possible groupings, taking into account the properties that each group possesses and why one or another product forming the group has them.

At the same time it is useful to know the *number* of products of the group that posses the respective properties. In this way it will be easy, given certain required characteristics, to know which group possesses them and by how many products they are possessed. For this we will resort to the clans theory.

As is well known the clans theory arose during the early 70's for the formal handling of files, but later it was found that it is particularly operative for the solution of many other problems linked to management. Let us now see how we can use it for our particular case.

From the previous matrix it can be established, very clearly, which are the products that posses each one of the characteristics or properties.

Therefore for C_j, $j = 1, 2, \ldots, 5$, we arrive at:

$$A_1^{(0.8)} = \{P_2, P_3, P_5\}$$
$$A_2^{(0.7)} = \{P_1, P_3, P_4, P_6\}$$
$$A_3^{(0.9)} = \{P_1, P_2, P_5, P_6\}$$
$$A_4^{(0.6)} = \{P_1, P_2, P_3, P_5\}$$
$$A_5^{(0.7)} = \{P_3, P_4, P_6\}$$

The set of these sub-sets will form what in the clans theory [5] is know as a <<family>>:

$$\begin{aligned} F &= \{A_1^{(0.8)}, A_2^{(0.7)}, A_3^{(0.9)}, A_4^{(0.6)}, A_5^{(0.7)}\} \\ &= \{\{P_2, P_3, P_5\}, \{P_1, P_3, P_4, P_6\}, \{P_1, P_2, P_5, P_6\}, \{P_1, P_2, P_3, P_5\}, \{P_3, P_4, P_6\}\} \end{aligned}$$

Again as is well known, from a family a <<clan>> can be produced by finding the mini-terms or <<atoms>>. For this all the possible intersections of $A_j^{(\alpha)*}$, $\alpha = 0, 0.1, 0.2, \ldots 0.9, 1$, $j = 1, 2, \ldots, 5$, in which:

$$A_j^{(\alpha)*} = A_j^{(\alpha)}, \quad \text{or} \quad A_j^{(\alpha)*} = \bar{A}_j^{(\alpha)}$$

that is to say:

$$A_1^{(\alpha)*} \cap A_2^{(\alpha)*} \cap A_3^{(\alpha)*} \cap A_4^{(\alpha)*} \cap A_5^{(\alpha)*}$$

The $A_j^{(\alpha)*}$ are:

$$\begin{aligned} A_1^{(0.8)} &= \{P_2, P_3, P_5\}, & \bar{A}_1^{(0.8)} &= \{P_1, P_4, P_6\} \\ A_2^{(0.7)} &= \{P_1, P_3, P_4, P_6\}, & \bar{A}_2^{(0.7)} &= \{P_2, P_5\} \\ A_3^{(0.9)} &= \{P_1, P_2, P_5, P_6\}, & \bar{A}_3^{(0.9)} &= \{P_3, P_4\} \\ A_4^{(0.6)} &= \{P_1, P_2, P_3, P_5\}, & \bar{A}_4^{(0.6)} &= \{P_4, P_6\} \\ A_5^{(0.7)} &= \{P_3, P_4, P_6\}, & \bar{A}_5^{(0.7)} &= \{P_1, P_2, P_5\} \end{aligned}$$

In this way we have grouped together in each of the sub-sets $A_j^{(\alpha)*}$, the financial products that comply, at the required level, the requirements for each characteristic or property, and also grouped together are the products which do not comply at the required level.

When taking into account the fact that the operator of the intersection represents in some way the word <<and>>, it is possible to group the sub-sets $A_j^{(\alpha)*}$ in all ways and with this know the most elemental groups that can be formed, in such a way that each one of them will include the products which posses <<and>> do not posses the characteristic or properties. In short what we are trying to do is to find the mini-terms or atoms.

Below we arrive at the corresponding atoms of our case[6]:

$$A_1 \cap A_2 \cap A_3 \cap A_4 \cap A_5 = \varnothing$$

$$A_1 \cap A_2 \cap A_3 \cap A_4 \cap \bar{A}_5 = \varnothing$$

$$A_1 \cap A_2 \cap A_3 \cap \bar{A}_4 \cap A_5 = \varnothing$$

$$A_1 \cap A_2 \cap \bar{A}_3 \cap A_4 \cap A_5 = \{P_3\}$$

$$A_1 \cap \bar{A}_2 \cap A_3 \cap A_4 \cap A_5 = \varnothing$$

$$\bar{A}_1 \cap A_2 \cap A_3 \cap A_4 \cap A_5 = \varnothing$$

$$A_1 \cap A_2 \cap A_3 \cap \bar{A}_4 \cap \bar{A}_5 = \varnothing$$

$$A_1 \cap A_2 \cap \bar{A}_3 \cap A_4 \cap \bar{A}_5 = \varnothing$$

$$A_1 \cap \bar{A}_2 \cap A_3 \cap A_4 \cap \bar{A}_5 = \{P_2, P_5\}$$

$$\bar{A}_1 \cap A_2 \cap A_3 \cap A_4 \cap \bar{A}_5 = \{P_1\}$$

$$A_1 \cap A_2 \cap \bar{A}_3 \cap \bar{A}_4 \cap A_5 = \varnothing$$

$$A_1 \cap \bar{A}_2 \cap A_3 \cap \bar{A}_4 \cap A_5 = \varnothing$$

$$\bar{A}_1 \cap A_2 \cap A_3 \cap \bar{A}_4 \cap A_5 = \{P_6\}$$

$$A_1 \cap \bar{A}_2 \cap \bar{A}_3 \cap A_4 \cap A_5 = \varnothing$$

$$\bar{A}_1 \cap A_2 \cap \bar{A}_3 \cap A_4 \cap A_5 = \varnothing$$

$$\bar{A}_1 \cap \bar{A}_2 \cap A_3 \cap A_4 \cap A_5 = \varnothing$$

$$A_1 \cap A_2 \cap \bar{A}_3 \cap \bar{A}_4 \cap \bar{A}_5 = \varnothing$$

$$A_1 \cap \bar{A}_2 \cap A_3 \cap \bar{A}_4 \cap \bar{A}_5 = \varnothing$$

$$\bar{A}_1 \cap A_2 \cap A_3 \cap \bar{A}_4 \cap \bar{A}_5 = \varnothing$$

$$A_1 \cap \bar{A}_2 \cap \bar{A}_3 \cap A_4 \cap \bar{A}_5 = \varnothing$$

$$\bar{A}_1 \cap A_2 \cap \bar{A}_3 \cap A_4 \cap \bar{A}_5 = \varnothing$$

$$\bar{A}_1 \cap \bar{A}_2 \cap A_3 \cap A_4 \cap \bar{A}_5 = \varnothing$$

$$A_1 \cap \bar{A}_2 \cap \bar{A}_3 \cap \bar{A}_4 \cap A_5 = \varnothing$$

$$\bar{A}_1 \cap A_2 \cap \bar{A}_3 \cap \bar{A}_4 \cap A_5 = \{P_4\}$$

$$\bar{A}_1 \cap \bar{A}_2 \cap A_3 \cap \bar{A}_4 \cap A_5 = \varnothing$$

$$\bar{A}_1 \cap \bar{A}_2 \cap \bar{A}_3 \cap A_4 \cap A_5 = \varnothing$$

$$A_1 \cap \bar{A}_2 \cap \bar{A}_3 \cap \bar{A}_4 \cap \bar{A}_5 = \varnothing$$

$$\bar{A}_1 \cap A_2 \cap \bar{A}_3 \cap \bar{A}_4 \cap \bar{A}_5 = \varnothing$$

$$\bar{A}_1 \cap \bar{A}_2 \cap A_3 \cap \bar{A}_4 \cap \bar{A}_5 = \varnothing$$

$$\bar{A}_1 \cap \bar{A}_2 \cap \bar{A}_3 \cap A_4 \cap \bar{A}_5 = \varnothing$$

$$\bar{A}_1 \cap \bar{A}_2 \cap \bar{A}_3 \cap \bar{A}_4 \cap A_5 = \varnothing$$

$$\bar{A}_1 \cap \bar{A}_2 \cap \bar{A}_3 \cap \bar{A}_4 \cap \bar{A}_5 = \varnothing$$

In this way, we have obtained certain occupied mini-terms that allow us to establish the formation of elemental groups of financial products which posses a certain number of common characteristics or properties. The representative sets of each group of products have the property of being disjunctive, although the properties are not. In fact:

$\{P_1\}$ possesses the set of properties $\{C_2, C_3, C_4\}$, and not the others
$\{P_2, P_5\}$ posses the set of properties $\{C_2, C_3, C_4\}$, and not the others
$\{P_3\}$ possesses the set of properties $\{C_1, C_2, C_4, C_5\}$, and not the others
$\{P_4\}$ posses the set of properties $\{C_2, C_5\}$, and not the others
$\{P_6\}$ posses the set of properties $\{C_2, C_3, C_5\}$, and not the others

We emphasise the fact the in the sub-sets we found, the property of possessing certain characteristics and *not* the others is complied with, therefore this constitutes a differential fact relative to other algorithms.

These results are easily verifiable visually in the boolean matrix $[B]$.

In order to be able to obtain the <<clan>> engendered by family F, it is sufficient to take the occupied atoms and all their possible links, adding $\varnothing$.

In our case we arrive at:

$$K(F) = \varnothing, \{P_1\}, \{P_3\}, \{P_4\}, \{P_6\}, \{P_2, P_5\}, \{P_1, P_3\}, \{P_1, P_4\}, \{P_1, P_6\}, \{P_1, P_2, P_5\},$$
$$\{P_3, P_4\}, \{P_3, P_6\}, \{P_2, P_3, P_5\}, \{P_4, P_6\}, \{P_2, P_4, P_5\}, \{P_2, P_5, P_6\},$$
$$\{P_1, P_3, P_4\}, \{P_1, P_3, P_6\}, \{P_1, P_2, P_3, P_5\}, \{P_1, P_3, P_4, P_6\},$$
$$\{P_1, P_2, P_3, P_4, P_5\}, \{P_1, P_4, P_6\}, \{P_1, P_2, P_4, P_5\}, \{P_1, P_2, P_5, P_6\},$$
$$\{P_1, P_2, P_3, P_5, P_6\}, \{P_1, P_2, P_4, P_5, P_6\}, \{P_3, P_4, P_6\}, \{P_2, P_3, P_4, P_5\},$$
$$\{P_2, P_3, P_5, P_6\}, \{P_2, P_3, P_4, P_5, P_6\}, \{P_2, P_4, P_5, P_6\}, E\}$$

It can be seen that the set of the parts $K(F)$ complies with the necessary conditions for the existence of a clan, that is to say:

1. $E \in K(F)$.
2. $(H \in K(F)) \Rightarrow (\bar{H} \in K(F))$ where H is one of any of the subsets comprising $K(F)$.
3. $(H_1, H_2, ..., H_{32} \in K(F)) \Rightarrow (H_1 \cup H_2 \cup \cdots \cup H_{32} \in K(F))$.

by which the following are also verified:

4. $\varnothing \in K(F)$
5. $(H_1, H_2, ..., H_{32} \in K(F)) \Rightarrow (H_1 \cap H_2 \cap \cdots \cap H_{32} \in K(F))$

Now we could well ask ourselves, what is the interest acquired by obtaining the <<clan>> in our problem for financing an investment process. We feel that the answer is obvious, if we take into account the fact that the financial means must not always come from a single elemental group of products (a single mini-term in the language of the clans) but that it is possible to get them from several, if so needed by the required characteristics or properties. On making the link of the mini-terms or atoms in all possible ways, we manage to bring to light the possible groupings *in an exhaustive manner*.

The clan permits an in depth analysis for the financial products existing in the market for the effects of their use in the investment process, on providing the differentiation, for each group (formative sub-set of the clan) between the characteristics or properties that one or/and the other product posses, those that are not possessed by any of them, as well as the number of times that a characteristic is possessed by the components of the group. In other words, the differentiation of an element from another of the clan takes place through the qualities that its components posses and do not posses, or by *the number of times* in which a characteristic or property is repeated in them. Thus, $\{P_3\}$ and $\{P_3, P_4\}$, for example posses characteristics C_1, C_2, C_4, C_5 and not C_3, but, on the other hand, while C_2 and C_5 is possessed by $\{P_3\}$ only once (and it is obvious that this should be so), in $\{P_3, P_4\}$ it is repeated twice.

We are now going to present, a complete table of the relations existing between the elements of the clan (sub-sets of financial products) and the characteristics in their three variations: possessed, not possessed and number of times they are possessed. The super-indices of the C_j in parenthesis will designate the number of times that a characteristic or property is repeated in a sub-set (element of the clan). Thus $C_4^{(2)}$ will show that characteristic C_4 is repeated twice in the group of products, that is to say it is possessed by two financial products of the group. The table is reproduced below:

Elements of clan	Possessed characteristic or properties	Non-possessed characteristics or properties	Repeated characteristics or properties	
$\emptyset$	C_1, C_2, C_3, C_4, C_5	$\emptyset$	C_1, C_2, C_3, C_4, C_5	
$\{P_1\}$	C_2, C_3, C_4	C_1, C_5	C_2, C_3, C_4	
$\{P_3\}$	C_1, C_2, C_4, C_5	C_3	C_1, C_2, C_4, C_5	
$\{P_4\}$	C_2, C_5	C_1, C_3, C_4, C_6	C_2, C_5	←
$\{P_6\}$	C_2, C_3, C_5	C_1, C_4	C_2, C_3, C_5	
$\{P_2, P_5\}$	C_1, C_3, C_4	C_2, C_5	$C_1^{(2)}, C_3^{(2)}, C_4^{(2)}$	
$\{P_1, P_3\}$	C_1, C_2, C_3, C_4, C_5	$\emptyset$	$C_2^{(2)}, C_4^{(2)}$	
$\{P_1, P_4\}$	C_2, C_3, C_4, C_5	C_1	$C_2^{(2)}$	←
$\{P_1, P_6\}$	C_2, C_3, C_4, C_5	C_1	$C_2^{(2)}, C_3^{(2)}$	
$\{P_1, P_2, P_5\}$	C_1, C_2, C_3, C_4	C_5	$C_1^{(2)}, C_3^{(3)}, C_4^{(3)}$	

$\{P_3, P_4\}$	C_1, C_2, C_4, C_5	C_3	$C_2^{(2)}, C_5^{(2)}$	←
$\{P_3, P_6\}$	C_1, C_2, C_3, C_4, C_5	$\varnothing$	$C_2^{(2)}, C_5^{(2)}$	←
$\{P_2, P_3, P_5\}$	C_1, C_2, C_3, C_4, C_5	$\varnothing$	$C_5^{(2)}, C_1^{(3)}, C_4^{(3)}$	
$\{P_4, P_6\}$	C_2, C_3, C_5	C_1, C_4	$C_2^{(2)}, C_5^{(2)}$	←
$\{P_2, P_4, P_5\}$	C_1, C_2, C_3, C_4, C_5	$\varnothing$	$C_1^{(2)}, C_3^{(2)}, C_4^{(2)}$	
$\{P_2, P_5, P_6\}$	C_1, C_2, C_3, C_4, C_5	$\varnothing$	$C_1^{(2)}, C_3^{(3)}, C_4^{(2)}$	←
$\{P_1, P_3, P_4\}$	C_1, C_2, C_3, C_4, C_5	$\varnothing$	$C_2^{(3)}, C_4^{(2)}, C_5^{(2)}$	←
$\{P_1, P_3, P_6\}$	C_1, C_2, C_3, C_4, C_5	$\varnothing$	$C_2^{(3)}, C_3^{(2)}, C_4^{(2)}, C_5^{(2)}$	←
$\{P_1, P_2, P_3, P_5\}$	C_1, C_2, C_3, C_4, C_5	$\varnothing$	$C_1^{(3)}, C_2^{(2)}, C_3^{(3)}, C_4^{(4)}$	
$\{P_1, P_3, P_4, P_6\}$	C_1, C_2, C_3, C_4, C_5	$\varnothing$	$C_2^{(4)}, C_3^{(2)}, C_4^{(2)}, C_5^{(3)}$	
$\{P_1, P_2, P_3, P_4, P_5\}$	C_1, C_2, C_3, C_4, C_5	$\varnothing$	$C_1^{(3)}, C_2^{(3)}, C_3^{(3)}, C_4^{(4)}, C_5^{(2)}$	
$\{P_1, P_4, P_6\}$	C_2, C_3, C_4, C_5	C_1	$C_2^{(3)}, C_3^{(2)}, C_5^{(2)}$	←
$\{P_1, P_2, P_4, P_5\}$	C_1, C_2, C_3, C_4, C_5	$\varnothing$	$C_1^{(2)}, C_2^{(2)}, C_3^{(3)}, C_4^{(3)}$	
$\{P_1, P_2, P_5, P_6\}$	C_1, C_2, C_3, C_4, C_5	$\varnothing$	$C_1^{(2)}, C_2^{(2)}, C_3^{(4)}, C_4^{(3)}$	
$\{P_1, P_2, P_3, P_5, P_6\}$	C_1, C_2, C_3, C_4, C_5	$\varnothing$	$C_1^{(3)}, C_2^{(3)}, C_3^{(4)}, C_4^{(4)}, C_5^{(2)}$	
$\{P_1, P_2, P_4, P_5, P_6\}$	C_1, C_2, C_3, C_4, C_5	$\varnothing$	$C_1^{(2)}, C_2^{(3)}, C_3^{(4)}, C_4^{(3)}, C_5^{(2)}$	
$\{P_3, P_4, P_6\}$	C_1, C_2, C_3, C_4, C_5	$\varnothing$	$C_2^{(3)}, C_5^{(3)}$	
$\{P_2, P_3, P_4, P_5\}$	C_1, C_2, C_3, C_4, C_5	$\varnothing$	$C_1^{(3)}, C_2^{(2)}, C_3^{(2)}, C_4^{(3)}, C_5^{(2)}$	
$\{P_2, P_3, P_5, P_6\}$	C_1, C_2, C_3, C_4, C_5	$\varnothing$	$C_1^{(3)}, C_2^{(2)}, C_3^{(3)}, C_4^{(3)}, C_5^{(2)}$	
$\{P_2, P_3, P_4, P_5, P_6\}$	C_1, C_2, C_3, C_4, C_5	$\varnothing$	$C_1^{(3)}, C_2^{(3)}, C_3^{(3)}, C_4^{(3)}, C_5^{(3)}$	
$\{P_2, P_4, P_5, P_6\}$	C_1, C_2, C_3, C_4, C_5	$\varnothing$	$C_1^{(2)}, C_2^{(2)}, C_3^{(3)}, C_4^{(2)}, C_5^{(2)}$	
E	C_1, C_2, C_3, C_4, C_5	$\varnothing$	$C_1^{(3)}, C_2^{(4)}, C_3^{(4)}, C_4^{(4)}, C_5^{(3)}$	

We have included in the column of repeated characteristics or properties those that only exist once, in the elements of the clan formed by a sole financial product and we have left them out, when they are formed by two or more, in order to be able to visualise the chart more clearly. In this way we have considered the word repeated in the widest possible sense.

The above table, in our opinion, allows for a very complete analysis of the financial products that are suitable for the investment process. In fact, not only do we get to know the products to which recourse has to be made when needing to cover certain characteristics or properties (second column) but the number of products of the group that do posses them (fourth column) is brought to light.

Obtaining affinities and the use of codes

Having reached this stage of the problem, it would seem convenient to turn our attention to an aspect of relevant interest. This is those cases in which the number of repetitions of a characteristic C_j (its super-index) is equal to the number of products P_i composing the corresponding element of the clan. This indicates that *all* the products of the sub-set without exception, posses the specific characteristic. If we look at the fourth column of the above table it will be seen that this requirement is complied with by those characteristics contained within a continuous line. It is obvious that this will *always* occur in those characteristics or properties relative to the elements of the clan comprising a single product, in this case $\{P_1\}$, $\{P_3\}$, $\{P_4\}$, and $\{P_6\}$.

If we consider each characteristic or property C_j, $j = 1, 2, ..., 5$, or group of characteristics or properties, highlighted with a line in the fourth column (these are possessed by all the financial products), it will be seen:

a) A same characteristic or property, can be possessed by *several* elements of the clan (groups of products) and by all the products of the group. In our case:

C_2 is possessed by $\{P_1, P_4\}$, $\{P_1, P_3, P_4\}$, $\{P_1, P_3, P_6\}$, $\{P_1, P_4, P_6\}$, $\{P_1, P_3, P_4, P_6\}$
C_3 is possessed by $\{P_2, P_3, P_6\}$, $\{P_1, P_2, P_5, P_6\}$
C_4 on the other hand is only possessed by all the products of $\{P_1, P_2, P_3, P_5\}$

b) The same occurs in the case of two characteristics or properties. In our case:

C_2, C_5 are possessed by $\{P_4\}$, $\{P_3, P_4\}$, $\{P_3, P_6\}$, $\{P_4, P_6\}$, $\{P_3, P_4, P_6\}$
C_1, C_4 on the other hand are only possessed by all the products of $\{P_2, P_3, P_5\}$
C_2, C_3 are possessed by $\{P_1, P_6\}$
C_2, C_4 are possessed by $\{P_1, P_3\}$
C_3, C_4 are possessed by $\{P_1, P_2, P_5\}$

c) In the case of three characteristics or properties, we have:

C_1, C_3, C_4 are only possessed by $\{P_2, P_5\}$
C_2, C_3, C_5 are only possessed by $\{P_6\}$
C_2, C_3, C_4 are only possessed by $\{P_1\}$

d) In the case of four characteristics or properties it will be:

C_1, C_2, C_4, C_5 are only possessed by $\{P_3\}$

e) And finally it will be seen that the five characteristics or properties are not exclusively possessed by any of the financial products, thus the symbol of vacant which appears in the first column of the table above.

In view of this information deduced from the $K(F)$ clan consideration should be given, in the case that it were to be necessary that all the characteristics or properties were present in the products which form the group, if it is desired to finance the investment with the *least* number of products possible or with the *most*, obviously if the possibility of selection were to exist. If we are dealing with the least, the decision must fall to one of the elements of the clan highlighted in the fourth column with an arrow pointing to the corresponding row. On the other hand, if the most is preferred, the choice falls to those elements with rows without arrows, which in our case will be 12 elements, which are the following:

$\{P_1\} \rightarrow \{C_2, C_3, C_4\}$	$\{P_1, P_2, P_5\} \rightarrow \{C_3, C_4\}$
$\{P_3\} \rightarrow \{C_1, C_2, C_4, C_5\}$	$\{P_2, P_3, P_5\} \rightarrow \{C_1, C_4\}$
$\{P_6\} \rightarrow \{C_2, C_3, C_5\}$	$\{P_3, P_4, P_6\} \rightarrow \{C_2, C_5\}$
$\{P_2, P_5\} \rightarrow \{C_1, C_3, C_4\}$	$\{P_1, P_2, P_3, P_5\} \rightarrow \{C_4\}$
$\{P_1, P_3\} \rightarrow \{C_2, C_4\}$	$\{P_1, P_2, P_5, P_6\} \rightarrow \{C_3\}$
$\{P_1, P_6\} \rightarrow \{C_2, C_3\}$	$\{P_1, P_3, P_4, P_6\} \rightarrow \{C_2\}$

We have now arrived at certain groupings of financial products by their common characteristics or properties that constitute maximum sub-relations, in the sense that, for each characteristic or property we have found the greatest number of products that posses the same. And these relations that have been obtained are none other than <<affinity relations>>. What we have tried to do is to form homogeneous groups, the interest of which resides in the fact that it is possible to choose *any one* of the financial products of the group, since each of these posses the characteristics marked by correspondence.

There is another much shorter way for obtaining affinity relations, which we will take a look at later on. Here what we have tried to do is to bring to light the possibility of arriving at the same, also by means of the clan theory.

What we have done so far, has as its objective the presentation in the most general way possible, of the panorama that arises before an investor seeking one or several financial products capable of covering the requirements of the process, by means of certain characteristics or properties which, in some way, are required for harmonising the finance-investment binomial. For this we have obtained a table in which, for each one of the elements of the clan, the three fundamental aspects of their characteristics are shown.

But the model we have presented also permits arriving at other objectives, starting out from the desires or specific requirements expressed by means of the characteristics or properties required and/or by others that are not required.

In fact, it is quite often the case that we need to select a financial product by formulating a chain of characteristics linked by an <<and>>, <<or/and>>, <<no>>. In this case, the clan method will provide a solution to this problem. For this, we can make recourse to $A_j^{(\alpha)*}$, $j = 1, 2, \ldots, 5$ which, if we remember, in our example were:

$$
\begin{aligned}
&A_1^{(0.8)} = \{P_2, P_3, P_5\}, && \overline{A}_1^{(0.8)} = \{P_1, P_4, P_6\} \\
&A_2^{(0.7)} = \{P_1, P_3, P_4, P_6\}, && \overline{A}_2^{(0.7)} = \{P_2, P_5\} \\
&A_3^{(0.9)} = \{P_1, P_2, P_5, P_6\}, && \overline{A}_3^{(0.9)} = \{P_3, P_4\} \\
&A_4^{(0.6)} = \{P_1, P_2, P_3, P_5\}, && \overline{A}_4^{(0.6)} = \{P_4, P_6\} \\
&A_5^{(0.7)} = \{P_3, P_4, P_6\}, && \overline{A}_5^{(0.7)} = \{P_1, P_2, P_5\}
\end{aligned}
$$

Let us take a look at some examples:

1. The financial product should include the following requirements: flexibility in availability (and) adaptable to possibilities of repayment (and) an adequate financial cost. The other characteristics are indifferent:

   It is clear that we shall have to use the intersection operator $\cap$. This then will be:

$$A_1 \cap A_2 \cap A_3 = \{P_2, P_3, P_5\} \cap \{P_1, P_3, P_4, P_6\} \cap \{P_1, P_2, P_5, P_6\} = \varnothing$$

   The conclusion then is that there is no single financial product that complies the required condition.

2. We are looking for a financial product with the following conditions: flexible in time availability (and) with an adequate financial cost (and) harmony with the financial institution, although also acceptable would be (or/and) a product with adaptability in the possibilities of repayment (and) compatible financial cost (and) a good period of grace. For each alternative we can do without the other characteristics.

   In this case the operators to be used are the intersection $\cap$ and union $\cup$. We arrive at:

$$
\begin{aligned}
(A_1 \cap A_3 \cap A_4) \cup (A_2 \cap A_3 \cap A_5) &= (\{P_2, P_3, P_5\} \cap \{P_1, P_2, P_5, P_6\} \cap \{P_1, P_2, P_3, P_5\}) \cup \\
&\cup (\{P_1, P_3, P_4, P_6\} \cap \{P_1, P_2, P_5, P_6\} \cap \{P_3, P_4, P_6\}) \\
&= \{P_2, P_5\} \cup \{P_6\} = \{P_2, P_5, P_6\}
\end{aligned}
$$

We have now found three financial products that are suitable for the entrusted mission, P_2, P_5, P_6, taking into account that for the first part of the conditions chain, linked by an <<and>>, there are two products and for the second part, the third.

3. As pure speculation we will now use the tree operators $\cap$, $\cup$, $^{-}$, with which we add negation to those already used. The financial product could, for example, have the following conditions: Adequate financial cost (and) *no* harmony with the financial institution (arid discussions are foreseen in the future, therefore an institution with fewer relations in the future is preferable) (and) adaptability in the possibility of repayment, but also accepted is (or/and) flexibility in time availability (and) adequate financial cost (and) no harmony with the financial institution. In each case the other characteristics are left out.
   Below let us take a look at our case. It will be:

$$
\begin{aligned}
(A_3 \cap \bar{A}_4 \cap A_2) \cup (A_1 \cap A_3 \cap \bar{A}_4) &= (\{P_1, P_2, P_5, P_6\} \cap \{P_4, P_6\} \cap \{P_1, P_3, P_4, P_6\}) \cup \\
&\cup (\{P_1, P_3, P_5\} \cap \{P_1, P_2, P_5, P_6\} \cap \{P_4, P_6\}) = \\
&= \{P_6\} \cup \varnothing = \{P_6\}
\end{aligned}
$$

The result of these conditions leave us with only one financial product, P_6, as apt for financing the investment process.

We could continue with a varied and large quantity of assumptions for which we could find a solution, from the proposed scheme. We feel therefore, the proposed model has great flexibility and is adaptable, both of which are fundamental conditions for it to be useful in a context of uncertainty.

Grouping the characteristics of the products by means of the Moore closing

In the previous section, we made a very brief reference to affinity as a basic element for obtaining homogenous groupings of financial products apt for use in investment activities. The usefulness of grouping financial products characteristics or properties that are common to all those forming the group, is unquestionable when making an adequate analysis of financial products for their later selection, since with this we obtain clarification, on separating certain products from others and in this way show the <<indifference>> within a group at the same time as the possible <<preference>> of the components of the group over the others. These are justifying reasons, we feel, for dedicating special attention to this aspect.

What we are going to do, stems from the notion of a <<Moore family>>[7]. As is known if one has a referential E and a set of its parts or <<power set>> $\Pi(E)$, then a family $F(E) \subset \Pi(E)$ complying with two conditions:

1. $E \in F(E)$.
2. $(A \in F(E), B \in F(E)) \Rightarrow (A \cap B \in F(E))$.

is a Moore family.

From a Moore family a <<Moore closing>> can be constructed. The Moore closing is a functional application in which to each element of E, $A \subset E$, a functional application MA is made to correspond so that:

$$MA = \bigcap_{\Phi \in F_A(E)} \Phi$$

where:

— $F(E)$ is a Moore family
— $F_A(E)$ the sub-set of $F(E)$ formed by those parts of $F(E)$ containing A.
— Φ all the elements of $F_A(E)$.

From a mathematical point of view, it is said that a Moore closing exists, if the corresponding functional application complies with the properties of extensiveness, idempower and isotonicity.

a) Extensiveness: $\forall A \in \Pi(E) \ : \ A \subset MA$
b) Idempower: $\forall A \in \Pi(E) \ : \ M(MA) = A$
c) Isotonicity: $\forall A, B \in \Pi(E) \ : \ (A \subset B) \Rightarrow (MA \subset MB)$

Relative to the handling of the problem of grouping financial products for the investment process, the first of these properties, that is extensiveness is worth highlighting. This property brings to light the fact that, given a functional application M of $\Pi(E)$ in $\Pi(E)$, all the components of any part of $A \subset \Pi(E)$ have a functional application MA in which from among its components the A appear (as well as others, if pertinent). Thus, if $A = \{a, b\}$, for example, in MA a and b should exist without a doubt. As a consequence of the extensiveness, one always arrives at, in a Moore closing where $ME = E$. Also it is customary to do (although not necessary) $M\varnothing = \varnothing$.

In the Moore closings the following properties occur:

1. Elements of $\Pi(E)$ which are the image of another element, are also images of their own. These elements are called <<closed>>.
2. The sub-set $C(E)$ of the closed elements of a Moore closing, form a Moore family.
3. The image of any element $A \in \Pi(E)$ is the smallest closed element con-

taining it.

Having seen these basic elements, we are now ready to pass on to the study of the Moore closing of a fuzzy graph.

As is well known, every fuzzy graph can be represented, among other things, by the arrow form or matrix form. Given its matrix form its analysis normally takes place by means of the α-cuts. Now, on certain occasions, as is the case with which we are concerned, its study is conditioned by a sub-set of thresholds that convert the fuzzy relation into a boolean matrix.

Having found the boolean matrix, either by means of the α-cuts or of a sub-set of thresholds, the concepts are defined of <<connection to the right>> and <<connection to the left>> as follows.

We name, connection to the right R^+, the sub-set of elements of referential E, such that for every $A \in \Pi(E)$, R^+ are the successors to every element belonging to A. We write it as:

$$\forall x \in A \ : \ R^+ A = \{y \in E/(x, y) \in [B]\}, \ \text{where} \ \ R^+\varnothing = E$$

$[B]$ being the boolean matrix.

We name, connection to the left R^-, the sub-set of elements of referential E such that, for every $A \in \Pi(E)$, R^- are the predecessors of every element belonging to A. This will be:

$$\forall x \in A \ : \ R^- A = \{y \in E/(y, x) \in [B]\}, \ \text{where} \ \ R^-\varnothing = E$$

$[B]$ being the boolean matrix.

Given the connections to the right, R^+, and the connections to the left, R^-, of a boolean matrix B, the Moore closings of $\Pi(E)$ are:

$$M^{(1)} = R^- \circ R^+ \quad , \quad M^{(2)} = R^+ \circ R^-$$

where $\circ$ is the maxmin.

The definitions of $R^+ A$ and $R^- A$ allow for the following properties to be enunciated.

$$\forall x \in A \in \Pi(E) \ : \begin{cases} R^+ A = \bigcap\limits_{x \in A} R^+ \{x\} \\ R^- A = \bigcap\limits_{x \in A} R^- \{x\} \end{cases}$$

These two properties, which are totally obvious, are important since they permit us to obtain by direct reading $R^+ A$ and $R^- A$, by making the corresponding intersections in the boolean matrix $[B]$. We can verify this with our example, after making certain considerations relative to rectangular relations.

Up to now we have developed the necessary aspects for obtaining Moore closings when the fuzzy relation and subsequent boolean matrix is square and such that $[B] \subset E \times E$. However this scheme is susceptible to generalisation in the case in which $[B] \subset E_1 \times E_2$, where $E_1 \neq E_2$. Let us say, therefore, that when $E_1 = E_2 = E$ (as we have seen up to now), we are dealing with a special case.

In order to develop this general model, we feel we have sufficient theoretical basis with what has been stated prior to this, so that we propose to continue with our subject in its application to resolving the problem of grouping financial products that are suitable for use in the investment process, using for this, the example we have been using throughout this chapter. To these effects, we will take the boolean matrix $[B]$ again as the basis for later development. Let us remember that it was from this matrix that we initiated the model by using the clan theory. Now we will follow another path, that of the Moore families, with which we intend to arrive at the same answer. Let us reproduce the boolean matrix in

$[B] =$	P_1	P_2	P_3	P_4	P_5	P_6
C_1	0	1	1	0	1	0
C_2	1	0	1	1	0	1
C_3	1	1	0	0	1	1
C_4	1	1	1	0	1	0
C_5	0	0	1	1	0	1

order to keep it in sight.

By simply looking at it we can obtain R^+ and R^-. For this the <<power set>> will be established of referential set C and we will make the intersection of all the elements of the corresponding rows of the matrix correspond to each of its elements in accordance with the already expressed formula. For R^+ we arrive at:

$$\begin{array}{ll}
\varnothing \rightarrow P_1P_2P_3P_4P_5P_6 & C_1C_2C_3 \rightarrow \varnothing \\
C_1 \rightarrow P_2P_3P_5 & C_1C_2C_4 \rightarrow P_3 \\
C_2 \rightarrow P_1P_3P_4P_6 & C_1C_3C_4 \rightarrow P_2P_5 \\
C_3 \rightarrow P_1P_2P_5P_6 & C_2C_3C_4 \rightarrow P_1 \\
C_4 \rightarrow P_1P_2P_3P_5 & C_1C_2C_5 \rightarrow P_3 \\
C_5 \rightarrow P_3P_4P_6 & C_1C_3C_5 \rightarrow \varnothing \\
C_1C_2 \rightarrow P_3 & C_1C_4C_5 \rightarrow P_3 \\
C_1C_3 \rightarrow P_2P_5 & C_2C_3C_5 \rightarrow P_6 \\
C_1C_4 \rightarrow P_2P_3P_5 & C_2C_4C_5 \rightarrow P_3 \\
C_1C_5 \rightarrow P_3 & C_3C_4C_5 \rightarrow \varnothing \\
C_2C_3 \rightarrow P_1P_6 & C_1C_2C_3C_4 \rightarrow \varnothing
\end{array}$$

$$C_2C_4 \to P_1P_3 \qquad C_1C_2C_3C_5 \to \varnothing$$
$$C_2C_5 \to P_3P_4P_6 \qquad C_1C_2C_4C_5 \to P_3$$
$$C_3C_4 \to P_1P_2P_5 \qquad C_1C_3C_4C_5 \to \varnothing$$
$$C_3C_5 \to P_6 \qquad C_2C_3C_4C_5 \to \varnothing$$
$$C_4C_5 \to P_3 \qquad C_1C_2C_3C_4C_5 \to \varnothing$$

From this combining analysis we have brought to light a first grouping of the financial products according to whether they include any one, two, three, four or all the characteristics or properties.

A first aspect to be considered arises from the fact that when certain characteristics are required jointly no products exists complying with them. For example this happens for C_1, C_2, C_3; C_1, C_2, C_5, ..., which is expressed by the symbol $\varnothing$.

A second aspect refers to the fact that a same financial product or certain same financial products posses groups of different characteristics. This happens, for example, with P_3 or with P_2P_5. It will be seen, in these cases, that there is *always* a grouping of characteristics or properties which include the rest. Thus, for P_3 the grouping C_1, C_2, C_4, C_5 includes any of the characteristics of the other relations concerning financial products P_3 exclusively.

Take a look, for example, at C_2, C_4, C_5 or C_1, C_5, where:

$$\{C_2, C_4, C_5\} \in \{C_1, C_2, C_4, C_5\}$$
$$\{C_1, C_5\} \in \{C_1, C_2, C_4, C_5\}$$

Therefore, this phase for concluding with definite results is not sufficient. We will continue with obtaining $R^{\cdot}$. We arrive at:

$$\varnothing \to C_1C_2C_3C_4C_5 \qquad P_2P_3P_4 \to \varnothing$$
$$P_1 \to C_2C_3C_4 \qquad P_2P_3P_5 \to C_1C_4$$
$$P_2 \to C_1C_3C_4 \qquad P_2P_3P_6 \to \varnothing$$
$$P_3 \to C_1C_2C_4C_5 \qquad P_2P_4P_5 \to \varnothing$$
$$P_4 \to C_2C_5 \qquad P_2P_4P_6 \to \varnothing$$
$$P_5 \to C_1C_3C_4 \qquad P_2P_5P_6 \to C_3$$
$$P_6 \to C_2C_3C_5 \qquad P_3P_4P_5 \to \varnothing$$
$$P_1P_2 \to C_3C_4 \qquad P_3P_4P_6 \to C_2C_5$$
$$P_1P_3 \to C_2C_4 \qquad P_3P_5P_6 \to \varnothing$$
$$P_1P_4 \to C_2 \qquad P_4P_5P_6 \to \varnothing$$
$$P_1P_5 \to C_3C_4 \qquad P_1P_2P_3P_4 \to \varnothing$$

$P_1P_6 \rightarrow C_2C_3$
$P_2P_3 \rightarrow C_1C_4$
$P_2P_4 \rightarrow \emptyset$
$P_2P_5 \rightarrow C_1C_3C_4$
$P_2P_6 \rightarrow C_1$
$P_3P_4 \rightarrow C_2C_5$
$P_3P_5 \rightarrow C_1C_4$
$P_3P_6 \rightarrow C_2C_5$
$P_4P_5 \rightarrow \emptyset$
$P_4P_6 \rightarrow C_2C_5$
$P_1P_2P_3 \rightarrow C_4$
$P_1P_2P_4 \rightarrow \emptyset$
$P_1P_2P_5 \rightarrow C_3C_4$
$P_1P_2P_6 \rightarrow C_3$
$P_1P_3P_4 \rightarrow C_4$
$P_1P_3P_5 \rightarrow C_2$
$P_1P_3P_6 \rightarrow C_2$
$P_1P_4P_5 \rightarrow \emptyset$
$P_1P_4P_6 \rightarrow C_2$
$P_1P_5P_6 \rightarrow C_3$

$P_1P_2P_3P_5 \rightarrow C_4$
$P_1P_2P_3P_6 \rightarrow \emptyset$
$P_1P_2P_4P_5 \rightarrow \emptyset$
$P_1P_2P_4P_6 \rightarrow \emptyset$
$P_1P_2P_5P_6 \rightarrow C_3$
$P_1P_3P_4P_5 \rightarrow \emptyset$
$P_1P_3P_4P_6 \rightarrow C_2$
$P_1P_3P_5P_6 \rightarrow \emptyset$
$P_1P_4P_5P_6 \rightarrow \emptyset$
$P_2P_3P_4P_5 \rightarrow \emptyset$
$P_2P_3P_4P_6 \rightarrow \emptyset$
$P_2P_3P_5P_6 \rightarrow \emptyset$
$P_2P_4P_5P_6 \rightarrow \emptyset$
$P_3P_4P_5P_6 \rightarrow \emptyset$
$P_1P_2P_3P_4P_5 \rightarrow \emptyset$
$P_1P_2P_3P_4P_6 \rightarrow \emptyset$
$P_1P_2P_3P_5P_6 \rightarrow \emptyset$
$P_1P_2P_4P_5P_6 \rightarrow \emptyset$
$P_1P_3P_4P_5P_6 \rightarrow \emptyset$
$P_2P_3P_4P_5P_6 \rightarrow \emptyset$
$P_1P_2P_3P_4P_5P_6 \rightarrow \emptyset$

By means of this relation we have managed to bring to light the characteristics concurring in each product and in all possible groupings of products.

Also in this case, the absence of characteristics for certain groupings of products possessing one or some of the same characteristic or properties will be seen. Once again, we have the case that there always exists a relation in which the group of products contains the remaining groupings with the same characteristic or characteristics.

From this connection to the right R^+, and connection to the left R^- the corresponding Moore closings $M^{(1)}$ and $M^{(2)}$ can be found. For this we are going to make recourse, as we mentioned before, to the maxmin compositions $R^- \circ R^+$ and $R^+ \circ R^-$. So as not to make the graphic schemes we are going to use too confusing, we are going to do without those superfluous relations for which there are no complete connections.

We will begin by showing in a first figure (figure 4.1.) the composition and

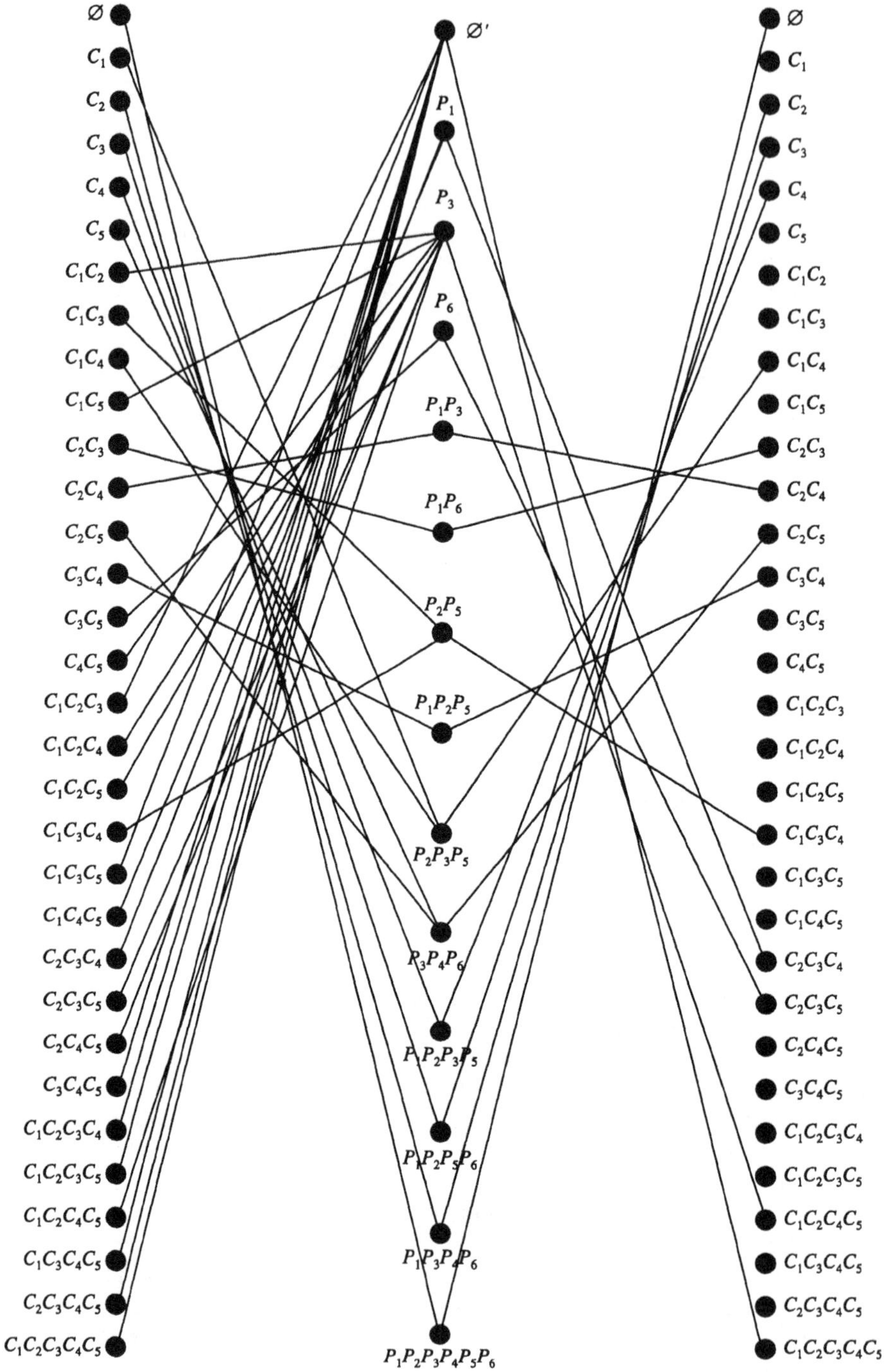
∅
C_1
C_2
C_3
C_4
C_5
C_1C_2
C_1C_3
C_1C_4
C_1C_5
C_2C_3
C_2C_4
C_2C_5
C_3C_4
C_3C_5
C_4C_5
$C_1C_2C_3$
$C_1C_2C_4$
$C_1C_2C_5$
$C_1C_3C_4$
$C_1C_3C_5$
$C_1C_4C_5$
$C_2C_3C_4$
$C_2C_3C_5$
$C_2C_4C_5$
$C_3C_4C_5$
$C_1C_2C_3C_4$
$C_1C_2C_3C_5$
$C_1C_2C_4C_5$
$C_1C_3C_4C_5$
$C_2C_3C_4C_5$
$C_1C_2C_3C_4C_5$
∅'
P_1
P_3
P_6
P_1P_3
P_1P_6
P_2P_5
$P_1P_2P_5$
$P_2P_3P_5$
$P_3P_4P_6$
$P_1P_2P_3P_5$
$P_1P_2P_5P_6$
$P_1P_3P_4P_6$
$P_1P_2P_3P_4P_5P_6$
∅
C_1
C_2
C_3
C_4
C_5
C_1C_2
C_1C_3
C_1C_4
C_1C_5
C_2C_3
C_2C_4
C_2C_5
C_3C_4
C_3C_5
C_4C_5
$C_1C_2C_3$
$C_1C_2C_4$
$C_1C_2C_5$
$C_1C_3C_4$
$C_1C_3C_5$
$C_1C_4C_5$
$C_2C_3C_4$
$C_2C_3C_5$
$C_2C_4C_5$
$C_3C_4C_5$
$C_1C_2C_3C_4$
$C_1C_2C_3C_5$
$C_1C_2C_4C_5$
$C_1C_3C_4C_5$
$C_2C_3C_4C_5$
$C_1C_2C_3C_4C_5$

Figure 4.1.

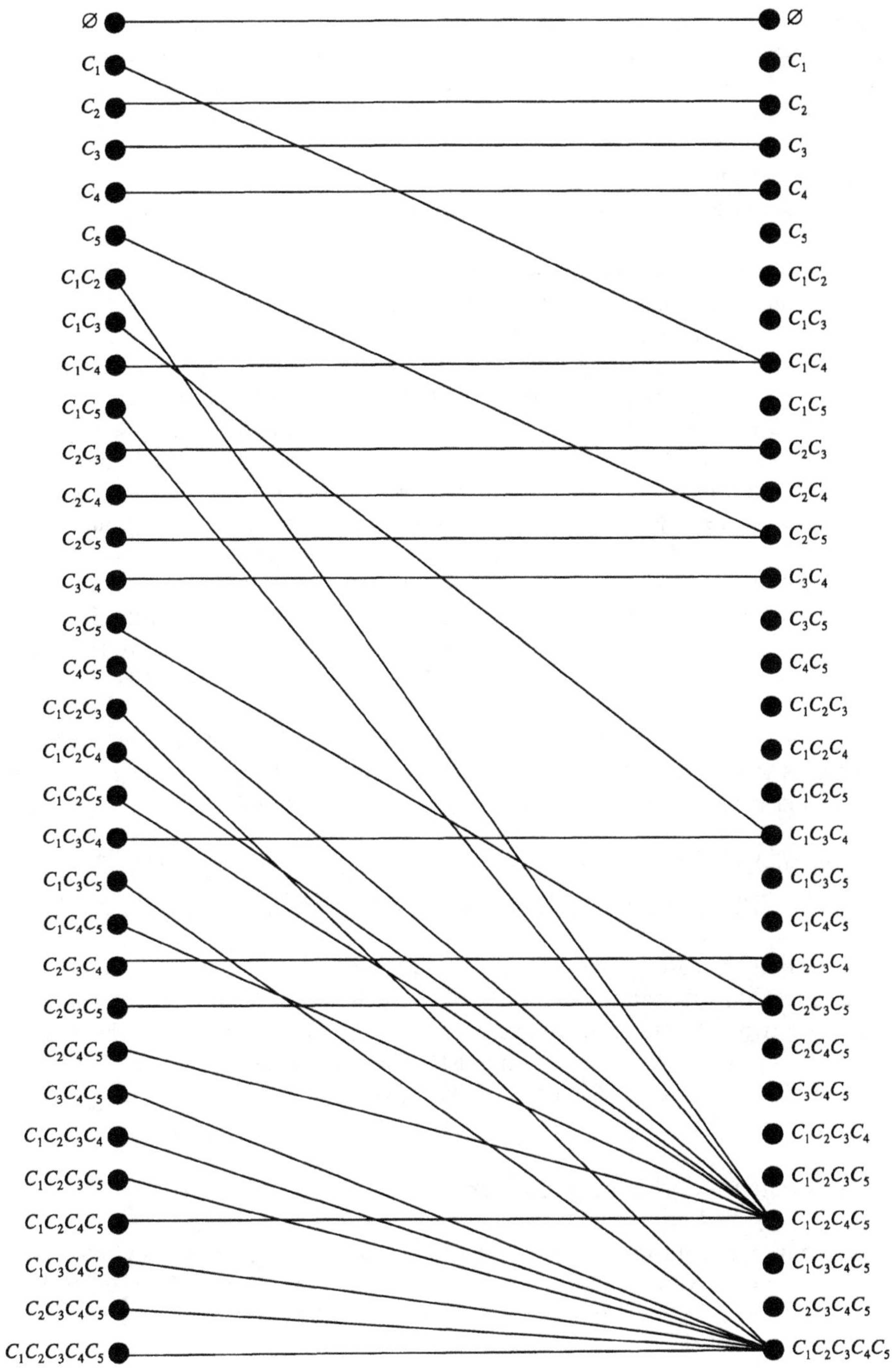

∅
C_1
C_2
C_3
C_4
C_5
C_1C_2
C_1C_3
C_1C_4
C_1C_5
C_2C_3
C_2C_4
C_2C_5
C_3C_4
C_3C_5
C_4C_5
$C_1C_2C_3$
$C_1C_2C_4$
$C_1C_2C_5$
$C_1C_3C_4$
$C_1C_3C_5$
$C_1C_4C_5$
$C_2C_3C_4$
$C_2C_3C_5$
$C_2C_4C_5$
$C_3C_4C_5$
$C_1C_2C_3C_4$
$C_1C_2C_3C_5$
$C_1C_2C_4C_5$
$C_1C_3C_4C_5$
$C_2C_3C_4C_5$
$C_1C_2C_3C_4C_5$

Figure 4.2.

$R^+ \circ R^-$, by establishing the connections existing between each other, of the elements of the <<power set>> of referential C representative of the characteristics or properties, by making intervene as elements that play the role of intermediaries, those elements that are significant in the <<power set>> of referential E of the financial products.

In the second figure (figure 4.2.) the results obtained, which make up the Moore closing, are presented. In it we can easily find the properties that we listed previously.

This Moore closing brings to light the widest group of which all the elements of the <<power set>> of referential C form a part. In other words, the relation existing between all possible groups of characteristics or properties and the largest group of which they form a part, taking into account existing financial products. We therefore arrive, for example, at the fact that characteristic C_2 can only be grouped with itself, while on the other hand, C_3C_5 can form a part of the group $C_2C_3C_5$ which is the largest possible group, if we are looking for the intervention of C_3 and C_5. This gives rise to certain <<closed>> groups.

In fact, as can be seen, in the last graph there are six closed groups $\{C_1, C_4\}$, $\{C_2, C_5\}$, $\{C_1, C_3, C_4\}$, $\{C_2, C_3, C_5\}$, $\{C_1, C_2, C_4, C_5\}$, $\{C_1, C_2, C_3, C_4, C_5\}$. In this respect it is particularly interesting to see that the image of any element of the <<power set>> of C is the smallest close group containing it (third property). Thus, for example, C_5 is contained in closed groups $\{C_2, C_5\}$, $\{C_2, C_3, C_5\}$, $\{C_1, C_2, C_4, C_5\}$, $\{C_1, C_2, C_3, C_4, C_5\}$ and obviously its image is $\{C_2, C_5\}$.

On the other hand and in short, when in a closed group several elements converge, there is always one which is its own image. Therefore, the grouping is represented precisely by this image. In our case the groupings are:

$$\emptyset, \{C_2\}, \{C_3\}, \{C_4\}, \{C_1, C_4\}, \{C_2, C_3\}, \{C_2, C_4\}, \{C_2, C_5\}, \{C_3, C_4\},$$
$$\{C_1, C_3, C_4\}, \{C_2, C_3, C_4\}, \{C_2, C_3, C_5\}, \{C_1, C_2, C_4, C_5\}, \{C_1, C_2, C_3, C_4, C_5\}$$

Each one of these groups is a support to one or several financial products, in the sense that the linked characteristics are so by means of one or some of them. The two extreme cases $\emptyset$ and $\{C_1, C_2, C_3, C_4, C_5\}$, acquire a theoretical sense as they represent <<no grouping>> for all the products and <<all the grouped characteristics>> for none of the products.

From product grouping to affinities

We now move on to show in the following graphs (figures 4.3 and 4.4) respectively, the maxmin composition $R^- \circ R^+$ and the second Moore closing corresponding to it. For this we will continue with the same procedure as in the

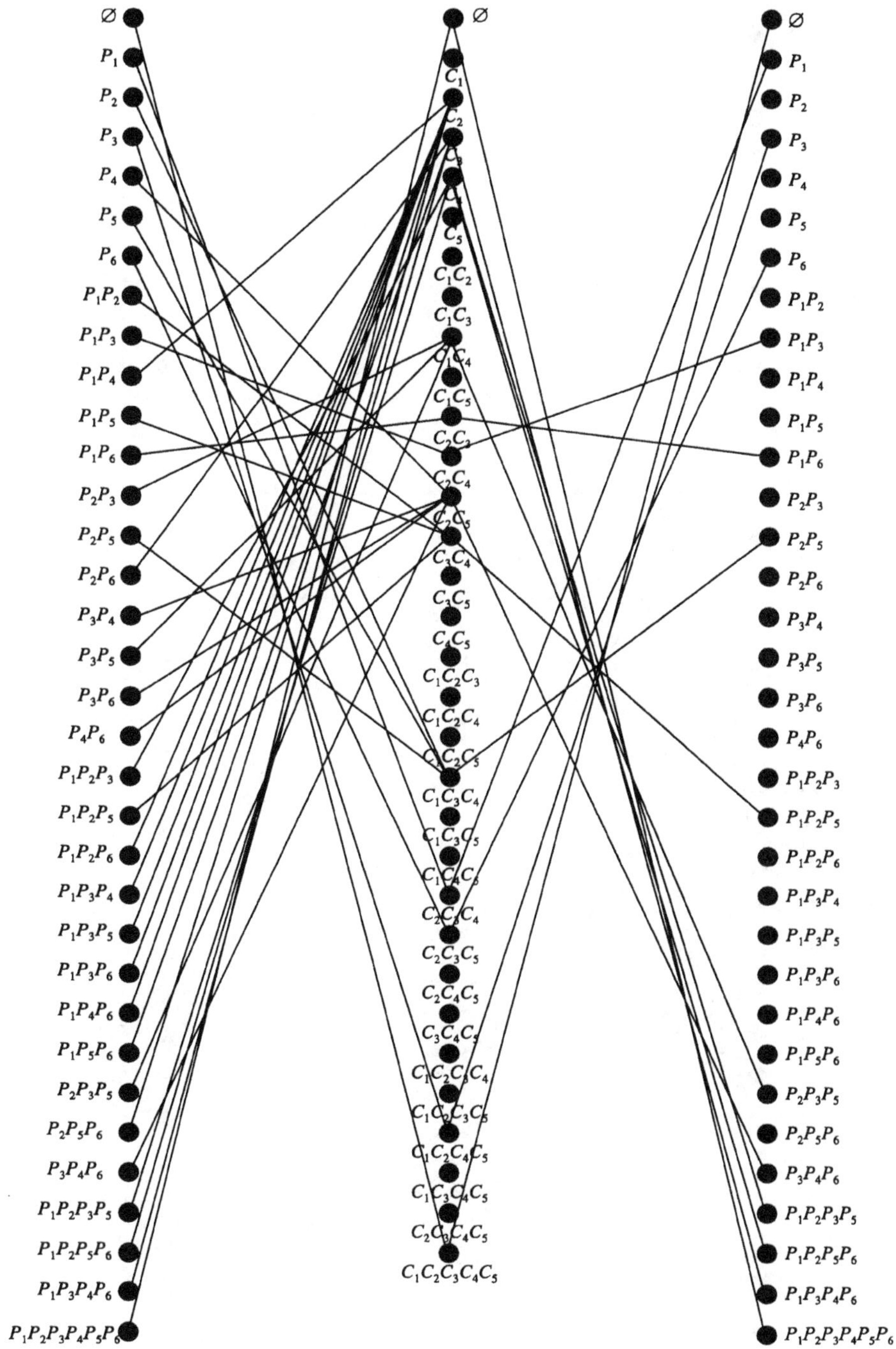
∅
P_1
P_2
P_3
P_4
P_5
P_6
P_1P_2
P_1P_3
P_1P_4
P_1P_5
P_1P_6
P_2P_3
P_2P_5
P_2P_6
P_3P_4
P_3P_5
P_3P_6
P_4P_6
$P_1P_2P_3$
$P_1P_2P_5$
$P_1P_2P_6$
$P_1P_3P_4$
$P_1P_3P_5$
$P_1P_3P_6$
$P_1P_4P_6$
$P_1P_5P_6$
$P_2P_3P_5$
$P_2P_5P_6$
$P_3P_4P_6$
$P_1P_2P_3P_5$
$P_1P_2P_5P_6$
$P_1P_3P_4P_6$
$P_1P_2P_3P_4P_5P_6$
∅
C_1
C_2
C_3
C_4
C_5
C_1C_2
C_1C_3
C_1C_4
C_1C_5
C_2C_3
C_2C_4
C_2C_5
C_3C_4
C_3C_5
C_4C_5
$C_1C_2C_3$
$C_1C_2C_4$
$C_1C_2C_5$
$C_1C_3C_4$
$C_1C_3C_5$
$C_1C_4C_5$
$C_2C_3C_4$
$C_2C_3C_5$
$C_2C_4C_5$
$C_3C_4C_5$
$C_1C_2C_3C_4$
$C_1C_2C_3C_5$
$C_1C_2C_4C_5$
$C_1C_3C_4C_5$
$C_2C_3C_4C_5$
$C_1C_2C_3C_4C_5$
∅
P_1
P_2
P_3
P_4
P_5
P_6
P_1P_2
P_1P_3
P_1P_4
P_1P_5
P_1P_6
P_2P_3
P_2P_5
P_2P_6
P_3P_4
P_3P_5
P_3P_6
P_4P_6
$P_1P_2P_3$
$P_1P_2P_5$
$P_1P_2P_6$
$P_1P_3P_4$
$P_1P_3P_5$
$P_1P_3P_6$
$P_1P_4P_6$
$P_1P_5P_6$
$P_2P_3P_5$
$P_2P_5P_6$
$P_3P_4P_6$
$P_1P_2P_3P_5$
$P_1P_2P_5P_6$
$P_1P_3P_4P_6$
$P_1P_2P_3P_4P_5P_6$

Figure 4.3.

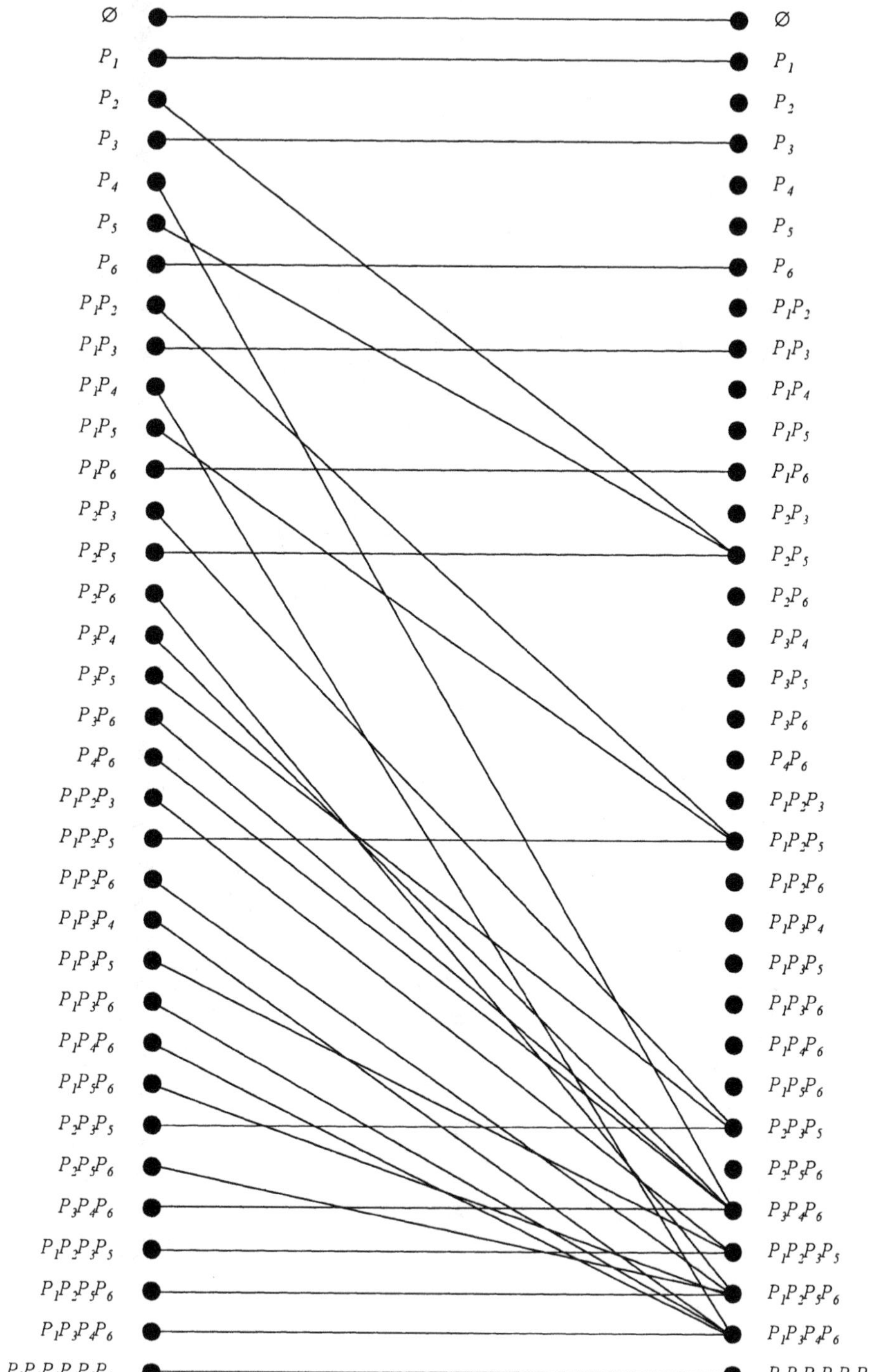
Ø
P1
P2
P3
P4
P5
P6
P1P2
P1P3
P1P4
P1P5
P1P6
P2P3
P2P5
P2P6
P3P4
P3P5
P3P6
P4P6
P1P2P3
P1P2P5
P1P2P6
P1P3P4
P1P3P5
P1P3P6
P1P4P6
P1P5P6
P2P3P5
P2P5P6
P3P4P6
P1P2P3P5
P1P2P5P6
P1P3P4P6
P1P2P3P4P5P6

Figure 4.4.

previous case although interchanging the columns. We arrive at:

It will also be seen in this case that we have done away with those elements of the <<power set>> of referential E that have no significant meaning as their image is $\emptyset$. An exception has been made of $\{P_1, P_2, P_3, P_4, P_5, P_6\}$ so as to keep the visual aspect of the Moore closing. On the other hand, in the first of these latter figures, we have kept the <<power set>> of referential C complete, as we feel it creates no confusion in the correspondences. Let us move on to comment on the results.

This Moore closing brings to light the groupings of products that can be made taking into account the characteristics or properties possessed by each one of them, in such a way that depending on the characteristics required, one grouping or another will be arrived at.

From a technical point of view, in the last of the figures, the existence of seven closed groups can be seen, $\{P_2, P_5\}$, $\{P_1, P_2, P_5\}$, $\{P_2, P_3, P_5\}$, $\{P_3, P_4, P_6\}$, $\{P_1, P_2, P_3, P_5\}$, $\{P_1, P_2, P_5, P_6\}$, $\{P_1, P_3, P_4, P_6\}$, although in reality an eighth should be added, $\{P_1, P_2, P_3, P_4, P_5, P_6\}$ which does not appear in the figure as a consequence of having eliminated the elements of the <<power set>> of E which have as their image $\emptyset$. Therefore, the real existence of closed groups is eight. These closed groups, in conjunction with the elements that have as their only correspondence their own image, give us all the possible groupings of financial products. In our case, these are:

$$\emptyset, \{P_1\}, \{P_3\}, \{P_6\}, \{P_1, P_3\}, \{P_1, P_6\}, \{P_2, P_5\}, \{P_1, P_2, P_5\}, \{P_2, P_3, P_5\}, \{P_3, P_4, P_6\},$$
$$\{P_1, P_2, P_3, P_5\}, \{P_1, P_2, P_5, P_6\}, \{P_1, P_3, P_4, P_6\}, \{P_1, P_2, P_3, P_4, P_5, P_6\}$$

We repeat once again, that each one of these groupings has as a support the same characteristics or properties for all the products comprising the same.

Therefore, it is not only interesting but essential, to automatically know which are the characteristics comprising each group. It is true that for this one can make recourse to the figure relative to the process of maxmin composition, however, we feel it is particularly advantageous to use, in this sense, the property according to which the Moore families resulting from compositions $R^- \circ R^+$ and $R^+ \circ R^-$ constitute isomorphic lattices.

It is true that the families resulting from the Moore closings[8] have the same number of elements (they have the same cardinal), in our example fourteen for $M^{(1)}$ and $M^{(2)}$. Likewise to every element of $M^{(1)}$ one and only one element of $M^{(2)}$, to which one and only one element of $M^{(1)}$ corresponds. The correspon-

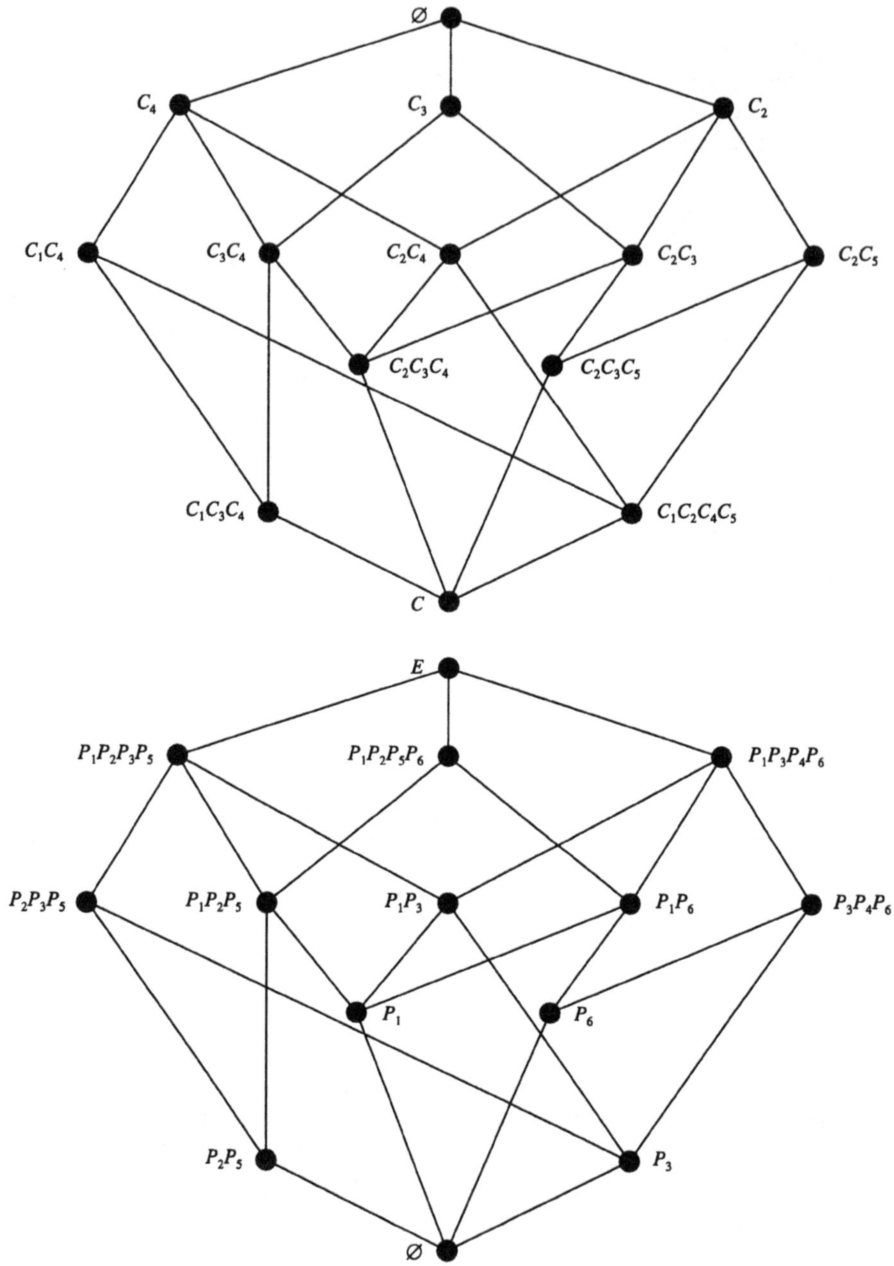
Ø
C_4
C_3
C_2
C_1C_4
C_3C_4
C_2C_4
C_2C_3
C_2C_5
$C_2C_3C_4$
$C_2C_3C_5$
$C_1C_3C_4$
$C_1C_2C_4C_5$
C
E
$P_1P_2P_3P_5$
$P_1P_2P_5P_6$
$P_1P_3P_4P_6$
$P_2P_3P_5$
$P_1P_2P_5$
P_1P_3
P_1P_6
$P_3P_4P_6$
P_1
P_6
P_2P_5
P_3
Ø

Figure 4.5.

ding lattices are (figure 4.5):

It can be seen that we have drawn the lattices inverted, in order to be able to show the isomorphism clearly. In this way, in the formation of groups, the financial products for the investment are accompanied by the characteristics or properties they posses. For example, products $\{P_2, P_3, P_5\}$ posses properties $\{C_1, C_4\}$; products $\{P_1, P_3, P_4, P_6\}$ only posses (all of them) characteristic $\{C_2\}$; and so on for all the groupings.

One aspect is worthy of special attention. As one moves from below to above, the number of financial products increases and the number of characteristics they posses decreases. By joining the same vertices of the two lattices, the products and their common characteristics are joined. Let us now see the results of our case:

$$\emptyset \rightarrow \{C_1, C_2, C_3, C_4, C_5\}$$
$$\{P_3\} \rightarrow \{C_1, C_2, C_4, C_5\}$$
$$\{P_6\} \rightarrow \{C_2, C_3, C_5\}$$
$$\{P_1\} \rightarrow \{C_2, C_3, C_4\}$$
$$\{P_1, P_3\} \rightarrow \{C_2, C_4\}$$
$$\{P_1, P_6\} \rightarrow \{C_2, C_3\}$$
$$\{P_2, P_5\} \rightarrow \{C_1, C_3, C_4\}$$
$$\{P_1, P_2, P_5\} \rightarrow \{C_3, C_4\}$$
$$\{P_2, P_3, P_5\} \rightarrow \{C_1, C_4\}$$
$$\{P_3, P_4, P_6\} \rightarrow \{C_2, C_5\}$$
$$\{P_1, P_2, P_3, P_5\} \rightarrow \{C_4\}$$
$$\{P_1, P_2, P_5, P_6\} \rightarrow \{C_3\}$$
$$\{P_1, P_3, P_4, P_6\} \rightarrow \{C_2\}$$
$$\{P_1, P_2, P_3, P_4, P_5, P_6\} \rightarrow \emptyset$$

It can be seen that the result coincides with the result obtained from the clan theory, although on this occasion we have added to the effective groupings, the theoretical ones which arise from joining the referentials with the vacancies.

It is obvious that, for practical reasons, it is not particularly operative to obtain the following affinities from either of the models presented. For this we have drawn up an algorithm[9] from which the path is shortened and the desired results are obtained. The following are the steps to take:

1. A selection is made between referentials E and C of the one possessing the least number of elements. In our case C with a cardinal of 5
2. The set is constructed of all parts of C, that is its <<power set>> $\Pi(C)$. This is:

$$\emptyset, \{C_1\}, \{C_2\}, \{C_3\}, \{C_4\}, \{C_5\}, \{C_1, C_2\}, \{C_1, C_3\}, \{C_1, C_4\}, \{C_1, C_5\}, \{C_2, C_3\}, \{C_2, C_4\}, \{C_2, C_5\}, \{C_3, C_4\}, \{C_3, C_5\}, \{C_4, C_5\}, \{C_1, C_2, C_3\}, \{C_1, C_2, C_4\}, \{C_1, C_3, C_4\}, \{C_2, C_3, C_4\}, \{C_1, C_2, C_5\}, \{C_1, C_3, C_5\}, \{C_2, C_3, C_5\}, \{C_3, C_4, C_5\}, \{C_1, C_2, C_3, C_4\}, \{C_1, C_2, C_3, C_5\}, \{C_1, C_2, C_4, C_5\}, \{C_1, C_3, C_4, C_5\}, \{C_2, C_3, C_4, C_5\}$$

3. The <<connection to the right>> R^+, is obtained in the sense that, for all $A \in \Pi(C)$, R^+ includes the successors existing simultaneously in all elements of A. We arrive at:

$\varnothing = \{P_1, P_2, P_3, P_4, P_5, P_6\}$
$C_1 = \{P_2, P_3, P_5\}$
$C_2 = \{P_1, P_3, P_4, P_6\}$
$C_3 = \{P_1, P_2, P_5, P_6\}$
$C_4 = \{P_1, P_2, P_3, P_5\}$
$C_5 = \{P_3, P_4, P_6\}$
$C_1C_2 = \{P_3\}$
$C_1C_3 = \{P_2, P_5\}$
$C_1C_4 = \{P_2, P_3, P_5\}$
$C_1C_5 = \{P_3\}$
$C_2C_3 = \{P_1, P_6\}$
$C_2C_4 = \{P_1, P_3\}$
$C_2C_5 = \{P_3, P_4, P_6\}$
$C_3C_4 = \{P_1, P_2, P_5\}$
$C_3C_5 = \{P_6\}$
$C_4C_5 = \{P_3\}$
$C_1C_2C_3 = \varnothing$
$C_1C_2C_4 = \{P_3\}$
$C_1C_2C_5 = \{P_3\}$
$C_1C_3C_4 = \{P_2, P_5\}$
$C_1C_3C_5 = \varnothing$
$C_1C_4C_5 = \{P_3\}$
$C_2C_3C_4 = \{P_1\}$
$C_2C_3C_5 = \{P_6\}$
$C_2C_4C_5 = \{P_3\}$
$C_2C_3C_5 = \{P_6\}$
$C_2C_4C_5 = \{P_3\}$
$C_3C_4C_5 = \varnothing$
$C_1C_2C_3C_4 = \varnothing$
$C_1C_2C_3C_5 = \varnothing$
$C_1C_2C_4C_5 = \{P_3\}$
$C_1C_3C_4C_5 = \varnothing$
$C_2C_3C_4C_5 = \varnothing$
$E = \varnothing$

4. For every non-vacant set of R^+, the one corresponding to A possessing the greatest number of elements, is chosen. We arrive at:

$\varnothing \rightarrow \{C_1, C_2, C_3, C_4, C_5\}$
$\{P_1\} \rightarrow \{C_2, C_3, C_4\}$
$\{P_3\} \rightarrow \{C_1, C_2, C_4, C_5\}$
$\{P_6\} \rightarrow \{C_2, C_3, C_5\}$
$\{P_1, P_3\} \rightarrow \{C_2, C_4\}$
$\{P_1, P_6\} \rightarrow \{C_2, C_3\}$
$\{P_2, P_5\} \rightarrow \{C_1, C_3, C_4\}$
$\{P_1, P_2, P_5\} \rightarrow \{C_3, C_4\}$
$\{P_2, P_3, P_5\} \rightarrow \{C_1, C_4\}$
$\{P_3, P_4, P_6\} \rightarrow \{C_2, C_5\}$
$\{P_1, P_2, P_3, P_5\} \rightarrow \{C_4\}$
$\{P_1, P_2, P_5, P_6\} \rightarrow \{C_3\}$
$\{P_1, P_3, P_4, P_6\} \rightarrow \{C_2\}$
$\{P_1, P_2, P_3, P_4, P_5, P_6\} \rightarrow \varnothing$

From this very simple algorithm we have arrived at the desired result, cutting the process down by a great deal. Let us not forget, however, that the groupings obtained allow us to determine certain sets of financial products each of which can be found by those possessing the same characteristics or properties at certain determined levels, which have been previously established. In this way, the financial analyst posses important information: any product of one and the same group is indifferent to him for the desired objective. On the other hand each group of products has a different interest as the characteristics or properties possessed by it are different.

But, as we have seen, this is not the only question that arises in the currently rich financial panorama. The possibility of having recourse to several sources of financing simultaneously, or of having access to more than one financial product to cover investment needs, makes the set of required properties able to be covered by several products, some possessing some of them and the remainder the rest. This is when the model based on the clans theory acquires all its interest. As we have been able to see, the groups formed by means of this theory, after taking the products in their entirety, include all the desired characteristics.

In our understanding, these two aspects cover a wide spectre of the phenomena arising in this day and age, and therefore, the elements described acquire an ever increasing and recognised utility,

There is one last aspect to be studied: the selection of financial products, the last phase after the analysis we have just looked at, which has cleared the way for this study. Obviously we could now describe the potentially valid variety of techniques for a treatment of this sort. However we do not do so taking into account the fact that the problem of selection of financial products is just one more of the cases in which a tool-box, common to the one we employed in the selection of investments, is used. Having tackled this particular aspect we feel that the other is also covered.

Let us immediately continue with developing a wide spectre of models for the selection of investments, particularly emphasising the diverse uncertain elements concurring in the same. As is well known, uncertainty can only be limited, in certain cases structured and estimated therefore by means of some type of uncertain number, and even uncertainty can reach such a dimension, that the estimate of economic parameters were useless even through valuations. All of this is possible in the convulsed universe that will be inherited by the next millennium. And our task is to attempt to explain it in the most suitable way possible, in order to be able to handle it in a better way.

References

[1] A. M. Gil Lafuente: <<Técnicas de selección de un instrumento financiero>> Article published in the Proceedings of the Vth. Hispano-Portuguese Conference on Scientific Management, Vigo, September, 1990.

[2] E. Pichat: <<Algorithm for finding the maximal elements of a finite universal algebra>>. *Inform Processing 68,* Published North Holland, 1969. A. Kaufmann and J. Gil Aluja: *<<Técnicas de gestión de empresas. Previsiones, decisiones y estrategias,* Pirámide, Madrid, 1992, pages 395-398.

[3] M. Courtillot: <<Structure canonique des fichiers>>, *AIER-AFCET* volume 7, January, 1973, pages 2-15. E.Wang and T.C. Chang: *Canonical structures in attribute based on file organization* , CACM, September, 1981.

[4] J. Lafosse-Marin:<<Moore closing and fuzzy graph>>, internal document, Mathematics Department, University of Algiers (no date).

[5] A. Kaufmann and J. Gil Aluja: *Técnicas operativas de gestión para el tratamiento de la incertidumbre,* Hispano Europea, Barcelona, 1987, page 236.

[6] From this point on we will do without the super-index in order to avoid a too complex representation, which is unnecessary.

[7] For greater detail, consult A. Kaufmann and J- Gil Aluja: *Técnicas de gestión de empresa. Previsiones, decisiones y estrategias,* Pirámide, Madrid, 1992, pages 347-405.

[8] As is well known, every Moore closing is a Moore family.

[9] This algorithm is based on the development carried out by A. Kaufmann and J. Gil Aluja: *Técnicas de gestión de empresa. Previsiones, decisiones y estrategias,* Pirámide, Madrid, 1992, pages 395-398.

SECOND PART
Selection

5 A first approximation to selection models

Updating of monetary currents

From a very general perspective it can be said that, if a determined interest rate is admitted as valid for the basis for calculation, it is accepted that an investment object is convenient from an economic point of view, if the updated current of collections is no less than the updated current of payments. In other words, when the updated difference between collections and payments is not negative. Certain authors normally call this updated difference <<capital value of an investment>>.

On the assumption that several investment objects exist, on which the decision to invest may fall by following economic criteria, selection will be made of the one, the updated difference of which (positive, of course) is greater, which stated in another way, means a greater capital value.

Let us pass on to develop a very simple case. We will deal with a company wishing to acquire industrial equipment A (investment object), in order to develop its production process and it wishes to know if its purchase will be suitable from an economic point of view. The experts consulted consider that the *useful life* of this investment object is of n years. Payment for the purchase of the machine, made at initial moment 0 is equal to M_A, payments arising from exploitation of the investment object will be a_j, $j = 1, 2, ..., n$, while collections from the sale of the products and/or services produced by the machine are estimated at b_j, $j = 1, 2, ..., n$.

Following this criterion, it can be said that the investment is convenient if the updated value of collections at an annual interest rate i is greater than or equal to that of payments, that is:

$$\sum_{j=1}^{n} b_j(1+i)^{-j} \geqslant M_A + \sum_{j=1}^{n} a_j(1+i)^{-j}$$

and also when:

$$\sum_{j=1}^{n} (b_j - a_j)(1+i)^{-j} - M_A \geqslant 0$$

known expression of the current value, in this case relative to moment 0, of a series of income, which is likewise written:

$$V_A = \sum_{j=1}^{n} \frac{b_j - a_j}{(1+i)^j} - M_A$$

The difference b_j - a_j can also be expressed by M_j and then V_A will be:

$$V_A = \sum_{j=1}^{n} M_j(1+i)^{-j} - M_A$$

where M_A and the M_j are the net values. There lies the reason V_A is the <<net updated value>>.

In the case of an investment, the M_j include the differences between collections and payments, and the updated algebraic addition of the same takes on the nature of a certain total updated profit. With this procedure a series of future capitals is reduced to a single value, so that updating resolves the problem of the order of preference between a series of capitals.

The updating technique presupposes, therefore, comparison between a series of capitals (either collections or payments) which by common sense it is not possible to classify due to the different rhythm of their expiry. This technique leads to <<a complete order>> between all the possible series of capitals.

In the scheme of action that we are proposing, and once it has been determined that an investment object is suitable from an economic point of view, it should be compared with the other objects that are subject to selection.

In accordance with what has already been mentioned, the fundamental criterion in this case can also be expressed in this way: on the assumption that a request can be made and any amount of money given at the rate of interest set for calculation purposes, *it will be convenient to choose the investment for which the capital value is the greatest.*

The above condition is necessary due to the fact that two different investment objects do not necessarily imply payments and collects of the same amount, nor do they have the same duration. Therefore we can play around with two alternatives:

1. The mass of money that corresponds to the lower expenses of one of the investments and make another complementary investment.
2. As there is less time to tie up the money, we can have it available for a differential time in order to carry out another investment that can be called complementary.

This is why when the listed condition is not complied with we must compare V_A and $V_{A'}$, on the one hand, with V_B on the other, which represents the capital value of an investment B, different from A. In this case, A', will be the complement of investment A. In this way we bring up the problem of the reinvestment of net cash flows.

Only when the rate of interest, at which a request is made for or a loan is given for A' is the interest rate for calculation purposes or calculatory interest, do we arrive at the fact that its capital value is equal to 0. This is when it is sufficient to do the comparison between V_A and V_B. In fact if, in order to simplify matters, we assume that the complementary investment A' consists in placing a monetary mass M' at moment 0 in order to recuperate it at moment n, will we arrive at the fact that the capital value $V_{A'}$ will be:

$$V_{A'} = -M' + \frac{iM'}{(1+i)} + \frac{iM'}{(1+i)^2} + \dots + \frac{iM'}{(1+i)^n} + \frac{M'}{(1+i)^n} =$$

$$= -M' + iM' \frac{(1+i)^n - 1}{(1+i)^n \cdot i} + \frac{M'}{(1+i)^n} =$$

$$= -M' + M' \frac{(1+i)^n}{(1+i)^n} - \frac{M'}{(1+i)^n} + \frac{M'}{(1+i)^n} = 0$$

As can be seen then, this condition for the validity of the method always appears necessarily when attempting to compare several possibilities for investment. Although adaptation to reality brings up important difficulties, any attempt to eliminate it causes serious inconveniences to arise. This is what happens when trying to introduce what could be called <<profitability ratio of invested capital>> which arises through the relation existing between the capital value and the updated value of payments. Representing three investments classified in increasing order of payments 1, 2, and 3, can be done in the form of a graph (figure 5.1).

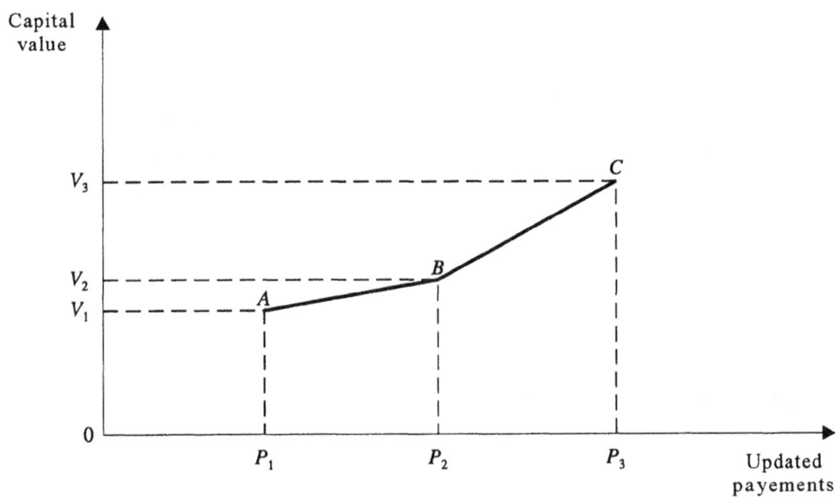

Figure 5.1.

The similarity of this concept with that of capital yield is quite obvious.

Given the fact that both V and P are updated values, this concept allows us to determine both the investment making the maximum V, that is to say, the capital value in an absolute sense, and also the mean capital value, understanding that the updated unit of payment is the capital value.

The comparison should be made between:

$$\frac{V_1}{P_1}, \quad \frac{V_2}{P_2} \text{ and } \frac{V_3}{P_3}$$

It would appear quite correct to acquire investment 2 if:

$$\frac{V_2}{P_2} > \frac{V_1}{P_1} \text{ and } \frac{V_2}{P_2} > \frac{V_3}{P_3}$$

Leaving aside what we have just stated, and, on the assumption that two possibilities exist for investment in two investment objects A and B, it can be said, with the limitations we have pointed out, that:

When $V_A > V_B$, investment in object A is appropriate; and on the contrary, then investment in object B is the case.

These conditions can be written as follows:

$$V_A - V_B \gtrless 0 \quad \begin{matrix} \text{A is advisavle} \\ \text{B is advisable} \end{matrix}$$

But $V_A - V_B$ is nothing else but the difference between the updating of the collection and payment currents of one or the other investment. This value can be called <<capital value of the investment by difference>>, and be written as V_{A-B}.

In this case it can be said that *an investment A is more advantageous than another investment B when the capital value of the investment by difference* V_{A-B} *is positive.* B will be more advantageous when this figure is negative.

In fact, for the two investments A and B, the capital value of each will be:

$$V_A = \sum_{j=1}^{n} M_j(1+i)^{-j} - M_A$$

$$V_B = \sum_{j=1}^{n} M_j'(1+i)^{-j} - M_B$$

If $V_A > V_B$, investment A is more favourable and $V_{A-B} > 0$ is complied with.

$$V_{A-B} = V_A - V_B = \sum_{j=1}^{n} (M_j - M_j')(1+i)^{-j} - (M_A - M_B)$$

When $V_{A-B} > 0$,overall what will happen is that collections less updated payments of investment A are higher than the difference between collections and updated payments of investment B.

As can be seen the form taken on by V_{A-B} is noticeably equal to that of the capital value on an individual investment where the M_j, will be the collections and the M'_j the payments and $(M_A - M_B)$ the initial payment at moment 0.

Let us now move on to take a look at a practical example in which the previous scheme is used. This highly suitable example has been taken from reality. We are dealing with an industrial company with several production centres between which material transfers take place.

Between two of these centres, A_1 and A_2, runs a roadway which prevents transport of materials by land, so that the transfer of raw materials and semi-finished products must be done by an overhead conveyor belt (elevated a few meters), at least up to an intermediate point B.

Technical studies reveal the existence of two possibilities for carrying out this transport task:

1. Solution I consists in the acquisition and installation of a conveyor belt to cover the distance from A_1 to A_2, some 3,100 meters.
2. Solution II divides the distance into two parts, the first where a conveyor belt is used of some 1,800 meters (from A_1 to B) which passes over the roadway, and the second part which is done by wheeled transport with traction vehicles and trailers from B to A_2. At point B the conveyor belt is unloaded and the trailer vehicles loaded.

Since the end sought is to determine which is the most advantageous investment from an economic point of view, the payment currents arising from the decision to invest in each of the alternatives must be obtained and compared. The decision will fall to the *lowest*.

In this case, as in many others which can be considered, the collection currents are not taken into account, because the result is the same whichever object is chosen (the task carried out with either one of the alternatives produces the same result).

In order to simplify data handling, we will only take into account the differential payments for each investment object, in this way doing away with those that appear for the same amount and at the same time, in one or other alternative.

Having made all the pertinent enquiries the following data has been taken as certain:

Alternative I

- Purchase and installation of a 3,100 meter conveyor belt for 51 million monetary units and a useful life of 12 years.
- Maintenance of the conveyor belt was valued as a percentage of its cost

price, starting out with 1 percent for the first year and increasing this figure by 0.5 per cent per year.

Alternative II

- Purchase and installation of a 1,800 meter conveyor belt for 29 million monetary units and a useful life of 12 years.
- Purchase of towing vehicles for 240,000 monetary units and a useful life of 3 years.
- Purchase of trailers for 1 million monetary units and a useful life of 6 years.
- Maintenance for the conveyor belt was valued at the same percentages as alternative I, that for the vehicles by a percentage of 5 percent for the first year, 10 percent for the second and 30 percent for the third. There is no maintenance for the trailers.
- Payments for purchase of fuel for the vehicles has been estiated at 200,000 monetary units per annum.
- Salaries paid per year to the drivers of the vehicles is for an amount of 600,000 monetary units per annum.
- Salaries paid to guard personnel at point *B* for unloading and loading is for 100,000 per annum.

With this data the following table can be constructed:

Moment	Alternative I			Alternative II							
	Payment for conveyor belt	Mainte-nance conveyor belt	Total	Payment for conveyor belt	Purchase trailer vehicles	Mainte-nance conveyor belt	Mainte-nance vehicles	Fuel	Drivers salaries	Point B personnel salaries	Total
0	51.000		51.000	29.000	1.240						30.240
1		510	510			290	12	200	600	100	1.020
2		765	765			435	24	200	600	100	1.359
3		1.020	1.020		240	580	72	200	600	100	1.792
4		1.275	1.275			725	12	200	600	100	1.637
5		1.530	1.530			870	24	200	600	100	1.794
6		1.785	1.785		1.240	1.015	72	200	600	100	3.227
7		2.040	2.040			1.160	12	200	600	100	2.072
8		2.295	2.295			1.305	24	200	600	100	2.229
9		2.550	2.550		240	1.450	72	200	600	100	2.662
10		2.805	2.805			1.595	12	200	600	100	2.507
11		3.060	3.060			1.740	24	200	600	100	2.664
12		3.315	3.315			1.885	72	200	600	100	2.757

Summarising the results it can be seen that the payment currents for Alternative I and II are the following:

Moment of useful life	0	1	2	3	4	5	6	7	8	9	10	11	12
Alternat. I	51.000	510	765	1.020	1.275	1.530	1.785	2.040	2.295	2.550	2.805	3.060	3.315
Alternat. II	30.240	1.202	1.359	1.792	1.637	1.794	3.227	2.072	2.229	2.662	2.507	2.664	2.757

On the assumption of considering that the rate of interest taken as a basis for calculation is 10 per cent, the following net updated values will be obtained:

Moment of useful life	Updating coefficient 0.1	Alternative I		Alternative II	
		Net values	Net updated value	Net values	Net updated value
0	1	51.000	51.000	30.240	30.240
1	.9090	510	464	1.202	1.092
2	.8264	765	632	1.359	1.123
3	.7513	1.020	766	1.792	1.346
4	.6830	1.275	870	1.637	1.118
5	.6209	1.530	950	1.794	1.113
6	.5644	1.785	1.007	3.227	1.821
7	.5131	2.040	1.046	2.072	1.063
8	.4665	2.295	1.070	2.229	1.039
9	.4240	2.550	1.081	2.662	1.128
10	.3855	2.805	1.081	2.507	966
11	.3504	3.060	1.071	2.664	933
12	.3186	3.315	1.056	2.757	878
$M + \sum a_j(1+i)^{-j}$			62.094		43.860

From the comparison of the data obtained it can be seen that <<alternative II>> is more advantageous, since 43,860 > 62,094.

These calculations can be simplified by operating with the net updated values by difference. In fact, as has been pointed out before, when $V_A > V_B$ is complied with, obviously then $V_{A-B} > 0$. In this case we arrive at:

Moment of useful life	Net values			Difference Net values I-II	Difference updated values	
	Updating coefficient 0.1	Alternative I	Alternative II		Positive	Negative
0	1	51.000	30.240	+20.760	20.760	
1	.909	510	1.202	-692		629
2	.8264	765	1.359	-594		490
3	.7513	1.020	1.792	-772		580
4	.683	1.275	1.637	-362		247
5	.6209	1.530	1.794	-264		163
6	.5644	1.785	3.227	-1.442		813
7	.5131	2.040	2.072	-32		16
8	.4665	2.295	2.229	+66	30	
9	.424	2.550	2.662	-112		47
10	.3855	2.805	2.507	+298	114	
11	.3504	3.060	2.664	+396	138	
12	.3186	3.315	2.757	+558	177	
Updated value by difference					21.219	2.985

The algebraic addition, as could not be any other way, provides us with the same previously obtained result. In effect, we arrive at:

$$62{,}094 - 43{,}860 = 21{,}219 - 2{,}219 = 18{,}234$$

which constitutes the highest updated profits by the fact of taking the decision to invest in Alternative II in stead of doing so in Alternative I.

The problems, both formal and real, brought up by using the so called method of capital value as has been formulated, are evident. Suffice it to analyse this example, even just superficially, for us to realise the difficulties existing in estimating with certainty some of the components of the monetary currents, in determining the rate of interest for calculation purposes for future periods as well as the lack of adequacy to reality on doing without items such as technical progress and the inflationary process, for example.

Incorporation of the lack of precision of interest rates

In a first approximation, we have started out from the hypothesis according to which the interest rate that is taken as a basis for calculation for obtaining a criterion of selection was known with certainty and considered equal for all periods making up the economic horizon. Therefore from this:

$$i_1 = i_2 = i_3 = \cdots = i_n = i$$

It is obvious that in an economic context such as we are living in today, these assumptions are untenable. Fortunately, abandoning this does not add any complementary difficulties. Thus, in relation to the equality of rates in time, if the rest of the hypothesis is maintained, the net updated value (capital value) will become, for an investment object A:

$$V_A = -M + M_1(1+i_1)^{-1} + M_2(1+i_1)^{-1}(1+i_2)^{-1} + \cdots +$$
$$+ M_n(1+i_1)^{-1}(1+i_2)^{-1} + \cdots + (1+i_n)^{-1}$$

Now, in spite of the fact that this formula allows us to incorporate the supposed *future* variations of the interest rate, let us consider that it is particularly difficult to estimate these with any kind of exactitude and that, in certain changing situations such as at present, it is more honest the major part of the time, to incorporate the lack of precision into the model by means of confidence intervals, triplets, quadruples, fuzzy triangular numbers, trapezoidals or any other numerical element representing this obligatory uncertainty.

We are now going to delve even deeper into this aspect, which has already been mentioned. For this we are going to assume that the experts supply their information relative to the hoped for interest rates, by means of fuzzy triangular numbers (FTN). Normally the experts we consulted furnish their FTN in the ternary form.

This then will be:

$$\underset{\sim}{I}_i = (r_i, m_i, s_i), \quad i = 1, 2, \ldots, n$$

n being the useful life of the investment object.

Now then, given the fact that the calculations for selection are not done directly with the interest rates, but through them, with the updated rates, it will be necessary to see the form acquired, in this case by the coefficients:

$$(1+i_1)^{-1},\ (1+i_1)^{-1}(1+i_2)^{-1},\ \ldots$$

At this point in time we feel it is necessary to make a prior warning. Taking into account that obtaining the updated rates includes certain quotients, in which the rate of interest appears in the denominator, the result of the operation (division) is not linear and, therefore, it is not correct to operate directly with the ternary form. It will be necessary that once the estimates (normally expressed in the ternary form) have been arrived at, that they be transformed into the α-cuts form.

As is known, if starting out from:

$$\underset{\sim}{I}_i = (r_i, m_i, s_i)$$

one arrives at in the α -cuts form:

$$I_{i\alpha} = [r_i + (m_i - r_i)\alpha,\ s_i - (s_i - m_i)\alpha], \quad \alpha \in [0, 1]$$

If the extremes of the interval are presented as follows:

$$r_i + (m_i - r_i)\alpha = r(\alpha)$$
$$s_i - (s_i - m_i)\alpha = s(\alpha)$$

We arrive at:

$$I_{i\alpha} = [r(\alpha), s(\alpha)]$$

where evidently, $r(\alpha)$ and $s(\alpha)$ are linear functions.

Once these considerations have been made, we are in a position to pass on from the interest rate to the updating coefficient. Let us remember, once again, that:

$$\frac{1}{1 + i_1}$$

is the updating rate, in certainty, corresponding to the first year.

By keeping the same expression, on expressing the rate of interest i_1 by means of a FTN in the form of α-cuts, we arrive at:

$$\frac{1}{1 + [r(\alpha), s(\alpha)]}$$

where the interval has been substituted by a crisp number.

On the other hand, the crisp number 1 can be represented by a confidence interval [1, 1]. By adding the two confidence intervals of the denominator we will obtain:

$$\frac{1}{[1, 1] (+) [r(\alpha), s(\alpha)]} = \frac{1}{[1 + r(\alpha), 1 + s(\alpha)]}$$

As the numerator can also be expressed by the confidence interval [1, 1], the following division will be made and we will arrive at:

$$\frac{[1, 1]}{[1 + r(\alpha), 1 + s(\alpha)]} = [1, 1] (:) [1 + r(\alpha), 1 + s(\alpha)] = \left[\frac{1}{1 + s(\alpha)}, \frac{1}{1 + r(\alpha)}\right]$$

With which we have expressed the updating rate by means of a fuzzy number expressed by the pair, confidence interval-level of presumption.

Obtaining the updating rates for the following periods is simple for those knowing the arithmetic of the FTN in the field of positive reals.

Thus, if we start out from:

$$\frac{1}{1+i_1} \cdot \frac{1}{1+i_2}$$

which represents the crisp updating for the second year, we arrive at in uncertainty:

$$\left[\frac{1}{1+s_1(\alpha)}, \frac{1}{1+r_1(\alpha)}\right] (\cdot) \left[\frac{1}{1+s_2(\alpha)}, \frac{1}{1+r_2(\alpha)}\right]$$

that is:

$$\left[\frac{1}{1+s_1(\alpha)} \cdot \frac{1}{1+s_2(\alpha)}, \frac{1}{1+r_1(\alpha)} \cdot \frac{1}{1+r_2(\alpha)}\right]$$

Let us finish by saying that:

$$\frac{1}{1+i_1} \cdot \frac{1}{1+i_2} \cdot \frac{1}{1+i_3}$$

is the updating for the third year, in the sphere of precision.

On passing over to the FTN it will be:

$$\left[\frac{1}{1+s_1(\alpha)}, \frac{1}{1+r_1(\alpha)}\right] (\cdot) \left[\frac{1}{1+s_2(\alpha)}, \frac{1}{1+r_2(\alpha)}\right] (\cdot) \left[\frac{1}{1+s_3(\alpha)}, \frac{1}{1+r_3(\alpha)}\right]$$

That is to say:

$$\left[\frac{1}{1+s_1(\alpha)} \cdot \frac{1}{1+s_2(\alpha)} \cdot \frac{1}{1+s_3(\alpha)}, \frac{1}{1+r_1(\alpha)} \cdot \frac{1}{1+r_2(\alpha)} \cdot \frac{1}{1+r_3(\alpha)}\right]$$

One of the first applications which have been made of the updating technique in uncertainty has taken place in the field of investment selection[1] through the criterion of <<capital value of an investment>> or <<net updated value>> presented in the previous section. For handling an investment problem with uncertain interest rates expressed by FTN, one will arrive at the fact that the net updated income $\underset{\sim}{V}_n$ would be given by:

$$\underset{\sim}{V}_n = -M[1, 1] \ (+) \ M_1 \left[\frac{1}{1+s_1(\alpha)}, \frac{1}{1+r_1(\alpha)}\right] (+)$$

$$(+) \ M_2 \left[\frac{1}{(1+s_1(\alpha))(1+s_2(\alpha))}, \frac{1}{(1+r_1(\alpha))(1+r_2(\alpha))}\right] (+) \cdots (+)$$

$$(+) \ M_n \left[\frac{1}{(1+s_1(\alpha))(1+s_2(\alpha)) \cdots (1+s_n(\alpha))}, \frac{1}{(1+r_1(\alpha))(1+r_2(\alpha)) \cdots (1+r_n(\alpha))}\right]$$

This expression allows us to obtain all the possible existing updated <<profits>>, among which the result arrived at in reality will be found. It will also be possible to know each of the possible results, expressed in intervals, to which all levels of presumption will be associated.

The hypothesis of known net values and fuzzy rate of interest

With the object of showing the practical possibilities of all we have pointed out, we are going to develop a simple example, in which the net values relative to each year M_j are assumed as known with certainty, while the interest rates will be expressed by means of FTN.

An economic horizon of three years will be considered:

$$j \in \{0, 1, 2, 3\}$$

As the initial quantity (payment at moment 0) M is known, it is not taken into account at this point, but it will be sufficient to add it at the end of the calculations, subtracting from it the result obtained. The following will be:

$M_1 = 3.000$ monetary units, $(r_1, m_1, s_1) = (6, 8, 10)$ in percentage

$M_2 = 2.000$ monetary units, $(r_2, m_2, s_2) = (3, 6, 9)$ in percentage

$M_3 = 4.000$ monetary units, $(r_3, m_3, s_3) = (5, 7, 8)$ in percentage

With this initial data we arrive at:

$$1 + r_1(\alpha) = 1 + r_1 + (m_1 - r_1)\alpha = 1 + 0.06 + (0.08 - 0.06)\alpha = 1.06 + 0.02\alpha$$

$$1 + r_2(\alpha) = 1 + r_2 + (m_2 - r_2)\alpha = 1 + 0.03 + (0.06 - 0.03)\alpha = 1.03 + 0.03\alpha$$

$$1 + r_3(\alpha) = 1 + r_3 + (m_3 - r_3)\alpha = 1 + 0.05 + (0.07 - 0.05)\alpha = 1.05 + 0.02\alpha$$

And, from here we obtain:

$$(1+r_1(\alpha))(1+r_2(\alpha)) = (1.06+0.02\alpha)(1.03+0.03\alpha)$$
$$(1+r_1(\alpha))(1+r_2(\alpha))(1+r_3(\alpha)) = (1.06+0.02\alpha)(1.03+0.03\alpha)(1.05+0.02\alpha)$$

On the other hand:

$$1+s_1(\alpha) = 1+s_1-(s_1-m_1)\alpha = 1+0.10-(0.1-0.08)\alpha = 1.1-0.02\alpha$$
$$1+s_2(\alpha) = 1+s_2-(s_2-m_2)\alpha = 1+0.09-(0.09-0.06)\alpha = 1.09-0.03\alpha$$
$$1+s_3(\alpha) = 1+s_3-(s_3-m_3)\alpha = 1+0.08-(0.08-0.07)\alpha = 1.08-0.01\alpha$$

And from here we obtain:

$$(1+s_1(\alpha))(1+s_2(\alpha)) = (1.1-0.02\alpha)(1.09-0.03\alpha)$$
$$(1+s_1(\alpha))(1+s_2(\alpha))(1+s_3(\alpha)) = (1.1-0.02\alpha)(1.09-0.03\alpha)(1.08-0.01\alpha)$$

In this way, giving values to α using the hendecadarion system in [0, 1], a fuzzy updating rate will be obtained for each period.

Therefore for the first year:

α	FTN		Fuzzy numbers	
	$1.06+0.02\alpha$	$1.1-0.02\alpha$	$\frac{1}{1.1-0.02\alpha}$	$\frac{1}{1.06+0.02\alpha}$
0	1.060	1.100	0.9090	0.9433
0.1	1.062	1.098	0.9107	0.9416
0.2	1.064	1.096	0.9124	0.9398
0.3	1.066	1.094	0.9140	0.9380
0.4	1.068	1.092	0.9157	0.9363
0.5	1.070	1.090	0.9174	0.9345
0.6	1.072	1.088	0.9191	0.9328
0.7	1.074	1.086	0.9208	0.9310
0.8	1.076	1.084	0.9225	0.9293
0.9	1.078	1.082	0.9242	0.9276
1	1.080	1.080	0.9259	0.9259

It can be seen that, although the fuzzy number representing the rate of interest is effectively a FTN, the same is not true for the updating rate. In fact, their respective graphic representations show this clearly (figure 5.2).

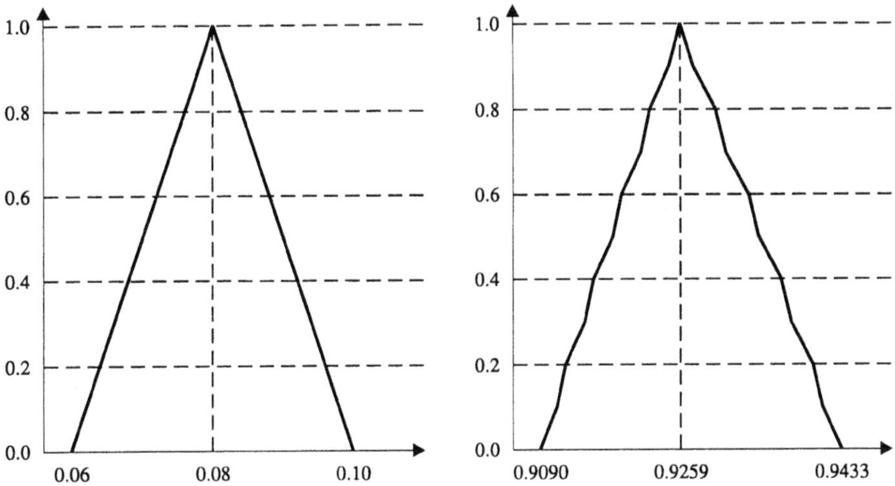

Fuzzy triangular number representing the rate of interest

Fuzzy non-triangular number representing updating

Figure 5.2.

For the second year we resort to the same procedure and the result shown in the following table is arrived at:

α	$1.03 + 0.03$	$1.09 - 0.03$	$\frac{1}{1.09 - 0.03\alpha}$	$\frac{1}{1.03 + 0.03\alpha}$	$\frac{1}{1.1 - 0.02\alpha} \cdot \frac{1}{1.09 - 0.03\alpha}$	$\frac{1}{1.06 + 0.02\alpha} \cdot \frac{1}{1.03 + 0.03\alpha}$
0	1.030	1.090	0.9174	0.9709	0.8340	0.9159
0.1	1.033	1.087	0.9200	0.9681	0.8379	0.9115
0.2	1.036	1.084	0.9225	0.9653	0.8417	0.9072
0.3	1.039	1.081	0.9251	0.9625	0.8456	0.9029
0.4	1.042	1.078	0.9276	0.9597	0.8495	0.8986
0.5	1.045	1.075	0.9302	0.9569	0.8534	0.8943
0.6	1.048	1.072	0.9328	0.9542	0.8574	0.8901
0.7	1.051	1.069	0.9355	0.9515	0.8614	0.8859
0.8	1.054	1.066	0.9381	0.9488	0.8654	0.8818
0.9	1.057	1.063	0.9407	0.9461	0.8694	0.8776
1	1.060	1.060	0.9434	0.9434	0.8735	0.8735
	FTN		Fuzzy NON-triangular numbers			

The same for the third year we will obtain:

α	$1.05+0.02\alpha$	$1.08-0.01\alpha$	$\frac{1}{1.08-0.01\alpha}$	$\frac{1}{1.05+0.02\alpha}$	$\frac{1}{1.1-0.02\alpha}\cdot\frac{1}{1.09-0.03\alpha}\cdot\frac{1}{1.08-0.01\alpha}$	$\frac{1}{1.06+0.02\alpha}\cdot\frac{1}{1.03+0.03\alpha}\cdot\frac{1}{1.05+0.02\alpha}$
0	1.050	1.080	0.9259	0.9524	0.7722	0.8723
0.1	1.052	1.079	0.9268	0.9506	0.7765	0.8665
0.2	1.054	1.078	0.9276	0.9488	0.7808	0.8607
0.3	1.056	1.077	0.9285	0.9470	0.7851	0.8550
0.4	1.058	1.076	0.9294	0.9452	0.7895	0.8493
0.5	1.060	1.075	0.9302	0.9434	0.7939	0.8437
0.6	1.062	1.074	0.9311	0.9416	0.7983	0.8381
0.7	1.064	1.073	0.9320	0.9398	0.8028	0.8326
0.8	1.066	1.072	0.9328	0.9381	0.8073	0.8272
0.9	1.068	1.071	0.9337	0.9363	0.8118	0.8217
1	1.070	1.070	0.9346	0.9346	0.8164	0.8164
	FTN		Fuzzy number (non-triangular)		Fuzzy number (non-triangular)	

With this data and returning to the previous updating formula the net updating value can be presented as follows:

$$V_\alpha = -M\,(+)\,M_1\left[\frac{1}{1.1-0.02\alpha}\cdot\frac{1}{1.06+0.02\alpha}\right](+)$$

$$(+)\,M_2\left[\frac{1}{1.1-0.02\alpha}\cdot\frac{1}{1.09-0.03\alpha}\cdot\frac{1}{1.06+0.02\alpha}\cdot\frac{1}{1.03+0.03\alpha}\right](+)$$

$$(+)\,M_3\left[\frac{1}{1.1-0.02\alpha}\cdot\frac{1}{1.09-0.03\alpha}\cdot\frac{1}{1.08-0.01\alpha}\cdot\frac{1}{1.06+0.02\alpha}\cdot\frac{1}{1.03+0.03\alpha}\cdot\frac{1}{1.05+0.02\alpha}\right]$$

Assuming that M = 7,000 monetary units and by assigning the corresponding data, we arrive at:

α	7000[1, 1]	3000 [1/(1.1 – 0.02α), 1/(1.06 + 0.02α)]	2000 · [1/(1.1 – 0.02α) · · 1/(1.09 – 0.03α), 1/(1.06 + 0.02α) · · 1/(1.03 + 0.03α)]	4000 · [1/(1.1 – 0.02α) · · 1/(1.09 – 0.03α) · · 1/(1.08 – 0.01α), 1/(1.06 + 0.02α) · · 1/(1.03 + 0.03α) · · 1/(1.05 + 0.02α)]	Total V_α
0	7000	[2727, 2830]	[1668, 1832]	[3089, 3489]	[484, 1151]
0.1	7000	[2732, 2825]	[1676, 1823]	[3106, 3466]	[514, 1114]
0.2	7000	[2737, 2820]	[1683, 1814]	[3123, 3443]	[544, 1077]
0.3	7000	[2742, 2814]	[1691, 1806]	[3141, 3420]	[574, 1040]
0.4	7000	[2747, 2809]	[1699, 1797]	[3158, 3397]	[604, 1003]
0.5	7000	[2752, 2804]	[1707, 1789]	[3176, 3375]	[635, 967]
0.6	7000	[2757, 2799]	[1715, 1780]	[3193, 3353]	[665, 931]
0.7	7000	[2762, 2793]	[1723, 1772]	[3211, 3331]	[696, 896]
0.8	7000	[2768, 2788]	[1731, 1764]	[3229, 3309]	[727, 860]
0.9	7000	[2773, 2783]	[1739, 1755]	[3247, 3287]	[759, 825]
1	7000	[2778, 2778]	[1747, 1747]	[3265, 3265]	[790, 790]

If the manner of presenting the fuzzy number V_α is inverted by putting level 0 in the lower part and 1 in the upper, the following figure can be shown (figure 5.3):

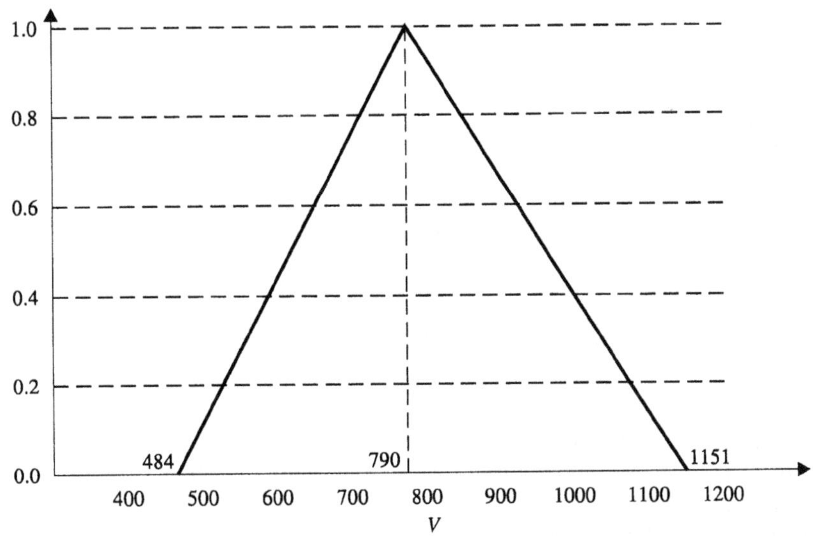

Figure 5.3.

It can be seen that the result obtained gets very close, in its form, to a fuzzy triangular number. This is not mere chance because while the number of periods (years) is not particularly high, a result very close to FTN is always arrived at.

The calculation we made could have been done much faster, by taking for this data the ternary form. Now, as is known, while $I = (r, m, s)$ and that $(1 + r, 1 + m, 1 + s)$ constitute a FTN, the reverse of the latter is not, although on certain occasions it can come very close. When this happens, for any year, for example for period 2, the following can be written:

$$\left(\frac{1}{1+s_1}, \frac{1}{1+m_1}, \frac{1}{1+r_1}\right) (\cdot) \left(\frac{1}{1+s_2}, \frac{1}{1+m_2}, \frac{1}{1+r_2}\right) \simeq$$

$$\simeq \left(\frac{1}{1+s_1} \cdot \frac{1}{1+s_2}, \frac{1}{1+m_1} \cdot \frac{1}{1+m_2}, \frac{1}{1+r_1} \cdot \frac{1}{1+r_2}\right)$$

In any event:

$\dfrac{1}{1+s_1} \cdot \dfrac{1}{1+s_2}$ will be the lower extreme

$\dfrac{1}{1+m_1} \cdot \dfrac{1}{1+m_2}$ will be the maximum presumption

$\dfrac{1}{1+r_1} \cdot \dfrac{1}{1+r_2}$ will be the upper extreme

If this simplification is admitted, the previous example could be expressed as follows:

$$V'_\alpha = -7000 + 3000 \left(\frac{1}{1.10}, \frac{1}{1.08}, \frac{1}{1.06}\right) (+)\, 2000 \left(\frac{1}{1.1990}, \frac{1}{1.1448}, \frac{1}{1.0918}\right) (+)$$

$$(+)\, 4000 \left(\frac{1}{1.29492}, \frac{1}{1.22493}, \frac{1}{1.14639}\right) = (482, 787, 1148)$$

These calculations are much shorter, but for a computer the time for obtaining the answers is negligible either for one or the other of these procedures.

The objective sought with the introduction of this simple scheme within the sphere of investment selection, is an attempt to arrive at a formalisation more in accord with reality, avoiding wherever possible its traditional deformation when a numerical precision is resorted to.

The works dealing with problems arising from investments in companies, otherwise particularly valuable contain a great variety of mathematical models, the basis of which can be found in the need of a certain exactness in their estimates. But it has also been found that this requirement for exactitude makes their schemes noticeably remote from the real world, which is characterised by multiple uncertainties. The complexity of the problems and the lack of clarity of situations, make it advisable to introduce more flexible schemes that are more adapted to reality. The model developed here is only a very first approximation.

References

1 A. Kaufmann and J. Gil Aluja: *Introducción a la teoría de los subconjuntos borrosos a la gestión de las empresas,* Milladoiro, 1986, chapter 4.

6 Selection of investments in an economy with inflaction

Estimate of monetary currents at constant prices

It is particularly well known that the word inflation can be found in the majority of works by neo-classical economists such as Marshall, Edgeworth, Jevons, Menger, Paretto and Walras, among others. In fact, during the First World War, an article by Edgeworth appeared in the English magazine, *The Economic Journal*, on inflation, in which this concept is identified with the increase in prices caused by war expenses. Having said this, we would like to sate that this section does not have as its object to arrive at a single concept of inflation, valid and accepted with a general nature, but explicitly our intention consists in introducing the effects that the latter causes in the monetary currents of collections and payments arising from the decision to invest, based on a representation of the inflation phenomena.

Let us pass on then to the technical aspects for determining how this concept can be introduced into the investment studies of the company, which in other terms is equivalent to establishing what indices should be used for incorporating the inflation phenomena into the monetary currents of collections and payments, when the economic system is immersed in a context of uncertainty.

In the first place we feel it is particularly necessary to point out the importance that the selection of the index used for quantifying inflation acquires, not only because it constitutes a basic element in making financial studies, but by the fact that it serves as the basis for calculating economic parameters that are used periodically by businessmen, workers, consumers, active and passive classes, etc., etc. The use of one or other of the existing indices can give rise to notably different results.

Among the measurements more frequently used is the consumer price index. The discussions caused by this index are particularly well known. Even when admitting the solidity of the corresponding methods for data collation and processing, it is obvious that, in each country, results are directly conditioned upon the composition of the <<shopping basket>>, and by the representative nature of the sample that serves as the basis for the same. If the consumer habits of the population change or if the socio-economic composition of the latter changes, this index can show notable differences in its results. Other indicators can also be used, such as the wholesale price index, the implicit deflator of the national product, etc.

We are conscious of the complexity that measuring the inflation process involves. Therefore, provided certain minimum requirements of homegeneousness are respected in the comparative analyses, the more well known indicators available should not present any spectacular differences, therefore being sufficiently orientative for translating the degree and evolution of the inflation process in an economy.

The eternal concern shown both by the authorities and businessmen on the incidence of the inflation process on investments, is the reason why it is necessary to reconsider the validity of the traditional methods for investment selection, relative as to whether it is possible to use them under changing economic situations. And this is so, because the classical criterion according to which an investment is favourable when the collection current at least compensates that of payments plus any accrued interest on the same, should be the subject for revision.

In fact, the incidence of inflation makes both collections and payments as time goes by loose their purchasing power, to a greater or lesser degree. In principal it should not come as a surprise then, that the aforesaid criterion should be substituted by one, according to which, an investment object is convenient when the collection current allows for not only recuperating payments but also compensating at least the current rate of interest and the effects of inflation.

Also, given the perspective that inflation will not disappear totally from economic life makes it necessary, in handling the microeconomic problem of investments, to place this phenomenon in a preferential place, in order to include it in a fundamental manner in those processes seeking to model it.

Now, the incorporation of the inflation effect in selection studies, has its requirements, since it is necessary to establish without a doubt, the sense that the value should acquire, in monetary terms, resulting from the study of whether an investment is an economic viability or not. And this is so because the latter can be expressed, from a very general perspective, in nominal values or representing a figure that maintains the same purchasing power as the one existing at the time of initiating the investment (referential moment).

When the monetary masses relative to each period have been estimated at prices at the time of initiating the investment (referential moment), indicating that the inflation process has not been taken into account, then the result obtained will reflect a monetary mass at initial prices. In this case the monetary units intervening in the process will maintain the same purchasing power.

The capital value of an investment in this case acquires the already known form of:

$$V = -M + \sum_{j=1}^{n} (b_j - a_j)(1 + i)^{-j}$$

where:

M: Payment of the investment object at moment 0.
b_j: Collections from exploitation.
a_j: Payments of exploitation.
n: Useful life of the investment object
i: Calculatory rate of interest.

Value V express the updated profit obtained by means of the investment object and expressed in monetary units with the same purchasing power.

In the more general case, when the interest rate is estimated for each period, we arrive at:

$$V = -M + (b_1 - a_1)(1+i_1)^{-1} + (b_2 - a_2)(1+i_1)^{-1}(1+i_2)^{-1} + \cdots +$$
$$+ (b_j - a_j)(1+i_1)^{-1} \cdots (1+i_j)^{-1} + \cdots + (b_n - a_n)(1+i_1)^{-1} \cdots (1+i_j)^{-1} \cdots (1+i_n)^{-1}$$

As we saw in the previous chapter, this proposal can be adapted to a context of uncertainty. On this occasion we are going to make other elements, such as carriers of uncertain economic parameters intervene, although also in this case recourse will be made to fuzzy triangular numbers.

In this sense, by means of these uncertain numbers, we are going to consider collections, payments and inflation rates, all of which are economic parameters located in the future.

On passing from certainty to uncertainty:

b_j will be converted into $(b_j^{(1)}, b_j^{(2)}, b_j^{(3)})$
a_j will be converted into $(a_j^{(1)}, a_j^{(2)}, a_j^{(3)})$
i_j will be converted into $(i_j^{(1)}, i_j^{(2)}, i_j^{(3)})$

M and n are going to be assumed as known, by means of certain parameters. If the FTN are expressed in the form of α-cuts we will arrive at, respectively:

$$[b_j^{(1)} + (b_j^{(2)} - b_j^{(1)})\alpha,\ b_j^{(3)} - (b_j^{(3)} - b_j^{(2)})\alpha]$$
$$[a_j^{(1)} + (a_j^{(2)} - a_j^{(1)})\alpha,\ a_j^{(3)} - (a_j^{(3)} - a_j^{(2)})\alpha]$$
$$[i_j^{(1)} + (i_j^{(2)} - i_j^{(1)})\alpha,\ i_j^{(3)} - (i_j^{(3)} - i_j^{(2)})\alpha]$$

On passing over from the rate of interest to the updating rate we will have:

$$\frac{1}{1\,(+)\,[i_j^{(1)} + (i_j^{(2)} - i_j^{(1)})\alpha,\ i_j^{(3)} - (i_j^{(3)} - i_j^{(2)})\alpha]} = \left[\frac{1}{1 + i_j^{(3)} - (i_j^{(3)} - i_j^{(2)})\alpha},\ \frac{1}{1 + i_j^{(1)} + (i_j^{(2)} - i_j^{(1)})\alpha}\right]$$

$$j = 1, 2, \ldots, n$$

Therefore the capital value in uncertainty, will take the form of:

$$V = -M (+) [b_1^{(1)} - a_1^{(3)} + (b_1^{(2)} - b_1^{(1)} + a_1^{(3)} - a_1^{(2)})\alpha, b_1^{(3)} - a_1^{(1)} - (b_1^{(3)} - b_1^{(2)} + a_1^{(2)} - a_1^{(1)})\alpha] (\cdot)$$

$$(\cdot) \left[\frac{1}{1 + i_1^{(3)} - (i_1^{(3)} - i_1^{(2)})\alpha}, \frac{1}{1 + i_1^{(1)} + (i_1^{(2)} - i_1^{(1)})\alpha} \right] (+) \cdots$$

$$\cdots (+) [b_n^{(1)} - a_n^{(3)} + (b_n^{(2)} - b_n^{(1)} + a_n^{(3)} - a_n^{(2)})\alpha, b_n^{(3)} - a_n^{(1)} - (b_n^{(3)} - b_n^{(2)} + a_n^{(2)} - a_n^{(1)})\alpha] (\cdot)$$

$$(\cdot) \left[\frac{1}{1 + i_1^{(3)} - (i_1^{(3)} - i_1^{(2)})\alpha}, \frac{1}{1 + i_1^{(1)} + (i_1^{(2)} - i_1^{(1)})\alpha} \right] (\cdot) \cdots (\cdot)$$

$$(\cdot) \cdots (\cdot) \left[\frac{1}{1 + i_n^{(3)} - (i_n^{(3)} - i_n^{(2)})\alpha}, \frac{1}{1 + i_n^{(1)} + (i_n^{(2)} - i_n^{(1)})\alpha} \right]$$

Let us move on now to develop an example. An investment object is acquired with a useful life of $n = 3$ years and an acquisition cost of $M = 4000$ monetary units payment in total at the initial moment of the process (referential). Also the following estimates are made:

n	$(b_j^{(1)}, b_j^{(2)}, b_j^{(3)})$	$(a_j^{(1)}, a_j^{(2)}, a_j^{(3)})$	$(i_j^{(1)}, i_j^{(2)}, i_j^{(3)})$
1	(3500, 3800, 4500)	(2000, 2500, 2800)	(0.06, 0.08, 0.10)
2	(4000, 4500, 5500)	(2200, 2800, 3000)	(0.03, 0.06, 0.09)
3	(4200, 5000, 6000)	(2300, 3000, 3200)	(0.05, 0.07, 0.08)

From where we will obtain:

$$V = -4000 (+) [700 + 600\alpha, 2500 - 1200\alpha] (\cdot) \left[\frac{1}{1.1 - 0.02\alpha}, \frac{1}{1.06 + 0.02\alpha} \right] (+)$$

$$(+) [1000 + 700\alpha, 3300 - 1600\alpha] (\cdot) \left[\frac{1}{1.1 - 0.02\alpha}, \frac{1}{1.06 + 0.02\alpha} \right] (\cdot)$$

$$(\cdot) \left[\frac{1}{1.09 - 0.03\alpha}, \frac{1}{1.03 + 0.03\alpha} \right] (+) [1000 + 1000\alpha, 3700 - 1700\alpha] (\cdot)$$

$$(\cdot) \left[\frac{1}{1.1 - 0.02\alpha}, \frac{1}{1.06 + 0.02\alpha} \right] (\cdot) \left[\frac{1}{1.09 - 0.03\alpha}, \frac{1}{1.03 + 0.03\alpha} \right] (\cdot)$$

$$(\cdot) \left[\frac{1}{1.08 - 0.01\alpha}, \frac{1}{1.05 + 0.02\alpha} \right]$$

This apparently tedious expression constitutes an important source of information, when applying the hendecadarian system to the α-cuts.

Therefore, relative to the updating rates we will arrive at:

α	$\left[\frac{1}{1.1-0.02\alpha}, \frac{1}{1.06+0.02\alpha}\right]$	$\left[\frac{1}{1.1-0.02\alpha}\cdot\frac{1}{1.09-0.03\alpha}, \frac{1}{1.06+0.02\alpha}\cdot\frac{1}{1.03+0.03\alpha}\right]$	$\left[\frac{1}{1.1-0.02\alpha}\cdot\frac{1}{1.09-0.03\alpha}\cdot\frac{1}{1.08-0.01\alpha}, \frac{1}{1.06+0.02\alpha}\cdot\frac{1}{1.03+0.03\alpha}\cdot\frac{1}{1.05+0.02\alpha}\right]$
0	[0.9091, 0.9434]	[0.8340, 0.9159]	[0.7722, 0.8723]
0.1	[0.9107, 0.9416]	[0.8379, 0.9115]	[0.7765, 0.8665]
0.2	[0.9124, 0.9398]	[0.8417, 0.9072]	[0.7808, 0.8607]
0.3	[0.9141, 0.9381]	[0.8456, 0.9029]	[0.7851, 0.8550]
0.4	[0.9158, 0.9363]	[0.8495, 0.8986]	[0.7895, 0.8493]
0.5	[0.9174, 0.9346]	[0.8534, 0.8943]	[0.7939, 0.8437]
0.6	[0.9191, 0.9328]	[0.8574, 0.8901]	[0.7983, 0.8381]
0.7	[0.9208, 0.9311]	[0.8614, 0.8859]	[0.8028, 0.8326]
0.8	[0.9225, 0.9294]	[0.8654, 0.8818]	[0.8073, 0.8272]
0.9	[0.9242, 0.9276]	[0.8694, 0.8776]	[0.8118, 0.8217]
1	[0.9259, 0.9259]	[0.8735, 0.8735]	[0.8164, 0.8164]

By doing the same to the expressions representing the profits from exploitation, we arrive at:

α	$[700 + 600\alpha, 2500 - 1200\alpha]$	$[1000 + 700\alpha, 3300 - 1600\alpha]$	$[1000 + 1000\alpha, 3700 - 1700\alpha]$
0	[700, 2500]	[1000, 3300]	[1000, 3700]
0.1	[760, 2380]	[1070, 3140]	[1100, 3530]
0.2	[820, 2260]	[1140, 2980]	[1200, 3360]
0.3	[880, 2140]	[1210, 2820]	[1300, 3190]
0.4	[940, 2020]	[1280, 2660]	[1400, 3020]
0.5	[1000, 1900]	[1350, 2500]	[1500, 2850]
0.6	[1060, 1780]	[1420, 2340]	[1600, 2680]
0.7	[1120, 1660]	[1490, 2180]	[1700, 2510]
0.8	[1180, 1540]	[1560, 2020]	[1800, 2340]
0.9	[1240, 1420]	[1630, 1860]	[1900, 2170]
1	[1300, 1300]	[1700, 1700]	[2000, 2000]

And finally we do the algebraic addition of the corresponding products, level by level, arriving at the capital value for the investment:

α	$\underset{\sim}{V}$
0	[–1757.36, 4608.55]
0.1	[–1557.17, 4161.97]
0.2	[–1355.32, 3719.48]
0.3	[–1151.79, 3281.04]
0.4	[–946.56, 2846.60]
0.5	[–739.62, 2416.12]
0.6	[–530.95, 1989.54]
0.7	[–320.53, 1566.82]
0.8	[–108.34, 1147.92]
0.9	[105.64, 732.80]
1	[321.42, 321.42]

The fuzzy number $\underset{\sim}{V}$, under this hendecadarian form, presents us with very extensive information on the economic viability of the investment object. In fact, the study level by level allows us to show that the estimate obtained does not take us to an unmistakable decision to acquire or not to acquire the investment object because, although the existence of profit can be conceived it can be seen that under unfavourable circumstances it is also possible that there may be losses.

When certain circumstances such as we have described occur, we propose to resort to one of the following calculations:

A) Criterion of possibility

With the object of simplifying the operation we are going to accept the <<triangular approximation>> as representative of the fuzzy number $\underset{\sim}{V}$ which will be, in this case (-1757.36, 321.42, 4608.55), the graphic representation of which is the following (figure 6.1):

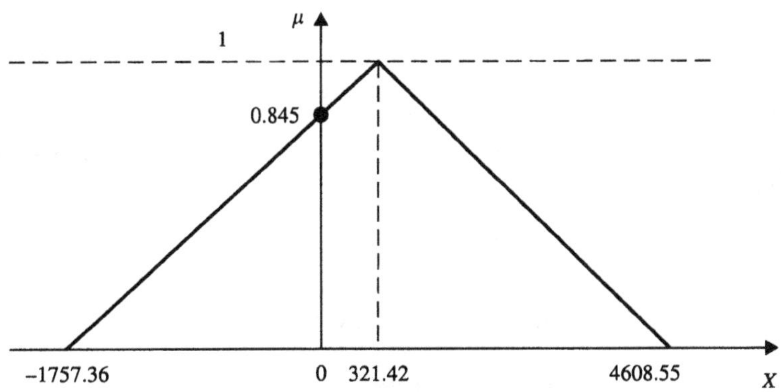

Figure 6.1.

The <<possibility>> of obtaining a loss will be shown by the intersection of the left side of the FTN with the ordinal axis, which in this case will be:

$$-1757.36 + 2078.78\alpha = 0$$

$$\alpha = \frac{1757.36}{2078.78} = 0.845$$

It can be said, therefore, and according to this criterion, and given the possibility that 0.845 is high, it could be admitted that the investment object is not convenient from an economic point of view.

In order to find the possibility of obtaining profits it will be sufficient to calculate the complement of the unit of α, that is to say, in this case:

$$\alpha' = 1 - \alpha = 1 - 0.845 = 0.155$$

B) *Index of consent*

The index of consent, or decision index, is obtained by dividing the part of the area of the triangle which is in the positive quadrant and the total area representing the FTN. In this case we will have:

— Area fourth quadrant triangle: $\dfrac{0.845 \times 1757.36}{2} = 742.48$

— Area corresponding to FTN: $\dfrac{6365.91 \times 1}{2} = 3182.95$

— Area first quadrant: $3182.95 - 742.48 = 2440.47$

$$\beta = \frac{2440.47}{3182.95} = 0.766$$

The use of this criterion includes, in this case, an indicator that supplies a very much higher number than that obtained by means of the calculation of <<possibility>> (remember the result $\alpha' = 0.155$). The use of one or other technique will depend in great measure on the specific circumstances relative to each situation.

Estimate of the monetary currents at prices for each period

Let us now move on to study the case in which monetary masses are calculated, for each period, at prices in force at each respective time. That is, inflation has an incidence year after year on the monetary currents of collections and payments. In this case, the result obtained will reflect a monetary mass that, as it is the algebraic addition of elements with different purchasing powers, will have *in real terms* a heterogeneous nature, although nominally it is a homogeneous result if we leave aside its purchasing power. Therefore, the known expression of capital value remains described in nominal terms. Only when it is intended to pass over to real terms will it be necessary to adopt certain updating rates that include both the discount rate and the inflation rate.

In fact, when we situate ourselves in the field of determinism, if the payment and collection currents estimated at each moment are M, a'_1, a'_2, ..., a'_n; b'_1, b'_2, ..., b'_n we will have as the capital value:

$$V' = -M + \sum_{j=1}^{n} (b'_j - a'_j)(1+i)^{-j}$$

the variation of which, when the interest rate changes for each period, will obtain a form which is parallel to that we obtained before.

The expression of the profit now takes place in monetary terms, since its mass will be constituted by amounts with different purchasing powers.

When tackling the problem of the incorporation of the inflation rate in an explicit manner[1], the formalisation process can take place in a different manner according to how estimating the monetary currents of collections and payments is done. Therefore it is a prior requirement that the significance of the monetary masses on which it will be operated should be established.

In fact, classical studies limited themselves to showing that a unit today in the money or capitals market can be changed for $(1 + i)$ units within a year, i being the unitary interest rate. Nowadays this overall statement is not sufficient, because the number should include or make reference to another: the number representing the rate of inflation.

The single consideration of the updating coefficient $(1 + i)^{-j}$, is only valid if starting out from the hypothesis of a stationary system and perfect estimate, when assuming that the interest rate is constantly equal throughout all the years, and there are no economic movements that have an incidence on the purchasing power of the collections and payments monetary currents. But reality shows us that a variation in the rates of interest takes place and that there is a process of inflation which makes booth collections and payments increase, as a consequence of price increases.

The <<explicit>> incorporation of the inflation rate can be done:

1. If starting out from certain payment and collection currents arising from the investment, estimated at their initial prices and it is assumed that an annual interest rate exists equal to s_j, $j = 1, 2, \ldots, n$, we will arrive at certain quantities to be <<collected>> and <<paid>> *at each moment in time* in the following amounts:

$$(b_j^{(1)}, b_j^{(2)}, b_j^{(3)})\,(\cdot)\,(1 + s_1^{(1)}, 1 + s_1^{(2)}, 1 + s_1^{(3)})\,(\cdot) \cdots (\cdot)\,(1 + s_j^{(1)}, 1 + s_j^{(2)}, 1 + s_j^{(3)})$$

$$(a_j^{(1)}, a_j^{(2)}, a_j^{(3)})\,(\cdot)\,(1 + s_1^{(1)}, 1 + s_1^{(2)}, 1 + s_1^{(3)})\,(\cdot) \cdots (\cdot)\,(1 + s_j^{(1)}, 1 + s_j^{(2)}, 1 + s_j^{(3)})$$

which give rise to the following exploitation profits:

$$\underset{\sim}{B}'_j = (b_j^{(1)} - a_j^{(3)}, b_j^{(2)} - a_j^{(2)}, b_j^{(3)} - a_j^{(1)})\,(\cdot)\,(1 + s_1^{(1)}, 1 + s_1^{(2)}, 1 + s_1^{(3)})\,(\cdot) \cdots (\cdot)$$
$$(\cdot)\,(1 + s_j^{(1)}, 1 + s_j^{(2)}, 1 + s_j^{(3)})$$

which expressed as α-cuts will be:

$$B'_j = [(b_j^{(1)} - a_j^{(3)}) + (b_j^{(2)} - a_j^{(2)} - b_j^{(1)} + a_j^{(3)})\alpha,\ (b_j^{(3)} - a_j^{(1)}) - (b_j^{(3)} - a_j^{(1)} - b_j^{(2)} + a_j^{(2)})\alpha]\,(\cdot)$$
$$(\cdot)\,[1 + s_1^{(1)} + (s_1^{(2)} - s_1^{(1)})\alpha,\ 1 + s_1^{(3)} - (s_1^{(3)} - s_1^{(2)})\alpha]\,(\cdot) \cdots (\cdot)$$
$$(\cdot)\,[1 + s_j^{(1)} + (s_j^{(2)} - s_j^{(1)})\alpha,\ 1 + s_j^{(3)} - (s_j^{(3)} - s_j^{(2)})\alpha]$$

$$j = 1, 2, \ldots, n$$

The significance of $\underset{\sim}{B}'_j$ is obvious: it constitutes the <<exploitation profit>> which will be arrived at in year j, estimated at prices for year j, always on the assumption that, in reality, inflation keeps in line with estimates. If it is wished to know the updated value of $\underset{\sim}{B}'_j$, it will be sufficient to include the corresponding updating rates, forming the following product:

$$\underset{\sim}{B}'_j\,(\cdot)\left[\frac{1}{1+i_1^{(3)}-(i_1^{(3)}-i_1^{(2)})\alpha},\ \frac{1}{1+i_1^{(1)}+(i_1^{(2)}-i_1^{(1)})\alpha}\right](\cdot)\cdots$$

$$\cdots(\cdot)\left[\frac{1}{1+i_j^{(3)}-(i_j^{(3)}-i_j^{(2)})\alpha},\ \frac{1}{1+i_j^{(1)}+(i_j^{(2)}-i_j^{(1)})\alpha}\right]$$

Let us now see what happens in the case of the previous example, assuming that the estimated inflation rates are:

n	$(1+s_j^{(1)},\ 1+s_j^{(2)},\ 1+s_j^{(3)})$
1	(1.05, 1.06, 1.07)
2	(1.02, 1.04, 1.08)
3	(1.03, 1.05, 1.06)

which will give rise to the following fuzzy numbers, expressed in the hendecadarian system:

α	$[1.05+0.01\alpha,\ 1.07-0.01\alpha]$	$[1.05+0.01\alpha,\ 1.07-0.01\alpha](\cdot)$ $(\cdot)[1.02+0.02\alpha,\ 1.08-0.04\alpha]$	$[1.05+0.01\alpha,\ 1.07-0.01\alpha](\cdot)$ $(\cdot)[1.02+0.02\alpha,\ 1.08-0.04\alpha](\cdot)$ $(\cdot)[1.03+0.02\alpha,\ 1.06-0.01\alpha]$
0	[1.05, 1.07]	[1.0710, 1.1556]	[1.1031, 1.2249]
0.1	[1.051, 1.069]	[1.0741, 1.1502]	[1.1085, 1.2181]
0.2	[1.052, 1.068]	[1.0772, 1.1449]	[1.1139, 1.2113]
0.3	[1.053, 1.067]	[1.0804, 1.1396]	[1.1193, 1.2045]
0.4	[1.054, 1.066]	[1.0835, 1.1342]	[1.1247, 1.1977]
0.5	[1.055, 1.065]	[1.0867, 1.1289]	[1.1301, 1.1910]
0.6	[1.056, 1.064]	[1.0898, 1.1236]	[1.1356, 1.1843]
0.7	[1.057, 1.063]	[1.0929, 1.1183]	[1.1410, 1.1775]
0.8	[1.058, 1.062]	[1.0961, 1.1130]	[1.1465, 1.1709]
0.9	[1.059, 1.061]	[1.0992, 1.1077]	[1.1520, 1.1642]
1	[1.06, 1.06]	[1.1024, 1.1024]	[1.1575, 1.1575]

If we compose[2] the product of the updating rate and the rate of inflation we obtain, for levels $\alpha \in [0, 1]$:

α	Moment 1	Moment 2	Moment 3
0	[0.9545, 1.0094]	[0.8932, 1.0584]	[0.8519, 1.0685]
0.1	[0.9572, 1.0066]	[0.9000, 1.0485]	[0.8608, 1.0555]
0.2	[0.9599, 1.0038]	[0.9067, 1.0386]	[0.8697, 1.0426]
0.3	[0.9625, 1.0009]	[0.9136, 1.0289]	[0.8788, 1.0299]
0.4	[0.9652, 0.9981]	[0.9204, 1.0192]	[0.8879, 1.0173]
0.5	[0.9679, 0.9953]	[0.9274, 1.0096]	[0.8972, 1.0049]
0.6	[0.9706, 0.9925]	[0.9344, 1.0001]	[0.9065, 0.9926]
0.7	[0.9733, 0.9898]	[0.9414, 0.9907]	[0.9160, 0.9805]
0.8	[0.9760, 0.9870]	[0.9485, 0.9814]	[0.9255, 0.9685]
0.9	[0.9787, 0.9842]	[0.9557, 0.9721]	[0.9352, 0.9567]
1	[0.9815, 0.9815]	[0.9630, 0.9630]	[0.9450, 0.9450]

The conjunction of the updating rate on the one hand, and the rate of inflation on the other, gives rise to certain new fuzzy numbers which make up certain coefficients to be applied to the profits from exploitation for each period. A quick look at the table above brings to light the fact that the major part of the intervals relative to the different levels of α are included in the segment [0, 1]. This constitutes a rule of a general nature, admitted above all in the field of certainty, because an adequate economic policy requires that the interest rate be greater than the rate of inflation.

Now, as we acquaint ourselves with the context of uncertainty, it may happen, and sometimes does happen, that under extreme situations there are rates of inflation that do exceed interest rates. In these cases the joint coefficient exits in the [0, 1] segment and gives values that are higher than the unit.

In this case the paradox appears where the monetary masses considered as nominal give rise to greater updated values, as they move out in time. In this way one could acquire any product totally on credit and sell in the future with no greater risk than that arising from the possible effectiveness of the sale. These then are situations that abound in speculation.

We feel that these realities should be taken into account by scientific studies, although always taken in their true context.

Let us now move on to obtaining the capital value for the investment, using as estimates the collections, payments and interest rates of the FTN from the previous section. By doing the corresponding calculations, we arrive at:

α	$\underset{\sim}{V}'$
0	[–1586.68, 5969.93]
0.1	[–1362.75, 5413.76]
0.2	[–1135.59, 4866.71]
0.3	[–905.18, 4328.66]
0.4	[–671.46, 3799.46]
0.5	[–434.39, 3278.98]
0.6	[–193.92, 2767.10]
0.7	[50.00, 2263.67]
0.8	[297.41, 1768.58]
0.9	[548.35, 1281.69]
1	[802.89, 802.89]

This table reflects the updated profits expressed in nominal terms (monetary masses with different purchasing powers). In this way, starting out from certain currents expressed in <<real terms>> we have obtained a result in <<nominal terms>>. And this was possible thanks to the incorporation of inflation coefficients.

The comparison between two fuzzy numbers $\underset{\sim}{V}'$ and $\underset{\sim}{V}$ permits us to verify that the inflation effect gives rise to a greater nominal economic viability in $\underset{\sim}{V}'$ than in $\underset{\sim}{V}$ as $\underset{\sim}{V}' > \underset{\sim}{V}$, as is easily verified, without this changing the purchasing power of the monetary surpluses provided by the investment.

2. When starting out from the estimate of the monetary currents of collections and payments, at prices current at any given time, it is possible to obtain, in turn, results in real terms (profits which are homogeneous relative to the purchasing power of the monetary masses making them up).

In order for this path to have any sense, it would be necessary for the experts to be capable of estimating, the future economic parameters of collections and payments, directly at nominal prices. In fact, if they were to start out with constant prices (relative to the initial moment), indexing them for inflation, there would be no sense in their going back later to reflect the result in real terms, since it would be sufficient to establish the calculation by means of the economic parameters just as if inflation did not exist.

In order to verify the identity of this scheme with the one presented previously, let us assume that the experts consulted were to have given their estimates of the exploitation profits $\underset{\sim}{b}_j' - \underset{\sim}{a}_j'$, $j = 1, 2, ..., n$, in the form of α-cuts. If it were not like this, it would be difficult for the results to coincide, taking into account the non linear form of the function of relevance in the product of the two FTN. Just as an example let us take a look at this for period 1:

$$
\begin{aligned}
(\underset{\sim}{b}_1 - \underset{\sim}{a}_1)\,(\cdot)\,(1 + \underset{\sim}{s}_1) &= (700,\ 1300,\ 2500)\,(\cdot)\,(1.05,\ 1.06,\ 1.07) = \\
&= [700 + 600\alpha,\ 2500 - 1200\alpha]\,(\cdot)\,[1.05 + 0.01\alpha,\ 1.07 - 0.01\alpha] = \\
&= [(700 + 600\alpha)(1.05 + 0.01\alpha),\ (2500 - 1200\alpha)(1.07 - 0.01\alpha)]
\end{aligned}
$$

Once again it will be seen that the resulting functions for the lower and upper extremes of the interval are not linear. If we were to take the estimate in a ternary form, the product would only be a triangular approximation and the only points of coincidence would be limited to the two extremes and maximum assumption.

The approximation would also be for period 1:

$$
(\underset{\sim}{b}_1 - \underset{\sim}{a}_1)\,(\cdot)\,(1 + \underset{\sim}{s}_1) \cong (700 \times 1.05,\ 1300 \times 1.06,\ 2500 \times 1.07) \cong (735,\ 1378,\ 2675)
$$

while the estimates agreeing with the previous case should be

α	$\underset{\sim}{b}_1{}' - \underset{\sim}{a}_1{}' = (\underset{\sim}{b}_1 - \underset{\sim}{a}_1)\,(\cdot)\,(1 + \underset{\sim}{s}_1)$	$\underset{\sim}{b}_2{}' - \underset{\sim}{a}_2{}' = (\underset{\sim}{b}_2 - \underset{\sim}{a}_2)\,(\cdot)\,(\cdot)\,(1 + \underset{\sim}{s}_1)\,(\cdot)\,(1 + \underset{\sim}{s}_2)$	$\underset{\sim}{b}_3' - \underset{\sim}{a}_3' = (\underset{\sim}{b}_3 - \underset{\sim}{a}_3)\,(\cdot)\,(\cdot)\,(1 + \underset{\sim}{s}_1)\,(\cdot)\,(\cdot)\,(1 + \underset{\sim}{s}_2)\,(\cdot)\,(1 + \underset{\sim}{s}_3)$
0	[735.00, 2675.00]	[1071.00, 3813.48]	[1103.13, 4532.26]
0.1	[798.76, 2544.22]	[1149.31, 3611.77]	[1219.34, 4299.92]
0.2	[862.64, 2413.68]	[1228.06, 3411.79]	[1336.65, 4069.97]
0.3	[926.64, 2283.38]	[1307.26, 3213.55]	[1455.05, 3842.39]
0.4	[990.76, 2153.32]	[1386.90, 3017.04]	[1574.56, 3617.18]
0.5	[1055.00, 2023.50]	[1466.98, 2822.25]	[1695.17, 3394.32]
0.6	[1119.36, 1893.92]	[1547.50, 2629.19]	[1816.90, 3173.81]
0.7	[1183.84, 1764.58]	[1628.48, 2437.84]	[1939.75, 2955.64]
0.8	[1248.44, 1635.48]	[1709.90, 2248.21]	[2063.71, 2739.79]
0.9	[1313.16, 1506.62]	[1791.76, 2060.29]	[2188.81, 2526.26]
1	[1378.00, 1378.00]	[1874.08, 1874.08]	[2315.04, 2315.04]

It seems difficult to imagine that in reality, experts could supply the data in this form directly (without making calculations). Let us assume, then, that these have been expressed in the ternary form and the results would in this way be approximate. We would have:

$b'_1 - a'_1$	$b'_2 - a'_2$	$b'_3 - a'_3$
(735, 1378, 2675)	(1071, 1874.08, 3813.48)	(1103.13, 2315.04, 4532.26)

If these then are the starting out estimates, for obtaining the capital value in real terms it will be necessary to pass them over to the α-cuts form, affecting, in the first place, the resulting fuzzy numbers by certain coefficients which would allow their deflation.

If in the field of certainty these <<deflation rates>> coincide with the reverse of inflation rates, in the sphere of uncertainty it will be necessary to use a different operator from normal division.

For the sole effect of verification, let us suppose that as initial estimates we have been given those expressed previously in α-cuts in stead of doing it by means of triangular approximations. If we choose as an example the first period, we will arrive at the following fuzzy number:

$$[1.05 + 0.01\alpha,\ 1.07 - 0.01\alpha]^{-1} = \left[\frac{1}{1.07 - 0.01\alpha},\ \frac{1}{1.05 + 0.01\alpha}\right]$$

which on multiplication by the fuzzy number $(\underset{\sim}{b}'_1 - \underset{\sim}{a}'_1)$ does not give us the result we had obtained on estimating the economic parameters in real terms. In fact, for $\alpha = 0$ it would be:

$$\frac{735}{1.07} = 686.91 \neq 700$$

$$\frac{2675}{1.05} = 2547.61 \neq 2500$$

In order to arrive at the same result, it would be necessary to divide the lower extremes of the intervals representing the nominally estimated exploitation profits, corresponding to each level, by the lower extremes of the rates of inflation and the upper extremes by the corresponding upper extremes. Therefore, for $\alpha = 0$, for example, we would arrive at:

$$\frac{735}{1.05} = 700 \quad ; \quad \frac{2675}{1.07} = 2500$$

This leads us to the need to operate with the lower and upper extremes independently, in such a way that for each level α we would have, for moment 1:

α	Moment 1	
	Lower extreme	Upper extreme
0	$735.00 \times 1.05^{-1} = 700$	$2675.00 \times 1.07^{-1} = 2500$
0.1	$798.76 \times 1.051^{-1} = 760$	$2544.22 \times 1.069^{-1} = 2380$
0.2	$862.64 \times 1.052^{-1} = 820$	$2413.68 \times 1.068^{-1} = 2260$
0.3	$926.64 \times 1.053^{-1} = 880$	$2283.38 \times 1.067^{-1} = 2140$
0.4	$990.76 \times 1.054^{-1} = 940$	$2153.32 \times 1.066^{-1} = 2020$
0.5	$1055.00 \times 1.055^{-1} = 1000$	$2023.50 \times 1.065^{-1} = 1900$
0.6	$1119.36 \times 1.056^{-1} = 1060$	$1893.92 \times 1.064^{-1} = 1780$
0.7	$1183.84 \times 1.057^{-1} = 1120$	$1764.58 \times 1.063^{-1} = 1660$
0.8	$1248.44 \times 1.058^{-1} = 1180$	$1635.48 \times 1.062^{-1} = 1540$
0.9	$1313.16 \times 1.059^{-1} = 1240$	$1506.62 \times 1.061^{-1} = 1420$
1	$1378.00 \times 1.06^{-1} = 1300$	$1378.00 \times 1.06^{-1} = 1300$

which evidently, coincides with the result obtained before, when the calculation was done in real terms, setting aside the inflation process.

For moment 2 we would arrive at:

α	Moment 2	
	Lower extreme	Upper extreme
0	$1071.00 \times 1.0710^{-1} = 1000$	$3813.48 \times 1.1556^{-1} = 3300$
0.1	$1149.31 \times 1.0741^{-1} = 1070$	$3611.77 \times 1.1502^{-1} = 3140$
0.2	$1228.06 \times 1.0772^{-1} = 1140$	$3411.79 \times 1.1449^{-1} = 2980$
0.3	$1307.26 \times 1.0804^{-1} = 1210$	$3213.55 \times 1.1396^{-1} = 2820$
0.4	$1386.90 \times 1.0835^{-1} = 1280$	$3017.04 \times 1.1342^{-1} = 2660$
0.5	$1466.98 \times 1.0867^{-1} = 1350$	$2822.25 \times 1.1289^{-1} = 2500$
0.6	$1547.50 \times 1.0898^{-1} = 1420$	$2629.19 \times 1.1236^{-1} = 2340$
0.7	$1628.48 \times 1.0929^{-1} = 1490$	$2437.84 \times 1.1183^{-1} = 2180$
0.8	$1709.90 \times 1.0961^{-1} = 1560$	$2248.21 \times 1.1130^{-1} = 2020$
0.9	$1791.76 \times 1.0992^{-1} = 1630$	$2060.29 \times 1.1077^{-1} = 1860$
1	$1874.08 \times 1.1024^{-1} = 1700$	$1874.08 \times 1.1024^{-1} = 1700$

Once again we see the equivalence of the results.

Finally for moment 3, it would be:

α	Moment 3	
	Lower extreme	Upper extreme
0	$1103.13 \times 1.1031^{-1} = 1000$	$4532.26 \times 1.2249^{-1} = 3700$
0.1	$1219.34 \times 1.1085^{-1} = 1100$	$4299.92 \times 1.2181^{-1} = 3530$
0.2	$1336.65 \times 1.1139^{-1} = 1200$	$4069.97 \times 1.2113^{-1} = 3360$
0.3	$1455.05 \times 1.1193^{-1} = 1300$	$3842.39 \times 1.2045^{-1} = 3190$
0.4	$1574.56 \times 1.1247^{-1} = 1400$	$3617.18 \times 1.1977^{-1} = 3020$
0.5	$1695.17 \times 1.1301^{-1} = 1500$	$3394.32 \times 1.1910^{-1} = 2850$
0.6	$1816.90 \times 1.1356^{-1} = 1600$	$3173.81 \times 1.1843^{-1} = 2680$
0.7	$1939.75 \times 1.1410^{-1} = 1700$	$2955.64 \times 1.1775^{-1} = 2510$
0.8	$2063.71 \times 1.1465^{-1} = 1800$	$2739.79 \times 1.1709^{-1} = 2340$
0.9	$2188.81 \times 1.1520^{-1} = 1900$	$2526.26 \times 1.1642^{-1} = 2170$
1	$2315.04 \times 1.1575^{-1} = 2000$	$2315.04 \times 1.1575^{-1} = 2000$

It can be seen that in this case the process to be followed brings up not only certain reservations relative to the adequacy of the scheme to the situations of expertise which take place in reality, but also determined problems relative to the calculation procedure, which however have a solution, although this is not particularly elegant.

The hypothesis of different rates of inflation

A situation could be imagined in which the prices of the elements intervening both in the collections current and in the payments current do no increase in the same amount as the general price index. In this case the <<particular rate of inflation>> relative to a company does not coincide with the <<general rate of inflation>>.

In the sphere of certainty it is assumed that both collections and payments increase cumulatively through a unitary rate $u_j \neq s_j$. Evidently when $u_j = s_j$, for all $j = 1, 2. \ldots, n$, we find ourselves faced with a particular case which we have studied before in this chapter. When passing over to a context of uncertainty it will be necessary to take into account two aspects. The first of these refers to the possibility that total or partial dominion exists of one index over another; the second is tied to the fact that $\underset{\sim}{u}_j \lesseqgtr \underset{\sim}{s}_j$. Both aspects can concur simultaneously, that is that one situation would give partial dominion with $\underset{\sim}{u}_j < \underset{\sim}{s}_j$, for example.

A more general supposition, would mean the consideration of an index for increasing prices in the payments of the company $\underset{\sim}{u}_j^{(p)}$, different from the index for increasing the prices of collections $\underset{\sim}{u}_j^{(c)}$. We will do without this hypothesis in order not to increase the complexity of the exposition. The reader will pass over easily to this case, if so desiring, starting out from what we are going to state below.

Let us assume, once again, that the estimates of the indices for increase of company prices are expressed by means of FTN, and that the estimate of the remaining economic parameters is the same as used in previous examples. Thus, the experts have given for the u_j, $j = 1, 2, 3$:

n	$(1 + u_j^{(1)}, 1 + u_j^{(2)}, 1 + u_j^{(3)})$
1	(1.06, 1.08, 1.10)
2	(1.04, 1.05, 1.07)
3	(1.02, 1.04, 1.05)

Passing from the ternary form to the α-cuts form, by means of the hendecadarian system, we arrive at:

α	$[1.06+0.02\alpha, 1.10-0.02\alpha]$	$[1.06+0.02\alpha, 1.10-0.02\alpha](\cdot)$ $(\cdot)[1.04+0.01\alpha, 1.07-0.02\alpha]$	$[1.06+0.02\alpha, 1.10-0.02\alpha](\cdot)$ $(\cdot)[1.04+0.01\alpha, 1.07-0.02\alpha](\cdot)$ $(\cdot)[1.02+0.02\alpha, 1.05-0.01\alpha]$
0	[1.060, 1.100]	[1.1024, 1.1770]	[1.1244, 1.2359]
0.1	[1.062, 1.098]	[1.1055, 1.1727]	[1.1299, 1.2301]
0.2	[1.064, 1.096]	[1.1087, 1.1683]	[1.1353, 1.2244]
0.3	[1.066, 1.094]	[1.1118, 1.1640]	[1.1407, 1.2187]
0.4	[1.068, 1.092]	[1.1150, 1.1597]	[1.1462, 1.2131]
0.5	[1.070, 1.090]	[1.1182, 1.1554]	[1.1517, 1.2074]
0.6	[1.072, 1.088]	[1.1213, 1.1511]	[1.1572, 1.2018]
0.7	[1.074, 1.086]	[1.1245, 1.1468]	[1.1627, 1.1961]
0.8	[1.076, 1.084]	[1.1276, 1.1425]	[1.1682, 1.1905]
0.9	[1.078, 1.082]	[1.1308, 1.1383]	[1.1738, 1.1849]
1	[1.080, 1.080]	[1.1340, 1.1340]	[1.1794, 1.1794]

If we now obtain the quotient between the index for increase in company prices and the index for inflation, we will arrive at a fuzzy number for each period, which on multiplying this by exploitation profits estimated at prices for moment 0, we will arrive at the capital value of the investment in real terms (all its monetary units will have the same purchasing power).

We can now ask ourselves what type of quotient should be used. Well, if it is assumed that a correspondence exists between the pessimistic positions (and the optimistic) in the estimate for company price increases, it will be necessary to proceed just as before on deflating profits in nominal terms in order to convert them into real terms: the lower extremes will be divided with lower extremes and the upper extremes with the upper extremes of the representative intervals of the respective fuzzy numbers.

But if the hypothesis is adopted which says it is possible for cohabitation in the same period of low increases in price for the company and high rates of inflation, and vice versa, the quotient to be used will be the normal one in the sphere of the arithmetic of uncertainty, which implies dividing by crossing over the extremes of the intervals. This more general case includes the previous one and in any case the results which are obtained by it are more uncertain.

Let us continue with this by starting out from the last hypothesis.

α	$(1+\underset{\sim}{u}_1)\,(:)\,(1+\underset{\sim}{s}_1)$	$(1+\underset{\sim}{u}_1)(1+\underset{\sim}{u}_2)$ $(:)$ $(1+\underset{\sim}{s}_1)(1+\underset{\sim}{s}_2)$	$(1+\underset{\sim}{u}_1)(1+\underset{\sim}{u}_2)(1+\underset{\sim}{u}_3)$ $(:)$ $(1+\underset{\sim}{s}_1)(1+\underset{\sim}{s}_2)(1+\underset{\sim}{s}_3)$
0	[0.9907, 1.0476]	[0.9540, 1.0990]	[0.9180, 1.1203]
0.1	[0.9935, 1.0447]	[0.9611, 1.0917]	[0.9276, 1.1097]
0.2	[0.9963, 1.0418]	[0.9684, 1.0846]	[0.9373, 1.0992]
0.3	[0.9991, 1.0389]	[0.9757, 1.0774]	[0.9471, 1.0889]
0.4	[1.0019, 1.0361]	[0.9830, 1.0703]	[0.9570, 1.0786]
0.5	[1.0047, 1.0332]	[0.9905, 1.0633]	[0.9670, 1.0684]
0.6	[1.0075, 1.0303]	[0.9980, 1.0563]	[0.9771, 1.0583]
0.7	[1.0103, 1.0274]	[1.0055, 1.0493]	[0.9874, 1.0483]
0.8	[1.0132, 1.0246]	[1.0132, 1.0424]	[0.9978, 1.0384]
0.9	[1.0160, 1.0217]	[1.0209, 1.0355]	[1.0083, 1.0286]
1	[1.0189, 1.0189]	[1.0287, 1.0287]	[1.0189, 1.0189]

One quick look at this table allows us to make certain considerations that will lead to a different conception of this problem, relative to its handling within the sphere of certainty. Let us just point out in the first place, that the quotient between both indices, brings to light the purchasing power of the monetary masses both paid and collected, as a consequence of acquiring an investment object, which are affected by increases in prices.

In a determinist context, it is accepted that when in each one of the periods, $j = 1, 2, \ldots, n$, the percentage price increases in the company u_j, are greater than the percentages for inflation s_j, the monetary masses located in the future have a purchasing power that is greater in relation to those estimated at initial prices, in an amount equal to the quotient of the products of their respective indices:

$$\frac{(1+\underset{\sim}{u}_1)(1+\underset{\sim}{u}_2)\cdots(1+\underset{\sim}{u}_j)}{(1+\underset{\sim}{s}_1)(1+\underset{\sim}{s}_2)\cdots(1+\underset{\sim}{s}_j)} \qquad j = 1, 2, \ldots, n$$

If in all the periods this quotient complies with being lower than the unit, the purchasing power is evidently lower. Both in one and the other case, and on the assumption that the investment process generated profits (necessary hypothesis for taking the decision to invest), it will be clear that the profits are not only greater (lesser) in the second case in nominal terms, but also relative to their purchasing power. When in certain periods the quotient is greater than 1 and in other lesser, the sense of overall profit will depend on the volume of profit for each period and the amount of the respective quotients.

Let us move on to the field of uncertainty. If we look at the fuzzy number resulting from the quotient $(1+\underset{\sim}{u}_1)\ (:)\ (1+\underset{\sim}{s}_1)$, corresponding to the first year, it will be seen that a part of the same is located to the left of the line representing the unit. In fact, for making it easier, we substitute the fuzzy number $(1+\underset{\sim}{u}_1)\ (:)\ (1+\underset{\sim}{s}_1)$, for its triangular approximation (0.9907, 1.0189, 1.0476), we arrive at (figure 6.2):

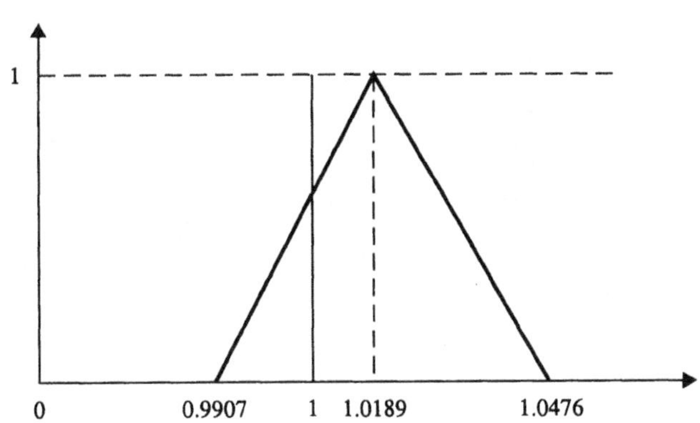

Figure 6.2.

The use of any of the indices we have used before, <<criterion of possibility>> and <<index of consent>>, or any other that can be imagined, will permit estimation of the degree of possibility that the price increases give rise, within a certain period, to a *lower* purchasing power of the monetary masses (exploitation profit or loss) that the investment process frees up or absorbs.

Finally let us move on to obtaining the capital value for an investment, when inflation causes situations such as we have described. For this we will resort once again to our didactic example, but on this occasion, in order not to repeat certain calculations which have already been made on several occasions, we will limit ourselves to obtaining approximate results, by resorting to triangular approximations.

If we consider that the estimate for collections and payments, made at the initial moment, is:

$$(b_1^{(1)}, b_1^{(2)}, b_1^{(3)}) (-) (a_1^{(1)}, a_1^{(2)}, a_1^{(3)}) = [700 + 600\alpha, 2500 - 1200\alpha]$$
$$(b_2^{(1)}, b_2^{(2)}, b_2^{(3)}) (-) (a_2^{(1)}, a_2^{(2)}, a_2^{(3)}) = [1000 + 700\alpha, 3300 - 1600\alpha]$$
$$(b_3^{(1)}, b_3^{(2)}, b_3^{(3)}) (-) (a_3^{(1)}, a_3^{(2)}, a_3^{(3)}) = [1000 + 1000\alpha, 3700 - 1700\alpha]$$

we arrive at the fact that, for each of the periods $j = 1, 2, 3.$ of the useful life of the investment, the exploitation profit at real prices (the same purchasing power for all the monetary masses making it up), will be reflected by the following three fuzzy numbers:

α	$\underset{\sim}{M}_1''$	$\underset{\sim}{M}_2''$	$\underset{\sim}{M}_3''$
	$(\underset{\sim}{b}_1 - \underset{\sim}{a}_1)(\cdot)\dfrac{(1+\underset{\sim}{u}_1)}{(1+\underset{\sim}{s}_1)}$	$(\underset{\sim}{b}_2 - \underset{\sim}{a}_2)(\cdot)\dfrac{(1+\underset{\sim}{u}_1)(1+\underset{\sim}{u}_2)}{(1+\underset{\sim}{s}_1)(1+\underset{\sim}{s}_2)}$	$(\underset{\sim}{b}_3 - \underset{\sim}{a}_3)(\cdot)\dfrac{(1+\underset{\sim}{u}_1)(1+\underset{\sim}{u}_2)(1+\underset{\sim}{u}_3)}{(1+\underset{\sim}{s}_1)(1+\underset{\sim}{s}_2)(1+\underset{\sim}{s}_3)}$
0	[693.46, 2619.05]	[953.96, 3626.61]	[917.96, 4145.16]
0.1	[755.02, 2486.43]	[1028.42, 3428.07]	[1020.31, 3917.33]
0.2	[816.93, 2354.52]	[1103.95, 3231.98]	[1124.71, 3693.45]
0.3	[879.18, 2223.32]	[1180.57, 3038.31]	[1231.18, 3473.45]
0.4	[941.76, 2092.83]	[1258.30, 2847.05]	[1339.77, 3257.28]
0.5	[1004.69, 1963.03]	[1337.14, 2658.17]	[1450.51, 3044.88]
0.6	[1067.97, 1833.94]	[1417.13, 2471.65]	[1563.44, 2836.21]
0.7	[1131.59, 1705.54]	[1498.26, 2287.47]	[1678.58, 2631.21]
0.8	[1195.56, 1577.84]	[1580.56, 2105.60]	[1795.99, 2429.83]
0.9	[1259.87, 1450.84]	[1664.05, 1926.03]	[1915.70, 2232.02]
1	[1324.53, 1324.53]	[1748.73, 1748.73]	[2037.74, 2037.74]

In order to find the capital value at real prices, it will be necessary to affect each one of these fuzzy numbers with the respective updating coefficients (which will also be expressed in fuzzy numbers), obtained from the interest rates of our example, deducting a each level the payment at the initial moment M = 4000.

α	$\frac{\underset{\sim}{M}_1''}{(1+\underset{\sim}{i}_1)}$	$\frac{\underset{\sim}{M}_2''}{(1+\underset{\sim}{i}_1)(\cdot)(1+\underset{\sim}{i}_2)}$	$\frac{\underset{\sim}{M}_3''}{(1+\underset{\sim}{i}_1)(\cdot)(1+\underset{\sim}{i}_2)(\cdot)(1+\underset{\sim}{i}_3)}$	$-M$
0	[630.42, 2470.80]	[795.63, 3321.68]	[708.90, 3615.83]	–4000
0.1	[687.64, 2341.27]	[861.66, 3124.82]	[792.28, 3394.30]	–4000
0.2	[745.37, 2212.90]	[929.20, 2932.02]	[878.17, 3179.00]	–4000
0.3	[803.63, 2085.67]	[998.27, 2743.21]	[966.64, 2969.78]	–4000
0.4	[862.42, 1959.58]	[1068.91, 2558.33]	[1057.73, 2766.50]	–4000
0.5	[921.74, 1834.61]	[1141.15, 2377.29]	[1151.54, 2569.00]	–4000
0.6	[981.59, 1710.76]	[1215.03, 2200.04]	[1248.11, 2377.16]	–4000
0.7	[1041.98, 1588.03]	[1290.57, 2026.51]	[1347.52, 2190.82]	–4000
0.8	[1102.91, 1466.40]	[1367.81, 1856.62]	[1449.85, 2009.86]	–4000
0.9	[1164.39, 1345.86]	[1446.79, 1690.32]	[1555.17, 1834.15]	–4000
1	[1226.42, 1226.42]	[1527.54, 1527.54]	[1663.54, 1663.54]	–4000

If we do the algebraic addition level by level, we arrive at the capital value expressed in real terms represented by the following fuzzy number:

α	$\underset{\sim}{V}$
0	[−1856.05, 5408.31]
0.1	[−1658.42, 4860.39]
0.2	[−1447.26, 4323.92]
0.3	[−1231.46, 3798.66]
0.4	[−1010.93, 3284.40]
0.5	[−785.57, 2780.91]
0.6	[−555.28, 2287.96]
0.7	[−319.93, 1805.36]
0.8	[−79.43, 1332.88]
0.9	[166.34, 870.33]
1	[417.50, 417.50]

The comparison of this estimated result with the one obtained at the commencement of this subject, clearly shows all that has been mentioned before in the sense that the purchasing power of the monetary masses (either profits or losses) is, in this case, greater. More negative in the lower levels of the levels with loss and more positive in the upper levels.

We have seen that in this subject we have conscientiously used simple elements of fuzzy algebra, taking as the basis for the estimates fuzzy triangular numbers. We have done it this way for two main reasons: to obtain greater comprehension of the argument of the exposition, avoiding any distraction of attention with technical complications and bringing the theoretical scheme closer to the needs of reality. In the current state of the handling given in practice to the problem of investment selection (and presumably this will also be given in the immediate future) estimates through FTN expressed in ternary form constitute the normal communications link between executives and scientists. Let us consider this as a contribution to better understanding between these two worlds.

And finally, we would like to record that all that has been stated based on singular estimates, can be made general to the case when the opinion of several (or better still many) experts is available. In this case we would reduce the unavoidable component of subjectivity which every individual valuation entails. Fortunately, today we have available many good instruments that allow for efficient addition of uncertain economic parameters. The possibility of using expertons and R^+-expertons, is good proof of this.

References

1 J. Gil Aluja: <<The economic environment in the decision to invest within a context of uncertainty>> International Symposium on Fuzzy Systems in Economics and Engineering, 28-31 October, 1993, Iasi (Rumania).

2 For this composition the possibility that reduced rates of inflation can be compatible with high rates of interest has been considered.

7 Taxation in uncertainty

Handling the problem within the determinist sphere

The economic surroundings in which the activities of companies are carried out, is all the time getting more and more complex as a consequence of the effects to acquisition and operation costs of investment objects caused by elements such as the inflation process, technical progress and taxation.

Specialised works on the subject supply an abundant amount of models on which, from all sorts of different perspectives, the investment process is tackled when reality allows it to be situated in a sphere of certainty or chance. But the current situation, characterised by very rapid changes makes it particularly difficult, if not impossible to accept with the necessary precision, the hypotheses required for using traditional techniques based on determinist mathematics and in the calculation of probabilities. We repeat once again, that we are faced by certain economic systems in which the greater part of the time the future can only be seen in terms of uncertainty.

In this chapter we will present a scheme in which certain economic parameters will be incorporated, estimation of which takes place in an uncertain manner, just as happens in reality. Once again the results obtained will not be <<strict rules>> to direct the decisions of executives, but <<channels of action>> in which businessmen can move by making use of their freedom and exercising their power of imagination.

On the other side of the coin, it can be seen that as the economy of a country advances and the welfare of its citizens increases, the needs of public government also increase in order to satisfy the ever growing demand by the community for goods and services. Under these circumstances, just as occurs with domestic economies, companies contribute to collective requirements with a whole range of taxes. The tax on profits which commercial companies have to face each period, due to its important amount and significance, stands out among all these.

In a first approximation it can be said that profits subject to taxation are formed by the difference between any income during a determined year and expenses relative to the same period, among which are included operating, financial and depreciation expenses.

The objective we have set ourselves consists in drawing up a model that allows us to take the decision to invest in an investment object when explicitly taking into consideration the tax on corporate profits.

Modern fiscal instruments although possibly more socially just, have led to greater deductions from companies and have created a climate of complementary worry that has only added a new problem to those handled by the company. For this reason it would appear convenient to incorporate the taxation phenomena into the studies that are being carried out on investment selection, in order to show the importance this has in the decision to invest.

In the first place let us point out that the handling of the problem brought up by taxation before the decision to invest cannot be freed from two important aspects:

1. The difference existing between expense and payment and income and collection.
2. The method used for the depreciation process.

And this is so as a consequence of the fact that the tax, on taxing profits during a specific period, reinforces the importance of the policy of time-period adjustments because depreciation affects the amount for tax assessment.

It is a well-known fact that accounting, in the area relative to recording, considers that a payment can be booked, in the first place as an expense of the period in which it was incurred, in second place by spreading it out as an expense over several periods and, finally, a payment may not imply any expense whatsoever (land and property). It is evident, then, that the accounting method used will have an influence on the amount and time when the expense is incurred. But, although it is also particularly well known, that studies for the selection of investments are made by taking as their basis financial capitals, it will be necessary to take into account, for the mere effects of the calculations for payment of taxes, those expenses that accounting presents as deductible, in this way to be able to arrive at the tax assessment. Standing out among these expenses, is depreciation.

Faced with the possibility of acquiring an investment object, if one starts out from the hypothesis of the non-existence of corporate tax, capital value can be obtained as a difference between <<supplementary>> collections and payments incurred by the purchase of the referential object. The elimination of this hypothesis and the consequent intervention of the tax process will require a new hypothesis: <<payments>> and <<collections>> arising from exploitation will be made to coincide with <<expenses>> and <<income>> from exploitation.

The simplest scheme for selecting investments, in the event of incorporating taxes, takes as a basis the calculation, for each year, of the profit from exploitation less taxes, the sum of which updated throughout the useful life of the investment object will give rise to the so called capital value. The calculation of these annual profits can be done as follows:

Annual profits from exploitation less taxes =   = Exploitation income - Exploitation expenses - Taxes

and the tax would be:

Corporate tax = Tax rate · (Exploitation income - exploitation expenses - depreciation)

and finally we would have the expression:

Annual exploitation profit less taxes = (1- Tax rate) (Exploitation income - Exploitation expenses) +   + Tax rate · Depreciation.

In this expression it can be seen that as exploitation profit increases the larger depreciation applied to each period gets. Throughout the useful life of the investment object, the most advantageous procedure will be that which accumulates the higher quotas in the early periods, taking into account the fact that the updating factor, on decreasing as payments move further out in time, also reduces the positive component of the exploitation profit represented by the updating of the product of depreciation by the tax rate.

By the mere fact that current legislation, relative to depreciation deductible for tax reasons, allows a certain flexibility relative to depreciation percentages and times, the investor has the possibility of selecting from among several procedures for distributing fixed assets throughout the different periods of the useful life of the same.

On many occasions the selected procedure may well be decisive in the problem of investment selection. What would dominate would be what could be called <<comparison between savings in taxes>> for each possible procedure for depreciating.

The model we are initially proposing[1] starts out from the following bases: the interest rate for calculation purposes is assumed as known; the useful life of the machine is n; payment for the investment object is made at moment 0 and is equal to M; throughout the useful life certain payments and collections are made arising form exploitation of the acquired object.

The current of payments is characterised, then, by the initial payment M and certain payments arising from exploitation a_1, a_2, ..., a_n, which, evidently do not include depreciation.

On the other hand certain collections from exploitation are obtained, b_1, b_2, ..., b_n. The differences b_j - a_j will designate what is known, in investment literature, as exploitation profit.

It is assumed that the percentages of depreciation during the useful life of the machine, for each period, are:

$$\alpha_1, \alpha_2, \alpha_3, \ldots, \alpha_n$$

and that the following must be complied with:

$$\sum_{j=1}^{n} \alpha_j = 1$$

If the circumstance arose where the useful life of the machine were to be greater than the fiscal life, then certain α_j equal to 0 would exist.

As is known, the capital value of an investment, that is the economic excess obtained by carrying out the investment process, updated economic parameter, without taking into account the incidence of tax, will be designated by:

$$V = \sum_{j=1}^{n} (b_j - a_j)(1 + i)^{-j} - M$$

It is necessary to show that the elements composing the previous expression are real entry and exit flows, that is to say, payments and collections in the strict sense of the expressions. We are using, then, one of the basic assumptions of the investment theory.

At the time of making the tax element intervene, which we are limiting exclusively to corporate tax, a percentage on the profits for each year will be incorporated. If we call the tax rate f, the amount to be taken out in a year j will be:

$$I_j = f \cdot (b_j^* - a_j^* - \alpha_j M)$$

(Tax equal to tax rate for (exploitation income less exploitation expenses less depreciation))

Faced with this equality we should make an important remark. The first member constitutes an outgoing monetary flow (payment of the corporate tax to the Tax Authorities) that *has been calculated on accounting data*, in such a way that both a_j^* and la b_j^* as well as $\alpha_j M$ show accounting economic parameters which, in principal do not necessarily have to coincide with the a_j and b_j which are cash flows. In this way the problem is brought up of the differences existing between payments and expenses as well as that of exploitation income and exploitation collections. In order to simplify matters it can be assumed that:

$$a_j^* = a_j; \quad b_j^* = b_j$$

That is that exploitation collections and payments are equal to exploitation income and expenses.

Now it is possible to add a hypothesis giving more generality to the model. What we are trying to do is consider the case that, at least a part of the investment object is acquired by means of outside financing.

In any year let us assume that the percentage of outside financing is k_j at an interest rate i_j. In this case, tax for a year j, will be:

$$I_j = f \cdot (b_j - a_j - \alpha_j M - i_j \cdot k_j \cdot M_j)$$

M_j being the non-depreciated value, in year j, of the investment object.

Within the sphere of certainty it is customary to adopt the hypothesis of constancy of the interest rate over time, that is $i = i_1 = i_2 = \ldots = i_n$, by which the capital value of an investment, after deducting taxes, will then be:

$$V'' = -M + \sum_{j=1}^{n} (b_j - a_j)(1+i)^{-j} - f \cdot \sum_{j=1}^{n} [(b_j - a_j) - \alpha_j M - i \cdot k_j \cdot M_j](1+i)^{-j}$$

On passing over to the field of uncertainty we will leave this limiting hypothesis, since it is very difficult to accept in an economic system characterised by constant changes.

Adapting the model to the field of uncertainty

We will now pass on to the study of the case[2], obviously of a far more general nature, in which certain economic parameters that intervene in the investment process can only be estimated by means of confidence intervals.

In this case we will have:

— Interest rate: $[i_j^{(1)}, i_j^{(2)}]$

— Exploitation income = Collections: $[b_j^{(1)}, b_j^{(2)}]$

— Exploitation Expenses = payments: $[a_j^{(1)}, a_j^{(2)}]$

— Percentage of outside financing: $[k_j^{(1)}, k_j^{(2)}]$

(in any case, $j = 1, 2, \ldots, n$)

— Payment for acquisition of the investment object: $[M^{(1)}, M^{(2)}]$

With the object that certain economic parameters appear, we are going to assume that the company has established a depreciation policy in such a way that the α_j, $(j = 1, 2, \ldots, n)$ are known at the time of making the study for selection. Also, considered as known, are the tax rates for the following accounting periods, which will remain unaltered at level f. There is no need to insist on the fact that there is no problem passing these economic parameters to the sphere of uncertainty by converting them, for example, into confidence intervals.

In order to develop the proposed scheme, in the first place we are going to obtain the amount which it is estimated should be paid during each period for Corporate Income Tax.

This will be:

$$[I_j^{(1)}, I_j^{(2)}] = f(\cdot)\,([b_j^{(1)}, b_j^{(2)}]\,(-)\,[a_j^{(1)}, a_j^{(2)}]\,(-)\,\alpha\,(\cdot)\,[M^{(1)}, M^{(2)}]\,(-)$$
$$(-)\,[i_j^{(1)}, i_j^{(2)}]\,(\cdot)\,[k_j^{(1)}, k_j^{(2)}]\,(\cdot)\,[M_j^{(1)}, M_j^{(2)}])$$

That is to say, from estimated income $[b_j^{(1)}, b_j^{(2)}]$ the fiscally deductible expenses are subtracted. These are:

$$[a_j^{(1)}, a_j^{(2)}]\,(+)\,[\alpha M^{(1)}, \alpha M^{(2)}]\,(+)\,[i_j^{(1)} \cdot k_j^{(1)} \cdot M_j^{(1)}, i_j^{(2)} \cdot k_j^{(2)} \cdot M_j^{(2)}] =$$
$$= [a_j^{(1)} + \alpha_j M^{(1)} + i_j^{(1)} \cdot k_j^{(1)} \cdot M_j^{(1)},\; a_j^{(2)} + \alpha_j M^{(2)} + i_j^{(2)} \cdot k_j^{(2)} \cdot M_j^{(2)}]$$

If the investment object is totally financed by in-house funds it will be $[k_j^{(1)}, k_j^{(2)}] = 0$, therefore the deductible expenses will be reduced to:

$$[a_j^{(1)} + \alpha_j M^{(1)},\; a_j^{(2)} + \alpha_j M^{(2)}]$$

As has been done in the calculation, it will be seen that obtaining the deductible expenses is not a problem, because the formula from the field of certainty continues to be valid, with the condition of repeating the same operation twice, once for the optimistic position and the other for the pessimistic (one and the other extremes of the interval).

In this way, estimating the corporate tax corresponding to year j will be[3]:

$$[I_j^{(1)}, I_j^{(2)}] = f(\cdot)\,[b_j^{(1)} - a_j^{(2)} - \alpha_j M^{(2)} - i_j^{(2)} \cdot k_j^{(2)} \cdot M_j^{(2)},\; b_j^{(2)} - a_j^{(1)} - \alpha_j M^{(1)} - i_j^{(1)} \cdot k_j^{(1)} \cdot M_j^{(1)}]$$

Now it will be seen that the introduction of the subtraction for obtaining the taxable profit, separates this model from the one used in the sphere of certainty, as the extreme representing the optimistic (or pessimistic) hypothesis of collections, does not coincide with the extreme representing the optimistic (or pessimistic) hypothesis of payments.

The net value (exploitation profit) for year j will be[4]:

$$[B_j^{(1)}, B_j^{(2)}] = ([b_j^{(1)}, b_j^{(2)}]\,(-)\,[a_j^{(1)}, a_j^{(2)}])\,(\overline{m})\,[I_j^{(1)}, I_j^{(2)}] =$$
$$= [b_j^{(1)} - a_j^{(2)},\; b_j^{(2)} - a_j^{(1)}]\,(\overline{m})\,[I_j^{(1)}, I_j^{(2)}]$$

In the previous expression the Minkovski subtraction appears, as a consequence of the need to tie in the lesser (greater) profits with the lesser (greater) taxes.

In fact, $I_j^{(1)}$ will be paid when the exploitation profits (before taxes) are $b_j^{(1)} - a_j^{(2)}$, and $I_j^{(2)}$ will be paid when these profits are $b_j^{(2)} - a_j^{(1)}$.

The result, therefore will be:

$$[B_j^{(1)}, B_j^{(2)}] = [b_j^{(1)} - a_j^{(2)} - I_j^{(1)},\ b_j^{(2)} - a_j^{(1)} - I_j^{(2)}]$$

Finally we will pass on to obtaining the net updated value relative to period (year) j. Taking into account the fact that the unitary interest rates have been estimated by means of confidence intervals $[i_j^{(1)}, i_j^{(2)}]$, we will arrive at as the updated value:

For year 1:

$$\frac{1}{1\,(+)\,[i_1^{(1)}, i_1^{(2)}]} = \frac{[1, 1]}{[1, 1]\,(+)\,[i_1^{(1)}, i_1^{(2)}]} = \frac{[1, 1]}{[1 + i_1^{(1)}, 1 + i_1^{(2)}]} = \left[\frac{1}{1 + i_1^{(2)}}, \frac{1}{1 + i_1^{(1)}}\right]$$

For year 2:

$$\left[\frac{1}{1 + i_1^{(2)}}, \frac{1}{1 + i_1^{(1)}}\right] (\cdot) \left[\frac{1}{1 + i_2^{(2)}}, \frac{1}{1 + i_2^{(1)}}\right] = \left[\frac{1}{1 + i_1^{(2)}} \cdot \frac{1}{1 + i_2^{(2)}}, \frac{1}{1 + i_1^{(1)}} \cdot \frac{1}{1 + i_2^{(1)}}\right]$$

....

For year j:

$$\left[\frac{1}{1 + i_1^{(2)}} \cdot \frac{1}{1 + i_2^{(2)}} \cdot \ldots \cdot \frac{1}{1 + i_j^{(2)}}, \frac{1}{1 + i_1^{(1)}} \cdot \frac{1}{1 + i_2^{(1)}} \cdot \ldots \cdot \frac{1}{1 + i_j^{(1)}}\right]$$

....

For year n:

$$\left[\frac{1}{1 + i_1^{(2)}} \cdot \ldots \cdot \frac{1}{1 + i_j^{(2)}} \cdot \ldots \cdot \frac{1}{1 + i_n^{(2)}}, \frac{1}{1 + i_1^{(1)}} \cdot \ldots \cdot \frac{1}{1 + i_j^{(1)}} \cdot \ldots \cdot \frac{1}{1 + i_n^{(1)}}\right]$$

In the case that $[B_j^{(1)}, B_j^{(2)}]$ were to be a member of the field of the real positives, as the net updated value for year j we will have:

$$[V_j^{(1)}, V_j^{(2)}] = \left[\frac{1}{1 + i_1^{(2)}} \cdot \frac{1}{1 + i_2^{(2)}} \cdot \ldots \cdot \frac{1}{1 + i_j^{(2)}}, \frac{1}{1 + i_1^{(1)}} \cdot \frac{1}{1 + i_2^{(1)}} \cdot \ldots \cdot \frac{1}{1 + i_j^{(1)}}\right] (\cdot)$$

$$(\cdot)\ [b_j^{(1)} - a_j^{(2)} - I_j^{(1)},\ b_j^{(2)} - a_j^{(1)} - I_j^{(2)}] =$$

$$= \left[\frac{b_j^{(1)} - a_j^{(2)} - I_j^{(1)}}{(1 + i_1^{(2)})(1 + i_2^{(2)}) \cdots (1 + i_j^{(2)})}, \frac{b_j^{(2)} - a_j^{(1)} - I_j^{(2)}}{(1 + i_1^{(1)})(1 + i_2^{(1)}) \cdots (1 + i_j^{(1)})}\right]$$

This expression is correct provided the net value is a member of R^+. In the event that the lower extreme or both extremes of interval $[b_j^{(1)} - a_j^{(2)} - I_j^{(1)}, b_j^{(2)} - a_j^{(1)} - I_j^{(2)}]$ were negative, the product of the updating rate by the net value should follow the rule of choosing as the lower extreme, the smallest of all the possible products and as the upper extreme, the largest.

Let us now move on to develop an example in which we will incorporate certain interesting peculiarities.

Let us assume that an operating company considers the possibility of acquiring new equipment (investment object) with a useful life of 3 years, the cost of which, totally payable at moment 0 (commencement of the process), is estimated by means of the confidence interval:

$$[M^{(1)}, M^{(2)}] = [240, 300]$$

For greater simplicity we are going to establish that this machine will be depreciated by constant quotas throughout its useful life and, on the other hand, its incorporation into the production process will not change the sign of the overall results, which in any case will be positive (profits). The introduction of this last clause will allow for considering the possibility, that should there be losses in exploiting the machine during any given period, <negative taxation>> would be incurred relative to these partial results, which would reduce the amount the company obtains from other machines and therefore, the amount it must pay as tax on profits will be less than it would have paid had the machine not been acquired.

With regard to payment for the machine it can be assumed that this will be done in part by financing with company in-house funds and the rest with outside financing, which is estimated at between 20 and 30 per cent. The amount of this will also be returned in three years, with constant quotas. Thus we will arrive at:

$$[k_j^{(1)}, k_j^{(2)}] = [k_1^{(1)}, k_1^{(2)}] = [k_2^{(1)}, k_2^{(2)}] = [k_3^{(1)}, k_3^{(2)}] = [0.2, 0.3]$$

$$\underset{\sim}{M}_1 = \underset{\sim}{M} = [240, 300]$$

$$\underset{\sim}{M}_2 = 2/3 \,(\cdot)\, [240, 300] = [160, 200]$$

$$\underset{\sim}{M}_3 = 1/3 \,(\cdot)\, [240, 300] = [80, 100]$$

The tax rate on company profits is considered as a very stable economic parameters, therefore there is no problem in estimating it by means of a crisp number, such as:

$$f = 0.36$$

With the object of completing the necessary estimates so that the study permitting determination of the convenience of carrying out the investment in the machine can be made, an expert is asked to supply information relative to exploitation collections and payments with the machine, as well as the rate of interest for each of the periods of its useful life, which are as follows:

Period	Collections = Exploitation income	Payments = Exploitation expenses (without depreciation)	Interest rate
1	$\underset{\sim}{b}_1 = [120, 160]$	$\underset{\sim}{a}_1 = [30, 50]$	$\underset{\sim}{i}_1 = [0.10, 0.12]$
2	$\underset{\sim}{b}_2 = [200, 240]$	$\underset{\sim}{a}_2 = [40, 60]$	$\underset{\sim}{i}_2 = [0.12, 0.14]$
3	$\underset{\sim}{b}_3 = [250, 300]$	$\underset{\sim}{a}_3 = [60, 80]$	$\underset{\sim}{i}_3 = [0.12, 0.16]$

Firstly we are going to arrive at the net updated value corresponding to the first period. For this we will calculate taxation:

$$\underset{\sim}{I}_1 = 0.36\,(\cdot)\,[120 - 50 - 100 - 10.8,\ 160 - 30 - 80 - 4.8] = 0.36\,(\cdot)\,[-40{,}8,\ 45{,}2] =$$
$$= [-14.68,\ 16.27]$$

as:

$$[\alpha_1 M^{(1)},\ \alpha_1 M^{(2)}] = [1/3 \cdot 240,\ 1/3 \cdot 300] = [80, 100]$$

and

$$[i_1^{(1)} \cdot k_1^{(1)} \cdot M_1^{(1)},\ i_1^{(2)} \cdot k_1^{(2)} \cdot M_1^{(2)}] = [0.10 \times 0.20 \times 240,\ 0.12 \times 0.30 \times 300] = [4.8, 10.8]$$

Here we should pause and take a look at certain important aspects. The first of these refers to the fact of identifying, as mentioned before, $[M_1^{(1)}, M_1^{(2)}]$ with $[M^{(1)}, M^{(2)}]$, which is due to the fact that, whatever the rate of payback of the loan, it will be paid at the end of each period. Thus in the first year interest will have to be paid on the total, that is, on [0.20, 0.30] (·) [240, 300]. Secondly the same rate as the rate used for calculation purposes has been used as a cost of the debts, in order to satisfy the clause whereby, at this particular rate any quantity of money can be <<given>> or <<asked for>>.

The result obtained [-14.68, 16.27] just shows that at the most pessimistic position the losses of 40.5 will reduce the amount to be paid in taxes on the total profits of the company by 14.68 monetary units.

The same result is obtained as follows:

Income = Collections .... [120, 160]

Expenses = Payments [30, 50]

(+)

Depreciation .... [80, 100]

(+)

Interest on debts ...... [4.8, 10.8]

Expenses + Depreciation + Interest on debts = [114.8, 160.8]

[120, 160] (−) [114.8, 160.8] = [−40.8, 45.2]

From where:

$$\underset{\sim}{I}_1 = 0.36\ (\cdot)\ [-40.8, 45.2] = [-14.68, 16.27]$$

In summary, then, the net value corresponding to period 1 will be:

$$\underset{\sim}{B}_1 = ([120, 160]\ (-)\ [30, 50])\ (\overline{m})\ [-14.68, 16.27] = [70, 130]\ (\overline{m})\ [-14.68, 16.27] = \\ = [84.68, 113.73]$$

Having reached this particular point we would again like to emphasise the importance acquired by the correct use of the arithmetic of confidence intervals. In fact the operations carried out for finding result $\underset{\sim}{B}_1$ correspond to:

$$\underset{\sim}{B}_1 = ([b_1^{(1)}, b_1^{(2)}]\ (-)\ [a_1^{(1)}, a_1^{(2)}])\ (\overline{m})\ \{f(\cdot)\ ([b_1^{(1)}, b_1^{(2)}]\ (-)\ [a_1^{(1)}, a_1^{(2)}])\ (-) \\ (-)\ f(\cdot)\ [\alpha_1 M^{(1)} + i_1^{(1)} \cdot k_1^{(1)} \cdot M_1^{(1)},\ \alpha_1 M^{(2)} + i_1^{(2)} \cdot k_1^{(2)} \cdot M_1^{(2)}]\} = \\ = [70, 130]\ (\overline{m})\ \{0.36\ (\cdot)\ [70, 130]\ (-)\ 0.36\ (\cdot)\ [84.8, 110.8]\} = \\ = [70, 130]\ (\overline{m})\ [-14.68, 16.27] = [84.68, 113.73]$$

We would like to underline the interest acquired by the placing of the key {} which joins the necessary operations for calculating taxation. To forget this would cause one of the more frequent errors in schemes using confidence intervals, consequent upon, contrary to what happens when using classical arithmetic, what is complied with in uncertainty is that: minus Minkowski by less normal minus is different from plus $((\overline{m}) \cdot (-) \neq (+))$. The results would only coincide if uncertainty is reduced to certainty by making the entropy fall, that is, passing over from the general case of uncertainty to the particular case of certainty, showing once again that the arithmetic of certainty is none other than a particular case of the arithmetic of uncertainty. Let us take a look at it in this specific case. If we were to do (incorrect operation):

$$\underset{\sim}{B}'_1 = [70, 130]\ (\overline{m})\ 0.36\ (\cdot)\ [70, 130]\ (+)\ 0.36\ (\cdot)\ [84.8, 110.8] = \\ = [70, 130]\ (\overline{m})\ [25.2, 46.8]\ (+)\ [30.52, 39.88] = [75.32, 123.08]$$

in where it can be seen that $\underset{\sim}{B}_1 \neq \underset{\sim}{B}'_1$. Only by making the entropy fall, by doing:

$$\overline{\underset{\sim}{B}_1} = \frac{84.68 + 113.73}{2} = 99.2$$

and

$$\overline{\underset{\sim}{B}'_1} = \frac{75.32 + 123.08}{2} = 99.2$$

The results we have obtained by following the two paths, coincide.

But we will leave aside these aspects of the arithmetic of uncertainty and pass on quickly to obtain the *net updated value* corresponding to period 1, which will be:

$$\underset{\sim}{V}_1 = \left[\frac{1}{1.12}, \frac{1}{1.10}\right] (\cdot) [84.68, 113.73] = [75.60, 103.39]$$

since:

$$\frac{1}{1 (+) [i_1^{(1)}, i_1^{(2)}]} = \frac{[1, 1]}{[1.10, 1.12]} = \left[\frac{1}{1.12}, \frac{1}{1.10}\right]$$

Now we are going to arrive at the *net updated value* relative to period 2. For this let us calculate, in the first place, taxation $\underset{\sim}{I}_2$, which will be:

$$\underset{\sim}{I}_2 = 0.36 (\cdot) [200 - 60 - 100 - 8.40, 240 - 40 - 80 - 3.84] = 0.36 (\cdot) [31.60, 116.16] =$$
$$= [11.37, 41.81]$$

as:

$$[i_2^{(1)} \cdot k_2^{(1)} \cdot M_2^{(1)}, i_2^{(2)} \cdot k_2^{(2)} \cdot M_2^{(2)}] = [0.12 \times 0.20 \times 160, 0.14 \times 0.30 \times 200] = [3.84, 8.40]$$

The net value corresponding to period 2 will be, therefore:

$$\underset{\sim}{B}_2 = ([200, 240] (-) [40, 60]) (\overline{m}) [11.37, 41.81] = [140, 200] (\overline{m}) [11.37, 41.81] =$$
$$= [128.63, 158.19]$$

Finally, the *net updated value* corresponding to period 2 is:

$$\underset{\sim}{V}_2 = \left[\frac{1}{1.2768}, \frac{1}{1.2320}\right] (\cdot) [128.63, 158.19] = [100.774, 128.400]$$

because:

$$\frac{1}{1 (+) [i_1^{(1)}, i_1^{(2)}]} (\cdot) \frac{1}{1 (+) [i_2^{(1)}, i_2^{(2)}]} = \left[\frac{1}{1.12} \cdot \frac{1}{1.14}, \frac{1}{1.10} \cdot \frac{1}{1.12}\right] = \left[\frac{1}{1.2768}, \frac{1}{1.2320}\right]$$

Now we pass on to find the *net updated value* corresponding to period 3. We calculate the taxes to be paid for the third year, that is, $\underset{\sim}{I}_3$:

$$\underset{\sim}{I}_3 = 0.36 (\cdot) [250 - 80 - 100 - 4.80, 300 - 60 - 80 - 1.92] = 0.36 (\cdot) [65.20, 158.08] =$$
$$= [23.47, 56.90]$$

as:

$$[i_3^{(1)} \cdot k_3^{(1)} \cdot M_3^{(1)},\ i_3^{(2)} \cdot k_3^{(2)} \cdot M_3^{(2)}] = [0.12 \times 0.20 \times 80,\ 0.16 \times 0.30 \times 100] = [1.92, 4.80]$$

We will now arrive at the net value for the third period:

$$\underset{\sim}{B}_3 = ([250, 300]\ (-)\ [60, 80])\ (\overline{m})\ [23.47, 56.90] = [170, 240]\ (\overline{m})\ [23.47, 56.90] =$$
$$= [146.53, 183.10]$$

With which the *net updated value* for period 3 will be:

$$\underset{\sim}{V}_3 = \left[\frac{1}{1.481088}, \frac{1}{1.379840}\right] (\cdot)\ [146.53, 183.10] = [98.9340, 132.6965]$$

as:

$$\frac{1}{1\ (+)\ [i_1^{(1)}, i_1^{(2)}]}\ (\cdot)\ \frac{1}{1\ (+)\ [i_2^{(1)}, i_2^{(2)}]}\ (\cdot)\ \frac{1}{1\ (+)\ [i_3^{(1)}, i_3^{(2)}]} = \left[\frac{1}{1.481088}, \frac{1}{1.379840}\right]$$

In order to obtain the net updated value of the investment it is sufficient to do the arithmetical addition of the intervals found for each period, from which the estimate of the value of the investment object that is assumed paid at moment 0, is deducted.

That is:

$$\underset{\sim}{V} = \sum_{j=1}^{3} \underset{\sim}{V}_j\ (-)\ \underset{\sim}{M}$$

which in this specific case will be:

$$\underset{\sim}{V} = [75.60, 103.39]\ (+)\ [100.744, 128.400]\ (+)\ [98.9340, 132.6965]\ (-)\ [240, 300] =$$
$$= [-24.7220, 124.4865]$$

This result brings to light the fact that acquisition of the investment object can take place, considering the effects caused by Taxation on Corporate Profits, from a loss position of 24.7 monetary units right up to a profit position of 124.4 monetary units. It is obvious that this result, characterised by the low limitation of uncertainty, is hardly efficient at the time of taking a decision. This inconvenience, linked to the fact that the original data was the result of the opinion of a single expert and therefore loaded with a high degree of subjectivity, advises the use of *m*-expertons.

Reduction of uncertainty and subjectivity by using *m*-expertons

An *m*-experton is nothing other than an experton constructed by means of confidence quadruples or triplets, that is, what we are dealing with is a random fuzzy sub-set in which the valuations, level by level, are confidence quadruples or triplets. Therefore, at each level $\alpha = 0, 0.1, ..., 0.9, 1$, in the most general case a quadruple can be found, formed by:

$$\underset{\sim}{a} = (a_1, [a_2, a_3], a_4) \subset [0, 1]$$

The algebra of confidence quadruples, the same as for valuations in [0, 1] have a structure of a distributive lattice. All the *T*-norms, *T*-co-norms and inferences used for fuzzy variables can be used in confidence quadruples. And given the fact that the configuration of expertons and of *m*-expertons is that of the distributive lattices of confidence quadruples (always taking into account the essential inherent monotony of their construction) the properties of *T*-norms, *T*-co-norms and inferences can also be applied.

We are going to construct an *m*-experton using the hendecadarian system, which, as is sufficiently well known, means considering 11 equidistant positions of 0 to 1. For greater ease of calculation the opinion of 10 counter-experts who will be requested to express the same relative to the result of acquiring and operating the investment object. That is to say their positioning within the segment [-24, 124] which was obtained[6]. With the object of giving the greatest liberty possible in their opinions, they have been requested to express the same by means of confidence quadruples, in accordance with the following semantic correspondence:

0 .... (–24)
0.1 .... Practically (–24)
0.2 .... Nearly (–24)
0.3 .... Close to (–24)
0.4 .... Closer to (-24) than to (124)
0.5 .... As close to (-24) as to (124)
0.6 .... Closer to (124) than to (-24)
0.7 .... Close to (124)
0.8 .... Nearly (124)
0.9 .... Practically (124)
1 .... (124)

It is obvious that this correspondence only has an indicative nature and can be substituted, in each case, by any other considered more convenient.

Now continuing on with the process, the opinions of the 10 counter-experts is gathered and summarised in the following table:

Counter-expert	Estimates
1	(.4, [.6, .7], .9)
2	(.5, [.6, .8], .8)
3	(.6, [.7, .7], .9)
4	(.9, [.9, .9], .9)
5	(.3, [.5, .7], .7)
6	(.4, [.4, .5], .5)
7	(.6, [.9, .9], 1)
8	(.5, [.6, .7], .8)
9	(.4, [.5, .6], .7)
10	(.3, [.4, .5], .6)

A first analysis of these estimates brings to light certain peculiarities in some of them. The opinions of counter-experts 3 and 7 are reduced to the following confidence triplets (.6, .7, .9) and (.6, .9, 1) respectively. The opinion of counter-expert 4 is reduced to that of a crisp estimate (.9, .9, .9) = 0.9, while the opinion of counter-expert 6 can be reduced to interval [.4, .5].

On the other hand, on giving an opinion by means of the estimates stated in the previous table, counter-expert 1, for example, stated that, in his opinion, in the worst case the number will be closer to -24 than to 124, and in the best case could become practically 124, but that his maximum presumption is that it will be between closer to 124 than to -24 and close to 124. We will leave it up to the reader to make the semantic conversion of the other estimates, as well as to modify the scale for doing so, if he should consider this correct in order to make it more operative.

We will now move on to note down the number of times that each counter-expert gave the same valuation as a lower extreme of the quadruple, lower and upper extreme of the maximum presumption and upper extreme of the quadruple.

We arrive at:

[–24, 124]

0				
.1				
.2				
.3	2			
.4	3	2		
.5	2	2	2	1
.6	2	3	1	1
.7		1	4	2
.8			1	2
.9	1	2	2	3
1				1

From this statistic we obtain the normalised frequencies by dividing each number obtained by the number of counter-experts.

[–24, 124]

0	0	0	0	0
.1	0	0	0	0
.2	0	0	0	0
.3	.2	0	0	0
.4	.3	.2	0	0
.5	.2	.2	.2	.1
.6	.2	.3	.1	.1
.7	0	.1	.4	.2
.8	0	0	.1	.2
.9	.1	.2	.2	.3
1	0	0	0	.1

And finally, by means of complementary accumulation (from 1 to 0) we arrive at the following *m*-experton:

[–24, 124]

$\underset{\sim}{a}=$				
0	1	1	1	1
.1	1	1	1	1
.2	1	1	1	1
.3	1	1	1	1
.4	.8	1	1	1
.5	.5	.8	1	1
.6	.3	.6	.8	.9
.7	.1	.3	.7	.8
.8	.1	.2	.3	.6
.9	.1	.2	.2	.4
1	0	0	0	.1

One of the advantages of the *m*-experton, and also of expertons, is the wealth of information they contain. In them we can see in which way the opinion of the counter-experts (or experts in the event) leans, if these are all close or far apart, if there are any contra-experts (or experts in the event) who deviate from the majority opinions, etc.

Now, as in this case, we want to arrive at a single opinion that includes both the opinion of the expert and counter-experts, it will be necessary to use some kind of operator that allows us to present the information contained in the *m*-experton in a summarised manner. For this we will use mathematical probability.

Obtaining the mathematical probability is a simple operation. It is sufficient to add each of the four columns, without taking into account level $\alpha = 0$ (in which there is always a 1) and then divide the result by 10. We will arrive at:

$$\varepsilon(\underset{\sim}{a}) = (0.49, [0.61, 0.70], 0.78)$$

the semantic correspondence of which we leave up to the reader.

And finally, in order to arrive at the estimate of the capital value of the investment, we will set up the following equation:

$$\varepsilon(\underset{\sim}{V}) = -24 + (124 - (-24)) \cdot \varepsilon(\underset{\sim}{a})$$

which will give rise to:

$$\varepsilon(\underset{\sim}{V}) = (48.52, [66.28, 79.60], 91.44)$$

which constitutes the aggregation of the experts' opinion in the form of a confidence quadruple.

In the event that it were essential to present an exact value, the ordinary number closest to the quadruple found could be obtained. In this case it would be sufficient to arrive at a mean such as:

$$\overline{\underset{\sim}{V}} = \frac{48.52 + 2 \times 66.28 + 2 \times 79.60 + 91.44}{6} = 71.95$$

In this case then, the most adequate exact estimate, taking into account the opinion of the expert and counter-experts relative to the capital value of the investment is 71.95 monetary units.

We could arrive at the same result by following another path, in our opinion far more interesting, although it does require quite a few more calculation operations. It consists in the use of the same linear equation that was used for arriving at $\varepsilon(\underset{\sim}{V})$ in a direct way, making the *m*-experton intervene. It would now be:

$$\underset{\sim}{V} = -24 + (124 - (-24)) \cdot \underset{\sim}{a}$$

In this way we arrive at the following *R*-experton:

	α	$\underset{\sim}{a}$					α	$\underset{\sim}{V}$			
	0	1	1	1	1		0	124	124	124	124
	.1	1	1	1	1		.1	124	124	124	124
	.2	1	1	1	1		.2	124	124	124	124
	.3	1	1	1	1		.3	124	124	124	124
	.4	.8	1	1	1		.4	94.4	124	124	124
– 24 (+) 148 (·)	.5	.5	.8	1	1	=	.5	50	94.4	124	124
	.6	.3	.6	.8	.9		.6	20.4	64.8	94.4	109.2
	.7	.1	.3	.7	.8		.7	–9.2	20.4	79.6	94.4
	.8	.1	.2	.3	.6		.8	–9.2	5.6	20.4	64.8
	.9	.1	.2	.2	.4		.9	–9.2	5.6	5.6	35.2
	1	0	0	0	.1		1	–24	–24	–24	–9.2

Now let us obtain, the mathematical probability of the R-m-experton $\underset{\sim}{V}$ by using the same procedure as used for the m-experton. As a consequence of the linearity, the same result will be arrived at:

$$\varepsilon(\underset{\sim}{V}) = (48.52, [66.28, 79.60], 91.44)$$

On this occasion it has been considered that the depreciation rate α_j were known with certainty. We are now going to do away with this restriction and also assume that the depreciation rates are uncertain economic parameters.

Uncertainty in depreciation rates

Under these circumstances, when depreciation rates are initially expressed in the form of intervals instead of crisp values, it could be interesting to include in the model, as well as the rates of depreciation α_j, the unitary rates β_j, pending depreciation, that is to say the representative percentage of the residual value at each moment of the investment object.

Take into account, in this respect, that company balance sheets supply information on gross and net fixed assets (the difference between the value of the machine and its depreciation fund), which is nothing other than the residual value in absolute terms. In order to pass over to relative values, that is values in β_j, depends on a simple mathematical operation of division.

Let us look then at the incidences arising in the described process when including in the model in an explicit way, the percentage of the investment object pending depreciation.

If we write β_{j-1} to designate the unitary rate pending depreciation in period j, the following must be complied with:

$$\underset{\sim}{\beta}_0 = [1, 1]$$
$$\underset{\sim}{\beta}_1 = [1, 1] (-) [\alpha_1^{(1)}, \alpha_1^{(2)}] = [\beta_1^{(1)}, \beta_1^{(2)}]$$
$$\underset{\sim}{\beta}_2 = [1, 1] (-) ([\alpha_1^{(1)}, \alpha_1^{(2)}] (+) [\alpha_2^{(1)}, \alpha_2^{(2)}]) = [\beta_2^{(1)}, \beta_2^{(2)}]$$
$$\cdots\cdots\cdots\cdots\cdots\cdots\cdots\cdots\cdots\cdots\cdots\cdots\cdots\cdots$$
$$\underset{\sim}{\beta}_n = [0, 0]$$

It is necessary to see that the residual percentage in n must always be null and void, so that the depreciation rate $\underset{\sim}{\alpha}_n$ will be determined by the interval $\underset{\sim}{\beta}_{n-1}$, *without it constituting*, for this reason a confidence interval in the strict sense.

Let us now move on to develop an example by means of the previous variation. Let us assume that the company established, for certain industrial equipment with a useful life of $n = 3$, the depreciation policy according to the rates of depreciation $[\alpha_1^{(1)}, \alpha_1^{(2)}] = [.4, 5]$ for the first period, $([\alpha_2^{(1)}, \alpha_2^{(2)}] = [.3, .4]$ for the second and residual depreciation for the third. The relation between the annual rate of depreciation $\underset{\sim}{\alpha}_j$ and the residual rate $\underset{\sim}{\beta}_j$ will be the following:

$$\underset{\sim}{\beta}_0 = [1, 1]$$
$$\underset{\sim}{\beta}_1 = [1, 1]\ (-)\ [.4, .5] = [.5, .6]$$
$$\underset{\sim}{\beta}_2 = [1, 1]\ (-)\ ([.4, .5]\ (+)\ [.3, .4]) = [.1, .3]$$
$$\underset{\sim}{\beta}_3 = [0, 0]$$

which we reflect in the following figure:

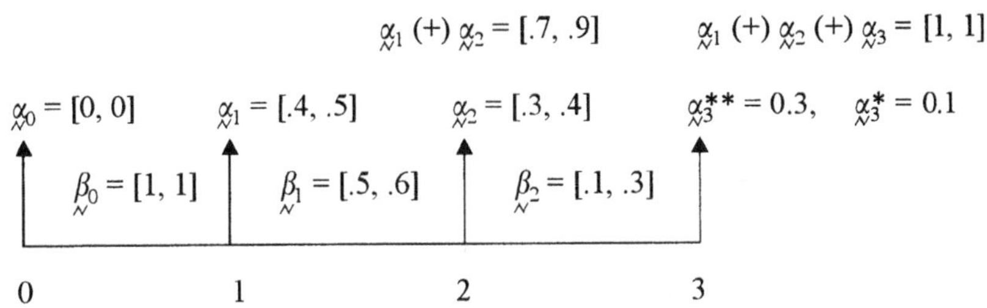

It is important to remember that the rate of residual depreciation, corresponding to α_n, cannot be expressed by an interval. Therefore, in this case, the accumulated depreciation for the second year would be $\underset{\sim}{\alpha}_1 + \underset{\sim}{\alpha}_2 = [.7, .9]$ so that we would arrive at a residual rate of $\underset{\sim}{\beta}_2 = [.1, .3]$ and in this way depreciation should be at a minimum of 0.1 and a maximum of 0.3. Under these circumstances, if we were to write $\underset{\sim}{\alpha}_3 = [.1, .3]$, we would arrive at:

$$\underset{\sim}{\beta}_2\ (\overline{m})\ \underset{\sim}{\alpha}_3 = [.1, .3]\ (\overline{m})\ [.1, .3] = [0, 0] = 0$$

but on the other hand:

$$\underset{\sim}{\alpha}_1\ (+)\ \underset{\sim}{\alpha}_2\ (+)\ \underset{\sim}{\alpha}_3 = [.4, .5]\ (+)\ [.3, .4]\ (+)\ [.1, .3] \neq [1, 1]$$

as a consequence of considering $\underset{\sim}{\alpha}_3$ as the residual depreciation (of the last year). In order for the operation of addition of the depreciation rates $\underset{\sim}{\alpha}_j$ to be equal to the unit to be complied with, it is necessary to add the rates $\underset{\sim}{\alpha}_1$, $\underset{\sim}{\alpha}_2$, ..., $\underset{\sim}{\alpha}_{n-1}$ and to add the lower extreme of the upper extreme of the residual rate $\underset{\sim}{\beta}_{n-1}$, and the upper extreme of the addition of the lower extreme of the said residual rate, that is to say, addition is done of the crossed over extremes.

In this case, as:

$$\underset{\sim}{\alpha}_1\ (+)\ \underset{\sim}{\alpha}_2 = [.7, .9]$$
$$\underset{\sim}{\beta}_2 = [.1, .3]$$

we will do:

$$\sum_{j=1}^{3} \underset{\sim}{\alpha}_j = [.7 + .3, .9 + .1] = [1, 1]$$

If acquisition of the investment object (industrial equipment) means a payment at the initial moment, equal to that considered in the previous section $[M^{(1)}, M^{(2)}] = = [240, 300]$, the capital invested, pending depreciation at each moment will be:

$$[M_j^{(1)}, M_j^{(2)}] = \underset{\sim}{\beta}_{j-1} (\cdot) [M^{(1)}, M^{(2)}]$$

and we arrive at:

$$[M_1^{(1)}, M_1^{(2)}] = [1, 1] (\cdot) [240, 300] = [240, 300]$$
$$[M_2^{(1)}, M_2^{(2)}] = [.5, .6] (\cdot) [240, 300] = [120, 180]$$
$$[M_3^{(1)}, M_3^{(2)}] = [.1, .3] (\cdot) [240, 300] = [24, 90]$$

If we continue by doing $[k_j^{(1)}, k_j^{(2)}] = [k_1^{(1)}, k_1^{(2)}] = [k_2^{(1)}, k_2^{(2)}] = [k_3^{(1)}, k_3^{(2)}] = [.2, .3]$, we arrive at:

$$[k_1^{(1)}, k_1^{(2)}] (\cdot) [M_1^{(1)}, M_1^{(2)}] = [.2, .3] (\cdot) [240, 300] = [48, 90]$$
$$[k_2^{(1)}, k_2^{(2)}] (\cdot) [M_2^{(1)}, M_2^{(2)}] = [.2, .3] (\cdot) [120, 180] = [24, 54]$$
$$[k_3^{(1)}, k_3^{(2)}] (\cdot) [M_3^{(1)}, M_3^{(2)}] = [.2, .3] (\cdot) [24, 90] = [4.8, 27]$$

it should be taken into account that $[M_j^{(1)}, M_j^{(2)}]$ is the estimate of the value of the investment object pending depreciation in period j, which means to say that depreciation has not been carried out in period j, because this accounting operation only takes place at the end of each period.

Notice that the incorporation of $[M_j^{(1)}, M_j^{(2)}]$ arises as a consequence of the need to calculate, in each period, the monetary mass corresponding to the payment of interest on outside capital, that is to say $[i_j^{(1)}, i_j^{(2)}] (\cdot) [k_j^{(1)}, k_j^{(2)}] (\cdot) [M_j^{(1)}, M_j^{(2)}]$.

Interest to be paid at the end of the first period, corresponds to the total capital which has been used during the first year. It is at this time when depreciation $[\alpha_1^{(1)}, \alpha_1^{(2)}] (\cdot) [M^{(1)}, M^{(2)}]$ is applied returning the part of the loan corresponding to the payment made during the first year which, in the second year, will no longer accrue interest. And this is what will happen period after period.

Let us assume that an expert has estimated the following data coinciding with that of the previous problem:

Estimated collections:

$$\underset{\sim}{\beta}_1 = [120, 160]; \quad \underset{\sim}{\beta}_2 = [200, 240]; \quad \underset{\sim}{\beta}_3 = [250, 300]$$

Estimated payments:

$$\underset{\sim}{a}_1 = [30, 50]; \quad \underset{\sim}{a}_2 = [40, 60]; \quad \underset{\sim}{a}_3 = [60, 80]$$

Estimated interest rates:

$$\underset{\sim}{i}_1 = [.10, .12]; \quad \underset{\sim}{i}_2 = [.12, .14]; \quad \underset{\sim}{i}_3 = [.12, .16]$$

Tax rate:

$$f = 0.36$$

With these estimates we can now find $\underset{\sim}{I}_j$, payments of the tax on profits, corresponding to each period:

$$\underset{\sim}{I}_1 = 0.36\,(\cdot)\,[120 - 50 - 150 - 10.8,\ 160 - 30 - 96 - 4.8] = 0.36\,(\cdot)\,[-90.8,\ 29.2] =$$
$$= [-32.68,\ 10.51]$$

as $[\alpha_1^{(1)} M^{(1)},\ \alpha_1^{(2)} M^{(2)}] = [96,\ 150]$:

$$[i_1^{(1)} \cdot k_1^{(1)} \cdot M_1^{(1)},\ i_1^{(2)} \cdot k_1^{(2)} \cdot M_1^{(2)}] = [4.8,\ 10.8]$$

$$\underset{\sim}{I}_2 = 0.36\,(\cdot)\,[200 - 60 - 120 - 7.56,\ 240 - 40 - 72 - 2.88] =$$
$$= 0.36\,(\cdot)\,[12.44,\ 125.12] = [4.47,\ 45.04]$$

as $[\alpha_2^{(1)} M^{(1)},\ \alpha_2^{(2)} M^{(2)}] = [72,\ 120]$:

$$[i_2^{(1)} \cdot k_2^{(1)} \cdot M_2^{(1)},\ i_2^{(2)} \cdot k_2^{(2)} \cdot M_2^{(2)}] = [2.88,\ 7.56]$$

$$\underset{\sim}{I}_3 = 0.36\,(\cdot)\,[250 - 80 - 30 - 4.32,\ 300 - 60 - 72 - 0.57] =$$
$$= 0.36\,(\cdot)\,[135.68,\ 167.43] = [48.84,\ 60.27]$$

as $\quad \alpha_3^{**} M^{(1)} = 0.3 \times 240 = 72$

$$\alpha_3^{*} M^{(2)} = 0.1 \times 300 = 30$$

$$[i_3^{(1)} \cdot k_3^{(1)} \cdot M_3^{(1)},\ i_3^{(2)} \cdot k_3^{(2)} \cdot M_3^{(2)}] = [0.576,\ 4.320]$$

In the calculation of the depreciation payment corresponding to the last period, we have avoided expressing the result by means of an interval, taking into account that the fundamental requirement, that the upper extreme be equal to or greater than the lower extreme, is not complied with. Under very special circumstances it could happen that the difference $\alpha_3^{**} M^{(1)} - \alpha_3^{*} M^{(2)} > 0$ were to be so large that it gave rise to the fact that the lower extreme of $\underset{\sim}{I}_3$ were larger than its upper extreme. These exceptional cases would bring up the problem of the impossibility of expressing $\underset{\sim}{I}_3$ in the form of a confidence interval, except in the event that the problem were to allow a revision of the starting out estimates and/or that the adequacy of the numbers were to give rise to a distance in which the results were of little significance. At this point we will leave this question as raised.

It is convenient to point out, also, that we have identified $[M_1^{(1)}, M_1^{(2)}]$ with $[M^{(1)}, M^{(2)}]$, since as has been said before, whatever the rate of depreciation of the loan, this is returned at the end of each period. For this reason, the first year interest on the total loan will have to paid, that is on [.2, .3] (·) [240, 300]. Finally it can be seen that in the result obtained for $\underset{\sim}{I}_1$ appear in the pessimistic position (lower extreme) certain losses of 32.68 (less profits), which number will reduce the amount to be paid as tax on profits for the whole company.

We are now in a position to obtain the net values relative to each of the periods. Thus:

$$\underset{\sim}{B}_1 = ([120, 160]\ (-)\ [30, 50])\ (\overline{m})\ [-32.68, 10.51] = [102.68, 119.49]$$

$$\underset{\sim}{B}_2 = ([200, 240]\ (-)\ [40, 60])\ (\overline{m})\ [4.47, 45.04] = [135.53, 154.96]$$

$$\underset{\sim}{B}_3 = ([250, 300]\ (-)\ [60, 80])\ (\overline{m})\ [48.84, 60.27] = [121.16, 179.73]$$

In order to obtain the net updated value of the investment it will be sufficient to do:

$$\underset{\sim}{V} = \left[\frac{1}{1.12}, \frac{1}{1.10}\right] (\cdot)\ [102.68, 119.49]\ (+) \left[\frac{1}{1.2768}, \frac{1}{1.2320}\right] (+)\ [135.53, 154.96]\ (+)$$

$$(+) \left[\frac{1}{1.481088}, \frac{1}{1.379840}\right] (\cdot)\ [121.16, 179.73]\ (-)\ [240, 300] =$$

$$= [91.67, 108.62]\ (+)\ [106.14, 125.77]\ (+)\ [81.80, 130.25]\ (-)\ [240, 300] =$$

$$= [-20.39, 124.64]$$

This result brings to light the fact that the acquisition of the investment object can give rise to, considering the effects caused by the tax on profits, from a loss of 20.39 monetary units to a profit of 124.64 monetary units in the most optimistic position. Even now this result is not particularly effective for aiding us in the decision.

With the object of avoiding excessive repetitions of calculations, we are going to assume that consultation of the counter-experts for an opinion relative to the result [-20.39, 124.64] has given rise to the same *m*-experton as in the previous section, that is:

[−20.39, 124.64]

	α				
	0	1	1	1	1
	.1	1	1	1	1
	.2	1	1	1	1
	.3	1	1	1	1
	.4	.8	1	1	1
$\underset{\sim}{a}=$	.5	.5	.8	1	1
	.6	.3	.6	.8	.9
	.7	.1	.3	.7	.8
	.8	.1	.2	.3	.6
	.9	.1	.2	.2	.4
	1	0	0	0	.1

To finally obtain the estimate of the capital value of the investment, we will establish the following equation, which is sufficiently well known:

$$\varepsilon(\underset{\sim}{V}) = -\,20.39 + (124.64 - (-20.39))\ (\cdot)\ \varepsilon(\underset{\sim}{a})$$

which will give rise to:

$$\varepsilon(\underset{\sim}{V}) = (50.67,\ [68.07,\ 81.13],\ 92.77)$$

which constitutes an aggregation of the opinion of the experts in the form of a confidence quadruple.

The result arrived at, either by means of the *m*-experton, by mathematical probability or vulgar number representing the same in a better way, allows for, within the limits imposed by uncertainty, preparing a decision on the convenience of acquiring an investment object when explicitly considering fiscal pressure, represented by Taxation on Corporate Profits.

With the object of arriving at certain results which are effective, in an attempt to instrument an aid for executives, two basic concepts have been used. The first are confidence intervals, the use of which requires a certain attention to be given, because of the peculiarities of their arithmetic, secondly the *m*-expertons or maximum presumption expertons. In these we have attempted to incorporate their more general aspects, when the counter-experts give their opinions by means of confidence quadruples. Now, if this interval constitutes the fact that the maximum presumption is so small that it can be confused by one point, the quadruple becomes a confidence triplet. This is why the triplet is a particular case of the confidence quadruple. The process, in the case of triplets would be the same as we have used for this last development.

Finally we would like to show that the scheme, primarily presented by means of a numerical example, can give rise to a large number of variations. Our objective, which we hope to have achieved, at least partially, has been to open up a new door giving way to future works, which we hope will be better perfected from a technical point of view and more useful from a professional perspective.

References

1 J. Gil Aluja: <<Incidencia de la fiscalidad en la decisión de invertir en un ambiente de incertidumbre>> Ist Congress on Management and Economy of the Company, Huelva, May, 1992

2 See in this respect: J. Gil Aluja: <<Investment decisions in a context of uncertainty>> II International Conference of BUFSA Karandeniz Technical University, Trabzon (Turkey), August 31-September 5, 1992. A. Kaufmann and J. Gil Aluja: *Técnicas especiales para la gestión de expertos,* Milladoiro, Santiago de Compostale, 1993, pages 353-367.

3 Again we can mention that the tax rate estimated by means of an interval, would mean substituting f for $[f^{(1)}, f^{(2)}]$, which introduces up no further complications for those having a knowledge of interval arithmetic.

4 It will be seen that in this subject we have changes the notations as we have designated with B_j the exploitation profit, with the object of not causing any confusion in the reader.

5 A confidence quadruple is a simplification of a trapezoidal fuzzy number, in which the membership function is disregarded from a_1 to a_2, and from a_3 to a_4, this then takes the valvue of 0 in a_1 and a_4, amd also the value of 1 (maximum presumption) in segment $[a_2, a_3]$

6 It will be seen that we have done without the decimals, since, in uncertainty, they are not relevant.

8 Wear and tear in the investment process

The study of wear and tear in determinist models

When handling the problem of selection of investments in industrial equipment, the analysis of one of the components of payment currents, wear and tear, acquires a special interest. And this is so, because operation and efficiency in economic terms depend, to a large degree, on the physical condition in which the investment object is at any given moment.

With the object of incorporating this element into the studies of economic viability, we propose to present a model, in uncertainty, which explicitly includes the phenomenon of wear and tear through its effects on payment monetary currents of the investment process[1] .

For this, we will commence by stating the problem in a determinist sphere and will designate by M payment at the initial moment, relative to acquisition, installation and start up of the investment object, and by a_j, $j = 1, 2, \ldots, n$ the payments arising from the costs of exploitation. When we talk about exploitations costs, it should be taken into account that the items making these up include exclusively, the costs of the corresponding work station, without considering indirect expenses which later have to be included for calculating total cost. Neither, obviously is the depreciation quota included.

It is generally accepted that as time goes by the equipments (investment object) gets older, and wear and tear makes maintenance and repairs more costly. This is one of the reasons why payments increase. As is sufficiently well known another of the reasons for the increase in exploitation payments as time goes by, is determined by the inflation process.

Therefore, the payment current arising from the decision to invest includes, apart from other concepts, one we would now like to point out: the payment current arising from maintenance and repair of the investment object. These payments can be included into the model for selection, either by assigning a number, increasing for each period, or by means of <<wear and tear indices>> $q_j = 1, 2, \ldots, n$, also know by the name of <<unitary wear and tear rates>>, which are multiplied period by period by a previously established figure.

In this sense, the wear and tear rates can be affected, for example, to the price paid for the investment object. But to make the q_j into a percentage of M, which increase as time goes by, means the need to define a q_j for each year of useful life, in such a way as if we call payments for repair and maintenance corresponding to year j, $a_j^{(q)}$ we will arrive at:

$$a_j^{(q)} = M \cdot q_j, \text{ where } q_1 < q_2 < q_3 \cdots < q_n$$

If instead of estimating n rates of wear and tear, only one, q is established which we apply as from the initial payment (for example, $M \cdot d$) and this is accumulated as time goes by, we can write:

$$\begin{aligned}
a_1^{(q)} &= M \cdot d \\
a_2^{(q)} &= M \cdot d(1+q) \\
a_3^{(q)} &= M \cdot d(1+q)^2 \\
&\cdots\cdots\cdots\cdots \\
a_n^{(q)} &= M \cdot d(1+q)^{n-1}
\end{aligned}$$

If we designated with $a^{(c)}$ (and it is considered for greater simplicity, that this is constant), all the payments for each period, excepting those for maintenance and repairs, and it is assumed, in a first approximation, that the inflation rate, s, can also be considered as constant throughout time, we will arrive at the fact that the payment current estimated for each period, could be written as:

$$M$$

$$\begin{aligned}
a_1' &= (a^{(c)} + a_1^{(q)})(1+s) = [a^{(c)} + M \cdot d](1+\mathrm{s}) \\
a_2' &= (a^{(c)} + a_2^{(q)})(1+s)^2 = [a^{(c)} + M \cdot d(1+\mathrm{q})](1+s)^2 \\
a_3' &= (a^{(c)} + a_3^{(q)})(1+s)^3 = [a^{(c)} + M \cdot d(1+\mathrm{q})^2](1+s)^3 \\
&\cdots\cdots\cdots\cdots\cdots\cdots\cdots\cdots \\
a_n' &= (a^{(c)} + a_n^{(q)})(1+s)^n = [a^{(c)} + M \cdot d(1+\mathrm{q})^{n-1}](1+s)^n
\end{aligned}$$

In this case, it has been considered that, setting aside the inflation process, the other payments are not modified by the mere passing of time. We can easily eliminate this hypothesis. It will be sufficient, in the previous formula, to substitute the $a^{(c)}$ for $a_j^{(c)}$, $j = 1, 2, \ldots, n$.

Finally, assuming that the interest rate is known and constant throughout time, we will arrive at the fact that the updated value of the payments current, to prices valid at any given moment, is:

$$P' = M + \sum_{j=1}^{n} a_j'(1+1)^{-j} = M + d^{(c)} \sum_{j=1}^{n} (1+s)^j(1+1)^{-j} + M \cdot d \sum_{j=1}^{n} (1+q)^{j-1}(1+s)^j(1+i)^{-j}$$

which finally can be written as:

$$\boxed{P' = M + \sum_{j=1}^{n} [a^{(c)} + M \cdot d(1+q)^{j-1}](1+s)^j(1+i)^{-j}}$$

With the object of verifying the practical validity of this scheme we are now going to present an example.

In order to generalise, let us assume that the investor has to select several industrial equipments of different characteristics and components. In order to avoid unnecessary operating complications we will limit ourselves to two investment objects, on the understanding that the scheme is automatically extendable to n equipments. Likewise, the estimated current for collections is considered equal for both equipments, therefore it is possible to do without this item for effects of this particular selection study. We will limit ourselves, therefore, to comparing updated payments for each investment object.

As often happens, the operation of both equipments can give rise to a group of payments which, by their very nature, acquire the same level for each equipment. In this case, it will be convenient to do without these payments in the calculations to be done. In this way we will be working with <<differential>> numbers for each object (those appearing by their concept or amount in one current and not the other).

With regard to the first equipment, we are going to assume that its characteristics are such that, apart from the payments in common with the other equipment, to which we referred in the previous paragraph, there are no others different from those arising from maintenance and repair of the investment object (effect of wear and tear). Thus on considering the value of $a^{(c)}$ as null and void for our effects, the previous expression will be reduced, in this case, to:

$$P_1' = M + M \cdot d \sum_{j=1}^{n} (1+q)^{j-1}(1+s)^j(1+i)^{-j}$$

Now we will continue with the numerical aggregation of the variables intervening in each of the formulae.

With regard to the first equipment, we assume an initial payment of M = 51000, and that the experts have considered for year 1, payments derived from wear and tear of 510. Thus, the amount of 510, constitutes the original figure from which we start out and which is in our example, 0.01 of the value of the equipment. For this then d = 0.01 in order for $M \cdot d$ = 510. From this initial estimate a percentage will be established which will allow us to show the growing development of payments for maintenance and repairs. On this occasion an accumulative increase of 21 per cent has been estimated, so that we arrive at: $q = 0.21$. An inflation rate of 5 per cent and an interest rate of 10 percent are considered.

There is another way of doing these estimates, that is quite adequate when reality requires the establishment of an increase that is constant in time for payments made for wear and tear. This consists in assuming, for example, an estimated increase for each period of 255 thousand monetary units. One can see that in our case the increases in payments for maintenance and repairs increase as the equipment gets older. It can be seen that if it were desired to maintain a constant increase in payments, by using this procedure the rate of wear and tear q_j should be considered as variable in time, and, therefore, in the case under study, the q_j will take on the following values:

$$q_2 = 0.50; \quad q_6 = 0.16; \quad q_{10} = 0.10$$
$$q_3 = 0.33; \quad q_7 = 0.14; \quad q_{11} = 0.09$$
$$q_4 = 0.25; \quad q_8 = 0.12; \quad q_{12} = 0.08$$
$$q_5 = 0.20; \quad q_9 = 0.11$$

Now let us move on to the second investment object. We can assume that it is formed by several components, for example 3, each with *a different useful life* and which require different maintenance and repairs (different rates of wear and tear). Let us imagine, in this case, that two of the components require maintenance and repairs of a different nature and that the other suffers no wear and tear whatsoever.

For all this, and this point is particularly important, it is not possible to assume that all payments from the initial moment remain unaltered by the passage of time, because there are substitutions made throughout the economic horizon of some of the components of the investment object. It will be necessary therefore, to separate the payments arising from the corresponding substitutions, from the rest of the exploitation payments.

Let us suppose that payments for acquisition of these components and their useful life are:

First component $\rightarrow M_1 = 29000, \quad n_1 = 12$

Second Component $\rightarrow M_2 = 240, \quad n_2 = 3$

Third component $\rightarrow M_3 = 1000, \quad n_3 = 6$

In this way renewal of the second component will take place every 3 years and of the third component, every 6 years.

Also, if the nature of the components is different a separation will have to be made between maintenance corresponding to each component of the investment object, apart from considering separately, those payments arising from exploitation and those that proceed from the substitutions. In this way we will have an initial payment for maintenance and repairs of the first component equal to $M_1 \cdot d_1$, another for the second component equal to $M_2 \cdot d_2$, and none for the third. In the event of developing this it is considered that they are:

$$M_1 \cdot d_1 = 290, \quad M_2 \cdot d_2 = 12, \quad M_3 \cdot d_3 = 0$$

For the first component we assume the same accumulative rate for wear and tear as for the other investment object, that is to say $q_1 = 0.21$, and for the second $q_2 = 1$.

If we finally assume that in this case $a^{(c)} = 900$ we can construct the following table, in which are detailed the calculations corresponding to the two investment objects.

Moment of the useful life	Updating rate (10 per cent)	Equipment I		
		Initial payment and maintenance ($q = 0,21$)	Payments current with inflation of 5 per cent	Updated payments
0	1	51000	51000	51000
1	0.9090	510	533	484
2	0.8264	617	680	561
3	0.7513	746	863	649
4	0.6830	903	1097	749
5	0.6209	1093	1394	865
6	0.5644	1322	1771	999
7	0.5131	1600	2251	1154
8	0.4665	1936	2860	1334
9	0.4240	2343	3634	1540
10	0.3855	2835	4617	1779
11	0.3504	3431	5868	2056
12	0.3186	4151	7454	2374
P'_I				65543

Moment of the useful life	Updating rate (10 per cent) component	Equipment II				
		Payments for components and constant payments	Maintenance first component Maintenance second	Total Payments current	Payments current wiht inflation of 5 per cent	Updated payments
0	1	30240		30240	30240	30240
1	0.9090	900	290 + 12	1202	1262	1147
2	0.8264	900	350 + 24	1274	1404	1160
3	0.7513	1140	424 + 48	1612	1866	1401
4	0.6830	900	513 + 12	1425	1732	1182
5	0.6209	900	621 + 24	1545	1971	1223
6	0.5644	2140	752 + 48	2940	3939	2223
7	0.5131	900	910 + 12	1822	2563	1315
8	0.4665	900	1101 + 24	2025	2991	1395
9	0.4240	1140	1332 + 48	2520	3909	1657
10	0.3855	900	1612 + 12	2524	4111	1584
11	0.3504	900	1950 + 24	2874	4915	1722
12	0.3186	900	2360 + 48	3308	5940	1892
P'_{II}						48141

As can be seen, with this data and based on the scheme we have described the conclusion is reached that as 48141< 65543, the decision to invest should fall to alternative II.

We insist on the fact that the way to introduce payments for maintenance and repairs depends on the nature of the investment object, which in certain cases can cause a more or less constant increase as it ages, while in others physical deterioration may occur causing progressive wear and tear.

The passage to a context of uncertainty

The case we have shown relative to incorporation of the problem of wear and tear into the investment process, has brought to light the fact that the supporting points for its study are various. This permits us to state that for handling the same situation and same objective it is possible to adopt different premises, the validity of which is subject to the greater or lesser importance of the incidence of the elements that have been explicitly considered in the model. In spite of this, it is difficult to find a determinist scheme that is suitable for representing what current reality requires when faced with a determined situation.

From here stems the interest for handling this problem with the aid of the arithmetic of uncertainty. Also, the passage from certainty to uncertainty, in considering the phenomenon of wear and tear, does not involve any particular problems.

In fact, let us assume that the experts we have consulted relative to the development of payments arising from the physical ageing of an investment object, do not consider it suitable to express their opinions in exact terms and make a request to do so by means of FTN, for example.

If the estimate is made by means of a percentage on the cost of the investment object, as we have used in the sphere of certainty, the problem is merely reduced to a very simple calculation of FTN arithmetic. This would result in:

$$\underset{\sim}{a}_j^{(q)} = M\,(\cdot)\,(q_j^{(1)}, q_j^{(2)}, q_j^{(3)}) = (M \cdot q_j^{(1)}, M \cdot q_j^{(2)}, M \cdot q_j^{(3)})$$
$$j = 1, 2, ..., n$$

on the condition that:

$$(q_1^{(1)}, q_1^{(2)}, q_1^{(3)}) \leqslant (q_2^{(1)}, q_2^{(2)}, q_2^{(3)}) \leqslant \cdots \leqslant (q_n^{(1)}, q_n^{(2)}, q_n^{(3)})$$

If, on the other hand, we start off with a single uncertain rate of wear and tear, $(q^{(1)}, q^{(2)}, q^{(3)})$, which accumulates with the ageing of the machine, applied to an initial payment (which can be exact) relative to the first period, assumption also presented in the case for certainty, we will arrive at certain consequences in the respective payments in the same sense as those arrived at when studying the effects of inflation. In fact, in the same way as the inflation process causes an accumulative increase in payments (and collections), the wear and tear process does also (although not necessarily for collections, if it is not possible to set them off).

In this case we would arrive at:

$$\underset{\sim}{a}_1^{(q)} = M \cdot d$$
$$\underset{\sim}{a}_2^{(q)} = M \cdot d\,(\cdot)\,(1 + q^{(1)}, 1 + q^{(2)}, 1 + q^{(3)})$$

....

$$\underset{\sim}{a}_j^{(q)} = M \cdot d\,(\cdot)\,\underbrace{(1 + q^{(1)}, 1 + q^{(2)}, 1 + q^{(3)})\,(\cdot) \cdots (\cdot)\,(1 + q^{(1)}, 1 + q^{(2)}, 1 + q^{(3)})}_{(j-1)\text{ times}}$$

....

$$\underset{\sim}{a}_n^{(q)} = M \cdot d\,(\cdot)\,\underbrace{(1 + q^{(1)}, 1 + q^{(2)}, 1 + q^{(3)})\,(\cdot) \cdots (\cdot)\,(1 + q^{(1)}, 1 + q^{(2)}, 1 + q^{(3)})}_{(n-1)\text{ times}}$$

Neither does consideration of the remaining payments arising from exploitation of the investment object present too many problems when passing from the sphere of uncertainty. Thus when expressing these by means of FTN that vary for every period, the following can be written:

$$\underset{\sim}{a}_1^{(c)} = (c_1^{(1)}, c_1^{(2)}, c_1^{(3)})$$

....

$$\underset{\sim}{a}_j^{(c)} = (c_j^{(1)}, c_j^{(2)}, c_j^{(3)})$$

....

$$\underset{\sim}{a}_n^{(c)} = (c_n^{(1)}, c_n^{(2)}, c_n^{(3)})$$

In this way the payment current, setting aside the inflation process, will be:

$$M$$

$$\underset{\sim}{a}_1 = [c_1^{(1)} + (c_1^{(2)} - c_1^{(1)})\alpha,\ c_1^{(3)} - (c_1^{(3)} - c_1^{(2)})\alpha]\ (+)\ M \cdot d$$

$$\underset{\sim}{a}_2 = [c_2^{(1)} + (c_2^{(2)} - c_2^{(1)})\alpha,\ c_2^{(3)} - (c_2^{(3)} - c_2^{(2)})\alpha]\ (+)$$
$$(+)\ M \cdot d\ (\cdot)\ [1 + q^{(1)} + (q^{(2)} - q^{(1)})\alpha,\ 1 + q^{(3)} - (q^{(3)} - q^{(2)})\alpha]$$

....

$$\underset{\sim}{a}_j = [c_j^{(1)} + (c_j^{(2)} - c_j^{(1)})\alpha,\ c_j^{(3)} - (c_j^{(3)} - c_j^{(2)})\alpha]\ (+)$$
$$(+)\ M \cdot d\ (\cdot)\ ([1 + q^{(1)} + (q^{(2)} - q^{(1)})\alpha,\ 1 + q^{(3)} - (q^{(3)} - q^{(2)})\alpha])^{j-1}$$

....

$$\underset{\sim}{a}_n = [c_n^{(1)} + (c_n^{(2)} - c_n^{(1)})\alpha,\ c_n^{(3)} - (c_n^{(3)} - c_n^{(2)})\alpha]\ (+)$$
$$(+)\ M \cdot d\ (\cdot)\ ([1 + q^{(1)} + (q^{(2)} - \mathrm{q}^{(1)})\alpha,\ 1 + q^{(3)} - (q^{(3)} - q^{(2)})\alpha])^{n-1}$$

The updating of this payment current is immediate. As this description is known by everyone we will amuse the reader by moving on to a numerical example.

Let us assume that an industrial equipment is put into operation the cost of which is 3000 monetary units and it has a useful life of 3 years. What is wanted is to study its economic <<behaviour>>, for which the opinion of an expert is requested, and he proposes the following:

- Raw materials, labour, power and sundry expenses:
  - Period 1: $(800, 900, 1100) = [800 + 100\alpha,\ 1100 - 200\alpha]$
  - Period 2: $(900, 1200, 1300) = [900 + 300\alpha,\ 1300 - 100\alpha]$
  - Period 3: $(1000, 1100, 1600) = [1000 + 100\alpha,\ 1600 - 500\alpha]$
- Maintenance with a wear and tear rate of (0.15, 0.20, 0.22)
  - Period 1: $M \cdot d = 300$
  - Period 2: $300\ (\cdot)\ (1.15, 1.20, 1.22) = 300\ (\cdot)\ [1.15 + 0.05\alpha,\ 1.22 - 0.02\alpha]$
  - Period 3: $300\ (\cdot)\ (1.15, 1.20, 1.22)\ (\cdot)\ (1.15, 1.20, 1.22) = 300\ (\cdot)\ [(1.15 + 0.05\alpha)(1.15 + 0.05\alpha),\ (1.22 - 0.02\alpha)(1.22 - 0.02\alpha)]$

These opinions are expressed by using the hendecadarian system:

$$[c_j^{(1)} + (c_j^{(2)} - c_j^{(1)})\alpha,\ c_j^{(3)} - (c_j^{(3)} - c_j^{(2)})\alpha]$$

α	$[800 + 100\alpha,$	$1100 - 200\alpha]$	$[900 + 300\alpha,$	$1300 - 100\alpha]$	$[1000 + 100\alpha,$	$1500 - 500\alpha]$
0	800	1100	900	1300	1000	1600
.1	810	1080	930	1290	1010	1550
.2	820	1060	960	1280	1020	1500
.3	830	1040	990	1270	1030	1450
.4	840	1020	1020	1260	1040	1400
.5	850	1000	1050	1250	1050	1350
.6	860	980	1080	1240	1060	1300
.7	870	960	1110	1230	1070	1250
.8	880	940	1140	1220	1080	1200
.9	890	920	1170	1210	1090	1150
1	900		1200		1100	

α	$M \cdot d$	$M \cdot d(\cdot)[1{,}15 + 0.05\alpha,\ 1{,}22 - 0.02\alpha]$ $[345 + 15\alpha,\ 366 - 6\alpha]$		$M \cdot d(\cdot)[1{,}15 + 0.05\alpha,\ 1{,}22 - 0.02\alpha]$ $(\cdot)\ [1{,}15 + 0.05\alpha,\ 1{,}22 - 0.02\alpha]$ $[345 + 15\alpha,\ 366 - 6\alpha]\ (\cdot)$ $[1{,}15 + 0.05\alpha,\ 1{,}22 - 0.02\alpha]$	
0	300	345	366	396.75	446.52
.1	300	346.5	365.4	400.20	445.05
.2	300	348	364.8	403.68	442.62
.3	300	349.5	364.2	407.16	441.89
.4	300	351	363.6	410.67	440.68
.5	300	352.5	363	414.18	439.23
.6	300	354	362.4	417.72	437.77
.7	300	355.5	361.8	421.26	436.33
.8	300	357	361.2	424.83	434.88
.9	300	358.5	360.6	428.40	433.44
1	300	360		432	

Below we obtain the total payments, corresponding to each period, arising from the acquisition and operation of the investment object.

α	Moment 0	Period 1		Period 2		Period 3	
	Ordinary number	FTN		FTN		Fuzzy number	
0	3000	1100	1400	1245	1666	1396.75	2046.52
.1	3000	1110	1380	1276.5	1655.4	1410.20	1995.05
.2	3000	1120	1360	1308	1544.8	1423.68	1942.62
.3	3000	1130	1340	1339.5	1634.2	1437.16	1891.89
.4	3000	1140	1320	1371	1623.6	1450.67	1840.68
.5	3000	1150	1300	1402.5	1613	1464.18	1789.23
.6	3000	1160	1280	1434	1602.4	1477.72	1737.77
.7	3000	1170	1260	1465.5	1591.8	1491.26	1686.33
.8	3000	1180	1240	1497	1581.2	1504.83	1634.88
.9	3000	1190	1220	1528.5	1570.6	1518.40	1583.44
1	3000	1200		1560		1532	

The estimate of the updated value of the payments, is now reduced to calculation of the product of the payments relative to each period by the updating rates. If the following are considered as unitary rates of interest for each period:

$$(i_1^{(1)}, i_1^{(2)}, i_1^{(3)}) = (0.08, 0.10, 0.11)$$
$$(i_2^{(1)}, i_2^{(2)}, i_2^{(3)}) = (0.06, 0.09, 0.11)$$
$$(i_3^{(1)}, i_3^{(2)}, i_3^{(3)}) = (0.05, 0.06, 0.10)$$

we arrive at, the following as fuzzy updating rates:

$$\frac{1}{1+\underset{\sim}{i}_1} = \left[\frac{1}{1.11 - 0.01\alpha}, \frac{1}{1.08 + 0{,}02\alpha}\right]$$

$$\frac{1}{1+\underset{\sim}{i}_1}\cdot\frac{1}{1+\underset{\sim}{i}_2} = \left[\frac{1}{1.11 - 0.01\alpha}\cdot\frac{1}{1.11 - 0.02\alpha}, \frac{1}{1.08 + 0.02\alpha}\cdot\frac{1}{1.06 + 0.03\alpha}\right]$$

$$\frac{1}{1+\underset{\sim}{i}_1}\cdot\frac{1}{1+\underset{\sim}{i}_2}\cdot\frac{1}{1+\underset{\sim}{i}_3} = \left[\frac{1}{1.11 - 0.01\alpha}\cdot\frac{1}{1.11 - 0.02\alpha}\cdot\frac{1}{1.10 - 0.04\alpha}, \frac{1}{1.08 + 0.02\alpha}\cdot\frac{1}{1.06 + 0.03\alpha}\cdot\frac{1}{1.05 + 0.01\alpha}\right]$$

In the case of using the hendecadarian system, we can write the following:

α	$1/(1+\underset{\sim}{i}_1)$		$[1/(1+\underset{\sim}{i}_1)]\,(\cdot)\,[1/(1+\underset{\sim}{i}_2)]$		$[1/(1+\underset{\sim}{i}_1)]\,(\cdot)\,[1/(1+\underset{\sim}{i}_2)]\,(\cdot)$ $(\cdot)\,[1/(1+\underset{\sim}{i}_3)]$	
0	0.9009	0.9259	0.8116	0.8735	0.7378	0.8319
.1	0.9017	0.9242	0.8138	0.8694	0.7425	0.8272
.2	0.9025	0.9225	0.8160	0.8653	0.7472	0.8226
.3	0.9033	0.9208	0.8182	0.8613	0.7520	0.8180
.4	0.9041	0.9191	0.8204	0.8573	0.7568	0.8134
.5	0.9049	0.9174	0.8227	0.8534	0.7617	0.8089
.6	0.9057	0.9157	0.8241	0.8494	0.7666	0.8044
.7	0.9066	0.9140	0.8272	0.8455	0.7716	0.7999
.8	0.9074	0.9124	0.8283	0.8417	0.7766	0.7955
.9	0.9082	0.9107	0.8317	0.8378	0.7817	0.7911
1	0.9090		0.8340		0.7868	

Now we can proceed to calculate the updated value of the payments current, carrying out the product, level by level, of the payments for each year of useful life of the investment object by the corresponding updating rate. We will arrive at:

α	Moment 0	Period 1		Period 2		Period 3		Total	
0	3000	990.99	1296.26	1010.44	1455.25	1030.52	1702.50	6031.95	7454.95
.1	3000	1000.88	1275.39	1038.81	1439.20	1047.07	1650.30	6086.76	7364.89
.2	3000	1010.80	1254.60	1067.32	1423.24	1063.77	1597.99	6141.89	7275.83
.3	3000	1020.72	1233.87	1095.97	1407.53	1080.74	1547.56	6197.43	7188.96
.4	3000	1030.67	1213.21	1124.76	1391.91	1097.86	1497.20	6253.29	7102.32
.5	3000	1040.63	1192.62	1153.83	1376.53	1115.26	1447.30	6309.72	7016.45
.6	3000	1050.61	1172.09	1181.75	1361.07	1132.82	1397.77	6365.18	6930.93
.7	3000	1060.72	1151.64	1212.26	1345.86	1150.65	1348.89	6423.63	6846.39
.8	3000	1070.73	1131.37	1239.96	1330.89	1168.65	1300.54	6479.34	6762.80
.9	3000	1080.75	1111.05	1271.25	1315.84	1186.93	1252.65	6535.93	6679.54
1	3000	1090.80		1301.04		1205.37		6597.21	

In this way we arrive at a result expressed by means of a fuzzy number (non-triangular) representing the estimate of the updated payments arising from the decision to invest. In this fuzzy number, it can be seen that the greatest uncertainty, at level $\alpha = 0$, is given by the interval [6031.95, 7454.05]. At the maximum level of assumption payments estimated at 6597.21 take place. This result can be graphically represented as follows (figure 8.1):

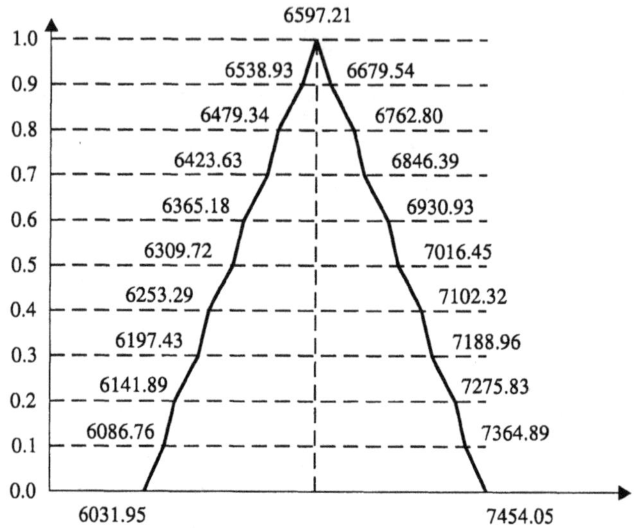

Figure 8.1.

The result we have arrived at through this process allows for an uncertain estimate of updated payments, among which payments arising from the wear and tear of the investment object have been individualised. This scheme, can well be extended if the inflation phenomenon were to be included. To include inflation is simple, so we are not going to detain ourselves on this aspect of the subject.

Different ways of expressing the opinion of counter-experts

With the development of the previous example it was seen that the results obtained depend, principally, on the initial estimates, frequently made by an expert. Again as we saw in the previous chapter, we now know how to obtain, a reduction in the degree of subjectivity that all individual opinions include, with a certain technical and operationally practical ease. For this it is sufficient to resort to *m*-expertons in order to obtain the aggregation of the counter-experts opinion from certain initial estimates. Although this is possible, and even in some cases sufficient, we are now going to propose a process that we feel could well give us good results. This is a procedure based on the separation of the opinion of the counter-experts, in which, different ways of representing their positioning relative to a pre-established result (fuzzy number obtained), are used.

Taking into account the difficulty normally represented by consulting counter-experts by asking them to give their position in the resulting fuzzy number, even though this were to be expressed in the form of α-cuts, we are going to consider a simplification, through a confidence interval given by the lower and upper extremes of the fuzzy number, which in our example is:

$$\underset{\sim}{P} = [6031.95,\ 7454.05] \simeq [6032,\ 7454]$$

Starting out then from this information we resort to the opinion of several counter-experts:

In summary their positions could be as follows:

1. They show agreement relative to the limiting of uncertainty that is to say with the extremes of the interval.
2. They believe that uncertainty is greater than that expressed in the estimate, therefore the interval forming the extremes should be extended.
3. They assume that the interval formed by the extremes is excessive, therefore they consider these should be positioned further within the interval, and in this way uncertainty would be reduced.
4. They feel that it is an estimate that is not situated in its just terms and wish to establish a <<transfer>> in block of the same (that is of the interval).

Let us now move on the see how to reflect each of these groups of opinions. For this it has to be admitted that the quality of the experts is proven and that their reasoning is sufficiently solid so as to be taken into account. On the contrary, it would be sufficient for, the position considered as not having a minimum of solvency, to be left out of the process.

- Relative to the first of the groups, given its coincidence with the result already obtained, its components show, in a certain way, a confirmation of the basic estimate. Only as an example, let us suppose that 3 experts are included in this line of thinking. Therefore, all of these would have given a *positioning* that could be reflected by means of interval [0, 1].
- With regard to the second group, here we have different positions which go from a reduction of the lower extreme of the interval to accepting the upper extreme or accepting the lower extreme and increasing the upper extreme, right up to an increase in both directions of the interval, which automatically means, in this letter case, an initial increase of the degree of uncertainty. Let us suppose in our didactic example, that 3 experts give their opinion in this sense, estimating as follows:

[5500, 6900]

[6500, 7500]

[6000, 7500]

Obviously, if these estimates are accepted as valid a modification of the base estimate will have occurred and this now becomes:

[5500, 7500]

- The experts of the third group can be positioned in different ways within the initial interval [6032, 7454], the most common being:

  a) Positioning in overall values. Let us assume that 2 experts give their opinion that their estimate is:

  [6500, 7000]

  [6200, 7200]

  b) Positioning by means of intervals in [0, 1] in accordance with the following semantic hendecadarian scale:

  0: For 6032
  .1: Practically 6032
  .2: Nearly 6032
  .3: Near to 6032
  .4: Nearer to 6032 than to 7454
  .5: As close to 6032 as to 7454
  .6: Nearer to 7454 than to 6032
  .7: Near to 7454
  .8: Nearly 7454
  .9: Practically 7454
  1: For 7454

In our hypothetical case, for example, there are 4 experts who select this procedure and give us:

[.5, .9], [.3, .7], [.6, .8], [.8, 1]

Up to now we have 12 experts who it can be considered will form a part of the three first groups. In order to obtain an aggregate opinion for all of them we can resort to several procedures. Let us first take a look at a very simple one, consisting of converting all the data into valuations of R^+ (overall estimate) and then obtaining the mean.

Since only the last 4 experts have expressed their opinion in [0, 1], we are going to convert this information into intervals in R^+. For this proportional positioning will be considered as valid, and this is expressed by:

$$[P_1, P_2] = [\alpha_1^{(j)}, \alpha_2^{(j)}]\ (\cdot)\ (7454 - 6032)\ (+)\ 6032 = [\alpha_1^{(j)}, \alpha_2^{(j)}]\ (\cdot)\ 1423\ (+)\ 6032$$

where $[\alpha_1^{(j)}, \alpha_2^{(j)}]$ is the valuation in [0, 1] of each expert.

We will arrive at the following for the 4 experts:

[6742.5, 7311.7]

[6457.9, 7027.1]

[6884.8, 7169.4]

[7169.4, 7454]

Finally we will move on to incorporate the opinions expressed by the fourth group of experts which, let us recall, wishes to make a transfer in block of the initial estimate given them for examination, which is [6032, 7454]. We are going to take an interval which is as wide as possible within what can reasonably be considered as viable, which obviously must include the interval that finally has been considered as the base of the counter-expertise [5500, 7500], for example, [5000, 8500]. A positioning expressed in [0, 1] would represent the fact that [6032, 7454] would mean a positioning equal to [.3, .7] in accordance with the linear equation expressed previously[2].

Now we will move on to a process of transfer, for which we will resort to parameterisation.

Using parameterisation requires detailed knowledge of certain aspects relative to the operation of this technique, in order to choose the most suitable operator for each case.

Many operators are known, which allow identified parameterisation. Simply as an indication we mention the following:

$$\underset{\sim}{p}^{(\lambda)} = \frac{\underset{\sim}{p}}{1 + \lambda\, \underset{\sim}{\bar{p}}} \quad , \lambda \in\,]-1, \infty)$$

$$\underset{\sim}{p}^{(\lambda)} = \frac{(1 + \lambda)\, \underset{\sim}{p}}{1 + \lambda\, \underset{\sim}{p}} \quad , \lambda \in\,]-1, \infty) \leftarrow$$

We will select the second, in rather an arbitrary fashion, stating at the same time that we have not been induced to this by anything else than the desire to make a fluid exposition that avoids an excess of breaks, such as would happen with a discussion on the best operator for each specific case[3].

Secondly we should explain to the group of counter-experts the sense they should give to their reply so that parameterisation responds in the most efficient way possible to their requirements. They should be advised that if they assign valuations to λ between 0 and -1 (negative) the values will decrease, while as the values get higher there will be an increase in their estimate.

Let us suppose that this last group of counter-experts is formed by 3 people giving to λ values of $\lambda = 2$, $\lambda = 0.75$ and $\lambda = -0.25$. By starting out from a positioning of [.3, .7] we will arrive at:

$$[p_1, p_2]^{(2)} = \left[\frac{(1+2)(.3)}{1+2(.3)}, \frac{(1+2)(.7)}{1+2(.7)} \right] = [.562, .875]$$

$$[p_1, p_2]^{(0.75)} = \left[\frac{(1+0.75)(.3)}{1+0.75(.3)}, \frac{(1+0.75)(.7)}{1+0.75(.7)} \right] = [.428, .803]$$

$$[p_1, p_2]^{(-0.25)} = \left[\frac{(1-0.25)(.3)}{1-0.25(.3)}, \frac{(1-0.25)(.7)}{1-0.25(.7)} \right] = [.243, .636]$$

If we now convert these intervals into values of R^+ we will arrive at, respectively:

$$5000 + 3500 \,(\cdot)\, [.562, .875] = [6967, 8063]$$

$$5000 + 3500 \,(\cdot)\, [.428, .803] = [6498, 7811]$$

$$5000 + 3500 \,(\cdot)\, [.243, .636] = [5850, 7226]$$

We can see then that in the first two cases the interval [6032, 7454] has undergone a transfer to the right while in the third the transfer has been to the left.

Aggregation of the opinion of the experts

Now let us gather together, in a homogeneous manner and in absolute values, the opinion of the 15 counter-experts. This will be:

Expert	*Valuation*[4]
1	[6032, 7454]
2	[6032, 7454]
3	[6032, 7454]
4	[5500, 6900]
5	[6500, 7500]
6	[6000, 7500]
7	[6500, 7000]
8	[6200, 7200]
9	[6742, 7312]
10	[6458, 7027]
11	[6885, 7169]
12	[7169, 7454]
13	[6967, 8063]
14	[6498, 7811]
15	[5850, 7226]

Taking into account the changes that have taken place in the lower and upper limits of the initial estimate, it is now necessary to expand the R^+ interval, within which the opinions move, which will now be, [5500, 8063]. If the intention is to present an aggregation of this result in a simple fashion, recourse could be made to the mean of the levels.

As is known the mean will be:

$$\overset{m}{\underset{\sim}{p}} = \left[\frac{1}{n} \sum_{i=1}^{n} p_i^{(1)}, \frac{1}{n} \sum_{i=1}^{n} p_i^{(2)} \right]$$

where $p_i^{(1)}$ and $p_i^{(2)}$ are respectively the upper and lower extremes of the intervals corresponding to counter-expert i.

This will be:

$$\overset{m}{\underset{\sim}{p}} = [6357, 7368]$$

In this way a first aggregate estimate of the opinion of all the experts is obtained.

Now we will pass on to study the process of aggregation based on the R^+-expertons. For this we will start out from the expanded interval [5500, 8063], in which all the counter-experts in [0, 1] can be positioned, by means of the hendecadarian system.

In this case it will be necessary to transform those estimates made in R^+, into estimates in [0, 1] by using the equation:

$$[\alpha_1, \alpha_2] = \frac{[P_1, P_2] \,(-)\, P_*}{P^* - P_*}$$

Where P_* and P^* are the extremes of the widest interval which, in this didactic example, are respectively, 5500 and 8063.

From the 15 absolute valuations we will arrive at:

$$[\alpha_1^{(1)}, \alpha_2^{(1)}] = [\alpha_1^{(2)}, \alpha_2^{(2)}] = [\alpha_1^{(3)}, \alpha_2^{(3)}] = \frac{[6032, 7454]\,(-)\,5500}{2563} = [0.20, 0.76] \cong [0.2, 0.8]$$

for the first experts:

$$[\alpha_1^{(4)}, \alpha_2^{(4)}] = \frac{[5500, 6900]\,(-)\,5500}{2563} = [0, 0.54] \cong [0, 0.5]$$

$$[\alpha_1^{(5)}, \alpha_2^{(5)}] = \frac{[6500, 7500]\,(-)\,5500}{2563} = [0.39, 0.79] \cong [0.4, 0.8]$$

$$[\alpha_1^{(6)}, \alpha_2^{(6)}] = \frac{[6000, 7500]\,(-)\,5500}{2563} = [0.19, 0.79] \cong [0.2, 0.8]$$

$$[\alpha_1^{(7)}, \alpha_2^{(7)}] = \frac{[6500, 7000]\,(-)\,5500}{2563} = [0.39, 0.58] \cong [0.4, 0.6]$$

$$[\alpha_1^{(8)}, \alpha_2^{(8)}] = \frac{[6200, 7200]\,(-)\,5500}{2563} = [0.27, 0.66] \cong [0.3, 0.7]$$

$$[\alpha_1^{(9)}, \alpha_2^{(9)}] = \frac{[6742, 7312]\,(-)\,5500}{2563} = [0.48, 0.71] \cong [0.5, 0.7]$$

$$[\alpha_1^{(10)}, \alpha_2^{(10)}] = \frac{[6458, 7027]\,(-)\,5500}{2563} = [0.37, 0.59] \cong [0.4, 0.6]$$

$$[\alpha_1^{(11)}, \alpha_2^{(11)}] = \frac{[6885, 7169]\,(-)\,5500}{2563} = [0.54, 0.65] \cong [0.5, 0.7]$$

$$[\alpha_1^{(12)}, \alpha_2^{(12)}] = \frac{[7169, 7454]\,(-)\,5500}{2563} = [0.65, 0.76] \cong [0.6, 0.8]$$

$$[\alpha_1^{(13)}, \alpha_2^{(13)}] = \frac{[6967, 8063]\,(-)\,5500}{2563} = [0.57, 1] \cong [0.6, 1]$$

$$[\alpha_1^{(14)}, \alpha_2^{(14)}] = \frac{[6498, 7811]\ (-)\ 5500}{2563} = [0.38, 0.90] \cong [0.4, 0.9]$$

$$[\alpha_1^{(15)}, \alpha_2^{(15)}] = \frac{[5850, 7226]\ (-)\ 5500}{2563} = [0.13, 0.67] \cong [0.1, 0.7]$$

So as not to move away from the hendecadarian system, we have rounded off the extremes of these intervals to tenths. This simplification in no way clouds the process, since this survives with the use of any other system it is desired to use[5].

We are fully aware of the manner of obtaining the corresponding experton. First the times that the experts have expressed the same valuation as the upper and lower extreme is calculated. In this way the following table will be constructed:

	[5500, 8063]	
0	1	
.1	1	
.2	4	
.3	1	
.4	4	
.5	2	1
.6	2	2
.7		4
.8		6
.9		1
1		1

From this statistic we can now obtain the normalised frequencies, by dividing each number by the number of experts (in this case fifteen). We then arrive at:

	[5500,	8063]
0	$0.06\widehat{6}$	
.1	$0.06\widehat{6}$	
.2	$0.26\widehat{6}$	
.3	$0.06\widehat{6}$	
.4	$0.26\widehat{6}$	
.5	$0.13\widehat{3}$	$0.06\widehat{6}$
.6	$0.13\widehat{3}$	$0.13\widehat{3}$
.7		$0.26\widehat{6}$
.8		0.400
.9		$0.06\widehat{6}$
1		$0.06\widehat{6}$

By means of complementary accumulation the corresponding experton $\underset{\sim}{\rho}$, is found, which will be:

	[5500,	8063]
0	1	1
.1	$0.93\widehat{3}$	1
.2	$0.86\widehat{6}$	1
.3	0.600	1
.4	$0.53\widehat{3}$	1
.5	$0.26\widehat{6}$	1
.6	$0.13\widehat{3}$	$0.93\widehat{3}$
.7	0	0.800
.8	0	$0.53\widehat{3}$
.9	0	$0.13\widehat{3}$
1	0	$0.06\widehat{6}$

the mathematical probability of which is:

$$\varepsilon(\underset{\sim}{p}) = [0.33\overset{\frown}{3}, 0.74\overset{\frown}{6}]$$

In order to pass over from the $\underset{\sim}{p}$ experton to the R^+-experton, and having accepted the linearity in the behaviour of the valuations, we do:

$$\underset{\sim}{P} = 5500 + 2563\,(\text{Experton}) = R^+\text{-experton}$$

α	Experton		R^+-experton	
0	1	1	8063	8063
.1	0.933	1	7892	8063
.2	0.866	1	7719	8063
.3	0.600	1	7038	8063
.4	0.533	1	6867	8063
.5	0.266	1	6183	8063
.6	0.133	0.933	5842	7892
.7	0	0.800	5500	7550
.8	0	0.533	5500	6867
.9	0	0.133	5500	5842
1	0	0.066	5500	5671

The mathematical probability of the R^+-experton will be:

$$\varepsilon(\underset{\sim}{P}) = [6354, 7414]$$

This result should coincide with the one obtained by using the same linear equation that was used before with the $\underset{\sim}{p}$, experton but now based on mathematical probabilities.

In effect:

$$\varepsilon(\underset{\sim}{P}) = 5500 + 2563\ (\cdot)\ \varepsilon(\underset{\sim}{p}) = 5500 + 2563\ (\cdot)\ [0.33\overset{\frown}{3}, 0.74\overset{\frown}{6}] = [6354, 7414]$$

In this way we obtain an estimate that includes, apart from the initial opinion, that of all the counter-experts[6].

The doubtless advantage, even in the case such as the one presented where we have abstained from using non-linear operators, is that with the use of the expertons information has been retained to the end. The entropy has only been made to fall in the last operations, due to the fact of having obtained the mathematical probability.

Having made these technical considerations aimed, wherever possible, at making the estimates, which by their very nature are subjective, more objective, let us return to the initial problem to conclude by saying that the problem of wear and tear in equipment, is one of the constants for analysis of investment selection for equipment assets. Its inclusion by economists in the modelling process, has not always taken place explicitly. On the other hand its study is very frequent within the sphere of reliability of material work means and in systems using advanced technology.

We feel that both aspects, technology and economy, should be made compatible in order for them to be complemented. It is true to say that wear and tear rates cannot be estimated efficiently if they are not preceded by technical studies (in all aspects) relative to the principal components and assembly of the same.

Now, the rapid changes in production and management systems, as well as the rhythm with which innovations occur makes it very difficult, both for engineers and economists, to make the relative study of elements having an incidence on wear and tear. The incorporation of fuzzy logic constitutes, in this sense, an invaluable aid for those having the responsibility in companies and institutions of managing this element, that is the decision to invest, so very basic for staying competitive.

References

1 J. Gil Aluja:<<El fenómeno de desgaste en un proceso de inversión>>, Proceedings of the III AEDEM Congress, Bucarest, 5-7 September, 1994.

2 We continue to express the opinions by means of the hendecadarian system.

3 Any reader interested in this problem can readily consult: A.Kaufmann and J. Gil Aluja: *Técnicas especiales para la gestión de expertos,* Milladoiro, Santiago de Compostela, 1993, section 16.

4 We have done away with the decimals, rounding off the corresponding numbers to whole numbers, for experts 9, 10, 11, and 12.

5 With the object of ensuring the opinions in a better way, in the case where 5 hundredths were obtained the tenth has been chosen which gives a greater extension to the interval (greater uncertainty) although with this the upper extreme of the mathematical probability which will be obtained will be somewhat larger than the number strictly corresponding to it.

6 Since no <<non linear>> operators have been used in the process, the result should be the same as that obtained through the means, but the simplifications used and the rounding up which was necessary to keep us within the hendecadarian system, have given rise to certain differences.

9 The incidence of technical progress on investments

Incorporation of technical progress

In latter years creativity is one of the elements, which has burst upon the economic field with the greatest impact. Modern techniques, drawn up for natural stimulus of the imagination[1], have been divulged in an environment that is favourable to innovative work as, businessmen and managers become aware that the survival of companies and institutions will only be possible with the strengthening of research activity aimed at obtaining new products, new processes and new organisations, permitting differentiating results (products and services, for example) and/or results that are economically more advantageous.

The process of permanent evolution (and even revolution) to which economic systems are subjected as a consequence of innovating activity means that the economic situation itself is impelled by these innovations, the result both of creation of new products and methods for manufacture and the start up of new organisations, and in general, the incorporation of new production and management methods.

Economic science has given a lot of attention to the concept of innovation almost since its very beginnings. In order to verify this it is sufficient to recall Schumpeter who talked about this way back in 1911. It is perhaps in the field of investment selection where there has been excessive delay, if we take into account the extraordinary importance that this element has always entailed, particularly for medium and long-term processes. But this interest is reinforced when rapid evolution of events takes place in economic realities. We are well aware of the difficulties involved in the incorporation of the innovative process in drawing up investment models. However we feel that, in a first approximation, the consideration, among other possible elements, of *technical progress* may give rise to fruitful thought, particularly when accompanied by a reduction in costs. Although this element is obviously not the only one representing this phenomenon in the company, we are talking about one of the most significant, because it takes part in a fundamental way in the yield of human labour, that is to say in productivity.

In our opinion all we have mentioned above will now allow us to enter upon the object of this chapter. For this we propose bringing attention to bear on the incidence of technical progress on the collection and payment currents arising from the decision to intervene in an investment object. Firstly let us say, that if the inflation phenomenon is set aside, there will be a consequent reduction in exploitation payments. We must also bear in mind that pressures by the consumer in the product market will give rise to price reductions for this reason, and therefore a reduction in the collection current.

On other occasions[2] we have attempted to draw up a model for selection in which technical progress appeared explicitly as an agglutinating agent for innovative activities causing reductions in costs and prices. The instruments known at that time impelled us to limit our studies to the sphere of determinism, by using the arithmetic of certainty for this. Today we believe that it is useful to generalise those schemes in order for them to be valid in systems governed by uncertainty, although for a better structural method of this chapter we feel that it could be useful to take a brief look at those works considered as classical.

If it is taken into account that the word innovation can be used for <<meaning new products and new methods of manufacturing the same; it also includes new markets and organisations and even new economic principals as guides lines to politics>>[3], at the same time innovations cause variations in technology which acquire so much importance in the normal development of business activities. And this is so because it constitutes the basic motor of all possible increases in labour productivity, which has an incidence, as can be deduced from what we have said before, both in the price of production factors, and in the maintenance cost of the same. It should not come as a surprise then when the conclusion is reached that <<investment without innovation, generally constitutes a waste>>[4].

Interest then, in studying the incidence that the inroad of *technical progress* has had on the investment process, would appear to be totally justified.

For this we feel that it would be useful if we incorporated the monetary consequences of technical progress into the currents of collections and payments arising from the decision to invest. Obviously, if the inflation phenomenon is set aside, a reduction in the acquisition price of the future investment objects and also in the exploitation payments should occur in consequence, always under the hypothesis that there is *no substantial variation* in the characteristics of the equipment, nor in the products or services made or rendered with the same.

We are going to call the annual unitary rate of technical progress k, which initially will be considered constant in time. Under the hypothesis according to which the effects of technical progress are felt even when no change exists in the investment object (technical progress refers to advances in organisation, management, raw materials, processes... and are quite capable of appearing with more or less antiquated equipment), and a payment or collection estimated for moment j would be affected, as a consequence of technical progress, by the coefficient:

$$(1 + k)^{-j}$$

When it is possible to estimate for each period a technical progress rate k_j, $j = 1, 2, \ldots, n$, then the coefficient would be:

$$(1 + k_1)^{-1}(1 + k_2)^{-1} \cdots (1 + k_j)^{-1}$$

We would hasten to state the difficulties to be found in estimating these economic parameters in the sphere of certainty. For this reason we are not going to entertain ourselves any more in this field and will pass on directly to the sphere of uncertainty.

For this, we are going to consider that the annual unitary rates of technical progress are expressed by fuzzy triangular numbers $(k_j^{(1)}, k_j^{(2)}, k_j^{(3)})$, $j = 1, 2, \ldots, n$.

If these FTN are expressed as α-cuts, they can be represented as follows.

$$[k_j^{(1)} + (k_j^{(2)} - k_j^{(1)})\alpha,\ k_j^{(3)} - (k_j^{(3)} - k_j^{(2)})\alpha], \quad j = 1, 2, \ldots, n$$

It can be assumed as a first approximation that technical progress affects exploitation collections and payments with the same intensity, whatever the period under consideration. The elimination of this hypothesis does not cause any greater problems.

Having accepted this clause and taking into account the reduction in costs and prices, it can be admitted that annual profits from exploitation for the first year, estimated at constant prices, will be affected by certain coefficients, as a consequence of technical progress:

$$\left[\frac{1}{1 + k_1^{(3)} - (k_1^{(3)} - k_1^{(2)})\alpha}, \frac{1}{1 + k_1^{(1)} + (k_1^{(2)} - k_1^{(1)})\alpha}\right]$$

For the second period we will have:

$$\left[\frac{1}{1 + k_1^{(3)} - (k_1^{(3)} - k_1^{(2)})\alpha} \cdot \frac{1}{1 + k_2^{(3)} - (k_2^{(3)} - k_2^{(2)})\alpha},\right.$$

$$\left., \frac{1}{1 + k_1^{(1)} + (k_1^{(2)} - k_1^{(1)})\alpha} \cdot \frac{1}{1 + k_1^{(1)} + (k_2^{(2)} - k_2^{(1)})\alpha}\right]$$

and so on successively.

The mechanics of the operations will be the same as used for interest rates, and we will have smaller values as the estimates of exploitation profits refer to more distant periods in time, if we are only considering the simple effect of technical progress.

We can now ask ourselves what would be the accumulated effect of the inflation and technical progress rates. Well, if we place ourselves in the certainty sphere, it can be said that, when inflation is greater than technical progress, there is an increase as time goes by in monetary masses of collections and payments, a quite normal phenomenon in latter years. But also the contrary effect could happen and that in a particular economic sector or for a particular product, inflation were to be surpassed by technical progress, and then we would have a decrease in prices even with a high rate of inflation. In preceding decades this was the case of certain products containing electronic components.

Placed in a context of uncertainty, the increase or decrease in prices for future periods, will depend on the accumulation of the products:

$$[1 + s_j^{(1)} + (s_j^{(2)} - s_j^{(1)})\alpha, 1 + s_j^{(3)} - (s_j^{(3)} - s_j^{(2)})\alpha](\cdot)$$

$$(\cdot)\left[\frac{1}{1 + k_j^{(3)} - (k_j^{(3)} - k_j^{(2)})\alpha}, \frac{1}{1 + k_j^{(1)} + (k_j^{(2)} - k_j^{(1)})\alpha}\right]$$

$$j = 1, 2, ..., n$$

Or, what comes to the same thing, since we are in the field of the R^+, of the successive accumulation, by means of products, of:

$$\left[\frac{1 + s_j^{(1)} + (s_j^{(2)} - s_j^{(1)})\alpha}{1 + k_j^{(3)} - (k_j^{(3)} - k_j^{(2)})\alpha}, \frac{1 + s_j^{(3)} - (s_j^{(3)} - s_j^{(2)})\alpha}{1 + k_j^{(1)} + (k_j^{(2)} - k_j^{(1)})\alpha}\right], \quad j = 1, 2, ..., n$$

Thus if we consider period 2 for example, we will have:

$$\left[\frac{1 + s_1^{(1)} + (s_1^{(2)} - s_1^{(1)})\alpha}{1 + k_1^{(3)} - (k_1^{(3)} - k_1^{(2)})\alpha} \cdot \frac{1 + s_2^{(1)} + (s_2^{(2)} - s_2^{(1)})\alpha}{1 + k_2^{(3)} - (k_2^{(3)} - k_2^{(2)})\alpha},\right.$$

$$\left., \frac{1 + s_1^{(3)} - (s_1^{(3)} - s_1^{(2)})\alpha}{1 + k_1^{(1)} + (k_1^{(2)} - k_1^{(1)})\alpha} \cdot \frac{1 + s_2^{(3)} - (s_2^{(3)} - s_2^{(2)})\alpha}{1 + k_2^{(1)} + (k_2^{(2)} - k_2^{(1)})\alpha}\right]$$

When the resulting corresponding fuzzy numbers are greater than the unit, that is that whatever the value of $\alpha \in [0, 1]$the lower extreme of any interval is >1, the estimate of inflation and technical progress will always give rise to an increase in profits. But when one or some of the intervals (although not all) situate the lower extreme below the unit, we could be faced with the phenomenon of a future reduction or an increase in prices. In order to find out to what degree either one or the other of these circumstances occur we will resort to any of the known criteria, among which can be mentioned the criterion of possibility and the index of consent which have already been considered. In the event that all the upper extremes of the interval were to be less than the unit, there would be a future reduction in profits.

Let us now move on to use the technical progress coefficients, in conjunction with those for inflation, within a criterion of selection. For this we are going to assume that both collections and payments arising from the decision to invest are estimated through FTN. Thus if we continue with the same symbols as were used in the previous chapter, we have:

$$\underset{\sim}{a}^{(c)} = \text{Constant payments for each period}$$

$$M(\cdot)\, d(\cdot)\, (1 + \underset{\sim}{q})^{j-1} = \text{Payments arising from wear and tear at moment } j.$$

$$\underset{\sim}{b}_j = \text{Collections estimated at moment } j..$$

Exploitation profits at a moment j can be expressed as:

$$\underset{\sim}{c}_j = \underset{\sim}{b}_j\, (-)\, [\underset{\sim}{a}^{(c)}\, (+)\, M(\cdot)\, d(\cdot)\, (1\, (+)\, \underset{\sim}{q})^{j-1}], \quad j = 1, 2, ..., n$$

Even when $\underset{\sim}{a}^{(c)}$, $\underset{\sim}{b}_j$ and $\underset{\sim}{q}$ are FTN, normally $\underset{\sim}{c}_j$ will not be, as a consequence of the non-linear operation $(1\, (+)\, \underset{\sim}{q})^{j-1}$. (Obviously, excepted are the cases in which $j = 1, 2$, as they are a FTN resulting from the product of a crisp number by a FTN). In spite of this, and with the object of not making later development excessively or unnecessarily complex, we will substitute the resulting fuzzy number by a triangular approximation. This will be:

$$\underset{\sim}{b}_j = (b_j^{(1)}, b_j^{(2)}, b_j^{(3)})$$

$$\underset{\sim}{a}^{(c)} = (a_1^{(c)}, a_2^{(c)}, a_3^{(c)})$$

$$\underset{\sim}{d}_j = M(\cdot)\, d(\cdot)\, (1\, (+)\, \underset{\sim}{q})^{j-1} = (d_j^{(1)}, d_j^{(2)}, d_j^{(3)}), \quad \text{triangular approximation}$$

$$\underset{\sim}{c}_j = (c_j^{(1)}, c_j^{(2)}, c_j^{(3)})$$

As a result of the corresponding operations, the FTN, $\underset{\sim}{c}_j$ should also be considered as a triangular approximation.

On expressing $\underset{\sim}{c}_j$ in the form of α-cuts, we arrive at:

$$c_j^{(\alpha)} = [c_j^{(1)} + (c_j^{(2)} - c_j^{(1)})\alpha,\; c_j^{(3)} - (c_j^{(3)} - c_j^{(2)})\alpha], \quad j = 1, 2, ..., n$$

Now we will include, inflation and technical progress, and profit for a period j:

$$[c_j^{(1)} + (c_j^{(2)} - c_j^{(1)})\alpha, c_j^{(3)} - (c_j^{(3)} - c_j^{(2)})\alpha](\cdot)$$

$$(\cdot)\left[\frac{1 + s^{(1)} + (s^{(2)} - s^{(1)})\alpha}{1 + k^{(3)} - (k^{(3)} - k^{(2)})\alpha}, \frac{1 + s^{(3)} - (s^{(3)} - s^{(2)})\alpha}{1 + k^{(1)} + (k^{(2)} - k^{(1)})\alpha}\right]^j, \quad j = 1, 2, ..., n$$

When the rates of inflation and technical progress vary on passing from one period to the next, which is the more general case, this expression should be adequately modified.

For period 1:

$$[c_1^{(1)} + (c_1^{(2)} - c_1^{(1)})\alpha, c_1^{(3)} - (c_1^{(3)} - c_1^{(2)})\alpha](\cdot)$$

$$(\cdot)\left[\frac{1 + s_1^{(1)} + (s_1^{(2)} - s_1^{(1)})\alpha}{1 + k_1^{(3)} - (k_1^{(3)} - k_1^{(2)})\alpha}, \frac{1 + s_1^{(3)} - (s_1^{(3)} - s_1^{(2)})\alpha}{1 + k_1^{(1)} + (k_1^{(2)} - k_1^{(1)})\alpha}\right]$$

For period 2:

$$[c_2^{(1)} + (c_2^{(2)} - c_2^{(1)})\alpha, c_2^{(3)} - (c_2^{(3)} - c_2^{(2)})\alpha](\cdot)$$

$$(\cdot)\left[\frac{1 + s_1^{(1)} + (s_1^{(2)} - s_1^{(1)})\alpha}{1 + k_1^{(3)} - (k_1^{(3)} - k_1^{(2)})\alpha} \cdot \frac{1 + s_2^{(1)} + (s_2^{(2)} - s_2^{(1)})\alpha}{1 + k_2^{(3)} - (k_2^{(3)} - k_2^{(2)})\alpha},\right.$$

$$\left., \frac{1 + s_1^{(3)} - (s_1^{(3)} - s_1^{(2)})\alpha}{1 + k_1^{(1)} + (k_1^{(2)} - k_1^{(1)})\alpha} \cdot \frac{1 + s_2^{(3)} - (s_2^{(3)} - s_2^{(2)})\alpha}{1 + k_2^{(1)} + (k_2^{(2)} - k_2^{(1)})\alpha}\right]$$

And so on successively, until the end of the useful life of the investment object. The consequent updating of exploitation profits for assignment by addition and subsequent deduction from the payment for acquisition of the invested asset for obtaining the net updated value is immediate. As this has been mentioned in previous chapters we will not do so here so as not to be excessively repetitive. But we will move on to a didactic example.

Let us assume that acquisition of an investment object requires a payment at the initial moment:

$$M = 80$$

After doing the corresponding calculations it is estimated, for its useful life of 5 years, that there will be certain profits from exploitation at constant prices, expressed by the following triangular approximations:

Year	Ternary form	α-cuts form
1	(24, 27, 28)	$[24 + 3\alpha, 28 - \alpha]$
2	(23, 25, 28)	$[23 + 2\alpha, 28 - 3\alpha]$
3	(21, 24, 26)	$[21 + 3\alpha, 26 - 2\alpha]$
4	(20, 23, 25)	$[20 + 3\alpha, 25 - 2\alpha]$
5	(18, 22, 24)	$[18 + 4\alpha, 24 - 2\alpha]$

Now we will express these triangular approximations by means of the hendecadarian system. We arrive at:

	Year 1		Year 2		Year 3		Year 4		Year 5	
α	$[24 + 3\alpha, 28 - \alpha]$		$[23 + 2\alpha, 28 - 3\alpha]$		$[21 + 3\alpha, 26 - 2\alpha]$		$[20 + 3\alpha, 25 - 2\alpha]$		$[18 + 4\alpha, 24 - 2\alpha]$	
1	27		25		24		23		22	
.9	26.7	27.1	24.8	25.3	23.7	24.2	22.7	23.2	21.6	22.2
.8	26.4	27.2	24.6	25.6	23.4	24.4	22.4	23.4	21.2	22.4
.7	26.1	27.3	24.4	25.9	23.1	24.6	22.1	23.6	20.8	22.6
.6	25.8	27.4	24.2	26.2	22.8	24.8	21.8	23.8	20.4	22.8
.5	25.5	27.5	24	26.5	22.5	25	21.5	24	20	23
.4	25.2	27.6	23.8	26.8	22.2	25.2	21.2	24.2	19.6	23.2
.3	24.9	27.7	23.6	27.1	21.9	25.4	20.9	24.4	19.2	23.4
.2	24.6	27.8	23.4	27.4	21.6	25.6	20.6	24.6	18.8	23.6
.1	24.3	27.9	23.2	27.7	21.3	25.8	20.3	24.8	18.4	23.8
0	24	28	23	28	21	26	20	25	18	24

The respective estimates for the rates of interest, inflation and technical progress are, already expressed in α-cuts (in percentages).

Year	Rates of interes	Rates of inflation	Rates of technical progress
1	$[8 + 2\alpha,\ 11 - \alpha]$	$[4 + \alpha,\ 7 - 2\alpha]$	$[2 + \alpha,\ 5 - 2\alpha]$
2	$[7 + 2\alpha,\ 11 - 2\alpha]$	$[3 + \alpha,\ 6 - 2\alpha]$	$[2 + \alpha,\ 4 - \alpha]$
3	$[6 + 3\alpha,\ 10 - \alpha]$	$[3 + \alpha,\ 5 - \alpha]$	$[2 + 2\alpha,\ 5 - \alpha]$
4	$[6 + 2\alpha,\ 10 - 2\alpha]$	$[2 + \alpha,\ 5 - 2\alpha]$	$[2 + 3\alpha,\ 6 - \alpha]$
5	$[5 + 2\alpha,\ 9 - 2\alpha]$	$[2 + \alpha,\ 4 - \alpha]$	$[3 + 2\alpha,\ 6 - \alpha]$

We are now going to tie together the rates expressed in so much by one, (inflation and technical progress) with the help of the hendecadarian system:

Year 1:

$(1\ (+)\ \underset{\sim}{s}_1)\ (:)\ (1\ (+)\ \underset{\sim}{k}_1)$

α	$[1.04 + 0.01\alpha,$	$1.07 - 0.02\alpha]$	$[1.02 + 0.01\alpha,$	$1.05 - 0.02\alpha]$	$[(1.04 + 0.01\alpha)/(1.05 - 0.02\alpha),$	$(1.07 - 0.02\alpha)/(1.02 + 0.01\alpha)]$
1	1.05		1.03		1.019	
.9	1.049	1.052	1.029	1.032	1.016	1.022
.8	1.048	1.054	1.028	1.034	1.013	1.025
.7	1.047	1.056	1.027	1.036	1.011	1.028
.6	1.046	1.058	1.026	1.038	1.008	1.031
.5	1.045	1.060	1.025	1.040	1.005	1.034
.4	1.044	1.062	1.024	1.042	1.002	1.037
.3	1.043	1.064	1.023	1.044	0.999	1.040
.2	1.042	1.066	1.022	1.046	0.996	1.043
.1	1.041	1.068	1.021	1.048	0.993	1.046
0	1.040	1.070	1.020	1.050	0.990	1.049

The resulting fuzzy number we will designated by $(1\ (+)\ \underset{\sim}{s}_1)\ (:)\ (1\ (+)\ \underset{\sim}{k}_1)$, and it expresses the rate of increase or decrease of prices through the joint action of inflation and technical progress during the first year.

Year 2:

			$(1\ (+)\ \tilde{s}_2)\ (:)\ (1\ (+)\ \tilde{k}_2)$	$(1\ (+)\ \tilde{s}_{12})\ (:)\ (1\ (+)\ \tilde{k}_{12})$
α	$[1.03 + 0.01\alpha,\ 1.06 - 0.02\alpha]$	$[1.02 + 0.01\alpha,\ 1.04 - 0.01\alpha]$	$[(1.03 + 0.01\alpha)/(1.04 - 0.01\alpha),\ (1.06 - 0.02\alpha)/(1.02 + 0.01\alpha)]$	$[(1\ (+)\ \tilde{s}_1)\ (:)\ (1\ (+)\ \tilde{k}_1)]\ (\cdot)\ (\cdot)\ [(1\ (+)\ \tilde{s}_2)\ (:)\ (1\ (+)\ \tilde{k}_2)]$
1	1.04	1.03	1.010	1.029
.9	1.039 1.042	1.029 1.031	1.008 1.013	1.024 1.035
.8	1.038 1.044	1.028 1.032	1.006 1.015	1.019 1.040
.7	1.037 1.046	1.027 1.033	1.004 1.018	1.015 1.046
.6	1.036 1.048	1.026 1.034	1.002 1.021	1.010 1.053
.5	1.035 1.050	1.025 1.035	1.000 1.024	1.005 1.059
.4	1.034 1.052	1.024 1.036	0.998 1.027	1.000 1.065
.3	1.033 1.054	1.023 1.037	0.996 1.030	0.995 1.071
.2	1.032 1.056	1.022 1.038	0.994 1.033	0.990 1.077
.1	1.031 1.058	1.021 1.039	0.992 1.036	0.985 1.084
0	1.030 1.060	1.020 1.040	0.990 1.039	0.980 1.090

The resulting fuzzy number $(1\ (+)\ \tilde{s}_{12})\ (:)\ (1\ (+)\ \tilde{k}_{12}) = [(1\ (+)\ \tilde{s}_1)\ (:)\ (1\ (+)\ \tilde{k}_1)]\ (\cdot)\ (\cdot)\ [(1\ (+)\ \tilde{s}_2)\ (:)\ (1\ (+)\ \tilde{k}_2)]$ allows us to see the increase or decrease in prices relative to the second year, in relation to moment 0, as a consequence of the joint action of inflation and technical progress.

Year 3:

			$(1\ (+)\ \tilde{s}_3)\ (:)\ (1\ (+)\ \tilde{k}_3)$	$(1\ (+)\ \tilde{s}_{123})\ (:)\ (1\ (+)\ \tilde{k}_{123})$
α	$[1.03 + 0.01\alpha,\ 1.05 - 0.01\alpha]$	$[1.02 + 0.02\alpha,\ 1.05 - 0.01\alpha]$	$[(1.03 + 0.01\alpha)/(1.05 - 0.01\alpha),\ (1.05 - 0.01\alpha)/(1.02 + 0.02\alpha)]$	$[(1\ (+)\ \tilde{s}_{12})\ (:)\ (1\ (+)\ \tilde{k}_{12})]\ (\cdot)\ (\cdot)\ [(1\ (+)\ \tilde{s}_3)\ (:)\ (1\ (+)\ \tilde{k}_3)]$
1	1.04	1.04	1	1.029
.9	1.039 1.041	1.038 1.041	0.998 1.003	1.022 1.038
.8	1.038 1.042	1.036 1.042	0.996 1.006	1.015 1.046
.7	1.037 1.043	1.034 1.043	0.994 1.009	1.009 1.055
.6	1.036 1.044	1.032 1.044	0.992 1.012	1.002 1.066
.5	1.035 1.045	1.030 1.045	0.990 1.014	0.995 1.074
.4	1.034 1.046	1.028 1.046	0.988 1.017	0.988 1.083
.3	1.033 1.047	1.026 1.047	0.987 1.020	0.982 1.092
.2	1.032 1.048	1.024 1.048	0.985 1.023	0.975 1.102
.1	1.031 1.049	1.022 1.049	0.983 1.026	0.968 1.112
0	1.030 1.050	1.020 1.050	0.981 1.029	0.961 1.122

Here we arrive at the fuzzy number $(1 (+) \underset{\sim}{s}_{123}) (:) (1 (+) \underset{\sim}{k}_{123}) = [(1 (+) \underset{\sim}{s}_{12}) (:) (:) (1 (+) \underset{\sim}{k}_{12})] (\cdot) [(1 (+) \underset{\sim}{s}_3) (:) (1 (+) \underset{\sim}{k}_3)]$ corresponding to the variations in prices for the third year in relation to the initial moment.

Year 4:

α	$[1.02 + 0.01\alpha, 1.05 - 0.02\alpha]$	$[1.02 + 0.03\alpha, 1.06 - 0.01\alpha]$	$(1 (+) \underset{\sim}{s}_4) (:) (1 (+) \underset{\sim}{k}_4)$ $[(1.02 + 0.01\alpha)/(1.06 - 0.01\alpha), (1.05 - 0.02\alpha)/(1.02 + 0.03\alpha)]$		$(1 (+) \underset{\sim}{s}_{1234}) (:) (1 (+) \underset{\sim}{k}_{1234})$ $[(1 (+) \underset{\sim}{s}_{123}) (:) (1 (+) \underset{\sim}{k}_{123})] (\cdot) (\cdot) [(1 (+) \underset{\sim}{s}_4) (:) (1 (+) \underset{\sim}{k}_4)]$	
1	1.03	1.05	0.981		1.009	
.9	1.029 1.032	1.047 1.051	0.979	0.986	1.000	1.023
.8	1.028 1.034	1.044 1.052	0.977	0.990	0.992	1.035
.7	1.027 1.036	1.041 1.053	0.975	0.995	0.984	1.050
.6	1.026 1.038	1.038 1.054	0.973	1.000	0.975	1.066
.5	1.025 1.040	1.035 1.055	0.971	1.005	0.966	1.079
.4	1.024 1.042	1.032 1.056	0.970	1.010	0.958	1.094
.3	1.023 1.044	1.029 1.057	0.968	1.014	0.950	1.107
.2	1.022 1.046	1.026 1.058	0.966	1.019	0.942	1.123
.1	1.021 1.048	1.023 1.059	0.964	1.024	0.933	1.139
0	1.020 1.050	1.020 1.060	0.962	1.029	0.924	1.154

The resulting fuzzy number $(1 (+) \underset{\sim}{s}_{1234}) (:) (1 (+) \underset{\sim}{k}_{1234}) = [(1 (+) \underset{\sim}{s}_{123}) (:) (:) (1 (+) \underset{\sim}{k}_{123})] (\cdot) [(1 (+) \underset{\sim}{s}_4) (:) (1 (+) \underset{\sim}{k}_4)]$ expresses the variations in prices for the fourth year in relation to moment zero.

Year 5:

α	$[1.02 + 0.01\alpha, 1.04 - 0.01\alpha]$	$[1.03 + 0.02\alpha, 1.06 - 0.01\alpha]$	$(1 (+) \underset{\sim}{s}_5) (:) (1 (+) \underset{\sim}{k}_5)$ $[(1.02 + 0.01\alpha)/(1.06 - 0.01\alpha), (1.04 - 0.01\alpha)/(1.03 + 0.02\alpha)]$		$(1 (+) \underset{\sim}{s}_{12345}) (:) (1 (+) \underset{\sim}{k}_{12345})$ $[(1 (+) \underset{\sim}{s}_{1234}) (:) (1 (+) \underset{\sim}{k}_{1234})] (\cdot) (\cdot) [(1 (+) \underset{\sim}{s}_5) (:) (1 (+) \underset{\sim}{k}_5)]$	
1	1.03	1.05	0.981		0.990	
.9	1.029 1.031	1.048 1.051	0.979	0.984	0.979	1.007
.8	1.028 1.032	1.046 1.052	0.977	0.987	0.969	1.021
.7	1.027 1.033	1.044 1.053	0.975	0.989	0.959	1.038
.6	1.026 1.034	1.042 1.054	0.973	0.992	0.949	1.057
.5	1.025 1.035	1.040 1.055	0.971	0.995	0.938	1.074
.4	1.024 1.036	1.038 1.056	0.970	0.998	0.929	1.092
.3	1.023 1.037	1.036 1.057	0.968	1.001	0.920	1.108
.2	1.022 1.038	1.034 1.058	0.966	1.004	0.910	1.127
.1	1.021 1.039	1.032 1.059	0.964	1.007	0.899	1.147
0	1.020 1.040	1.030 1.060	0.962	1.010	0.889	1.165

We have now found the fuzzy number $((1 \,(+)\, \underset{\sim}{s}_{12345}) \,(:)\, (1 \,(+)\, \underset{\sim}{k}_{12345})$ $= [(1 \,(+)\, \underset{\sim}{s}_{1234}) \,(:)\, (1 \,(+)\, \underset{\sim}{k}_{1234})] \,(\cdot)\, [(1 \,(+)\, \underset{\sim}{s}_5) \,(:)\, (1 \,(+)\, \underset{\sim}{k}_5)]$ that expresses the variations in prices for the fifth year relative to the initial moment.

Year 1:

$1 \,(:)\, (1 \,(+)\, \underset{\sim}{i}_1)$

α	$[1/(1.11 - 0.01\alpha),$ $1/(1.08 + 0.02\alpha]$	
1	0.909	
.9	0.908	0.911
.8	0.907	0.912
.7	0.907	0.914
.6	0.906	0.916
.5	0.905	0.917
.4	0.904	0.919
.3	0.903	0.921
.2	0.902	0.922
.1	0.902	0.924
0	0.901	0.926

The fuzzy number obtained $1 \,(:)\, (1 \,(+)\, \underset{\sim}{i}_1)$ permits updating the monetary masses from year 1 to the initial moment.

Year 2:

α	$1\ (:)\ (1\ (+)\ \underset{\sim}{i}_2)$ $[1/(1.11-0.02\alpha),$ $1/(1.07+0.02\alpha)]$		$1\ (:)\ (1\ (+)\ \underset{\sim}{i}_{12})$ $[1/(1\ (+)\ \underset{\sim}{i}_1)]\ (\cdot)$ $(\cdot)\ [1/(1\ (+)\ \underset{\sim}{i}_2)]$	
1	0.917		0.833	
.9	0.916	0.919	0.832	0.837
.8	0.914	0.921	0.829	0.840
.7	0.912	0.922	0.827	0.843
.6	0.911	0.924	0.825	0.846
.5	0.909	0.926	0.823	0.849
.4	0.907	0.928	0.820	0.853
.3	0.906	0.929	0.818	0.856
.2	0.904	0.931	0.815	0.858
.1	0.902	0.933	0.814	0.862
0	0.901	0.934	0.812	0.865

The result we have expressed symbolically by $1\ (:)\ (1\ (+)\ \underset{\sim}{i}_{12})$, allows for updating the monetary masses from moment 2 to moment 0.

Year 3:

α	$1\ (:)\ (1\ (+)\ \underset{\sim}{i}_3)$ $[1/(1.10-0.01\alpha),$ $1/(1.06+0.03\alpha)]$		$1\ (:)\ (1\ (+)\ \underset{\sim}{i}_{123})$ $[1/(1\ (+)\ \underset{\sim}{i}_{12})]\ (\cdot)$ $(\cdot)\ [1/(1\ (+)\ \underset{\sim}{i}_3)]$	
1	0.917		0.764	
.9	0.916	0.920	0.762	0.770
.8	0.916	0.922	0.759	0.774
.7	0.915	0.925	0.757	0.780
.6	0.914	0.928	0.754	0.785
.5	0.913	0.930	0.751	0.789
.4	0.912	0.933	0.748	0.796
.3	0.911	0.935	0.745	0.800
.2	0.911	0.938	0.742	0.805
.1	0.910	0.941	0.741	0.811
0	0.909	0.943	0.738	0.816

The fuzzy number 1 (:) (1 (+) $\underset{\sim}{i}_{123}$) allows us to update the monetary masses situated at moment 3.

Year 4:

	1 (:) (1 (+) $\underset{\sim}{i}_4$)		1 (:) (1 (+) $\underset{\sim}{i}_{1234}$)	
α	[1/(1.10 – 0.02α), 1/(1.06 + 0.02α)]		[1/(1 (+) $\underset{\sim}{i}_{123}$)] (·) (·) [1/(1 (+) $\underset{\sim}{i}_4$)]	
1	0.926		0.707	
.9	0.924	0.928	0.704	0.714
.8	0.922	0.929	0.700	0.719
.7	0.921	0.931	0.697	0.726
.6	0.919	0.933	0.693	0.732
.5	0.917	0.934	0.689	0.737
.4	0.916	0.936	0.685	0.745
.3	0.914	0.938	0.681	0.750
.2	0.912	0.940	0.677	0.757
.1	0.911	0.942	0.675	0.764
0	0.909	0.943	0.671	0.769

Here we have obtained, by means of the fuzzy number expressed by 1 (:) (1 (+) $\underset{\sim}{i}_{1234}$), the updating of the values at moment 4 to the initial moment.

Year 5:

	1 (:) (1 (+) $\underset{\sim}{i}_5$)		1 (:) (1 (+) $\underset{\sim}{i}_{12345}$)	
α	[1/(1.09 – 0.02α), 1/(1.05 + 0.02α)]		[1/(1 (+) $\underset{\sim}{i}_{1234}$)] (·) (·) [1/(1 (+) $\underset{\sim}{i}_5$)]	
1	0.934		0.660	
.9	0.933	0.936	0.657	0.668
.8	0.931	0.938	0.652	0.674
.7	0.929	0.940	0.647	0.682
.6	0.928	0.942	0.643	0.689
.5	0.926	0.943	0.638	0.695
.4	0.924	0.945	0.633	0.704
.3	0.922	0.947	0.628	0.710
.2	0.921	0.949	0.623	0.718
.1	0.919	0.950	0.620	0.726
0	0.917	0.952	0.615	0.732

The number expressed by $1 (:) (1 (+) \underset{\sim}{i}_{12345})$ allows us to update the monetary masses at moment 5 up to the initial period.

Having now obtained this information, we are in a position for finding the net updated value resulting from acquisition and operation of the investment object. For this we will calculate the net updated value period by period, and then carry out the addition and subtraction of the initial payment for acquisition of the investment object. This will be:

Year 1:

α	$\underset{\sim}{c}_1$		$(1 (+) \underset{\sim}{s}_1) (:) (1 (+) \underset{\sim}{k}_1)$		$1 (:) (1 (+) \underset{\sim}{i}_1)$		$\underset{\sim}{c}_1 (\cdot) [(1 (+) \underset{\sim}{s}_1) (:) (1 (+) \underset{\sim}{k}_1)] (\cdot) [1 (:) (1 (+) \underset{\sim}{i}_1)]$	
1	27		1.019		0.909		25.01	
.9	26.7	27.1	1.016	1.022	0.908	0.911	24.63	25.23
.8	26.4	27.2	1.013	1.025	0.907	0.912	24.26	25.43
.7	26.1	27.3	1.011	1.028	0.907	0.914	23.93	25.65
.6	25.8	27.4	1.008	1.031	0.906	0.916	23.56	25.88
.5	25.5	27.5	1.005	1.034	0.905	0.917	23.19	26.07
.4	25.2	27.6	1.002	1.037	0.904	0.919	22.83	26.30
.3	24.9	27.7	0.999	1.040	0.903	0.921	22.46	26.53
.2	24.6	27.8	0.996	1.043	0.902	0.922	22.10	26.73
.1	24.3	27.9	0.993	1.046	0.902	0.924	21.76	26.96
0	24	28	0.990	1.049	0.901	0.926	21.41	27.20

Year 2:

α	$\underset{\sim}{c}_2$		$(1 (+) \underset{\sim}{s}_{12}) (:) (1 (+) \underset{\sim}{k}_{12})$		$1 (:) (1 (+) \underset{\sim}{i}_{12})$		$\underset{\sim}{c}_2 (\cdot) [(1 (+) \underset{\sim}{s}_{12}) (:) (1 (+) \underset{\sim}{k}_{12})] (\cdot) [1 (:) (1 (+) \underset{\sim}{i}_{12})]$	
1	25		1.029		0.833		21.43	
.9	24.8	25.3	1.024	1.035	0.832	0.837	21.13	21.92
.8	24.6	25.6	1.019	1.040	0.829	0.840	20.78	22.36
.7	24.4	25.9	1.015	1.046	0.827	0.843	20.48	22.84
.6	24.2	26.2	1.010	1.053	0.825	0.846	20.16	23.34
.5	24	26.5	1.005	1.059	0.823	0.849	19.85	23.82
.4	23.8	26.8	1.000	1.065	0.820	0.853	19.52	24.35
.3	23.6	27.1	0.995	1.071	0.818	0.856	19.21	24.84
.2	23.4	27.4	0.990	1.077	0.815	0.858	18.88	25.32
.1	23.2	27.7	0.985	1.084	0.814	0.862	18.60	25.88
0	23	28	0.980	1.090	0.812	0.865	18.30	26.40

Year 3:

α	$\underset{\sim}{c}_3$		$(1 (+)\underset{\sim}{s}_{123}) (:) (:) (1 (+)\underset{\sim}{k}_{123})$		$1 (:) (1 (+)\underset{\sim}{i}_{123})$		$\underset{\sim}{c}_3 (\cdot) [(1 (+)\underset{\sim}{s}_{123}) (:) (1 (+)\underset{\sim}{k}_{123})] (\cdot) (\cdot) [1 (:) (1 (+)\underset{\sim}{i}_{123})]$	
1	24		1.029		0.764		18.87	
.9	23.7	24.2	1.022	1.038	0.762	0.770	18.46	19.34
.8	23.4	24.4	1.015	1.046	0.759	0.774	18.03	19.75
.7	23.1	24.6	1.009	1.055	0.757	0.780	17.64	20.24
.6	22.8	24.8	1.002	1.066	0.754	0.785	17.22	20.75
.5	22.5	25	0.995	1.074	0.751	0.789	16.81	21.18
.4	22.2	25.2	0.988	1.083	0.748	0.796	16.41	21.72
.3	21.9	25.4	0.982	1.092	0.745	0.800	16.02	22.19
.2	21.6	25.6	0.975	1.102	0.742	0.805	15.63	22.71
.1	21.3	25.8	0.968	1.112	0.741	0.811	15.28	23.27
0	21	26	0.961	1.122	0.738	0.816	14.89	23.80

Year 4:

α	$\underset{\sim}{c}_4$		$(1 (+)\underset{\sim}{s}_{1234}) (:) (:) (1 (+)\underset{\sim}{k}_{1234})$		$1 (:) (1 (+)\underset{\sim}{i}_{1234})$		$\underset{\sim}{c}_4 (\cdot) [(1 (+)\underset{\sim}{s}_{1234}) (:) (1 (+)\underset{\sim}{k}_{1234})] (\cdot) (\cdot) [1 (:) (1 (+)\underset{\sim}{i}_{1234})]$	
1	23		1.009		0.707		16.41	
.9	22.7	23.2	1.000	1.023	0.704	0.714	15.98	16.94
.8	22.4	23.4	0.992	1.035	0.700	0.719	15.55	17.41
.7	22.1	23.6	0.984	1.050	0.697	0.726	15.16	17.99
.6	21.8	23.8	0.975	1.066	0.693	0.732	14.73	18.57
.5	21.5	24	0.966	1.079	0.689	0.737	14.31	19.08
.4	21.2	24.2	0.958	1.094	0.685	0.745	13.91	19.72
.3	20.9	24.4	0.950	1.107	0.681	0.750	13.52	20.26
.2	20.6	24.6	0.942	1.123	0.677	0.757	13.14	20.91
.1	20.3	24.8	0.933	1.139	0.675	0.764	12.78	21.58
0	20	25	0.924	1.154	0.671	0.769	12.40	22.18

Year 5:

α	$\underset{\sim}{c}_5$		$(1\ (+)\underset{\sim}{s}_{12345})\ (:)\ (:)\ (1\ (+)\underset{\sim}{k}_{12345})$		$1\ (:)\ (1\ (+)\underset{\sim}{i}_{12345})$		$\underset{\sim}{c}_5\ (\cdot)\ [(1\ (+)\underset{\sim}{s}_{12345})\ (:)\ (1\ (+)\underset{\sim}{k}_{12345})]\ (\cdot)\ (\cdot)\ [1\ (:)\ (1\ (+)\underset{\sim}{i}_{12345})]$	
1	22		0.990		0.660		14.37	
.9	21.6	22.2	0.979	1.007	0.657	0.668	13.89	14.93
.8	21.2	22.4	0.969	1.021	0.652	0.674	13.39	15.41
.7	20.8	22.6	0.959	1.038	0.647	0.682	12.90	16.00
.6	20.4	22.8	0.949	1.057	0.643	0.689	12.45	16.60
.5	20	23	0.938	1.074	0.638	0.695	11.97	17.17
.4	19.6	23.2	0.929	1.092	0.633	0.704	11.52	17.83
.3	19.2	23.4	0.920	1.108	0.628	0.710	11.09	18.41
.2	18.8	23.6	0.910	1.127	0.623	0.718	10.66	19.10
.1	18.4	23.8	0.899	1.147	0.620	0.726	10.25	19.82
0	18	24	0.889	1.165	0.615	0.732	9.84	20.47

The last column of the above tables shows us the fuzzy numbers representing net exploitation profits updated to moment zero, in which inflation and technical progress have been explicitly taken into account. In order to find the capital value or Net Updated Value it will be sufficient to do the corresponding addition to which the payment made for acquisition of the investment object should be deducted, in this case estimated at $M = 80$. We will show this in the following table in which we express the crisp number 80 in the form of a fuzzy number, also using the hendecadarian system.

α	Year 0		Year 1		Year 2		Year 3		Year 4		Year 5		NUV	
1	80		25.01		21.43		18.87		16.41		14.37		16.09	
.9	80	80	24.63	25.23	21.13	21.92	18.46	19.34	15.98	16.94	13.89	14.93	14.09	18.36
.8	80	80	24.26	25.43	20.78	22.36	18.03	19.75	15.55	17.41	13.39	15.41	12.01	20.36
.7	80	80	23.93	25.65	20.48	22.84	17.64	20.24	15.16	17.99	12.90	16.00	10.11	22.72
.6	80	80	23.56	25.88	20.16	23.34	17.22	20.75	14.73	18.57	12.45	16.60	8.12	25.14
.5	80	80	23.19	26.07	19.85	23.82	16.81	21.18	14.31	19.08	11.97	17.17	6.13	27.32
.4	80	80	22.83	26.30	19.52	24.35	16.41	21.72	13.91	19.72	11.52	17.83	4.19	29.92
.3	80	80	22.46	26.53	19.21	24.84	16.02	22.19	13.52	20.26	11.09	18.41	2.30	32.23
.2	80	80	22.10	26.73	18.88	25.32	15.63	22.71	13.14	20.91	10.66	19.10	−0.41	34.77
.1	80	80	21.76	26.96	18.60	25.88	15.28	23.27	12.78	21.58	10.25	19.82	−1.33	37.51
0	80	80	21.41	27.20	18.30	26.40	14.89	23.80	12.40	22.18	9.84	20.47	−3.16	40.05

The result presented in this fashion, possesses a wealth of information which allows us to make a wide range of interpretations, given the possibility of placing ourselves at the different levels of α. Therefore, if we select, for example, level $\alpha = 0.7$ we have a capital value for the investment given by the interval [10.11, 22.72], if we consider level $\alpha = 0.6$ interval [8.12, 25.14] The greatest uncertainty appears, obviously, at level $\alpha = 0$ with an interval of [-3.16, 40.05] where even a negative Net Updated Value is possible in the most pessimistic positions. The maximum assumption, $\alpha = 1$ gives rise to a net updated value of 16.09.

We hope that this long process, which we have shown in full detail, is useful for systemisation of the operations to be followed and allows for full comprehension of the structure of the problem. During its development highly suggestive elements arise which allow us to make some interesting reflections on the role played above all by inflation and technical progress, when both phenomena appear in conjunction.

Consideration of a long-term economic horizon.

Up to this point we have studied the case in which technical progress has an incidence on the monetary currents of collections and payments even with the use of a single investment object. Now we are going to look at a new aspect of this problem that arises when we take into account a wider economic horizon than the economic life of an investment object. This means considering a manufacturing programme, in which the well-known phenomenon of renovation will occur, linked in some way to the concept of *chains of investments*.

The mere fact of studying the management of a long-term programme, in no way means forcing the sense of investment analysis, because if we consider that one of the objects of the company is the wealth of the shareholders from optimisation of profits, compatible with other ends, this requires taking into account several and even a large number of periods.

Before presenting a model, in which, initially all the economic parameters taking part will be assumed as known with absolute certainty, we will make certain considerations relative to terminology, although we cannot, as of now, elude pointing out the important restriction of this hypothesis since in reality and with ever more frequency, certain elements appear which can only be considered in an uncertain fashion. Among these can be mentioned *technical progress*, which, in a certain way, will represent the phenomenon of innovation in the investment process.

Therefore it can be said that the inclusion of the concept of <<technical progress>>, in the sphere of management, gives a certain sense to the study of investments within a medium and long-term economic horizon.

Let us move on to describe certain of the more common terms used in the field of investment decision, such as the concepts of investment <<series>> and <<chains>>.

In the event of the existence of two possibilities for investing in two basic objects A and B, in such a way that throughout a wide economic horizon successive purchases of the same initial objects (they are repeated) are considered and, although the duration of these were not to be the same, renewal takes place at the same times, either if the useful life of the object were to have ended or not, what we are faced with is a <<series>> of investments.

Let us clarify this concept with figure 9.1:

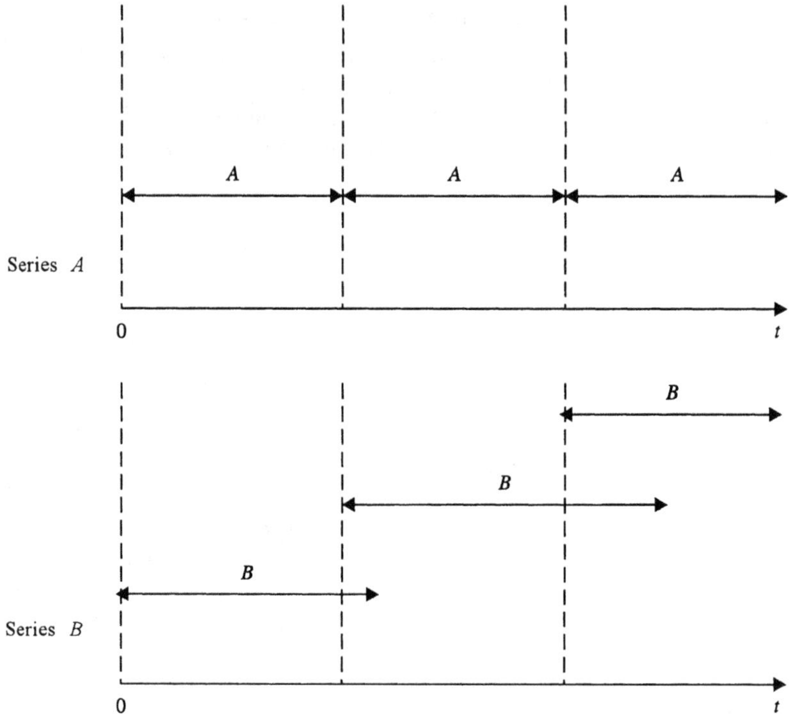

Figure 9.1.

If we consider only one of the investments forming the series and we obtain the capital value of the investment, it could happen for example that:

$$V_A > V_B$$

It can be accepted in this case that *investment A* is more favourable than B and also *that the investment <<series>> formed by the repetition of investment A is better than the investment <<series>> formed by the repetition of investment B.*

On the other hand the study of individual investments can be conceived that repeat themselves in such a way that <<the moment of repetition>> does not coincide. In this case simple comparison is not sufficient between the capital values of the basic individual investments. A particularly interesting case is that in which the commencement of each investment takes place at the time when the previous investment ends. In this case it is said that we are faced with a <<chain of investments>>.

The graphic representation of this hypothesis can be done as follows (figure 9.2):

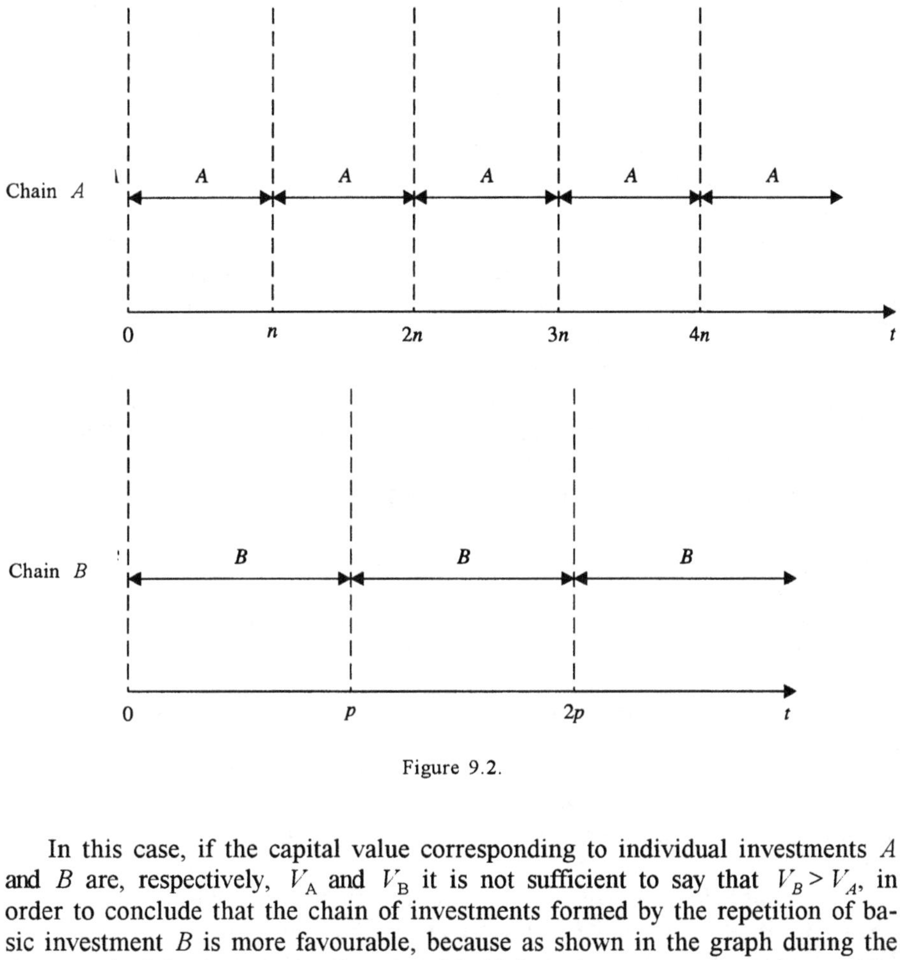

Figure 9.2.

In this case, if the capital value corresponding to individual investments A and B are, respectively, V_A and V_B it is not sufficient to say that $V_B > V_A$, in order to conclude that the chain of investments formed by the repetition of basic investment B is more favourable, because as shown in the graph during the time required for investment B, one and half times investment A can be completed.

In a general case in which repetition takes place over a period of time corresponding to a wide economic horizon, it will be necessary to find the capital value *of each one of the chains.*

Let us suppose that the duration of one of the individual investments A is n years and the programme covers a duration of m x n years. The capital value of the A chain will be, under the hypothesis of a stationary economic system:

$$V_{CA} = V_A + \frac{V_A}{(1+i)^n} + \frac{V_A}{(1+i)^{2n}} + \cdots + \frac{V_A}{(1+i)^{(m-1)n}} =$$

$$= V_A \frac{1 - \dfrac{1}{(1+i)^{(m-1)n} \cdot (1+i)^n}}{1 - \dfrac{1}{(1+i)^n}} = V_A \frac{(1+i)^{(m+1)n} - (1+i)^n}{(1+i)^{(m+1)n} - (1+i)^{mn}}$$

If $V_{CA} > V_{CB}$ is complied with it will be more convenient to select the chain of investments, the basic investment of which is A, although eventually $V_B > V_A$ could be complied with.

Up to this point we have not taken into account the innovation factor for the investment object, nor for the production or management processes. We are now going to make our first incursion into this field by including, in some way, technical progress in the case of the chains of investments. We have seen that, when the decision to invest in an individual object (limited economic horizon) is studied, technical progress is included immediately into the currents, that is to say right from the very first moment of operation of the object. Therefore, it is not necessary to acquire a new object in order to improve costs and sales prices (there is no dependence between improvements and production and/or management processes and the characteristic of the equipment).

Nevertheless, on many occasions, the <<subjection>> of costs to the production equipment is so great that technical progress can only be incorporated by purchasing a new object. In this way, technical progress will only have an incidence on the monetary currents of collections and payments at the time that each of the machines is acquired. In this way,<<technical progress, does not affect the investment process until such time as the new object of the chain is purchased>>.

Let us move on to study the form acquired by the model, in which inflation and wear and tear are considered, if this case is admitted. For this we will start out with a chain of investments formed by m equipments each one of which has a useful life of n periods.

As we did before we will consider that k is the unitary annual technical progress rate. In this case if M is the payment for acquisition of the investment object at moment 0, when the new equipment is acquired at moment n, its cost (and therefore, payment) will be:

$$M(1+k)^{-n}$$

Assuming that technical progress affects the cost of the equipment with the same intensity as exploitation profits, in any period j relative to the second equipment, that is to say in a period $n + j$ after the investment process, profits will be:

$$c_j(1+s)^{(n+j)}(1+k)^{-(n+j)}$$

if technical progress has an incidence independently of the equipment we are working with.

And these will be:

$$c_j(1+s)^{(n+j)}(1+k)^{-n}$$

if they are conditioned by each equipment, in the sense that once acquired it is impossible to carry out any improvements in the production process during their useful life.

We will now adopt this latter hypothesis: we will consider that technical progress is only included with the purchase of a new equipment, affecting at that time both the purchase cost of the same and its operating costs, but that once equipment is acquired, during its useful life no complementary reductions in costs as a consequence of technical progress are generated, that do not affect the investment until purchase of the new equipment in the chain.

Let us consider then as we have done previously, a chain of investments formed by m equipments with a useful life of n periods for each one. For the object of the chain we arrive at:

$$V_1 = -M + \sum_{j=1}^{n} [b_j - (a^{(c)} + M \cdot d \cdot (1+q)^{j-1})](1+s)^j(1+i)^{-j} =$$

$$= -M + \sum_{j=1}^{n} c_j(1+s)^j(1+i)^{-j}$$

For the second object:

$$V_2 = \{ -M + \sum_{j=1}^{n} [b_j - (a^{(c)} + M \cdot d \cdot (1+q)^{j-1})](1+s)^j(1+i)^{-j} \}(1+s)^n(1+k)^{-n}(1+i)^{-n} =$$

$$= [-M + \sum_{j=1}^{n} c_j(1+s)^j(1+i)^{-j}](1+s)^n(1+k)^{-n}(1+i)^{-n}$$

And so on successively until object m for which we arrive at:

$$V_m = \{ -M + \sum_{j=1}^{n} [b_j - (a^{(c)} + M \cdot d \cdot (1+q)^{j-1})](1+s)^j(1+i)^{-j} \}(1+s)^{(m-1)n} \cdot$$

$$(1+k)^{-(m-1)n} \cdot (1+i)^{-(m-1)n} =$$

$$= [-M + \sum_{j=1}^{n} c_j(1+s)^j(1+i)^{-j}](1+s)^{(m-1)n} \cdot (1+k)^{-(m-1)n} \cdot (1+i)^{-(m-1)n}$$

The net updated value of the chain can be written in a summarised manner, as follows:

$$V_c = \sum_{g=1}^{m} V_g = [-M + \sum_{j=1}^{n} c_j(1+s)^j(1+i)^{-j}] \cdot \sum_{g=0}^{m-1} (1+s)^{gn} \cdot (1+k)^{-gn} \cdot (1+i)^{-gn}$$

Now we can move on to the sphere of uncertainty, by developing an example, with the information from the previous section, although somewhat adapted now to the new hypothesis. Obviously the interest and inflation rates, as well as the technical progress rate, are assumed variable in time.

First, we will calculate the net updated values for year 1. Taking the estimates from the previous section we have:

α	$\underset{\sim}{c}_1$		$(1\,(+)\,\underset{\sim}{s}_1)$		$1\,(:)\,(1\,(+)\,\underset{\sim}{i}_1)$		$\underset{\sim}{c}_1\,(\cdot)\,(1\,(+)\,\underset{\sim}{s}_1)\,(\cdot)\,[1\,(:)\,(1\,(+)\,\underset{\sim}{i}_1)]$	
1	27		1.05		0.909		25.77	
.9	26.7	27.1	1.049	1.052	0.908	0.911	25.43	25.97
.8	26.4	27.2	1.048	1.054	0.907	0.912	25.09	26.14
.7	26.1	27.3	1.047	1.056	0.907	0.914	24.78	26.35
.6	25.8	27.4	1.046	1.058	0.906	0.916	24.45	26.55
.5	25.5	27.5	1.045	1.060	0.905	0.917	24.11	26.73
.4	25.2	27.6	1.044	1.062	0.904	0.919	23.78	26.94
.3	24.9	27.7	1.043	1.064	0.903	0.921	23.45	27.14
.2	24.6	27.8	1.042	1.066	0.902	0.922	23.12	27.32
.1	24.3	27.9	1.041	1.068	0.902	0.924	22.82	27.53
0	24	28	1.040	1.070	0.901	0.926	22.49	27.74

Now we move on to year 2. In this case, not all data to be used are from the previous section since $1\,(+)\,\underset{\sim}{s}_{12}$ does not figure there, although obtaining it is easy by the simple multiplication $(1\,(+)\,\underset{\sim}{s}_1)\,(\cdot)\,(1\,(+)\,\underset{\sim}{s}_2) = (1\,(+)\,\underset{\sim}{s}_{12})$. We have done this in the following table.

α	$\underset{\sim}{c}_2$		$(1\,(+)\,\underset{\sim}{s}_{12})$		$1\,(:)\,(1\,(+)\,\underset{\sim}{i}_{12})$		$\underset{\sim}{c}_2\,(\cdot)\,(1\,(+)\,\underset{\sim}{s}_{12})\,(\cdot)\,[1\,(:)\,(1\,(+)\,\underset{\sim}{i}_{12})]$	
1	25		1.092		0.833		22.74	
.9	24.8	25.3	1.090	1.096	0.832	0.837	22.49	23.21
.8	24.6	25.6	1.088	1.100	0.829	0.840	22.19	23.65
.7	24.4	25.9	1.086	1.104	0.827	0.843	21.91	24.10
.6	24.2	26.2	1.084	1.109	0.825	0.846	21.64	24.58
.5	24	26.5	1.082	1.113	0.823	0.849	21.37	25.04
.4	23.8	26.8	1.079	1.117	0.820	0.853	21.06	25.53
.3	23.6	27.1	1.077	1.121	0.818	0.856	20.79	26.00
.2	23.4	27.4	1.075	1.126	0.815	0.858	20.50	26.47
.1	23.2	27.7	1.073	1.130	0.814	0.862	20.26	26.98
0	23	28	1.071	1.134	0.812	0.865	20.00	27.46

When moving on to year three and successive years, it is necessary to take into account the same considerations relative to the inflation rate $(1\ (+)\ \underset{\sim}{s}_{123})$. This then will be:

α	$\underset{\sim}{C}_3$		$(1\ (+)\ \underset{\sim}{s}_{123})$		$1\ (:)\ (1\ (+)\ \underset{\sim}{i}_{123})$		$\underset{\sim}{C}_3\ (\cdot)\ (1\ (+)\ \underset{\sim}{s}_{123})\ (\cdot)$ $(\cdot)\ [1\ (:)\ (1\ (+)\ \underset{\sim}{i}_{123})]$	
1	24		1.136		0.764		20.83	
.9	23.7	24.2	1.132	1.141	0.762	0.770	20.44	21.26
.8	23.4	24.4	1.129	1.146	0.759	0.774	20.05	21.64
.7	23.1	24.6	1.126	1.151	0.757	0.780	19.69	22.08
.6	22.8	24.8	1.123	1.158	0.754	0.785	19.30	22.54
.5	22.5	25	1.120	1.163	0.751	0.789	18.92	22.94
.4	22.2	25.2	1.116	1.168	0.748	0.796	18.53	23.43
.3	21.9	25.4	1.112	1.174	0.745	0.800	18.14	23.85
.2	21.6	25.6	1.109	1.180	0.742	0.805	17.77	24.32
.1	21.3	25.8	1.106	1.185	0.741	0.811	17.46	24.79
0	21	26	1.103	1.191	0.738	0.816	17.09	25.27

Year 4:

α	$\underset{\sim}{C}_4$		$(1\ (+)\ \underset{\sim}{s}_{1234})$		$1\ (:)\ (1\ (+)\ \underset{\sim}{i}_{1234})$		$\underset{\sim}{C}_4\ (\cdot)\ (1\ (+)\ \underset{\sim}{s}_{1234})\ (\cdot)$ $(\cdot)\ [1\ (:)\ (1\ (+)\ \underset{\sim}{i}_{1234})]$	
1	23		1.170		0.707		19.02	
.9	22.7	23.2	1.165	1.177	0.704	0.714	18.62	19.50
.8	22.4	23.4	1.161	1.185	0.700	0.719	18.20	19.94
.7	22.1	23.6	1.156	1.192	0.697	0.726	17.81	20.42
.6	21.8	23.8	1.152	1.202	0.693	0.732	17.40	20.94
.5	21.5	24	1.148	1.209	0.689	0.737	17.00	21.38
.4	21.2	24.2	1.143	1.217	0.685	0.745	16.60	21.94
.3	20.9	24.4	1.137	1.226	0.681	0.750	16.18	22.43
.2	20.6	24.6	1.133	1.234	0.677	0.757	15.80	22.98
.1	20.3	24.8	1.129	1.242	0.675	0.764	15.47	23.53
0	20	25	1.125	1.250	0.671	0.769	15.10	24.03

Finally we find the net updated value for year 5:

α	$\underset{\sim}{C}_5$		$(1\ (+)\ \underset{\sim}{s}_{12345})$		$1\ (:)\ (1\ (+)\ \underset{\sim}{i}_{12345})$		$\underset{\sim}{C}_5\ (\cdot)\ (1\ (+)\ \underset{\sim}{s}_{12345})\ (\cdot)$ $(\cdot)\ [1\ (:)\ (1\ (+)\ \underset{\sim}{i}_{12345})]$	
1	22		1.205		0.660		17.50	
.9	21.6	22.2	1.199	1.213	0.657	0.668	17.01	17.99
.8	21.2	22.4	1.193	1.223	0.652	0.674	16.49	18.46
.7	20.8	22.6	1.187	1.231	0.647	0.682	15.97	18.97
.6	20.4	22.8	1.182	1.243	0.643	0.689	15.50	19.53
.5	20	23	1.177	1.251	0.638	0.695	15.02	20.00
.4	19.6	23.2	1.170	1.261	0.633	0.704	14.51	20.59
.3	19.2	23.4	1.163	1.271	0.628	0.710	14.02	21.12
.2	18.8	23.6	1.158	1.281	0.623	0.718	13.56	21.71
.1	18.4	23.8	1.153	1.290	0.620	0.726	13.15	22.29
0	18	24	1.147	1.300	0.615	0.732	12.70	22.84

We now gather the fuzzy numbers obtained in order to carry out their addition on a level to level basis, obviously deducting the initial payment for the purchase of the investment object $M = 80$. In this way we can find the net updated value in which, at this point in the calculations, technical progress has not yet been included, in accordance with the hypothesis established according to which this phenomenon does not appear in the process until acquisition of new equipment (investment object).

Below we show the result:

α	Year 0		Year 1		Year 2		Year 3		Year 4		Year 5		NUV	
1	80		25.77		22.74		20.83		19.02		17.50		25.86	
.9	80	80	25.43	25.97	22.49	23.21	20.44	21.26	18.62	19.50	17.01	17.99	23.99	27.93
.8	80	80	25.09	26.14	22.19	23.65	20.05	21.64	18.20	19.94	16.49	18.46	22.02	29.83
.7	80	80	24.78	26.35	21.91	24.10	19.69	22.08	17.81	20.42	15.97	18.97	20.16	31.92
.6	80	80	24.45	26.55	21.64	24.58	19.30	22.54	17.40	20.94	15.50	19.53	18.29	34.14
.5	80	80	24.11	26.73	21.37	25.04	18.92	22.94	17.00	21.38	15.02	20.00	16.42	36.09
.4	80	80	23.78	26.94	21.06	25.53	18.53	23.43	16.60	21.94	14.51	20.59	14.48	38.43
.3	80	80	23.45	27.14	20.79	26.00	18.14	23.85	16.18	22.43	14.02	21.12	12.58	40.54
.2	80	80	23.12	27.32	20.50	26.47	17.77	24.32	15.80	22.98	13.56	21.71	10.75	42.80
.1	80	80	22.82	27.53	20.26	26.98	17.46	24.79	15.47	23.53	13.15	22.29	9.16	45.12
0	80	80	22.49	27.74	20.00	27.46	17.09	25.27	15.10	24.03	12.70	22.84	7.38	47.34

Before continuing with this process, we feel we should make a couple of observations.

The first refers to the fact, which can occur with certain frequency (the previous example is representative of this), for which the investment object is *totally* advisable if technical progress is not taken into account, because the Net Updated Value is within the positive field of reality, in the R^+, while on making this phenomenon intervene, the decision to invest may become economically inadequate, because in part or totally, the fuzzy number representing the capital value of the investment is in R^-. When displacement to the left gives rise to the fact that only a part of the referential is within the field of the negative reals, then only the pessimistic positions will not advise the acquisition of the investment object.

This leads us on to the second consideration, linked of course, to the first: the Net Updated Value *without* technical progress is greater than the Net Updated Value *with* technical progress, when this phenomenon has an incidence of the same intensity on collections and payments. The question is now brought up as to why incorporate any technical progress to the production process. The reply is obvious. Only if we board the train of progress will it be possible to maintain a competitive position, if other companies reduce their sales prices. On the contrary, maintenance of collections and the reduction in payments (caused by technical progress) will determine an increase in the Net Updated Value. In other words, without resorting to technical progress, it is difficult to imagine maintaining sales quotas, because a reduction in price, which the other companies will certainly do, will not be possible.

Having made these comments we will continue with our calculations. For this we are going to assume an economic horizon of 15 years, for which it will be necessary to use 3 investment objects.

If we use, for the first 5 years, the same rates for technical progress as used in the previous section, $1\,(+)\,\underset{\sim}{k}^{(1)}_{12345}$, we will have to use the same inflation rates $1\,(+)\,\underset{\sim}{s}^{(1)}_{12345}$ and interest rates $1\,(+)\,\underset{\sim}{i}^{(1)}_{12345}$ for making the <<transfer>> of the capital value from period 5 to period 0, but on the other hand, even though the <<structure>> of the cost of acquisition and exploitation of the equipment were to be the same, for the first and for the rest, there is no reason why, inflation and interest rates should be equal, and they normally are not, during the years of life of the second equipment, to the years of life of the first. Let us see how we can solve this riddle.

a) With regard to the inflation process for years 6 through 10 it can be assumed, for example, that the experts consider certain numbers that are relatively moderate as a consequence of the consolidation of the European Union, the end of the run up period to the single currency and the development of financial policies, although certain contraindications and frictions that will not permit figures as low as is desired are foreseen. They offer as an orienting annual estimate the FTN $\underset{\sim}{s}^{(2)} = (1.6, 2, 2.5)$ as a percentage. For the accumulation we feel it is possible to abandon the ordinary products that break triangulation, taking into account the experience arrived at from the calculations made for the first investment object in which we have seen the low deviation there was of the triangular approximation relative to the fuzzy numbers obtained by <<regular operation>>. Therefore we accept the following triangular approximations[5].

	$1 (+) \underset{\sim}{s}_{1}^{(2)}$	$1 (+) \underset{\sim}{s}_{12}^{(2)}$	$1 (+) \underset{\sim}{s}_{123}^{(2)}$	$1 (+) \underset{\sim}{s}_{1234}^{(2)}$	$1 (+) \underset{\sim}{s}_{12345}^{(2)}$
α	(1.016, 1.020, 1.025)	(1.032, 1.040, 1.051)	(1.048, 1.061, 1.077)	(1.065, 1.082, 1.104)	(1.082, 1.104, 1.132)
1	1.020	1.040	1.061	1.082	1.104
.9	1.020 1.020	1.039 1.041	1.060 1.063	1.080 1.084	1.102 1.107
.8	1.019 1.021	1.038 1.042	1.058 1.064	1.079 1.086	1.100 1.110
.7	1.019 1.021	1.038 1.043	1.057 1.066	1.077 1.089	1.097 1.112
.6	1.018 1.022	1.037 1.044	1.056 1.067	1.075 1.091	1.095 1.115
.5	1.018 1.022	1.036 1.045	1.054 1.069	1.073 1.093	1.093 1.118
.4	1.018 1.023	1.035 1.047	1.053 1.071	1.072 1.095	1.091 1.121
.3	1.017 1.023	1.034 1.048	1.052 1.072	1.070 1.097	1.089 1.124
.2	1.017 1.024	1.034 1.049	1.051 1.074	1.068 1.100	1.086 1.126
.1	1.016 1.024	1.033 1.050	1.049 1.075	1.067 1.102	1.084 1.129
0	1.016 1.025	1.032 1.051	1.048 1.077	1.065 1.104	1.082 1.132

b) With regard to the rates of interest, generally speaking, the same considerations, as made for inflation rates, are valid. In this sense, the experts have estimated a rate of interest, for years 6 through 10, of $\underset{\sim}{i}^{(2)} = (3, 4, 4.5)$ in percentage. The following FTN can be accepted then, as triangular approximations of the respective capitalisation coefficients:

α	$1 (+) \underset{\sim}{i}_1^{(2)}$		$1 (+) \underset{\sim}{i}_{12}^{(2)}$		$1 (+) \underset{\sim}{i}_{123}^{(2)}$		$1 (+) \underset{\sim}{i}_{1234}^{(2)}$		$1 (+) \underset{\sim}{i}_{12345}^{(2)}$	
	(1.030, 1.040, 1.045)		(1.061, 1.082, 1.092)		(1.093, 1.125, 1.141)		(1.126, 1.170, 1.192)		(1.160, 1.217, 1.246)	
1	1.040		1.082		1.125		1.170		1.217	
.9	1.039	1.040	1.080	1.083	1.122	1.127	1.166	1.172	1.211	1.220
.8	1.038	1.041	1.078	1.084	1.119	1.128	1.161	1.174	1.206	1.223
.7	1.037	1.041	1.076	1.085	1.115	1.130	1.157	1.177	1.200	1.226
.6	1.036	1.042	1.074	1.086	1.112	1.131	1.152	1.179	1.194	1.229
.5	1.035	1.042	1.071	1.087	1.109	1.133	1.148	1.181	1.188	1.231
.4	1.034	1.043	1.069	1.088	1.106	1.135	1.144	1.183	1.183	1.234
.3	1.033	1.043	1.067	1.089	1.103	1.136	1.139	1.185	1.177	1.237
.2	1.032	1.044	1.065	1.090	1.099	1.138	1.135	1.188	1.171	1.240
.1	1.031	1.044	1.063	1.091	1.096	1.139	1.130	1.190	1.166	1.243
0	1.030	1.045	1.061	1.092	1.093	1.141	1.126	1.192	1.160	1.246

With the results we have obtained for inflation and capitalisation relative to the useful life of the second investment object, we are now ready to find the net updated values for each period, from the estimates of the exploitation profits estimated in the previous section.

We will take a look at the results for the first year, and on this occasion so as to vary the calculations, we will do so by means of the division[6] between the inflation rate and the capitalisation rate.

α	$\underset{\sim}{\mathcal{C}}_1$		$1 (+) \underset{\sim}{s}_1^{(2)}$		$1 (+) \underset{\sim}{i}_1^{(2)}$		$\underset{\sim}{\mathcal{C}}_1 (\cdot) (1 (+) \underset{\sim}{s}_1^{(2)}) (:) (1 (+) \underset{\sim}{i}_1^{(2)})$	
1	27		1.02		1.04		26.48	
.9	26.7	27.1	1.020	1.020	1.039	1.040	26.19	26.60
.8	26.4	27.2	1.019	1.021	1.038	1.041	25.84	26.75
.7	26.1	27.3	1.019	1.021	1.037	1.041	25.55	26.88
.6	25.8	27.4	1.018	1.022	1.036	1.042	25.20	27.03
.5	25.5	27.5	1.018	1.022	1.035	1.042	24.91	27.15
.4	25.2	27.6	1.018	1.023	1.034	1.043	24.59	27.31
.3	24.9	27.7	1.017	1.023	1.033	1.043	24.28	27.43
.2	24.6	27.8	1.017	1.024	1.032	1.044	23.96	27.58
.1	24.3	27.9	1.016	1.024	1.031	1.044	23.65	27.71
0	24	28	1.016	1.025	1.030	1.045	23.33	27.86

With regard to the second year we arrive at:

α	$\tilde{C}_2$		$1 \,(+)\, \tilde{s}_{12}^{(2)}$		$1 \,(+)\, \tilde{i}_{12}^{(2)}$		$\tilde{C}_2 \,(\cdot)\, (1 \,(+)\, \tilde{s}_{12}^{(2)}) \,(:)\, (1 \,(+)\, \tilde{i}_{12}^{(2)})$	
1	25		1.040		1.082		24.03	
.9	24.8	25.3	1.039	1.041	1.080	1.083	23.79	24.39
.8	24.6	25.6	1.038	1.042	1.078	1.084	23.56	24.74
.7	24.4	25.9	1.038	1.043	1.076	1.085	23.34	25.10
.6	24.2	26.2	1.037	1.044	1.074	1.086	23.11	25.47
.5	24	26.5	1.036	1.045	1.071	1.087	22.87	25.86
.4	23.8	26.8	1.035	1.047	1.069	1.088	22.64	26.25
.3	23.6	27.1	1.034	1.048	1.067	1.089	22.41	26.62
.2	23.4	27.4	1.034	1.049	1.065	1.090	22.20	26.99
.1	23.2	27.7	1.033	1.050	1.063	1.091	21.97	27.36
0	23	28	1.032	1.051	1.061	1.092	21.74	27.74

Now we move on to the third year:

α	$\tilde{C}_3$		$1 \,(+)\, \tilde{s}_{123}^{(2)}$		$1 \,(+)\, \tilde{i}_{123}^{(2)}$		$\tilde{C}_3 \,(\cdot)\, (1 \,(+)\, \tilde{s}_{123}^{(2)}) \,(:)\, (1 \,(+)\, \tilde{i}_{123}^{(2)})$	
1	24		1.061		1.125		22.63	
.9	23.7	24.2	1.060	1.063	1.122	1.127	22.29	22.93
.8	23.4	24.4	1.058	1.064	1.119	1.128	21.95	23.20
.7	23.1	24.6	1.057	1.066	1.115	1.130	21.61	23.52
.6	22.8	24.8	1.056	1.067	1.112	1.131	21.29	23.80
.5	22.5	25	1.054	1.069	1.109	1.133	20.93	24.10
.4	22.2	25.2	1.053	1.071	1.106	1.135	20.60	24.40
.3	21.9	25.4	1.052	1.072	1.103	1.136	20.28	24.69
.2	21.6	25.6	1.051	1.074	1.099	1.138	19.95	25.02
.1	21.3	25.8	1.049	1.075	1.096	1.139	19.62	25.30
0	21	26	1.048	1.077	1.093	1.141	19.29	25.62

We do the calculations for the fourth year:

α	$\underset{\sim}{C}_4$		$1 (+) \underset{\sim}{s}^{(2)}_{1234}$		$1 (+) \underset{\sim}{i}^{(2)}_{1234}$		$\underset{\sim}{C}_4 (\cdot) (1 (+) \underset{\sim}{s}^{(2)}_{1234} (:) (1 (+) \underset{\sim}{i}^{(2)}_{1234})$	
1	23		1.082		1.170		21.27	
.9	22.7	23.2	1.080	1.084	1.166	1.172	20.92	21.57
.8	22.4	23.4	1.079	1.086	1.161	1.174	20.59	21.89
.7	22.1	23.6	1.077	1.089	1.157	1.177	20.22	22.21
.6	21.8	23.8	1.075	1.091	1.152	1.179	19.88	22.54
.5	21.5	24	1.073	1.093	1.148	1.181	19.53	22.85
.4	21.2	24.2	1.072	1.095	1.144	1.183	19.21	23.16
.3	20.9	24.4	1.070	1.097	1.139	1.185	18.87	23.50
.2	20.6	24.6	1.068	1.100	1.135	1.188	18.52	23.84
.1	20.3	24.8	1.067	1.102	1.130	1.190	18.20	24.18
0	20	25	1.065	1.104	1.126	1.192	17.87	24.51

And finally we obtain the net updated value for the fifth year:

α	$\underset{\sim}{C}_5$		$1 (+) \underset{\sim}{s}^{(2)}_{12345}$		$1 (+) \underset{\sim}{i}^{(2)}_{12345}$		$\underset{\sim}{C}_5 (\cdot) (1 (+) \underset{\sim}{s}^{(2)}_{12345}) (:) (1 (+) \underset{\sim}{i}^{(2)}_{12345})$	
1	22		1.104		1.217		19.96	
.9	21.6	22.2	1.102	1.107	1.211	1.220	19.51	20.29
.8	21.2	22.4	1.100	1.110	1.206	1.223	19.07	20.62
.7	20.8	22.6	1.097	1.112	1.200	1.226	18.61	20.94
.6	20.4	22.8	1.095	1.115	1.194	1.229	18.17	21.29
.5	20	23	1.093	1.118	1.188	1.231	17.76	21.64
.4	19.6	23.2	1.091	1.121	1.183	1.234	17.33	21.98
.3	19.2	23.4	1.089	1.124	1.177	1.237	16.90	22.35
.2	18.8	23.6	1.086	1.126	1.171	1.240	16.46	22.69
.1	18.4	23.8	1.084	1.129	1.166	1.243	16.05	23.04
0	18	24	1.082	1.132	1.160	1.246	15.63	23.42

Once we have obtained the duly updated exploitation profits, we can find the Net Updated Value of the second object of the chain, taking into account that the value arrived at is situated at the end of the fifth year (or if needs be at the beginning of year 6). We now do the presentation in the same way as we did for the first investment object.

α	Year 0	Year 1	Year 2	Year 3	Year 4	Year 5	NUV
1	−80	26.48	24.03	22.63	21.27	19.96	34.37
.9	−80 −80	26.19 26.60	23.79 24.39	22.29 22.93	20.92 21.57	19.51 20.29	32.70 35.78
.8	−80 −80	25.84 26.75	23.56 24.74	21.95 23.20	20.59 21.89	19.07 20.62	31.01 37.20
.7	−80 −80	25.55 26.88	23.34 25.10	21.61 23.52	20.22 22.21	18.61 20.94	29.33 38.65
.6	−80 −80	25.20 27.03	23.11 25.47	21.29 23.80	19.88 22.54	18.17 21.29	27.65 40.13
.5	−80 −80	24.91 27.15	22.87 25.86	20.93 24.10	19.53 22.85	17.76 21.64	26.00 41.60
.4	−80 −80	24.59 27.31	22.64 26.25	20.60 24.40	19.21 23.16	17.33 21.98	24.37 43.10
.3	−80 −80	24.28 27.43	22.41 26.62	20.28 24.69	18.87 23.50	16.90 22.35	22.74 44.59
.2	−80 −80	23.96 27.58	22.20 26.99	19.95 25.02	18.52 23.84	16.46 22.69	21.09 46.12
.1	−80 −80	23.65 27.71	21.97 27.36	19.62 25.30	18.20 24.18	16.05 23.04	19.49 47.59
0	−80 −80	23.33 27.86	21.74 27.74	19.29 25.62	17.87 24.51	15.63 23.42	17.86 49.15

The net updated value obtained in this way constitutes a sort of profit situated at the end of the fifth year. In order to <<transfer>> this to the initial period it is necessary to take into account the inflation there was during the first five years (coefficient $\underset{\sim}{s}_{12345}$), as well as technical progress occurring during the first five year period (according to our hypothesis $\underset{\sim}{k}_{12345}$). Obviously it will be necessary to apply the updating coefficient (in this case $1\ (:)\ (1\ (+)\ \underset{\sim}{i}_{12345})$). We arrive at:

α	NUV	$(1\ (+)\underset{\sim}{s}_{12345})\ (:)\ (1\ (+)\ \underset{\sim}{k}_{12345})$	$1\ (:)\ (1\ (+)\ \underset{\sim}{i}_{12345})$	NUV initial moment
1	34.37	0.990	0.660	22.46
.9	32.70 35.78	0.979 1.007	0.657 0.668	21.03 24.07
.8	31.01 37.20	0.969 1.021	0.652 0.674	19.59 25.60
.7	29.33 38.65	0.959 1.038	0.647 0.682	18.20 27.36
.6	27.65 40.13	0.949 1.057	0.643 0.689	16.87 29.22
.5	26.00 41.60	0.938 1.074	0.638 0.695	15.56 31.05
.4	24.37 43.10	0.929 1.092	0.633 0.704	14.33 33.13
.3	22.74 44.59	0.920 1.108	0.628 0.710	13.14 35.08
.2	21.09 46.12	0.910 1.127	0.623 0.718	11.96 37.32
.1	19.49 47.59	0.899 1.147	0.620 0.726	10.86 39.63
0	17.86 49.15	0.889 1.165	0.615 0.732	9.76 41.91

Finally we are left to tackle the study of the third and last investment object in the chain. It would seem normal, given the instability of economic systems, to accept as estimated for the medium and long-term, orienting overall figures that are valid for all the years. And this is more certain as the economic parameters refer to a much wider horizon. In this sense we must repeat, for the period from 11 to 15 years, the same process that we carried out for the second object. We feel that is not necessary to do the same calculations, although perhaps with different numbers, as no element is contributed that is complementary to those used up to now. For this we propose to consider the same rates of inflation and interest as those estimated for the second investment object, which will take us to obtaining a Net Updated Value situated at the end of period 10, equal to the one at the end of period 5. On accepting this assumption all that remains is to transfer the Net Updated Value from period 10 to period 0, by using the coefficients that we will designate by $\underset{\sim}{s}_{1234567890}$ and $\underset{\sim}{i}_{1234567890}$. Let us move on and see how this information can be obtained.

With the object of not stretching this development out excessively we are going to continue operating with triangular approximations.

1. Relative to inflation we have arrived at:

$$(1\ (+)\,\underset{\sim}{s}_{12345}) = (1.147,\ 1.205,\ 1.300)$$
$$(1\ (+)\,\underset{\sim}{s}^{(2)}_{12345}) = (1.082,\ 1.104,\ 1.132)$$

We can accept:

$$(1\ (+)\,\underset{\sim}{s}_{1234567890}) = (1\ (+)\,\underset{\sim}{s}_{12345})\ (\cdot)\ (1\ (+)\,\underset{\sim}{s}^{(2)}_{12345}) \cong (1.241,\ 1.330,\ 1.472)$$

2. Relative to interest rates, we know:

$$1\ (:)\ (1\ (+)\,\underset{\sim}{i}_{12345}) = (0.615,\ 0.660,\ 0.732)$$
$$1\ (:)\ (1\ (+)\,\underset{\sim}{i}^{(2)}_{12345}) = 1\ (:)\ (1.160,\ 1.217,\ 1.246) \cong (0.802,\ 0.822,\ 0.862)$$

Then we can accept:

$$1\ (:)\ (1\ (+)\,\underset{\sim}{i}_{1234567890}) = [1\ (:)\ (1\ (+)\,\underset{\sim}{i}_{12345})]\ (\cdot)\ [1\ (:)\ (1\ (+)\,\underset{\sim}{i}^{(2)}_{12345})] \cong$$
$$\cong (0.493,\ 0.542,\ 0.631)$$

And in α-cuts:

$$[0.493 + 0.049\alpha,\ 0.631 - 0.089\alpha]$$

We now have to estimate the technical progress rate that will have occurred during the first ten years of the investment process, which can be included with the third object of the chain. With this known information we have the technical progress rates for the first 5 years. In effect:

$$(1\ (+)\ \underset{\sim}{k}_1) = (1.02,\ 1.03,\ 1.05)$$

$$(1\ (+)\ \underset{\sim}{k}_2) = (1.02,\ 1.03,\ 1.04)$$

$$(1\ (+)\ \underset{\sim}{k}_3) = (1.02,\ 1.04,\ 1.05)$$

$$(1\ (+)\ \underset{\sim}{k}_4) = (1.02,\ 1.05,\ 1.06)$$

$$(1\ (+)\ \underset{\sim}{k}_5) = (1.03,\ 1.05,\ 1.06)$$

We arrive at:

$$(1\ (+)\ \underset{\sim}{k}_{12345}) = (1\ (+)\ \underset{\sim}{k}_1)\ (\cdot)\ (1\ (+)\ \underset{\sim}{k}_2)\ (\cdot) \cdots (\cdot)\ (1\ (+)\ \underset{\sim}{k}_5) = (1.115,\ 1.216,\ 1.288)$$

Now we must establish the basis for estimating the technical progress rate for the second five-year period. From all points of view all reasonable hypotheses are acceptable. For example, the hypothesis that it is expected that during this period an important innovation will be introduced, with a rate of:

$$(1\ (+)\ \underset{\sim}{k}^{(2)}_{12345}) = (1.15,\ 1.25,\ 1.30)$$

In this case, we would accept:

$$(1\ (+)\ \underset{\sim}{k}_{1234567890}) = (1\ (+)\ \underset{\sim}{k}_{12345})\ (\cdot)\ (1\ (+)\ \underset{\sim}{k}^{(2)}_{12345}) \cong (1.282,\ 1.520,\ 1.674)$$

All this allows us to <<transfer>> the Net Update Value situated at moment 10 to moment 0. Let us remember in this respect the hypothesis of constancy the conditions under which the economic activity unfolds during the useful life of invesment objects 2 and 3 (except relative to technical progress).

The quotient between inflation rate and technical progress can be expressed by a triangular approximation.

$$(1\ (+)\ \underset{\sim}{s}_{1234567890})\ (:)\ (1\ (+)\ \underset{\sim}{k}_{1234567890}) \cong (0.741,\ 0.875,\ 1.148)$$

Expressed in α-cuts, it is:

$$[0.741 + 0.134\alpha,\ 1.148 - 0.273\alpha]$$

In the following table we have shown the result obtained:

α	NUV		$(1\ (+)\ \underset{\sim}{s}_{1234567890})\ (:)$ $(:)\ (1\ (+)\ \underset{\sim}{k}_{1234567890})$		$1\ (:)\ (1\ (+)\ \underset{\sim}{i}_{1234567890})$		NUV initial moment	
1	34.37		0.875		0.542		16.30	
.9	32.70	35.78	0.862	0.902	0.537	0.551	15.14	17.78
.8	31.01	37.20	0.848	0.930	0.532	0.560	13.99	19.37
.7	29.33	38.65	0.835	0.957	0.527	0.569	12.91	21.05
.6	27.65	40.13	0.821	0.984	0.522	0.578	11.85	22.82
.5	26.00	41.60	0.808	1.011	0.517	0.586	10.86	24.64
.4	24.37	43.10	0.795	1.039	0.513	0.595	9.94	26.64
.3	22.74	44.59	0.781	1.066	0.508	0.604	9.02	28.71
.2	21.09	46.12	0.768	1.093	0.503	0.613	8.15	30.90
.1	19.49	47.59	0.754	1.121	0.498	0.622	7.32	33.18
0	17.86	49.15	0.741	1.148	0.493	0.631	6.52	35.60

Having found the net updated value, relative to period zero of the three objects forming the investment chain, it will now be sufficient to carry out the addition in order to obtain the net updated value of the chain, which in our case is:

α	NUV first object		NUV second object		NUV third object		NUV chain	
1	25.86		22.46		16.30		64.62	
.9	23.99	27.93	21.03	24.07	15.14	17.78	60.16	69.78
.8	22.02	29.83	19.59	25.60	13.99	19.37	55.60	74.80
.7	20.16	31.92	18.20	27.36	12.91	21.05	51.27	80.33
.6	18.29	34.14	16.87	29.22	11.85	22.82	47.01	86.18
.5	16.42	36.09	15.56	31.05	10.86	24.64	42.84	91.78
.4	14.48	38.43	14.33	33.13	9.94	26.64	38.75	98.20
.3	12.58	40.54	13.14	35.08	9.02	28.71	34.74	104.33
.2	10.75	42.80	11.96	37.32	8.15	30.90	30.86	111.02
.1	9.16	45.12	10.86	39.63	7.32	33.18	27.34	117.93
0	7.38	47.34	9.76	41.91	6.52	35.60	23.66	124.85

In the event of having to make a decision in terms of investing or not in a chain, the result arrived at will be sufficiently indicative for considering the economic convenience of its acquisition. The simple and very much outlined reasoning would be: in the worst of cases I shall obtain an updated <<profit>> of

23.66, in the best of case 124.85 and the best assumption will be found in 64.62. However, it is not a rare occurrence to contemplate the existence of several (or many) possible chains of investment with very different basic individual objects. In this case, as already mentioned, it will be necessary to calculate the value of all the chains subject to analysis and determine which of them is the most convenient. Therefore, the technical problem is reduced to the comparison between fuzzy numbers, an operation that is sufficiently well known and used.

From another point of view in the didactic example we have developed, the existence of a high degree of uncertainty in the fuzzy number obtained with the net updated value of the chain can be seen. This fact should come as no surprise, if the lengthy period considered as the economic horizon (15 years) is taken into account, since with the passage of time the number of operations increases and with them the <<base>> (interval at level 0) of the fuzzy number is widened. As we are well aware there are a wide variety of techniques in existence for reducing uncertainty. We have used some of them in previous chapters of this book. Also our predilection (we feel not arbitrary) is known for the use of counter-expertise by means of R^+-expertons. We propose their consideration, out of need or simply convenience, convinced of their excellent results.

Finally let us say, in justification, that the detail used in developing this case seeks a methodological and didactic end. In effect, this chapter is the last of a series devoted to the problem of the selection of investments in uncertainty, in which a set of models has been presented drawn up through the transformation or adaptation of classical schemes in certainty, based on the updating of the monetary currents of collections and payments arising from the decision to invest. It would seem then adequate to include the whole and systemised process by means of the corresponding tables, in this way allowing, the transition with no problems for those who are not accustomed to operating with fuzzy numbers. The simultaneous or successive use of FTN, triangular approximations or simply fuzzy numbers, is intended to show the interest of these uncertain numbers in realities or perspectives which are difficult to estimate exactly, and also to emphasise the oft repeated assertion, that in a context of profound changes, a decision is possible even when not having available information that is acceptable as certain, because the mere approximation is a sufficient source of valid elements for framing our objectives.

The schemes we have presented allow for the drawing up of a large number of variations. It is sufficient to explicitly introduce, into any of the monetary currents, economic parameters that represent the many elements that form them. In our case we have limited ourselves to incorporating technical progress, inflation and wear and tear, but the way is open for the entry of many other phenomena that have an incidence on the monetary consequences of the decision to invest.

References

1 See, for example, A. Kaufmann, J. Gil Aluja and A. M. Gil Lafuente: *La creatividad en la gestión de las empresas,* Pirámide, Madrid, 1994.

2 J. Gil Aluja: *Inversiones, Certeza, riesgo e incertidumbre. I. Certeza,* Faculty of Economic and Business Sciences, Barcelona, 1992, pages 76-84.

3 Stephen Enke: *Economia para el desarrollo,* Uteha, Mexico, 1966, page 77.

4 Stephen Enke: *Economia para el desarrollo,* Uteha, Mexico, 1966, page 120.

5 The necessary rounding off to three decimal figures does not allow regularity in the numbers and moving through the different levels.

6 Just remember that to divide intervals in the field of R^+, it is sufficient to cross the extremes.

10 Estimating economic parameters in investment

General description of the model

Investment processes comprise a complex reality that companies today approach with considerable difficulties as a consequence of the intervention of many aspects of a diverse nature. It is paradoxical, however, that this complexity can arise from initial structures, the simplicity of which later on causes surprise when delving deeper into the intricacies of the investment network.

Indeed, under any study carried out taking into account the traditional schemes for the decision to invest, an underlying principal can be found: the collection current arising from acquisition and operation of an investment object must <<at least>> compensate the payments current incurred by the same. Here, in a very summarised manner, we have, on the one hand, the collections arising as a consequence of production and sale of the goods and/or services made with the investment object (in the event equipment) and on the other, payments frequently separated into several categories which can by summarised in two: those arising out of the acquisition of the investment object and those that are a consequence of its operation (raw materials, labour, maintenance costs...).

It has been seen that with these initial bases or other similar ones, specialists on the subject have drawn up a wide range of models that include a very extensive variety of aspects taken from reality that permit a more or less adequate treatment of the needs of our executives. There are many elements that are included implicitly or explicitly in models for investment selection, forming a part of or having an influence on collection and payment currents. Just to mention a few of them, we can refer to inflation, technical progress, wear and tear (already studied by us) and a long etcetera. The <<manner>> in which the corresponding numbers are arrived at, the monetary reflection of these phenomena, is not uniform in every context and is normally quite different from company to company.

We should not be shocked if we notice that with an enormous degree of frequency this particular <<data>> of the problem is estimated in a not very rigorous manner and sometimes it is even based on the simple intuition of those supplying the information. We have repeated over and over again that these <<amounts>>, included as <<data>> for models are not normally the result of objective calculations and therefore they are not <<measurements>>, but are the result of subjective estimates, that is to say <<valuations>>. Then of course it will not be suitable to use hard operators in the model, as these are only valid within the sphere of certainty or probability, and the use will be imposed of those operators called soft, that are suitable for handling subjectivity and imprecision.

Located in this context, in which rapid social and economic changes lead to an environment of uncertainty, we feel that it is advantageous and up to a certain point necessary, to search in the secrets of this act of the human operator that means subjective estimating of an amount, although behind the latter, and as a support, exist technical knowledge, experience, intuition and even genius.

For this we are going to imagine that in a company the need is brought up for acquiring equipment (investment object) that exists in the market, which, by its technological characteristics, does not permit estimating, with the desired exactitude, the collections and/or payments corresponding to all or part of these that intervene in the monetary currents arising from its eventual purchase. This is a necessary condition for determining the economic viability of the investment by means of a selection criterion which has been previously accepted and in this way take a decision based on the instruments supplied by traditional economic logic.

Faced with this possibility, the responsible executive of the company requests the advice of an expert, who with the data supplied by the company selling the equipment, his personal experience and that of the technical personnel of the purchasing company, and after having made a survey of the situation, needs and prospects of the market for the product or service resulting from the use of the investment object, makes certain estimates, considered acceptable, of the ranges within which the economic parameter sought could be (payments and/or collections or any of their component parts) in all and each one of the periods of useful life of the investment object.

As a consequence of habitual social and economic instability, the expert does not wish to express his opinion by means of crisp numbers, but does so by means of confidence intervals, in this way opting for greater freedom of expression. With this, the expert has the intention of covering all the possibilities that could arise, on resorting to a <<finite set of intervals *E*>>, valid for all and each of the periods under consideration. In this *E* set, the value of the economic parameter under study is also included at the time of initiating the investment process.

Let us assume that the expert establishes the following as possible intervals:

$$E = \{\underset{\sim}{A}, \underset{\sim}{B}, \underset{\sim}{C}, \underset{\sim}{D}, \underset{\sim}{E}, \underset{\sim}{F}\}$$

where:

$$\underset{\sim}{A} = [a_1, a_2], \quad \underset{\sim}{B} = [b_1, b_2], \quad \underset{\sim}{C} = [c_1, c_2]$$

$$\underset{\sim}{D} = [d_1, d_2], \quad \underset{\sim}{E} = [e_1, e_2], \quad \underset{\sim}{F} = [f_1, f_2]$$

Simply as an example we are going to accept valuation $\underset{\sim}{A} = [a_1, a_2]$ as the starting out point.

Before commencing with the presentation of the model, let us point out that the elements of set E can be expressed by crisp valuations, confidence intervals, triplets, fuzzy numbers or any other estimate considered as suitable for the reality of the object under study.

Once the elements of the E set are established, the need arises for assigning to each period, the valuations reflecting the real phenomena in a better way. In the first place an estimate could be proposed, equal for every period, that included any of the figures included in the E set. In the case under study, what would be found as a result would be an interval such that it would have as the lower extreme the lowest of the lower extremes and as the upper extreme the highest of the upper extremes of the intervals representing the set of estimates. It would be:

$$\underset{\sim}{X} = [x_1, x_2]$$

where:

$$x_1 = a_1 \wedge b_1 \wedge c_1 \wedge d_1 \wedge e_1 \wedge f_1$$

$$x_2 = a_2 \vee b_2 \vee c_2 \vee d_2 \vee e_2 \vee f_2$$

It would appear to be unnecessary to insist on the fact that in a great many cases interval $[x_1, x_2]$ can be very wide and, therefore, inoperative due to its very high degree of uncertainty.

Except on very rare occasions, in practice this path would appear to be particularly inoperative.

Now let us move on and propose a new scheme the object of which, in a certain fashion, is to gather together determined aspects that are implicit in direct estimates. For this, the expert is asked to establish new estimates by assigning a level of assumption on the <<passage>> of an element of set E in a period t to another, or the same, within period $t + 1$. In other words he is asked to establish certain new valuations for [0, 1], corresponding to the possibility of transfer or passage of one valuation to another. Obtaining this information gives rise to a matrix or fuzzy relation of transfer, such as the following:

$[\underset{\sim}{R}] =$

	$\underset{\sim}{A}$	$\underset{\sim}{B}$	$\underset{\sim}{C}$	$\underset{\sim}{D}$	$\underset{\sim}{E}$	$\underset{\sim}{F}$
$\underset{\sim}{A}$	Γ_{AA}	Γ_{AB}	Γ_{AC}	Γ_{AD}	Γ_{AE}	Γ_{AF}
$\underset{\sim}{B}$	Γ_{BA}	Γ_{BB}	Γ_{BC}	Γ_{BD}	Γ_{BE}	Γ_{BF}
$\underset{\sim}{C}$	Γ_{CA}	Γ_{CB}	Γ_{CC}	Γ_{CD}	Γ_{CE}	Γ_{CF}
$\underset{\sim}{D}$	Γ_{DA}	Γ_{DB}	Γ_{DC}	Γ_{DD}	Γ_{DE}	Γ_{DF}
$\underset{\sim}{E}$	Γ_{EA}	Γ_{EB}	Γ_{EC}	Γ_{ED}	Γ_{EE}	Γ_{EF}
$\underset{\sim}{F}$	Γ_{FA}	Γ_{FB}	Γ_{FC}	Γ_{FD}	Γ_{FE}	Γ_{FF}

This fuzzy relation of transition, in the first place, can be considered valid for any period of the economic horizon. What we have here then is a stationary economic system.

Finally, the expert is requested to express an opinion relative to the valuations of the economic parameter sought for the first period of start up of the investment object. This will give rise to a situation vector such as the following:

	$\underset{\sim}{A}$	$\underset{\sim}{B}$	$\underset{\sim}{C}$	$\underset{\sim}{D}$	$\underset{\sim}{E}$	$\underset{\sim}{F}$
$[\underset{\sim}{q}(0)] =$	v_A	v_B	v_C	v_D	v_E	v_F

From these estimates the situation vectors for each period can be obtained by means of successive convolutions:

$$[\underset{\sim}{q}(1)] = [\underset{\sim}{q}(0)] \bullet [\underset{\sim}{R}]$$
$$[\underset{\sim}{q}(2)] = [\underset{\sim}{q}(1)] \bullet [\underset{\sim}{R}] = [\underset{\sim}{q}(0)] \bullet [\underset{\sim}{R}]^2$$
$$\cdots\cdots\cdots\cdots\cdots\cdots\cdots\cdots\cdots\cdots\cdots\cdots$$
$$[\underset{\sim}{q}(n)] = [\underset{\sim}{q}(n-1)] \bullet [\underset{\sim}{R}] = [\underset{\sim}{q}(0)] \bullet [\underset{\sim}{R}]^n$$

An important differentiating fact between probability and uncertainty should be mentioned.

While in the probabilistic sphere, when transitions or passages are measured by probabilities, convergence towards a limit, when this exists, is represented by $[M]^n$ when $[M]^n = [M]^s$, $n > s$ being, in the sphere of uncertainty the limit position is expressed by the transitive closure $[\hat{\underset{\sim}{R}}]$ where, as is known:

$$[\hat{\underset{\sim}{R}}] = [\underset{\sim}{R}] \cup [\underset{\sim}{R}]^2 \cup \cdots \cup [\underset{\sim}{R}]^n$$

Now, as we have just mentioned, the existence or not of convergence in the limit, as well as the behaviour of the successive convoluted fuzzy relations $[\underset{\sim}{R}]^j$ give rise to a casuistic the study of which can supply valuable elements in the attempt for shedding light on the subject in question.

With the object of making this exposition simpler, we are going to resort to numerical examples that are capable of covering the widest range of situations that real problems present.

The hypothesis of the existence of equivalency classes

Let us return to the beginning of the problem, and situate ourselves at the time when the expert must assign the corresponding valuations. He starts out from the E set:

$$E = \{[10, 20], [21, 25], [26, 30], [31, 35], [36, 40], [41, 50]\}$$

It will be seen that with all the intervals, a segment [10, 50], considered excessively wide, is covered.

Following on this the following fuzzy relation of transition is supplied:

$[\underset{\sim}{R}] =$

	[10, 20]	[21, 25]	[26, 30]	[31, 35]	[36, 40]	[41, 50]
[10, 20]		.8	.6			
[21, 25]		.6	1	.8		
[26, 30]		.6	.8	1	.9	
[31, 35]			.8	1	.8	
[36, 40]			.4	.6	.8	
[41, 50]					1	.8

which can also be presented by an arrow form graph associated to this relation, such as the following (figure 10.1):

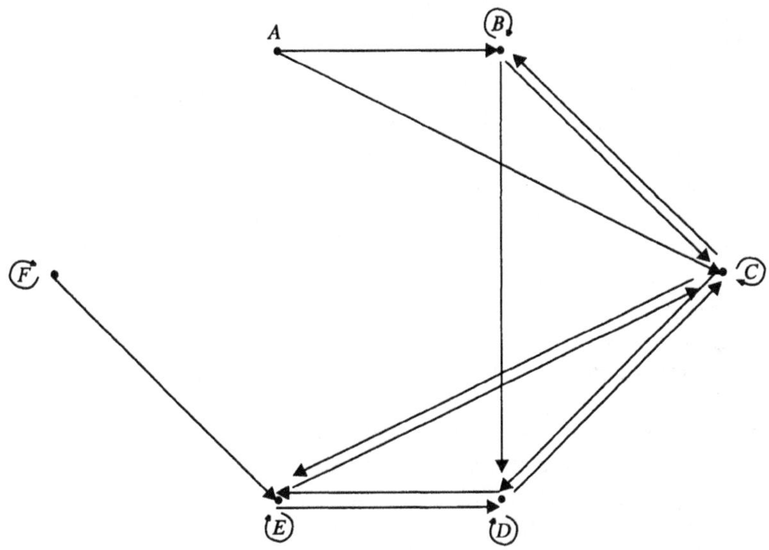

Figure 10.1.

Finally we arrive at the initial situation vector:

$[\underset{\sim}{q}(0)] =$

[10, 20]	[21, 25]	[26, 30]	[31, 35]	[36, 40]	[41, 50]
1	.9	.8	.6	.2	.1

Once we have the valuations supplied by the expert, we are going to develop the process that allows us to make a valid estimate of the economic parameters required for studying the investment. For this we will follow a procedure[1] the first phase of which consists in normalising the fuzzy relation of transition $[\underset{\sim}{R}]$, which in turn will give rise to $[\underset{\sim}{N}]$ [2].

$[\underset{\sim}{N}] =$

	$\underset{\sim}{A}$	$\underset{\sim}{B}$	$\underset{\sim}{C}$	$\underset{\sim}{D}$	$\underset{\sim}{E}$	$\underset{\sim}{F}$
$\underset{\sim}{A}$		1	.75			
$\underset{\sim}{B}$		.6	1	.8		
$\underset{\sim}{C}$		.6	.8	1	.9	
$\underset{\sim}{D}$			.8	1	.8	
$\underset{\sim}{E}$			.5	.75	1	
$\underset{\sim}{F}$					1	.8

Few variations can be seen in the valuations of each box between fuzzy relations $[\underset{\sim}{R}]$ and $[\underset{\sim}{N}]$. This is the reason why these are assumed as accepted by the expert. The circumstance could arise that in one row there could be no valuations near to the unit. In this case, normalisation would give rise to substantial differences between valuations in the passage from one state to the other of the fuzzy relation $[\underset{\sim}{R}]$ and $[\underset{\sim}{N}]$. When this happens, it would be wise, even using the proposed process, to do the normalisation of the transitive closure $[\hat{\underset{\sim}{R}}]$ if considered necessary, which is not the case in this and many other problems arising in the filed of management. The formal advantages are sufficiently well known, for using normalised fuzzy relations as a consequence of the bi-directional correspondence between conjecturable and normal fuzzy relations[3].

Having made these comments, we will continue with the process for determining which are the intervals which can <<succeed>> other confidence intervals, that is, which economic parameters of the E set can take place after others of the same set. For this we are going to determine, in the first place if any <<circuits>> exist or not in the arrow form graph.

Therefore, supposing, for example, that in one period the economic parameter were to be found in [26, 30], to see if it is possible to pass over, in other periods, to [31, 35] or [21, 25], etc., and return to [26, 30]. For this, we will show the associated boolean matrix $[B]$, below which two rows have been added[4]:

$[\underset{\sim}{B}] =$

	$\underset{\sim}{A}$	$\underset{\sim}{B}$	$\underset{\sim}{C}$	$\underset{\sim}{D}$	$\underset{\sim}{E}$	$\underset{\sim}{F}$
$\underset{\sim}{A}$		1	1			
$\underset{\sim}{B}$		1	1	1		
$\underset{\sim}{C}$		1	1	1	1	
$\underset{\sim}{D}$			1	1	1	
$\underset{\sim}{E}$			1	1	1	
$\underset{\sim}{F}$					1	1

	$\underset{\sim}{A}$	$\underset{\sim}{B}$	$\underset{\sim}{C}$	$\underset{\sim}{D}$	$\underset{\sim}{E}$	$\underset{\sim}{F}$	
Λ_0	0	3	5	4	4	1	$\underset{\sim}{A}$

	$\underset{\sim}{A}$	$\underset{\sim}{B}$	$\underset{\sim}{C}$	$\underset{\sim}{D}$	$\underset{\sim}{E}$	$\underset{\sim}{F}$	
Λ_1	•	2	4	4	4	1	No zeros exist

In the first of these rows Λ_0, in each box we put the result of adding the ones from each of the columns $\underset{\sim}{A}$, $\underset{\sim}{B}$,... . Since in Λ_0 there is a zero in $\underset{\sim}{A}$,, we arrive at the fact that through this vertex <<no>> circuit passes. We now remove this row and column $\underset{\sim}{A}$, from matrix $[B]$ the columns are again added after suitably marking (in this case with a point) the box (or boxes in general) in which there is a zero. In this way we arrive at row Λ_1 in which it can be seen that *no zero appears*. This fact indicates the existence of circuits in this graph and, therefore, it is not possible to order the circuits of the states of the E set.

The interest arising from establishing an order is given by the fact that once leaving the system of a state (here it means that the economic parameter has abandoned an interval) it does not return to it, passing on to others, so that the state can be called temporary, except the final state or states.

Now, in spite of the fact that it is not possible in this case, to order the state because of the circuits, it is possible to gather several states together in the so called <<equivalency classes>>, the principal characteristic of which is the fact that all the states are members of a same circuit, that is to say, they can pass over from any state to any other along a path (therefore from one interval of E to another), but that once leaving this circuit they cannot return to it. This characteristic allows for ordering the equivalency classes. By definition, equivalency classes correspond in the graph theory to <<strongly connected sub-graphs>>. We are now going to arrive at equivalency classes by using the Malgrange[5] algorithm.

We will start off from the associated boolean matrix $[B]$ and for a vertex, chosen arbitrarily, for example $\underset{\sim}{A}$, the transitive closure $\hat{\Gamma}\{\underset{\sim}{A}\}$ and the inverted transitive closure $\hat{\Gamma}^{-}\{\underset{\sim}{A}\}$, will be found. The intersection of both will give us the formative elements of the equivalency class of which $\underset{\sim}{A}$ is a member. This will be:

	$\underset{\sim}{A}$	$\underset{\sim}{B}$	$\underset{\sim}{C}$	$\underset{\sim}{D}$	$\underset{\sim}{E}$	$\underset{\sim}{F}$	$\hat{\Gamma}\{\underset{\sim}{A}\}$
$\underset{\sim}{A}$		1	1				0
$\underset{\sim}{B}$		1	1	1			1
$\underset{\sim}{C}$		1	1	1	1		1
$\underset{\sim}{D}$			1	1	1		2
$\underset{\sim}{E}$			1	1	1		2
$\underset{\sim}{F}$					1	1	x
$\hat{\Gamma}^{-}\{\underset{\sim}{A}\}$	0	x	x	x	x	x	

From where:

$$\hat{\Gamma}\{\underset{\sim}{A}\} \cap \hat{\Gamma}^{-}\{\underset{\sim}{A}\} = \{\underset{\sim}{A}\}$$

We now eliminate row and column $\underset{\sim}{A}$ and commence the process again with another vertex, for example $\underset{\sim}{B}$. We now arrive at:

	$\underset{\sim}{B}$	$\underset{\sim}{C}$	$\underset{\sim}{D}$	$\underset{\sim}{E}$	$\underset{\sim}{F}$	$\hat{\Gamma}\{\underset{\sim}{B}\}$
$\underset{\sim}{B}$	1	1	1			0
$\underset{\sim}{C}$	1	1	1	1		1
$\underset{\sim}{D}$		1	1	1		1
$\underset{\sim}{E}$		1	1	1		2
$\underset{\sim}{F}$				1	1	x
$\hat{\Gamma}^{-}\{\underset{\sim}{B}\}$	0	1	2	2	3	

From where:

$$\hat{\Gamma}\{\underset{\sim}{B}\} \cap \hat{\Gamma}^{-}\{\underset{\sim}{B}\} = \{\underset{\sim}{B}, \underset{\sim}{C}, \underset{\sim}{D}, \underset{\sim}{E}\}$$

Finally we are left with $\underset{\sim}{F}$ which itself forms another equivalency class.

In this way we will arrive at the following equivalency classes, numbered arbitrarily:

$$C_1 = \{\underset{\sim}{A}\}$$
$$C_2 = \{\underset{\sim}{B}, \underset{\sim}{C}, \underset{\sim}{D}, \underset{\sim}{E}\}$$
$$C_3 = \{\underset{\sim}{F}\}$$

If we take into account the initial graph, this graph can be shown by means of the following <<class graph>> (figure 10.2):

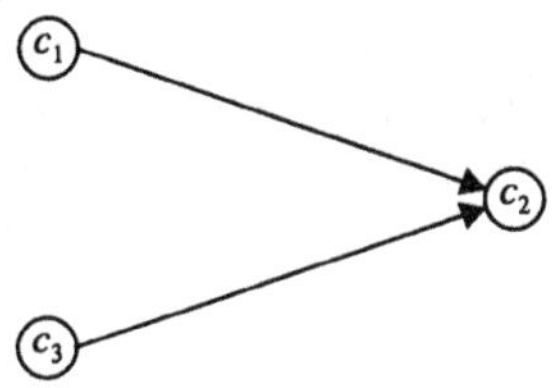

Figure 10.2.

We have been able to see that in this class graph no circuits exist, therefore it will be possible to find the <<ordinal function>> of equivalency classes C_1, C_2, C_3. On using the same procedure as used before for the states of E, we arrive at:

	C_1	C_2	C_3
C_1		1	
C_2			
C_3		1	

					Level
0	2	0	C_1, C_3	→	N_0
•	0	•	C_2	→	N_1

In this way we can verify the first intuitive vision resulting from a quick glance at the class graph: the order, in this partial case, is:

$$C_1 > C_2, \quad C_3 > C_2$$

which is written as:

$$\{\underset{\sim}{B}, \underset{\sim}{C}, \underset{\sim}{D}, \underset{\sim}{E}\} < \{\underset{\sim}{A}\}$$
$$\{\underset{\sim}{B}, \underset{\sim}{C}, \underset{\sim}{D}, \underset{\sim}{E}\} < \{\underset{\sim}{F}\}$$

This brings to light the fact that when the system leaves the valuations represented by $\underset{\sim}{A} = [10, 20]$ y $\underset{\sim}{F} = [41, 50]$, whatever the time gone by, it will never return to these intervals.

Now let us move on to see if the normal fuzzy relation allows us, through the use of suitable operators, to obtain successive estimates of the corresponding economic parameter, for each one of the periods of useful life of the investment object. In order to obtain an ordered structure of the relations, we are going to conveniently interchange rows and columns, in this way arriving at a fuzzy relation of normalised transition, expressed in the usual manner. For this, those elements of E, which are members of the same class of equivalence[6], will be grouped together

$[\underset{\sim}{N}] =$

	$\underset{\sim}{F}$	$\underset{\sim}{A}$	$\underset{\sim}{B}$	$\underset{\sim}{C}$	$\underset{\sim}{D}$	$\underset{\sim}{E}$
$\underset{\sim}{F}$	.8					1
$\underset{\sim}{A}$			1	.75		
$\underset{\sim}{B}$			.6	1	.8	
$\underset{\sim}{C}$			.6	.8	1	.9
$\underset{\sim}{D}$				.8	1	.8
$\underset{\sim}{E}$				.5	.75	1

Following this we immediately find the transitive closure $[\hat{\underset{\sim}{N}}]$ obtaining successively:

$[\underset{\sim}{N}]^2 =$

	$\underset{\sim}{F}$	$\underset{\sim}{A}$	$\underset{\sim}{B}$	$\underset{\sim}{C}$	$\underset{\sim}{D}$	$\underset{\sim}{E}$
$\underset{\sim}{F}$	.8			.5	.75	1
$\underset{\sim}{A}$			.6	1	.8	.75
$\underset{\sim}{B}$			.6	.8	1	.9
$\underset{\sim}{C}$			.6	.8	1	.9
$\underset{\sim}{D}$			.6	.8	1	.8
$\underset{\sim}{E}$			.5	.75	.75	1

$[\underset{\sim}{N}]^3 =$

	$\underset{\sim}{F}$	$\underset{\sim}{A}$	$\underset{\sim}{B}$	$\underset{\sim}{C}$	$\underset{\sim}{D}$	$\underset{\sim}{E}$
$\underset{\sim}{F}$	.8		.5	.75	.75	1
$\underset{\sim}{A}$			.6	.8	1	.9
$\underset{\sim}{B}$			.6	.8	1	.9
$\underset{\sim}{C}$			.6	.8	1	.9
$\underset{\sim}{D}$			.6	.8	1	.8
$\underset{\sim}{E}$			.6	.75	.75	1

$[\underset{\sim}{N}]^4 =$

	$\underset{\sim}{F}$	$\underset{\sim}{A}$	$\underset{\sim}{B}$	$\underset{\sim}{C}$	$\underset{\sim}{D}$	$\underset{\sim}{E}$
$\underset{\sim}{F}$	.8		.6	.75	.75	1
$\underset{\sim}{A}$			.6	.8	1	.9
$\underset{\sim}{B}$			.6	.8	1	.9
$\underset{\sim}{C}$			.6	.8	1	.9
$\underset{\sim}{D}$			.6	.8	1	.8
$\underset{\sim}{E}$			.6	.75	.75	1

$[\underset{\sim}{N}]^5 =$

	$\underset{\sim}{F}$	$\underset{\sim}{A}$	$\underset{\sim}{B}$	$\underset{\sim}{C}$	$\underset{\sim}{D}$	$\underset{\sim}{E}$
$\underset{\sim}{F}$	.8		.6	.75	.75	1
$\underset{\sim}{A}$			.6	.8	1	.9
$\underset{\sim}{B}$			.6	.8	1	.9
$\underset{\sim}{C}$			.6	.8	1	.9
$\underset{\sim}{D}$			.6	.8	1	.8
$\underset{\sim}{E}$			.6	.75	.75	1

Taking into account that $[\underset{\sim}{N}]^4 = [\underset{\sim}{N}]^5$ we stop the process in order to obtain the transitive closure:

$$[\hat{\underset{\sim}{N}}] = [\underset{\sim}{N}] \cup [\underset{\sim}{N}]^2 \cup [\underset{\sim}{N}]^3 \cup [\underset{\sim}{N}]^4 \cup [\underset{\sim}{N}]^5$$

And we arrive at:

$[\hat{\underset{\sim}{N}}] =$

	$\underset{\sim}{F}$	$\underset{\sim}{A}$	$\underset{\sim}{B}$	$\underset{\sim}{C}$	$\underset{\sim}{D}$	$\underset{\sim}{E}$
$\underset{\sim}{F}$	.8		.6	.75	.75	1
$\underset{\sim}{A}$			1	1	1	.9
$\underset{\sim}{B}$			.6	1	1	.9
$\underset{\sim}{C}$			.6	.8	1	.9
$\underset{\sim}{D}$			.6	.8	1	.8
$\underset{\sim}{E}$			.6	.75	.75	1

the associated graph of which is (figure 10.3):

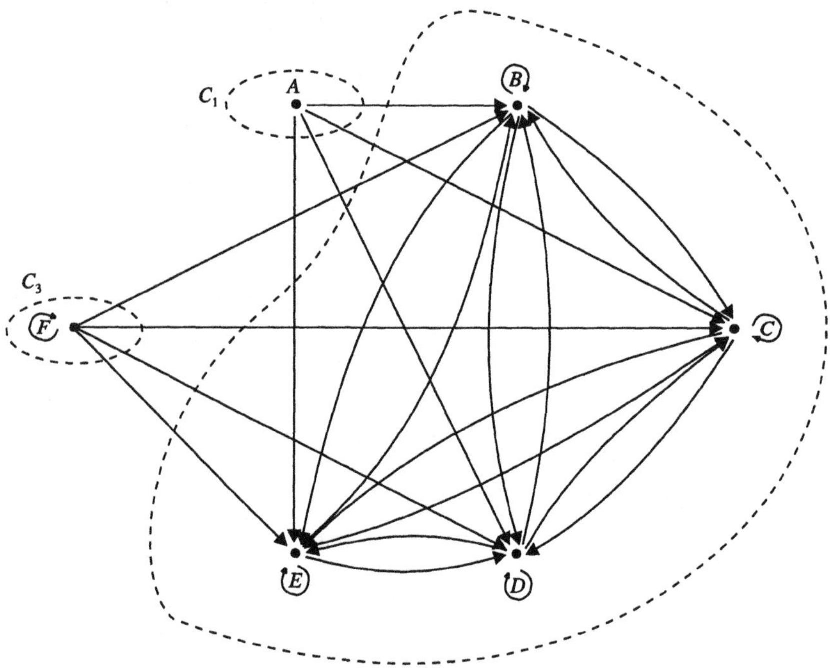

Figure 10.3.

As it could not be otherwise, it will be seen that the same classes of equivalence in the transitive closure are maintained. This indicates that the states of A and F are transitory states and that once leaving them it is impossible to return. In our case, situated in any type of state different to $\underset{\sim}{A} = [10, 20]$ and $\underset{\sim}{F} = [41, 50]$, in no later period can the valuations these positions signify be arrived at. On the contrary, with greater or lesser possibility, the corresponding economic parameter can move between one year and another between $\underset{\sim}{B}$, $\underset{\sim}{C}$, $\underset{\sim}{D}$ y $\underset{\sim}{E}$.

Starting out now from the estimates made by the expert relative to the position at initial moment 0 (relative to a future moment where the process is initiated) given by the vector $[\underset{\sim}{q}(0)]$, we arrive at:

$$[\underset{\sim}{q}(0)] \circ [\hat{\underset{\sim}{N}}] = [\underset{\sim}{q}(n)]$$

Vector $[\underset{\sim}{q}(n)]$ shows the long-term possibilities. Let us now move on to the estimates for each period.

Valuation of the economic parameter for each period

In order to make a relative estimate to the desired economic parameter for all periods making up the useful life of the investment object, it will be sufficient to apply successive fuzzy relations $[\underset{\sim}{N}]^j$, $j = 1, 2, 3, \ldots, n$, to the vector of the initial situation $[\underset{\sim}{q}(0)]$, through the maxmin operator, and in this way arrive at $[\underset{\sim}{q}(1)]$, $[\underset{\sim}{q}(2)]$, ..., $[\underset{\sim}{q}(n)]$. In our case these will be:

$[\underset{\sim}{q}(1)] =$

$\underset{\sim}{A}$	$\underset{\sim}{B}$	$\underset{\sim}{C}$	$\underset{\sim}{D}$	$\underset{\sim}{E}$	$\underset{\sim}{F}$
1	.9	.8	.6	.2	.1

$\circ$

	$\underset{\sim}{A}$	$\underset{\sim}{B}$	$\underset{\sim}{C}$	$\underset{\sim}{D}$	$\underset{\sim}{E}$	$\underset{\sim}{F}$
$\underset{\sim}{A}$		1	.75			
$\underset{\sim}{B}$		.6	1	.8		
$\underset{\sim}{C}$		.6	.8	1	.9	
$\underset{\sim}{D}$			.8	1	.8	
$\underset{\sim}{E}$			.5	.75	1	
$\underset{\sim}{F}$					1	.8

$=$

$\underset{\sim}{A}$	$\underset{\sim}{B}$	$\underset{\sim}{C}$	$\underset{\sim}{D}$	$\underset{\sim}{E}$	$\underset{\sim}{F}$
0	1	.9	.8	.8	.1

It will be seen, in the result we have arrived at, that the estimate for the first period entails a maximum of presumption in $\underset{\sim}{B} = [21, 25]$ and also a presumption of $\alpha = 0.9$ in $\underset{\sim}{C} = [26, 30]$.

Presumption descends in intervals $\underset{\sim}{D} = [31, 35]$ y $\underset{\sim}{E} = [36, 40]$ to a level of $\alpha = 0.8$. Taking into account the high level reached in these intervals, in a first instance it would seem wise to accept as an estimate of the economic parameter *for this period, the interval [21, 40]*, in spite of the existence of a high degree of uncertainty.

We now pass on to the second period:

$[\underset{\sim}{q}(2)] =$

$\underset{\sim}{A}$	$\underset{\sim}{B}$	$\underset{\sim}{C}$	$\underset{\sim}{D}$	$\underset{\sim}{E}$	$\underset{\sim}{F}$
1	.9	.8	.6	.2	.1

$\circ$

	$\underset{\sim}{A}$	$\underset{\sim}{B}$	$\underset{\sim}{C}$	$\underset{\sim}{D}$	$\underset{\sim}{E}$	$\underset{\sim}{F}$
$\underset{\sim}{A}$		.6	1	.8	.75	
$\underset{\sim}{B}$		.6	.8	1	.9	
$\underset{\sim}{C}$		.6	.8	1	.9	
$\underset{\sim}{D}$		.6	.8	1	.8	
$\underset{\sim}{E}$		.5	.75	.75	1	
$\underset{\sim}{F}$			.5	.75	1	.8

$=$

$\underset{\sim}{A}$	$\underset{\sim}{B}$	$\underset{\sim}{C}$	$\underset{\sim}{D}$	$\underset{\sim}{E}$	$\underset{\sim}{F}$
0	.6	1	.9	.9	.1

We will accept, for the *second period interval [26, 40]* given the high presumption of $\underset{\sim}{C}$, $\underset{\sim}{D}$ y $\underset{\sim}{E}$.

For the third period we will have:

$[\underset{\sim}{q}(3)] =$

$\underset{\sim}{A}$	$\underset{\sim}{B}$	$\underset{\sim}{C}$	$\underset{\sim}{D}$	$\underset{\sim}{E}$	$\underset{\sim}{F}$
1	.9	.8	.6	.2	.1

$\circ$

	$\underset{\sim}{A}$	$\underset{\sim}{B}$	$\underset{\sim}{C}$	$\underset{\sim}{D}$	$\underset{\sim}{E}$	$\underset{\sim}{F}$
$\underset{\sim}{A}$		.6	.8	1	.9	
$\underset{\sim}{B}$		.6	.8	1	.9	
$\underset{\sim}{C}$		.6	.8	1	.9	
$\underset{\sim}{D}$		.6	.8	1	.8	
$\underset{\sim}{E}$		.6	.75	.75	1	
$\underset{\sim}{F}$		.5	.75	.75	1	.8

$=$

$\underset{\sim}{A}$	$\underset{\sim}{B}$	$\underset{\sim}{C}$	$\underset{\sim}{D}$	$\underset{\sim}{E}$	$\underset{\sim}{F}$
0	.6	.8	1	.9	.1

In spite of the fact that the maximum presumption changes relative to the second period, we can continue to accept for the *third period interval [26, 40]*.

For the fourth period it will be:

$[\underset{\sim}{q}(4)] =$

$\underset{\sim}{A}$	$\underset{\sim}{B}$	$\underset{\sim}{C}$	$\underset{\sim}{D}$	$\underset{\sim}{E}$	$\underset{\sim}{F}$
1	.9	.8	.6	.2	.1

$\circ$

	$\underset{\sim}{A}$	$\underset{\sim}{B}$	$\underset{\sim}{C}$	$\underset{\sim}{D}$	$\underset{\sim}{E}$	$\underset{\sim}{F}$
$\underset{\sim}{A}$		.6	.8	1	.9	
$\underset{\sim}{B}$		.6	.8	1	.9	
$\underset{\sim}{C}$		.6	.8	1	.9	
$\underset{\sim}{D}$		.6	.8	1	.8	
$\underset{\sim}{E}$		.6	.75	.75	1	
$\underset{\sim}{F}$		.6	.75	.75	1	.8

$=$

$\underset{\sim}{A}$	$\underset{\sim}{B}$	$\underset{\sim}{C}$	$\underset{\sim}{D}$	$\underset{\sim}{E}$	$\underset{\sim}{F}$
0	.6	.8	1	.9	.1

It will be seen that the result coincides with that obtained for the previous period, which takes us to accept the *same interval [26, 40]* for this and successive periods.

In summary we will have:

Period 1: [21, 40], with $[\underset{\sim}{q}(1)] =$

$\underset{\sim}{A}$	$\underset{\sim}{B}$	$\underset{\sim}{C}$	$\underset{\sim}{D}$	$\underset{\sim}{E}$	$\underset{\sim}{F}$
0	1	.9	.8	.8	.1

Period 2: [26, 40], with $[\underset{\sim}{q}(2)] =$

$\underset{\sim}{A}$	$\underset{\sim}{B}$	$\underset{\sim}{C}$	$\underset{\sim}{D}$	$\underset{\sim}{E}$	$\underset{\sim}{F}$
0	.6	1	.9	.9	.1

Period 3: [26, 40], with $[\underset{\sim}{q}(3)] =$

$\underset{\sim}{A}$	$\underset{\sim}{B}$	$\underset{\sim}{C}$	$\underset{\sim}{D}$	$\underset{\sim}{E}$	$\underset{\sim}{F}$
0	.6	.8	1	.9	.1

If the transitive closure $[\hat{\underset{\sim}{N}}]$ is used, for a long-term situation, an extension of the interval under consideration will be seen, as a consequence of the increase in the degree of presumption for each one of the possible positions. Thus we arrive at:

$[\underset{\sim}{q}(n)] =$

$\underset{\sim}{A}$	$\underset{\sim}{B}$	$\underset{\sim}{C}$	$\underset{\sim}{D}$	$\underset{\sim}{E}$	$\underset{\sim}{F}$
1	.9	.8	.6	.2	.1

$\circ$

	$\underset{\sim}{A}$	$\underset{\sim}{B}$	$\underset{\sim}{C}$	$\underset{\sim}{D}$	$\underset{\sim}{E}$	$\underset{\sim}{F}$
$\underset{\sim}{A}$		1	1	1	.9	
$\underset{\sim}{B}$		.6	1	1	.9	
$\underset{\sim}{C}$		.6	.8	1	.9	
$\underset{\sim}{D}$		.6	.8	1	.8	
$\underset{\sim}{E}$		.6	.75	.75	1	
$\underset{\sim}{F}$		.6	.75	.75	1	.8

$=$

$\underset{\sim}{A}$	$\underset{\sim}{B}$	$\underset{\sim}{C}$	$\underset{\sim}{D}$	$\underset{\sim}{E}$	$\underset{\sim}{F}$
0	1	1	1	.9	.1

In the event of extreme caution, this fact would entail considering the confidence interval [21, 40].

Technical elements for a reduction of uncertainty

In the results we arrived at from the didactic example we were able to see certain estimates imbued with a high degree of uncertainty, which is reflected in the width of the intervals or, in the event of selecting fuzzy sub-sets $[\underset{\sim}{q}(r)]$, $r = 1, 2, 3, \ldots, n$, in the high degree of presumption that several intervals have in each period (nearly always $\underset{\sim}{C}$, $\underset{\sim}{D}$ y $\underset{\sim}{E}$). This is not a special or isolated case, but a phenomenon present in wide range of situations arising in reality.

With the object of reducing uncertainty and at the same time reducing the degree of subjectivity inherent in all estimates made by an expert, recourse can be made to a technique we have already used: counter-expertise using R^+-expertons. For this we are going to start out from the interval arrived at for one of the periods such as [21, 40] or [26, 40] of the case we have developed. For effects of generalisation, we will designate:

$$\underset{\sim}{M} = [M_*, M^*] \subset R^+$$

Since the process we are following is known, we are going to avoid the technical aspects that justify the validity of this scheme[7] and pass directly on to more operative aspects. For this we are going to ask a certain number of experts to give their opinion relative to the interval arrived at $[M_*, M^*]$ (assuming this is accepted by them all, since, otherwise, this interval should be extended to a more uncertain $[M'_*, M^{*\prime}] \supset [M_*, M^*]$).

With the aid of a semantic scale such as:

0: For M_*
0.1: Practically M_*
0.2: Nearly M_*
0.3: Near to M_*
0.4: Nearer to M_* than to M^*
0.5: As close to M_* as to M^*
0.6: Nearer to M^* than to M_*
0.7: Near to M^*
0.8: Nearly M^*
0.9: Practically M^*
1: For M^*

In order to give greater liberty the counter-experts are allowed to express their opinions by mean of an interval $[\alpha_{i1}, \alpha_{i2}] \subset [0, 1]$, $i = 1, 2, ..., m$ counter-experts. If the principal is accepted of linearity in positioning within the interval $[M_*, M^*]$ we will arrive at the fact that the opinion of a counter-expert i, $[m_{i1}, m_{i2}]$ will be given by:

$$[m_{i1}, m_{i2}] = M* + (M^* - M*) (\cdot) [\alpha_{i1}, \alpha_{i2}]$$

If we select one of the intervals arrived at for a period, for example, [26, 40] for period 3, and the opinion is asked of eight counter-experts (this number, obviously, is arbitrary) through a positioning in the hendecadarian scale, certain intervals $[\alpha_{i1}, \alpha_{i2}]$, $i = 1, 2, \ldots, 8$. In our example these could be as follows:

Expert 1: [.6, .8]	Expert 5: [.2, .7]
Expert 2: [.4, .5]	Expert 6: [.1, .4]
Expert 3: .6	Expert 7: [.6, .9]
Expert 4: [.3, .5]	Expert 8: [0, .3]

From this information it is necessary to find the statistic of the number of times the experts have given the same valuation for the lower extreme and for the upper extreme. We pass on immediately to calculate the normalised frequencies, by dividing each figure of the table by 8, the number of counter-experts consulted. We will arrive at the following:

	Statistic	
0	1	
.1	1	
.2	1	
.3	1	1
.4	1	1
.5		2
.6	3	1
.7		1
.8		1
.9		1
1		

Statistic

	Normalised Frequency	
0	.125	
.1	.125	
.2	.125	
.3	.125	.125
.4	.125	.125
.5		.250
.6	.375	.125
.7		.125
.8		.125
.9		.125
1		

Normalised Frequency

From the normalised frequencies and by doing an accumulation from $\alpha = 1$ to $\alpha = 0$ experton $\underset{\sim}{\alpha}_j$, is arrived at, where j is the period considered (in this case $j = 3$).

	Expertón $\underset{\sim}{\alpha}_j$	
0	1	1
.1	.875	1
.2	.750	1
.3	.625	1
.4	.500	.875
.5	.375	.750
.6	.375	.500
.7	0	.375
.8	0	.250
.9	0	.125
1	0	0

Expertón $\underset{\sim}{\alpha}_j$

Finally in order to arrive at the aggregate opinion of all the experts, the R^+-experton is found from equation:

$$\underset{\sim}{m}_j = M_* + (M^* - M_*) (\cdot) \underset{\sim}{\alpha}_j$$

which in this case is:

$\underset{\sim}{m}_3 = 26 + (40 - 26) (\bullet)$

α	Experton in [0, 1]		=	α	Experton in R^+	
0	1	1		0	40	40
.1	.875	1		.1	38.25	40
.2	.750	1		.2	36.50	40
.3	.625	1		.3	34.75	40
.4	.500	.875		.4	33	38.25
.5	.375	.750	=	.5	31.25	36.50
.6	.375	.500		.6	31.25	33
.7	0	.375		.7	26	31.25
.8	0	.250		.8	26	29.50
.9	0	.125		.9	26	27.75
1	0	0		1	26	26

The experton arrived at in R^+, also called R^+-experton, provides all the available information relative to the aggregate opinion of the expert and all the counter-experts. With this one of the fundamental requirements of management in uncertainty has been complied with: maintaining all the information, although also the uncertainty, throughout the whole process and making the entropy fall as late as possible.

But now we have arrived at the final point. It is possible, therefore, to reduce uncertainty by finding the mathematical probability of the R^+-experton. For this it will be sufficient to add the columns to the left, on the one hand, and those on the right, on the other (excepting level $\alpha = 0$) and divide both results by 10. We will arrive at:

$$\varepsilon(\underset{\sim}{m}_3) = [30.90, 34.22]$$

What we have for period 3, which we took as an example, is an estimate [30.90, 34.22], now finding a less uncertain interval than the start out interval [26, 40].

It is obvious, in this case, that the same result would be arrived at without the need of passing through the stage of using expertons, by only calculating the mean (that is to make the entropy fall) at the beginning, with the direct estimates of the experts. In effect, the mean of the valuations is:

$$1/8 \,(\cdot)\, ([.6, .8] \,(+)\, [.4, .5] \,(+)\, [.6, .6] \,(+)\, [.3, .5] \,(+)\, [.2, .7] \,(+)\, [.1, .4] \,(+)$$
$$(+)\, [.6, .9] \,(+)\, [0, .3]) = [0.350, 0.5875]$$

and the sought after estimate:

$$26 + (40\text{-}26)\,(.)\,[0.350, 0.5875] = [30.90, 34.22]$$

This then is the same result as found by means of the R^+-expertons.

In this and many other cases, it is said that there is no special interest for passing through a more complex technique when obtaining the same result by means of a simple elementary calculation. This would be true if not taking an important element into consideration, which is information. If the entropy is made to fall at the beginning, information is lost, as it would not be carried over into the successive calculations, and we would arrive at the end with only the mean. Obviously, it could be argued that, in a case as the one we have just studied in which only 8 counter-experts exist, there is not much use for the summarised information (but very complete) of the R^+-experton, as this also exists in the table summarising the intervals provided initially by the 8 counter-experts. However, the same does not occur when there is a large number of counter-experts, as would be the more normal case.

On the other hand, it often happens that the calculations do not end with arriving at the mathematical probability, as this constitutes summarised information of an intermediary nature and the R^+-experton is submitted to later calculations. If the operators used in these calculations are all linear, the final result will always be the same using means rather than R^+-expertons. We insist, once again, in the loss of information as the only differentiating phenomenon. But if non-linear operators are used (for example max ($\vee$) or min ($\wedge$)) then the means will no longer be valid and some other technique must be used: the R^+-expertons. Our desire for greater generalisation through the use of didactic examples, has led us to choose the path we have described.

This scheme, thought out for arriving at economic parameters relative to the process of investment, starts out from an elemental premise, perfectly well known by all those who have lived through the problems of investment reality in the company: it is not easy to estimate the formative elements of the currents of collections and payments arising from the decision to invest, quantitatively, nor even in uncertain terms. From here stems the object of this chapter, which could well constitute a new element for working out the complex puzzle called investment process.

The path we have followed for drawing up the proposed model, is based upon sequential techniques, the basis of which are laid down by starting out from pseudo-markovian theories, developed at the time in conjunction with Professor Kaufmann, as well as in the use of methods of assignment arising from the expertons theory. We are conscious of the fact of not having exhausted the subject, treated here voluntarily in an incomplete fashion. With it we have only intended to draw attention to the problem, all too often brought to light by reality and very often evaded by management researchers. We can only hope that others in future works, will know how to create better ways that will allow an advancement in the task of renewing techniques for handling investments, in order to bring then into line for handling in the convulsed reality of our times.

References

1 A. Kaufmann and J. Gil Aluja: *Nuevas técnicas para la dirección estratégica*, Barcelona University Publications, Barcelona, 1991, pages 132-133

2 For greater ease, from now onwards we are going to use symbols $\underset{\sim}{A}$, $\underset{\sim}{B}$ ..., in place of detailing the corresponding intervals [10, 20], [21, 50],....

3 See in this respect: A. Kaufmann and J. Gil Aluja: *Nuevas técnicas para la dirección estratégica*, PUB Barcelona, 1991, pages 118-123.

4 In this case it is sufficient to add two rows, in others the number of rows to be added below the boolean matrix would be different.

5 Ives Malgrange: <<Décomposition d'un graphe en sous-graphes fortement connexes maximaux>>, Internal memo of the Cie. Machines Bull, Paris, 1967.

6 In this specific example there would be no need to change the order. We have done so in order to show a more general example.

7 For greater detail consult: A. Kaufmann and J. Gil Aluja: *Técnicas de gestión de empresa, Previsiones, decisiones y estrategias,* Pirámide, Madrid, 1992, pages 236-265.

11 Investment selection based on diversified criteria

Some preliminary aspects

As has been seen repeatedly, studies on investment selection lay special emphasis on the importance, for taking investment decisions, acquired by the fact that the collection currents <<taken overall>> be greater than those for payments, also considered jointly. From this a varied range of models arise, some of which have been studied, that allow under certain conditions, to carry out studies of economic viability. What can be inferred from these is a fundamental element, if not the only one for taking decisions, which possesses a strictly monetary nature.

Now, the complexity of the situations in which the company moves in this day and age, make this method, even though necessary, perhaps not sufficient in the majority of cases. In fact, one of the mobilising constants of management policies and strategies is to obtain the greatest possible wealth for the company and its shareholders, but this objective in not only reached as a consequence of are direct or indirect causality, but also intervening, and in no insignificant manner, indirect or second generation effects[1] .

This reasoning has made us dwell upon the suitability of drawing up a scheme[2] in which, the different aspects that take part in the decision to invest, which will be known from now on as <<decision elements>>, are brought to light in an explicit manner.

The scheme we are proposing below will start out from the existence of a set:

$$C = \{C_1, C_2, ..., C_n\}$$

that includes the mobilising elements of the decision to invest.

In an attempt to arrive at the greatest possible degree of generalisation, we are going to assume that each C_i, i = 1, 2, ..., n, is estimated through a different evaluation and that even among them a high degree of heterogeneity may exist. Therefore, their calculation is normally made by means of substantially different measurable or evaluable concepts.

Also the existence is assumed of a relationship between these decision elements and the potential objects of decision. These can also be included in another set:

$$E = \{E_1, E_2, ..., E_m\}$$

formed by all those objects to which the decision to invest could fall.

This relation can be expressed by means of a matrix that, in its most general formulation, will take the form of a fuzzy relation $\underset{\sim}{R}$, such as:

$$\underset{\sim}{R} = \begin{array}{c|c|c|c|c|c|} & E_1 & E_2 & E_3 & & E_m \\ \hline C_1 & r_{11} & r_{12} & r_{13} & \cdots & r_{1m} \\ \hline C_2 & r_{21} & r_{22} & r_{23} & \cdots & r_{2m} \\ \hline C_3 & r_{31} & r_{32} & r_{33} & \cdots & r_{3m} \\ \hline & \vdots & \vdots & \vdots & & \vdots \\ \hline C_n & r_{n1} & r_{n2} & r_{n3} & \cdots & r_{nm} \\ \hline \end{array}$$

For an easier description of the proposed process we are going to consider the case of the decision to invest in industrial equipment. Obviously this model can be used for any type of investment, provided it is suitably adapted.

A finite number of machines m exist in the market, that are suitable for the activity to be carried out, which in this case we will assume equal to 7 and these will be expressed by E_i, i = 1, 2, ... 7. Also, a finite number of decision elements n should be taken into account, which we will assume equal to 5 and these will be represented by C_j, j = *1, 2, ..., 5.*

Merely as an indication, the following are listed as decision elements:

C_1: Capital value of an investment (NUV).
C_2: Degree of capitalisation of the machine (initial financial requirements).
C_3: Financial conditions (division of payments for the machine).
C_4: Ease of obtaining technical assistance (repairs and spare parts).
C_5: Possibility of selling estimated production from the equipment.

Evidently, under different circumstance and in each company, many different elements may appear, incorporation of which may be necessary for making a decision to invest, which could easily increase or decrease the number taken as an example.

The different nature of the decision elements conditions the unit of measurement or valuation in which each relation formed by the pair, type of equipment-decision element, is expressed.

Therefore each row of the relation will be expressed in different terms, such as: monetary units, in terms of time and even as estimated in [0, 1], for example. In order to specify this important prior aspect, we are going to establish a numerical example merely for didactic effects. We will continue with our 5 decision elements and 7 equipments to which the decision to invest may fall, and we will fill in the boxes of the $\underset{\sim}{R}$ relation of estimates, the rows of which, obviously, will be of a different nature. Let us assume then, that for C_1 (*capital value*) we have obtained:

$$E_1 = 60, \quad E_2 = 54, \quad E_3 = 12, \quad E_4 = 48, \quad E_5 = 25, \quad E_6 = 70, \quad E_7 = 63$$

net updated value, expressed in millions of monetary units.

C_2 (*cost of the equipment*) the following is estimated:

$$E_1 = 12000, \quad E_2 = 20000, \quad E_3 = 8000, \quad E_4 = 18000$$
$$E_5 = 16000, \quad E_6 = 25000, \quad E_7 = 28000$$

expressed in millions of monetary units.

For C_3 (*financial conditions*) the following have been established:

E_1 = Cash

E_2 = 20 per cent initial payment + 3 years

E_3 = 30 per cent initial payment + 2 years

E_4 = 50 per cent initial payment + 1 year

E_5 = 0 per cent initial payment + 2 years

E_6 = 20 per cent initial payment + 2 years

E_7 = 40 per cent initial payment + 3 years

For C_4 (speed of technical assistance) the following:

$$E_1 = 5, \quad E_2 = 3, \quad E_3 = 14, \quad E_4 = 10, \quad E_5 = 1, \quad E_6 = 2, \quad E_7 = 8$$

expressed in hours required for commencing revision or repair.

With regard to C_5 (*possibility of selling production*) is should be taken into account that this element depends on the production capacity of each equipment and of the absorption capacity for the manufactured product in the market. In order to take into account both circumstances we propose calculating the

<<possibility indices>> for each product relative to a law of absorption of the product into the market. For this the hoped for production units for each machine is estimated by means of fuzzy triangular numbers (FTN) and the law of limitation (capacity of absorption of the product) by means of a linear function. In this case we are going to assume the following:

Equipment	*Production en FTN*
E_1	$(250, 300, 380) = \underset{\sim}{P}_1$
E_2	$(180, 220, 250) = \underset{\sim}{P}_2$
E_3	$(60, 70, 90) = \underset{\sim}{P}_3$
E_4	$(190, 200, 230) = \underset{\sim}{P}_4$
E_5	$(80, 120, 140) = \underset{\sim}{P}_5$
E_6	$(350, 400, 420) = \underset{\sim}{P}_6$
E_7	$(320, 350, 370) = \underset{\sim}{P}_7$

Law of absorption into the market:

$$\mu(x) = \begin{cases} 1 & , \quad x \leqslant 150 \\ \dfrac{500 - x}{350} & , \quad 150 \leqslant x \leqslant 500 \\ 0 & , \quad x \geqslant 500 \end{cases}$$

Given that $x = 500 - 350\alpha$, for $150 \leqslant x \leqslant 500$, it will be possible to arrive at the intersection points of the left sides of each triangle representing the FTN with the commercial limitation law. Firstly let us take a look at this in figure 11.1.

It can be seen that there are two triangles, representing the FTN $\underset{\sim}{P}_3$ and $\underset{\sim}{P}_5$, which are <<totally>> to the left of the line representing the market limitation. For these the <<possibility>> of absorption of the product is total. For this reason then they will be assigned an index with a maximum value of 1. In which they will be:

$$\text{pos } \underset{\sim}{P}_3 = 1$$

$$\text{pos } \underset{\sim}{P}_5 = 1$$

For the remaining FTN the solution to the corresponding equations will be arrived at and we will have:

$$\underset{\sim}{P}_4 = [190 + 10\alpha, 230 - 30\alpha]$$

$$500 - 350\alpha = 190 + 10\alpha$$

$$360\alpha = 310$$

$$\text{pos } \underset{\sim}{P}_4 = \frac{310}{360} = 0.861$$

$$\underset{\sim}{P}_2 = [180 + 40\alpha, 250 - 30\alpha]$$

$$500 - 350\alpha = 180 + 40\alpha$$

$$390\alpha = 320$$

$$\text{pos } \underset{\sim}{P}_2 = \frac{320}{390} = 0.820$$

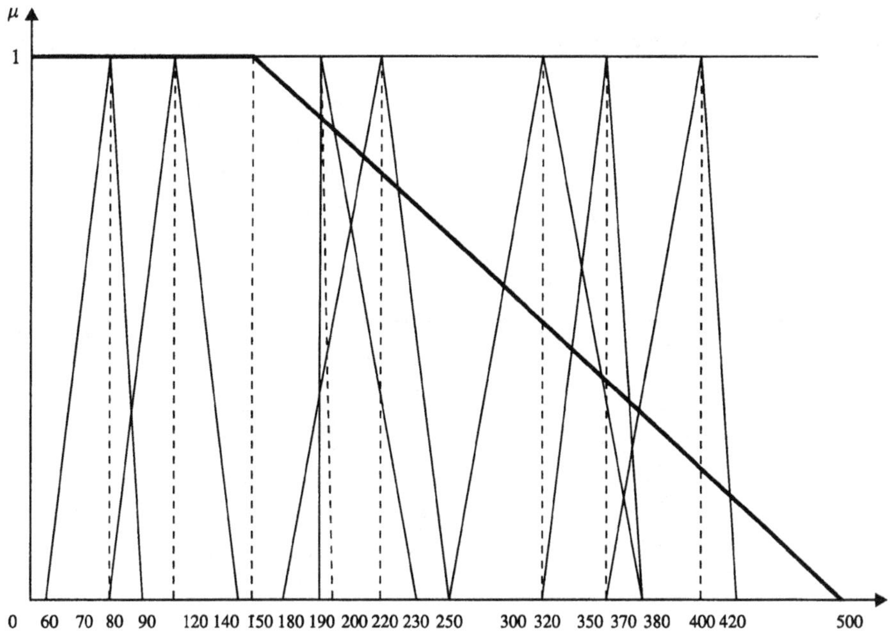

Figure 11.1

$$\underset{\sim}{P}_1 = [250 + 50\alpha,\ 380 - 80\alpha]$$

$$500 - 350\alpha = 250 + 50\alpha$$

$$400\alpha = 250$$

$$\text{pos } \underset{\sim}{P}_1 = \frac{250}{400} = 0.625$$

$$\underset{\sim}{P}_7 = [320 + 30\alpha,\ 370 - 20\alpha]$$

$$500 - 350\alpha = 320 + 30\alpha$$

$$380\alpha = 180$$

$$\text{pos } \underset{\sim}{P}_7 = \frac{180}{380} = 0.473$$

$$\underset{\sim}{P}_6 = [350 + 50\alpha,\ 420 - 20\alpha]$$

$$500 - 350\alpha = 350 + 50\alpha$$

$$400\alpha = 150$$

$$\text{pos } \underset{\sim}{P}_6 = \frac{150}{400} = 0.375$$

In short we arrive at for C_5 (*possibility of absorption*):

$E_1 = 25/40, \quad E_2 = 32/39, \quad E_3 = 1, \quad E_4 = 31/36, \quad E_5 = 1, \quad E_6 = 15/40, \quad E_7 = 18/38$

expressed in terms of <<possibility indices>>. For resolving this problem we could resort to another type of index, for example, the <<index of consent>> among others[3].

We now move on to present, in summary, a table in the form of a matrix that includes the heterogeneous estimates established for the relations set up between the set of decision elements and the eventual investment objects.

↱	E_1	E_2	E_3	E_4	E_5	E_6	E_7
C_1	60	54	12	48	25	70	63
C_2	12000	20000	8000	18000	16000	25000	28000
C_3	100% initial	20% init. + 3 years	30% init. + 2 years	50% init. + 1 year	0% init. + 2 years	20% inic. + 2 years	40% init. + 3 years
C_4	5	3	14	10	1	2	8
C_5	25/40	32/39	1	31/36	1	15/40	18/38

From this table we are going to arrive at certain valuations from certain rules, which will substitute the heterogeneous data, in order to allow us to operate with fuzzy relations. For this we propose a procedure the use of which has given excellent results in other fields.

Obtaining a fuzzy relation

In order to arrive at the valuations corresponding to each element of a fuzzy relation capable of bringing to light the links existing between decision elements and equipment, we are going to construct a matrix $[C_i]$, $i = 1, 2, \ldots, 5$ for each decision element formed from data contained in the table above, considering those corresponding to each row independently and establishing a preference between each one of the estimates of the elements making it up.

Therefore, for example, for C_1 (capital value) there will be preference for the highest value, relative to C_4 (technical assistance) for the least possible time,... And so on for each of the rows, the element corresponding to each box will be arrived at, by means of the quotient between the value taken as a reference and the initial data of the table.

Once each of the matrices $[C_i]$, $i = 1, 2, \ldots, 5$ are found we shall proceed with successive maxmin compositions, commencing with the $[C_i]\,(\cdot)\,[1]$ in order to arrive at the corresponding particular vector and particular dominant value.

We will then follow this same process for each of the decisions elements C_i.

For C_1 (capital value), the fuzzy relation will be:

	E_1	E_2	E_3	E_4	E_5	E_6	E_7
E_1	1	60/54	60/12	60/48	60/25	60/70	60/63
E_2	54/60	1	54/12	54/48	54/25	54/70	54/63
E_3	12/60	12/54	1	12/48	12/25	12/70	12/63
E_4	48/60	48/54	48/12	1	48/25	48/70	48/63
E_5	25/60	25/54	25/12	25/48	1	25/70	25/63
E_6	70/60	70/54	70/12	70/48	70/25	1	70/63
E_7	63/60	63/54	63/12	63/48	63/25	63/70	1

And from the above table we arrive at:

$[C_1] \cdot [1] =$

	E_1	E_2	E_3	E_4	E_5	E_6	E_7
E_1	1	60/54	60/12	60/48	60/25	60/70	60/63
E_2	54/60	1	54/12	54/48	54/25	54/70	54/63
E_3	12/60	12/54	1	12/48	12/25	12/70	12/63
E_4	48/60	48/54	48/12	1	48/25	48/70	48/63
E_5	25/60	25/54	25/12	25/48	1	25/70	25/63
E_6	70/60	70/54	70/12	70/48	70/25	1	70/63
E_7	63/60	63/54	63/12	63/48	63/25	63/70	1

$\cdot$

1
1
1
1
1
1
1

$=$

12.570
11.313
2.514
10.056
5.237
14.665
13.199

$= 14.665 \cdot$

0.857
0.771
0.171
0.685
0.357
1
0.900

$= 14.665 \cdot [A_1]$

$$[C_1] \cdot [A_1] = \begin{bmatrix} 5.996 \\ 5.396 \\ 1.199 \\ 4.796 \\ 2.498 \\ 6.995 \\ 6.245 \end{bmatrix} = 6.995 \cdot \begin{bmatrix} 0.857 \\ 0.771 \\ 0.171 \\ 0.685 \\ 0.357 \\ 1 \\ 0.900 \end{bmatrix} \rightarrow \lambda_1 = 6.995$$

The corresponding particular vector arrived at will be the first row of the sought after fuzzy relation.

For C_2 (equipment cost), since this is a minimising preference we will have:

$[C_2] \cdot [1] =$

	E_1	E_2	E_3	E_4	E_5	E_6	E_7
E_1	1	20/12	8/12	18/12	16/12	25/12	28/12
E_2	12/20	1	8/20	18/20	16/20	25/20	28/20
E_3	12/8	20/8	1	18/8	16/8	25/8	28/8
E_4	12/18	20/18	8/18	1	16/18	25/18	28/18
E_5	12/16	20/16	8/16	18/16	1	25/16	28/16
E_6	12/25	20/25	8/25	18/25	16/25	1	28/25
E_7	12/28	20/28	8/28	18/28	16/28	25/28	1

$$\cdot \begin{bmatrix} 1 \\ 1 \\ 1 \\ 1 \\ 1 \\ 1 \\ 1 \end{bmatrix} =$$

$$= \begin{bmatrix} 10.583 \\ 6.350 \\ 15.875 \\ 7.055 \\ 7.937 \\ 5.080 \\ 4.535 \end{bmatrix} = 15.875 \cdot \begin{bmatrix} 0.666 \\ 0.400 \\ 1 \\ 0.444 \\ 0.499 \\ 0.320 \\ 0.285 \end{bmatrix} = 15.875 \cdot [A_2]$$

$$[C_2] \cdot [A_2] = \begin{bmatrix} 4.662 \\ 2.797 \\ 6.993 \\ 3.108 \\ 3.496 \\ 2.237 \\ 1.998 \end{bmatrix} = 6.993 \cdot \begin{bmatrix} 0.666 \\ 0.400 \\ 1 \\ 0.444 \\ 0.499 \\ 0.320 \\ 0.285 \end{bmatrix} \rightarrow \lambda_2 = 6.993$$

In this way we arrive at the corresponding particular vector which will constitute the second row of the fuzzy relation.

For C_3 (financial conditions) it will be necessary to carry out certain adaptations, taking into account the manner in which the initial information is expressed. We propose the following:

1. With the data obtained a scale of preference is set up. In this case the following:

Preference: 1.°: E_5
2.°: E_2
3.°: E_6
4.°: E_3
5.°: E_7
6.°: E_4
7.°: E_1

2. The degree of preference is sought, which can be estimated by the number of times a type of breakdown into fractions is preferred over the rest. In this case E_5 is preferred 2 times over E_2, 3 times over E_6,... and so on successively one could arrive at a table such as the one we have included below.

Times preferred:

	E_5 ↓	E_2 ↓	E_6 ↓	E_3 ↓	E_7 ↓	E_4 ↓
E_5	a					
E_2	2	a				
E_6	3	2	a			
E_3	4	3	2	a		
E_7	6	5	3	2	a	
E_4	8	6	5	4	3	a
E_1	10	8	7	6	5	3

3. With this information the following matrix can be set up which we form with vector [1]:

$[C_3] \cdot [1] =$

	E_1	E_2	E_3	E_4	E_5	E_6	E_7
E_1	1	1/8	1/6	1/3	1/10	1/7	1/5
E_2	8	1	3	6	1/2	2	5
E_3	6	1/3	1	4	1/4	1/2	2
E_4	3	1/6	1/4	1	1/8	1/5	1/3
E_5	10	2	4	8	1	3	6
E_6	7	1/2	2	5	1/3	1	3
E_7	5	1/5	1/2	3	1/6	1/3	1

$\cdot$

1
1
1
1
1
1
1

$=$

2.067
25.500
14.083
5.075
34.000
18.833
10.200

$= 34 \cdot$

0.060
0.750
0.414
0.149
1
0.553
0.300

$= 34 \cdot [A_3]$

Compositions $[C_3] \cdot [A_3]$, $[C_3] \cdot [A_3^{\mathrm{I}}]$, $[C_3] \cdot [A_3^{\mathrm{II}}]$, $[C_3] \cdot [A_3^{\mathrm{III}}]$ and finally $[C_3] \cdot [A_3^{\mathrm{IV}}]$ are done successively, and we arrive at:

$[C_3] \cdot [A_3^{\mathrm{IV}}] =$

0.421
4.888
2.093
0.728
7.279
3.135
1.360

$= 7.279 \cdot$

0.057
0.671
0.287
0.100
1
0.430
0.186

$\rightarrow \lambda_3 = 7.279$

This new corresponding particular vector will constitute the third row of the sought after fuzzy relation.

For C_4 (speed of technical assistance) a reverse order of preference to duration can be established, from which $[C_4]$ is arrived at:

$[C_4] \cdot [1] =$

	E_1	E_2	E_3	E_4	E_5	E_6	E_7
E_1	1	3/5	14/5	10/5	1/5	2/5	8/5
E_2	5/3	1	14/3	10/3	1/3	2/3	8/3
E_3	5/14	3/14	1	10/14	1/14	2/14	8/14
E_4	5/10	3/10	14/10	1	1/10	2/10	8/10
E_5	5	3	14	10	1	2	8
E_6	5/2	3/2	14/2	10/2	1/2	1	8/2
E_7	5/8	3/8	14/8	10/8	1/8	2/8	1

$\cdot$

1
1
1
1
1
1
1

$=$

8.6		0.2
14.333		0.333
3.071		0.071
4.3	$= 43 \cdot$	0.100
43		1
21.5		0.500
5.375		0.125

$= 43 \cdot [A_4]$

$[C_4] \cdot [A_4] =$

1.394		0.2
2.322		0.333
0.497		0.071
0.699	$= 6.968 \cdot$	0.1
6.968		1
3.484		0.500
0.871		0.125

$\rightarrow \lambda_4 = 6.968$

The corresponding vector will be the fourth row of the fuzzy relation.

Now, for this same decision element C_4, a grading of preferences could be established differing from proportionality, which could be as follows:

Times that E_i prefers E_j:

	E_5 ↓					
E_5	prefers	E_6 ↓				
E_6	2	prefers	E_2 ↓			
E_2	3	2	prefers	E_1 ↓		
E_1	5	4	2	prefers	E_7 ↓	
E_7	10	6	4	2	prefers	E_4 ↓
E_4	12	8	5	4	2	prefers
E_3	14	12	8	5	4	2

In this way we arrive at the reciprocal matrix $[C_4]$ which we submit to a process of convolution.

$[C_4] \cdot [1] =$

	E_1	E_2	E_3	E_4	E_5	E_6	E_7
E_1	1	1/2	5	4	1/5	1/4	2
E_2	2	1	8	5	1/3	1/2	4
E_3	1/5	1/8	1	1/2	1/14	1/12	1/4
E_4	1/4	1/5	2	1	1/12	1/8	1/2
E_5	5	3	14	12	1	2	10
E_6	4	2	12	8	1/2	1	6
E_7	1/2	1/4	4	2	1/10	1/6	1

$\cdot$

1
1
1
1
1
1
1

$=$

12.950
20.833
2.229
4.158
47.000
33.500
8.016

$= 47.000 \cdot$

0.275
0.443
0.047
0.088
1
0.712
0.170

$= 47.000 \cdot [A_4]$

$$[C_4] \cdot [A_4] = \begin{bmatrix} 1.801 \\ 3.178 \\ 0.374 \\ 0.596 \\ 8.542 \\ 5.486 \\ 1.000 \end{bmatrix} = 8.542 \cdot \begin{bmatrix} 0.210 \\ 0.372 \\ 0.043 \\ 0.069 \\ 1 \\ 0.642 \\ 0.117 \end{bmatrix} = 8.542 \cdot [A_4']$$

$$[C_4] \cdot [A_4'] = \begin{bmatrix} 1.481 \\ 2.603 \\ 0.320 \\ 0.503 \\ 7.050 \\ 4.496 \\ 0.832 \end{bmatrix} = 7.050 \cdot \begin{bmatrix} 0.210 \\ 0.369 \\ 0.045 \\ 0.071 \\ 1 \\ 0.637 \\ 0.118 \end{bmatrix} = 7.050 \cdot [A_4'']$$

$$[C_4] \cdot [A_4''] = \begin{bmatrix} 1.498 \\ 2.627 \\ 0.322 \\ 0.509 \\ 7.093 \\ 4.531 \\ 0.843 \end{bmatrix} = 7.093 \cdot \begin{bmatrix} 0.211 \\ 0.370 \\ 0.045 \\ 0.071 \\ 1 \\ 0.638 \\ 0.118 \end{bmatrix} \rightarrow \lambda_4 = 7.093$$

In this way we will arrive at a new corresponding particular vector, which we will take as the fourth row of the matrix.

Let us suppose that the nature of the specific problem treated determines the selection between two particular vectors and the second is selected. In this case, for the fourth row we would take:

0.211
0.370
0.045
0.071
1
0.638
0.118

For C_5 (sales possibility) we propose to take as values for the fuzzy relation, the possibilities we arrived at before, since the <<index of possibility>> is, in itself, a valuation.

We now have available all the valuations for constructing the sought after fuzzy matrix. It will be as follows:

$[\underset{\sim}{R}] =$

	E_1	E_2	E_3	E_4	E_5	E_6	E_7
C_1	0.85	0.77	0.17	0.68	0.35	1	0.90
C_2	0.66	0.40	1	0.44	0.49	0.32	0.28
C_3	0.05	0.67	0.28	0.10	1	0.43	0.18
C_4	0.21	0.37	0.04	0.07	1	0.63	0.11
C_5	0.62	0.82	1	0.86	1	0.37	0.47

From this fuzzy relation, we can now commence the selection process.

Determination of relations of affinity

We are going to treat the fuzzy relation $\underset{\sim}{R}$ in such a way as to permit us to visibly bring to light, the whole range of possibilities arising for the investing subject, and to permit the taking of a decision according to the importance which may be given to each of the decision elements.

For this we will establish a <<threshold>> by means of a fuzzy sub-set, such as:

C_1	0.80
C_2	0.40
C_3	0.25
C_4	0.10
C_5	0.60

From the point of intervention of this threshold the fuzzy relation $\underset{\sim}{R}$ is converted into a boolean matrix. The assignment of values to each element of decision C_i, $i = 1, 2, \ldots 5$ indicates that when, a valuation equal to or higher than the threshold established for that criterion exists in the relation, the equipment has the required level and, therefore, we will assign a 1 to the associated boolean matrix. If it is lower, it is considered that the minimum requirement is not met and therefore we will place a 0 or leave a space in the boolean matrix.

The levels of the threshold, obviously in this case arbitrary, are 0.80 for C_1, 0.40 for C_2, ... Therefore the following boolean matrix is arrived at:

$[B]$ =

	A	*B*	*C*	*D*	*E*	*F*	*G*
a	1					1	1
b	1	1	1	1	1		
c		1	1		1	1	
d	1	1			1	1	1
e	1	1	1	1	1		

For handling and operating this matrix we will resort to the notion of affinity[4] which we used previously.

In order to establish <<relations of affinity>> recourse can be made, among others, to the so called method of elimination.

Let us recall the existence of two sets, which in our case are:

$$E = \{E_1, E_2, E_3, E_4, E_5, E_6, E_7\}$$

corresponding to the eventual equipment and,

$$C = \{C_1, C_2, C_3, C_4, C_5\}$$

which refers to the elements of decision.

For easier development we are going to use a new notation resulting from doing:

$$E_1 = A,\quad E_2 = B,\quad \ldots,\quad E_7 = G \quad \text{y} \quad C_1 = a,\quad C_2 = b,\quad \ldots,\quad C_5 = e$$

From these two sets, the one with the least elements is chosen, in this case C, and with it the largest possible set is constructed with them (the so called <<power set>> of C). In our case it will be:

$$P(C) = \{\phi, a, b, c, d, e, ab, ac, ad, ae, bc, bd, be, cd, ce, de, abc, abd, abe, acd, ace, ade, bcd, bce, bde, cde, abcd, abce, abde, acde, bcde, E^{(2)}\}$$

To each element of $P(C)$ the element or elements will be made to correspond from the set of the parts of the other set, $P(E)$, constructed with elements of E for the established α levels, according to the previous boolean matrix.

The non-vacant elements of $P(E)$ and sub-sets of C not included in others will be taken into account. In this case we will arrive at:

$a \to AFG,\quad be \to ABCDE,\quad bcd \to BE,$

$b \to ABCDE,\quad cd \to BEF,\quad bce \to BCE,$

$c \to BCEF,\quad ce \to BCE,\quad bde \to ABE,$

$d \to ABEFG,\quad de \to ABE,\quad cde \to BE,$

$e \to ABCDE,\quad abc \to \phi,\quad abcd \to \phi,$

$ab \to A,\quad abd \to A,\quad abce \to \phi,$

$ac \to F,\quad abe \to A,\quad abde \to A,$

$ad \to AFG,\quad acd \to F,\quad acde \to \phi,$

$ae \to A,\quad ace \to \phi,\quad bcde \to BE,$

$bc \to BCE,\quad ade \to A,\quad abcde \to \phi$

$bd \to ABE$

Now we select, for each group of the right hand column (upper case letters) the element of the <<power set>> of C with the largest number of elements (greatest number of lower case letters). We arrive at:

$A \to abde,\quad BCE \to bce,$

$F \to acd,\quad BEF \to cd,$

$BE \to bcde,\quad BCEF \to c,$

$ABE \to bde,\quad ABCDE \to be,$

$AFG \to ad,\quad ABEFG \to d$

From this the following affinities arise:

$$(abde, A),\quad (acd, F),\quad (bcde, BE),\quad (bde, ABE),\quad (ad, AFG),\quad (bce, BCE),$$
$$(cd, BEF),\quad (c, BCEF),\quad (be, ABCDE),\quad (d, ABEFG)$$

We can now ask ourselves, if the possibility exists for carrying out a different treatment of the boolean matrix [B] in order to arrive at a result which allows for the taking of a decision for investing in an object. For this we are going to consider, again as an example, the matrix we used before:

	A	B	C	D	E	F	G
a	1					1	1
b	1	1	1	1	1		
c		1	1		1	1	
d	1	1			1	1	1
e	1	1	1	1	1		

Let us now see what happens if we resort to the theory of clans. As is known, given a boolean matrix a <<clan>> K can be constructed from the <<mini-terms>> or <<atoms>>. First, let us move on to obtain the atoms:

$$\{a, b, c, d, e\} = \phi,\quad \{a, b, c, d, \bar{e}\} = \phi,\quad \{a, b, c, \bar{d}, e\} = \phi,\quad \{a, b, \bar{c}, d, e\} = \{A\},$$
$$\{a, \bar{b}, c, d, e\} = \phi,\quad \{\bar{a}, b, c, d, e\} = \{B, E\},\quad \ldots\quad \{a, \bar{b}, c, d, \bar{e}\} = \{F\},\quad \ldots$$
$$\{\bar{a}, b, c, \bar{d}, e\} = \{C\},\quad \ldots ,$$
$$\{a, \bar{b}, \bar{c}, d, \bar{e}\} = \{G\},\quad \ldots\quad \{\bar{a}, b, \bar{c}, \bar{d}, e\} = \{D\},\quad \ldots$$

It can be seen that the non vacant mini-terms or atoms are $\{A\}$, $\{B, E\}$, $\{C\}$, $\{D\}$, $\{F\}$, $\{G\}$, the correspondence of which is the following:

$$\{A\} \rightarrow \{a, b, d, e\}$$
$$\{B, E\} \rightarrow \{b, c, d, e\}$$
$$\{C\} \rightarrow \{b, c, e\}$$
$$\{D\} \rightarrow \{b, e\}$$
$$\{F\} \rightarrow \{a, c, d\}$$
$$\{G\} \rightarrow \{a, d\}$$

The set formed by the atoms, all their possible unions and ϕ will form a clan.

If on establishing the corresponding unions of the elements to the left (A, B, ..., G) the intersection of the elements to the right (a, b, c, d, e) are done, the following unoccupied[5] correspondences are arrived at:

$$\{A, B, E\} \to \{b, d, e\} \quad \{A, C\} \to \{b, e\} \quad \{A, D\} \to \{b, e\}$$
$$\{A, F\} \to \{a, d\} \quad \{A, G\} \to \{a, d\} \quad \{B, C, E\} \to \{b, c, e\}$$
$$\{B, D, E\} \to \{b, e\} \quad \{B, E, F\} \to \{c, d\} \quad \{B, E, G\} \to \{d\}$$
$$\{C, D\} \to \{b, e\} \quad \{C, F\} \to \{c\} \quad \{F, G\} \to \{a, d\}$$
$$\{A, B, C, E\} \to \{b, e\} \quad \{A, B, D, E\} \to \{b, e\} \quad \{A, B, E, F\} \to \{d\}$$
$$\{A, B, E, G\} \to \{d\} \quad \{A, C, D\} \to \{b, e\} \quad \{B, C, D, E\} \to \{b, e\}$$
$$\{B, C, E, F\} \to \{c\} \quad \{A, F, G\} \to \{a, d\} \quad \{A, B, C, D, E\} \to \{b, e\}$$
$$\{A, B, E, F, G\} \to \{d\}$$

Therefore, it is these elements, in conjunction with the unoccupied atoms we arrived at previously and the ϕ that form clan K. Now, if all the sets are brought together with the same elements to the right and from among these the greatest from the left is selected, it will be seen that it possesses all the elements existing in the rest. The result coincides with the correspondence found in the previous section. In effect:

$$\{A\} \to \{a, b, d, e\} \leftarrow$$
$$\{B, E\} \to \{b, c, d, e\} \leftarrow$$
$$\{F\} \to \{a, c, d\} \leftarrow$$

From:

$$\{C\} \to \{b, c, e\}$$
$$\{B, C, E\} \to \{b, c, e\}$$

the following are selected:

$$\{B, C, E\} \to \{b, c, e\} \leftarrow$$

$$\{A, B, E\} \to \{b, d, e\} \leftarrow$$

From:

$$\{G\} \rightarrow \{a, d\}$$
$$\{A, F\} \rightarrow \{a, d\}$$
$$\{A, G\} \rightarrow \{a, d\}$$
$$\{F, G\} \rightarrow \{a, d\}$$
$$\{A, F, G\} \rightarrow \{a, d\}$$

the following are selected:

$$\{A, F, G\} \rightarrow \{a, d\} \leftarrow$$

$$\{B, E, F\} \rightarrow \{c, d\} \leftarrow$$

From:

$$\{C, F\} \rightarrow \{c\}$$
$$\{B, C, E, F\} \rightarrow \{c\}$$

the following are selected:

$$\{B, C, E, F\} \rightarrow \{c\} \leftarrow$$

From:

$$\{D\} \rightarrow \{b, e\}$$
$$\{B, E, D\} \rightarrow \{b, e\}$$
$$\{C, D\} \rightarrow \{b, e\}$$
$$\{A, B, C, E\} \rightarrow \{b, e\}$$
$$\{A, C\} \rightarrow \{b, e\}$$
$$\{A, B, D, E\} \rightarrow \{b, e\}$$
$$\{A, C, D\} \rightarrow \{b, e\}$$
$$\{A, D\} \rightarrow \{b, e\}$$
$$\{B, C, D, E\} \rightarrow \{b, e\}$$
$$\{A, B, C, D, E\} \rightarrow \{b, e\}$$

the following is selected:

$$\{A, B, C, D, E\} \rightarrow \{b, e\} \leftarrow$$

From:

$$\{B, E, G\} \rightarrow \{d\}$$
$$\{A, B, E, F\} \rightarrow \{d\}$$
$$\{A, B, E, G\} \rightarrow \{d\}$$
$$\{A, B, E, F, G\} \rightarrow \{d\}$$

the following is selected:

$$\{A, B, E, F, G\} \rightarrow \{d\} \leftarrow$$

In this way we have arrived at the relations of affinity, which make an important base for studying investment selection from the point of view of the different criteria selected as decision elements.

In fact, the relations of affinity arrived at in this way can be presented in the form of a Galois lattice.

The establishment of preferences by means of Galois lattices

Let us remember that in an algebraic configuration or structure a set T can be considered along with two laws of internal composition $*$ and $*'$ in T.

If:

$$\forall x, y, z \in T$$

the properties of commutability, associability, idempotence, and absorption are complied with:

$$\left.\begin{array}{r} x * y = y * x \\ x *' y = y *' x \end{array}\right\} \text{Commutability}$$

$$\left.\begin{array}{r} x * (y * z) = (x * y) * z \\ x *' (y *' z) = (x *' y) *' z \end{array}\right\} \text{Associativity}$$

$$\left.\begin{array}{r} x * x = x \\ x *' x = x \end{array}\right\} \text{Idempotence}$$

$$\left.\begin{array}{r} x * (x *' y) = x \\ x *' (x * y) = x \end{array}\right\} \text{Absorption}$$

the T set is called a lattice.

This idea plays an important role in nearly all spheres of mathematics in which the concept of an ordered set is considered.

A variety of lattice types are known that correspond to peculiarities of configuration the use of which is certain in applied mathematics. We are going to pay particular attention to one type of lattice, because of its participation in forming affinities: the Galois lattice.

For this we are going to consider two finite sets E and C and their respective sets of the parts $P(E)$ and $P(C)$.

We will now establish two relations of order defined as follows:

$$\forall X, X' \in P(E) \quad , \quad \forall Y, Y' \in P(C):$$
$$((X, Y) \leqslant (X', Y')) \quad \Leftrightarrow \quad (X \subset X', Y \supset Y')$$

The upper extreme of (X, Y) will be designated by $X \nabla Y$ and the lower extreme by $X \Delta Y$. These extremes are induced by the relation of order $\leqslant$.

In the same way the opposing relation of order is introduced:

$$\forall X, X' \in P(E) \quad , \quad \forall Y, Y' \in P(C):$$
$$((X, Y) \geqslant (X', Y')) \quad \Leftrightarrow \quad (X \supset X', Y \subset Y')$$

The upper extreme of (X, Y) will be designated by $(X \nabla Y)$ and the lower extreme by $(X \Delta Y)$. These extremes are induced by the previous relation of order.

The pairs (ϕ, C) and (E, ϕ) are introduced respectively as the lower and upper extremes.

When the following properties are verified, the T set possessing them has a configuration known as a << Galois lattice>>.

$$(U, V) = (X, Y) \nabla (X', Y')$$
$$(U \supset X \cup X' \quad \text{and} \quad V \subset Y \cap Y')$$

and also:

$$(Z, S) = (X, Y) \Delta (X', Y')$$
$$(Z \subset X \cap X' \quad \text{and} \quad S \supset Y \cup Y')$$

When in a relation $\underset{\sim}{R} \subset E \times C$ a level or levels α, are chosen as we have done in order to arrive at $[B]$, the maximum sub-relations which have been joined by (ϕ, C) and (E, ϕ), form a Galois lattice. The study of a lattice of this type shows very explicitly how certain affinities are situated relative to others.

In fact, if a lattice is constructed with the affinities we arrived at, in accordance with the relations of order defined previously, the following Galois lattice is arrived at (figure 11.2):

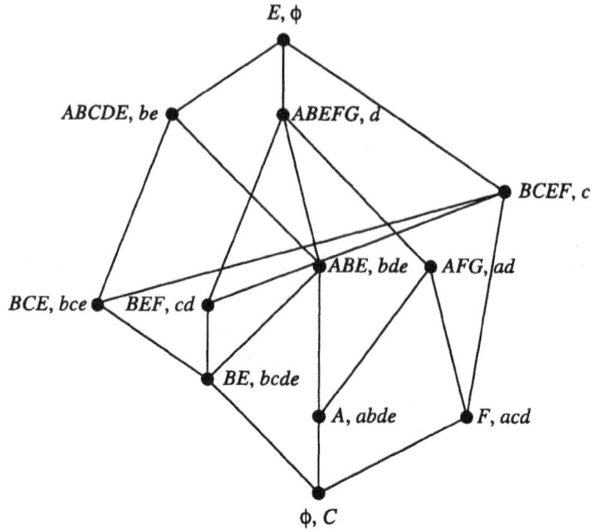

Figure 11.2.

This lattice structure allows us to visualise the affinities existing between the different investment objects relative to the elements of decision. According to the importance that the deciding subjects assign to each one of them, one or other of the groups of objects formed can be considered as interesting.

In this way, when, for example, decision elements b, c, d and e are considered as essential, only equipment B and E comply with the same at the required levels. And so on successively, all the possible combinations will arise for decision elements and equipment.

The use of this presentation in the form of Galois lattices is obvious. It can be seen how the groupings are made alternatively either through the progressive association of decision elements (starting out from below to above) or of the specific objects of the investment (from above to below). On the other hand the existence of changes in the configuration of the lattice could be verified when the α levels were modified, as required by the different decision subjects.

Relative estimate of the decision elements

We will now move on to study, based on the scheme already used in this chapter, another way of considering the fact that the investing subject does not estimate the same level for each of the decision elements, as a consequence of assigning to them a different weight and importance at the time of deciding the hypothetical acquisition of an investment object.

At the same time an order and degree of priority for each element over all the others should be established, which in our hypothetical case could be the following:

- Element C_1 is estimated as worth 2 times C_2, 3 times C_3, 4 times C_4, and 1/2 times C_5.
- Element C_2 is estimated as worth 2 times C_3, 3 times C_4, and 1/3 times C_5.
- Element C_3 is estimated as worth 2 times C_4, and 1/5 times C_5.
- Element C_4 is estimated as worth 1/6 times C_5.

This allows presenting the following reciprocal matrix.

$[C] =$

	C_1	C_2	C_3	C_4	C_5
C_1	1	2	3	4	1/2
C_2	1/2	1	2	3	1/3
C_3	1/3	1/2	1	2	1/5
C_4	1/4	1/3	1/2	1	1/6
C_5	2	3	5	6	1

From matrix $[C]$ we move on to obtain the dominant particular value and corresponding vector.

We initiate the process by:

$$[C] \cdot [1] = \begin{bmatrix} 10.500 \\ 6.833 \\ 4.033 \\ 2.250 \\ 17.000 \end{bmatrix} = 17.000 \cdot \begin{bmatrix} 0.617 \\ 0.401 \\ 0.237 \\ 0.132 \\ 1 \end{bmatrix} = 17.000 \cdot [B]$$

$$[C] \cdot [B] = \begin{bmatrix} 3.158 \\ 1.912 \\ 1.107 \\ 0.705 \\ 5.414 \end{bmatrix} = 5.414 \cdot \begin{bmatrix} 0.583 \\ 0.353 \\ 0.204 \\ 0.130 \\ 1 \end{bmatrix} = 5.414 \cdot [B']$$

$$[C] \cdot [B'] = \begin{bmatrix} 2.921 \\ 1.775 \\ 1.034 \\ 0.662 \\ 5.025 \end{bmatrix} = 5.025 \cdot \begin{bmatrix} 0.581 \\ 0.353 \\ 0.205 \\ 0.131 \\ 1 \end{bmatrix} = 5.025 \cdot [B'']$$

Arriving finally at:

$$[C] \cdot [B''] = \begin{bmatrix} 2.926 \\ 1.779 \\ 1.037 \\ 0.663 \\ 5.032 \end{bmatrix} = 5.032 \cdot \begin{bmatrix} 0.581 \\ 0.353 \\ 0.206 \\ 0.131 \\ 1 \end{bmatrix} = 5.032 \cdot [B''']$$

$$\rightarrow \lambda = 5.032$$

$[B''']$ is normalised. For this we will do:

$$\sum_{j=1}^{5} c_j = 0.581 + 0.353 + 0.206 + 0.131 + 1 = 2.271$$

For each c_j, j = 1, 2, 3, 4, 5, we arrive at:

$$\frac{c_j}{\sum_{j=1}^{5} c_j}$$

which will give rise to vector $[L]$:

$$[L] = \begin{bmatrix} 0.256 \\ 0.155 \\ 0.091 \\ 0.058 \\ 0.440 \end{bmatrix}$$

the vector elements of which can be considered as the weights for weighting each of the decision elements.

From fuzzy relation $[\underset{\sim}{R}]$, we obtain the sum of the elements of each of its rows:

$[\underset{\sim}{R}] =$

	E_1	E_2	E_3	E_4	E_5	E_6	E_7	*Sum rows*
C_1	0.85	0.77	0.17	0.68	0.35	1	0.90	4.72
C_2	0.66	0.40	1	0.44	0.49	0.32	0.28	3.59
C_3	0.05	0.67	0.28	0.10	1	0.43	0.18	2.71
C_4	0.21	0.37	0.04	0.07	1	0.63	0.11	2.43
C_5	0.62	0.82	1	0.86	1	0.37	0.47	5.14

with the object of normalising, in the probabilistic sense, each of the rows in such a way that the sum of the values arrived at for each of them, is equal to the unit.

This will be:

$[\underset{\sim}{N}] =$

	E_1	E_2	E_3	E_4	E_5	E_6	E_7
C_1	0.18	0.16	0.04	0.15	0.07	0.21	0.19
C_2	0.18	0.11	0.28	0.12	0.14	0.09	0.08
C_3	0.02	0.25	0.10	0.03	0.37	0.16	0.07
C_4	0.09	0.15	0.01	0.03	0.41	0.26	0.05
C_5	0.12	0.16	0.19	0.17	0.20	0.07	0.09

Now we will multiply this fuzzy relation $[\underset{\sim}{N}]$ to the right by the normalised vector $[L]$ obtained before, which will give rise to:

$[\underset{\sim}{L}] \cdot [\underset{\sim}{N}] =$

C_1	C_2	C_3	C_4	C_5
0.256	0.155	0.091	0.058	0.440

$\cdot$

	E_1	E_2	E_3	E_4	E_5	E_6	E_7
C_1	0.18	0.16	0.04	0.15	0.07	0.21	0.19
C_2	0.18	0.11	0.28	0.12	0.14	0.09	0.08
C_3	0.02	0.25	0.10	0.03	0.37	0.16	0.07
C_4	0.09	0.15	0.01	0.03	0.41	0.26	0.05
C_5	0.12	0.16	0.19	0.17	0.20	0.07	0.09

=

E_1	E_2	E_3	E_4	E_5	E_6	E_7
0.133	0.159	0.147	0.136	0.185	0.128	0.110

This result can be expressed as a normal fuzzy sub-set:

	E_1	E_2	E_3	E_4	E_5	E_6	E_7
$\underset{\sim}{E}=$	0.718	0.859	0.794	0.735	1	0.691	0.594

Now it can be seen that the following order of priority has been obtained from among the investment objects E_i, $i = 1, 2, \ldots, 7$:

$$E_5 > E_2 > E_3 > E_4 > E_1 > E_6 > E_7$$

As the reader can now verify, the order established also constitutes an order of preference in the selection process. Likewise the greater or lesser distance of the value of the membership function with regard to the unit, will also represent the greater or lesser potential distancing of the investment object from its possibility of being chosen.

The techniques we have used constitute therefore certain useful instruments for aiding in investment selection, when the criterion of economic viability is not the only criterion to be taken into account in order to take the decision to invest.

References

1 Let us point out in this respect the interest that the theory of forgotten effects may have, included in A.Kaufmann and J. Gil Aluja: *Modelos para la investigación de efectos olvidados,* Milladoiro, Santiago de Compostela, 1987.

2 A first consideration on this subject can be found in J. Gil Aluja: <<Selección multicriterio de inversiones mediante retículos de Galois>> included in the work in homage to Professor López Moreno *Dirección de empresas de los noventa,* Civitas, Madrid, 1995, pages 139-157.

3 For more information relative to this subject, consult: A. Kaufmann and J. Gil Aluja: *Técnicas de Gestión de empresa. Previsiones, decisiones y estrategias,* Pirámide, Madrid, 1992.

4 J. Gil Aluja:<<El concepto de afinidad en el nuevo paradigma de la teoría de decisión>>, Speech made at the act of incorporation into the Universidad Rovira i Virgili as Doctor <<Honoris Causa>>, Tarragona, May 16, 1997 (published).

5 With the object of not drawing this exposition out unnecessarily we have omitted those relations the intersection of which gives rise to Ø.

12 Investment in the event of non-specified criteria

Presentation of the problem

Within the spheres of determinism or probability, it is becoming ever more difficult to estimate monetary currents of collections and payments that constitute the monetary consequences of the decision to invest. During the last few years, in conjunction with Professor Kaufmann, we developed various techniques based on multivalent logic, which permitted handling this problem under contexts of uncertainty[1] .

However, current reality presents situations that surpass all limits, in themselves particularly wide, in which these models can be used. Under these circumstances, and being conscious of the need for showing the way to those who invariably must make the decision to invest, when not having available estimates relative to the monetary currents arising from the hypothetical acquisition and operation of the investment object, we propose to draw up certain schemes that are valid when the uncertainty of monetary currents of collections and payments do not even allow for their limits to be determined. What we are dealing with is a situation of absolute ignorance or impossibility for valuation.

Accumulated experience has shown that the case we have brought up is going to be ever more frequent, as it becomes more difficult, when not impossible, to make any <<valuations>> with the minimum guarantees of solvency, even when resorting to estimates by means of uncertain numbers.

On the other hand, with the uncertainty reigning in society today, on quite a few occasions it becomes even difficult to explain the basic criteria of the decision to invest, either because of the lack of information relative to the supposedly important aspects in the future, or of the total ignorance of the degree of interest of certain criteria with regard to others. For whatever the reason, the need has been seen with ever greater frequency, for drawing up a process that avoids the incorporation <<in an explicit manner>> of traditional selection criteria, leaving the task of establishing the basic information of the decision to invest, to the qualities and intuition of experts. Under these circumstances the importance of the concepts of comparison and ordering appear with total clarity, to the detriment of normally used purely quantitative notions.

The solution to the problem of selection under this context can take place by means of various paths and the use of very varied techniques. In a work done some time ago, we presented one of these[2] the most significant characteristic of which is its high degree of flexibility and adaptability. On this occasion, we have set our objective to seeking a parallel path to the one already found, which, obviously leads to similar results. We feel that its comparison can be quite enriching.

In a first approximation we start out with the opinion of an expert, capable of comparing, two by two, the set of m investment objects E_i, $i = 1, 2, \dots, m$ in order to form an boolean matrix (and its associated graph if necessary) as follows: when an object E_i is preferred to E_j put a 1 in box (E_i, E_j), $i, j = 1, 2, \dots, m$. (in the graph an arc is drawn from E_i to E_j). If E_i is preferable to E_j and also E_j is preferred to E_i there will be equivalence between objects E_i and E_j (in the graph a circuit occurs). It is possible that in this comparative process other groupings into classes (other cycles) exist such as is the case where E_i is preferred to E_j, E_j is preferred to E_k and E_k is preferred to E_i. When this happens the study of equivalence must be made by means of adequate algorithms for obtaining equivalency classes.

In the resulting boolean matrix, as shown below, no account is taken of the boxes of the principal diagonal, because an investment object cannot be preferred over itself. It is normal, to place a symbol such as x in these boxes:

$$[E] = \begin{array}{c|cccccc} & E_1 & E_2 & E_3 & & E_m \\ \hline E_1 & x & e_{12} & e_{13} & \cdots & e_{1m} \\ E_2 & e_{21} & x & e_{23} & \cdots & e_{2m} \\ E_3 & e_{31} & e_{32} & x & \cdots & e_{3m} \\ & \vdots & \vdots & \vdots & & \vdots \\ E_m & e_{m1} & e_{m2} & e_{m3} & \cdots & x \end{array}$$

where $e_{ij} \in \{0, 1\}$, $i, j = 1, 2, \dots, m$; $i \neq j$.

The treatment of the boolean matrix $[E]$ should be commenced, therefore, with obtaining the equivalency classes from which a class matrix can be constructed. In it equivalences occur (the corresponding class graph has no circuits). From this matrix (or associated graph) the different levels will be sought. Although in each level several classes may exist, this does not imply the existence of equivalence but of indifference.

By obtaining a functional ordinal we can establish an <<order>> of the classes, although this order may be a <<partial order>> contrary to the case of levels in which a <<total order>> occurs.

For the time being we will do without the development of these ideas by means of the corresponding algorithms, as we feel it is much more useful to do this in the case of a boolean matrix obtained from the aggregation of opinions from several experts. What we will have, in this case, will be a generalising case of the previous scheme.

Let us move on then to the existence of several experts whose opinion is sought relative to their preferences with regard to the investment objects considered on a two by two basis, as was already stated for the case of a single expert. In this event, we will arrive at as many boolean matrices $[E]$ as experts are consulted.

In order to obtain an aggregate opinion a new matrix can be arrived at in which each of the elements r_{ij} corresponding to the pair $[E_i, E_j]$will include the simple mean (the weighted mean could be taken into account if it were considered that the experts possessed different qualifications) of the valuations established individually by the experts. In this way we arrive at a matrix with valuations in [0, 1], that is, a fuzzy relation $[\underset{\sim}{R}]$, since all its elements r_{ij} are located in the interval [0, 1]:

$$
[\underset{\sim}{R}] = \begin{array}{c|cccccc|}
 & E_1 & E_2 & E_3 & & E_m \\
\hline
E_1 & x & r_{12} & r_{13} & \cdots & r_{1m} \\
E_2 & r_{21} & x & r_{23} & \cdots & r_{2m} \\
E_3 & r_{31} & r_{32} & x & \cdots & r_{3m} \\
\vdots & \vdots & \vdots & \vdots & & \vdots \\
E_m & r_{m1} & r_{m2} & r_{m3} & \cdots & x \\
\hline
\end{array}
$$

where $r_{ij} \in [0, 1]$.

This fuzzy relation is treated by means of α-cuts. For each α-cut a boolean matrix $[R_\alpha]$ (or associated graph) representing the preference or equivalence for each α level is obtained. Studies are normally limited to the high α levels, where there are greater presumptions, that is to say, the greatest predominance

Once the desired level has been determined, it is necessary to arrive at the equivalency classes (strongly connected sub-graphs). For this several paths can be followed, among which we propose one[3] that consists in arriving at the transitive closure $\hat{\Gamma}\{E_i\}$ and the inverted transitive closure $\hat{\Gamma}^{-}\{E_i\}$, and carry out the intersection between both for any element E_i, $i = 1, 2, ..., m$. With this we arrive at all the objects included in the same equivalency class of which E_i is a member. We now eliminate from matrix $[R_\alpha]$ the rows and columns corresponding to the class already arrived at, in this way leaving a matrix of a lower order. By the same process we arrive at a new class and so on successively until the matrix is emptied.

Once all the classes are formed, we are ready to establish an order (partial or total) between the same. The concept capable of carrying out this ordering is called a <<functional ordinal>>.

Development of the model by means of expert opinions

We now continue to develop the stated ideas with a didactic case in which the decision to invest must be taken on a limited number of objects $\{A, B, C, D, E\}$. Several experts, in this case 10, whom it is assumed have the same qualifications, are asked to express their opinions in the way we have explained up to now. The results are the following boolean matrices:

Expert 1

	A	*B*	*C*	*D*	*E*
A	*x*	1	1	1	0
B	0	*x*	1	0	0
C	0	1	*x*	1	1
D	1	1	0	*x*	1
E	1	1	0	0	*x*

Expert 2

	A	*B*	*C*	*D*	*E*
A	*x*	0	1	0	1
B	1	*x*	1	0	1
C	0	0	*x*	1	1
D	0	1	0	*x*	1
E	0	1	0	0	*x*

Expert 3

↱	*A*	*B*	*C*	*D*	*E*
A	*x*	0	1	1	0
B	1	*x*	1	0	1
C	0	0	*x*	1	1
D	0	1	0	*x*	0
E	1	0	0	1	*x*

Expert 4

↱	*A*	*B*	*C*	*D*	*E*
A	*x*	1	1	0	1
B	0	*x*	1	0	1
C	0	0	*x*	0	1
D	1	1	1	*x*	0
E	0	0	0	1	*x*

Expert 5

↱	*A*	*B*	*C*	*D*	*E*
A	*x*	1	0	0	1
B	0	*x*	1	0	0
C	1	0	*x*	1	1
D	1	1	0	*x*	0
E	0	1	0	1	*x*

Expert 6

↱	*A*	*B*	*C*	*D*	*E*
A	*x*	1	0	0	0
B	1	*x*	1	0	0
C	1	0	*x*	1	1
D	1	1	0	*x*	1
E	1	1	0	0	*x*

Expert 7

↱	*A*	*B*	*C*	*D*	*E*
A	*x*	0	0	1	1
B	1	*x*	1	0	0
C	1	0	*x*	1	1
D	0	1	1	*x*	1
E	0	1	0	0	*x*

Expert 8

↱	*A*	*B*	*C*	*D*	*E*
A	*x*	1	1	0	1
B	0	*x*	1	0	1
C	0	1	*x*	1	1
D	1	1	0	*x*	1
E	0	0	0	1	*x*

Expert 9

↱	*A*	*B*	*C*	*D*	*E*
A	*x*	1	0	1	1
B	1	*x*	1	0	0
C	1	0	*x*	1	1
D	0	1	0	*x*	0
E	0	1	0	1	*x*

Expert 10

↱	*A*	*B*	*C*	*D*	*E*
A	*x*	1	0	1	1
B	0	*x*	1	0	1
C	1	0	*x*	1	1
D	1	1	0	*x*	1
E	0	0	0	0	*x*

By adding the values of each box and dividing the result by the number of experts we arrive at the following fuzzy relation:

$[\underset{\sim}{R}]$ =

	A	B	C	D	E
A	x	0.7	0.5	0.5	0.7
B	0.5	x	1	0	0.5
C	0.5	0.2	x	0.9	1
D	0.6	1	0.2	x	0.6
E	0.3	0.6	0	0.5	x

Now it is necessary to select a determined level of presumption, which will constitute the <<decision risk>> position accepted by the investor.

As happens with all fuzzy relations, it is possible to carry out a treatment by means of its α-cuts. In this way we arrive at 11 matrices corresponding to the α = 1, 0.9, ..., 0.1, 0 levels, by using the hendecadarian system. As is customary the study is limited to the high levels, where the greatest presumption exists, that is to say, the strongest predominance.

For operative reasons let us assume that the selection falls to α= 0.7, in this case we will arrive at a new boolean matrix $[R_{0.7}]$:

$[R_{0.7}]$ =

	A	B	C	D	E
A	x	1			1
B		x	1		
C			x	1	1
D		1		x	
E					x

the corresponding associated graph of which is shown as figure 12.1.

With it we can immediately visualise at least one <<circuit>>. Under these circumstances it is impossible to establish an order between the investment objects, because the circuit shows the equivalence between the vertices (objects) that make it up.

This example brings to light the need to state as a prior requirement, the possibility of the appearance of circuits. For this we must first verify of any crossings, in which case there is a circuit. If there are no crossings, it should be verified that in the process for arriving at classes, each class is formed by a single vertex.Only in this way does the absence of circuits exist. Therefore, in second place, it is necessary to arrive at the <<equivalency class>>.

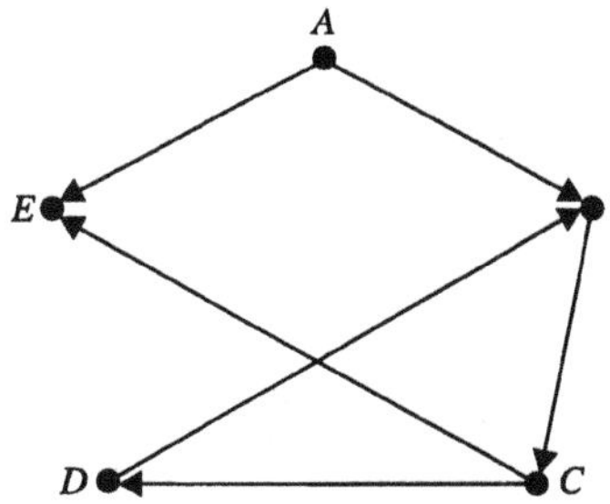

Figure 12.1.

As we have already pointed out, for this it will be necessary to establish the transitive closure $\hat{\Gamma}\{E_j\}$ and the inverted transitive closure $\hat{\Gamma}^{-}\{E_j\}$, by selecting any element E_j in order to carry out the intersection of both. In this way we arrive at all the elements of the class of which E_j is a member. We will then proceed to eliminate the rows and columns corresponding to the elements included in the class we arrived at from matrix $[R_{0.7}]$, in which case a lower order matrix will remain. Continue in this way until the matrix is empty.

Let us begin the process with vertex B, for example. We arrive at:

	A	B	C	D	E	$\hat{\Gamma}\{B\}$
A		1			1	
B			1			0
C				1	1	1
D		1				2
E						2
$\hat{\Gamma}^{-}\{B\}$	1	0	2	1		

Vertex B was selected arbitrarily. We place a column $\hat{\Gamma}\{B\}$ alongside the matrix and underneath a row $\hat{\Gamma}^{-}\{B\}$. In row $\hat{\Gamma}^{-}\{B\}$ we place a 0 in box B a 1 in A and in D because in column B of the matrix there were ones in these boxes. In column D there is a 1 in C, therefore in box C of row $\hat{\Gamma}^{-}\{B\}$ we place a 2. In column C of the matrix there is a 1 in B, but as box B has already been filled, the process is closed. We now arrive at:

$$\hat{\Gamma}^{-}\{B\} = \{A, B, C, D\}$$

We now move on to $\hat{\Gamma}\{B\}$. In row B there is C, therefore we place a 0 in B and a 1 in C in the column next to the matrix. In C we find D and E; we place a 2 in the corresponding boxes. In D we find B, already marked, while row E is vacant. We stop here and arrive at:

$$\hat{\Gamma}\{B\} = \{B, C, D, E\}$$

The class for B is:

$$C_1(B) = \hat{\Gamma}\{B\} \cap \hat{\Gamma}^{-}\{B\} = \{B, C, D, E\} \cap \{A, B, C, D\} = \{B, C, D\}$$

We now eliminate rows B, C and D from the matrix and we remain with $\{A, E\}$. E is selected arbitrarily, and by following the same process we arrive at:

	A	E	$\hat{\Gamma}\{E\}$
A		1	
E			0
$\hat{\Gamma}^{-}\{E\}$	1	0	

$$C_2(E) = \hat{\Gamma}\{E\} \cap \hat{\Gamma}^{-}\{E\} = \{E\} \cap \{A, E\} = \{E\}$$

We are now only left with vertex A which by itself forms a class: $C_3(A) = \{A\}$. Finally we have:

$$C_1(B) = \{B, C, D\}$$
$$C_2(E) = \{E\}$$
$$C_3(A) = \{A\}$$

To conclude we arrive at the fact that investment objects B, C and D, according to the aggregate opinion of the experts, are equivalent.

Having now obtained the equivalency classes (heavily connected sub-graphs) it may be useful to show a graph associated to relation $[R_{0.7}]$, by explicitly showing the vertices forming each equivalency class C_1, C_2 and C_3 (figure 12.2).

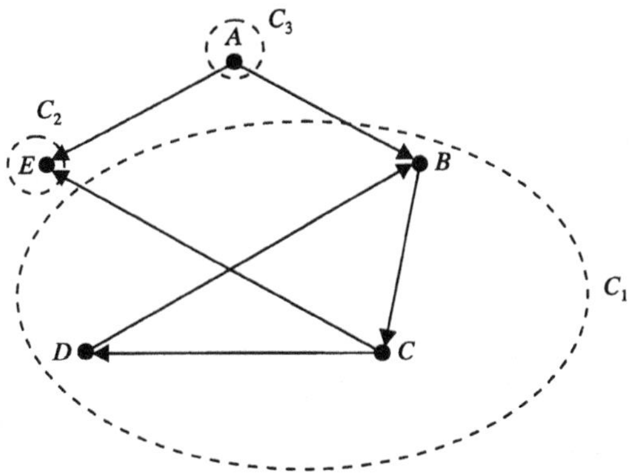

Figure 12.2.

The result obtained allows us to draw the following class graph, which in this case is particularly simple (figure 12.3).

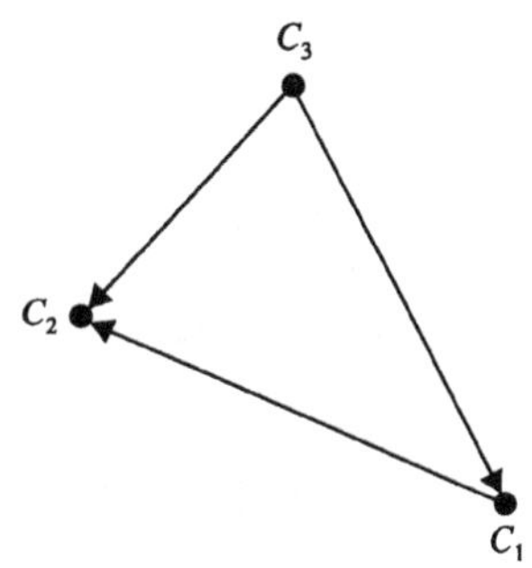

Figure 12.3.

The following boolean class matrix corresponds to the above graph:

	C_1	C_2	C_3
C_1		1	
C_2			
C_3	1	1	

Once the equivalency classes have been found, it is necessary to arrive at an order between them by using any of the known algorithms. When a class includes only one element and the order is total there is no difficulty for determining the order of preference between investment objects. But this does not always happen and then, as in the case we are looking at, it is only possible to obtain a partial order under the very best of conditions.

Order of preference by means of the Latin composition method.

Several algorithms are known for finding an order among equivalency classes (class graph with no circuits). In this sphere it may be suitable to point out that, while in certain cases each of the classes is composed of a single object (case of a graph without circuits in which each vertex forms a class by itself), in others it is formed by several. In one case the order will be individually established between objects and in the other between the classes. Algorithms exist that start out from the matrix and others from its associated graph (arrow diagram). We will now move on to briefly describe one of the former.

So as to be able to establish an order of preference between several investment objects, when this order is not strict, that is to say, when in a matrix classes of equivalence appear (or in the associated graph, heavily connected sub-graphs) in which one or more of them contain several objects (there are one or several sub-graphs with more than one vertex) it may be useful to resort to numbering the elementary paths of a graph from N_0 to N_r.

In order to arrive at this objective certain algorithms have been drawn up, among which we would like to emphasise the one based on the so-called method of the <<P-Latin composition>>[4].

A finite sequence of vertices $(E_{i1}, E_{i2}, ..., E_{in})$ that forms a path possessing property P in the graph $G = (E, \Gamma)$ is called <<Latin sequence of property P>> or simply <<P-Latin sequence>>.

Let us assume two paths, one with a longitude of p and the other a longitude of q, which include property P and are represented, respectively by the P-Latin sequences:

$$s_1 = (E_{i1}, E_{i2}, ..., E_{ip}, E_k)$$
$$s_2 = (E_1, E_{j1}, E_{j2}, ..., E_{jp})$$

A binary operation * is then considered such that:

$$s_1 * s_2 = (E_{i1}, E_{i2}, ..., E_{ip}, E_k, E_{j1}, E_{j2}, ..., E_{jp})$$

if: $E_k = E_1$; and if: the sequence is P-latin

$$= \varnothing$$

if it is not.

With the object of numbering the paths[5], we will start off from the notion of a Latin matrix $[L]^1$, the elements of which are formed by the description of the

Latin letters corresponding to the row and column defining each element. By construction, this Latin matrix $[L]^1$ numbers the paths, obviously elementary in this case, of a longitude of 1. Likewise the matrix $[L']^1$ is defined equal to the previous matrix which has deprived the element of each box of its respective initial letters.

The composition $[L]^1 \circ [L']^1$ gives us $[L]^2$ which numbers the elementary paths of a longitude of 2 when the property required is that of an elementary path. After making successive compositions we arrive at:

$$[L]^2 \circ [L']^1 = [L]^3$$
$$[L]^3 \circ [L']^1 = [L]^4$$
$$\dots\dots\dots\dots$$
$$[L]^{r-1} \circ [L']^1 = [L]^r$$
$$\dots\dots\dots\dots$$

This allows for the numbering of the elementary paths of a longitude of 1, 2, ..., r, without omission or repetition. For this it is essential that the fundamental relation is complied with.

$$s_1 * s_2 = s_1 \cdot s_2' \quad , \quad \text{if } s_1 \cdot s_2' \text{ is an elementary path}$$
$$= \varnothing \quad , \quad \text{on the contrary}$$

We now move on to use this algorithm in the simple case of the class boolean matrix arrived at. The Latin matrix will be, in this case:

$[L]^1 =$

	C_1	C_2	C_3
C_1		C_1C_2	
C_2			
C_3	C_3C_1	C_3C_2	

and the matrix with its initial letters removed will be:

$[L']^1 =$

	C_1	C_2	C_3
C_1		C_2	
C_2			
C_3	C_1	C_2	

We now arrive at the following elementary paths of a longitude of 2:

$[L]^2 = [L]^1 \circ [L'] =$

↱	C_1	C_2	C_3
C_1		C_1C_2	
C_2			
C_3	C_3C_1	C_3C_2	

$\circ$

↱	C_1	C_2	C_3
C_1		C_2	
C_2			
C_3	C_1	C_2	

$=$

↱	C_1	C_2	C_3
C_1			
C_2			
C_3		$C_3C_1C_2$	

In this way we find the existence of a single elementary path of the order of 2 (order between investment objects or groups of investment objects):

— With regard to classes: $C_3 \rightarrow C_1 \rightarrow C_2$

— With regard to objects: $A \rightarrow B \rightarrow E$, $A \rightarrow C \rightarrow E$, $A \rightarrow D \rightarrow E$

We can now consider the case of the existence of a single element in each equivalency class (heavily connected sub-graphs all of which are formed by a single vertex), as is the case of the following matrix:

↱	A	B	C	D	E
A	x		1		
B		x			1
C			x	1	1
D		1		x	
E					x

The corresponding Latin matrix and amputated Latin are:

$[L]^1$	A	B	C	D	E
A			AC		
B					BE
C				CD	CE
D		DB			
E					

$[L']^1$	A	B	C	D	E
A			C		
B					E
C				D	E
D		B			
E					

The elementary paths of a longitude of 2 and 3 are numbered:

$[L]^2$	A	B	C	D	E
A				ACD	ACE
B					
C		CDB			
D					DBE
E					

$[L]^3$	A	B	C	D	E
A		ACDB			
B					
C					CDBE
D					
E					

And, finally, we see the existence of a single elementary path of a longitude of 4:

$[L]^4$	A	B	C	D	E
A					ACDBE
B					
C					
D					
E					

The order of preference between the investment objects will be:

$$A \rightarrow C \rightarrow D \rightarrow B \rightarrow E$$

Before finishing this section, it would appear convenient to reiterate a fact, which is highly obvious: a class graph does not posses any circuits since, to the contrary, the classes could not be ordered.

Arriving at the ordinal function of a graph

When in order to establish an order between investment objects or classes of objects one starts out from the notion of a graph, an important aspect makes its presence felt: the ordinal function.

What this means is to break down, a graph of investment objects or classes of objects without circuits, into levels, in such a way that a vertex E_j preferred to another vertex E_i, is never at a preceding level to E_i (the same happens with classes C_i and C_j).

First let us carry out a theoretical formulation of the notion of ordinal function.

We consider a graph (either of objects or classes) without circuits $G = (E, \Gamma)$, for which sub-sets N_0, N_1, ..., N_r, which we will call <<levels>>, is established. These sub-sets are defined as follows:

$$N_0 = \{E_i / \Gamma^{-1}\{E_i\} = \varnothing\}$$
$$N_1 = \{E_i / (\Gamma^{-1}\{E_i\} \subset N_0) - N_0\}$$
$$N_2 = \{E_i / (\Gamma^{-1}\{E_i\} \subset N_0 \cup N_1) - N_0 \cup N_1\}$$

....

$$N_r = \{E_i / (\Gamma^{-1}\{E_i\} \subset N_0 \bigcup_{k=0}^{r-1} N_k) - \bigcup_{k=0}^{r-1} N_1\}$$

Where r is the lowest whole number, for which:

$$\Gamma N_r = \varnothing$$

It is easily shown that by construction sub-sets N_k, $k = 1, 2, ..., r$, form a partition of E and are totally ordered by the relation:

$$(N_k < N_{k'}) \Leftrightarrow (k < k')$$

The function $O(E)$ defined by:

$$(E_i \in N_k) \Leftrightarrow (O(E_i) = k)$$

is called <<ordinal function of the graph without circuits>>.

In short what we are trying to do is to break down the set of vertices of the graph without circuits into disjointed sub-sets and ordered, in such a way that if one vertex is a member of one of these sub-sets having been assigned a number k, every vertex after the vertex under consideration should be placed in a sub-set having a number greater than k.

To put it in another way, in the graph all the vertices without a predecessor are sought and with them level N_0 is formed. In the graph all vertices and arcs leaving from the same that are members of N_0 are crossed out. In the new graph we look for the vertices with no predecessors, with which we form level N_1. In the new graph, obtained by eliminating the vertices and arcs leaving from the same in N_1, we now look for the vertices with no predecessors, which will then form N_2. And so on successively until the graph disappears.

In this way we arrive at the establishment of an order among the investment objects or classes of objects. When the class includes a single element, the order is rigid, and there is no difficulty in determining a preference among the investment objects. But as we have seen it does not always occur in this way and, then, it is only possible to arrive at a non-rigid order, in which case the deciding subject must take the initiative in many cases in order to justify the object to which the decision to invest will fall.

The use of this concept is very simple. First let us take a look at the simpler case of the class graph associated to the boolean matrix of our example (figure 12.4):

	C_1	C_2	C_3
C_1		1	
C_2			
C_3	1	1	

Class matrix

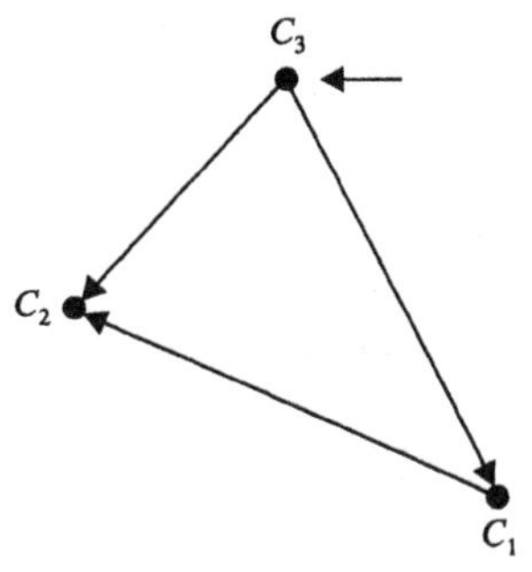

Figure 12.4.—Class graph

In order to obtain the ordinal function of the classes a process can be followed consisting in indicating the vertices with no predecessor with an arrow. The first of these is C_3, which forms level 0. We eliminate vertex C_3 and all the arcs (in this case one) that leave from it. In this way we arrive at figure 12.5:

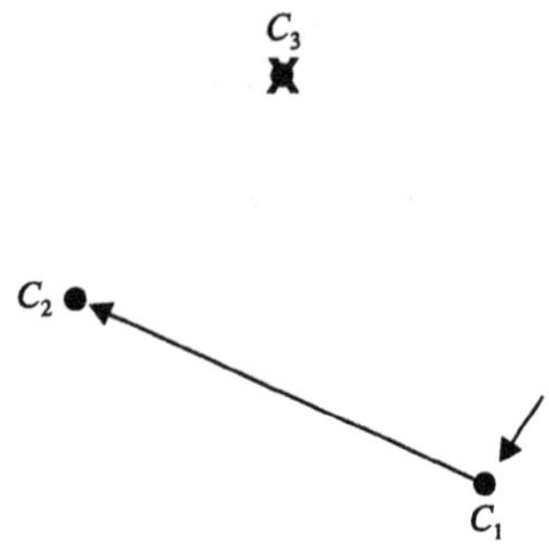

Figure 12.5.

The only vertex with no predecessor is now C_1. This then will form level 1. On eliminating the arc leaving from it we arrive at vertex C_2 in this way arriving at level 2 (figure 12.6):

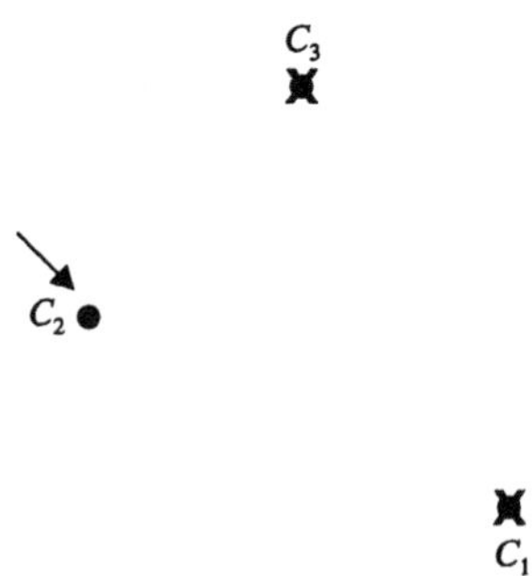

Figure 12.6.

In this way the same graph, associated to the boolean matrix $[R_{0.7}]$ we drew, can be constructed, taking into account the three levels we found (figure 12.7):

$$N_0 = \{A\}$$
$$N_1 = \{B, C, D\}$$
$$N_2 = \{E\}$$

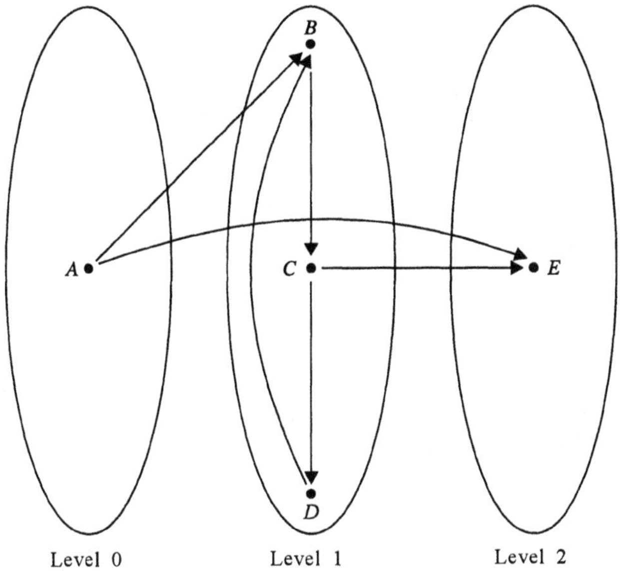

Figure 12.7.

It is necessary to take into account that fact that the levels are not classes, as they only indicate the order in which the vertices can be selected by following the direction of the arcs.

Now we will pass on to the hypothetical case of each class composing a single element. For this we follow again the example of the previous section, with the following matrix and associated graph (figure 12.8):

	A	*B*	*C*	*D*	*E*
A	*x*		1		
B		*x*			1
C			*x*	1	1
D		1		*x*	
E					*x*

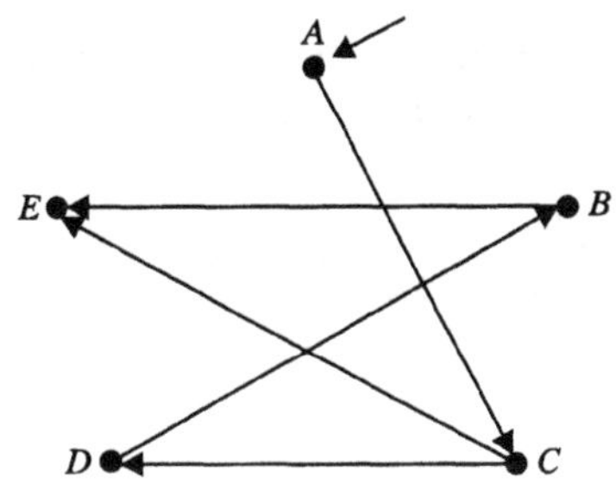

Figure 12.8.

In the above graph, the vertex without a predecessor is indicated with an arrow. This is *A* that forms level 0. We eliminate the arc leaving from it and we arrive at figure 12.9.

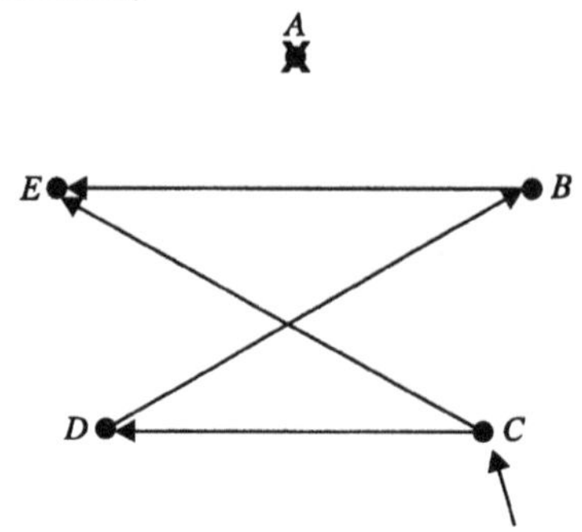

Figure 12.9.

The vertex with no predecessor is now C marked with an arrow, and this forms level 1. We eliminate this vertex and the arcs leaving from it (figure 12.10):

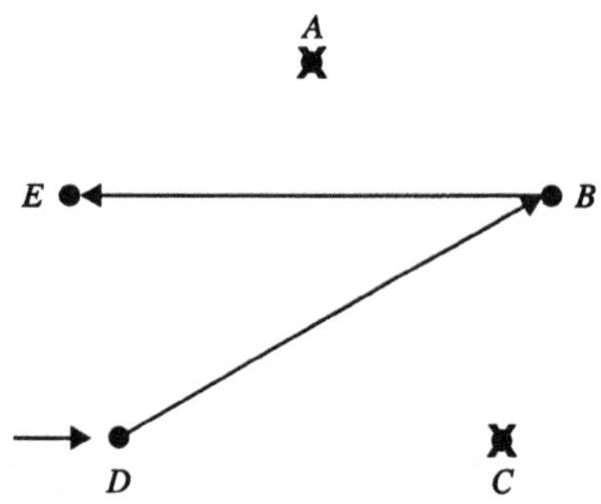

Figure 12.10.

The vertex with no predecessor is now D giving rise to level 2. This is marked with an arrow and the arc leaving from it is eliminated (figure 12.11):

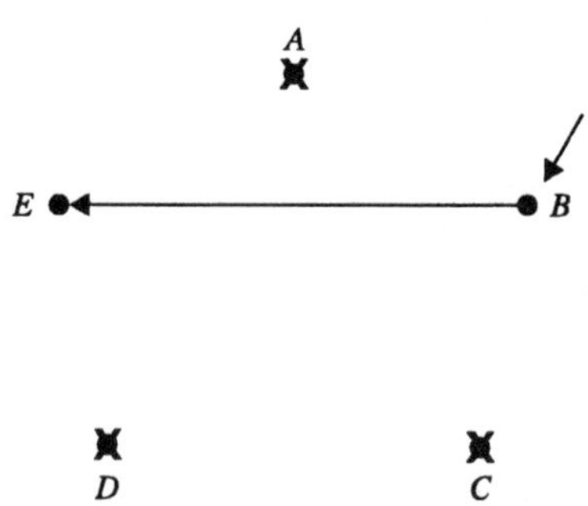

Figure 12.11.

Vertex B has no predecessor, and therefore, forms level 3. The arc leaving B is eliminated. Finally vertex E remains, and we arrive at level 4 (figure 12.12).

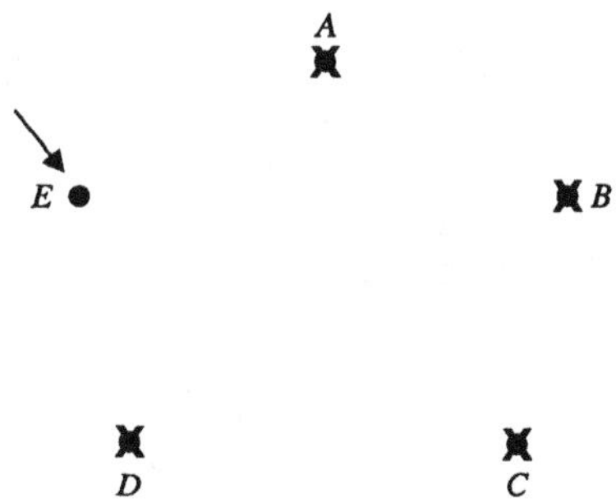

Figure 12.12.

The order is established by taking into account the five levels (figure 12.13).

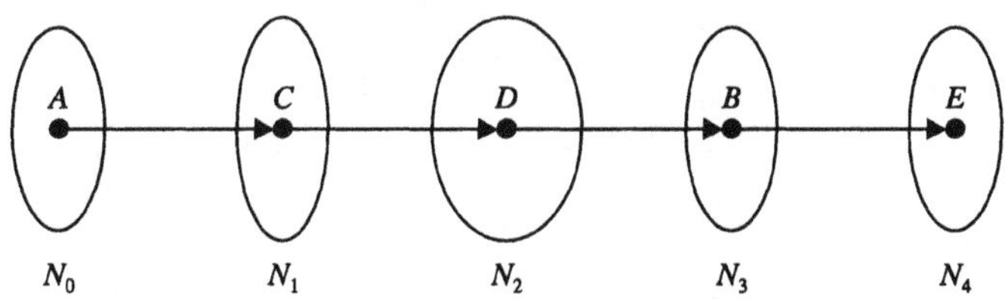

Figure 12.13.

What we have just arrived at by the intuitive visual method can also be found by means of a matrix form algorithm. This calculation procedure is, as we have seen, frequently used. First we present the boolean matrix associated to the class graph used in our example.

	C_1	C_2	C_3
C_1		1	
C_2			
C_3	1	1	

Although we are assuming that the proposed scheme is already known, we are going to develop it again in order to establish its operative aspects more solidly.

A sufficient number of rows Λ_i, $i = 0, 1, 2, \ldots$, are added to the corresponding matrix, where as many boxes as elements of the matrix appear (3 in this case), In row Λ_0 each box is filled in with the number resulting from adding the 1s of each column. The 0s of Λ_0 supply the elements (vertices if the graph) without predecessor, that is to say C_3 forming level N_0. We now remove from the matrix the 1s of the boxes of row C_3 and we arrive at Λ_1 where the 0 of Λ_0 has been substituted with a x. The 0 that appears in Λ_1 gives rise to an element without a predecessor when C_3 is eliminated. This is C_1 forming level N_1, We remove from the matrix the 1 in the corresponding box of row C_1, placing an x in the 0 of Λ_1. This gives rise to the appearance in Λ_2 of a 0 in C_2 that forms the last level N_2. As only 0 and x remain in this row, the process has concluded.

	C_1	C_2	C_3
C_1		1	
C_2			
C_3	1	1	

	C_1	C_2	C_3	
Λ_0	1	2	0	C_3

	C_1	C_2	C_3	
Λ_1	0	1	x	C_1

	C_1	C_2	C_3	
Λ_2	x	0	x	C_2

As is obvious, the same result is arrived at:

$$C_3 \rightarrow C_1 \rightarrow C_2$$

If the graph had at least one circuit, a row would exist in which it would be impossible for a new 0 to appear. This then is an automatic means of verifying if the graph has or has no circuits, that is to say, the existence or not of any equivalence between two or more investment objects.

Lastly let us move on to briefly describe this algorithm in the case of equivalency classes formed by a single element. For this we will take advantage of the boolean matrix of the previous section, to which the corresponding Λ_i rows are added. We arrive at:

	A	B	C	D	E
A			1		
B					1
C				1	1
D		1			
E					

	A	B	C	D	E	
Λ_0	0	1	1	1	2	$\{A\}$

	A	B	C	D	E	
Λ_1	x	1	0	1	2	$\{C\}$

	A	B	C	D	E	
Λ_2	x	1	x	0	1	$\{D\}$

	A	B	C	D	E	
Λ_3	x	0	x	x	1	$\{B\}$

	A	B	C	D	E	
Λ_4	x	x	x	x	0	$\{E\}$

The order we have obtained is:

$$A \rightarrow C \rightarrow D \rightarrow B \rightarrow E$$

Obviously this result coincides with the solution found by following the previously described processes.

In this example we have arrived, by the proposed method, at a total order. As can well be imagined, in other cases it is possible to find a relation of partial order and also a relation of vacant order. In certain cases the causes that prevent a total or partial order are studied and the experts are asked to accept certain modifications in order to arrive at a solution.

Throughout the pages of this chapter we have attempted to materialise certain processes that mean a profound change relative to the classical models for selecting investments. The schemes we have presented have no intention of being closed and complete works, but they only constitute certain lines of conduct for future advancement in this field. In this sense we have described some of the many techniques that are available in order for our objectives to be successful. By the very nature of this work we have limited ourselves to developing two paths which we have included schematically in figure 12.14:

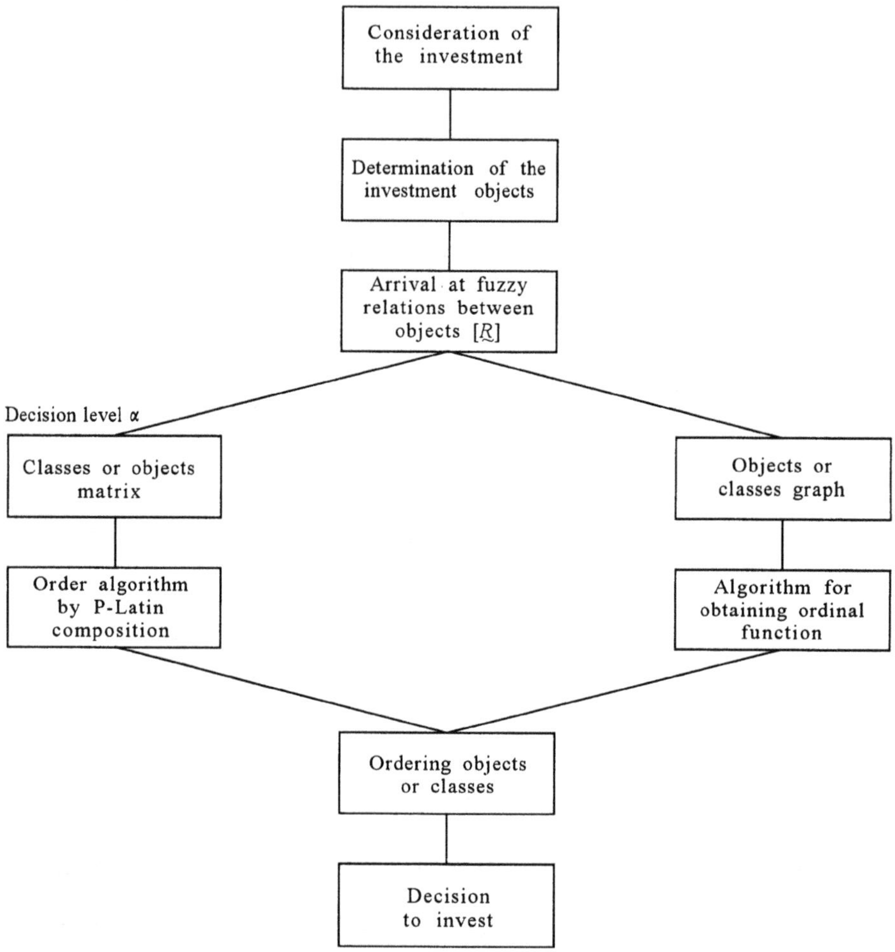

Figure 12.14.

This scheme only constitutes one of the many alternatives that arise under cover of these techniques, the possibilities of which, as we have seen, exceed the limits of investment selection

References

1 In this respect see: A. Kaufmann and J. Gil Aluja: *Introducción a la teoria de los subconjuntos borrosos a la gestión de las empresas*. Milladorio, Santiago de Compostela, 3rd. ed, 1992; A. Kaufmann and J. Gil Aluja: *Técnicas operativas de gestión para el tratamiento de la incertidumbre*, Hispano Europea, Barcelona, 1987, and A. Kaufmann and J.Gil Aluja: *Técnicas especiales para la gestión de expertos*, Milladorio, Santiago de Compostela, 1993.

2 J. Gil Aluja: *Modelo de selección de inversiones con desconocimiento de las magnitudes económico-financieras*, VI Jornadas Luso-Espanholas de Gestao Científica, Funchal, 10-12 December, 1992, volume I.

3 A. Kaufmann and J. Gil Aluja: *Técnicas especiales para la gestión de expertos*, Milladorio, Santiago de Compostela, 1993, pages 307-311.

4 For greater detail on this algorithm see: A. Kaufmann and J. Gil Aluja: *Nuevas técnicas para la dirección etsratégica*, Universidad de Barcelona, Barcelona, 1991, section 6.

5 An elemental path is formed by a succession of vertices without any repetition of any of them occurring, taking into account the arcs of the graph.

13 Optimum distribution of financial resources

Handling distribution by means of dynamic programming

One of the questions that arises with most frequency within the sphere of investment selection refers to the need of placing a determined monetary mass for a certain period of time, which can be affected to several investment objects overall or split into fractions, by distributing the total sum between all or only a part of them. Obviously, the investor wishes to gain the maximum profit, the nature of which has to be specified.

From a traditional standpoint, this problem can be resolved by following different techniques. In this chapter we are going to tackle it with the aid of an instrument which has been particularly efficient on a large number of occasions: dynamic programming.

As is sufficiently well known, the principle of optimisation requires for its use, that the phenomenon under study posses a monoid structure and be monotonous, that is to say, that it complies with the following properties:

— Associativity: if a, b, and c are successively articulated <<segments>> of a determined economic parameter, then $(a * b) * c = a * (b * c)$.

— Existence of a neutral: if a <<vacant segment>> exists, which is designated by $\varnothing$ for every <<segment>> a it will be $a * \varnothing = \varnothing * a = a$.

— Monotony: if the criterion is of optimisation, as in this case, when a <<segment>> τ includes another τ', the gollowing must be complied with $v(\tau) \geqslant v(\tau')$.

We will call <<segment>> the part of the monetary mass placed in a determined investment object.

With the object of making the presentation of the model we are proposing easier, we are going to assume the existence of a finite number of objects to which the decision to invest could fall: $A, B, C, D, ..., K$. Likewise we will designate by X the monetary mass available to be distributed (or not) between several options, in which case it would give rise to certain $x_1, x_2, ..., x_k$, on condition that the following were to be complied: $X = \sum_{j=1}^{k} x_j$.

Placing an amount x_j in an object D, for example, will give rise to an updated net profit (UNP) which can be designated by $f_D(x_j)$. Therefore we will have:

$f_A(x_j)$: UNP function relative to object A.

$f_B(x_j)$: UNP function relative to object B.

....

$f_K(x_j)$: UNP function relative to object K.

$$j = 1, 2, ..., k$$

Taking into account the fact that the objective consists in arriving at a maximum profit (optimisation) the following should be arrived at successively:

$F_{A,B}(X)$: Maximum profit when placing X monetary units jointly in A and B.

$F_{A,B,C}(X)$: Maximum profit when placing X monetary units jointly in A, B and C.

....

$F_{A,B,...,K}(X)$: Maximum profit when placing X monetary units jointly in A, B, ..., K.

It is easy to see for this problem, stated as we have done, that apart from the properties of a monoid, it possess commutability, therefore the order has no importance whatsoever, because optimisation could commence with B and C for example, to continue with B, C, D, ..., finalising with A, B, C, ..., K, without the result undergoing any variation.

In order to arrive at maximisation, we will use the principle of dynamic programming[1], by finding successively:

$$F_{A,B}(X) = \max_{x_i + x_j = X} (f_A(x_i) + f_B(x_j)) \qquad \begin{cases} X = 1, 2, ..., P \\ i,j = 1, 2, ..., k \end{cases}$$

$$F_{A,B,C}(X) = \max_{x_i + x_j = X} (F_{A,B}(x_i) + f_C(x_j)) \qquad \begin{cases} X = 1, 2, ..., P \\ i,j = 1, 2, ..., k \end{cases}$$

....

$$F_{A,B,...,K}(X) = \max_{x_i + x_j = X} (F_{A,B,...,J}(x_i) + f_K(x_j)) \qquad \begin{cases} X = 1, 2, ..., P \\ i,j = 1, 2, ..., k \end{cases}$$

In this way, the principle by which <<an optimum trajectory can only be formed by optimum sub-trajectories>> becomes truly meaningful.

We will now move on to develop an example. For this we are going to assume that an investor has available, as a maximum, a monetary mass of $X = 1000$ which can be place in 3 investment objects A, B, and C. In a first approximation and with the object of making this very simple, we will start out with the hypothesis that states that the unit cost is equal for each of the objects at 100. In this way, the investor can select from 11 possible investments which are, respectively, 0, 100, 200, ..., 900, 1000. That is to say he must constrain himself until he has invested all his possibilities.

For greater generalisation it will be assumed that the net updated value does not grow proportionally to the monetary mass invested in each object, that is to say that for example: $f_A(300) \neq 3 \cdot f_A(100)$, $f_B(400) \neq 4 \cdot f_B(100)$, ..., because in the case of proportionality the problem would be reduced to an elementary process.

We will start off then from the knowledge that the UNP (since this is the type of profit selected) relative to each placing of 100 units in each of the objects A, B and C, and we will assume as current the principle of the decrease in marginal profit.

The following table shows all data relative to the placing of 100 complementary units and their respective accumulation:

Order	Units		*A*		*B*		*C*	
	Partial	X_i	Partial	f_A	Partial	f_B	Partial	f_C
Ø	0	0	0	0	0	0	0	0
1	100	100	2	2	2	2	1.3	1.3
2	100	200	1.8	3.8	1.6	3.6	1.2	2.5
3	100	300	1.6	5.4	1.5	5.1	1.1	3.6
4	100	400	1.4	6.8	1.5	6.6	0.9	4.5
5	100	500	1.2	8	1.4	8	0.8	5.3
6	100	600	0.8	8.8	1.2	9.2	0.7	6
7	100	700	0.4	9.2	0.7	9.9	0.5	6.5
8	100	800	0.3	9.5	0.6	10.5	0.4	6.9
9	100	900	0.2	9.7	0.2	10.7	0.3	7.2
10	100	1000	0.1	9.8	0.1	10.8	0.3	7.5

The first phase for optimisation of the process

We begin the optimisation process by placing the first block of 100 monetary units, and see that the same figure is obtained both through A and B. In effect:

$F_A(X)$, if $X = 100$ is equal to $F_B(X)$

$$F_A(100) = F_B(100) = f_A(x_1) = f_B(x_1) = \underset{\uparrow}{2}$$

We are now going to consider A and B jointly in order to obtain $F_{A,B}(X)$.

If $X = 200$:

$$\begin{aligned} F_{A,B}(200) &= \text{Max}\ \{(f_A(200) + f_B(0)),\ (f_A(100) + f_B(100)),\ (f_A(0) + f_B(200))\} \\ &= \text{Max}\ \{(3.8 + 0),\ (2 + 2),\ (0 + 3.6)\} \\ &= \text{Max}\ \{3.8,\ \underset{\uparrow}{4},\ 3.6\} = f_A(100) + f_B(100) \end{aligned}$$

If $X = 300$:

$$\begin{aligned} F_{A,B}(300) &= \text{Max}\ \{(f_A(300) + f_B(0)),\ (f_A(200) + f_B(100)),\ (f_A(100) + f_B(200)), \\ &\quad (f_A(0) + f_B(300))\} \\ &= \text{Max}\ \{(5.4 + 0),\ (3.8 + 2),\ (2 + 3.6),\ (0 + 5.1)\} \\ &= \text{Max}\ \{5.4,\ \underset{\uparrow}{5.8},\ 5.6,\ 5.1\} = f_A(200) + f_B(100) \end{aligned}$$

If $X = 400$:

$$\begin{aligned} F_{A,B}(400) &= \text{Max}\ \{(f_A(400) + f_B(0)),\ (f_A(300) + f_B(100)),\ (f_A(200) + f_B(200)), \\ &\quad (f_A(100) + f_B(300)),\ (f_A(0) + f_B(400))\} \\ &= \text{Max}\ \{(6.8 + 0),\ (5.4 + 2),\ (3.8 + 3.6),\ (2 + 5.1),\ (0 + 6.6)\} \\ &= \text{Max}\ \{6.8,\ \underset{\uparrow}{7.4},\ \underset{\uparrow}{7.4},\ 7.1,\ 6.6\ \} \\ &= \{(f_A(300) + f_B(100)),\ (f_A(200) + f_B(200))\} \end{aligned}$$

If $X = 500$:

$$\begin{aligned} F_{A,B}(500) &= \text{Max}\ \{(f_A(500) + f_B(0)),\ (f_A(400) + f_B(100)),\ (f_A(300) + f_B(200)), \\ &\quad (f_A(200) + f_B(300)),\ (f_A(100) + f_B(400)),\ (f_A(0) + f_B(500))\} \\ &= \text{Max}\ \{(8 + 0),\ (6.8 + 2),\ (5.4 + 3.6),\ (3.8 + 5.1),\ (2 + 6.6),\ (0 + 8)\} \\ &= \text{Max}\ \{8,\ 8.8,\ \underset{\uparrow}{9},\ 8.9,\ 8.6,\ 8\} \\ &= f_A(300) + f_B(200) \end{aligned}$$

If $X = 600$:

$$\begin{aligned} F_{A,B}(600) &= \text{Max } \{(f_A(600)+f_B(0)), (f_A(500)+f_B(100)), (f_A(400)+f_B(200)), \\ &\quad (f_A(300)+f_B(300)), (f_A(200)+f_B(400)), (f_A(100)+f_B(500)), \\ &\quad (f_A(0)+f_B(600))\} \\ &= \text{Max } \{(8.8+0), (8+2), (6.8+3.6), (5.4+5.1), (3.8+6.6), \\ &\quad (2+8), (0+9.2)\} \\ &= \text{Max } \{8.8, 10, 10.4, \underset{\uparrow}{10.5}, 10.4, 10, 9.2\} \\ &= f_A(300)+f_B(300) \end{aligned}$$

If $X = 700$:

$$\begin{aligned} F_{A,B}(700) &= \text{Max } \{(f_A(700)+f_B(0)), (f_A(600)+f_B(100)), (f_A(500)+f_B(200)), \\ &\quad (f_A(400)+f_B(300)), (f_A(300)+f_B(400)), (f_A(200)+f_B(500)), \\ &\quad (f_A(100)+f_B(600)), (f_A(0)+f_B(700))\} \\ &= \text{Max } \{(9.2+0), (8.8+2), (8+3.6), (6.8+5.1), (5.4+6.6), \\ &\quad (3.8+8), (2+9.2), (0+9.9)\} \\ &= \text{Max } \{9.2, 10.8, 11.6, 11.9, \underset{\uparrow}{12}, 11.8, 11.2, 9.9\} \\ &= f_A(300)+f_B(400) \end{aligned}$$

If $X = 800$:

$$\begin{aligned} F_{A,B}(800) &= \text{Max } \{(f_A(800)+f_B(0)), (f_A(700)+f_B(100)), (f_A(600)+f_B(200)), \\ &\quad (f_A(500)+f_B(300)), (f_A(400)+f_B(400)), (f_A(300)+f_B(500)), \\ &\quad (f_A(200)+f_B(600)), (f_A(100)+f_B(700)), (f_A(0)+f_B(800))\} \\ &= \text{Max } \{(9.5+0), (9.2+2), (8.8+3.6), (8+5.1), (6.8+6.6), \\ &\quad (5.4+8), (3.8+9.2), (2+9.9), (0+10.5)\} \\ &= \text{Max } \{9.5, 11.2, 12.4, 13.1, \underset{\uparrow}{13.4}, \underset{\uparrow}{13.4}, 13, 11.9, 10.5\} \\ &= \{(f_A(400)+f_B(400)), (f_A(300)+f_B(500))\} \end{aligned}$$

If $X = 900$:

$$\begin{aligned}F_{A,B}(900) = \text{Max}\ \{&(f_A(900)+f_B(0)),\ (f_A(800)+f_B(100)),\ (f_A(700)+f_B(200)),\\ &(f_A(600)+f_B(300)),\ (f_A(500)+f_B(400)),\ (f_A(400)+f_B(500)),\\ &(f_A(300)+f_B(600)),\ (f_A(200)+f_B(700)),\ (f_A(100)+f_B(800)),\\ &(f_A(0)+f_B(900))\}\\ = \text{Max}\ \{&(9.7+0),\ (9.5+2),\ (9.2+3.6),\ (8.8+5.1),(8+6.6),\\ &(6.8+8),\ (5.4+9.2),\ (3.8+9.9),\ (2+10.5),\ (0+10.7)\}\\ = \text{Max}\ \{&9.7,\ 11.5,\ 12.8,\ 13.9,\ 14.6,\ \underset{\uparrow}{14.8},\ 14.6,\ 13.7,\ 12.5,\ 10.7\}\\ = f_A&(400)+f_B(500)\end{aligned}$$

If $X = 1000$:

$$\begin{aligned}F_{A,B}(1000) = \text{Max}\ \{&(f_A(1000)+f_B(0)),\ (f_A(900)+f_B(100)),\ (f_A(800)+f_B(200)),\\ &(f_A(700)+f_B(300)),\ (f_A(600)+f_B(400)),\ (f_A(500)+f_B(500),\\ &(f_A(400)+f_B(600)),\ (f_A(300)+f_B(700)),\ (f_A(200)+f_B(800)),\\ &(f_A(100)+f_B(900)),\ (f_A(0)+f_B(1000))\}\\ = \text{Max}\ \{&(9.8+0),\ (9.7+2),\ (9.5+3.6),\ (9.2+5.1),\ (8.8+6.6),\\ &(8+8),\ (6.8+9.2),\ (5.4+9.9),\ (3.8+10.5),\ (2+10.7),\ (0+10.8)\}\\ = \text{Max}\ \{&9.8,\ 11.7,\ 13.1,\ 14.3,\ 15.4,\ \underset{\uparrow}{16},\ \underset{\uparrow}{16},\ 15.3,\ 14.3,\ 12.7,\ 10.8\}\\ = \{&(f_A(500)+f_B(500)),\ (f_A(400)+f_B(600))\}\end{aligned}$$

In this way we obtain the optimum placement of resources in the case of only considering investment objects A and B.

The scheme we have described can now be represented by means of a graph expressed with vertices and arcs, such as we have included below (figure 13.1). In the same it can be seen that the optimum combinations have been drawn with a thick line.

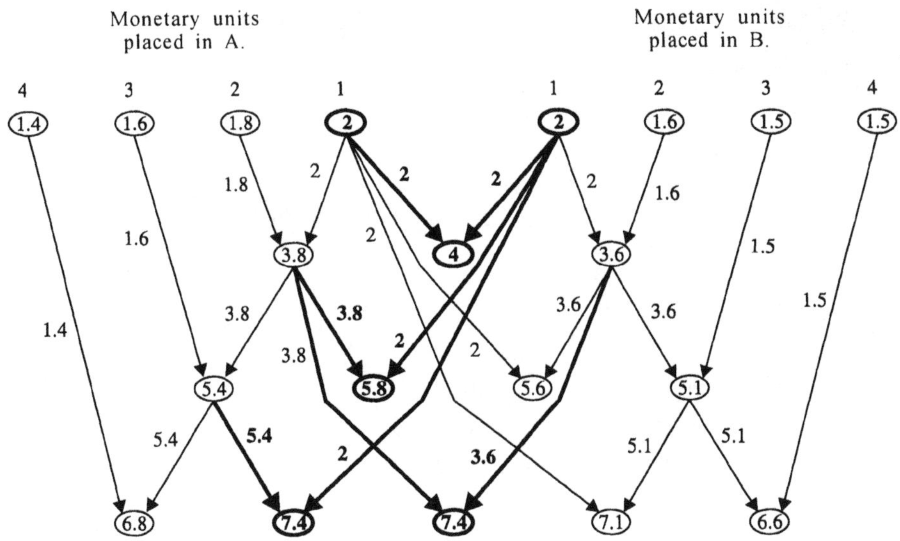

Figure 13.1.

Obtaining the optimum under the hypothesis of certainty

In the table, we now set down the optimums when the monetary masses are invested in A and B, $F_{A,B}(X)$ as well as the UNP relative to C, that is to say $f_c(x_i)$. We arrive at:

X	$F_{A,B}(X)$	$f_C(x_i)$
0	0	0
100	2	1.3
200	4	2.5
300	5.8	3.6
400	7.4	4.5
500	9	5.3
600	10.5	6
700	12	6.5
800	13.4	6.9
900	14.8	7.2
1000	16	7.5

We now make the calculations for finding $F_{A,B,C}(X)$.

For $X = 100$:

$$\begin{aligned} F_{A,B,C}(100) &= \text{Max}\ \{(F_{A,B}(0) + f_C(100)), (F_{A,B}(100) + f_C(0))\} \\ &= \text{Max}\ \{(0 + 1.3), (2 + 0)\} \\ &= \text{Max}\ \{1.3, \underset{\uparrow}{2}\} = F_{A,B}(100) + f_C(0) \end{aligned}$$

For $X = 200$:

$$\begin{aligned} F_{A,B,C}(200) &= \text{Max}\ \{(F_{A,B}(0) + f_C(200)), (F_{A,B}(100) + f_C(100)), (F_{A,B}(200) + f_C(0))\} \\ &= \text{Max}\ \{(0 + 2.5), (2 + 1.3), (4 + 0)\} \\ &= \text{Max}\ \{2.5, 3.3, \underset{\uparrow}{4}\} = F_{A,B}(200) + f_C(0) \end{aligned}$$

For $X = 300$:

$$\begin{aligned} F_{A,B,C}(300) &= \text{Max}\ \{(F_{A,B}(0) + f_C(300)), (F_{A,B}(100) + f_C(200)), (F_{A,B}(200) + f_C(100)), \\ &\qquad (F_{A,B}(300) + f_C(0))\} \\ &= \text{Max}\ \{(0 + 3.6), (2 + 2.5), (4 + 1.3), (5.8 + 0)\} \\ &= \text{Max}\ \{3.6, 4.5, 5.3, \underset{\uparrow}{5.8}\} = F_{A,B}(300) + f_C(0) \end{aligned}$$

For $X = 400$:

$$\begin{aligned} F_{A,B,C}(400) &= \text{Max}\ \{(F_{A,B}(0) + f_C(400)), (F_{A,B}(100) + f_C(300)), (F_{A,B}(200) + f_C(200)), \\ &\qquad (F_{A,B}(300) + f_C(100)), (F_{A,B}(400) + f_C(0))\} \\ &= \text{Max}\ \{(0 + 4.5), (2 + 3.6), (4 + 2.5), (5.8 + 1.3), (7.4 + 0)\} \\ &= \text{Max}\ \{4.5, 5.6, 6.5, 7.1, \underset{\uparrow}{7.4}\} = F_{A,B}(400) + f_C(0) \end{aligned}$$

For $X = 500$:

$$\begin{aligned} F_{A,B,C}(500) &= \text{Max}\ \{(F_{A,B}(0) + f_C(500)), (F_{A,B}(100) + f_C(400)), (F_{A,B}(200) + f_C(300)), \\ &\qquad (F_{A,B}(300) + f_C(200)), (F_{A,B}(400) + f_C(100)), (F_{A,B}(500) + f_C(0))\} \\ &= \text{Max}\ \{(0 + 5.3), (2 + 4.5), (4 + 3.6), (5.8 + 2.5), (7.4 + 1.3), (9 + 0)\} \\ &= \text{Max}\{5.3, 6.5, 7.6, 8.3, 8.7, \underset{\uparrow}{9}\} = F_{A,B}(500) + f_C(0) \end{aligned}$$

For $X = 600$:

$$\begin{aligned} F_{A,B,C}(600) &= \text{Max}\ \{(F_{A,B}(0)+f_C(600)), (F_{A,B}(100)+f_C(500)), (F_{A,B}(200)+f_C(400)),\\ &\quad (F_{A,B}(300)+f_C(300)), (F_{A,B}(400)+f_C(200)), (F_{A,B}(500)+f_C(100)),\\ &\quad (F_{A,B}(600)+f_C(0))\}\\ &= \text{Max}\ \{(0+6), (2+5.3), (4+4.5), (5.8+3.6), (7.4+2.5), (9+1.3),\\ &\quad (10.5+0)\}\\ &= \text{Max}\ \{6, 7.3, 8.5, 9.4, 9.9, 10.3, \underset{\uparrow}{10.5}\} = F_{A,B}(600)+f_C(0) \end{aligned}$$

For $X = 700$:

$$\begin{aligned} F_{A,B,C}(700) &= \text{Max}\ \{(F_{A,B}(0)+f_C(700)), (F_{A,B}(100)+f_C(600)), (F_{A,B}(200)+f_C(500)),\\ &\quad (F_{A,B}(300)+f_C(400)), (F_{A,B}(400)+f_C(300)), (F_{A,B}(500)+f_C(200)),\\ &\quad (F_{A,B}(600)+f_C(100)), (F_{A,B}(700)+f_C(0))\}\\ &= \text{Max}\ \{(0+6.5), (2+6), (4+5.3), (5.8+4.5), (7.4+3.6), (9+2.5),\\ &\quad (10.5+1.3), (12+0)\}\\ &= \text{Max}\ \{6.5, 8, 9.3, 10.3, 11, 11.5, 11.8, \underset{\uparrow}{12}\} = F_{A,B}(700)+f_C(0) \end{aligned}$$

For $X = 800$:

$$\begin{aligned} F_{A,B,C}(800) &= \text{Max}\ \{(F_{A,B}(0)+f_C(800)), (F_{A,B}(100)+f_C(700)), (F_{A,B}(200)+f_C(600)),\\ &\quad (F_{A,B}(300)+f_C(500)), (F_{A,B}(400)+f_C(400)), (F_{A,B}(500)+f_C(300)),\\ &\quad (F_{A,B}(600)+f_C(200)), (F_{A,B}(700)+f_C(100)), (F_{A,B}(800)+f_C(0))\}\\ &= \text{Max}\ \{(0+6.9), (2+6.5), (4+6), (5.8+5.3), (7.4+4.5), (9+3.6),\\ &\quad (10.5+2.5), (12+1.3), (13.4+0)\}\\ &= \text{Max}\ \{6.9, 8.5, 10, 11.1, 11.9, 12.6, 13, 13.3, \underset{\uparrow}{13.4}\}\\ &= F_{A,B}(800)+f_C(0) \end{aligned}$$

For $X = 900$:

$$\begin{aligned} F_{A,B,C}(900) &= \text{Max}\ \{(F_{A,B}(0)+f_C(900)), (F_{A,B}(100)+f_C(800)), (F_{A,B}(200)+f_C(700)),\\ &\quad (F_{A,B}(300)+f_C(600)), (F_{A,B}(400)+f_C(500)), (F_{A,B}(500)+f_C(400)),\\ &\quad (F_{A,B}(600)+f_C(300)), (F_{A,B}(700)+f_C(200)), (F_{A,B}(800)+f_C(100)),\\ &\quad (F_{A,B}(900)+f_C(0))\}\\ &= \text{Max}\ \{(0+7.2), (2+6.9), (4+6.5), (5.8+6), (7.4+5.3), (9+4.5),\\ &\quad (10.5+3.6), (12+2.5), (13.4+1.3), (14.8+0)\} \end{aligned}$$

$$= \text{Max}\{7.2, 8.9, 10.5, 11.8, 12.7, 13.5, 14.1, 14.5, 14.7, \underset{\uparrow}{14.8}\}$$

$$= F_{A,B}(900) + f_C(0)$$

For $X = 1000$:

$$F_{A,B,C}(1000) = \text{Max}\{(F_{A,B}(0)+f_C(1000)), (F_{A,B}(100)+f_C(900)), (F_{A,B}(200)+f_C(800)), (F_{A,B}(300)+f_C(700)), (F_{A,B}(400)+f_C(600)), (F_{A,B}(500)+f_C(500)), (F_{A,B}(600)+f_C(400)), (F_{A,B}(700)+f_C(300)), (F_{A,B}(800)+f_C(200)), (F_{A,B}(900)+f_C(100)), (F_{A,B}(1000)+f_C(0))\}$$

$$= \text{Max}\{(0+7.5), (2+7.2), (4+6.9), (5.8+6.5), (7.4+6), (9+5.3), (10.5+4.5), (12+3.6), (13.4+2.5), (14.8+1.3), (16+0)\}$$

$$= \text{Max}\{7.5, 9.2, 10.9, 12.3, 13.4, 14.3, 15, 15.6, 15.9, \underset{\uparrow}{16.1}, 16\}$$

$$= F_{A,B}(900) + f_C(100)$$

Arriving at the following result:

X	$F_{A,B,C}(X)$	$F_{A,B}(x_i) + f_C(x_j)$	$f_A(x_k) + f_B(x_l) + f_C(x_m)$
0	0	$F_{A,B}(0) + f_C(0)$	$f_A(0) + f_B(0) + f_C(0)$
100	2	$F_{A,B}(100) + f_C(0)$	$\{(f_A(100), f_B(100)\} + f_C(0)$
200	4	$F_{A,B}(200) + f_C(0)$	$f_A(100) + f_B(100) + f_C(0)$
300	5.8	$F_{A,B}(300) + f_C(0)$	$f_A(200) + f_B(100) + f_C(0)$
400	7.4	$F_{A,B}(400) + f_C(0)$	$\{f_A(300) + f_B(100), f_A(200) + f_B(200)\} + f_C(0)$
500	9	$F_{A,B}(500) + f_C(0)$	$f_A(300) + f_B(200) + f_C(0)$
600	10.5	$F_{A,B}(600) + f_C(0)$	$f_A(300) + f_B(300) + f_C(0)$
700	12	$F_{A,B}(700) + f_C(0)$	$f_A(300) + f_B(400) + f_C(0)$
800	13.4	$F_{A,B}(800) + f_C(0)$	$\{f_A(400) + f_B(400), f_A(300) + f_B(500)\} + f_C(0)$
900	14.8	$F_{A,B}(900) + f_C(0)$	$f_A(400) + f_B(500) + f_C(0)$
1000	16.1	$F_{A,B}(900) + f_C(100)$	$f_A(400) + f_B(500) + f_C(100)$

In the above table, it will be seen that up to the moment of investing a figure equal to 900 monetary units it is only convenient to invest in objects *A* and *B*. Only when arriving at 1000 units does optimisation appear for *C*, with an amount of 100 units.

As we did before, we are going to show below a graph in which the process followed for obtaining the two optimums at each investment level appears (figure 13.2).

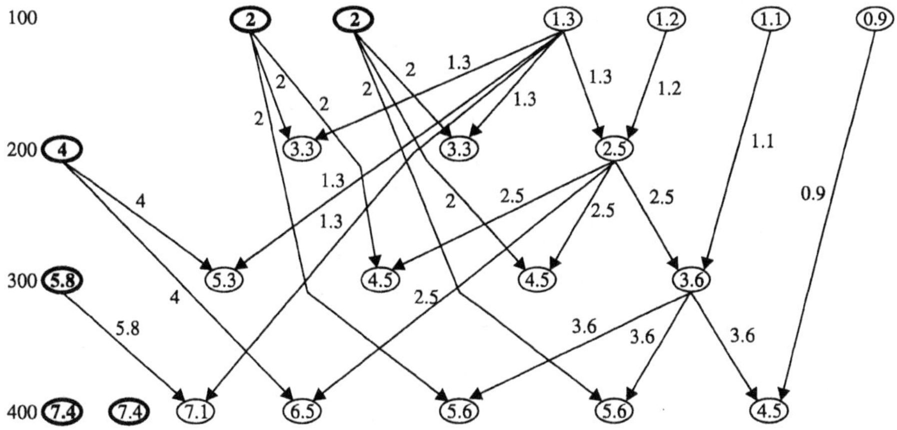

Figure 13.2.

We can now ask ourselves what happens in the event of following a process by commencing optimisation of $f_A(x_i)$ and $f_C(x_j)$, in stead of doing it (just as we have presented it up to now) with $f_A(x_i)$ and $f_B(x_j)$. As it could be in no other way, compliance of the announced property of associativity, can now be seen. In effect, if we move on to the summarising tables, we have:

X	$f_A(x_i)$	$f_C(x_j)$	Decomposition $F_{A,C}(X)$	$F_{A,C}(X)$
0	0	0	$\varnothing$	0
100	2	1.3	$f_A(100) + f_C(0)$	2
200	3.8	2.5	$f_A(200) + f_C(0)$	3.8
300	5.4	3.6	$f_A(300) + f_C(0)$	5.4
400	6.8	4.5	$f_A(400) + f_C(0)$	6.8
500	8	5.3	$f_A(400) + f_C(100)$	8.1
600	8.8	6	$\{(f_A(500) + f_C(100), (f_A(400) + f_C(200))\}$	9.3
700	9.2	6.5	$f_A(500) + f_C(200)$	10.5
800	9.5	6.9	$f_A(500) + f_C(300)$	11.6
900	9.7	7.2	$f_A(500) + f_C(400)$	12.5
1000	9.8	7.5	$\{(f_A(600) + f_C(400), (f_A(500) + f_C(500))\}$	13.3

X	$F_{A,C}(X)$	$f_B(x_j)$	Decomposition $F_{A,B,C}(X)$	$F_{A,B,C}(X)$
0	0	0	$\varnothing$	$\varnothing$
100	2	2	$\{(F_{A,C}(100)+f_B(0),\ (F_{A,C}(0)+f_B(100))\}$	2
200	3.8	3.6	$F_{A,C}(100)+f_B(100)$	4
300	5.4	5.1	$F_{A,C}(200)+f_B(100)$	5.8
400	6.8	6.6	$\{(F_{A,C}(300)+f_B(100),\ (F_{A,C}(200)+f_B(200))\}$	7.4
500	8.1	8	$F_{A,C}(300)+f_B(200)$	9
600	9.3	9.2	$F_{A,C}(300)+f_B(300)$	10.5
700	10.5	9.9	$F_{A,C}(300)+f_B(400)$	12
800	11.6	10.5	$\{(F_{A,C}(300)+f_B(500),\ (F_{A,C}(400)+f_B(400))\}$	13.4
900	12.5	10.7	$F_{A,C}(400)+f_B(500)$	14.8
1000	13.3	10.8	$F_{A,C}(500)+f_B(500)$	16.1

It can be seen then that the results for $F_{A,B,C}(X)$ are the same. Therefore we can write:

$$\underset{x_i+x_j=X}{\text{Max}}\{F_{A,B}(x_i)+f_C(x_j)\} = \underset{x_i+x_j=X}{\text{Max}}\{F_{A,C}(x_i)+f_B(x_j)\}$$

Finally let us see how the monetary units are invested in an optimum manner for each X level of investment.

X	Decomposition $F_{A,C}(x_i)+f_B(x_j)$	Description $f_A(x_i)+f_B(x_j)+f_C(x_k)$
0	$\varnothing$	$\varnothing$
100	$\{(F_{A,C}(100)+f_B(0)),\ (F_{A,C}(0)+f_B(100))\}$	$\{(f_A(100)+f_B(0)+f_C(0)),\ (f_A(0)+f_B(100)+f_C(0))\}$
200	$F_{A,C}(100)+f_B(100)$	$f_A(100)+f_B(100)+f_C(0)$
300	$F_{A,C}(200)+f_B(100)$	$f_A(200)+f_B(100)+f_C(0)$
400	$\{(F_{A,C}(300)+f_B(100)),\ (F_{A,C}(200)+f_B(200))\}$	$\{(f_A(300)+f_B(100)+f_C(0)),\ (f_A(200)+f_B(200)+f_C(0))\}$
500	$F_{A,C}(300)+f_B(200)$	$f_A(300)+f_B(200)+f_C(0)$
600	$F_{A,C}(300)+f_B(300)$	$f_A(300)+f_B(300)+f_C(0)$
700	$F_{A,C}(300)+f_B(400)$	$f_A(300)+f_B(400)+f_C(0)$
800	$\{(F_{A,C}(300)+f_B(500)),\ (F_{A,C}(400)+f_B(400))\}$	$\{(f_A(300)+f_B(500)+f_C(0)),\ (f_A(400)+f_B(400)+f_C(0))\}$
900	$F_{A,C}(400)+f_B(500)$	$f_A(400)+f_B(500)+f_C(0)$
1000	$F_{A,C}(500)+f_B(500)$	$f_A(400)+f_B(500)+f_C(100)$

Again as it could be in no other way, the description of $f_A(x_i) + f_B(x_j) + f_C(x_k)$, relative to the initial optimisation of A and C, for each level of investment, indicates the same units invested in each object A, B and C as those arrived at from the initial optimisation of A and B.

Transition to a context of uncertainty

From the previously described conceptual and technical elements, we are now going to develop a model in which we commence the inclusion of uncertain economic parameters. In a first approximation, uncertainty is represented by the expected profits from hypothetical investments of means of payment and expressed by means of fuzzy triangular numbers[2]. In this way we will arrive at the fact that functions $f_A(x_j)$, $f_B(x_j)$, ..., $f_K(x_j)$ will be:

$$\underset{\sim}{f_A}(x_j) = (a_1(x_j),\ a_2(x_j),\ a_3(x_j))$$
$$\underset{\sim}{f_B}(x_j) = (b_1(x_j),\ b_2(x_j),\ b_3(x_j))$$
$$\cdots\cdots\cdots\cdots\cdots\cdots\cdots\cdots$$
$$\underset{\sim}{f_K}(x_j) = (k_1(x_j),\ k_2(x_j),\ k_3(x_j))$$

As we saw in the sphere of certainty, in each of the segments in which investment of a monetary mass X is desired, it is necessary to make a *comparison* between the different possibilities of combining the partial quantities assigned to each investment object A, B, ..., K. In a determinist context, there is no problem whatsoever in carrying out this task, but the same is not true when handling uncertain numbers, as is the particular case of the FTN, in which case it is necessary to resort to certain criteria of comparison.

In this sense, we are going to recall certain of these that are used frequently.

In the first place if we have two FTN:

$$\underset{\sim}{M} = (m_1(x_j),\ m_2(x_j),\ m_3(x_j))$$
$$\underset{\sim}{N} = (n_1(x_j),\ n_2(x_j),\ n_3(x_j))$$

if:

$$\left.\frac{m_1(x_j) + 2m_2(x_j) + m_3(x_j)}{4} > \frac{n_1(x_j) + 2n_2(x_j),\ n_3(x_j)}{4}\right) \Rightarrow (\underset{\sim}{M} > \underset{\sim}{N})$$

In the event we were to arrive at equality in the weighted means, which would prevent separation of $\underset{\sim}{M}$ and $\underset{\sim}{N}$ based on this first criterion, we would have to resort to a second criterion which could be considering as the greatest the least uncertain fuzzy number, that is:

$$(m_3(x_j) - m_1(x_j) < n_3(x_j) - n_1(x_j)) \Rightarrow (\underset{\sim}{M} > \underset{\sim}{N})$$

What we have here is a slightly arbitrary criterion, but highly useful in real problems. We could consider a third, fourth, etc. usable complementary criterion provided that the previous ones were not sufficient for determining the order to be arrived at.

Having made this brief comment, we will move on to develop a scheme shown by means of a numerical example.

In order to be as nearly parallel to the sphere of certainty we will consider as the maximum supposition of the FTN, the crisp value established in the previously developed example.

Let us assume, then, that the *accumulated* doses invested in each object A, B, and C give us the following updated profits (as they occur, net updated values).

Units	A	B	C
x_j	$\underset{\sim}{f}_A(x_j)$	$\underset{\sim}{f}_B(x_j)$	$\underset{\sim}{f}_C(x_j)$
0	0	0	0
100	(1.8, 2, 2.5)	(1.8, 2, 2.8)	(1, 1.3, 1.8)
200	(3.4, 3.8, 4)	(3.2, 3.6, 4)	(2, 2.5, 2.8)
300	(5, 5.4, 5.6)	(4.8, 5.1, 5.5)	(3.2, 3.6, 4)
400	(6.5, 6.8, 7.2)	(6.2, 6.6, 7)	(4.4, 4.5, 4.9)
500	(7.8, 8, 8.5)	(7.7, 8, 8.2)	(5, 5.3, 5.7)
600	(8.7, 8.8, 9)	(9, 9.2, 9.5)	(5.6, 6, 6.2)
700	(8.6, 9.2, 9.4)	(9.4, 9.9, 10.2)	(6.1, 6.5, 7)
800	(9.2, 9.5, 9.8)	(10, 10.5, 10.8)	(6.6, 6.9, 7.4)
900	(9.6, 9.7, 10)	(10.4, 10.7, 11)	(7, 7.2, 7.6)
1000	(9.7, 9.8, 10.2)	(10.5, 10.8, 11.4)	(7.3, 7.5, 8)

Just as we did before, we are going to designated the investment of 100 monetary units respectively in objects A, B, and C by $\underset{\sim}{f}_A(100)$, $\underset{\sim}{f}_B(100)$ y $\underset{\sim}{f}_C(100)$. By $\underset{\sim}{E}_{A,B}(X)$ the maximum updated profits when X monetary units are invested in A and B, as well as by $\underset{\sim}{E}_{A,B,C}(X)$those obtained by the investment of X in A, B, and C.

By following the same process as for the sphere of certainty we will arrive at:

$$\underset{\sim}{f}_A(100) = (1.8, 2, 2.5)$$
$$\underset{\sim}{f}_B(100) = (1.8, 2, 2.8) \leftarrow$$
$$\underset{\sim}{f}_C(100) = (1, 1.3, 1.8)$$

As $\underset{\sim}{f}_B(100) > \underset{\sim}{f}_A(100) > \underset{\sim}{f}_C(100)$, in the event of only investing 100 monetary units, these would be invested in object B, with an updated profit of no less than 1.8, nor greater than 2.8 and with a maximum presumption of 2 monetary units. This would be then $\underset{\sim}{f}_B(100) = \underset{\sim}{F}_B(100)$ (optimum investment).

When considering object A and B, it will be necessary to arrive at $\underset{\sim}{F}_{A,B}(X)$, X = 200, 300, ..., 1000.

For X = 200:

$$\begin{aligned}\underset{\sim}{F}_{A,B}(200) &= \text{Max}\,\{(\underset{\sim}{f}_A(200)\,(+)\,\underset{\sim}{f}_B(0)),\ (\underset{\sim}{f}_A(100)\,(+)\,\underset{\sim}{f}_B(100)),\ (\underset{\sim}{f}_A(0) + \underset{\sim}{f}_B(200))\}\\ &= \text{Max}\,\{(3.4, 3.8, 4)\,(+)\,(0),\ (1.8, 2, 2.5)\,(+)\,(1.8, 2, 2.8),\ (0)\,(+)\\ &\quad (+)\,(3.2, 3.6, 4)\}\\ &= \text{Max}\,\{(3.4, 3.8, 4),\ \underset{\uparrow}{(3.6, 4, 5.3)},\ (3.2, 3.6, 4)\}\\ &= \underset{\sim}{f}_A(100) + \underset{\sim}{f}_B(100)\end{aligned}$$

Because according to the first comparison criterion established, as:

$$\frac{3.4 + 2 \times 3.8 + 4}{4} = 3.750$$
$$\frac{3.6 + 2 \times 4 + 5.3}{4} = 4.225$$
$$\frac{3.2 + 2 \times 3.6 + 4}{4} = 3.600$$

the following order takes place:

$$(\underset{\sim}{f}_A(100)\,(+)\,\underset{\sim}{f}_B(100)) > (\underset{\sim}{f}_A(200)\,(+)\,\underset{\sim}{f}_B(0)) > (\underset{\sim}{f}_A(0)\,(+)\,\underset{\sim}{f}_B(200))$$

In this case investment should be made of 100 monetary units in object A and 100 monetary units in object B.

We would continue to do the same calculations for $X = 300$, $X = 400$, ..., $X =$ 1000, starting out from the expression:

$$\underset{\sim}{F}_{A,B}(X) = \underset{x_i + x_j = X}{\text{Max}}\,(\underset{\sim}{f}_A(x_i)\,(+)\,\underset{\sim}{f}_B(x_j))$$

arriving at the following results:

X	$\underset{\sim}{E}_{A,B,C}(X)$	Optimum investments
100	(1.8, 2, 2.8)	$\underset{\sim}{f}_A(0)+\underset{\sim}{f}_B(100)$
200	(3.6, 4, 5.3)	$\underset{\sim}{f}_A(100)+\underset{\sim}{f}_B(100)$
300	(5.2, 5.8, 6.8)	$\underset{\sim}{f}_A(200)+\underset{\sim}{f}_B(100)$
400	(6.8, 7.4, 8.4)	$\underset{\sim}{f}_A(300)+\underset{\sim}{f}_B(100)$
500	(8.3, 8.8, 10)	$\underset{\sim}{f}_A(400)+\underset{\sim}{f}_B(100)$
600	(9.8, 10.5, 11.5)	$\underset{\sim}{f}_A(300)+\underset{\sim}{f}_B(300)$
700	(11.2, 12, 12.6)	$\underset{\sim}{f}_A(300)+\underset{\sim}{f}_B(400)$
800	(12.7, 13.4, 14.2)	$\underset{\sim}{f}_A(400)+\underset{\sim}{f}_B(400)$
900	(14.2, 14.8, 15.4)	$\underset{\sim}{f}_A(400)+\underset{\sim}{f}_B(500)$
1000	(15.5, 16, 16.7)	$\underset{\sim}{f}_A(500)+\underset{\sim}{f}_B(500)$ $\underset{\sim}{f}_A(400)+\underset{\sim}{f}_B(600)$

It will be seen that under the investment of 400 m.u. there is a single optimum combination, contrary to what happened in certainty when two different investments were possessed giving the same result. This is because of the different uncertainties (width of the bases of the triangles representing the FTN).

Obtaining a different combination for 500 m.u. in certainty and in uncertainty is also as a consequence of the different distances between the maximum supposition and the extremes between the FTN.

In the investment for 700 m.u. we obtain as results (11.3, 11.9, 12.7) when investing 400 m.u. in A and 300 m.u. in B, as well as (11.2, 12, 12.6) by investing 300 m.u. in A and 400 in B. With the first criterion the separation will be:

$$\frac{11.3+2\times 11.9+12.7}{4}=\frac{11.2+2\times 12+12.6}{4}=11.95$$

Given the fact that this criterion is not sufficient, recourse must be made to the second by means of which:

$$12.7-11.3=12.6-11.2=1.4$$

Neither is this second criterion sufficient to allow an ordering, it is necessary to resort to the third which can be, for example, to consider the upper number as the maximum presumption. We could also take as a reference, the largest of the lower extremes (conservative hypothesis). This would be as follows:

$$(11.2, 12, 12.6) > (11.3, 11.9, 12.7)$$

In this case, we cannot act in the same way as we did in certainty, because the results expressed by means of FTN are different, although they may be the same crisp number (11.95) on making the entropy fall.

The same does not happen when investing 1000 monetary units, because in this case we arrive at *the same* fuzzy triangular number, (15.5, 16, 16.7) from two different combinations: by investing 500 m.u. in A and in B, as well as by investing 400 m.u. in A and 600 m.u. in B.

Before starting with calculations for arriving at $\underset{\sim}{F}_{A,B,C}(X)$ we are going to construct a table in which we include $\underset{\sim}{F}_{A,B}(x_j)$ and also $\underset{\sim}{f}_C(x_j)$.

X	$\underset{\sim}{F}_{A,B}(x_j)$	$\underset{\sim}{f}_C(x_j)$
100	(1.8, 2, 2.8)	(1, 1.3, 1.8)
200	(3.6, 4, 5.3)	(2, 2.5, 2.8)
300	(5.2, 5.8, 6.8)	(3.2, 3.6, 4)
400	(6.8, 7.4, 8.4)	(4.4, 4.5, 4.9)
500	(8.3, 8.8, 10)	(5, 5.3, 5.7)
600	(9.8, 10.5, 11.1)	(5.6, 6, 6.2)
700	(11.2, 12, 12.6)	(6.1, 6.5, 7)
800	(12.7, 13.4, 14.2)	(6.6, 6.9, 7.4)
900	(14.2, 14.8, 15.4)	(7, 7.2, 7.6)
1000	(15.5, 16, 16.7)	(7.3, 7.5, 8)

We are now ready to optimise the process in an overall manner, by incorporating investment objects A, B, and C, by finding $\underset{\sim}{F}_{A,B,C}(X)$, $X = 200, 300, ..., 1000$.

For $X = 200$.

$$\begin{aligned}\underset{\sim}{F}_{A,B,C}(200) &= \text{Max}\,\{(\underset{\sim}{F}_{A,B}(200)\,(+)\,\underset{\sim}{f}_C(0)),\ (\underset{\sim}{F}_{A,B}(100)\,(+)\,\underset{\sim}{f}_C(100)),\\ &\quad (\underset{\sim}{F}_{A,B}(0)\,(+)\,\underset{\sim}{f}_C(200))\}\\ &= \text{Max}\,\{((3.6, 4, 5.3)\,(+)\,0),\ ((1.8, 2, 2.8)\,(+)\,(1, 1.3, 1.8)),\\ &\quad (0\,(+)\,(2, 2.5, 2.8))\}\end{aligned}$$

$$= \text{Max}\ \{(3.6, 4, 5.3), (2.8, 3.3, 4.6), (2, 2.5, 2.8)\}$$
$$\uparrow$$
$$= \underset{\sim}{E}_{A,B}(200)\ (+)\ \underset{\sim}{f}_C(0) = \underset{\sim}{f}_A(100)\ (+)\ \underset{\sim}{f}_B(100)\ (+)\ \underset{\sim}{f}_C(0)$$ [3]

in accordance with the first criterion we established for separation. We now continue with $X = 300$:

$$\underset{\sim}{E}_{A,B,C}(300) = \text{Max}\ \{(\underset{\sim}{E}_{A,B}(300)\ (+)\ \underset{\sim}{f}_C(0)), (\underset{\sim}{E}_{A,B}(200)\ (+)\ \underset{\sim}{f}_C(100)),$$
$$(\underset{\sim}{E}_{A,B}(100)\ (+)\ \underset{\sim}{f}_C(200)), (\underset{\sim}{E}_{A,B}(0)\ (+)\ \underset{\sim}{f}_C(300))\}$$
$$= \text{Max}\ \{((5.2, 5.8, 6.8)\ (+)\ 0), ((3.6, 4, 5.3)\ (+)\ (1, 1.3, 1.8)),$$
$$((1.8, 2, 2.8)\ (+)\ (2, 2.5, 2.8)), (0\ (+)\ (3.2, 3.6, 4))\}$$
$$= \text{Max}\ \{(5.2, 5.8, 6.8), (4.6, 5.3, 7.1), (3.8, 4.5, 5.6), (3.2, 3.6, 4)\}$$
$$\uparrow$$
$$= \underset{\sim}{E}_{A,B}(300)\ (+)\ \underset{\sim}{f}_C(0) = \underset{\sim}{f}_A(200)\ (+)\ \underset{\sim}{f}_B(100)\ (+)\ \underset{\sim}{f}_C(0)$$ [4]

And by continuing this process we would arrive at the following table by using the expression:

$$\underset{\sim}{E}_{A,B,C}(X) = \underset{x_i + x_j = X}{\text{Máx}}\ (\underset{\sim}{E}_{A,B}(x_i)\ (+)\ \underset{\sim}{f}_C(x_j))$$

X	$\underset{\sim}{E}_{A,B,C}(X)$	Optimum placements
100	(1.8, 2, 2.8)	$\underset{\sim}{f}_A(0) + \underset{\sim}{f}_B(100) + \underset{\sim}{f}_C(0)$
200	(3.6, 4, 5.3)	$\underset{\sim}{f}_A(100) + \underset{\sim}{f}_B(100) + \underset{\sim}{f}_C(0)$
300	(5.2, 5.8, 6.8)	$\underset{\sim}{f}_A(200) + \underset{\sim}{f}_B(100) + \underset{\sim}{f}_C(0)$
400	(6.8, 7.4, 8.4)	$\underset{\sim}{f}_A(300) + \underset{\sim}{f}_B(100) + \underset{\sim}{f}_C(0)$
500	(8.3, 8.8, 10)	$\underset{\sim}{f}_A(400) + \underset{\sim}{f}_B(100) + \underset{\sim}{f}_C(0)$
600	(9.8, 10.5, 11.1)	$\underset{\sim}{f}_A(300) + \underset{\sim}{f}_B(300) + \underset{\sim}{f}_C(0)$
700	(11.2, 12, 12.6)	$\underset{\sim}{f}_A(300) + \underset{\sim}{f}_B(400) + \underset{\sim}{f}_C(0)$
800	(12.7, 13.4, 14.2)	$\underset{\sim}{f}_A(400) + \underset{\sim}{f}_B(400) + \underset{\sim}{f}_C(0)$
900	(14.2, 14.8, 15.4)	$\underset{\sim}{f}_A(400) + \underset{\sim}{f}_B(500) + \underset{\sim}{f}_C(0)$
1000	(15.2, 16.1, 17.2)	$\underset{\sim}{f}_A(400) + \underset{\sim}{f}_B(500) + \underset{\sim}{f}_C(100)$

Under the investment of 900 m.u. one could think, at a glance, in the intervention of investment object C with 100 m.u. But by using the first criterion of comparison, it will be seen that:

For $\underset{\sim}{E}_{A,B}(900)\ (+)\ \underset{\sim}{f}_C(0)$ this is:

$$\frac{14.2 + 2 \times 14.8 + 15.4}{4} = 14.800$$

while for $\underset{\sim}{E}_{A,B}(800)\ (+)\ \underset{\sim}{f}_C(100)$ it will be:

$$\frac{13.7 + 2 \times 14.7 + 16}{4} = 14.775$$

where:

$$(14.2, 14.8, 15.4) > (13.7, 14.7, 16)$$

therefore it will be necessary to consider $\underset{\sim}{E}_{A,B}(900)\ (+)\ \underset{\sim}{f}_C(0)$.

This latter table may suggest other specific considerations, which we leave up to the common sense and imagination of the reader.

From a general perspective, it can be concluded that the use of Bellman's principle of optimisation allows us to find a good solution to the problem of optimum investment of financial resources when the economic system is plunged into a context of uncertainty. The possibilities of divided distribution of the available monetary mass, also constitutes an element in the search for management instruments which can not be easily set aside when what is required of them are the necessary qualities of flexibility and adaptability.

References

[1] For greater detail see: A. Kaufmann and J. Gil Aluja: *Nuevas técnicas para la dirección estratégica*, Universidad de Barcelona, Barcelona, 1990, pages 189 and following.

[2] This case has been dealt with in: A. Kaufmann and J. Gil Aluja: *Técnicas operativas de gestión para el tratamiento de la incertidumbre, Hispano-Europea, Barcelona, 1987, pages 393-405.*

[3] Given the fact that $\underset{\sim}{F}_{A,B}(200) = \underset{\sim}{f}_A(100)\ (+)\ \underset{\sim}{f}_B(100)$.

[4] Taking into account that $\underset{\sim}{F}_{A,B}(300) = \underset{\sim}{f}_A(200)\ (+)\ \underset{\sim}{f}_B(100)$.

14 Neural networks in investment

Basic elements of neuromimetics

The study of the problem of investment selection, handled by means of a sequential process such as that described in the previous chapter and resolved with the aid of dynamic programming, can now be contemplated from a new perspective by making use of the basic elements of neuromimetics.

Indeed, the handling of this problem by means of Bellman's optimisation principle has its support in the operation of a graph. And, from a certain point of view, a graph is a network and vice-versa. For this reason, it can clarify the attempt to bring both approaches closer and at the same time is interesting in the development of a model based on neural networks. Perhaps in this manner we will be able to open up a new way for the solution of the problem of optimum financial investment.

Before delving into the hub of the matter, we will make a brief reference to certain elementary concepts on neural networks, in order to establish a nexus with the theory of graphs. In fact as a starting off point, it is particularly interesting and useful for the construction of artificial neural networks, to study the electro-chemical operation of nervous systems in living beings. But as from this very moment let us state the fact that nature does not always allow itself to be copied, even though all the time we are getting to know it better.

The central element of nervous systems is the <<neuron>>. There are different kinds of neurons in the different species, all of which carry out very diverse functions, although they do have certain common characteristics which allow us to define a prototype, at the same time admitting its generalised nature.

The neuron is a cell composed of a cellular body and a nucleus. The cellular body, called <<soma>>, branches out forming <<dendrites>> that are usually quite numerous. Information proceeding from a neuron arrives at the soma of another neuron through the dendrites. Certain complex electro-chemical operations take place in the neuron through ionic channels that open and close according to the electrical power flowing in through the dendrites. Leaving the neuron is a single<<axon>>, a prolongation of the neuron itself, which then branches out into millions of dendrites connected to other neurons. The link between one neuron and another is called <<synapses>>. A diagram, obviously simplified, could be the following (figure 14.1):

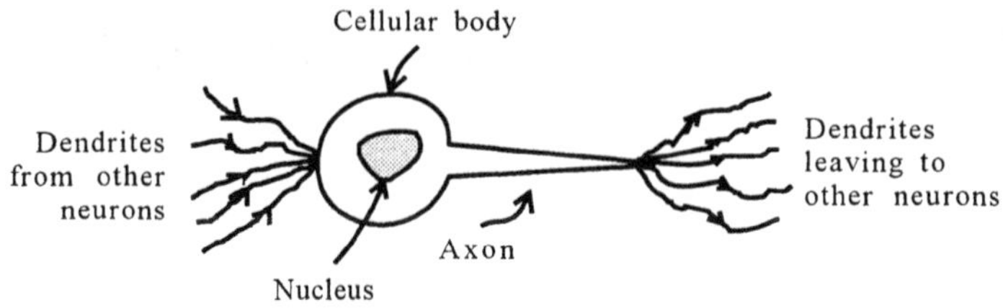

Figure 14.1.

If we simplify this drawing even further, as we have done in the graph below (figure 14.2) we will arrive at a possibility of associating the same with concepts of the theory of graphs.

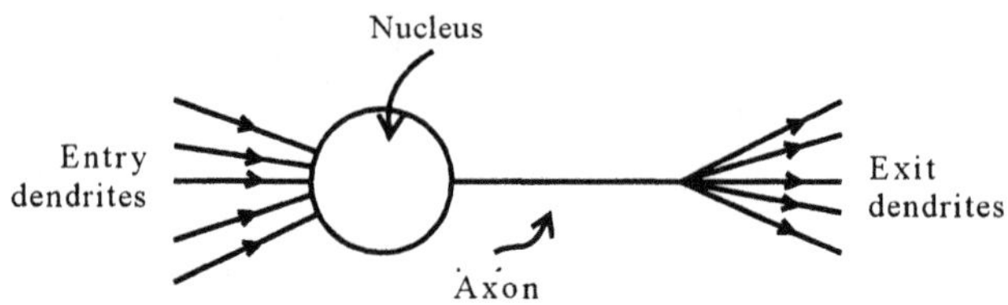

Figure 14.2.

The following could be a simplified correspondence between the nervous system and a graph:

— Neuron and axon: Vertex of the graph.

— Entry dendrites: Arcs arriving at the vertex.

— Exit dendrites: Arcs leaving the vertex.

When signals arrive at a neuron through the dendrites what occurs is an <<aggregation>> (addition or any other operation). In the event that this addition were to be adequate, a single signal leaves the neuron along the axon which is transmitted to other neurons by the exit dendrites.

In one way and another many models have been thought out in order to reproduce nature. Among the better known we will mention that of Mc.Culloch and Pitts[1], the representation of which we show below in figure 14.3.

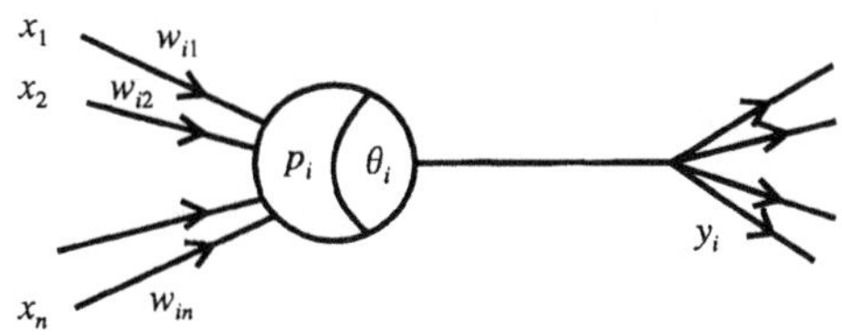

Figure 14.3.

The entry signals are $x_1, x_2, ..., x_n$. Each entry dendrite allows passage of one signal supposedly equal to +1 (excitement) or -1 (inhibition). Each of the entry dendrites is affected by a synaptic weight w_{ij}, $j = 1, 2, ..., n$. These weights are established in such a way that their addition is equal to the unit (convex weighting). Operations can be summarised as follows:

x_j: Entry stimulus (signal), $x_j \in \{-1, 1\}$.

w_{ij}: Synaptic weight of the signal x_j destined for neuron i

θ_i: Threshold of neuron i.

p_i: Potential of neuron i, $p_i \in \{-1, 1\}$

y_i: exit potential, $y_i \in \{-1, 1\}$

$$p_i = \sum_{j=1}^{n} w_{ij} \cdot x_j \begin{cases} \text{if: } p_i > \theta_i : y_i = +1 \\ \text{if: } p_i \leqslant \theta_i : y_i = -1 \end{cases}$$

For each of the stimuli or signals of the model {0, 1} can be chosen instead of {-1, 1}without this noticeably changing the proposed scheme.

Description of the model and network architecture

This very brief and obviously incomplete summary, has as its sole objective, that of an introduction, and in the event a reminder of those elementary concepts that can be incorporated in the proposed model. We are now ready to begin the process.

As happened in the previous chapter we start out from the need or convenience of investing <<up to>> 1000 monetary units in three possible investment objects *A*, *B*, and *C*. In order to simplify the scheme it is assumed that this investment can be made in blocks of 100 monetary units. The yield expressed by the UNP (or any other concept of calculation or addition) for each block is of 2 monetary units <<if certain determined circumstances were to be carried out>> (considered as optimum) that are rarely complied with. For this a coefficient must be affected to each investment of 100 units with a theoretical yield of 2 (<<sig-

nal>>), which is normally (although not exclusively) reducing, w_i will be therefore $0 \leqslant w_i \leqslant 1$ (<<synaptic weight>>)[2].

With the object of continuing with the parallelism between the model classically considered, exclusively based on dynamic programming, and the model presented now, we are going to establish certain weights that will make the figures used in the example of the previous chapter coincide with those used in this chapter. They should be:

Dosis	1	2	3	4	5	6	7	8	9	10
w_A	1	0.90	0.80	0.70	0.60	0.40	0.20	0.15	0.10	0.05
w_B	1	0.80	0.75	0.75	0.70	0.60	0.35	0.30	0.10	0.05
w_C	0.65	0.60	0.55	0.45	0.40	0.35	0.25	0.20	0.15	0.15

We are now ready to describe the process, which we will develop with the use of the terminology peculiar to neural networks. Thus each vertex of the graph will be attributed a <<potential>> (signal) subject to being transmitted to other vertices (neurons). In a very general case, these functions of transfer can be of a very diverse nature. In this development they will be very simple.

As a first hypothesis we will establish the fact that every entry arc (dendrite) transmits the potential of the vertex (neuron) from which it leaves.

This potential is submitted to a modification as a consequence of external elements. In the case of the investment process under study modifications to the <<potential>> are due to the greater or lesser <<effectiveness>> of each invested monetary mass. In order to reflect this phenomenon, we resort to a weighting process, by assigning a <<weight>> to each exit potential.

When a vertex (neuron) receives more than one dendrite (arc) a process of aggregation of the diverse potentials received takes place. In our specific case this aggregation takes the more simple form of an addition. The neuron is now in a position to emit (or not) its potential by means of its axon towards the axonic dendrites (arcs leaving the vertex) which then end up in another or other neurons. However, in order for this impulse to be able to leave the neuron to the exterior, it must exceed a <<threshold>> previously established and designated by θ. The role of the threshold in natural neurons is performed by the <<axon>>. The potential acquired by a neuron can be transmitted by the exit dendrites to several others.

This can all be represented by a neural graph, which we have attempted to construct following a parallelism with the one we used for dynamic programming.

During the first phase we will only take into account the area of the <<brain>> relative to neurons $A = \{x_1^{(1)}, x_1^{(2)}, ..., x_1^{(10)}\}$ and the $B = \{y_1^{(1)}, y_1^{(2)}, ..., y_1^{(10)}\}$, that is to say the yields of the monetary masses susceptible to being invested in investment objects A and B.

Each impulse of the <<initial>> neurons implies the transmission of 2 monetary units, although they will not always keep this amount on arrival at the next neuron or neurons, as a consequence of the assignment of a weight w_{Ai}, w_{Bj} and w_{Ck} to each dendrite (arc).

In order to be able to visualise the process better, the neural network shown below is only formed by four <<levels>>, on the understanding that the complete neural graph would be formed by ten levels, if we were to follow the parallelism with the previous scheme, taking into account the case considered originally in which we could have invested 10 blocks of 100 monetary units each. For this, we have only drawn four neurons in each of the original two sets A and B and only those receiving one impulse, in the other levels (figure 14.4).

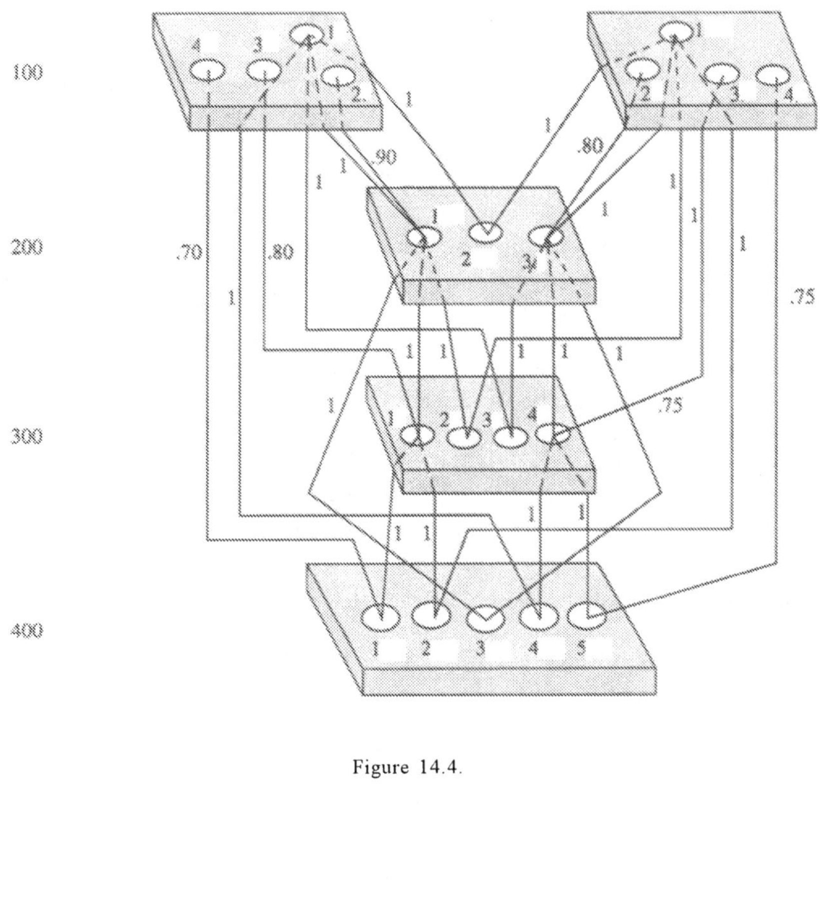

Figure 14.4.

We will now move on to describe the process.

Transfer from the first level to the second

Firstly we will consider neuron sub-set A, $x_1^{(i)}$, $i = 1, 2, \ldots, 10$ that forms a part of the original level. From the first neuron $x_1^{(1)}$, several <<impulses>> leave (in our specific case 10, which we can also call <<signals>>) which with the object of simplification we have always assumed as equal to $e_{Aj}^{(i)} = 2$. Of these, for the time being, we will only consider those that arrive at the neurons of the second level. Two can be seen to arrive at different neurons. The weight w_{A1} is in all the impulses of the first neuron equal to 1, therefore the arrival neurons will receive the same impulse as the exit neuron. Therefore:

$$e_{A1}^{(1)} \cdot w_{A1}^{(1)} = e_{A1}^{(1)} = 2$$ [3]

The first neuron of the second level also receives an impulse from the second neuron of the first level, but as the weight, in this case is $w_{A1}^{(2)} = 0.9$ the arrival potential along this path will be:

$$e_{A1}^{(2)} \cdot w_{A1}^{(2)} = 2 \times 0.9 = 1.8$$

Since the aggregation of potential takes place by means of simple addition, the overall potential of the first neuron of the second level will be:

$$e_{A1}^{(1)} \cdot w_{A1}^{(1)} + e_{A1}^{(2)} \cdot w_{A1}^{(2)} = 2 + 1.8 = 3.8 = h_{A2}^{(1)}$$

If we now take into account, the B set of neurons $y_1^{(i)}$, $i = 1, 2, \ldots, 10$, which also form a part of the original level, it can be seen that, among others, impulses with a potential of $f_{B1}^{(1)} = 2$ and a weight of $w_{B1}^{(1)} = 1$ leave from the first neuron $y_1^{(1)}$. These will be received by the second and third neurons of the second level. Another signal leaves the second neuron of the first level of this set B arriving at the third neuron of the second level with a weight of $w_{B1}^{(2)} = 0.8$. The arriving potentials will be:

$$f_{B1}^{(1)} \cdot w_{B1}^{(1)} = f_{B1}^{(1)} = 2$$

$$f_{B1}^{(2)} \cdot w_{B1}^{(2)} = 2 \times 0.8 = 1.6$$

The third neuron of the second level will receive a potential of:

$$f_{B1}^{(1)} \cdot w_{B1}^{(1)} + f_{B1}^{(2)} \cdot w_{B1}^{(2)} = 2 + 1.6 = 3.6 = h_{B2}^{(3)}$$

Taking into account that the second neuron of the second level receives the impulses from the first neuron A and the first B, the arrival potential will be:

$$e_{A1}^{(1)} \cdot w_{A1}^{(1)} + f_{B1}^{(1)} \cdot w_{B1}^{(1)} = 2 + 2 = 4 = h_{AB2}^{(2)} \quad \leftarrow^{4}$$

It can be seen that the maximum potential occurs in the second neuron with a value of 4. We will leave this potential and continue with the other neurons (the first and the third).

Transfer to the third level

With a simple glance at the neural graph, we can look at the arrival at the neurons of the third level of the dendrites from the second level, as well as from the first level. As a simplifying hypothesis we now establish that the weights of the dendrites from the previous level (except the first) do not modify the exit potentials[5].

From the first neuron of the second level, among others, three axonic dendrites leave of which two are connected with the entry dendrites in the first and second neuron of the third level.

Also, in the first, a dendrite arrives proceeding from the third neuron of set A of the first level. In the second a dendrite arrives proceeding from the first neuron of set B (first level). Taking into account that the respective weights are:

$$w_{A2}^{(1)} = 1, \quad w_{A1}^{(3)} = 0.8, \quad w_{B1}^{(2)} = 1 \quad ^{6}$$

we arrive at entry potentials from the first and second neurons of the third level of:

$$h_{A2}^{(1)} \cdot w_{A2}^{(1)} + e_{A1}^{(3)} \cdot w_{A1}^{(3)} = 3.8 \times 1 + 2 \times 0.8 = 5.4 = l_{A3}^{(3)}$$
$$h_{A2}^{(1)} \cdot w_{A2}^{(1)} + f_{B1}^{(1)} \cdot w_{B1}^{(1)} = 3.8 \times 1 + 2 \times 1 = 5.8 = l_{AB3}^{(2)} \quad \leftarrow$$

From the third neuron of the second level, among others, three axonic dendrites leave, of which two go to the third and fourth neurons, respectively, of the third level. At the third a dendrite also arrives proceeding from the first neuron of sub-set A (first level) and to the fourth which has its exit through the synapses of the third neuron of sub-set B (first level). As the weights are:

$$w_{A1}^{(1)} = 1, \quad w_{B2}^{(3)} = 1, \quad w_{B1}^{(3)} = 0.75$$

the third and fourth neurons of the third level will have the following entry potentials:

$$e_{A1}^{(1)} \cdot w_{A1}^{(1)} + h_{B2}^{(3)} \cdot w_{B2}^{(3)} = 2 \times 1 + 3.6 \times 1 = 5.6 = l_{AB3}^{(3)}$$
$$h_{B2}^{(3)} \cdot w_{B2}^{(3)} + f_{B1}^{(3)} \cdot w_{B1}^{(3)} = 3.6 \times 1 + 2 \times 0.75 = 5.1 = l_{B3}^{(4)}$$

The maximum potential occurs in the second neuron with a value of 5.8, followed by the maximum potential for the third neuron of 5.6. We will leave these neurons for the time being, in order to continue with the fourth level.

Transfer to the fourth level

In the graph can be seen the arrival at the neurons of the fourth level of dendrites proceeding from all the previous levels. In order to simplify we are going to assume that the weights of the dendrites proceeding from the axons of neurons that are members of the intermediary levels have a weight of 1. We will spare the reader of any comments relative to the dendritic connections and move on directly to the operating process.

With regard to the first neuron, the weights are:

$$w_{A1}^{(4)} = 0.70, \quad w_{A3}^{(1)} = 1$$

and we will have an entry potential of:

$$e_{A1}^{(4)} \cdot w_{A1}^{(4)} + l_{A3}^{(1)} \cdot w_{A3}^{(1)} = 2 \times 0.7 + 5.4 \times 1 = 6.8 = m_{A4}^{(1)}$$

For the second neuron, the weights are:

$$w_{A3}^{(1)} = 1, \quad w_{B1}^{(1)} = 1$$

entry potential:

$$l_{A3}^{(1)} \cdot w_{A3}^{(1)} + f_{B1}^{(1)} \cdot w_{B1}^{(1)} = 5.4 \times 1 + 2 \times 1 = 7.4 = m_{AB4}^{(2)} \quad \leftarrow$$

For the third neuron the weights are:

$$w_{A2}^{(1)} = 1, \quad w_{B2}^{(3)} = 1$$

entry potential:

$$h_{A2}^{(1)} \cdot w_{A2}^{(1)} + f_{B2}^{(3)} \cdot w_{B2}^{(3)} = 3.8 \times 1 + 3.6 \times 1 = 7.4 = m_{AB4}^{(3)} \quad \leftarrow$$

For the fourth neuron the weights are:

$$w_{A1}^{(1)} = 1, \quad w_{B3}^{(4)} = 1$$

entry potential:

$$e_{A1}^{(1)} \cdot w_{A1}^{(1)} + l_{B3}^{(4)} \cdot w_{B3}^{(4)} = 2 \times 1 + 5.1 \times 1 = 7.1 = m_{AB4}^{(4)}$$

For the fifth neuron the weights are:

$$w_{B3}^{(4)} = 1, \quad w_{B1}^{(4)} = 0.75$$

entry potential:

$$l_{B3}^{(4)} \cdot w_{B3}^{(4)} + f_{B1}^{(4)} \cdot w_{B1}^{(4)} = 5.1 \times 1 + 2 \times 0.75 = 6.6 = \mathrm{m_{B4}}^{(5)}$$

The maximum values of the entry potentials of the neurons under consideration in the fourth level take place in the second and third neurons. In order to continue with the process we will set aside these neurons and move on with the first and fifth, that is to say with those that <<only>> receive impulses from a single intitial sub-set either *A* or *B*. And the process will continue, during this first phase, until all levels are emptied.

The second phase of the model means incorporating the set of neurons $C = \{z_1{}^{(1)}, z_1{}^{(2)}, ..., z_1{}^{(10)}\}$, representing the yields obtained as a consequence of investing the monetary masses in investment object *C*. In the same way as presented in the first phase, when we only considered two sub-sets of initial neurons *A* and *B*, we are now also going to consider the process through a neural graph, in which the connections existing between the different levels will be described, but on this occasion including all the relations of causality occurring from the three sets.

For this, and for the only reason of visual simplicity, for sets *A* and *B* we will only draw the axonic connections relative to those neurons from which a potential leaves and we will not consider those that do not later transmit any signal whatsoever. In this way we will reduce the number of arcs of the part of the neural graph corresponding to the one we have already shown, which in itself was complete for the first four levels.

In the fragments of the <<brain>> we already know we now add another relative to connections existing (always for the first four levels) between the neurons that commence their activity in those of sub-set *C* and the neurons commencing in *A* and *B*. In this way we form a new neural network that includes as one of its parts, the one represented previously. With these premises the following graph is arrived at figure 14.5:

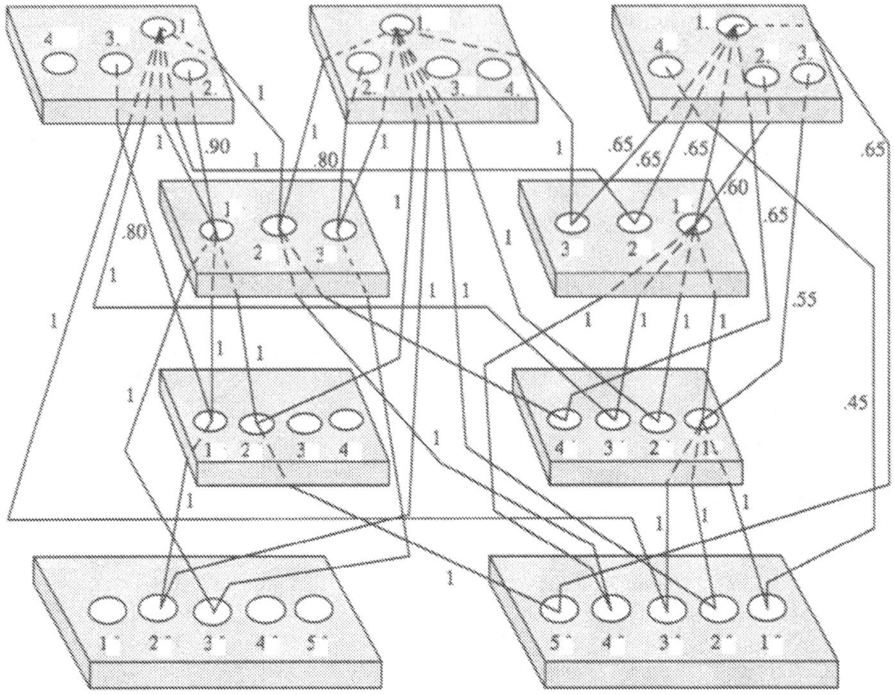

Figure 14.5.

Once again we are in a position to proceed to the calculation of the potential flowing in the network. For this we will commence the process at the first level, and carry on with successive levels, always taking into consideration the optimums arrived at in the first phase.

Transfer from the first to the second level

We take into consideration neurons of sub-set $C = \{z_1^{(i)} / \; i = 1, 2, ..., 10\}$, that also form the original level, as well as the first neuron of set A and the first of set B *which allowed the maximum potential* in the first stage.

In order to form an investment of 200 monetary units in which sub-set C always intervenes, we can only resort to the following combinations:

- Two neurons (first and second) from sub-set C.
- One neuron (the first) from sub-set A and one (the first) from sub-set C.
- One neuron (the first) from sub-set B and one (the first) from sub-set C.

Using the same nomenclature as for the first stage and designating as $g_1^{(i)}$, $i = 1, 2, ..., 10$ the exit potential of the first level of sub-set C, we arrive at the following potentials for the respective neurons of the second level.

First neuron of the second level:

$$g_{C1}^{(1)} \cdot w_{C1}^{(1)} + g_{C1}^{(2)} \cdot w_{C1}^{(2)} = 2 \times 0.65 + 2 \times 0.60 = 2.5 = p_{C2}^{(1)}$$

Second neuron of the second level

$$e_{A1}^{(1)} \cdot w_{A1}^{(1)} + g_{C1}^{(1)} \cdot w_{C1}^{(1)} = 2 \times 1 + 2 \times 0.65 = 3.3 = p_{AC2}^{(2)}$$

Third neurona of the second level:

$$f_{B1}^{(1)} \cdot w_{B1}^{(1)} + g_{C1}^{(1)} \cdot w_{C1}^{(1)} = 2 \times 1 + 2 \times 0.65 = 3.3 = p_{BC2}^{(3)}$$

If we now compare the potentials of all neurons appearing in the second phase with the optimum of the first, we arrive at the fact that the maximum will be:

$$\text{Max } \{h_{AB2}^{(2)}, p_{C2}^{(1)}, p_{AC2}^{(2)}, p_{BC2}^{(3)}\} = \text{Max } \{4, 2.5, 3.3, 3.3\} = 4 \quad \leftarrow$$

The maximum profitability in the second level will take place in the combination of 100 monetary units invested in object A and 100 in object B.

Transfer from the second to the third level

As a result of the incorporation of sub-set C activity has appeared in four neurons in the third level. We will set aside describing the entry dendrite of the same, as they appear quite clearly in the neural graph. Potentials for these neurons are as follows:

First neuron, third level:

$$p_{C2}^{(1)} \cdot w_{C2}^{(1)} + g_{C1}^{(3)} \cdot w_{C1}^{(3)} = 2.5 \times 1 + 2 \times 0.55 = 3.6 = q_{C3}^{(1)}$$

Second neuron, third level:

$$p_{C2}^{(1)} \cdot w_{C2}^{(1)} + f_{B1}^{(1)} \cdot w_{B1}^{(3)} = 2.5 \times 1 + 2 \times 1 = 4.5 = q_{BC3}^{(2)}$$

Third neuron, third level:

$$p_{C2}^{(1)} \cdot w_{C2}^{(1)} + e_{A1}^{(1)} \cdot w_{A1}^{(3)} = 2.5 \times 1 + 2 \times 1 = 4.5 = q_{AC3}^{(3)}$$

Fourth neuron, third level:

$$g_{C1}^{(1)} \cdot w_{C1}^{(1)} + h_{AB2}^{(2)} \cdot w_{AB2}^{(2)} = 2 \times 0.65 + 4 \times 1 = 5.3 = q_{ABC3}^{(4)}$$

If we obtain the maximum from among the potentials of the active neurons in this second phase and the maximum of the previous phase, relative to the third level we have:

$$\text{Max}\ \{l^{(2)}_{AB3}, q^{(1)}_{C3}, q^{(2)}_{BC3}, q^{(3)}_{AC3}, q^{(4)}_{ABC3}\} = \text{Max}\ \{5.8, 3.6, 4.5, 4.5, 5.3\} = 5.8 \quad \leftarrow$$

In this way, the higher profitability for investment of 300 monetary units occurs when investing 200 units in object A and 100 in B.

Transfer from the third to the fourth level

Consideration of the sub-set of C neurons makes five new neurons acquire activity in the fourth level. Let us now do the calculation of the corresponding potentials of these new neurons.

First neuron, fourth level:

$$q^{(1)}_{C3} \cdot w^{(1)}_{C3} + g^{(4)}_{C1} \cdot w^{(4)}_{C1} = 3.6 \times 1 + 2 \times 0.45 = 4.5 = r^{(1)}_{C4}$$

Second neuron, fourth level:

$$q^{(1)}_{C3} \cdot w^{(1)}_{C3} + f^{(1)}_{B1} \cdot w^{(1)}_{B1} = 3.6 \times 1 + 2 \times 1 = 5.6 = r^{(2)}_{BC4}$$

Third neuron, fourth level:

$$q^{(1)}_{C3} \cdot w^{(1)}_{C3} + e^{(1)}_{A1} \cdot w^{(1)}_{A1} = 3.6 \times 1 + 2 \times 1 = 5.6 = r^{(3)}_{AC4}$$

Fourth neuron, fourth level:

$$p^{(1)}_{C2} \cdot w^{(1)}_{C2} + h^{(2)}_{AB2} \cdot w^{(2)}_{AB2} = 2.5 \times 1 + 4 \times 1 = 6.5 = r^{(4)}_{ABC4}$$

Fifth neuron, fourth level:

$$g^{(1)}_{C1} \cdot w^{(1)}_{C1} + l^{(2)}_{AB3} \cdot w^{(2)}_{AB3} = 2 \times 0.65 + 5.8 \times 1 = 7.1 = r^{(5)}_{ABC4}$$

We now obtain the maximum from among the potentials of the new active neurons and the highest value found in the first phase of the fourth level. This will be:

$$\text{Max}\ \{m^{(2)}_{AB4}, m^{(3)}_{AB4}, r^{(1)}_{C4}, r^{(2)}_{BC4}, r^{(3)}_{AC4}, r^{(4)}_{ABC4}, r^{(5)}_{ABC4}\} =$$
$$= \text{Max}\ \{7.4, 7.4, 4.5, 5.6, 5.6, 6.5, 7.1\} = 7.4 \quad \leftarrow$$

The highest profitability for the fourth level will take place when one of the following combinations is followed:

- Investment of 200 monetary units in investment object A and 200 in object B.

- Investment of 300 monetary units in investment object A and 100 in object B.

In either of the cases a <<profit>> of 7.4 monetary units is obtained.

The process continues by following the same path until finishing with the number of established levels, which in this specific case are ten.

Incorporating uncertainty

We will now move on to develop a model when certain amounts, such as yields (UNP) arising from investment in financial means are estimated by means of uncertain amounts. In a first approximation we will consider the use of confidence triplets[7].

Here again let us suppose that the impulses emitted by all neurons of the same sub-set have the same intensity, estimated by means of triplets:

$$e_{Aj}^{(i)} = (1.8, 2, 2.5), \quad f_{Bj}^{(i)} = (1.8, 2, 2.8), \quad g_{Cj}^{(i)} = (1.5, 2, 2.8)$$ [8]

and that the respective synaptic weights are the same as for the previous case when we were dealing in the sphere of certainty.

With these bases, we can calculate the impulses emitted and received by the neurons of the network. Therefore, in the first level the optimum appears in the first neuron of sub-set B, with $f_{B1}^{(1)} = (1.8, 2, 2.8)$.

In the transfer of the first level to the second, we will have:

For the first neuron:

$$e_{A1}^{(1)} (\cdot) w_{A1}^{(1)} = (1.8, 2, 2.5) (\cdot) 1 = (1.8, 2, 2.5)$$

$$e_{A1}^{(2)} (\cdot) w_{A1}^{(2)} = (1.8, 2, 2.5) (\cdot) 0.9 = (1.62, 1.80, 2.25)$$

$$h_{A2}^{(1)} = e_{A1}^{(1)} (\cdot) w_{A1}^{(1)} (+) e_{A1}^{(2)} (\cdot) w_{A1}^{(2)} = (3.42, 3.80, 4.75)$$

For the second neuron:

$$e_{A1}^{(1)} (\cdot)\, w_{A1}^{(1)} = (1.8, 2, 2.5) (\cdot)\, 1 = (1.8, 2, 2.5)$$

$$f_{B1}^{(1)} (\cdot)\, w_{B1}^{(1)} = (1.8, 2, 2.8) (\cdot)\, 1 = (1.8, 2, 2.8)$$

$$h_{AB2}^{(2)} = e_{A1}^{(1)} (\cdot)\, w_{A1}^{(1)} (+) f_{B1}^{(1)} (\cdot)\, w_{B1}^{(1)} = (3.60, 4, 5.3) \quad \leftarrow$$

For the third neuron:

$$f_{B1}^{(1)} (\cdot)\, w_{B1}^{(1)} = (1.8, 2, 2.8) (\cdot)\, 1 = (1.8, 2, 2.8)$$

$$f_{B1}^{(2)} (\cdot)\, w_{B1}^{(2)} = (1.8, 2, 2.8) (\cdot)\, 0.8 = (1.44, 1.60, 2.24)$$

$$h_{B2}^{(3)} = f_{B1}^{(1)} (\cdot)\, w_{B1}^{(1)} (+) f_{B1}^{(2)} (\cdot)\, w_{B1}^{(2)} = (3.24, 3.60, 5.04)$$

With the object of finding the neuron that receives the maximum potential we will establish a comparison by means of an already known criterion. Therefore:

$$\overline{h}_{A2}^{(1)} = \frac{3.42 + 2 \times 3.80 + 4.75}{4} = 3.942$$

$$\overline{h}_{AB2}^{(2)} = \frac{3.60 + 2 \times 4 + 5.3}{4} = 4.225$$

$$\overline{h}_{AB2}^{(3)} = \frac{3.24 + 2 \times 3.60 + 5.04}{4} = 3.870$$

Taking into account that:

$$\overline{h}_{AB2}^{(2)} > \overline{h}_{A2}^{(1)} > \overline{h}_{AB2}^{(3)}$$

the optimum will occur in the second neuron with an estimate of $h_{AB}{}^{(2)}{}_{2} = (3.60, 4, 5.30)$.

In order to pass on from the second level to the third we will do:

Relative to the first neuron:

$$e_{A1}^{(3)} (\cdot)\, w_{A1}^{(3)} = (1.8, 2, 2.5) (\cdot)\, 0.8 = (1.44, 1.6, 2)$$

$$h_{A2}^{(1)} (\cdot)\, w_{A2}^{(1)} = (3.42, 3.8, 4.75) (\cdot)\, 1 = (3.42, 3.80, 4.75)$$

$$l_{A3}^{(1)} = e_{A1}^{(3)} (\cdot)\, w_{A1}^{(3)} (+)\, h_{A2}^{(1)} (\cdot)\, w_{A2}^{(1)} = (4.86, 5.40, 6.75)$$

For the second neuron:

$$h_{A2}^{(1)} (\cdot)\, w_{A2}^{(1)} = (3.42, 3.80, 4.75) (\cdot)\, 1 = (3.42, 3.80, 4.75)$$

$$f_{B1}^{(1)} (\cdot)\, w_{B1}^{(1)} = (1.8, 2, 2.8) (\cdot)\, 1 = (1.8, 2, 2.8)$$

$$l_{AB3}^{(2)} = h_{A2}^{(1)} (\cdot)\, w_{A2}^{(1)} (+) f_{B1}^{(1)} (\cdot)\, w_{B1}^{(1)} = (5.22, 5.80, 7.55) \quad \leftarrow$$

$$f_{B1}^{(1)}\ (\cdot)\ w_{B1}^{(1)} = (1.8, 2, 2.8)\ (\cdot)\ 1 = (1.8, 2, 2.8)$$

$$l_{AB3}^{(2)} = h_{A2}^{(1)}\ (\cdot)\ w_{A2}^{(1)}\ (+)\ f_{B1}^{(1)}\ (\cdot)\ w_{B1}^{(1)} = (5.22, 5.80, 7.55) \quad \leftarrow$$

For the third neuron:

$$e_{A1}^{(1)}\ (\cdot)\ w_{A1}^{(1)} = (1.8, 2, 2.5)\ (\cdot)\ 1 = (1.8, 2, 2.5)$$

$$h_{B2}^{(3)}\ (\cdot)\ w_{B2}^{(3)} = (3.24, 3.60, 5.04)\ (\cdot)\ 1 = (3.24, 3.60, 5.04)$$

$$l_{AB3}^{(3)} = e_{A1}^{(1)}\ (\cdot)\ w_{A1}^{(1)}\ (+)\ h_{B2}^{(3)}\ (\cdot)\ w_{B2}^{(3)} = (5.04, 5.60, 7.54)$$

For the fourth neuron:

$$h_{B2}^{(3)}\ (\cdot)\ w_{B2}^{(3)} = (3.24, 3.60, 5.04)\ (\cdot)\ 1 = (3.24, 3.60, 5.04)$$

$$f_{B1}^{(3)}\ (\cdot)\ w_{B1}^{(3)} = (1.8, 2, 2.8)\ (\cdot)\ 0.75 = (1.35, 1.50, 2.10)$$

$$l_{B3}^{(4)} = h_{B2}^{(3)}\ (\cdot)\ w_{B2}^{(3)}\ (+)\ f_{B1}^{(1)}\ (\cdot)\ w_{B1}^{(1)} = (4.59, 5.10, 7.14)$$

The optimum for this level will take place in the second neuron with an estimate of $l_{AB3}^{(2)} = (5.22, 5.80, 7.55)$.

When passing from the third level to the fourth we have:

For the first neuron:

$$e_{A1}^{(4)}\ (\cdot)\ w_{A1}^{(4)} = (1.8, 2, 2.5)\ (\cdot)\ 0.7 = (1.26, 1.40, 1.75)$$

$$l_{A3}^{(1)}\ (\cdot)\ w_{A3}^{(1)} = (4.86, 5.40, 6.75)\ (\cdot)\ 1 = (4.86, 5.40, 6.75)$$

$$m_{A4}^{(1)} = e_{A1}^{(4)}\ (\cdot)\ w_{A1}^{(4)}\ (+)\ l_{A3}^{(1)}\ (\cdot)\ w_{A3}^{(1)} = (6.12, 6.80, 8.50)$$

For the second neuron:

$$l_{A3}^{(1)}\ (\cdot)\ w_{A3}^{(1)} = (4.86, 5.40, 6.75)\ (\cdot)\ 1 = (4.86, 5.40, 6.75)$$

$$f_{B1}^{(1)}\ (\cdot)\ w_{B1}^{(1)} = (1.8, 2, 2.8)\ (\cdot)\ 1 = (1.8, 2, 2.8)$$

$$m_{AB4}^{(2)} = l_{A3}^{(1)}\ (\cdot)\ w_{A3}^{(1)}\ (+)\ f_{B1}^{(1)}\ (\cdot)\ w_{B1}^{(1)} = (6.66, 7.40, 9.55)$$

For the third neuron:

$$h_{A2}^{(1)}\ (\cdot)\ w_{A2}^{(1)} = (3.42, 3.80, 4.75)\ (\cdot)\ 1 = (3.42, 3.80, 4.75)$$

$$h_{B2}^{(3)}\ (\cdot)\ w_{B2}^{(3)} = (3.24, 3.60, 5.04)\ (\cdot)\ 1 = (3.24, 3.60, 5.04)$$

$$m_{AB4}^{(3)} = h_{A2}^{(1)}\ (\cdot)\ w_{A2}^{(1)}\ (+)\ h_{B2}^{(3)}\ (\cdot)\ w_{B2}^{(3)} = (6.66, 7.40, 9.79) \quad \leftarrow$$

For the fourth neuron:

$$e_{A1}^{(1)}\ (\cdot)\ w_{A1}^{(1)} = (1.8, 2, 2.5)\ (\cdot)\ 1 = (1.8, 2, 2.5)$$

For the fifth neuron:

$$l_{B3}^{(4)} (\cdot) w_{B3}^{(4)} = (4.59, 5.10, 7.14) (\cdot) 1 = (4.59, 5.10, 7.14)$$

$$f_{B1}^{(4)} (\cdot) w_{B1}^{(4)} = (1.8, 2, 2.8) (\cdot) 0.75 = (1.35, 1.50, 2.10)$$

$$m_{B4}^{(5)} = l_{B3}^{(4)} (\cdot) w_{B3}^{(4)} (+) f_{B1}^{(4)} (\cdot) w_{B1}^{(4)} = (5.94, 6.60, 9.24)$$

The optimum can be observed in the third neuron. In fact, although it possesses the same lower extreme and the same maximum presumption as the second neuron, its upper extreme is larger. In this way the following is complied with:

$$\overline{m}_{AB4}^{(3)} > \overline{m}_{AB4}^{(2)}$$

The estimate is:

$$\overline{m}_{AB4}^{(3)} = (6.60, 7.40, 9.79)$$

The process will continue until such time as the ten levels making up this neural network are depleted.

Once we have finished this phase of the calculation, we are going to incorporate the neurons of sub-set C to the optimum neurons of each phase.

Taking into account that for the first level only one optimum $f_{B1}^{(1)} = (1.8, 2, 2.8)$ appears, initially we will only consider the first neuron of sub-set B, on the contrary to what happened in certainty, where we considered both the first neuron of sub-set A and the first of sub-set B, as both were representative of an optimum for an initial investment with a profitability (UNP) as a simplifying hypothesis of 2. In this way the second neuron of sub-set C (second level)[9] disappears from the network of <<active>> neurons.

Having made this observation, valid for all levels when this phenomenon takes place, we move on to detail the calculations for the first four levels.

Transfer from the first to the second level

For the first neuron:

$$g_{C1}^{(1)} (\cdot) w_{C1}^{(1)} = (1.5, 2, 2.8) (\cdot) 0.65 = (0.975, 1.300, 1.820)$$

$$g_{C1}^{(2)} (\cdot) w_{C1}^{(2)} = (1.5, 2, 2.8) (\cdot) 0.60 = (0.90, 1.20, 1.68)$$

$$p_{C2}^{(1)} = g_{C1}^{(1)} (\cdot) w_{C1}^{(1)} (+) g_{C1}^{(2)} (\cdot) w_{C1}^{(2)} = (1.875, 2.500, 3.500)$$

For the third neuron:

$$g_{C1}^{(1)} (\cdot)\, w_{C1}^{(1)} = (1.5, 2, 2.8) (\cdot)\, 0.65 = (0.975, 1.300, 1.820)$$
$$f_{B1}^{(1)} (\cdot)\, w_{B1}^{(1)} = (1.8, 2, 2.8) (\cdot)\, 1 = (1.8, 2, 2.8)$$
$$p_{BC2}^{(3)} = g_{C1}^{(1)} (\cdot)\, w_{C1}^{(1)} (+) f_{B1}^{(1)} (\cdot)\, w_{B1}^{(1)} = (2.775, 3.300, 4.620)$$

For arriving at the optimum in the second level it will be sufficient to obtain the maximum between the first stage and the potentials of this second stage. We will arrive at:

$$\text{Max}\, \{h_{AB2}^{(2)}, p_{C2}^{(1)}, p_{BC2}^{(3)}\} = \text{Max}\, \{\underset{\uparrow}{(3.6, 4, 5.3)}, (1.875, 2.5, 3.5), (2.775, 3.30, 4.62)\} =$$
$$= (3.6, 4, 5.3) = h_{AB2}^{(2)}$$

Transfer from the second to the third level

For the first neuron:

$$p_{C2}^{(1)} (\cdot)\, w_{C2}^{(1)} = (1.875, 2.500, 3.500) (\cdot)\, 1 = (1.875, 2.500, 3.500)$$
$$g_{C1}^{(3)} (\cdot)\, w_{C1}^{(3)} = (1.5, 2, 2.8) (\cdot)\, 0.55 = (0.825, 1.100, 1.540)$$
$$q_{C3}^{(1)} = p_{C2}^{(1)} (\cdot)\, w_{C2}^{(1)} (+)\, g_{C1}^{(3)} (\cdot)\, w_{C1}^{(3)} = (2.700, 3.600, 5.040)$$

For the second neuron:

$$p_{C2}^{(1)} (\cdot)\, w_{C2}^{(1)} = (1.875, 2.500, 3.500) (\cdot)\, 1 = (1.875, 2.500, 3.500)$$
$$f_{B1}^{(1)} (\cdot)\, w_{B1}^{(1)} = (1.8, 2, 2.8) (\cdot)\, 1 = (1.8, 2, 2.8)$$
$$q_{BC3}^{(2)} = p_{C2}^{(1)} (\cdot)\, w_{C2}^{(1)} (+) f_{B1}^{(1)} (\cdot)\, w_{B1}^{(1)} = (3.675, 4.500, 6.300)$$

For the fourth neuron:

$$g_{C1}^{(1)} (\cdot)\, w_{C1}^{(1)} = (1.5, 2, 2.8) (\cdot)\, 0.65 = (0.975, 1.300, 1.820)$$
$$h_{AB2}^{(2)} (\cdot)\, w_{AB2}^{(2)} = (3.6, 4, 5.3) (\cdot)\, 1 = (3.6, 4, 5.3)$$
$$q_{ABC3}^{(4)} = g_{C1}^{(1)} (\cdot)\, w_{C1}^{(1)} (+)\, h_{AB2}^{(2)} (\cdot)\, w_{AB2}^{(2)} = (4.575, 5.300, 7.120)$$

The optimum of the third level is obtained by means of the maximum between the optimum of the first phase and the potentials of this second phase. Therefore:

$$\text{Max}\, \{l_{AB3}^{(2)}, q_{C3}^{(1)}, q_{BC3}^{(2)}, q_{ABC3}^{(4)}\} = \text{Max}\, \{\underset{\uparrow}{(5.22, 5.80, 7.55)}, (2.700, 3.600, 5.040),$$
$$(3.675, 4.500, 6.300), (4.575, 5.300, 7.120)\}$$
$$= (5.22, 5.80, 7.55) = l_{AB3}^{(2)}$$

Transfer from the third to the fourth level

For the first neuron:

$$q_{C3}^{(1)}\ (\cdot)\ w_{C3}^{(1)} = (2.700, 3.600, 5.040)\ (\cdot)\ 1 = (2.700, 3.600, 5.040)$$
$$g_{C1}^{(4)}\ (\cdot)\ w_{C1}^{(4)} = (1.5, 2, 2.8)\ (\cdot)\ 0.45 = (0.675, 0.900, 1.260)$$
$$r_{C4}^{(1)} = q_{C3}^{(1)}\ (\cdot)\ w_{C3}^{(1)}\ (+)\ g_{C1}^{(4)}\ (\cdot)\ w_{C1}^{(4)} = (3.375, 4.500, 6.300)$$

For the second neuron:

$$q_{C3}^{(1)}\ (\cdot)\ w_{C3}^{(1)} = (2.700, 3.600, 5.040)\ (\cdot)\ 1 = (2.700, 3.600, 5.040)$$
$$f_{B1}^{(1)}\ (\cdot)\ w_{B1}^{(1)} = (1.8, 2, 2.8)\ (\cdot)\ 1 = (1.8, 2, 2.8)$$
$$r_{BC4}^{(2)} = q_{C3}^{(1)}\ (\cdot)\ w_{C3}^{(1)}\ (+) f_{B1}^{(1)}\ (\cdot)\ w_{B1}^{(1)} = (4.500, 5.600, 7.840)$$

For the fourth neuron:

$$p_{C2}^{(1)}\ (\cdot)\ w_{C2}^{(1)} = (1.875, 2.500, 3.500)\ (\cdot)\ 1 = (1.875, 2.500, 3.500)$$
$$h_{AB2}^{(2)}\ (\cdot)\ w_{AB2}^{(2)} = (3.6, 4, 5.3)\ (\cdot)\ 1 = (3.6, 4, 5.3)$$
$$r_{ABC4}^{(4)} = p_{C2}^{(1)}\ (\cdot)\ w_{C2}^{(1)}\ (+)\ h_{AB2}^{(2)}\ (\cdot)\ w_{AB2}^{(2)} = (5.475, 6.500, 8.800)$$

For the fifth neuron:

$$g_{C1}^{(1)}\ (\cdot)\ w_{C1}^{(1)} = (1.5, 2, 2.8)\ (\cdot)\ 0.65 = (0.975, 1.300, 1.820)$$
$$l_{AB3}^{(2)}\ (\cdot)\ w_{AB3}^{(2)} = (5.22, 5.80, 7.55)\ (\cdot)\ 1 = (5.22, 5.80, 7.55)$$
$$r_{ABC4}^{(5)} = g_{C1}^{(1)}\ (\cdot)\ w_{C1}^{(1)}\ (+)\ l_{AB3}^{(2)}\ (\cdot)\ w_{AB3}^{(2)} = (6.195, 7.100, 9.370)$$

Obtaining the optimum in the fourth stage will take place by means of the maximisation of the optimum of the first phase and the potentials of the neurons that have taken place in this second phase. Therefore we will do:

$$\begin{aligned} \text{Max}\ \{m_{AB4}^{(3)}, r_{C4}^{(1)}, r_{BC4}^{(2)}, r_{ABC4}^{(4)}, r_{ABC4}^{(5)}\} &= \text{Max}\ \{(\underset{\uparrow}{6.66}, 7.40, 9.79), (3.375, 4.500, 6.300), \\ &\quad (4.500, 5.600, 7.840), (5.475, 6.5, 8.8), \\ &\quad (6.195, 7.1, 9.37)\} \\ &= (6.66, 7.40, 9.79) = m_{AB4}^{(4)} \end{aligned}$$

The process will continue in the same way until all levels are depleted, which in our didactic example is limited to ten.

Below we show the neural network in which the <<electro-chemical impulses>> emitted and received by those neurons with an essential role in the desired optimisation can be clearly seen. It can now be verified that, by the mere fact of incorporating uncertainty (even when this only intervenes by means of confidence triplets) potentials are separated that resulted equivalent in the sphere of certainty giving rise then to more than one optimum in a determined level. On passing over to uncertainty and incorporating a <<maximum of presumption>> the extremes of the triplets (not always equal in the different neurons) are automatically defined as different uncertain potentials. This is the reason that in the network shown below certain neurons without an active role appear, when in the neural graph for certainty they played an essential role figure 14.6).

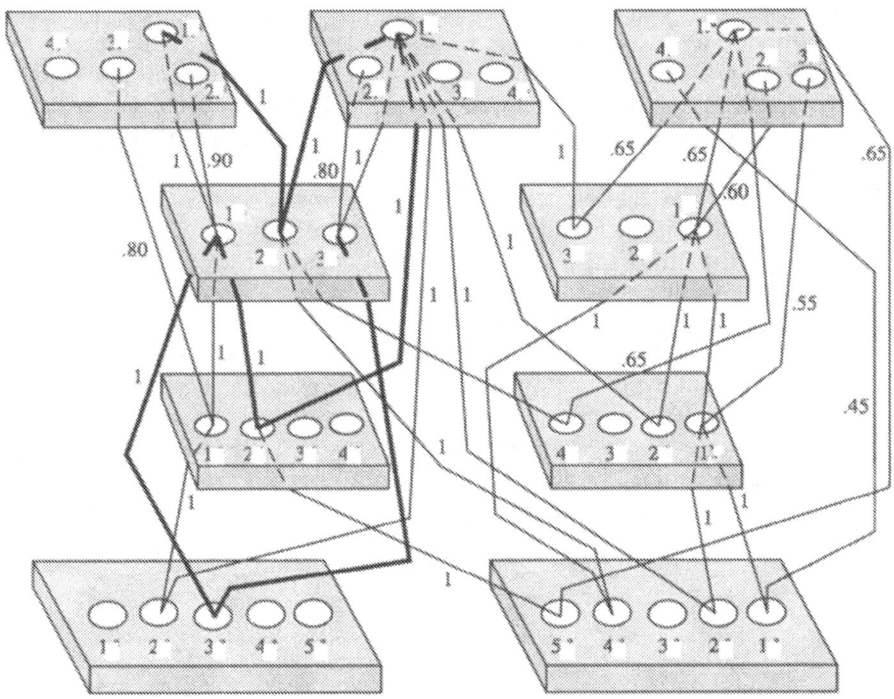

Figure 14.6.

Below we have summarised the results obtained through the optimisations arising from the principle of dynamic programming and those developed by means of the fundamental concepts of neuromimetics.

Dose	Maximum profit	Optimum combination	Symbol for optimum profit
1	(1.8, 2, 2.8)	1 dose B	$f_{B1}^{(1)}$
2	(3.6, 4, 5.3)	1 dose A + 1 dose B	$h_{AB2}^{(2)}$
3	(5.22, 5.80, 7.55)	2 doses A + 1 dose B	$l_{AB3}^{(2)}$
4	(6.66, 7.40, 9.79)	2 doses A + 2 doses B	$m_{AB4}^{(3)}$
5	...	...	...

We have described in detail, the process that would be followed for adopting a criterion for investment when incorporating techniques based on concepts arising from neuro-mimetics and estimates are made based on uncertain economic parameters. As we have followed a sequential process, Bellman's principle of optimisation, that is the basis of dynamic programming, has been particularly adequate and has been useful for acquiring greater awareness of the algorithm.

Most of the time the restrictive hypotheses that implicitly or explicitly have been adopted throughout the development of the calculations do not invalidate the validity of the model. However, we are conscious of the fact of the possibility of making a generalisation if new elements are introduced in an active manner, such as the concept of the threshold, which perhaps would allow a wider vision on the causes motivating the activity or inactivity of neurons.

We have avoided this and other aspects of the problem in order to arrive at greater simplicity and obtain a comparison, as homogenous as possible, between classical and fuzzy handling of this selection criterion. We have only attempted to show a brief outline, an elementary proposal that will serve as the basis for new and more profound studies which, may be carried out, perhaps by us or others.

References

1 W.S. Mc Culloch and N. Pitts: <<A logical calculus of the ideas immanent in nervous systems>>, *Bulletin of mathematical Biophysics*, number 5, 1943, pages 115-133.

2 Here can be seen the incorporation of the concept of weight, which does not appear in the case carried out based on dynamic programming.

3 In the $e_{Aa}^{(b)}$ we have represented the number of the level by the sub-index (a) and the specific neuron for each level by upper-index (b).

4 Letters A and B have been included as sub-indices of h, and these correspond to the sub-sets of neurons from which the entry potentials proceed.

5 The elimination of this hypothesis, established for greater simplicity in calculation, does not modify the validity of the model.

6 We have kept the letter of the sub-index of the w when all the dendrites proceed from the same sub-set (A or B).

7 Generalisation to triangular fuzzy numbers created no additional problems for those having knowledge of fuzzy arithmetic.

8 For greater differentiation we will change the letters as we pass from one level to the following (when j takes on the values 1, 2, ..., 10).
We will no longer place the symbol $\sim$ under the letters representing triplets, as in this case it is superfluous as no error whatsoever is induced.

9 In spite of the fact that this second neuron is inactive we will keep it in the graphic representation of the network, for the effects of clarity in comparison between certainty and uncertainty.

PART THREE

Handling the problem of equipment

15 Economic renewal of industrial equipment

The company and the needs for renewal

In order for a modern industry to be able to carry out its productive function it must have recourse to certain means or production factors, among which equipment stands out. The classical consideration as fixed assets that these items have warranted from an accounting point of view, in present times has a relative sense. In fact, the rapid changes there have been in the life of companies convert this concept of fixed or permanence into a relative concept.

The reasons for this relativity are numerous and oblige the economic subject to determine at what exact time the best conditions will occur for equipment to be withdrawn from service and replaced with another.

The economic aspect of this problem is tackled by a part of business studies known under the name of <<economic renewal of industrial equipment>>.

As a prior hypothesis, the existence of equipment is considered and the possibility examined for its removal from service either by substitution or renovation, which leads to the need of making a quantitative study in order to determine if withdrawing the same is necessary or not. Obviously the old equipment will have lost its economical-functional value when the new equipment allows for production at much reduced costs. It is here that economic viability studies on renewal come into play. The criteria on which these studies are based are real studies and not accounting studies, and for this reason the fact that the available equipment has or has not been depreciated in the books <<lacks all significance>>[1].

In a very general fashion, it can be stated that the problem of renewal of industrial equipment is considered under two very distinct ways. The first refers to obtaining an optimum chain, that is, the best programme from an initial moment, to a final moment in the future, which are representative of what is technically known as *economic horizon*. The second way consists in tackling the problem of renewal in the sense of determining at what future moment equipment should be withdrawn from service following economic criteria.

In any event, the high cost incurred by the withdrawal from service of equipment is obvious, whether it is included in a chain or not.

For this reason the problem of renewal has a particular interest for the businessman.

On the other hand, the duration of the useful life of equipment and, consequently, the time for its renewal, exert an influence that at times is decisive in the costs. From this stems the well-known classification of companies taking as a basis the age of equipment in operation. In this sense, one can consider certain companies with average production equipment, compared to companies called *burgeoning companies*, the equipment of which is very young in age, and companies in recession, with old equipment, that is to say, equipment having had a long life. Obviously, the operating costs of these companies are generally varied, above all if an element of utmost importance in current economic systems, called <<technical progress>> exists.

The general structure of the problem of *renewal*, can be described by taking two aspects as its basis:

1. Causes for renewal

2. Techniques for the optimum treatment of renewal

With regard to the first of these two aspects, Abraham and Thomas[2] give their opinion that renewal, <<can be justified by three principal reasons that become inexorably mixed up together in practice: physical destruction, wear and tear and obsolescence>>.

1. The first case, concerns equipment in a situation of <<all or nothing>> or equipment subject to irreparable breakdowns. This becomes manifest when the cost of the repair is higher than purchase price of a new unit.
2. Wear and tear justifies withdrawal when maintenance expenses required for perfect operation exceed a certain point.
3. Obsolescence is one of the more characteristic phenomena of our industrial civilisation; <<equipment is renewed even though still useable, because more modern materials have appeared on the market>>.

If we make a summary of what we have just stated, we reach the conclusion of the appearance of two fundamental facts, which determine the question of renewal: *functional ageing* and *economic ageing*.

Terborgh, establishes an important definition relative to the causes for equipment renewal. This is the so-called *inferiority of service*. This term includes not only the situation in which the equipment may be from an operational point of view, but it also includes the problem of obsolescence. The concept of inferiority of service makes an attempt to manifest a comparison between old equipment, equipment currently in service and the best equipment that could be acquired at this current moment in time. In short what we are trying to do is to determine the greatest profit, or loss, estimated by the fact of using old or antiquated equipment relative to new and modern equipment.

Normally, industrial equipment is the object of repairs and modifications that, obviously, lengthen its useful life. However, the existence of the phenomenon of obsolescence entails the need not only of comparing the consequences of acquiring new equipment in place of old machinery of the same characteristics, but with other equipment capable of carrying out the same function entrusted to it, under the best possible conditions. Traditionally it has been recommended that special attention should be paid to technical development, in order to consider the convenience and possibilities of introducing modifications or substitutions in equipment used in productive processes.

In order to summarise these ideas we are going to resort to a graphic representation presented by Desrousseaux[3], which with certain modifications allows us to highlight the most important concepts relative to the problem of renewal.

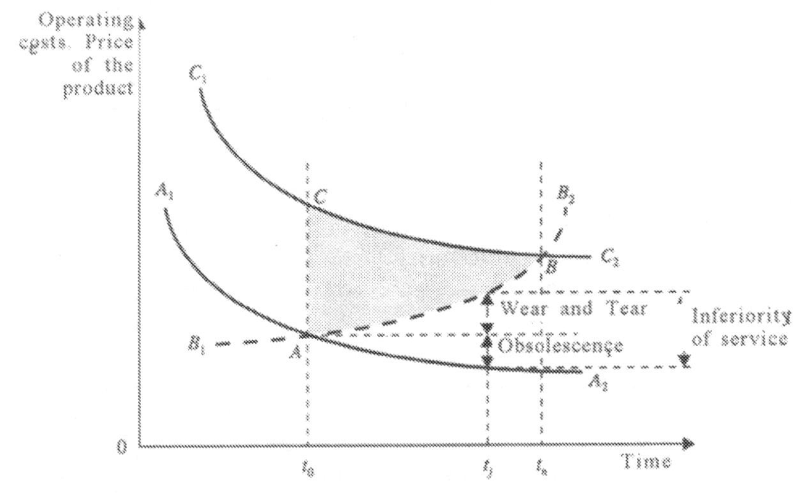

C_1C_2 = Mean product cost = Sales price

B_1B_2 = Operating cost with equipment acquired at t_0 which we designate by $C(0, t)$.

A_1A_2 = Mean operating costs with the use, at all times, of the best new equipment. Designated by $C(t, t)$.

ABC = Net profit which should be higher than the cost of the equipment.

Figure 15.1.

Analysing this graph allows us to make the following considerations:

Starting out from the assumption of the sales by a company, at a given time t_0, of the production carried out by equipment, at its mean cost. If technical progress exists, the mean cost for companies competing in the market will decrease with the passage of time. If the sales price is exactly consistent with the mean cost of the product, a reduction in the same will take place, provided that one starts out from the hypothesis of the non-existence of an inflationary process. The development of a sales price over a length of time, is expressed by the curve C_1C_2.

However, the acquisition of equipment at moment t_0 includes the fact that operating costs, among which as is well known depreciation is not included, will undergo increases because of the wear and tear of the equipment. This is the reason why equipment acquired at moment t_0 generates an operating cost, the evolution of which follows curve B_1B_2.

Also the fact can be considered that equipment may render a <<lesser service>> as a consequence not only of its own wear and tear, but also as a result of the phenomenon of obsolescence by the appearance in the market of new equipment. If there is no inflation process, operating costs for the first units manufactured with new highly perfected equipment will decrease. This requires us to admit the hypothesis of the existence of technical progress. The development of these costs over a period of time is represented by the curve A_1A_2.

If the three curves are compared, it can be seen at a moment t_j, between t_0 and t_n, that there is a difference between the mean operating costs, depending on whether the operation is carried out with old or with new equipment. This difference is what Terborgh calls inferiority of service. As can be seen, this inferiority can be separated into two parts: one referring to wear and tear and the other to obsolescence.

From another point of view it can be seen that, in the case of acquiring equipment at moment t_0, operating costs will increase until they reach moment t_n, when operating costs are higher than the sales price. This point t_n constitutes the latest time for removing the equipment from service.

Finally, if the operating cost, which (we repeat once again) does not include equipment depreciation, develops as reflected in B_1B_2, and the sales price by curve C_1C_2, there will be an area, ABC which constitutes a gross profit in which depreciation has not been taken into account. This allows us to determine the hypothetical profit for operation of the equipment, the figure for which will only be positive if the amounts reflected by this area, updated at moment t_0, are higher than the cost of acquiring the equipment.

If physical wear and tear and breakdowns determine functional ageing, the phenomenon of obsolescence appears, principally when one of the following circumstances occurs:

1. Appearance in the market of *technological variations* that introduce the belief that with them increases in profit will be attained.
   The introduction of technological innovations places in the market new equipment that is capable of faster production and/or manufacturing goods of a higher quality.
2. Technological changes caused by the increase in price of a certain production factor, making the machinery with a different productive factor efficient.
3. Reorganisation of the company, the new processes of which could include the need for new equipment differing from existing equipment.

Whatever type of ageing exists, the need arises for becoming aware of a situation requiring a decision that could consist of proceeding or not with renewal.

Renewal in management studies

In order to take one or other path in the dilemma of renewal, a *prior study*, that current economic literature has acquired the custom of separating from the strict ambience of investment selection, becomes more necessary as time goes by.

Studies for renewal, from the most traditional to the most modern, have been carried out from the elaboration of certain models that attempt to avoid excessive simplification of reality. In this sense the following can be considered:

- Models for an economic system governed by certainty
- Models for the field of probability.
- Models for the sphere of uncertainty.

Given the current situation, characterised by very rapid changes, the way has been closed to the use of certain of these schemes. The lack of adaptation of these models, formally of particular perfection, to complex realities makes then inoperative for executives who require at every moment to know whether renewal is required or not.

However, let us take a very brief bird's eye view of the techniques to which recourse can be made for the treatment of the problem of renewal in the field of certainty.

We will commence with the so-called <<theory of adverse minimum method>> the development and divulging of which is due to the works of Terborgh. The basis of this can be found in the determination, for a particular part of equipment, of the costs arising from <<inferiority of service>>. This is an important concept in which, as is known, wear and tear is included, if we are dealing with a stationary economic system, or wear and tear and obsolescence, as a consequence of the appearance of technical progress, if we are dealing with an evolutionary economic system

As a basic concept the existence of a lower profit is considered as the inferiority of service for equipment arises relative to what is appearing in the market in a evolutionary economic system, or in relation to new equipment, as a consequence of wear and tear in a stationary economic system. From this proposal a quantitative study is initiated by obtaining the *mean cost arising from the inferiority of service*. The minimum adverse situation of equipment is the lowest value of this mean cost, relative to time. The moment that this cost becomes minimum will determine the optimum time for renewal.

Also in classical works on the subject, for example in the works of Schneider[4], treatment is given to the optimum moment for renewal when considering a stationary economic system, either for the case of equipment that <<must be renewed a finite number of times>> or for the theory of renewal <<to infinity>>. In these models, wear and tear takes on a predominant role, and as no consideration is given to the phenomenon of obsolescence its use in evolutionary economic systems is reduced. In this respect, it is significant that, in these studies, renewal should be made for identical equipment and that both the sales current and prices of the factors, including equipment are considered as constant in spite of the incorporation of a function of payments for exploitation dependent upon time. In this way, optimisation can be obtained by reducing payments, since collections are invariable as a consequence of the constancy of sales.

There can be no doubt about the interest there is in technical progress when taking a decision to renew. In fact, even assuming the continued use of certain equipment, which would mean important wear and tear, technical progress can modify the time at which it should be retired from service. If technical progress is slow, the equipment will not become obsolete in a short time, therefore there is a certain interest in acquiring equipment that is particularly resistant to wear and tear. Finally when technical progress is particularly fast, the use of the equipment is reduced over time. In this latter case, it would appear more convenient to acquire equipment that is susceptible to frequent renewal, laying aside equipment considered <<strong>> in the case that its economic viability were not to be less than equipment with slower wear and tear.

When we delve deeper into those quantitative studies considered as traditional, it will be seen that they take as their basis a certain knowledge of the economic parameters intervening in the problem of renewal. It is quite logical to think along the lines of the use of crisp numbers, when these reflect a perfect knowledge of reality.

Now then, the difficulties of obtaining exact information has lead to resorting to the concept of probability, which has revived the old problem of validity, within the field of business, of objective probabilities. To the well known obstacles arising from the need to:

a) Knowing favourable cases and possible cases; or

b) That all cases are equally probable; or

c) That a series of observations of a repeatable phenomenon are available;

is added the problem arising from the possibility of adopting, in our opinion wrongly named, <<subjective>> probabilities, that is to say, those arising from psychological axioms.

The difficulties of method arising from these considerations however have not prevented the systematic use of the calculation of probabilities in the theory of renewal of industrial equipment. In fact, the appearance of the principles of modern statistics in management has contributed certain results, on opening up new perspectives for old problems, and at the same time in certain useful cases, supplying solutions for renewal decisions.

But the lack of historical data and the fog with which the future is surrounded, makes us more and more often place more confidence in new applications of the theory of fuzzy sub-sets and their multiple variations. Within the sphere of uncertainty, it is perhaps discontinuous processes, because of their adaptation to current reality, which in latter times have captured the attention of those interested in this path.

The opening up of these new perspectives has allowed for giving current orientation to works on renewal. Certain new models have arisen in this way based on the framework of an evolutionary economic system that allows for treatment of the problems arising from the use of modern equipment. For this there are available, apart from the classical techniques, those derived from the development of multivalent logic, which as they have done in other fields represent an important advance on the formal handling of business problems. In fact over the last few years in publications relative to management, the first systematic uses of this theory have appeared, when the phenomena under study are immersed in a context of uncertainty[5].

This brief summary which, as such has no intention of being exhaustive, has as its objective the presentation of the instruments available to the executive when, having resolved the important matter of the supply of payment means, wishes to obtain from his money the maximum possible result in a specific field of action: equipment renewal. The businessman is not left alone with only his genius or intuition, but now has available valued assistance represented by operative management techniques. Nevertheless, in order for this assistance to become an ever more fruitful reality, the situations through which the normal course of events of the company pass must be analysed and revised, in order to establish the necessary bridge between theory and reality.

Terborgh's <<Adverse Minimum Method>>

The concept of adverse minimum is tied to the works of George Terborgh. His first contribution took place in 1946, with the publication of a work[6], the development and applications of which were made within the framework of the research service of the Machinery and Allied Products Institute (MAPI) which Terborgh directed.

Study of the performance of the investment object during its useful life can be found in the basis of the works carried out at MAPI[7]. In a first approximation it can be seen that equipment has a limited physical life, but this physical limitation cannot be confused with its own capacity for carrying out the activity entrusted to it. On determined occasions the useful life ends before the finalisation of its <<total>> capacity for work that arises among other things, as a consequence of the phenomenon of wear and tear.

The use of production equipment, acquired at any determined time, includes, therefore, certain physical wear and tear. As time goes by an increase in maintenance costs occurs, due to the needs of greater effort for its preservation and to the existence of an increasing number of breakdowns. But it also means less profit relative to the technically better equipment appearing on the market due to technical progress.

The introduction of the concept of time implies elaborating a model, the basis of which can be supplied by the following hypotheses:

- Acquisition of new equipment requires a payment, which we shall call M, at a given time zero.
- The <<efficiency>>, in monetary terms, of this equipment will be less than that for equipment appearing on the market the following year as a consequence of wear and tear and obsolescence. There will exist, therefore, a difference between exploitation profits obtained by using the acquired equipment and those obtained by using new equipment, which will be expressed by means of growth function $d(t)$ for continuous analysis and shall be considered equal to d_1, d_2, ..., in years 1, 2, ..., following the initial zero, in the field of discontinuity.

From an economic point of view the objective to be arrived at is to determine *the time for withdrawing equipment with which work is commenced at time zero*. If continuing with the equipment, less annual exploitation profits will be obtained compared to those which would be obtained, in the event of replacing the equipment every year, by other more modern and newer equipment; however, what would be avoided would be the payments for acquiring the equipment that would appear every year.

Therefore, from an economic point of view, two very different currents can be quantified during the passing of time, relative to the equipment:

a) Increase in payments due to inferiority of service.

b) Decrease in financial charges due to recuperation in part of the investment, through exploitation profits.

From an intuitive point of view two factors arise that should be taken into account:

- The existence of a tendency to renewal for newer machinery given the fact that it may be more technically advanced.
- Limitation to the purchase of new equipment, as a consequence of the need for a monetary payment.

If equipment is considered that will be acquired at a future time zero, at the end of each year there will be a decrease in exploitation profits, apart from the cost of the initial payment equal to M, given the fact that as from the year following start up, the equipment will provide inferior service, <<operating inferiority>>, with respect to new and more modern equipment.

On this basis George Terborgh drew up his so-called <<Theory of the Adverse Minimum>>. In it the following hypotheses is observed:

- All equipment appearing in the future will have an adverse minimum.
- The inferiority of service of equipment increases in time.

In the initial study by Terborgh, these two hypotheses are made even more restrictive, being reduced to the following:

- All future equipment has the same adverse minimum as current equipment.
- Inferiority of service increases in a linear manner over time.

Relative to this latter hypothesis, it can be seen that, in the diagrams for twelve categories of equipment submitted by Terborgh, the cost of repairs increases approximately in a linear fashion in relation to time. For obsolescence, practice demonstrates that, although technical progress takes place <<in leaps and bounds>>, in the long term and considering a mean tendency, the incidence in the monetary currents of this, could be represented by means of an exponential. But in the medium term, and as an approximation, the mean tendency is admissible as the simplest.

In a general case, adversity can be formalised by means of a model in the hypothesis of continuity, which can be described by means of the following formula:

$$P = M + \sum_{j=1}^{t} d_j(1 + i)^{-j}$$

This expression brings to light the fact that acquisition of an investment object at moment zero, required the payment of a monetary mass at that time equal to M. At the end of a year, this equipment will be the reason for <<less profit>> d_1, difference between the profit produced by new equipment (challenger) and that which will be given by equipment in operation for a year (defender). Also existing will be certain d_2, d_3, ..., d_t; that is to say, certain lower profits referring to years 2, 3, ..., t.

If we wish to arrive at an annual mean <<adversity>>, which we will call x, for all the period of time from 0 to t, from the so-called annuities method, we can write:

$$x\left[\frac{1}{1+i} + \cdots + \frac{1}{(1+i)^t}\right] = M + \sum_{j=1}^{t} d_j(1+i)^{-j}$$

where:

$$x(t) = \frac{M + \sum_{j=1}^{t} \frac{d_j}{(1+i)^j}}{\sum_{j=1}^{t} \frac{1}{(1+i)^j}}$$

But as:

$$\sum_{j=1}^{t} \frac{1}{(1+i)^j} = \frac{\frac{1}{1+i} - \frac{1}{(1+i)^{t+1}}}{1 - \frac{1}{1+i}} = \frac{(1+i)^t - 1}{(1+i)^t \cdot i}$$

this will be:

$$x(t) = \left[M + \sum_{j=1}^{t} \frac{d_j}{(1+i)^j}\right] \frac{(1+i)^t \cdot i}{(1+i)^t - 1}$$

The adverse minimum will be that which, in relation to time, makes the mean adversity less, expressed by $x(t)$, that is to say:

$$m = \text{Min } x(t)$$

When adopting the restrictive hypothesis, according to which inferiority of service increases proportionally as time goes by, in the discontinuous field, the following would be complied with:

$$d_t = d \cdot (t - 1)$$

where it is assumed that the inferiority of service is nil during the first year.

It is customary to call coefficient d the <<gradient>> of the inferiority of service[8].

As has already been pointed out, from a general aspect, the mean adversity is given by:

$$x(t) = \frac{M + \sum_{j=1}^{t} d_j(1+i)^{-j}}{\sum_{i=1}^{t} (1+i)^{-j}}$$

but when consideration is given to the inferiority of service, as $d_j = d \cdot (j-1)$ we will arrive at:

$$x(t) = \frac{M + d \cdot \sum_{j=2}^{t} (j-1)(1+i)^{-j}}{\sum_{i=1}^{t} (1+i)^{-j}}$$

With the object of arriving at an easier acceptance of this method by company executives, certain simplifying calculation procedures have been drawn up. Among these we can mention the one that substitutes the inferiority of service, considered as a constant annuity, by the arithmetical mean, which grows in a linear fashion from 0 to $d(t - 1)$ (on assuming that inferiority of service is nil throughout the first year).

In order to arrive at the mean adversity, the mean capital charges are added to this figure, formed by constant depreciation plus certain mean interest charges <<on the initial investment>>.

This can be expressed as follows:

$$x(t) = \frac{d \cdot (t-1)}{2} + \frac{M}{t} + \frac{M \cdot i}{2}$$

Mean of the inferiority of service. — Capital charges

As can be seen, although the interest rate is introduced relative to the monetary mass required for acquiring the investment object, this is not calculated for the amount of money that measures the inferiority of service.

Optimisation will occur when the <<adversity>> measured by x is minimum in relation to time.

By resorting, perhaps in an abusive fashion, to differential calculation, we will arrive at the fact that the necessary condition requires:

$$\frac{dx}{dt} = 0$$

But the derivative of x with regard to t is

$$\frac{dx}{dt} = \frac{d}{2} - \frac{M}{t^2} = 0$$

therefore:

$$\boxed{t = \sqrt{\frac{2M}{d}}}$$

In this way we arrive at a simple expression which in practice allows us to obtain the optimum time for renewal.

As we have seen, the treatment we carried out starts off from the hypothesis that an economic system exists in which the economic parameters can be estimated in terms of certainty. Transition to uncertainty does not entail any excessive complications if a basic knowledge of fuzzy mathematics exists.

Below we are going to carry out an adaptation of this scheme in order to be able to use it in a context of uncertainty. For this we will resort initially to the expression of uncertain estimates by means of confidence triplets.

The <<Fuzzy Adverse Minimum Method>> (FAMM)

Let us move on then to the field of uncertainty[9]. For this we are going to assume that the inferiority of service cannot be estimated in crisp terms. The experts express their opinion by means of confidence triplets. In this way we will arrive at the fact that the d_j will be substituted by:

$$(d_j^{(1)}, d_j^{(2)}, d_j^{(3)})$$

If the interest rate is also estimated by means of triplets $(i_j^{(1)}, i_j^{(2)}, i_j^{(3)})$, total adversity, if payment for acquisition of the equipment is known with certainty as equal to M, will be:

$$P = M(+)(d_1^{(1)}, d_1^{(2)}, d_1^{(3)})(\cdot)\left(\frac{1}{1+i_1^{(3)}}, \frac{1}{1+i_1^{(2)}}, \frac{1}{1+i_1^{(1)}}\right)(+)(d_2^{(1)}, d_2^{(2)}, d_2^{(3)})(\cdot)$$

$$(\cdot)\left(\frac{1}{1+i_1^{(3)}}\cdot\frac{1}{1+i_2^{(3)}}, \frac{1}{1+i_1^{(2)}}\cdot\frac{1}{1+i_2^{(2)}}, \frac{1}{1+i_1^{(1)}}\cdot\frac{1}{1+i_2^{(1)}}\right)(+)\cdots(+)(d_t^{(1)}, d_t^{(2)}, d_t^{(3)})(\cdot)$$

$$(\cdot)\left(\frac{1}{1+i_1^{(3)}}\cdots\frac{1}{1+i_t^{(3)}}, \frac{1}{1+i_1^{(2)}}\cdots\frac{1}{1+i_t^{(2)}}, \frac{1}{1+i_1^{(1)}}\cdots\frac{1}{1+i_t^{(1)}}\right)$$

We can write:

$$P = M(+)\left(\frac{d_1^{(1)}}{1+i_1^{(3)}}, \frac{d_1^{(2)}}{1+i_1^{(2)}}, \frac{d_1^{(3)}}{1+i_1^{(1)}}\right)(+)$$

$$(+)\left(\frac{d_2^{(1)}}{(1+i_1^{(3)})\cdot(1+i_2^{(3)})}, \frac{d_2^{(2)}}{(1+i_1^{(2)})\cdot(1+i_2^{(2)})}, \frac{d_2^{(3)}}{(1+i_1^{(1)})\cdot(1+i_2^{(1)})}\right)(+)\cdots(+)$$

$$(+)\cdots(+)\left(\frac{d_t^{(1)}}{(1+i_1^{(3)}\cdot(1+i_2^{(3)})\cdots(1+i_t^{(3)})}, \frac{d_t^{(2)}}{(1+i_1^{(2)})\cdot(1+i_2^{(2)})\cdots(1+i_t^{(2)})},\right.$$

$$\left.\frac{d_t^{(3)}}{(1+i_1^{(1)})\cdot(1+i_2^{(1)})\cdots(1+i_t^{(1)})}\right)$$

Total adversity remains, then, also expressed by means of a confidence triplet.

Under these assumptions, mean adversity, which under certainty we designated by x will now be:

$$P = (x^{(1)}, x^{(2)}, x^{(3)})(\cdot)\left(\frac{1}{1+i_i^{(3)}}, \frac{1}{1+i_i^{(2)}}, \frac{1}{1+i_i^{(1)}}\right)(+)(x^{(1)}, x^{(2)}, x^{(3)})(\cdot)$$

$$(\cdot)\left(\frac{1}{(1+i_1^{(3)})\cdot(1+i_2^{(3)})}, \frac{1}{(1+i_1^{(2)})\cdot(1+i_2^{(2)})}, \frac{1}{(1+i_1^{(1)})\cdot(1+i_2^{(1)})}\right)(+)\cdots(+)$$

$$(+)\cdots(+)(x^{(1}, x^{(2)}, x^{(3)})(\cdot)\left(\frac{1}{(1+i_1^{(3)})\cdot(1+i_2^{(3)})\cdots(1+i_t^{(3)})},\right.$$

$$\left.\frac{1}{(1+i_1^{(2)})\cdot(1+i_2^{(2)})\cdots(1+i_t^{(2)})}, \frac{1}{(1+i_1^{(1)})\cdot(1+i_2^{(1)})\cdots(1+i_t^{(1)})}\right)$$

We now have total adversity expressed by means of these two triplet additions. We are now going to attempt to arrive at, the mean adversity $(x^{(1)}, x^{(2)}, x^{(3)})$. For this we will resort to an example.

Let us suppose that an expert has estimated the following valuations:

t	M	$(d_j^{(1)}, d_j^{(2)}, d_j^{(3)})$	$(i_j^{(1)}, i_j^{(2)}, i_j^{(3)})$
0	70	—	—
1	—	(20, 25, 40)	(0.10, 0.12, 0.13)
2	—	(40, 50, 80)	(0.08, 0.10, 0.12)
3	—	(60, 75, 120)	(0.06, 0.07, 0.10)
4	—	(80, 100, 160)	(0.06, 0.07, 0.10)
…	…	…	…

On this occasion we have started out from the assumption that the inferiority of service already takes place as from the first year. Suppression of this circumstance does not cause any complementary problem whatsoever.

It will be seen from the previous estimates:

$$(d_t^{(1)}, d_t^{(2)}, d_t^{(3)}) = (d_1^{(1)}, d_1^{(2)}, d_1^{(3)}) \,(\cdot)\, t = (20, 25, 40) \,(\cdot)\, t \quad ; \quad t = 1, 2, \ldots$$

In this case this will be:

$$P = 70\,(+)\left(\frac{20}{1.13}, \frac{25}{1.12}, \frac{40}{1.10}\right)(+)\left(\frac{40}{1.13\cdot 1.12}, \frac{50}{1.12\cdot 1.10}, \frac{80}{1.10\cdot 1.08}\right)(+)$$

$$(+)\left(\frac{60}{1.13\cdot 1.12\cdot 1.10}, \frac{75}{1.12\cdot 1.10\cdot 1.07}, \frac{120}{1.10\cdot 1.08\cdot 1.06}\right)(+)$$

$$(+)\left(\frac{80}{1.13\cdot 1.12\cdot 1.10\cdot 1.10}, \frac{100}{1.12\cdot 1.10\cdot 1.07\cdot 1.07}, \frac{160}{1.10\cdot 1.08\cdot 1.06\cdot 1.06}\right)(+)\cdots$$

And this can also be written as:

$$P = (x^{(1)}, x^{(2)}, x^{(3)})\,(\cdot)\left(\frac{1}{1.13}, \frac{1}{1.12}, \frac{1}{1.10}\right)(+)\,(x^{(1)}, x^{(2)}, x^{(3)})\,(\cdot)$$

$$(\cdot)\left(\frac{1}{1.13\cdot 1.12}, \frac{1}{1.12\cdot 1.10}, \frac{1}{1.10\cdot 1.08}\right)(+)\,(x^{(1)}, x^{(2)}, x^{(3)})\,(\cdot)$$

$$(\cdot)\left(\frac{1}{1.13\cdot 1.12\cdot 1.10}, \frac{1}{1.12\cdot 1.10\cdot 1.07}, \frac{1}{1.10\cdot 1.08\cdot 1.06}\right)(+)\cdots =$$

$$= (x^{(1)}, x^{(2)}, x^{(3)})\,(\cdot)\left[\left(\frac{1}{1.13}, \frac{1}{1.12}, \frac{1}{1.10}\right)(+)\left(\frac{1}{1.13\cdot 1.12}, \frac{1}{1.12\cdot 1.10}, \frac{1}{1.10\cdot 1.08}\right)(+)\right.$$

$$\left.(+)\left(\frac{1}{1.13\cdot 1.12\cdot 1.10}, \frac{1}{1.12\cdot 1.10\cdot 1.07}, \frac{1}{1.10\cdot 1.08\cdot 1.06}\right)(+)\cdots\right]$$

As is well known, in the field of certainty, in order to obtain the mean adversity, it is sufficient to equal the two equations and clear the x, in this way arriving at a function of time, which later on it is necessary to minimise. On passing over to the sphere of uncertainty, we are going to maintain the general lines of this process by attempting to adapt them to the needs of their particular arithmetic.

The first question that arises refers to the type of quotient to be used. Taking into account the fact that the problem that has arisen consists in the resolution of an equation, the Minkowski quotient will have to be used. Therefore we arrive at:

$$(x^{(1)}, x^{(2)}, x^{(3)}) = \Big[70\,(+)\left(\frac{20}{1.13}, \frac{25}{1.12}, \frac{40}{1.10}\right)(+)\left(\frac{40}{1.13\cdot 1.12}, \frac{50}{1.12\cdot 1.10}, \frac{80}{1.10\cdot 1.08}\right)(+)$$

$$(+)\left(\frac{60}{1.13\cdot 1.12\cdot 1.10}, \frac{75}{1.12\cdot 1.10\cdot 1.07}, \frac{120}{1.10\cdot 1.08\cdot 1.06}\right)(+)\cdots\Big]$$

$$(\dot{m})\Big[\left(\frac{1}{1.13}, \frac{1}{1.12}, \frac{1}{1.10}\right)(+)\left(\frac{1}{1.13\cdot 1.12}, \frac{1}{1.12\cdot 1.10}, \frac{1}{1.10\cdot 1.08}\right)(+)$$

$$(+)\left(\frac{1}{1.13\cdot 1.12\cdot 1.10}, \frac{1}{1.12\cdot 1.10\cdot 1.07}, \frac{1}{1.10\cdot 1.08\cdot 1.06}\right)(+)\cdots\Big]$$

Let us not forget that the objective sought consists in finding the moment in time that minimises this expression. For this we will follow a sequential process in which, starting out from the mean adversity corresponding to the first period, we will continue to find successive mean adversities for each of the following periods, by adding to the adversities of a moment j - 1 the adversity corresponding to the following moment j. And so on until we arrive at the desired minimum. We will find successively:

For the first year:

$$(x^{(1)}, x^{(2)}, x^{(3)})^{(1)} = \left[70\,(+)\left(\frac{20}{1.13}, \frac{25}{1.12}, \frac{40}{1.10}\right)\right](\dot{m})$$

$$(\dot{m})\left(\frac{1}{1.13}, \frac{1}{1.12}, \frac{1}{1.10}\right)$$

For year 2:

$$(x^{(1)}, x^{(2)}, x^{(3)})^{(2)} = \Big[70\,(+)\left(\frac{20}{1.13}, \frac{25}{1.12}, \frac{40}{1.10}\right)(+)$$

$$(+)\left(\frac{40}{1.13\cdot 1.12}, \frac{50}{1.12\cdot 1.10}, \frac{80}{1.10\cdot 1.08}\right)\Big](\dot{m})$$

$$(\dot{m})\Big[\left(\frac{1}{1.13}, \frac{1}{1.12}, \frac{1}{1.10}\right)(+)\left(\frac{1}{1.13\cdot 1.12}, \frac{1}{1.12\cdot 1.10}, \frac{1}{1.10\cdot 1.08}\right)\Big]$$

For year 3:

$$(x^{(1)}, x^{(2)}, x^{(3)})^{(3)} = \Big[70\,(+)\left(\frac{20}{1.13}, \frac{25}{1.12}, \frac{40}{1.10}\right)(+)$$

$$(+)\left(\frac{40}{1.13\cdot 1.12}, \frac{50}{1.12\cdot 1.10}, \frac{80}{1.10\cdot 1.08}\right)(+)$$

$$(+)\left(\frac{60}{1.13\cdot 1.12\cdot 1.10}, \frac{75}{1.12\cdot 1.10\cdot 1.07}, \frac{120}{1.10\cdot 1.08\cdot 1.06}\right)\Big](\dot{m})$$

$$\left(\dot{\overline{m}}\right)\left[\left(\frac{1}{1.13}, \frac{1}{1.12}, \frac{1}{1.10}\right)(+)\left(\frac{1}{1.13\cdot 1.12}, \frac{1}{1.12\cdot 1.10}, \frac{1}{1.10\cdot 1.08}\right)(+)\right.$$

$$\left.(+)\left(\frac{1}{1.13\cdot 1.12\cdot 1.10}, \frac{1}{1.12\cdot 1.10\cdot 1.07}, \frac{1}{1.10\cdot 1.08\cdot 1.06}\right)\right]$$

And so on until we arrive at the desired minimum.

We now proceed to compare $(x^{(1)}, x^{(2)}, x^{(3)})^{(1)}$, $(x^{(1)}, x^{(2)}, x^{(3)})^{(2)}$, $(x^{(1)}, x^{(2)}, x^{(3)})^{(3)}$, ..., taking the lowest triplet, which will determine the optimum time for renewal.

Having made the necessary calculations we arrive at:

$$\begin{aligned}(x^{(1)}, x^{(2)}, x^{(3)})^{(1)} &= (87.699, 92.321, 106.363)\left(\dot{\overline{m}}\right)(0.884, 0.892, 0.909) = \\ &= (99.207, 103.498, 117.011)\end{aligned}$$

$$\begin{aligned}(x^{(1)}, x^{(2)}, x^{(3)})^{(2)} &= (119.304, 132.905, 173.703)\left(\dot{\overline{m}}\right)(1.673, 1.702, 1.750) = \\ &= (71.311, 78.087, 99.258)\end{aligned}$$

$$\begin{aligned}(x^{(1)}, x^{(2)}, x^{(3)})^{(3)} &= (162.402, 189.799, 268.995)\left(\dot{\overline{m}}\right)(2.391, 2.460, 2.544) = \\ &= (67.922, 77.154, 105.737)\end{aligned}$$

From comparison of the triplet corresponding to year 2 and year 3, it will be seen that no total dominion exists. When this happens it will be necessary to use the already known criteria, in order to arrive at an order among the same, that is to say, between $(x^{(1)}, x^{(2)}, x^{(3)})^{(2)}$ y $(x^{(1)}, x^{(2)}, x^{(3)})^{(3)}$.

On making the entropy fall, we arrive at:

$$\overline{|(x^{(1)}, x^{(2)}, x^{(3)})^{(2)}|} = \frac{71.311 + 2 \times 78.087 + 99.258}{4} = 81.685$$

$$\overline{|(x^{(1)}, x^{(2)}, x^{(3)})^{(3)}|} = \frac{67.922 + 2 \times 77.154 + 105.737}{4} = 81.991$$

Therefore one can conclude that under this criterion it will be:

$$(x^{(1)}, x^{(2)}, x^{(3)})^{(3)} > (x^{(1)}, x^{(2)}, x^{(3)})^{(2)}$$

Therefore, the optimum will be found at moment 2, or in any case, will be found between moment 2 and moment 3.

But we will continue in order to verify the result at the following moment 4. This will be:

$$\begin{aligned}(x^{(1)}, x^{(2)}, x^{(3)})^{(4)} &= (214.642, 260.695, 388.859)\left(\dot{\overline{m}}\right)(3.044, 3.168, 3.293) = \\ &= (70.513, 82.290, 118.086)\end{aligned}$$

Now clearly superior to $(x^{(1)}, x^{(2)}, x^{(3)})^{(3)}$. We can now halt the process.

We now compare the result arrived at with the one which we could find in the event of using a simplifying procedure consisting in substituting the inferiority of service by an arithmetical mean that increases in a linear fashion, and consider as capital charges a constant depreciation and mean interest on the initial investment.

$$(x^{(1)}, x^{(2)}, x^{(3)}) = \frac{(20, 25, 40)(\cdot)\,t}{2}(+)\frac{70}{t}(+)\frac{70\,(\cdot)\,(0.07, 0.08, 0.11)}{2}{}_{;1\,0}$$

$$\frac{d[(x^{(1)}, x^{(2)}, x^{(3)})]}{dt} = \frac{(20, 25, 40)}{2} - \frac{70}{t^2} = 0$$

$$t = \left[\frac{2 \times 70}{(20, 25, 40)}\right]^{1/2}$$

This expression coincides with the expression arrived at under certainty:

$$t = \sqrt{\frac{2M}{d}}$$

Thus as we are situated in uncertainty we arrive at:

$$(t^{(1)}, t^{(2)}, t^{(3)})^{\mathrm{opt}} = \left[\frac{2 \times 70}{(20, 25, 40)}\right]^{1/2} = \left[\frac{140}{(20, 25, 40)}\right]^{1/2} = \sqrt{(3.5, 5.6, 7)}$$

Now, as is known, if $(d^{(1)}, d^{(2)}, d^{(3)})$ is a triplet in R^+, we can write:

$$\sqrt{d^{(1)}, d^{(2)}, d^{(3)}} = \left(\sqrt{d^{(1)}}, \sqrt{d^{(2)}}, \sqrt{d^{(3)}}\right)$$

therefore:

$$(t^{(1)}, t^{(2)}, t^{(3)})^{\mathrm{opt}} = (1.870, 2.366, 2.645)$$

If we make the entropy fall then the optimum is:

$$\overline{(t^{(1)}, t^{(2)}, t^{(3)})^{(\mathrm{opt})}} = \frac{1.870 + 2.366 \times 2 + 2.645}{4} = 2.311$$

Which implies that the withdrawal from service must be done between the second and the third year. Therefore, this result coincides with the result arrived at with the model we described.

This model constitutes just one more example of the many possibilities that exist for adapting classical management techniques to the requirements of our day and age. In this case we have used confidence triplets as the carrying element for the experts' opinions, but the scheme will continue to be valid even if we were to use some other form of uncertain number, as we shall see in the following section.

The incorporation of fuzzy triangular numbers

Let us suppose that both the inferiority of service for each period, and the interest rates are expressed by means of FTN taken from the same triplets as the previous model, completed by the same valuations of the membership function between the extremes and the maximum presumption.

If these FTN are presented in the form of α-cuts, we arrive at:

t	M	$\underset{\sim}{d}_j$	$\underset{\sim}{i}_j$
0	70	—	—
1	—	[20 + 5α, 40 – 15α]	[0.10 + 0.02α, 0.13 –0.01α]
2	—	[40 + 10α, 80 –30α]	[0.08 + 0.02α, 0.12 –0.02α]
3	—	[60 + 15α, 120 – 45α]	[0.06 + 0.01α, 0.10 –0.03α]
4	—	[80 + 20α, 160 –60α]	[0.06 + 0.01α, 0.10 –0.03α]
...	...	...	...

In this way the mean adversities for each of the periods will be:

For year 1:

$$\underset{\sim}{x}_1 = \left(70\,(+)\,[20 + 5\alpha, 40 - 15\alpha]\,(\cdot)\left[\frac{1}{1.13 - 0.01\alpha}, \frac{1}{1.10 + 0.02\alpha}\right]\right)\left(\dot{\overline{m}}\right)$$

$$\left(\dot{\overline{m}}\right)\left[\frac{1}{1.13 - 0.01\alpha}, \frac{1}{1.10 + 0,02\alpha}\right] =$$

$$= \left[70 + \frac{20 + 5\alpha}{1.13 - 0.01\alpha}, 70 + \frac{40 - 15\alpha}{1.10 + 0.02\alpha}\right]\left(\dot{\overline{m}}\right)\left[\frac{1}{1.13 - 0.01\alpha}, \frac{1}{1.10 + 0.02\alpha}\right] =$$

$$= [70(1.13 - 0.01\alpha) + (20 + 5\alpha), 70(1.10 + 0.02\alpha) + (40 - 15\alpha)] =$$

$$= [79.10 - 0.7\alpha + 20 + 5\alpha, 77 + 1.4\alpha + 40 - 15\alpha] =$$

$$= [99.10 + 4.3\alpha, 117 - 13.6\alpha]$$

The result obtained, exceptionally in the first period, is a FTN.

For year 2:

$$\underset{\sim}{x}_2 = \left[70 + \frac{20+5\alpha}{1.13-0.01\alpha} + \frac{40+10\alpha}{(1.13-0.01\alpha)(1.12-0.02\alpha)},\right.$$
$$\left. 70 + \frac{40-15\alpha}{1.10+0.02\alpha} + \frac{80-30\alpha}{(1.10+0.02\alpha)(1.08+0.02\alpha)}\right] (\dot{m})$$
$$(\dot{m}) \left[\frac{1}{1.13-0.01\alpha} + \frac{1}{(1.13-0.01\alpha)(1.12-0.02\alpha)},\right.$$
$$\left. \frac{1}{1.10+0.02\alpha} + \frac{1}{(1.10+0.02\alpha)(1.08+0.02\alpha)}\right] =$$
$$= [A_*^{(2)}, A^{*(2)}] (\dot{m}) [B_*^{(2)}, B^{*(2)}]$$

It will be seen that $\underset{\sim}{x}_2$ is a fuzzy number, although not triangular.

For year 3:

$$\underset{\sim}{x}_3 = \left[70 + \frac{20+5\alpha}{1.13-0.01\alpha} + \frac{40+10\alpha}{(1.13-0.01\alpha)(1.12-0.02\alpha)} +\right.$$
$$+ \frac{60+15\alpha}{(1.13-0.01\alpha)(1.12-0.02\alpha)(1.10-0.03\alpha)}, 70 + \frac{40-15\alpha}{1.10+0.02\alpha} +$$
$$\left. + \frac{80-30\alpha}{(1.10+0.02\alpha)(1.08+0.02\alpha)} + \frac{120-45\alpha}{(1.10+0.02\alpha)(1.08+0.02\alpha)(1.06+0.01\alpha)}\right] (\dot{m})$$
$$(\dot{m}) \left[\frac{1}{1.13-0.01\alpha} + \frac{1}{(1.13-0.01\alpha)(1.12-0.02\alpha)} +\right.$$
$$+ \frac{1}{(1.13-0.01\alpha)(1.12-0.02\alpha)(1.10-0.03\alpha)}, \frac{1}{1.10+0.02\alpha} +$$
$$\left. + \frac{1}{(1.10+0.02\alpha)(1.08+0.02\alpha)} + \frac{1}{(1.10+0.02\alpha)(1.08+0.02\alpha)(1.06+0.01\alpha)}\right] =$$
$$= [A_*^{(3)}, A^{*(3)}] (\dot{m}) [B_*^{(3)}, B^{*(3)}]$$

And so on successively we will arrive at $\underset{\sim}{x}_4$, $\underset{\sim}{x}_5$, ..., $\underset{\sim}{x}_t$.

We are now going to express these results, by using the hendecadarian system. We will arrive at:

Mean adversity at the end of year 1

α	$99.10 + 4.3\alpha$	$117 - 13.6\alpha$
0	99.10	117
.1	99.53	115.64
.2	99.96	114.28
.3	100.39	112.92
.4	100.82	111.56
.5	101.25	110.20
.6	101.68	108.84
.7	102.11	107.48
.8	102.54	106.12
.9	102.97	104.76
1	103.4	

Mean adversity at the end of year 2

α	$\left[70 + \frac{20+5\alpha}{1.13-0.01\alpha} + \frac{40+10\alpha}{(1.13-0.01\alpha)(1.12-0.02\alpha)}\right]$ (:) $\left[\frac{1}{1.13-0.01\alpha} + \frac{1}{(1.13-0.01\alpha)(1.12-0.02\alpha)}\right]$	$\left[70 + \frac{40-15\alpha}{1.10+0.02\alpha} + \frac{80-30\alpha}{(1.10+0.02\alpha)(1.08+0.02\alpha)}\right]$ (:) $\left[\frac{1}{1.10+0.02\alpha} + \frac{1}{(1.10+0.02\alpha)(1.08+0.02\alpha)}\right]$
0	(70 + 17.699 + 31.605):(0.884 + 0.790)	(70 + 36.363 + 67.340):(0.909 + 0.841)
.1	(70 + 18.157 + 32.482):(0.885 + 0.792)	(70 + 34.936 + 64.577):(0.907 + 0.838)
.2	(70 + 18.617 + 33.386):(0.886 + 0.794)	(70 + 33.514 + 61.834):(0.905 + 0.835)
.3	(70 + 19.077 + 34.249):(0.887 + 0.796)	(70 + 32.097 + 59.111):(0.904 + 0.832)
.4	(70 + 19.538 + 35.140):(0.888 + 0.798)	(70 + 30.685 + 56.407):(0.902 + 0.829)
.5	(70 + 20 + 36.036):(0.888 + 0.800)	(70 + 29.279 + 53.723):(0.900 + 0.826)
.6	(70 + 20.462 + 36.936):(0.889 + 0.802)	(70 + 27.877 + 51.058):(0.899 + 0.823)
.7	(70 + 20.926 + 37.841):(0.890 + 0.805)	(70 + 26.481 + 48.411):(0.897 + 0.820)
.8	(70 + 21.390 + 38.750):(0.891 + 0.807)	(70 + 25.089 + 45.783):(0.896 + 0.817)
.9	(70 + 21.855 + 39.665):(0.892 + 0.809)	(70 + 23.703 + 43.174):(0.894 + 0.814)
1	(70 + 22.321 + 40.584):(0.892 + 0.811)	

α	$A_*^{(2)}/B_*^{(2)}$	$A^{*(2)}/B^{*(2)}$
0	71.268	99.258
.1	71.937	97.142
.2	72.620	95.027
.3	73.277	92.861
.4	73.948	90.752
.5	74.665	88.645
.6	75.338	86.489
.7	75.968	84.386
.8	76.643	82.237
.9	77.319	80.138
1	78.041	

Mean adversity at the end of year 3

α	$A_*^{(3)}/B_*^{(3)}$	$A^{*(3)}/B^{*(3)}$
0	67.893	105.737
.1	68.801	102.883
.2	69.728	100.033
.3	70.623	97.109
.4	71.539	94.268
.5	72.487	91.394
.6	73.408	88.524
.7	74.302	85.659
.8	75.228	82.798
.9	76.158	79.942
1	77.122	

And continuing on in the same way in order to obtain the mean adversity for years 4, 5, ...

The results we have obtained for the first three years (and the same would occur for the following), just brings to light the fact that in the levels of presumption $\alpha = 0$ and $\alpha = 1$ the figures arrived at coincide with those obtained by using confidence triplets (as it could not be any other way), except for small differences due to rounding off the decimal points. The difference existing in one or the other of these uncertain schemes, arises from the *information*, since in one case (triplets) this is limited to three values, while in the other (fuzzy triangular numbers) there exist in theory an infinite number of values resulting from the possible α-cuts. In our example, on using the hendecadarian system, we have been content with one step $\alpha = 0.1$ and for this reason the result has remained expressed by means of 11 intervals.

Once the successive mean adversities have been arrived at, the process continues, just as was done in the case of triplets, by establishing the comparison of the fuzzy numbers (obviously non-triangular), by choosing the one considered as the lowest. In this case what is required is an ordering from lower to higher.

There are several procedures for doing this, which we have stated on other occasions, which allow for the establishment of an order among uncertain numbers. Taking into account the objective we are seeking, we are now going to use one of these, very simple to be sure, even though we know that this may warrant certain criticism. It may be practically useful in this and many other cases: what it consists of is making the entropy fall, by obtaining the mean point of the intervals at each level and later adding the numbers arrived at. In this way we arrive at:

α	Mean adversity		
	Year 1	Year 2	Year 3
0	108.050	85.2630	86.8150
.1	107.580	84.5395	85.8420
.2	107.120	83.8235	84.8805
.3	106.655	83.0690	83.8660
.4	106.190	82.3500	82.9035
.5	105.725	81.6550	81.9405
.6	105.260	80.9135	80.9660
.7	104.795	80.1170	79.9805
.8	104.330	79.4400	79.0130
.9	103.865	78.7285	78.0500
1	103.400	78.0410	77.1220
Total	1162.97	898.0000	901.3790

In this table it will be seen that there is a reduction in the mean adversity on passing from the first to the second year and this later increases slightly on passing from the second to the third year. From this is can be concluded, once again, that the minimum mean adversity will take place between the second and third periods.

If the study is done level by level it will be seen that, for the lower levels the increase in the mean adversity is between years 2 and 3, but as we move on to higher levels the difference is reduced until level $\alpha = 0.7$ and following, where the adversity of the third year is lower than that for the second year. The logical reading of this fact once again brings to light the different solutions that appear in the field of uncertainty for one and the same phenomenon. For those executives situated in a position of moderation or extreme moderation and for this reason choose the levels with the greatest uncertainty (the lowest), the decision to renew should take place sooner, once the second year has commenced and prior to the third. But on the contrary those who assume the risk of choosing levels of high presumption or maximum presumption, will foresee renewal at a later date, that is once the third year has commenced.

On this subject we have attempted to bring to light the wide possibilities of fuzzy arithmetic for adapting classical models to the reality of our day and age. The use of triplets and fuzzy triangular numbers is only dependent on the modeller who believes they are more suitable to the problem under study. In each situation and specific time the use of one or another uncertain parameter will be convenient. The flexibility and adaptability of these schemes gives us then new added incentives to those that because of their novelty could be assigned.

The re-launching of techniques for handling the problem of equipment renewal constitutes in our opinion, a need for supplying companies with valid instruments in order for them to be able to defend and improve their respective positions in the future.

References

1 E. Schneider: *Economia politica y economia de la empresa,* Sagitario, Barcelona, 1968, page 397.

2 C. Abraham and A. Thomas: *Microéconomie: décisions optimales dans l'entreprise et dans la nation* Dunod, Paris, 1996, pages 325-327.

3 J. Desrousseaux: *L'évolution économique el le comportement industriel,* Dunod, Paris, 1965, page 176.

4 E. Schneider: *Teoría de la inversión,* Ateneo, Buenos Aires, 1956, pages 87 and following.

5 A. Kaufmann and J. Gil Aluja: *Introducción de la teoría de los subconjuntos borrosos a la gestión de las empresas,* Milladoiro, Santiago de Compostela, 1986.

6 G. Terborgh: *Dynamic Equipment Policy,* McGraw-Hill, New York, 1946.

7 G. Terborgh: *Business Investments Policy,* Machinery and Allied Products Institute, Washington, 1958. G. Terborgh: *Business Investment Management* Machinery and Allied Products Institute, Washington, 1967.

8 In literal terms, <<gradient>> is the variation of the barometric pressure between two points.

9 See in this respect J. Gil Aluja: <<FAMM>> (Fuzzy Adverse Minimum Method>>, presentation made at the European Congress of AEDEM and published in the proceedings of the same, Minsk, 20-23 September, 1993.

* A mean rate may be considered, or any other since it has no influence on the optimisation process.

16 Equipment performance

The life of industrial equipment

Industrial equipment is submitted throughout its life to an inevitable succession of incidents that affect performance and modify operating capacity. In order to maintain its entrusted activity under the best possible conditions, certain actions of maintenance and repairs take place which, in a some way, modify the conditions under which it carries out its work. Normally, knowledge of the elements forming the equipment and experience accumulated by those responsible for its operation, allows in some way for the establishment of certain estimates on the situation in which the equipment is at any given moment. When there is a need to formalise the <<experience>> through quantified information, it is customary to resort to gathering data on equipment performance by drawing up statistics which later will be used in many diverse ways, as this will be incorporated into the models that will be constructed, the nature of which will vary substantially depending on the objectives sought.

But present day reality, we repeat once again, characterised by a very rapid evolution of events, the greater part of the time does not allow taking into consideration any data from the past, even if immediate, in order to be able to establish a sufficiently valid forecast for future data. To stop and think about this reality inevitably means reconsidering the hypotheses on which the models are based, if it is desired that they allow for greater understanding of the operation of the equipment and that they should constitute a valid path for taking decisions with regard to the future.

When a certain level of information is available, it is possible to draw up models that in other circumstances if the required data was lacking could not be adapted to reality. And, in this sense, the existence of a preference in the construction of those formal schemes based on crisp and <<sure>> data obviously exists. However, these can be totally inoperative when reality does not allow us to obtain the same. With the object of bringing to light the possibility of modelling in the field of equipment renewal, we are going to reproduce an interesting classification of models, even if this were to be drawn up with a certain generalised nature, which we feel is valid for our particular effects.

Following a reverse order of preference five types of models can be considered[1] relative to the different levels of information:

1. Non-determinist model with unknown states.
2. Non-determinist model with known states but with non-valuable events (we know the possible states, but we do not know how to give them a subjective scale of values).
3. Non-determinist model with known states that are valuable but not measurable, (we know the possible states, we can give to each event of each state a valuation, taking into account that this value is not a measurement).
4. Non-determinist model with known states and with measurable events (we know the possible states and know how to affect a probability to their occurrence).
5. Determinist model (we know the states and hypothesise that the event of a specific state is known).

Preference for the models of the last level is obvious, but realities push us towards the use of those relative to the lowest levels. In this sense, on of the more important difficulties for the use of models based on certainty or probability, arises because of the need to have available certain data that the great majority of companies cannot obtain. Thus it would appear to be difficult for having sufficient data available for obtaining the following parameters considered as basic for traditional studies:

— Probability of survival. Probability that equipment can continue to carry out its production function after a determined year.

— Conditional probability of breakdown. Probability that the equipment, assuming that it had reached a certain year with no difficulty, <<were to die>> during the time from this particular year to the following.

Both concepts assume that the equipment suffers <<probable wear and tear>>. We will now move on to develop these basic elements of traditional studies[2] in certain detail.

The so-called <<law of survival>> of equipment, which will give rise to a survival curve, can be obtained if there are a sufficient number of identical cases available, of which the useful life is known. For this it will be sufficient to determine at each moment t which equipment is still in service. If we assume a continuous function, we arrive at a curve $n(t)$ that will show the <<live>> equipment for each period, which expressed in relative terms, gives us the <<survival curve>>. We will now take a look at a numerical example.

If we have sufficient identical cases available, for example 5000, for which we know the useful life, we can arrive at the following table:

Equipment duration			Equipment breaking down in each interval	Amount of equipment with breakdowns (accumulated)	Amount of equipment in service	Relative mortality
Intervals in years	Type of duration t	Duration t'	$n(t-1)-n(t)$		$n(t)$	$p(t)=[n(t-1)-n(t)]/n(0)$
—	0	—	—	0	5000	—
[0, 1]	1	0.5	10	10	4990	0.002
[1, 2]	2	1.5	30	40	4960	0.006
[2, 3]	3	2.5	80	120	4880	0.016
[3, 4]	4	3.5	180	300	4700	0.036
[4, 5]	5	4.5	320	620	4380	0.064
[5, 6]	6	5.5	400	1020	3980	0.080
[6, 7]	7	6.5	500	1520	3480	0.100
[7, 8]	8	7.5	700	2220	2780	0.140
[8, 9]	9	8.5	1200	3420	1580	0.240
[9, 10]	10	9.5	900	4320	680	0.180
[10, 11]	11	10.5	500	4820	180	0.100
[11, 12]	12	11.5	120	4940	60	0.024
[12, 13]	13	12.5	40	4980	20	0.008
[13, 14]	14	13.5	20	5000	0	0.004
[14, ∞)	—	—	0	5000	0	0

The amount of equipment in service at any given moment t can be seen in the corresponding column designated by $n(t)$. If we assume a continuous function we arrive at curve $n(t)$, which expressed relative to the amount of initial equipment (making a change of scale on the ordinate axis) gives rise to the <<survival curve>>:

$$\frac{n(t)}{n(0)} = v(t)$$

that represents, approximately, the probability of equipment survival at any given time.

Therefore the probability that any given equipment were to have a useful life greater than 5 years will be: 4380/5000 = 0.876, that is to say 87.6 per cent.

The survival curve, as well as the one that expresses the amount of equipment in service at any given time, with a change in ordinates, can be represented as follows (figure 16.1):

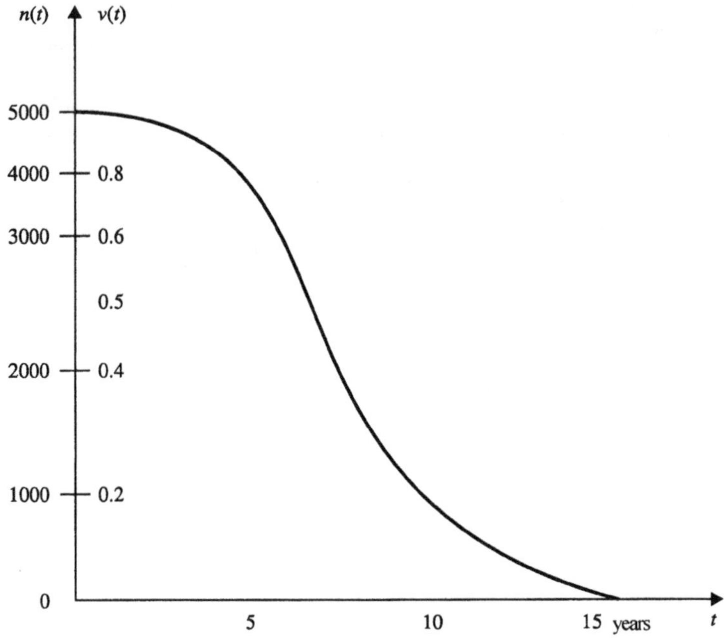

Figure 16.1.

The <<probability that any given equipment were to suffer a breakdown>>, between any given time and the next, that is to say the relative mortality, will be seen in the last column of the table, defined by:

$$p(t) = \frac{n(t-1) - n(t)}{n(0)} = \frac{n(t-1)}{n(0)} - \frac{n(t)}{n(0)} = v(t-1) - v(t)$$

Therefore the probability of breakdown between years 5 and 6 will be:

$$p(6) = \frac{4380 - 3980}{5000} = 0.08$$

as can be seen from the previous table.

What is known as the <<conditional breakdown probability>> of certain equipment at a precise moment t, $p_c(t)$, is the probability that this particular equipment, having reached t - 1 in good condition, were to suffer a breakdown between t - 1 and t.

The probability of breakdown of equipment between t - 1 and t is also defined $p(t)$ as the product of the probability that this equipment may have survived until t - 1, that is to say $v(t - 1)$ by the conditional breakdown probability $p_c(t)$. Therefore:

$$p(t) = v(t-1) \cdot p_c(t)$$

where it happens that:

$$p_c(t) = \frac{p(t)}{v(t-1)}$$

But as:

$$p(t) = \frac{n(t-1) - n(t)}{n(0)}$$

$$v(t-1) = \frac{n(t-1)}{n(0)}$$

it will be:

$$p_c(t) = \frac{n(t-1) - n(t)}{n(0)} \cdot \frac{n(0)}{n(t-1)} = \frac{n(t-1) - n(t)}{n(t-1)} = 1 - \frac{n(t)}{n(t-1)}$$

If for example we calculate $p_c(10)$ we arrive at:

$$p_c(10) = 1 - \frac{n(10)}{n(9)} = 1 - \frac{680}{1580} \cong 1 - 0{,}43 = 0{,}57$$

that indicates that 57 per cent of the equipment in service at the end of year 9 will suffer a breakdown between period 9 and 10.

It is logical to think that every type of equipment will have a corresponding survival curve and that if we know the form this takes, we can determine which type of equipment this represents.

All of this particular treatment is suitable for transfer to the sphere of uncertainty by means of the theory of fuzzy sub-sets[3]. For this it is assumed that the performance of the investment object during its useful life, can be expressed by a fuzzy number, that is to say, a normal and convex fuzzy subset $\underset{\sim}{A}$ in which the membership function $\mu_{\underset{\sim}{A}}(t)$ takes on values in [0, 1], as

$\underset{\sim}{A} \subset R^+$. If it is also established that $\mu_{\underset{\sim}{A}}(0) = 0$ that is, that the membership function is nil at moment zero, the fuzzy number $\underset{\sim}{A}$ can be considered as the *basis* of a <<law of possibility>> and, in this case, the possibility of a breakdown at moment t is represented by:

$$\pi(t) = \mu_{\underset{\sim}{A}}(t)$$

We now designate by θ the first date on which $\pi(t) = 1$ ($\underset{\sim}{A}$ is not inevitably unimodal and can have the form of a plateau). Therefore we will consider a law representing the possibility that certain equipment were to suffer a breakdown in the interval $[0, t] \subset R^+$. For this law the following would be written:

$$\varphi(t) = \bigvee_{t=0}^{t} \pi(t) \quad , \quad t \leqslant \theta$$
$$= 1 \quad , \quad t \geqslant \theta$$

To put it in another way, $\varphi(t) = \pi(t)$ until dateθ and $\varphi(t) = 1$ for $t = \theta$ and later dates.

Yet another law can be defined that represents the <<possibility that certain equipment is still in operation at moment t>>:

$$k(t) = 1 - \varphi(t)$$

Function $k(t)$ will have, in this theory, the same role as the survival curve in the probabilistic theory and will also be called <<survival curve>>.

These three laws can be represented graphically as follows (figure 16.2):

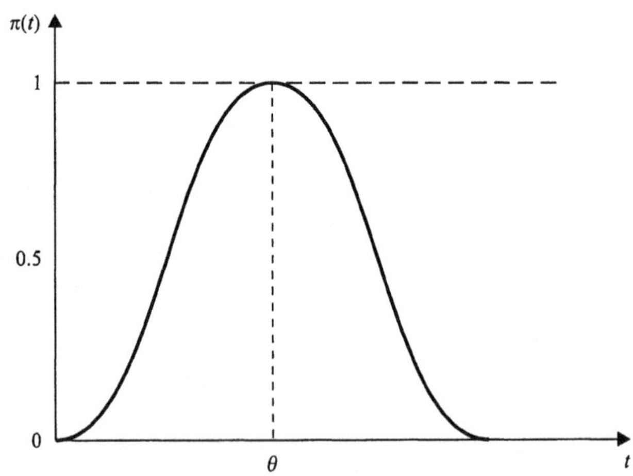

Figure 16.2.

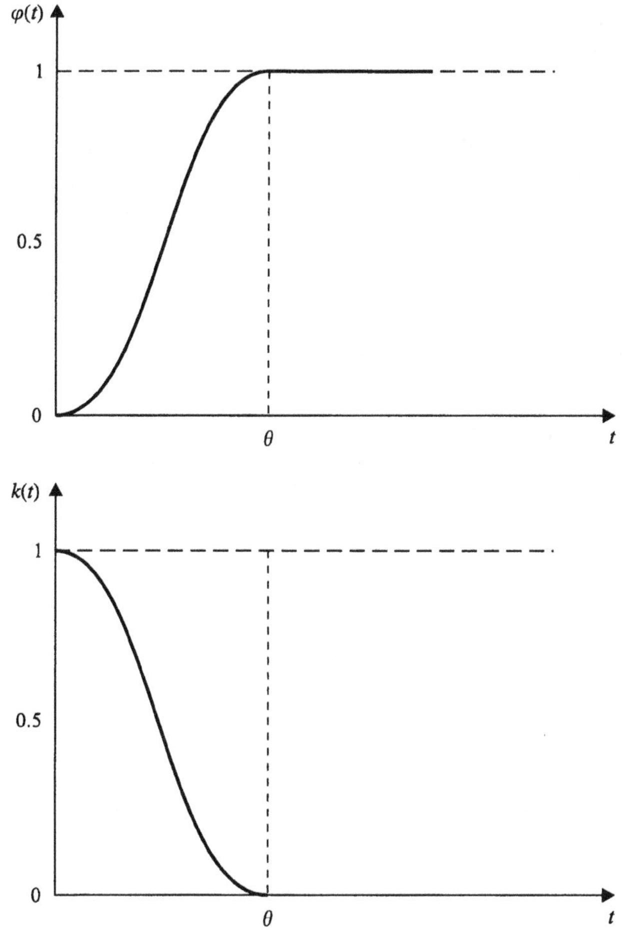

Figure 16.2. (cont.)

For the effects of simplification it is assumed that, in order to arrive at the law of possibility of breakdown, we start out from a fuzzy triangular number in R^+ such as $\underset{\sim}{A} = (0, b, 2b)$ the graphic representation of which would be that of figure 16.3.

This can also be expressed by means of the following equations:

$$\begin{aligned} \pi(t) &= \frac{t}{b} \quad , \quad 0 \leqslant t \leqslant b \\ &= 2 - \frac{t}{b} \quad , \quad b \leqslant t \leqslant 2b \\ &= 0 \quad , \quad t \geqslant 2b \end{aligned}$$

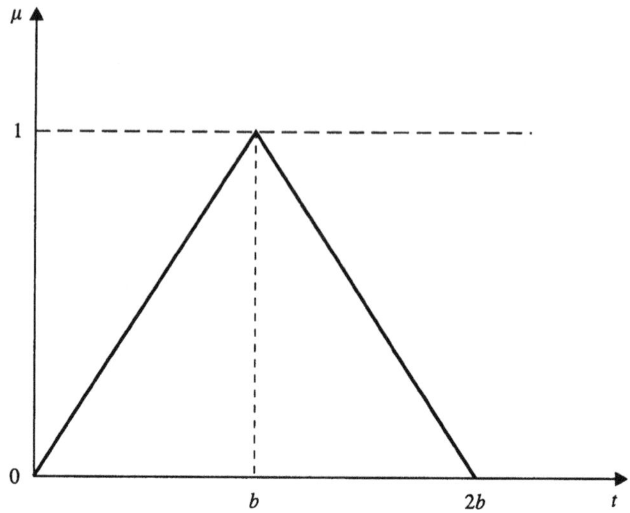

Figure 16.3.

The law of possibility of breakdown would be expressed by:

$$\varphi(t) = \frac{t}{b} \quad , \quad 0 \leqslant t \leqslant b$$
$$= 1 \quad , \quad t \geqslant b$$

And the law of survival:

$$k(t) = 1 - \frac{t}{b} \quad , \quad 0 \leqslant t \leqslant b$$
$$= 0 \quad , \quad t \geqslant b$$

As is known the fuzzy number $\underset{\sim}{A}$, which up to now we have expressed in the ternary form and in the form of three equations, can also take the form of confidence intervals associated to levels of presumption. Therefore, the previous fuzzy triangular number can be represented by:

$$[b\alpha, 2b - b\alpha]$$

it also being easy to arrive at the law of survival in the form of confidence intervals linked to levels of presumption, that is in the form of α-cuts.

Now let us look for the <<conditional possibility>> that the equipment having reached moment a were still to be in operation at a period t after a, that is to say that it were not to suffer a breakdown in the interval $[0, a + t]$. This could be written as:

$$k(t + a) = k(a) \cdot k_a(t)$$

where $k(t + a)$ is not a law of possibility since $k(a) < 1$ if $a > 0$. From the previous formula it can be deduced that:

$$k_a(t) = \frac{k(t + a)}{k(a)}$$

This formula corresponds to the law of survival of the equipment used to date a without breakdown and that it can attain moment $a + t$ without a breakdown. If we stretch t to 0, $k(a)$ can be taken as a type of breakdown.

Before continuing let us look at an example in the field of caution. For this we will assume the base function of the law of possibility of breakdown $\pi(t)$ is known:

	0	1	2	3	4	5	6	7	8	9
$\underset{\sim}{\pi}(t)$:	0	0.1	0.2	0.5	0.8	1	0.7	0.6	0.1	0

We have as the law of possibility of breakdown $\varphi(t)$:

	0	1	2	3	4	5	6
$\varphi(t)$:	0	0.1	0.2	0.5	0.8	1	1

and by means of complementation of the unit, $k(t) = 1 - \varphi(t)$:

	0	1	2	3	4	5	6
$k(t)$:	1	0.9	0.8	0.5	0.2	0	0

The conditional possibility of survival is $k_a(t) = k(t + a)/k(a)$, and if it is desired to know the possibility that the equipment, having arrived alive at moment $a = 2$, continues to survive $t = 0, 1, 2, 3, \ldots$ years, it will be:

$$k_2(t) = \frac{k(t + 2)}{k(2)}$$

In our example we will have:

$$k_2(0) = \frac{k(0+2)}{k(2)} = \frac{0.8}{0.8} = 1$$

$$k_2(1) = \frac{k(1+2)}{k(2)} = \frac{0.5}{0.8} = 0.625$$

and so on successively, we arrive at:

	0	1	2	3	4
$k_a(t)$: $a = 2$	1	0.625	0.25	0	0

In this section we have developed some of the basic elements concerning the life of equipment, by seeking the greatest possible parallelism between traditional studies and those relative to the field of uncertainty. We are going to leave this aspect now in order to tackle a concept of special interest which is equipment <<consumption>>.

The problem of consumption in the renewal of equipment

The use of certain mathematical models for the handling of problems of renewal and maintenance in the probabilistic environment, starts out from the case that survival curves are known from statistics on a sufficient number of breakdowns relative to known and operating equipment.

We start out then with the existence of n(0) equipment commencing activity at period $t = 0$. If $v(t)$ is the survival function of identical equipment, that will remain in service at moment t, if there has been no substitution:

$$n(t) = n(0) \cdot v(t)$$

since in the previous section $v(t)$ was defined as the quotient between $n(t)$ and $n(0)$.

We are now going to substitute this equipment taking into account that the amount of equipment in service follows a law $f(t)$ called <<law of utilisation>>[4]. Figure 16.4 shows a utilisation curve which, it is obvious, depends closely on the type of equipment used.

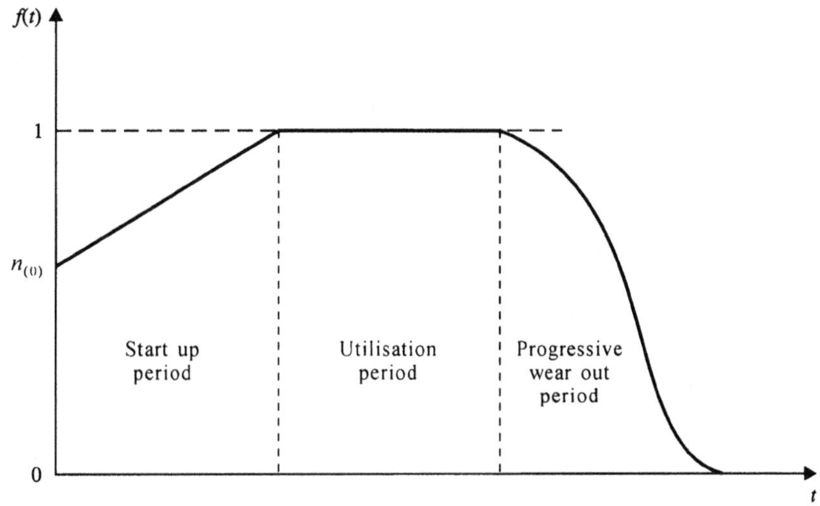

Figure 16.4.

If $r(u)$ is the amount of equipment substituted up to moment u, the amount:

$$p(u) = r(u) - r(u-1), \quad u = 1, 2, 3, 4, \ldots$$

shows the amount of equipment substituted in the interval u - 1 to u. Function $p(u)$ is called a <<supply rate>>.

The amount of equipment surviving at a future moment t proceeding from this supply will be:

$$p(u) \cdot v(t-u) = [r(u) - r(u-1)] \cdot v(t-u)$$

The amount of equipment in service at moment t is equal to the sum of the same surviving for each interval of time taken between $u = 1$ and $u = t$ obviously increased with the survivors from the $n(0)$ equipment put into service at the commencement and which has obeyed the same survival law. Therefore, the amount of equipment at moment t will be:

$$f(t) = n(0) \cdot v(t) + \sum_{u=1}^{t} p(u) \cdot v(t-u)$$

The formula allows for easy calculation of $p(t)$ by successive steps. Obviously we have:

$$f(0) = n(0)$$

We now calculate successively $p(1)$, $p(2)$, $p(3)$, ... when $v(t)$ and $f(t)$ are known:

$$f(1) = n(0) \cdot v(1) + p(1) \cdot v(0)$$
$$= n(0) \cdot v(1) + p(1) \qquad \text{since } v(0) = 1$$

where:

$$p(1) = f(1) - n(0) \cdot v(1)$$

We continue:

$$f(2) = n(0) \cdot v(2) + p(1) \cdot v(1) + p(2)$$

where:

$$p(2) = f(2) - n(0) \cdot v(2) - p(1) \cdot v(1)$$

$$f(3) = n(0) \cdot v(3) + p(1) \cdot v(2) + p(2) \cdot v(1) + p(3)$$

therefore:

$$p(3) = f(3) - n(0) \cdot v(3) - p(1) \cdot v(2) - p(2) \cdot v(1)$$

....

$$f(t) = n(0) \cdot v(t) + \sum_{u=1}^{t-1} p(u) \cdot v(t-u) + p(t)$$

$$u, t = 1, 2, 3, \ldots$$

$$p(t) = f(t) - n(0) \cdot v(t) - \sum_{u=1}^{t-1} p(u) \cdot v(t-u)$$

We will now look at a numerical example[5].

The column below is now considered and data from columns (1), (2) and (3) are taken. Since $n(0) = 0$ we arrive at:

$$p(t) = f(t) - \sum_{u=1}^{t-1} p(u) \cdot v(t-u)$$

t	$v(t)$	$f(t)/100$	
0	1	0	← we do $n(0) = 0$
1	.98	.17	
2	.91	.33	
3	.81	.50	
4	.69	.67	
5	.56	.83	
6	.43	1	← commencement of ceiling
7	.32	1	
8	.23	1	
9	.15	1	
10	.10	1	
11	.06	1	
12	.04	1	
13	.02	1	
14	.01	1	
15		1	
16		1	
17		1	
18		1	
19		1	
20		1	

t	$v(t)$	$f(t)/100$	
21		1	
22		1	
23		1	
24		1	
25		1	
26		1	
27		1	
28		1	
29		1	← commencement of extinction period
30		.97	
31		.95	
32		.92	
33		.87	
34		.83	
35		.77	
36		.72	
37		.66	
38		.60	
39		.54	
40		.48	

We arrive at successively by taking $p(t)/100$ in place of $p(t)$ and $f(t)/100$ in place of $f(t)$:

$$p(1) = f(1) = 0.170$$

$$p(2) = f(2) - p(1)v(1) = 0.330 - (0.170)(0.98) = 0.163$$

$$p(3) = f(3) - p(1)v(2) - p(2)v(1)$$
$$= 0.500 - (0.170)(0.91) - (0.163)(0.98) = 0.185$$

$$p(4) = f(4) - p(1)v(3) - p(2)v(2) - p(3)v(1) = 0.202$$

$$p(5) = f(5) - p(1)v(4) - p(2)v(3) - p(3)v(2) - p(4)v(1) = 0.214$$

....

At the same time in order to arrive at $r(t)$, always taking $r(t)/100$ we will do successively as:

$$r(u) = p(u) + r(u-1)$$
$$r(1) = p(1) + r(0) = 0.170$$
$$r(2) = p(2) + r(1) = 0.163 + 0.170 = 0.333$$
$$r(3) = p(3) + r(2) = 0.185 + 0.333 = 0.518$$
$$r(4) = p(4) + r(3) = 0.202 + 0.518 = 0.720$$
$$r(5) = p(5) + r(4) = 0.214 + 0.720 = 0.934$$

....

The law of considered survival $v(t)$, has the same form as the one we already know and which we reproduce below (figure 16.5):

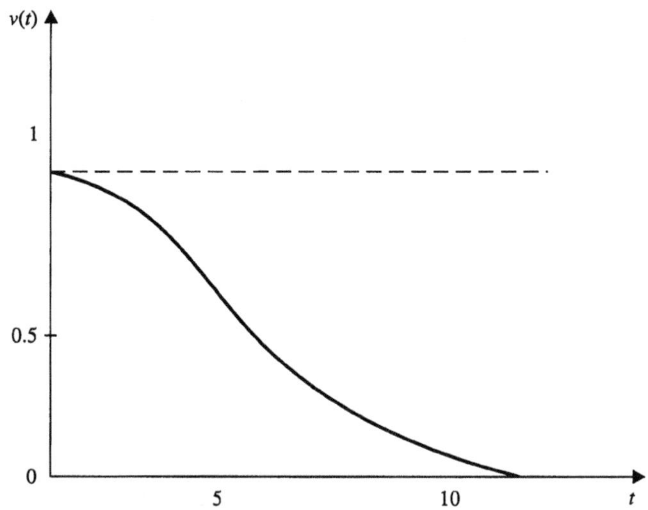

Figure 16.5.

The above exposition has allowed us to know $p(t)$ assuming that $v(t)$ and $f(t)$ are given, but we can also determine $v(t)$ by knowing $f(t)$ and $p(t)$. This is an indirect manner of studying $v(t)$. In this case we would be operating by recurrence.

The panorama we have just stated, relative to the probabilistic sphere is not intended to be complete but just a brief sample of a traditional approach of the so-called problem of equipment consumption. We will now pass on to present one of the many models that are suitable for study in uncertainty.

For this let us suppose, that certain new equipment forms a part of a set of equipment and is replaced at the time of a breakdown. We are now going to see what is the possibility $P_m(t)$ that there will be m substitutions of this type of equipment (for other identical new equipment) in the interval of time of 0 to t.

We will designate <<consumption>>, the amount of equipment incorporated during this interval of time.

The possibility of nil consumption, that is no substitution ($m = 0$) is obviously:

$$P_0(t) = k(t)$$

In order to calculate $P_1(t)$ it will be necessary to admit that there is one and only one breakdown in interval 0 to u and none in interval u to t. In this case then the following can be written for all u moments under consideration:

$$P_1(t) = \bigvee_{u=0}^{t} (\pi(u) \wedge \mathrm{k}(t-u))$$

That is to say, that for each value of u, we compare the possibility of breakdown between 0 and u with the possibility of survival (of the equipment incorporated in u) from u to t (that is, in the period t - u) and as a measure of caution the lowest is chosen. And so on for all values in u (and obviously in t - u). Of the lowest, the largest is chosen. This is no more than the addition of the maxmin convolution.

In this general manner, there is a relation that gives us $P_m(t)$ based on $\pi(t)$ and $P_{m-1}(t)$. In fact, in order for there to be a consumption of m equipment for 0 to t it is sufficient for there were to have been 1 substitution between 0 and u and then m - 1 substitutions in the time between u to t (or also the contrary m -1 and then 1). Therefore we arrive at:

$$P_m(t) = \bigvee_{u=0}^{t} (\pi(u) \wedge P_{m-1}(t-u)) = \bigvee_{u=0}^{t} (\pi(t-u) \wedge P_{m-1}(u))$$

In this way we arrive at the recurrence formulae:

$$P_1(t) = \bigvee_{u=0}^{t} (\pi(u) \wedge k(t-u))$$

$$P_2(t) = \bigvee_{u=0}^{t} (\pi(u) \wedge P_1(t-u))$$

$$P_3(t) = \bigvee_{u=0}^{t} (\pi(u) \wedge P_2(t-u))$$

....

$$P_m(t) = \bigvee_{u=0}^{t} (\pi(u) \wedge P_{m-1}(t-u))$$

Let us look at an example. If we take, as we did in the previous section for $p(t)$ and $k(t)$:

	0	1	2	3	4	5	6	7	8	⩾9
$\underset{\sim}{\pi}(t)$:	0	0.1	0.2	0.5	0.8	1	0.7	0.6	0.1	0

	0	1	2	3	4	5	6
$\underset{\sim}{k}(t)$:	1	0.9	0.8	0.5	0.2	0	0

this will be:

	0	1	2	3	4	5	6	7	8	⩾9	
$\underset{\sim}{P}_1(t)$:	0	0.1	0.2	0.5	0.8	1	0.7	0.6	0.1	0	(+)

	0	1	2	3	4	5	
(+)	1	0.9	0.8	0.5	0.2	0	=

	0	1	2	3	4	5	6	7	8	9	10	11	12	⩾13
=	0	0.1	0.2	0.5	0.8	1	0.9	0.8	0.7	0.6	0.5	0.2	0.1	0

	0	1	2	3	4	5	6	7	8	9	
$\underset{\sim}{P}_2(t)$:	0	0.1	0.2	0.5	0.8	1	0.7	0.6	0.1	0	(+)

	0	1	2	3	4	5	6	7	8	9	10	11	12	⩾13	
(+)	0	0.1	0.2	0.5	0.8	1	0.9	0.8	0.7	0.6	0.5	0.2	0.1	0	=

	0	1	2	3	4	5	6	7	8	9
=	0	0.1	0.1	0.2	0.2	0.2	0.5	0.5	0.8	0.8

10	11	12	13	14	15	16	17	18	19	20	⩾21
1	0.9	0.8	0.7	0.7	0.6	0.6	0.5	0.2	0.1	0.1	0

and so on successively.

It is also possible to develop another example, by now taking functions $\underset{\sim}{\pi}(t)$ and $\underset{\sim}{k}(t)$ in R^+, based on the fuzzy triangular number $\underset{\sim}{A} = (0, b, 2b)$.

The linearity of the addition operator makes arriving at $P_1(t)$, $P_2(t)$, ..., given the possibility of using the ternary form for the calculations.

We now arrive at, successively:

$$P_1(t) = (0, 0, b) (+) (0, b, 2b) = (0, b, 3b)$$

$$P_2(t) = (0, b, 3b) (+) (0, b, 2b) = (0, 2b, 5b)$$

$$P_3(t) = (0, 2b, 5b) (+) (0, b, 2b) = (0, 3b, 7b)$$

....

$$P_m(t) = (0, (m-1)b, (2m-1)b) (+) (0, b, 2b) = (0, mb, (2m+1)b)$$

These results can be expressed graphically as follows (figure 16.6):

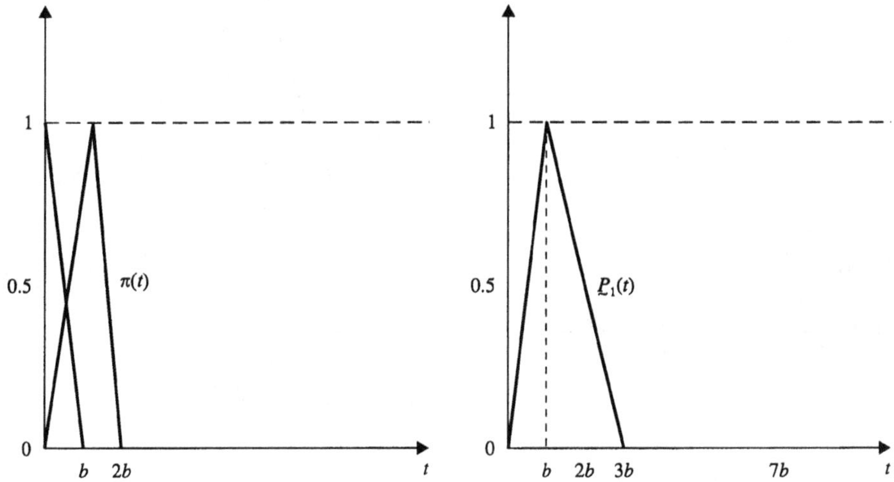

Obtaining $\underset{\sim}{P}_1(t)$

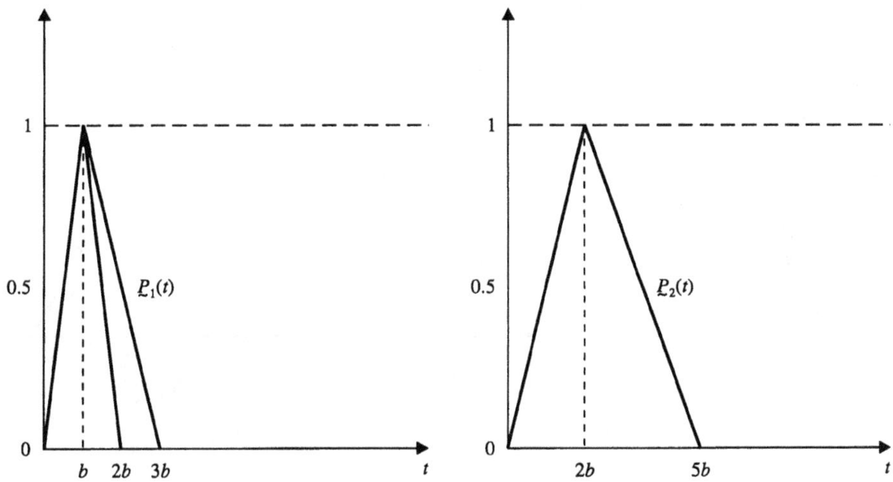

Obtaining $\underset{\sim}{P}_2(t)$

Figure 16.6.

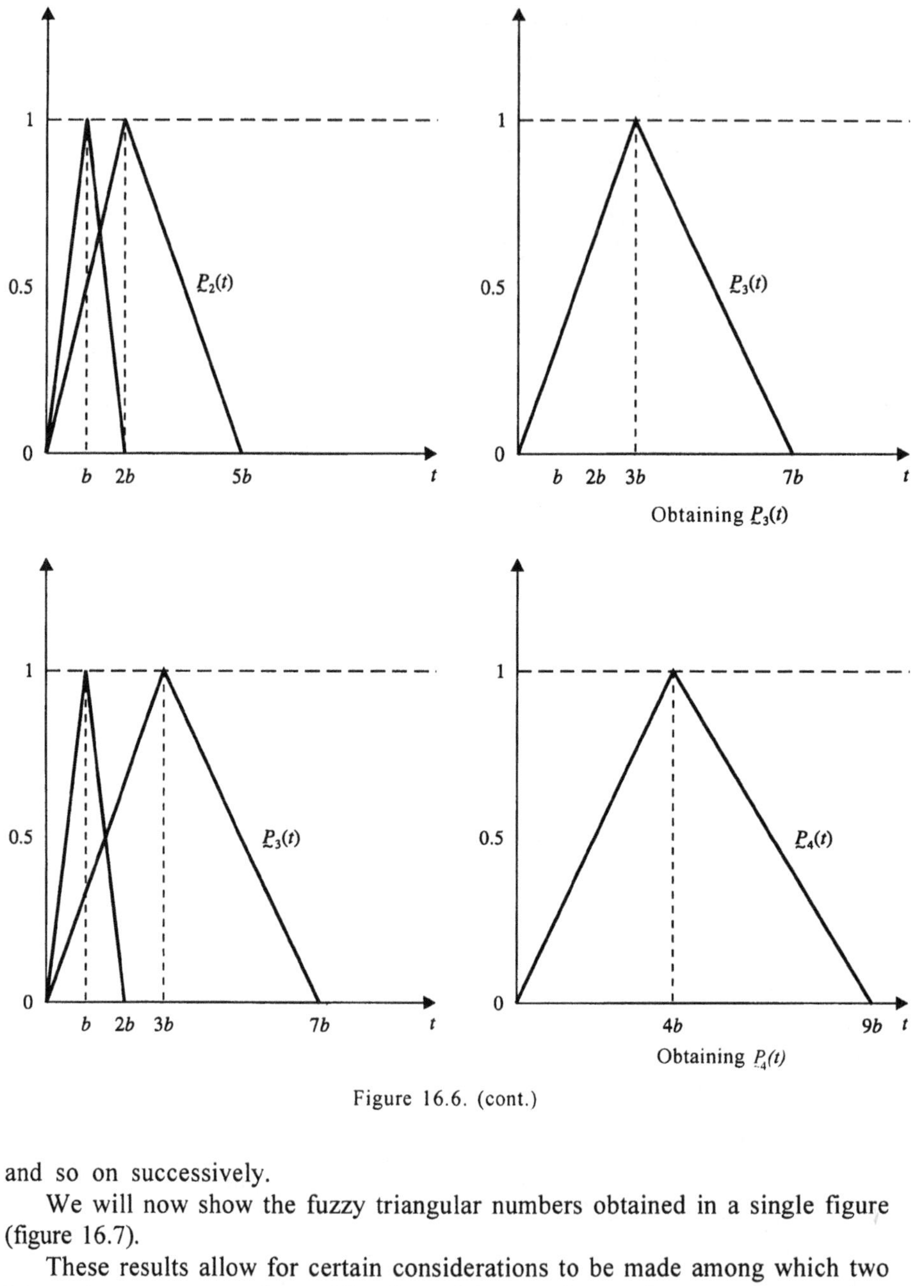

Figure 16.6. (cont.)

and so on successively.

We will now show the fuzzy triangular numbers obtained in a single figure (figure 16.7).

These results allow for certain considerations to be made among which two interesting aspects stand out. The first of these refers to the greater uncertainty as we pass from P_1, to P_4, that is to say when the amount of equipment consumed increases. In fact, at one and the same level of presumption, the correspon-

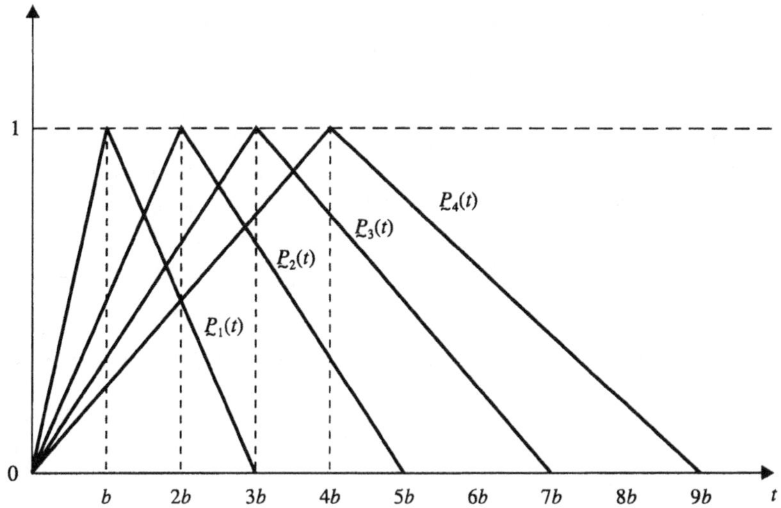

Figure 16.7.

ding interval is wider. The second confirms something that is intuitively perceptible and that is that for one and the same moment in time the possibility of consuming more equipment is less or equal to the case of consuming less. Let us clarify this statement with the help of the following graph that reproduces the significant parts of the previous figure (figure 16.8).

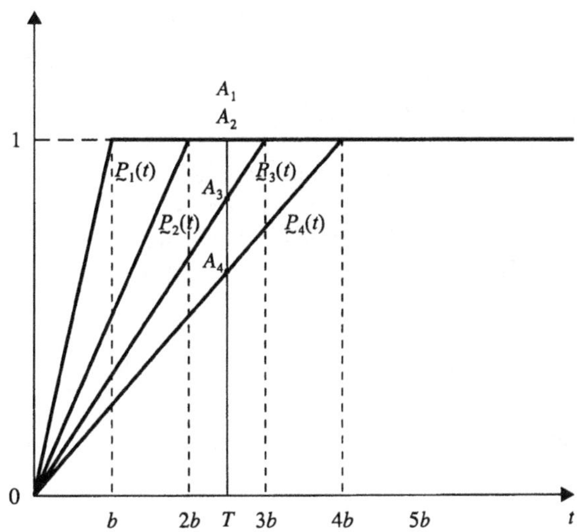

Figure 16.8.

Only the left hand side has been considered of the triangles representing the economic-technical sense of the process, lengthening it, as is logical, in level 1 to infinity. Therefore, if we consider a moment such as T, it will be seen that the possibility of consuming 1 and 2 sets of equipment is total (membership function equal to 1 as this is the value of the segments TA_1 and TA_2). Segment TA_3 is less, representing the possibility of consuming 3 sets of equipment in the period of time OT and segment TA_4 is even smaller, reflecting the possibility of consuming 4 sets of equipment in the same time OT.

We will leave off here and move on to another no less interesting problem.

Hypothesis of the existence of an equipment network

In production processes, equipment does not always carry out its entrusted tasks independently, but forming a network, the links of which are quite often of a very different nature.

The case of the existence of a network of equipment laid out differently, relative to the other, brings up a problem of formalisation, when making an attempt to describe operations. Literature relative to this subject normally separates the same into two kinds of structure: in <<series>> or <<parallel>>. Let us see now how we can treat this in a context of uncertainty. For this we will start off from the assumption according to which the possibility of retiring equipment from service is defined by a fuzzy number $\underset{\sim}{A}$. We will take a look at a simple case in which two sets of equipment E_1 and E_2 are available in such a way that the system only functions when both are in operation simultaneously and breakdown of one causes the system to cease to function. This equipment therefore, operates <<in series>>.

An alternative situation is the one where only if both sets of equipment breakdown the system ceases to function. In this case this equipment is operating <<in parallel>>.

We will now study how we can express the two types of operation that are most likely to be found in the production activity of a company, by means of the laws of possibility of breakdown based on fuzzy triangular numbers.

The first will be represented in the ternary form by:

$$\underset{\sim}{A}_1 = (0,\, b,\, 2b)$$

The second, also expressed in the ternary form, could be the following:

$$\underset{\sim}{A}_2 = \left(\frac{b}{3},\, \frac{2}{3}b,\, 3b\right)$$

If these two fuzzy numbers are expressed in the form of α-cuts we will have:

$$A_1(\alpha) = [b\alpha,\ 2b - b\alpha]$$

$$A_2(\alpha) = \left[\frac{b}{3}\alpha + \frac{b}{3},\ 3b - \frac{7b}{3}\alpha\right]$$

In order to make this exposition more accessible, we are going to give a value to parameter b, for example $b = 3$. In this case we will arrive at:

$$A_1(\alpha) = [3\alpha,\ 6 - 3\alpha]$$
$$A_2(\alpha) = [\alpha + 1,\ 9 - 7\alpha]$$

The following figure representation allows us to establish the points of intersection, between the two triangles (FTN) (figure 16.9):

$$(\alpha = 0.5,\ t = 3/2), \quad (\alpha = 0.75,\ t = 15/4)$$

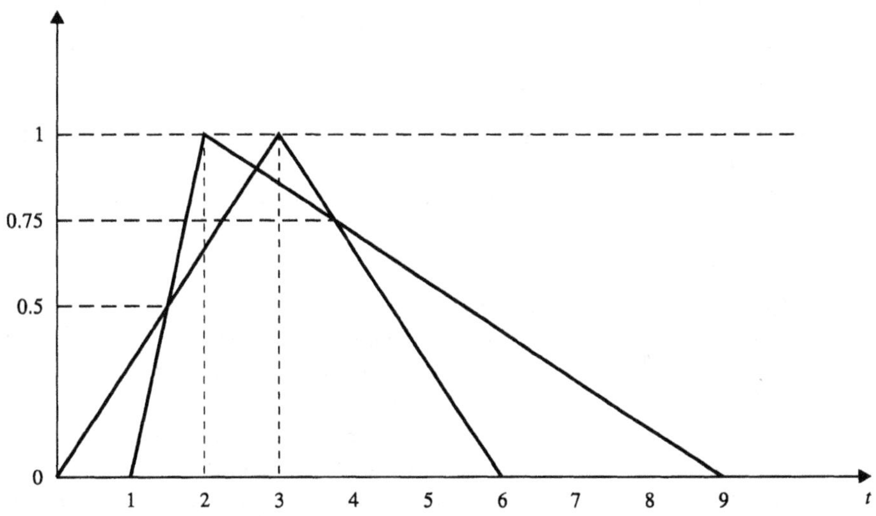

Figure 16.9.

Let us now express these FTN by means of the values of their membership functions only taking into consideration the whole numbers (obviously positive). Since:

$$\begin{aligned} \pi_1(t) &= 0 &&, \quad t = 0 \\ &= \frac{t}{3} &&, \quad 0 \leqslant t \leqslant 3 \\ &= 2 - \frac{t}{3}, && \quad 3 \leqslant t \leqslant 6 \\ &= 0 &&, \quad t \geqslant 6 \end{aligned}$$

and:

$$\begin{aligned} \pi_2(t) &= 0 \quad , \quad 0 \leqslant t \leqslant 1 \\ &= t-1 \quad , \quad 1 \leqslant t \leqslant 2 \\ &= \frac{9-t}{7} \quad , \quad 2 \leqslant t \leqslant 9 \\ &= 0 \quad , \quad t \geqslant 9 \end{aligned}$$

we will arrive at:

	0	1	2	3	4	5	6	7	8	9
$\underset{\sim}{A}_1$:	0	1/3	2/3	1	2/3	1/3	0	0	0	0

	0	1	2	3	4	5	6	7	8	9
$\underset{\sim}{A}_2$:	0	0	1	6/7	5/7	4/7	3/7	2/7	1/7	0

We are now ready and have the necessary means for delving into the heart of the problem.

In fact, if the values of the membership function of the fuzzy numbers that is the basis of the law of breakdown constitute at each moment the <<degree of possibility>> that this may occur, it is evident that:

a) In the <<in series>> operation the possibility that the system will function will be determined by the *greater* of the possibilities of all the equip-ment (in our example two sets), because the system depends on all the equipment making it up.

b) For the <<in parallel>> operation, the possibility that the system operates will be determined by the *lesser* of the possibilities of the two sets of equipment, because it is sufficient for only one of the machines to be live for the *system* to be live.

This can be represented in a diagram as follows (figure 16.10):

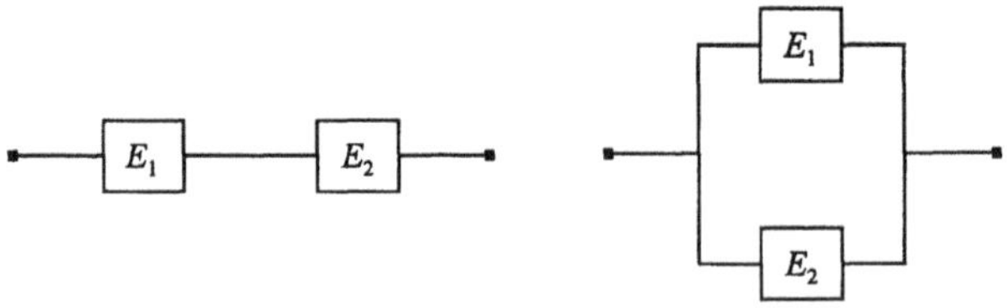

Assembly in series   Parallel assembly

Figure 16.10.

Our objective now is to formalise these two kinds of assembly by arriving at a fuzzy number representing the basis of a law of breakdown of the system, when this operates in series and in parallel.

Therefore for assembly in parallel we would have:

$$\underset{\sim}{A}_s = \underset{\sim}{A}_1 \,(\wedge)\, \underset{\sim}{A}_2$$

and for series assembly:

$$\underset{\sim}{A}_p = \underset{\sim}{A}_1 \,(\vee)\, \underset{\sim}{A}_2$$

for which we will use respectively the following maxmin convolutions:

$$\mu_{\underset{\sim}{A}_1 (\wedge) \underset{\sim}{A}_2}(t) = \bigvee_{t = u \wedge v} (\mu_{\underset{\sim}{A}_1}(u) \wedge \mu_{\underset{\sim}{A}_2}(v))$$

$$\mu_{\underset{\sim}{A}_1 (\vee) \underset{\sim}{A}_2}(t) = \bigvee_{t = u \vee v} (\mu_{\underset{\sim}{A}_1}(u) \wedge \mu_{\underset{\sim}{A}_2}(v))$$

Below we arrive at the result to be used:

$$\mu_{\underset{\sim}{A}_1 (\wedge) \underset{\sim}{A}_2}(t) = \bigvee_{t = u \wedge v} (\mu_{\underset{\sim}{A}_1}(u) \wedge \mu_{\underset{\sim}{A}_2}(v))$$

with the estimates of the previous example.

The combinations in which a $t = 0$ appears will always be zero

$\mu_{\underset{\sim}{A}_1}(1) \wedge \mu_{\underset{\sim}{A}_2}(1) = 0$ $\qquad$ $\mu_{\underset{\sim}{A}_1}(2) \wedge \mu_{\underset{\sim}{A}_2}(1) = 0$

$\mu_{\underset{\sim}{A}_1}(1) \wedge \mu_{\underset{\sim}{A}_2}(2) = 1/3$ $\qquad$ the remaining combinations in which $\mu_{\underset{\sim}{A}_2}(1)$ appears will be zero

$\mu_{\underset{\sim}{A}_1}(1) \wedge \mu_{\underset{\sim}{A}_2}(3) = 1/3$

$\mu_{\underset{\sim}{A}_1}(1) \wedge \mu_{\underset{\sim}{A}_2}(4) = 1/3$

$\mu_{\underset{\sim}{A}_1}(1) \wedge \mu_{\underset{\sim}{A}_2}(5) = 1/3$

$\mu_{\underset{\sim}{A}_1}(1) \wedge \mu_{\underset{\sim}{A}_2}(6) = 1/3$

$\mu_{\underset{\sim}{A}_1}(1) \wedge \mu_{\underset{\sim}{A}_2}(7) = 2/7$

$\mu_{\underset{\sim}{A}_1}(1) \wedge \mu_{\underset{\sim}{A}_2}(8) = 1/7$

The largest of all these numbers will be: 1/3

$\mu_{\underset{\sim}{A}_1}(2) \wedge \mu_{\underset{\sim}{A}_2}(2) = 2/3$ $\qquad$ $\mu_{\underset{\sim}{A}_1}(3) \wedge \mu_{\underset{\sim}{A}_2}(2) = 1$

$\mu_{\underset{\sim}{A}_1}(2) \wedge \mu_{\underset{\sim}{A}_2}(3) = 2/3$ $\qquad$ $\mu_{\underset{\sim}{A}_1}(4) \wedge \mu_{\underset{\sim}{A}_2}(2) = 2/3$

$\mu_{\underset{\sim}{A}_1}(2) \wedge \mu_{\underset{\sim}{A}_2}(4) = 2/3$ $\qquad$ $\mu_{\underset{\sim}{A}_1}(5) \wedge \mu_{\underset{\sim}{A}_2}(2) = 1/3$

$\mu_{\underset{\sim}{A}_1}(2) \wedge \mu_{\underset{\sim}{A}_2}(5) = 4/7$

$\mu_{\underset{\sim}{A}_1}(2) \wedge \mu_{\underset{\sim}{A}_2}(6) = 3/7$
$\mu_{\underset{\sim}{A}_1}(2) \wedge \mu_{\underset{\sim}{A}_2}(7) = 2/7$
$\mu_{\underset{\sim}{A}_1}(2) \wedge \mu_{\underset{\sim}{A}_2}(8) = 1/7$

the largest of all these numbers will be :1

$\mu_{\underset{\sim}{A}_1}(3) \wedge \mu_{\underset{\sim}{A}_2}(3) = 6/7$ $\qquad \mu_{\underset{\sim}{A}_1}(4) \wedge \mu_{\underset{\sim}{A}_2}(3) = 2/3$
$\mu_{\underset{\sim}{A}_1}(3) \wedge \mu_{\underset{\sim}{A}_2}(4) = 5/7$ $\qquad \mu_{\underset{\sim}{A}_1}(5) \wedge \mu_{\underset{\sim}{A}_2}(3) = 1/3$
$\mu_{\underset{\sim}{A}_1}(3) \wedge \mu_{\underset{\sim}{A}_2}(5) = 4/7$
$\mu_{\underset{\sim}{A}_1}(3) \wedge \mu_{\underset{\sim}{A}_2}(6) = 3/7$
$\mu_{\underset{\sim}{A}_1}(3) \wedge \mu_{\underset{\sim}{A}_2}(7) = 2/7$
$\mu_{\underset{\sim}{A}_1}(3) \wedge \mu_{\underset{\sim}{A}_2}(8) = 1/7$

the largest of all these numbers will be: 6/7

$\mu_{\underset{\sim}{A}_1}(4) \wedge \mu_{\underset{\sim}{A}_2}(4) = 2/3$ $\qquad \mu_{\underset{\sim}{A}_1}(5) \wedge \mu_{\underset{\sim}{A}_2}(4) = 1/3$
$\mu_{\underset{\sim}{A}_1}(4) \wedge \mu_{\underset{\sim}{A}_2}(5) = 4/7$
$\mu_{\underset{\sim}{A}_1}(4) \wedge \mu_{\underset{\sim}{A}_2}(6) = 3/7$
$\mu_{\underset{\sim}{A}_1}(4) \wedge \mu_{\underset{\sim}{A}_2}(7) = 2/7$
$\mu_{\underset{\sim}{A}_1}(4) \wedge \mu_{\underset{\sim}{A}_2}(8) = 1/7$

the largest of all these numbers will be: 2/3

$\mu_{\underset{\sim}{A}_1}(5) \wedge \mu_{\underset{\sim}{A}_2}(5) = 1/3$ $\qquad \mu_{\underset{\sim}{A}_1}(6) \wedge \mu_{\underset{\sim}{A}_2}(5) = 0$
$\mu_{\underset{\sim}{A}_1}(5) \wedge \mu_{\underset{\sim}{A}_2}(6) = 1/3$
$\mu_{\underset{\sim}{A}_1}(5) \wedge \mu_{\underset{\sim}{A}_2}(7) = 2/7$
$\mu_{\underset{\sim}{A}_1}(5) \wedge \mu_{\underset{\sim}{A}_2}(8) = 1/7$

the largest of all these numbers will be: 1/3

$\mu_{\underset{\sim}{A}_1}(6) \wedge \mu_{\underset{\sim}{A}_2}(6) = 0$ $\qquad \mu_{\underset{\sim}{A}_1}(7) \wedge \mu_{\underset{\sim}{A}_2}(6) = 0$

from here onwards it will always be zero.
The fuzzy number is $\underset{\sim}{A}_1 (\wedge) \underset{\sim}{A}_2$, since:

	0	1	2	3	4	5	6
$\underset{\sim}{A}_1 (\wedge) \underset{\sim}{A}_2$	0	1/3	1	6/7	2/3	1/3	0

In order to arrive at the fuzzy number $\underset{\sim}{A}_1 (\vee) \underset{\sim}{A}_2$ each $\mu_{\underset{\sim}{A}}(t)$ will be compared with the value of t lower than the other number. Below we show the results obtained:

$$\mu_{\underset{\sim}{A}_1 (\vee) \underset{\sim}{A}_2}(0) = 0 \qquad \mu_{\underset{\sim}{A}_1 (\vee) \underset{\sim}{A}_2}(3) = 1 \qquad \mu_{\underset{\sim}{A}_1 (\vee) \underset{\sim}{A}_2}(6) = 3/7$$
$$\mu_{\underset{\sim}{A}_1 (\vee) \underset{\sim}{A}_2}(1) = 0 \qquad \mu_{\underset{\sim}{A}_1 (\vee) \underset{\sim}{A}_2}(4) = 5/7 \qquad \mu_{\underset{\sim}{A}_1 (\vee) \underset{\sim}{A}_2}(7) = 2/7$$
$$\mu_{\underset{\sim}{A}_1 (\vee) \underset{\sim}{A}_2}(2) = 2/3 \qquad \mu_{\underset{\sim}{A}_1 (\vee) \underset{\sim}{A}_2}(5) = 4/7 \qquad \mu_{\underset{\sim}{A}_1 (\vee) \underset{\sim}{A}_2}(8) = 1/7$$

We arrive at therefore:

	1	2	3	4	5	6	7	8	9
$\underset{\sim}{A}_1 (\vee) \underset{\sim}{A}_2 =$	0	2/3	1	5/7	4/7	3/7	2/7	1/7	0

These results can be represented in a graph, by passing over to the continuous form, as follows (figure 16.11):

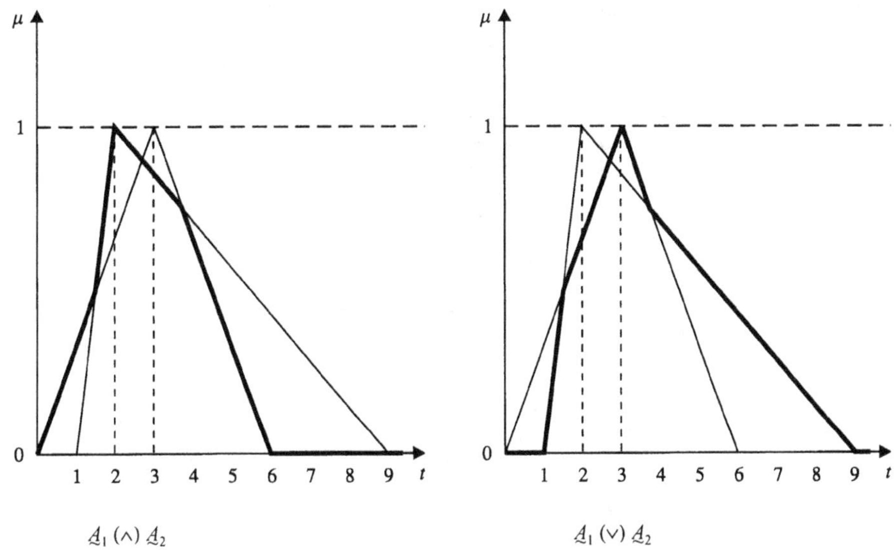

Figure 16.11.

Calculations are much easier if the FTN adopt the form of confidence intervals associated to levels of presumption. In this case it is sufficient to make the calculations level by level by determining for each α (level) the lower (respectively the greater) of the lower extremes and the lower (respectively the greater) of the upper extremes. The fuzzy number arrived at is also represented level by level, as can be seen from the calculations that follow, made with information from the previous example.

$$A_1 = (0, 3, 6) \qquad A_2 = (1, 2, 9)$$
$$A_1(\alpha) = [3\alpha,\ 6 - 3\alpha] \qquad A_2(\alpha) = [1 + \alpha,\ 9 - 7\alpha]$$

α	3α	$\alpha + 1$	$(3\alpha) \wedge (\alpha + 1)$	$(3\alpha) \vee (\alpha + 1)$
0	0	1	0	1
.1	0.3	1.1	0.3	1.1
.2	0.6	1.2	0.6	1.2
.3	0.9	1.3	0.9	1.3
.4	1.2	1.4	1.2	1.4
.5	1.5	1.5	1.5	1.5
.6	1.8	1.6	1.6	1.8
.7	2.1	1.7	1.7	2.1
.8	2.4	1.8	1.8	2.4
.9	2.7	1.9	1.9	2.7
1	3	2	2	3

α	$6 - 3\alpha$	$9 - 7\alpha$	$(6 - 3\alpha) \wedge (9 - 7\alpha)$	$(6 - 3\alpha) \vee (9 - 7\alpha)$
0	6	9	6	9
.1	5.7	8.3	5.7	8.3
.2	5.4	7.6	5.4	7.6
.3	5.1	6.9	5.1	6.9
.4	4.8	6.2	4.8	6.2
.5	4.5	5.5	4.5	5.5
.6	4.2	4.8	4.2	4.8
.7	3.9	4.1	3.9	4.1
.8	3.6	3.4	3.4	3.6
.9	3.3	2.7	2.7	3.3
1	3	2	2	3

α	$A_1(\alpha)\ (\wedge)\ A_2(\alpha)$	$A_1(\alpha)\ (\vee)\ A_2(\alpha)$
0	[0, 6]	[1, 9]
.1	[0.3, 5.7]	[1.1, 8.3]
.2	[0.6, 5.4]	[1.2, 7.6]
.3	[0.9, 5.1]	[1.3, 6.9]
.4	[1.2, 4.8]	[1.4, 6.2]
.5	[1.5, 4.5]	[1.5, 5.5]
.6	[1.6, 4.2]	[1.8, 4.8]
.7	[1.7, 3.9]	[2.1, 4.1]
.8	[1.8, 3.4]	[2.4, 3.6]
.9	[1.9, 2.7]	[2.7, 3.3]
1	2	3

What we have shown here is the oft-repeated interest in the fact of being able to represent a fuzzy number in different forms. Each one can be used under different circumstances as they permit a solution to a problem in the easiest fashion. This is the case we have just studied, in which we simplified the calculations very much by using the form of α-cuts.

All we have done for the fuzzy numbers, which constitute the support for the law of possibility of breakdown, is also valid for the law of survival $k(t)$ where we would obtain the following figure 16.12.

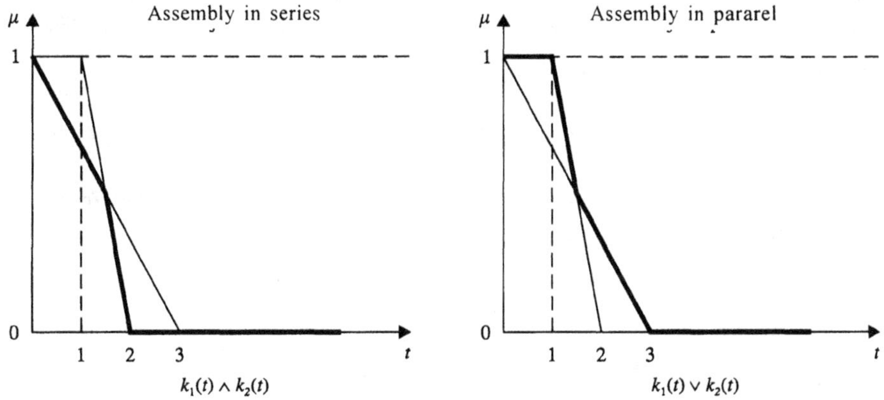

Figure 16.12.

This same process can be followed for truncated survival functions, as a consequence of actions such as preventive renewal or fixed date revision, among others.

Intervals of probability in the treatment of the life of equipment

Before finalising this chapter we are going to tackle the subject of equipment life, by means of the combination of the concept of probability and that of confidence intervals. For this there are several paths to follow. Selection of the process to follow depends principally on the nature of the machines and the manner of carrying out the expert survey.

We are justifying this path by admitting as normal the case of the expert who cannot evaluate a probability of breakdown for a machine, but on the other hand he can give to this probability a limit or lower extreme and a limit or upper extreme, that is:

$$\underset{\sim}{p} = [p_1, p_2], \quad p_1 < p_2, \quad p_1, p_2 \in [0, 1]$$

The interval of probability $\underset{\sim}{p}$ in not a probability, and neither can we talk about an uncertain probability because, from the strict point of view of the axiomatic of the theory of probabilities, an uncertain probability is excluded - the axiomatic of activity is not complied with, except in the case of the lower extremes (respectively upper) between each other - In spite of this, we are going to show the fact that the survival curves are monotonous and not increasing. This allows us to use the intervals of probability just as is done with probabilities in studies of reliability.

An expert is asked for two laws of survival for equipment, one pessimistic $v_*(t)$ and the other optimistic $v^*(t)$, just as represented in the figure below. This will give birth the a law of survival in the form of a confidence interval (figure 16.13):

$$\underset{\sim}{v} = [v_*(t), v^*(t)]$$

Let us remember that the survival curve of equipment is defined from the probabilistic point of view, by the probability:

$$v(t) = \text{pr}(T \geqslant t)$$

in which T is the instant or date of the breakdown.

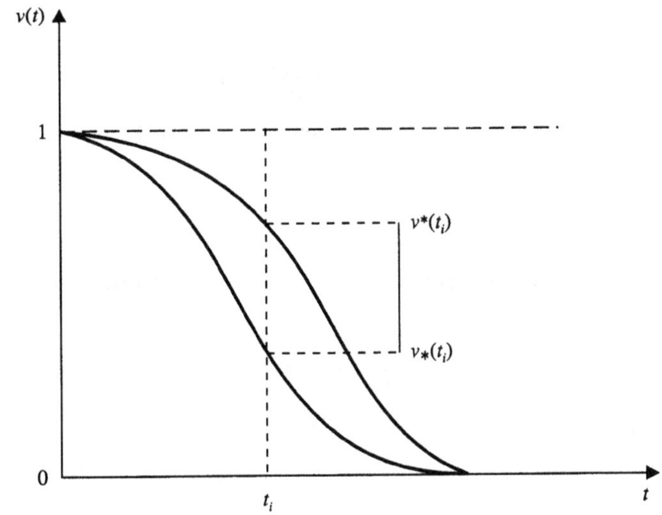

Figure 16.13.

Before continuing, let us take a look at an interesting aspect relative to survival curves.

It is quite logical to think that a survival curve would correspond to each type of equipment and knowing the form of this, one would be able to determine the type of equipment it represents. Also, it is demonstrated that as the form of the survival curve gets closer to a decreasing exponential, the probability of breakdown tends even more towards a constant. For this we start out from a survival function the form of which is that of a continuous exponential, as we have shown below.

$$v(t) = e^{-\lambda_0 t}$$

where λ_0 is a constant.

Now, with regard to all that was said in the first section of this chapter, the probability of renewal of equipment between t and $t + \Delta t$, it is:

$$v(t) - v(t + \Delta t)$$

When Δt is assumed as infinitely small, by definition it will be:

$$\lim_{\Delta t \to 0} \frac{v(t) - v(t + \Delta t)}{\Delta t} = - v'(t)$$

Therefore we arrive at:

$$-v'(t) \cdot \Delta t = v(t) - v(t + \Delta t)$$

Therefore, the probability that equipment is renewed between t and $t + \Delta t$ when $\Delta t \to 0$, is:

$$-v'(t) \cdot \Delta t$$

But by the definition itself of conditional breakdown probability, this same probability can be expressed as:

$$v(t) \cdot p_c(t) \cdot \Delta t$$

From where the following can be written:

$$-v'(t) \cdot \Delta t = v(t) \cdot p_c(t) \cdot \Delta t$$

Therefore the probability of renewal between t and $t + \Delta t$ is equal to the probability of survival in t because of the conditional breakdown probability between t and $t + \Delta t$.

In short the following is arrived at:

$$p_c(t) = -\frac{v'(t)}{v(t)}$$

If the previous exponential function is considered:

$$p_c(t) = -\frac{-\lambda_0 \cdot e^{-\lambda_0 t}}{e^{-\lambda_0 t}} = \lambda_0$$

Let us move on to a more general case, where:

$$v(t) = e^{-\lambda(t)}$$

For the monotonous non-growing and continuous laws of survival, if $v_*(t) \leqslant \leqslant v^*(t)$ we arrive at $\lambda^*(t) \geqslant \lambda_*(t)$ and also $-\lambda^*(t) \leqslant -\lambda_*(t)$, therefore in the general case we can write:

$$[v_*(t), v^*(t)] = [e^{-\lambda^*(t)}, e^{-\lambda_*(t)}] = e^{[-\lambda^*(t), -\lambda_*(t)]}$$

because the rate of breakdown $\lambda(t)$, in our hypothesis, is monotonous non-decreasing. This formula corresponds to a concept that is held intuitively: there is no decrease in the breakdown rate the longer time goes by.

Now, let us move on to the case of a network of equipment. In the probabilistic theory of reliability, the operator $(\cdot)$ is used, product, for a network in series and the operator $(\hat{+})$, algebraic sum, such as $a \hat{+} b = a + b - a \cdot b$, for a network in parallel.

Therefore:

$$v(t) = v_1(t) \cdot v_2(t) \text{ for the <<series>> case}^6$$
$$v(t) = v_1(t) \hat{+} v_2(t) = v_1(t) + v_2(t) - v_1(t) \cdot v_2(t) \text{ for the <<parallel>> case}^6$$

From here the whole theory relative to the reliability of systems that exist in the probabilistic hypothesis can be applied, to the case of intervals of survival probability. It will be seen that:

$$[v_*(t), v^*(t)] = [v_{1*}(t), v_1^*(t)] \, (\cdot) \, [v_{2*}(t), v_2^*(t)] = [v_{1*}(t) \cdot v_{2*}(t),\ v_1^*(t) \cdot v_2^*(t)]$$
$$[v_*(t), v^*(t)] = [v_{1*}(t), v_1^*(t)] \, (\hat{+}) \, [v_{2*}(t), v_2^*(t)] =$$
$$= [v_{1*}(t) + v_{2*}(t) - v_{1*}(t) \cdot v_{2*}(t),\ v_1^*(t) + v_2^*(t) - v_1^*(t) \cdot v_2^*(t)]$$

We are not going to go any further into the calculation and particularities relative to reliability networks. We will just take a look at an example (figure 16.14).

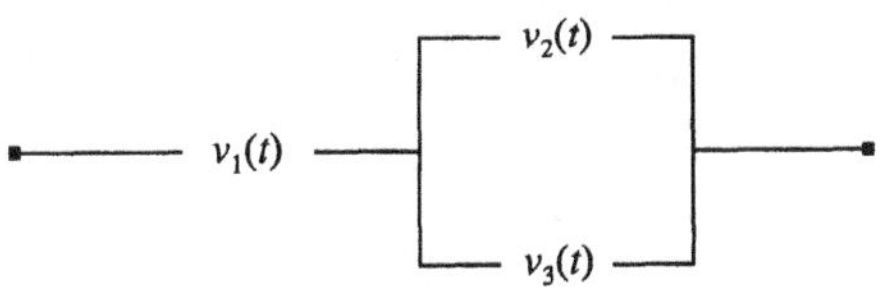

Figure 16.14.

$$\underset{\sim}{v}(t) = \underset{\sim}{v}_1(t) \, (\cdot) \, (\underset{\sim}{v}_2(t) \, (\hat{+}) \, \underset{\sim}{v}_3(t)) = [v_{1*}(t), v_1^*(t)] \, (\cdot) \, ([v_{2*}(t), v_2^*(t)] \, (\hat{+}) \, [v_{3*}(t), v_3^*(t)]) =$$
$$= [v_{1*}(t) \cdot (v_{2*}(t) \hat{+} v_{3*}(t)),\ v_1^*(t) \cdot (v_2^*(t) \hat{+} v_3^*(t))] =$$
$$= [v_{1*}(t) \cdot (v_{2*}(t) + v_{3*}(t) - v_{2*}(t) \cdot v_{3*}(t)),\ v_1^*(t) \cdot (v_2^*(t) + v_3^*(t) - v_2^*(t) \cdot v_3^*(t))]$$

When more complicated networks appear than the one we have just shown, it is customary to use binary variables.

$$x = x_1 \cdot x_2 = 0 \quad \begin{array}{l} \text{if } x_1 \text{ is in operation and } x_2 \text{ not.} \\ \text{if } x_1 \text{ is not in operation and } x_2 \text{ is} \\ \text{if } x_1 \text{ and } x_2 \text{ are not in operation} \end{array}$$

$$x = x_1 \hat{+} x_2 \quad \begin{array}{ll} = 1, & \text{if } x_1 \text{ and } x_2 \text{ are in operation} \\ = 0, & \text{if } x_1 \text{ and } x_2 \text{ are not in operation} \\ = 1, & \text{if } x_1 \text{ or } x_2 \text{ are in operation} \end{array}$$

The laws of substitution or maintenance of equipment, used for the probabilities of survival of identical equipment, continue to be the same for the intervals of survival probability.

In this way the function of survival is given in the form of a continuous function $v(t)$ and when there is no substitution, we arrive at, as we saw in the second section:

$$n(t) = n(0) \cdot v(t)$$

The function of established use has been called $f(t)$ and the amount of equipment substituted up to moment u is called $r(u)$. The differential:

$$r'(u)\, du$$

gives us the amount of equipment substituted in interval $u + du$. The function $r'(t)$ will be called <<supply rate>>[7].

The amount of equipment still alive, as a result of this supply at a future moment t, will be, in the event of continuity:

$$r'(u)\, du \cdot v(t-u) = r'(u) \cdot v(t-u)\, du$$

The amount of identical equipment in service at moment t, including the equipment in service at moment $t = 0$ (the first to be used) will in this case be:

$$f(t) = n(0) \cdot v(t) + \int_{u=0}^{t} r'(u) \cdot v(t-u)\, du$$

This integral equation, called Volterra integral, can be transposed with no special difficulty to those cases in which functions $v(t)$, $r'(t)$ y $f(t)$ are intervals $[v_*(t), v^*(t)]$, $[r'_*(t), r'^*(t)]$, $[f_*(t), f^*(t)]$, always taking into account the normal precautions of differential calculus and confidence intervals.

We will now conclude this chapter by pointing out that the new contributions there have been in the field of applied mathematics have added new elements to the problem for treating equipment, on incorporating new techniques which have allowed for a widening of research in the sphere of renewal.

These fragments linked by a conductor as solid as possible only intends to bring to light the study of an eternal problem, from a new perspective that may be adequate in surroundings in which companies may have to move in the very near future.

References

1 A. Kaufmann: *Modèles mathématiques pour la stimulation inventive*, Albin Michel París, 1979 page 53.

2 For this development we have followed the works of A. Kaufmann included mainly in: *Métodos y modelos de la investigación de operaciones*, Volume I, Cecsa, Mexico, 1972, pages 249-278.

3 A.Kaufmann and J. Gil Aluja: *Introducción a la teoría de los subconjuntos borrosos a la gestión de las empresas*, Milladoiro, Santiago de Compostela, 1986, pages 93-111.

4 These aspects were treated in A. Kaufmann: <<Le remplacement des équipements dans l'incertain>>, *Note de travail*, number 153, October, 1985, pages 1-5.

5 This data and corresponding example have been taken from A. Kaufmann: <<Le remplacement des équipements dans l'incertain>>, *Note de travail*, Number 153, October, 1985, page 4.

6 Obviously, operators $(\cdot)$ and $(\hat{+})$ maintain their increasing monotony.

7 In the continuous field function $r'(t)$ at the same time complies $p(u) = r(u) - r(u-1)$ as defined in the second section of this chapter.

17 Preventive maintenance of equipment in uncertainty

A brief reference to Dynamic Programming

Throughout this book constant reference has been made to the fact that with ever greater frequency uncertainty makes itself felt in social, economic and business phenomena, as a consequence of the rapid changes taking place not only in the field of technology, which has undergone spectacular advance in latter years, but also in the way we human beings conceive life, all of which has given rise to continuous changes in thought, customs, likes and dislikes and the scale of values.

The existence of unequal speed in one or other sphere can be accepted without a problem, as it is difficult for the mind to follow the vortex of physical changes. But there can be no doubt about the great effort made by men of science to interpret, study and treat this world in which we live, so changeable and therefore so uncertain.

All of us who direct our interest towards the problems of management, observe how the techniques used for handling the same, are not always sufficient if only the mathematics of certainty or probability are taken as their bases. The difficulties arising from their use prevent taking advantage of the fact that determinist mathematics, on the one hand, and the theory of probabilities on the other constitute a solid monolithic monument, which does not happen with the theories used in the handling of those problems for which information available is reduced, unfortunately, to uncertain levels.

Obviously in this chapter we do not propose to make an exposition of the techniques that are suitable for the treatment of equipment renewal in uncertainty, which has already been the object of other works[1] . Our objective will be limited to the exposition of a model that may be useful in those sequential processes that so often appear in phenomena of fixed asset management. In order for our exposition to be as clear as possible we will develop a numerical case relative to the handling of industrial equipment.

As we have already pointed out in other chapters[2], within the known sequential techniques, those included under the name of Dynamic Programming acquire special interest.

Nearly all sequential processes are based explicitly or implicitly on dynamic programming. Whether in certainty, probability or uncertainty, dynamic programming is very nearly an essential tool, which can acquire the most diverse nature and in which the most varied data and operators can be used, from operators as classical as addition and multiplication, to many others, recognised in ordinary or fuzzy sets. The principle according to which an optimum strategy can only be formed by optimum sub-strategies is a very important element, so much so, that it is used continuously without knowing. Expressed in this way it is particularly elemental, but it is precisely the simplest things that are also the most inspired. We are going to take advantage of this occasion to complete the practical aspects developed before, with certain general considerations.

Dynamic programming is the result of the work of Bellman and the Soviet scientist Pontryagin carried out more than 30 years ago, and has given rise to a very general method, which has taken shape in nearly all applications from mathematics to the most diverse sciences. Dynamic programming is linked to the calculation of variations by means of many common points and one can even return to the mathematics of the XVIII and XIX centuries to look for some of its grounds.

It may be convenient at this point to recall the meaning of certain terms frequently used in current language and even in certain scientific works in a rather indistinct manner. We are referring to the words: decision, policy, tactics and strategy. These are concepts that correspond to different ways of conceiving human intervention in a system with a number of finite or non-finite states.

Let us assume a system S in which the states in finite number, are $\varepsilon = \{E_1, E_2, ..., E_n\}$. If the system, at moment ν, in a state of E_i, and a human operator can decide and place it in state E_j, it can be said that we are faced with a <<decision>>. If these decisions take place at moments 1, 2, 3, ..., ν, ..., it can be said that the set of these decisions constitutes a policy. In this way, in a policy it is assumed that the system can only evolve from human decisions. Therefore, a policy will be defined by a sequence of states decided upon by the human operator: $(E_{i0}, E_{i1}, E_{i2}, ..., E_{i\nu}, ...)$. To put this in another way, evolution is not submitted either to probability or uncertainty. If a sequence of articulated decisions is considered, that form a part of a sequence of articulated decisions, we are faced with a <<sub-policy>>. The sub-policy is also known under the name of <<tactic>>.

Now let us consider a system S that can take on n states $\varepsilon = \{E_1, E_2, ..., E_n\}$. It is assumed that at a moment ν the system evolves by itself according to a stochastic process (such as exists in the Markov chains) and passes over from a state E_i to a state E_j at a time $\nu + \delta_\nu$ located between ν and $\nu + 1$, the human operator intervenes and makes the system pass over to state E_k; after this, by means of a stochastic mechanism, to state E_2; and then the human operator will act in order to pass it over to state E_m at moment $\nu + 1 + \delta_{\nu+1}$, located between $\nu + 1$ and $\nu + 2$. And so on successively. If the first evolution, at moment $\nu = 0$, is consequent upon the intervention of probability, it can be said that the system is of the <<probability-decision>> type and if the first intervention is a decision then it will be of the <<decision-probability>> type. But in many cases, intervention of probability and decision can take place simultaneously according to certain rules to be defined. The set of decisions associated to this way for the effects of probability, is called <<strategy>>.

In a strategy the human operator reasons as follows: if at any given moment n probability leads the system of E_i to E_j, I will take it to E_k and I have foreseen this for all periods. It is obvious that all these transitions, for policies or strategies, can be such that they have $E_k = E_j = E_i$, as they do not exclude repetition other than for very specific cases. If we consider these as sub-sequences of a strategy then we are now faced with a <<sub-strategy>>.

Now let us move on to express the principle of dynamic programming by means of a surface area within a space of n dimensions. In this surface area, which we assume as continuous, we take two points A and B and all lines possible are drawn joining A and B maintaining ourselves within the surface area. Let us assume the existence of a line *AMPNB* which is optimum according to a pre-established criterion. Then we consider the segment of the line *MPN* that forms a part of the optimum line *AMPNB*. We then consider the segment of the line *MQN* which takes on a value that is different from the value of *MPN*. Relative to the same criterion, the optimum line cannot be *AMQNB*. In fact, if this sub-trajectory were greater, the optimum trajectory would pass along it.

If we call <<trajectory in Σ>> a line that joins A and B (figure 17.1) the already known principle is stated: <<An optimum trajectory can only be formed by optimum sub-trajectories>>.

This is the principle of optimality. But this is only a principle and it is preferable, each time it is used, to draw up a theorem and show it, as happens in many cases, when it is not obvious. This theorem can only be applied when the concept of trajectory is interpreted as we have seen and possess the properties, expressed before of associativity, monotony and the existence of a neutral[3].

For this the monoïd structure and also monotony are necessary. In certain cases associativity and monotony are not apparent and should be shown.

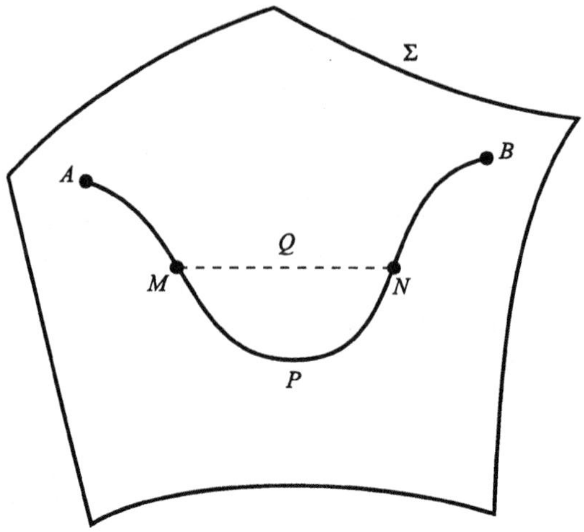

Figure 17.1.

Decision-probability processes

We now move on to bring up a probable, discreet and stationary case[4]. At each moment n, the system can be in a state $E_i \in \varepsilon$; a decision then takes this from state E_i to a state $E'_r \in \Gamma_D E_i \subset \varepsilon'$ at a moment n', $n < n' < n+1$; to each decision $E_i \rightarrow E'_r$ a value $\underset{\sim}{a}_{ir} = [a_{ir}^{(1)}, a_{ir}^{(2)}]$ is assigned (therefore a confidence interval); at moment n' probability intervenes and the system returns to states $E_j \in \Gamma_H E'_r \subset \varepsilon$ with a probability of p_{ij} and a value of $\underset{\sim}{b}_{rj} = [b_{rj}^{(1)}, b_{rj}^{(2)}]$. The interval of time between moment n and moment n + 1 will be called <<phase n>>.

Let us suppose that $[\bar{f}_i^{(1)}(N-n, N), \bar{f}_i^{(2)}(N-n, N)]$ is the optimum mathematical probability (a confidence interval) for the set of phases n, n +1, ... N - 1, N, when the system is in state E_i at moment i. Let us remember in this respect that when attempting to compare confidence intervals the mean value can be taken as the first criterion, as the second eventually the upper extreme or lower extreme according to the case that is being dealt with. This is written then as:

$$[\bar{f}_i^{(1)}(N-n, N), \bar{f}_i^{(2)}(N-n, N)] = \underset{E'_r \in \Gamma_D E_i}{\text{OPT}} \{[a_{ir}^{(1)}, a_{ir}^{(2)}] \, (+) \sum_{E_i \in \Gamma_H E'_r} p_{rj}([b_{rj}^{(1)}, b_{rj}^{(2)}] \, (+)$$

$$(+) \, [\bar{f}_j^{(1)}(N-n+1, N), \bar{f}_j^{(2)}(N-n+1, N)])\}$$

$$i = 1, 2, ..., M$$

$$n = 1, 2, ..., M$$

$$[\bar{f}_i^{(1)}(N, N), \bar{f}_i^{(2)}(N, N)] = [f_{0i}^{(1)}, f_{0i}^{(2)}]$$

given the confidence interval.

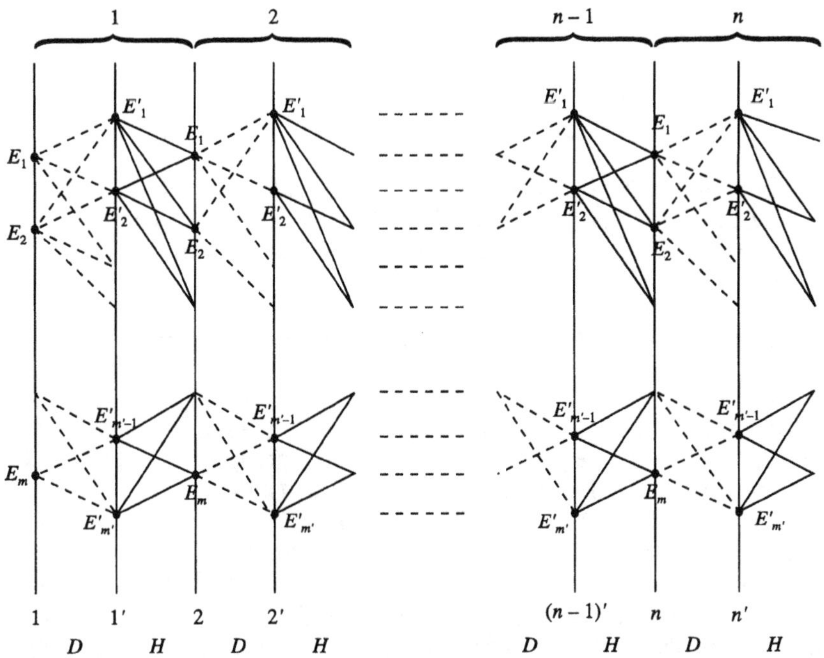

Figure 17.2. - Decision-probability process.

A system in which in each phase a contingent effect follows a decision and has its commencement in a decision called DH system[5]. These sequential optimisation formulae are susceptible to generalisation in non-stationary cases. We will arrive at then:

$$E_i(n) \in \varepsilon(n) \quad , \quad E_r'(n') \in \Gamma_D(n) E_i(n)$$
$$E_j(n) \in \varepsilon'(n) \quad , \quad E_j'(n+1) \in \Gamma_H(n') E_r'(n')$$

with $[a_{ir}^{(1)}(n), a_{ir}^{(2)}(n)]$, $p_{rj}(n)$, $[b_{rj}^{(1)}(n), b_{rj}^{(2)}(n)]$. In this way the previous expressions are converted into:

$$[\bar{f}_i^{(1)}(N-n, N), \bar{f}_i^{(2)}(N-n, N)] = \underset{E_r'(n) \in \Gamma_H(n) E_i(n)}{\text{OPT}} \{[a_{ir}^{(1)}(n), a_{ir}^{(2)}(n)] \ (+)$$

$$(+) \sum_{E_i(n) \in \Gamma_H(n) E_r'(n)} p_{rj}(n) \ ([b_{rj}^{(1)}(n), b_{rj}^{(2)}(n)] \ (+)$$

$$(+)\ [\overline{f}_j^{(1)}(N-n+1, N), \overline{f}_j^{(2)}(N-n+1, N)])\}$$
$$i = 1, 2, ..., M$$
$$n = 1, 2, ..., N$$
$$[\overline{f}_i^{(1)}(N, N), \overline{f}_i^{(2)}(N, N)] = [f_{0i}^{(1)}, f_{0i}^{(2)}]$$

In the non-stationary case the probabilities, confidence intervals representing uncertain values and the Γ_H and Γ_D, functions, dependent upon n, are expressed in the same way as was done for the seasonal hypothesis.

Proposal for a model for preventive maintenance

Having reviewed these technical aspects, we will now start out from the assumption of industrial equipment carrying out a production process, and we will pay particular attention to maintenance during its useful life.

As is particularly well known, when equipment is in operation it undergoes wear and tear that can be mitigated by certain periodic revisions. When doing preventive maintenance, the physical ageing and therefore breakdowns and operational difficulties decrease during periods succeeding its revision. Therefore it can be admitted that certain adequate revisions can avoid stoppages and repairs that make the cost of using the investment object more expensive. These revisions can take place preventively or when the equipment has not operated normally and has had to be repaired. The revision can be total or partial, and obviously incurs a cost. This simple question allows us to demonstrate a scheme with wide possibilities in application to a very extensive range of real situations. Let us now move on to a specific application.

We are considering a work means, that entered into service at a certain moment zero and has a useful life of 4 periods (years). Its activity is watched carefully throughout these years and prior to termination of each period, information is requested relative to its operation. The answer can be:

E_1 = It has had a major breakdown.
E_2 = There have been failures in its principal components.
E_3 = There have been operating difficulties.
E_4 = It has operated normally.

In this way we can consider a set of states:

$$\varepsilon = \{E_1, E_2, E_3, E_4\}$$

When an abnormal operation of the equipment takes place during a period (states E_1, E_2, E_3) a repair is made in order for it to continue with the production process. This implies a cost that it will be necessary to establish. In this case it is wise to make a later revision.

In the event that during a period the equipment were to have operated normally (state E_4), the decision can be twofold: on the one hand, make some sort of revision, or on the other, make no revision at all.

These alternatives arise during all the periods of the estimated life of the investment object.

From all we have stated above it can be deduced that at the end of each period three alternatives arise that include a decision leading to one of the following states:

E'_1= Equipment totally inspected
E'_2= Equipment partially inspected
E'_3= Equipment not inspected

In this way we arrive at another set of states:

$$\varepsilon' = \{E'_1, E'_2, E'_3\}$$

The states that the equipment can pass through, in one of the periods of its useful life can be represented as follows (figure 17.3):

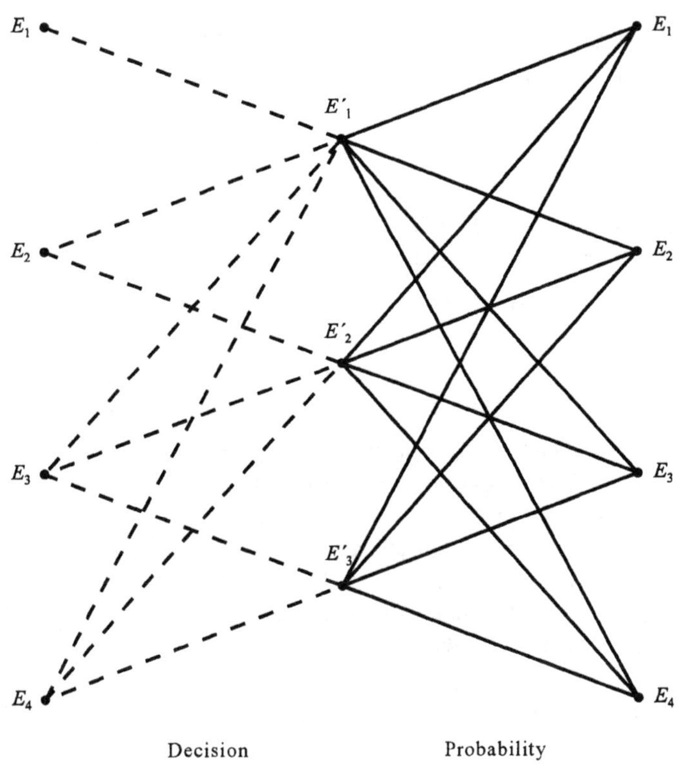

Figure 17.3.

The changes of state by decision ($E_i \rightarrow E'_j$) and their respective costs are established as follows:

$$E_1 \rightarrow E'_1 \quad [a^{(1)}_{11}, a^{(2)}_{11}] = [10, 12]$$
$$E_2 \rightarrow E'_1 \quad [a^{(1)}_{21}, a^{(2)}_{21}] = [8, 11]$$
$$E_2 \rightarrow E'_2 \quad [a^{(1)}_{22}, a^{(2)}_{22}] = [6, 8]$$
$$E_3 \rightarrow E'_1 \quad [a^{(1)}_{31}, a^{(2)}_{31}] = [7, 10]$$
$$E_3 \rightarrow E'_2 \quad [a^{(1)}_{32}, a^{(2)}_{32}] = [3, 5]$$
$$E_3 \rightarrow E'_3 \quad [a^{(1)}_{33}, a^{(2)}_{33}] = 0$$
$$E_4 \rightarrow E'_1 \quad [a^{(1)}_{41}, a^{(2)}_{41}] = [5, 7]$$
$$E_4 \rightarrow E'_2 \quad [a^{(1)}_{42}, a^{(2)}_{42}] = [2, 3]$$
$$E_4 \rightarrow E'_3 \quad [a^{(1)}_{43}, a^{(2)}_{43}] = 0$$

The changes of state as a consequence of probability ($E'_j \rightarrow E_k$) take place through the following probabilities:

	First period	Second period	Third period
$E'_1 \rightarrow E_1$	$p_{11}(1) = 0.1$	$p_{11}(2) = 0.1$	$p_{11}(3) = 0.1$
$E'_1 \rightarrow E_2$	$p_{12}(1) = 0.1$	$p_{12}(2) = 0.1$	$p_{12}(3) = 0.1$
$E'_1 \rightarrow E_3$	$p_{13}(1) = 0.1$	$p_{13}(2) = 0.2$	$p_{13}(3) = 0.2$
$E'_1 \rightarrow E_4$	$p_{14}(1) = 0.7$	$p_{14}(2) = 0.6$	$p_{14}(3) = 0.6$
$E'_2 \rightarrow E_1$	$p_{21}(1) = 0.2$	$p_{21}(2) = 0.2$	$p_{21}(3) = 0.2$
$E'_2 \rightarrow E_2$	$p_{22}(1) = 0.2$	$p_{22}(2) = 0.3$	$p_{22}(3) = 0.3$
$E'_2 \rightarrow E_3$	$p_{23}(1) = 0.2$	$p_{23}(2) = 0.3$	$p_{23}(3) = 0.3$
$E'_2 \rightarrow E_4$	$p_{24}(1) = 0.4$	$p_{24}(2) = 0.2$	$p_{24}(3) = 0.2$
$E'_3 \rightarrow E_1$	$p_{31}(1) = 0.3$	$p_{31}(2) = 0.4$	$p_{31}(3) = 0.5$
$E'_3 \rightarrow E_2$	$p_{32}(1) = 0.3$	$p_{32}(2) = 0.4$	$p_{32}(3) = 0.4$
$E'_3 \rightarrow E_3$	$p_{33}(1) = 0.3$	$p_{33}(2) = 0.1$	$p_{33}(3) = 0.1$
$E'_3 \rightarrow E_4$	$p_{34}(1) = 0.1$	$p_{34}(2) = 0.1$	$p_{34}(3) = 0$

A period prior or preliminary to the decision-probability process can be considered, in which no decision is taken but on the other hand does entail certain costs. This is the moment from start-up of the equipment to the instant of taking the first decision. For formal effects, this is normally considered as a period of time the duration of which is a year. During this period the same events as occur during the following periods can take place, and these must be assigned a probability. We therefore establish:

$$E'_1 \rightarrow E_1 \quad P_{11}(0) = 0.0$$
$$E'_1 \rightarrow E_2 \quad P_{12}(0) = 0.1$$
$$E'_1 \rightarrow E_3 \quad P_{13}(0) = 0.1$$
$$E'_1 \rightarrow E_4 \quad P_{14}(0) = 0.8$$

- Stoppage and repair costs due to major breakdowns ($E_j' \to E_1$), j = 1,2,3,4, are estimated by the interval:

$$[b_{j1}^{(1)}, b_{j1}^{(2)}] = [20, 25]$$

- Stoppage and repair costs for failure of principal components, ($E_j' \to E_2$), j= 1,2,3,4, are estimated by the interval:

$$[b_{j2}^{(1)}, b_{j2}^{(2)}] = [14, 18]$$

- Stoppage and repair costs caused by operating difficulties ($E_j' \to E_3$), j = 1,2,3,4, are estimated by means of the interval:

$$[b_{j3}^{(1)}, b_{j3}^{(2)}] = [11, 13]$$

- Stoppage and repair costs when the equipment operates normally ($E_j' \to E_4$), j = 1,2,3,4, are obviously nil, that is to say:

$$[b_{i4}^{(1)}, b_{i4}^{(2)}] = 0$$

Finally a calculatory interest rate is estimated i = 0.12 which will give rise to an updating rate:

$$\frac{1}{1+i} = 0.892$$

We will now look at, by means of the graph (figure 17.4), the sequentially complete scheme that comprises the useful life of the investment object. All the possible states through which the equipment may pass have been broken down into three phases.

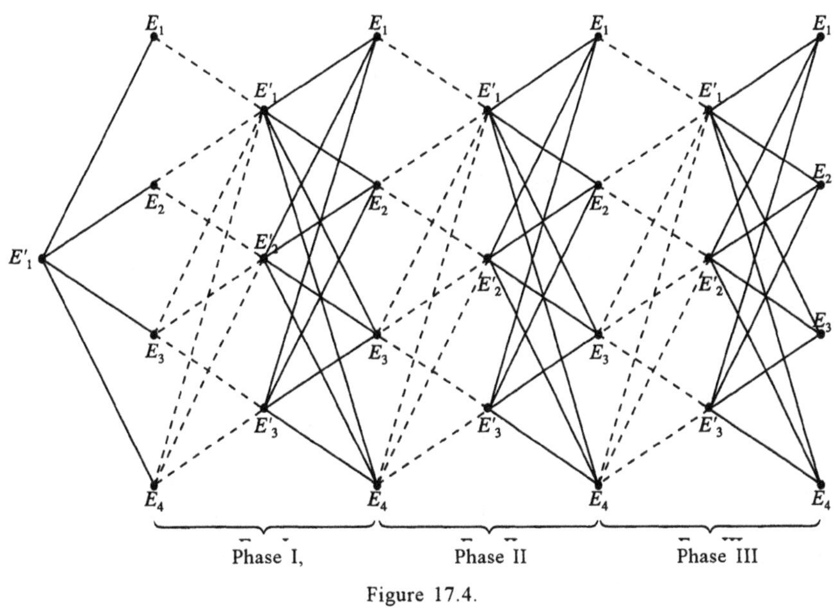

Figure 17.4.

Once the investment object has finished its production activity it must be physically separated from the place where it has rendered its services. Continuing with the example, there is a cost for disassembly of the equipment at the end of its useful life in order to leave the workshop in conditions for commencing activity with other equipment, equal to:

$$\begin{aligned}[3, 6] &= [f_{01}^{(1)}, f_{01}^{(2)}] \\ &= [f_{02}^{(1)}, f_{02}^{(2)}] \\ &= [f_{03}^{(1)}, f_{03}^{(2)}] \\ &= [f_{04}^{(1)}, f_{04}^{(2)}]\end{aligned}$$

Development of the sequential model

We now move on to carry out calculations by means of a sequential process leading to the establishment of the decisions to be taken at the end of each of the periods in order for management, relative to the operation of the equipment, to be correct.

For this, and as is so well known, we will commence with phase III. Thus we will arrive at:

Phase III

$$\begin{aligned}[a_{11}^{(1)}, a_{11}^{(2)}] \,(+)\, p_{11}(3)([b_{11}^{(1)}, b_{11}^{(2)}] \,(+)\, \frac{1}{1+i}\, [f_{01}^{(1)}, f_{01}^{(2)}]) \,(+) \\ (+)\, p_{12}(3)([b_{12}^{(1)}, b_{12}^{(2)}] \,(+)\, \frac{1}{1+i}\, [f_{02}^{(1)}, f_{02}^{(2)}]) \,(+) \\ (+)\, p_{13}(3)([b_{13}^{(1)}, b_{13}^{(2)}] \,(+)\, \frac{1}{1+i}\, [f_{03}^{(1)}, f_{03}^{(2)}]) \,(+) \\ (+)\, p_{14}(3)([b_{14}^{(1)}, b_{14}^{(2)}] \,(+)\, \frac{1}{1+i}\, [f_{04}^{(1)}, f_{04}^{(2)}]) = \\ = [10, 12](+)\, (0.1)([20, 25] \,(+)\, (0.892)[3, 6]) \,(+) \\ (+)\, (0.1)([14, 18] \,(+)\, (0.892)[3, 6]) \,(+) \\ (+)\, (0.2)([11, 13] \,(+)\, (0.892)[3, 6]) \,(+) \\ (+)\, (0.6)(0(+)(0.892)[3, 6]) = \\ = [10, 12](+)\, [2.267, 3.035] \,(+)\, [1.667, 2.335] \,(+) \\ (+)\, [2.735, 3.670] \,(+)\, [1.605, 3.211] = [18.274, 24.251]\end{aligned}$$

$$E_1 \rightarrow E_1'$$

Therefore we will take:

$$[\bar{f}_1^{(1)}(2, 3), \bar{f}_1^{(2)}(2, 3)] = [18.274, 24.251]$$

taking into account that the only way out when the equipment is in state E_1 is to pass over to E_1'. In this case the cost will be no less than 18.274 nor no more than 24.251.

Let us now look at what the decision to be taken will be in the same phase II when the equipment is at the beginning of state E_2. We will calculate:

$$\begin{aligned}
[a_{21}^{(1)}, a_{21}^{(2)}] \; (+) \; & p_{11}(3)([b_{11}^{(1)}, b_{11}^{(2)}] \; (+) \; \frac{1}{1+i} \; [f_{01}^{(1)}, f_{01}^{(2)}]) \; (+) \\
& (+) \; p_{12}(3)([b_{12}^{(1)}, b_{12}^{(2)}] \; (+) \; \frac{1}{1+i} \; [f_{02}^{(1)}, f_{02}^{(2)}]) \; (+) \\
& (+) \; p_{13}(3)([b_{13}^{(1)}, b_{13}^{(2)}] \; (+) \; \frac{1}{1+i} \; [f_{03}^{(1)}, f_{03}^{(2)}]) \; (+) \\
& (+) \; p_{14}(3)([b_{14}^{(1)}, b_{14}^{(2)}] \; (+) \; \frac{1}{1+i} \; [f_{04}^{(1)}, f_{04}^{(2)}]) = \\
& = [8, 11](+) \; [2.267, 3.035] \; (+) \; [1.667, 2.335] \; (+) \\
& (+) \; [2.735, 3.670] \; (+) \; [1.605, 3.211] = [16.274, 23.251]
\end{aligned}$$

$$E_2 \rightarrow E_1'$$

$$\begin{aligned}
[a_{22}^{(1)}, a_{22}^{(2)}] \; (+) \; & p_{21}(3)([b_{21}^{(1)}, b_{21}^{(2)}] \; (+) \; \frac{1}{1+i} \; [f_{01}^{(1)}, f_{01}^{(2)}]) \; (+) \\
& (+) \; p_{22}(3)([b_{22}^{(1)}, b_{22}^{(2)}] \; (+) \; \frac{1}{1+i} \; [f_{02}^{(1)}, f_{02}^{(2)}]) \; (+) \\
& (+) \; p_{23}(3)([b_{23}^{(1)}, b_{23}^{(2)}] \; (+) \; \frac{1}{1+i} \; [f_{03}^{(1)}, f_{03}^{(2)}]) \; (+) \\
& (+) \; p_{24}(3)([b_{24}^{(1)}, b_{14}^{(2)}] \; (+) \; \frac{1}{1+i} \; [f_{04}^{(1)}, f_{04}^{(2)}]) = \\
& = [6, 8](+) \; (0.2)([20, 25] \; (+) \; (0.892)[3, 6]) \; (+) \\
& (+) \; (0.3)([14, 18] \; (+) \; (0.892)[3, 6]) \; (+) \\
& (+) \; (0.3)([11, 13] \; (+) \; (0.892)[3, 6]) \; (+) \\
& (+) \; (0.2)(0 \; (+) \; (0.892)[3, 6]) = \\
& = [6, 8] \; (+) \; [4.535, 6.070] \; (+) \; [5.002, 7.005] \; (+) \\
& (+) \; [4.102, 5.505] \; (+) \; [0.535, 1.070] = [20.174, 27.650]
\end{aligned}$$

The comparison between [16.274, 23.251] and [20.174, 27.650] shows us that the selection should fall to:

$$[\bar{f}_2^{(1)}(2, 3), \bar{f}_2^{(2)}(2, 3)] = [16.274, 23.251]$$

From state E_3, we can arrive at E'_1, E'_2 and E'_3. It will be necessary, therefore to make the following calculations:

$$\begin{aligned}
[a_{31}^{(1)}, a_{31}^{(2)}] & (+) p_{11}(3)([b_{11}^{(1)}, b_{11}^{(2)}] (+) \frac{1}{1+i} [f_{01}^{(1)}, f_{01}^{(2)}]) (+) \\
& (+) p_{12}(3)([b_{12}^{(1)}, b_{12}^{(2)}] (+) \frac{1}{1+i} [f_{02}^{(1)}, f_{02}^{(2)}]) (+) \\
& (+) p_{13}(3)([b_{13}^{(1)}, b_{13}^{(2)}] (+) \frac{1}{1+i} [f_{03}^{(1)}, f_{03}^{(2)}]) (+) \\
& (+) p_{14}(3)([b_{14}^{(1)}, b_{14}^{(2)}] (+) \frac{1}{1+i} [f_{04}^{(1)}, f_{04}^{(2)}]) = \\
& = [7, 10] (+) [2.267, 3.035] (+) [1.667, 2.335] (+) \\
& (+) [2.735, 3.670] (+) [1.605, 3.211] = \\
& = [7, 10] (+) [8.274, 12.251] = [15.274, 22.251]
\end{aligned}$$

$$E_3 \rightarrow E'_1$$

$$\begin{aligned}
[a_{32}^{(1)}, a_{32}^{(2)}] & (+) p_{21}(3)([b_{21}^{(1)}, b_{21}^{(2)}] (+) \frac{1}{1+i} [f_{01}^{(1)}, f_{01}^{(2)}]) (+) \\
& (+) p_{22}(3)([b_{22}^{(1)}, b_{22}^{(2)}] (+) \frac{1}{1+i} [f_{02}^{(1)}, f_{02}^{(2)}]) (+) \\
& (+) p_{23}(3)([b_{23}^{(1)}, b_{23}^{(2)}] (+) \frac{1}{1+i} [f_{03}^{(1)}, f_{03}^{(2)}]) (+) \\
& (+) p_{24}(3)([b_{24}^{(1)}, b_{24}^{(2)}] (+) \frac{1}{1+i} [f_{04}^{(1)}, f_{04}^{(2)}]) = \\
& = [3, 5] (+) [14.174, 19.650] = [17.174, 24.650]
\end{aligned}$$

$$\begin{aligned}
[a_{33}^{(1)}, a_{33}^{(2)}] & (+) p_{31}(3)([b_{31}^{(1)}, b_{31}^{(2)}] (+) \frac{1}{1+i} [f_{01}^{(1)}, f_{01}^{(2)}]) (+) \\
& (+) p_{32}(3)([b_{32}^{(1)}, b_{32}^{(2)}] (+) \frac{1}{1+i} [f_{02}^{(1)}, f_{02}^{(2)}]) (+) \\
& (+) p_{33}(3)([b_{33}^{(1)}, b_{33}^{(2)}] (+) \frac{1}{1+i} [f_{03}^{(1)}, f_{03}^{(2)}]) (+)
\end{aligned}$$

$$(+)\ p_{34}(3)([b_{34}^{(1)}, b_{34}^{(2)}]\ (+)\ \frac{1}{1+i}\ [f_{04}^{(1)}, f_{04}^{(2)}]) =$$

$$= 0\ (+)\ (0.5)([20, 25]\ (+)\ (0.892)[3, 6])\ (+)$$
$$(+)\ (0.4)([14, 18]\ (+)\ (0.892)[3, 6])\ (+)$$
$$(+)\ (0.1)([11, 13]\ (+)\ (0.892)[3, 6])\ (+)$$
$$(+)\ 0(0\ (+)\ (0.892)[3, 6]) =$$
$$= 0\ (+)\ [11.338, 15.176]\ (+)\ [6.670, 9.340]\ (+)$$
$$(+)\ [1.367, 1.835]\ (+)\ [0, 0] = [19.375, 26.351]$$

It is obvious that, by taking into account the need to arrive at an optimisation by minimums, the choice will be between the confidence intervals:

$$[15.274, 22.251], \quad [17.174, 24.650], \quad [19.375, 26.351]$$

of the lowest and therefore consideration will be made of:

$$[\bar{f}_3^{(1)}(2, 3), \bar{f}_3^{(2)}(2, 3)] = [15.274, 22.251]$$

To state E_4 of this phase three situations can also be arrived at, E'_1, E'_2 and E'_3. Successive calculation therefore will be made:

$$[a_{41}^{(1)}, a_{41}^{(2)}]\ (+)\ p_{11}(3)([b_{11}^{(1)}, b_{11}^{(2)}]\ (+)\ \frac{1}{1+i}\ [f_{01}^{(1)}, f_{01}^{(2)}])\ (+)$$

$$(+)\ p_{12}(3)([b_{12}^{(1)}, b_{12}^{(2)}]\ (+)\ \frac{1}{1+i}\ [f_{02}^{(1)}, f_{02}^{(2)}])\ (+)$$

$$(+)\ p_{13}(3)([b_{13}^{(1)}, b_{13}^{(2)}]\ (+)\ \frac{1}{1+i}\ [f_{03}^{(1)}, f_{03}^{(2)}])\ (+)$$

$$(+)\ p_{14}(3)([b_{14}^{(1)}, b_{14}^{(2)}]\ (+)\ \frac{1}{1+i}\ [f_{04}^{(1)}, f_{04}^{(2)}]) =$$

$$= [5, 7]\ (+)\ [8.274, 12.251] = [13.274, 19.251]$$

$$E_4 \rightarrow E'_1$$

$$[a_{42}^{(1)}, a_{42}^{(2)}]\ (+)\ p_{21}(3)([b_{21}^{(1)}, b_{21}^{(2)}]\ (+)\ \frac{1}{1+i}\ [f_{01}^{(1)}, f_{01}^{(2)}])\ (+)$$

$$(+)\ p_{22}(3)([b_{22}^{(1)}, b_{22}^{(2)}]\ (+)\ \frac{1}{1+i}\ [f_{02}^{(1)}, f_{02}^{(2)}])\ (+)$$

$$(+)\ p_{23}(3)([b_{23}^{(1)}, b_{23}^{(2)}]\ (+)\ \frac{1}{1+i}\ [f_{03}^{(1)}, f_{03}^{(2)}])\ (+)$$

$$(+)\, p_{24}(3)([b_{24}^{(1)}, b_{24}^{(2)}]\ (+)\ \frac{1}{1+i}\ [f_{04}^{(1)}, f_{04}^{(2)}]) =$$

$$= [2, 3]\ (+)\ [14.174, 19.650] = [16.174, 22.650]$$

$$[a_{43}^{(1)}, a_{43}^{(2)}]\ (+)\ p_{31}(3)([b_{31}^{(1)}, b_{31}^{(2)}]\ (+)\ \frac{1}{1+i}\ [f_{01}^{(1)}, f_{01}^{(2)}])\ (+)$$

$$(+)\, p_{32}(3)([b_{32}^{(1)}, b_{32}^{(2)}]\ (+)\ \frac{1}{1+i}\ [f_{02}^{(1)}, f_{02}^{(2)}])\ (+)$$

$$(+)\, p_{33}(3)([b_{33}^{(1)}, b_{33}^{(2)}]\ (+)\ \frac{1}{1+i}\ [f_{03}^{(1)}, f_{03}^{(2)}])\ (+)$$

$$(+)\, p_{34}(3)([b_{34}^{(1)}, b_{34}^{(2)}]\ (+)\ \frac{1}{1+i}\ [f_{04}^{(1)}, f_{04}^{(2)}]) =$$

$$= 0\ (+)\ [19.375, 26.351] = [19.375, 26.351]$$

Comparison between the confidence intervals arrived at makes us take in this case:

$$[\bar{f}_4^{(1)}(2, 3), \bar{f}_4^{(2)}(2, 3)] = [13.274, 19.251]$$

In this way at commencement of phase III we have:

$$\begin{aligned}
[\bar{f}_1^{(1)}(2, 3), \bar{f}_1^{(2)}(2, 3)] &= [18.274, 24.251] \\
[\bar{f}_2^{(1)}(2, 3), \bar{f}_2^{(2)}(2, 3)] &= [16.274, 23.251] \\
[\bar{f}_3^{(1)}(2, 3), \bar{f}_3^{(2)}(2, 3)] &= [15.274, 22.251] \\
[\bar{f}_4^{(1)}(2, 3), \bar{f}_4^{(2)}(2, 3)] &= [13.274, 19.251]
\end{aligned}$$

and the sub-strategy for phase III will be:

$$E_1 \rightarrow E_1', \quad E_2 \rightarrow E_1', \quad E_3 \rightarrow E_1', \quad E_4 \rightarrow E_1'$$

Phase II

In order not to stretch this section out too long we will omit the calculations, which will only be repeating those for phase III, obviously with different figures.

The results arrived at give rise to obtaining at commencement of phase II:

$$\begin{aligned}
[\bar{f}_1^{(1)}(1, 3), \bar{f}_1^{(2)}(1, 3)] &= [28.509, 37.408] \\
[\bar{f}_2^{(1)}(1, 3), \bar{f}_2^{(2)}(1, 3)] &= [26.509, 36.408] \\
[\bar{f}_3^{(1)}(1, 3), \bar{f}_3^{(2)}(1, 3)] &= [25.509, 35.408] \\
[\bar{f}_4^{(1)}(1, 3), \bar{f}_4^{(2)}(1, 3)] &= [23.509, 32.408]
\end{aligned}$$

and the optimum sub-strategy for phase II will be:

$$E_1 \to E_1', \quad E_2 \to E_1', \quad E_3 \to E_1', \quad E_4 \to E_1'$$

One way or another, the initial state of phase II, the correct decision will consist, in this case in passage to situation E_1'.

Phase I

With regard to phase I we will also limit ourselves to showing the results. At commencement of this phase we will have:

$$[\bar{f}_1^{(1)}(0, 3), \bar{f}_1^{(2)}(0, 3)] = [36.361, 47.576]$$
$$[\bar{f}_2^{(1)}(0, 3), \bar{f}_2^{(2)}(0, 3)] = [34.361, 46.576]$$
$$[\bar{f}_3^{(1)}(0, 3), \bar{f}_3^{(2)}(0, 3)] = [33.361, 45.576]$$
$$[\bar{f}_4^{(1)}(0, 3), \bar{f}_4^{(2)}(0, 3)] = [31.361, 42.576]$$

and the optimum sub-strategy for phase I will be:

$$E_1 \to E_1', \quad E_2 \to E_1', \quad E_3 \to E_1', \quad E_4 \to E_1'$$

Repeated constantly in each of the phases with the assigned date has been the fact that the correct decision consists in always passing to state E_1'.

In fact, the sequential process decision-probability will end at the moment in which the optimum decisions have been arrived at for each of phases III, II and I. Nevertheless in this case we have a phase, designated as preliminary or prior, which means the transition to a state in which the equipment is recently acquired and, therefore, totally inspected, E_1' up to the possible states E_1, E_2, E_3, E_4 at commencement of phase I. This then is operation of the investment object during the first year of its useful life.

Transition from this moment that constitutes the origin of phase I to the origin of phase 0 <<preliminary>> is done by the following calculation:

$$p_{11}(0)([b_{11}^{(1)}, b_{11}^{(2)}] \,(+)\, \frac{1}{1+i}\,[\bar{f}_1^{(1)}(0, 3)\ \bar{f}_1^{(2)}(0, 3)]) \,(+)\, p_{12}(0)([b_{12}^{(1)}, b_{12}^{(2)}] \,(+)$$

$$(+)\, \frac{1}{1+i}\,[\bar{f}_2^{(1)}(0, 3), \bar{f}_2^{(2)}(0, 3)]) \,(+)\, p_{13}(0)([b_{13}^{(1)}, b_{13}^{(2)}] \,(+)$$

$$(+)\, \frac{1}{1+i}\,[\bar{f}_3^{(1)}(0, 3), \bar{f}_3^{(2)}(0, 3)]) \,(+)\, p_{14}(0)([b_{14}^{(1)}, b_{14}^{(2)}] \,(+)$$

$$(+)\, \frac{1}{1+i}\,[\bar{f}_4^{(1)}(0, 3), \bar{f}_4^{(2)}(0, 3)]) =$$

$$
\begin{aligned}
&= 0\,([20, 25]\ (+)\ (0.892)[36.361, 47.576])\ (+)\\
&(+)\ 0.1([14, 18]\ (+)\ (0.892)[34.361, 46.576])\ (+)\\
&(+)\ 0.1([11, 13]\ (+)\ (0.892)[33.361, 45.576])\ (+)\\
&(+)\ 0.8(0\ (+)\ (0.892)[31.361, 42.457]) =\\
&= [0, 0]\ (+)\ [4.465, 5.954]\ (+)\ [4.075, 5.365]\ (+)\\
&(+)\ [22.379, 30.382] = [30.919, 41.701]
\end{aligned}
$$

Consideration of this preliminary phase allows for bringing to light the costs of maintenance and repair of the machine in question. Thus in the example we have developed we arrive at the fact, if the strategy obtained is followed, that the aforementioned costs will be no less than 30.919 and no greater than 41.701.

We feel it important to point out that in this, as in other sequential processes, the incorporation of probability implies assigning of probabilities based on the Borel-Kolmogorov axiomatic and its use responds to the requirements of the same. However we ask ourselves the question, that if in a changing reality such as the one we live in and faced with the technological revolution which is occurring, it is possible to talk of the probabilities of determined events. In other words, will historically obtained data on operating equipment be valid when used for new equipment, normally more highly evolved with regard to the services it renders. At the very least this problem should provide food for thought. Humility that is the guide to every research work makes us think that science is constructed by adding minuscule grains of sand to the immense beach of knowledge. In this case the incorporation of an element of uncertainty has only just opened a door for future works a mere fraction. We hope that an interested reader may decide to open the door to its fullest extent.

References

[1] See as an example Kaufmann, A. and Gil Aluja, J.: *Las matemáticas del azar y de la incertidumbre*, Ceura, Madrid, 1989.

[2] We refer mainly to chapter 13 in which the optimum distribution of financial resources is mentioned.

[3] See the first section of chapter 13.

[4] This case was the object of a chapter in the work by Kaufmann, A. and Gil Aluja, J.: *Técnicas operativas para la dirección estratégica*, Universidad de Barcelona, Barcelona, 1991.

[5] This terminology was introduced by Companys, R. in his thesis at the University of Grenoble <<Contributions à la théorie mathématique des processus de décision séquentiel>>. In this case the DH processes introduce uncertain data (confidence intervals).

Conclusions

The work we have presented comprises an attempt to homogeneously gather together a set of techniques that are capable of explaining and treating the problem of investment, when the investor is face by a world governed by uncertainty. Throughout the pages of our work we have gradually introduced theoretical elements, available at this time, relative to numerical and non-numerical mathematics that we feel are capable of formalising uncertain systems in the best possible way. But all this would not have been possible without the support of traditional devices based on determinism and probability. On many occasions we have presented the classical model most commonly accepted by the research community, as a prior step to its transformation to the sphere of uncertainty. In this way, the comparison between both schemes has allowed us to reach the double objective of, on the one hand, facilitating comprehension and, on the other, permitting entry into the new formal world without excessive complications.

It is obvious that our work could not end here and therefore we have included new models, which are removed from the traditional models presented in texts on these studies, where estimates of future economic parameters are established with the required certainty. Let us say in any case that normally between these two cases there is no confrontation or contradiction but that one of them, determinism, is a particular case of the other, uncertainty. One particular item should be pointed out: all the time real situations in which certainty or probability are present are becoming less and therefore the use of classical schemes means forcing the limits of validity on which the models are based. However we will repeat once again, that when it is possible to use elements of determinism it would be madness not to do so. If when this is not so and on the other hand the conditions exist for using the mathematics of probability, then let us do so. Only in the event then that neither one nor the other is technically viable should we resort to certain theoretical elements of which unfortunately we do not have so many years of experience. Scientific honesty obliges, all the time with greater intensity, to resort to techniques that as yet we know very little about, when we contemplate the guarantees represented by many centuries of use and successes that support the others.

The models we have linked together throughout the text are the result of work carried out by the author over the last few years. Some of them were the subject of articles published in various scientific magazines. Others, submitted and defended as papers or communications at national and international conferences, have undergone the corresponding debates and exchanges of opinion. In both cases acceptance by the scientific community of the points of view make us feel confident relative to the results obtained. In one or the other we have been particularly careful to mention publications and meetings in order for the reader to be able to gather further information if so desiring. However, this book does not intend to be a compendium of works published by the author, but a compilation of the knowledge that comprises the subjects of the same. For this, even though subjects that have already been tackled have been included, these have had to be adapted to a greater or lesser degree in order to facilitate the main train of thought of the work. On the other hand everybody knows the different nature between a brief monographic investigation work and a part of a book that also should possess in our opinion, pedagogic overtones. Although seasoned with this type of work, we have written again chapter after chapter, thinking on the needs of those who have to take decisions on investments at the threshold of a new millennium, which has required reconsideration of a great many aspects that appeared to be assumed and consolidated.

We have divided this work into three parts, each of which has included elements, that we feel are complete in themselves by explaining and in many cases treating the aspects considered as the most significant in the investment process. Obviously the intensity and extent of coverage has not been the same for each one. The task commences with a group of subjects dedicated to the preparation of the investment process. Thus, after expounding on the conceptual and methodological elements, the technical aspects directed at materialising an investment programme have been tackled. Two fundamental aspects of this have been highlighted from a financial point of view: the inherent risk of investment and the analysis of financial products with a view to being able to face the payments undertaken throughout the length of the economic horizon covering the project. The logical and mathematical elements we have used are a component part, principally, of the non-numerical studies among which the theory of graphs and certain developments of topology and pre-topology have played a predominant role.

The second part includes the central problem of investment which is what the decision to invest monetary means in one or another object, that is to say the problem of selection. The group of chapters on this subject considered generically, have shown us a different treatment depending from which of the different hypothesis we started out relative to the knowledge of the factors having an incidence on the monetary masses intervening throughout the length of the investment process. Thus for a group of models we have considered the case in which the monetary current of payments and collections arising from the hypothetical purchase of the investment object were known more or less precisely or were susceptible to being estimated by means of some uncertain number. In these cases the transfer from certainty to uncertainty was possible thanks to the intervention of confidence intervals, fuzzy numbers, expertons, ... In this way the numerical mathematics of uncertainty has permitted approximations to solutions for the cases brought up. On the other hand the other group of models has been directed at obtaining solutions when uncertainty acquires its fullest sense, that is to say in those cases in which it is not even possible to demarcate, and consequently numerically structure events. In this case then it is necessary to resort to non-numerical mathematics. But on transferring from the numerical to the non-numerical there are many things that change, and concepts such as profitability, economic viability, etc., normally expressed by one or several numbers, no longer have the traditionally recognised central role, but leave the leading part to other new or redefined concepts among which stand out those of order and affinity. In these cases a fundamental change takes place in the conception of the investment problem on considering that selection does not necessarily mean precise or imprecise knowledge of a numerical economic parameter (it is not absolutely necessary to know the difference of the profits by buying one object in place of another) in order to take the decision, but it is sufficient, in the context of uncertainty, to obtain an order of preference (suffice it to earn more with one object than with the rest). Uncertainty therefore admits and sometimes requires certain nuances to be considered in order for an efficient economic-financial performance.

The third part has been dedicated to one of the most characteristic objects of industrial activity: equipment. We are conscious of the fact that the treatment of industrial equipment in its triple aspect of economic renewal, its insertion into a productive context and its maintenance, cannot be studied in depth in just a few chapters, since the knowledge of these subjects would require several volumes. In our work we have only wanted to present an outline, susceptible to later development by us or by any interested reader. In this way we have included a chapter dedicated to renewal based on the works of Terborgh and his group of researchers, from which we have constructed a model suitable for treatment of uncertainty. We have chosen this path as we feel it is adequate for presenting a sufficiently overall panorama of the renewal problem. A second chapter has as its object to show how to handle industrial equipment immersed in a production process when its characteristics do not allow for estimating its performance with sufficient precision. Finally in the last chapter we have shown in what way it is possible for better operability of equipment by means of more efficient maintenance in order to avoid or mitigate the effects of breakdowns and the consequent stoppages in the production process.

We are conscious of the fact that a work such as we have presented should in principal be incomplete. And this both by the nature itself of the work undertaken and by the limitation of the author. But in no case can we be denied the pleasure with which each page has been written and the very profound hope that our efforts will be of use to those having the responsibility of taking decisions. As our very much-missed teacher Arnold Kaufmann used to say *in our work we are guided by nothing else than to be useful to others.*

Bibliography

Abraham, C. and Thomas, A. (1966): *Microéconomie: décisions optionales dans l'entreprise et dans la nation,* Dunod Paris.

Barre, R. (1987): Preface to the work by A. Kaufmann and J.Gil Aluja: *Técnicas operativas de gestión para el tratamiento de la incertidumbre,* Hispano Europea, Barcelona.

Boulding, H. (1962): <<Análisis económico>>, *Rev. de Occidente,* 2nd Edition, Madrid.

Clark, W.W. (1994): *El gráfico Gantt en la dirección de empresas industriales y comerciales,* 2nd edition, Montesó, Barcelona.

Courtillot, M. (1973): <<Structure canonique des fichiers>>, AIER-AFCET, volume 7, January.

Demoocrom, M. (1964): Work submitted to Cie. des Machines Bull.

Desrousseaux, J. (1965): *L'évolution économique et le comportement industriel,* Dunod, Paris.

Dinh Xuân B. (1984): <<A method for estimating the membership function of a fuzzy set>>, *Revue Busefal,* number 19 L.S.I. Univers. Paul Sabatier, Toulouse.

Enke, S. (1966): *Economía para el desarrollo,* Uteha, Mexico.

Evants, H.F. (1965): *Introducción al PERT,* Sagitario.

Gil Aluja, J. (1967): <<El estudio dinámico de la selección de las inversiones>>, *Revista Técnica Contable,* February.

— (1990): <<Ensayo sobre un modelo de diagnóstico económico-financiero>> Proceedings of the V Hispano-Luso Conference on Scientific Management, Vigo, September.

— (1991): *Inversiones. Certeza, riesgo e incertidumbre. I. Certeza,* Faculty of Economic and Business Sciences, University of Barcelona.

—(1992): *The Economic Environment in the Decision to Invest within a Context of Uncertainty. Advances in Fuzzy Sets and Applications,* Universitauti IASI, Rumania.

— (1992): <<Incidencia de la fiscalidad en la decisión de invertir en un ambiente de incertidumbre>>, I European Congress on Company Management and Economy, Huelva.

— (1992); <<Modelo de selección de inversiones con desconocimiento de las magnitudes económico-financieras>> VI Hispano-Luso Conference on Scientific Management, volume 1, Funchal.

— (1994): <<La selección de inversiones en base a criterios diversificados>>, Proceedings of AEDEM Conference, Cáceres.

— (1994): <<La incertidumbre en la economía y gestión de empresas>>, Proceedings of the IV Congress of the Spanish Association on Fuzzy Technologies and Logic, Blanes, September 14.

— (1994): <<Criterial Selection of Investments within a Context of uncertainty>>, Fuzzy Systems and Neural Networks Symposium, AMSE Press, Lyon, July.

— (1994): <<El fenómeno de desgaste en un proceso de inversión>>, Proceedings of the III International AEDEM Congress, Bucarest.

— (1995): <<Spre o noua paradigma a teoriei deciziei>>, Induction Speech to the Rumanian Academy, September 27, *Rev. Academica, October.*

— (1995): <<Selección multicriterio de inversines mediante retículos de Galois>>, in *Dirección de empresas en los noventa,* Civitas, Madrid.

— (1996): <<Programming investment activities>>, Proceedings of the International Conference on Intelligent Technologies in Human-Related Sciences, León, July 5-7.

— (1996): <<Les Approches connexionistes dans le changement du paradigme de la théorie de la décision>>, 3rd. International Meeting of ACSEG, Nantes, October 25.

— (1997): <<El concepto de afinidad en el nuevo paradigma de la teoría de la decisión>>, Acceptance speech as <<Doctor Honoris Causa>>, University Rovira i Virgili, Tarragona.

Insolera, F. (1959): *Curso de matemática financiera y actuarial,* Aguilar, Madrid.

Kaufmann, A. (1985): <<Le remplacement des équipements dans l'incertain>>, Work note, number 153, October.

— (1972): *Métodos y modelos de la investigación de operaciones*, volume I, CECSA, Mexico.

— (1979): *Modèles mathématiques pour la stimulation inventive*, Albin Michel.

Kaufmann, A. and Desbazeille, G. (1965): *El método del camino crítico*, Sagitario, Barcelona. The original version in French was published by Dunod, 1964.

Kaufmann, A. and Gil Aluja, J. (1986): *Introducción a la teoría de los subconjuntos borrosos a la gestión de las empresas,* Milladoiro, Santiago de Compostela.

— (1987): *Técnicas operativas de gestión para el tratamiento de la incertidumbre*, Hispano-Europea, Barcelona.

— (1988): *Modelos para la investigación de efectos olvidados*, Milladoiro, Santiago de Compostela.

— (1990): *Matemáticas del azar y de la incertidumbre,* Ceura, Madrid.

— (1991): <<Selection of Affinities by means of Fuzzy Relations and Galois Lattices>>, Proceedings of the XI Euro O.R.Congress, Aachen, July 16-19.

— (1991): *Nuevas técnicas para la dirección estratégica,* Barcelona University Publications, Barcelona.

— (1992): *Técnicas de gestión de empresa. Previsiones, decisiones y estrategias,* Pirámide, Madrid.

— (1992): <<La programación de actividades por el método del semáforo>>, European Rewiev on Management and Economy, volume 1, April.

— (1993): *Técnicas especiales para la gestión de expertos*, Milladoiro, Santiago de Compostela.

— (1995): *Grafos neuronales para la economía y gestión de empresas*, Pirámide, Madrid.

Kaufmann, A,; Gil Aluja, J. and Gil Lafuente, A.M. (1994): *La creatividad en la gestión de las empresas*, Pirámide, Madrid.

Khun, T. (1981): *La estructura de las revoluciones científicas,* Fondo de Cultura Económica, Madrdi.

Lafosse-Marin, J: <<Moore Closure and Fuzzy Graph>>, internal document, Mathematics Department University of Algiers.

Laporeau, C. (1965): <<Evaluation des charges de contrôle de l'avancement des travaux par la méthode de cheminement critique>> *Revue de gestion,* October.

Masse, P. (1963): *La elección de las inversiones*, Sagitario, Barcelona.

Malgrange, Y. (1967): <<Décomposition d'un graphe en sous-graphes fortement connexes maximaux>>, internal memo Cie. des Machines Bull.

McCulloch, W.S. and Pitts, N. (1943): <<A Logical Calculus of the Ideas Immanent in Nervous Systems>>, *Bulletin of Mathematical Biophysics* number 5.

Pichat, E. (1969): <<Algorithm for Finding the Maximal Elements of a Finite Universal Algebra>>, Inform Processing 68 Publ. North Holland.

Popper, K. (1971): *La lógica de la investigación científica,* Tecnos, Madrid.

Rodríguez, A. (1983): *Matemática de la inversión*, Romargraf, Barcelona.

Saaty, T.L. (1978): <<Exploring the Interface Between Hierarchies, Multiple Objectives and Fuzzy Sets>>, *Fuzzy Sets and Systems,* vol I, num 1.

Schneider, E. (1956): *Teoría de la inversión. Calculo de la economicidad*, Ateneo, Buenos Aires.

— (1968): *Economía, política y economía de la empresa*, Sagitario, Barcelona.

Terborgh, G. (1946): *Dynamic Equipment Policy,* McGraw Hill, New York.

— (1958): *Business Investment Policy*, Machinery and Allied Products Institute, Washington.

— (1967): *Business Investment Policy*, Machinery and Allied Products Institute, Washington.

Wang, E. and Chang, T.C. (1981): <<Canonical Structures in Attribute Based on File Organization>>, *CACM*, September.

Applied Optimization

1. D.-Z. Du and D.F. Hsu (eds.): *Combinatorial Network Theory.* 1996 ISBN 0-7923-3777-8
2. M.J. Panik: *Linear Programming: Mathematics, Theory and Algorithms.* 1996 ISBN 0-7923-3782-4
3. R.B. Kearfott and V. Kreinovich (eds.): *Applications of Interval Computations.* 1996 ISBN 0-7923-3847-2
4. N. Hritonenko and Y. Yatsenko: *Modeling and Optimimization of the Lifetime of Technology.* 1996 ISBN 0-7923-4014-0
5. T. Terlaky (ed.): *Interior Point Methods of Mathematical Programming.* 1996 ISBN 0-7923-4201-1
6. B. Jansen: *Interior Point Techniques in Optimization.* Complementarity, Sensitivity and Algorithms. 1997 ISBN 0-7923-4430-8
7. A. Migdalas, P.M. Pardalos and S. Storøy (eds.): *Parallel Computing in Optimization.* 1997 ISBN 0-7923-4583-5
8. F.A. Lootsma: *Fuzzy Logic for Planning and Decision Making.* 1997 ISBN 0-7923-4681-5
9. J.A. dos Santos Gromicho: *Quasiconvex Optimization and Location Theory.* 1998 ISBN 0-7923-4694-7
10. V. Kreinovich, A. Lakeyev, J. Rohn and P. Kahl: *Computational Complexity and Feasibility of Data Processing and Interval Computations.* 1998 ISBN 0-7923-4865-6
11. J. Gil-Aluja: *The Interactive Management of Human Resources in Uncertainty.* 1998 ISBN 0-7923-4886-9
12. C. Zopounidis and A.I. Dimitras: *Multicriteria Decision Aid Methods for the Prediction of Business Failure.* 1998 ISBN 0-7923-4900-8
13. F. Giannessi, S. Komlósi and T. Rapcsák (eds.): *New Trends in Mathematical Programming.* Homage to Steven Vajda. 1998 ISBN 0-7923-5036-7
14. Ya-xiang Yuan (ed.): *Advances in Nonlinear Programming.* Proceedings of the '96 International Conference on Nonlinear Programming. 1998 ISBN 0-7923-5053-7
15. W.W. Hager and P.M. Pardalos: *Optimal Control.* Theory, Algorithms, and Applications. 1998 ISBN 0-7923-5067-7
16. Gang Yu (ed.): *Industrial Applications of Combinatorial Optimization.* 1998 ISBN 0-7923-5073-1
17. D. Braha and O. Maimon (eds.): *A Mathematical Theory of Design: Foundations, Algorithms and Applications.* 1998 ISBN 0-7923-5079-0

Applied Optimization

18. O. Maimon, E. Khmelnitsky and K. Kogan: *Optimal Flow Control in Manufacturing*. Production Planning and Scheduling. 1998 ISBN 0-7923-5106-1
19. C. Zopounidis and P.M. Pardalos (eds.): *Managing in Uncertainty: Theory and Practice*. 1998 ISBN 0-7923-5110-X
20. A.S. Belenky: *Operations Research in Transportation Systems:* Ideas and Schemes of Optimization Methods for Strategic Planning and Operations Management. 1998 ISBN 0-7923-5157-6
21. J. Gil-Aluja: *Investment in Uncertainty*. 1999 ISBN 0-7923-5296-3

KLUWER ACADEMIC PUBLISHERS – DORDRECHT / BOSTON / LONDON

CPSIA information can be obtained
at www.ICGtesting.com
Printed in the USA
LVHW011020120720
660448LV00016B/1148

9 780792 352969